A BEGINNING-INTERMEDIATE
GRAMMAR OF
HELLENISTIC GREEK

A BEGINNING-INTERMEDIATE GRAMMAR OF HELLENISTIC GREEK

Third Edition

Robert W. Funk

POLEBRIDGE PRESS

Salem, Oregon

p5n+
To all the students

s   2c   4b
//who / taught / me

i   4n
to attend / the text

C   i   pb6
(and) learn / from them

Design and production by Robaire Ream

Library of Congress Cataloging-in-Publication Data

Funk, Robert Walter, 1926-2005.
  A beginning-intermediate grammar of Hellenistic Greek / Robert W. Funk. -- Third edition.
    pages cm
 Includes bibliographical references and index.
  ISBN 978-1-59815-115-2 (alk. paper)
1. Greek language, Hellenistic (300 B.C.-600 A.D.)--Grammar. I. Title.
 PA617.F8 2013
 487'.4--dc23

2013015749

Table of Contents

Part Three: Short Syntax

Sentence Structure

The Subject

The Predicate

Function Words

Nominal Word Clusters

The Verb: Tense-Aspect/Mood/Infinitive

Foreword

Robert W. Funk (1926-2005) was a specialist in the languages and literature of early Christianity. He earned an A.B. in Classics at Butler University, a B.D. in the philosophy of religion at the Christian Theological Seminary, an M.A. in Semitics at Butler, and a Ph.D. in New Testament at Vanderbilt University. Because he was trained in both ancient Greek and the New Testament, Funk was thoroughly prepared to produce an innovative and comprehensive grammar of the Greek dialect that flourished during the Greco-Roman period.

As a graduate student in the early 1950s, Funk was encouraged by his Vanderbilt mentor, Kendrick Grobel—himself a linguist and translator—to translate Friedrich Blass and Albert Debrunner's *Grammatik des neutestamentlichen Griechisch,* the premier advanced New Testament reference grammar of the time. Funk started with the ninth edition (1954), but Debrunner sent Funk his notes for the projected tenth edition. Using Debrunner's notes, Funk produced a new translation and thorough revision of the ninth-tenth edition of Blass-Debrunner in 1961. Yale scholar Nils Dahl wrote that Blass-Debrunner-Funk, *A Greek Grammar of the New Testament and Other Early Christian Literature* "is one of those rare cases in which a translation is definitely better than the original." During this same time W. F. Arndt and F. W. Gingrich produced an English translation of the fourth edition of Walter Bauer's *Griechisch-Deutsches Wörterbuch zu den Schriften des Neuen Testaments und der übrigen urchristlichen Literatur* (1957). Both Bauer's dictionary and Funk's edition of the Blass-Debrunner grammar continue to be basic reference works for New Testament students and scholars. By his early thirties, Funk had already established himself as a solid scholar and major authority on the Greek New Testament.

Immediately following the publication of Blass-Debrunner-Funk in 1961, Funk began work on his own hellenistic Greek grammar. The Blass-Debrunner tradition was based on a classical philological approach to language analysis and pedagogy. During the 1950s a new approach to language called linguistics challenged the assumption of classical philology that meaning resides primarily in the lexical stock of a language. Funk also recognized that grammatical analysis at the word level is inadequate while writing his dissertation, "The Syntax of the Greek Article: Its Importance for Critical Pauline Problems" (1953). Funk was thus motivated by two overarching questions in designing his own grammar: Should New Testament Greek grammar be presented as a deviation, even corruption, of an earlier classical standard, or is it simply a distinctive dialect that deserves its own definition? What insights from modern linguistics and second-language pedagogy can improve the way New Testament Greek is taught and learned? In order to address these questions, Funk spent the next decade creating a new database, analyzing the essential features of hellenistic Greek, and writing *A Beginning-Intermediate Grammar of Hellenistic Greek* (1973).

The major innovative features of Funk's Grammar can be summarized as follows:

1. *It is both a lesson grammar and a reference grammar.* Reference grammars are encyclopedic treatments of all facets of a language, topically arranged and usually divided into three categories: phonology, morphology, and syntax. They are thus resources for those who already know the basics of the language. In contrast, lesson grammars jump around from topic to topic. They are not suitable as reference sources since various aspects of a topic are scattered throughout. Funk combines the two types, so that his grammar is useful for both beginning and advanced students. The material is arranged topically, but within each lesson a distinction is made between introductory content for beginning students and advanced material that can be skipped until later.

2. *It is a narrative grammar, not an outline of topics to be covered by the instructor.* Most lesson grammars assume that explanations of the content will be presented by the instructor. Funk's grammar includes clear explanations of each topic so that it can be assigned as reading before class meetings, thus allowing for student questions to the instructor and further elaboration of difficult issues during the limited time available in class. Conceivably, those wanting to learn Greek on their own could do so with Funk's grammar and a copy of the Greek New Testament.

3. *It employs actual texts, not artificial examples.* Greek illustrations of topics covered in Funk's grammar are actual sentences from the database of selected passages from the New Testament and other hellenistic Greek texts. Students thus are learning to read the New Testament from the start and assimilating its grammatical signals and patterns.

4. *It describes the Greek of the New Testament as a distinct dialect.* In the fifth century BCE, the Attic dialect of Athens came to be regarded as the normative form of Greek. Following Alexander the Great's conquest of the Middle East in the late fourth century, Attic Greek was transformed into a new dialect called

Koine (hellenistic Greek), which became the universal language of the Greco-Roman world for over a millennium. Later literary purists viewed this transformation of Attic as a corruption of the classical standard. Because of the notion that there is a pure form of a language, the European philological tradition has tended to treat the grammar of New Testament Greek as a series of notes about the changes from fifth-century Attic.

Modern linguists, however, regard all stages in the history of languages as distinct dialects and equally adept as vehicles for human communication. Greek grammars produced from this point of view are thus comprehensive descriptions of the bread-and-butter features of a particular phase in the history of a language. One implication of this view of languages is that students can learn hellenistic Greek without first having mastered classical Greek.

5. *It highlights syntactic structures rather than vocabulary.* The most significant feature of Funk's Grammar is his analysis of syntax. Funk identifies the six basic sentence patterns in hellenistic Greek and describes how all actual Greek sentences are derived, via various transformations, from these six patterns. This approach reflects the linguistic claim that there are regular patterns underlying all levels of human language. With respect to morphology, Funk identifies models for the inflection of nouns and verbs and then describes how one can decline nouns or conjugate verbs by applying predictable changes to the models. This approach eliminates the need for rote memorization of multiple paradigms and stresses the fact that adults who are learning a second language need to recognize its underlying patterns, rather than trying, often vainly, to memorize an array of random examples.

Scholars Press published the first edition of the complete three-volume Grammar for the Society of Biblical Literature in 1973, followed by a second, corrected edition in 1977. At Funk's request, I produced a student workbook with exercises, reading assignments, and translation notes to accompany the Grammar. It was published in 1976 and will be made available on-line from Polebridge Press.

Although Funk's Grammar went out of print in 1987, a loyal cadre of instructors continued to use it. But, as the original version of the Grammar was produced on a typewriter, there was no electronic version available. Jonathan Robie, list owner of the online Biblical Greek forum known as B-Greek (www.ibiblio.org/bgreek/forum), volunteered to facilitate the production of an electronic text, and members of the forum helped with its production, thus giving the Grammar new life until a reissue was possible. Carl W. Conrad of Washington University in St. Louis, a long-time co-chair of the B-Greek forum, encouraged the reissue of the Grammar, facilitated the process through the forum, and helped check the Greek in this edition. Ken Penner, St. Francis Xavier University of Nova Scotia, led the team that did the OCR scanning and prepared the initial HTML formatting of the text. And Louis L. Sorenson, a Biblical Greek forum administrator, heroically proofread the Greek, not just once but several times.

In addition, Robaire Ream, graphics designer for Polebridge Press, has done a masterful job of producing what he describes as the most complicated book he has designed. Mahlon H. Smith III, Rutgers University, offered valuable advice about the organization of heads and extracts in the new edition. Polebridge's proofreader, Jon Andreas, painstakingly checked the proofs against a printout of the second edition. We want to express our deep appreciation to all these friends of Funk's Grammar and others who gladly and skillfully assisted with the preparation of this new edition.

Despite the best efforts of so many dedicated people, errors will inevitably have made their way into these pages. We hope you will help us find and fix them by emailing corrections to: errata@westarinstitute.org.

Finally, Westar and Polebridge folks will not be surprised to learn that Char Matejovsky has spearheaded the effort to bring out a third edition of her late husband's Grammar. Both she and I believe that A Beginning-Intermediate Grammar of Hellenistic Greek is still an up-to-date and innovative approach to ancient Greek and so are delighted to see its reissue in a single volume for future generations of students.

Lane C. McGaughy
Westar Institute
Willamette University
May 27, 2013

Preface

A Personal Word to the Teacher and Students

The aim of this grammar is to introduce students to the structure of the Greek language in the briefest possible time. Notice that structure and Greek language are being emphasized. It is the language itself and not a grammar about that language that students who wish to learn to read Greek need to confront. For that reason, the grammar itself is suppressed wherever possible. And, if modern linguistics is correct in its fundamental affirmations, the one needful thing in learning a new language is familiarity with its grammatical structure. Such familiarity need not be explicit; learners need to "know" the structure and structure signals only in the sense that they are able, immediately and without deliberation, to respond to them.

More recent methods of grammatical analysis and language teaching bear directly upon a chronic condition I have mused as a teacher of Greek. Although in almost daily touch with some Greek text for twenty-five years, I find that each time I teach beginning Greek from a traditional grammar, it is necessary for me to recommit portions of that grammar to memory. There seems to be little correlation between my ability to read and understand a Greek text and the ability, say, to reproduce nominal and verbal paradigms by heart. I was puzzled by this discrepancy in myself, and by the fact that students who appeared to be able to handle a Greek text with facility often did poorly on examinations over Greek "grammar." The reverse condition has also frequently caught my attention: students who appear to know the "grammar" are not always able to read a Greek text with correlative ease. In the case of the former, the difficulty may have been that the students merely lacked the technical language with which to make their functional knowledge explicit. Yet I took it to be the case that more often than not those same students aspired to a working knowledge of the language and not to a grammarian's portfolio. In the case of the latter, knowledge of the "grammar" did not appear to guarantee knowledge of the language. It then occurred to me that traditional grammar might be something apart from the ability to read Greek, in fact, might be an impediment to such ability.

It was with some reluctance that I undertook to reassess the status of traditional Greek grammar. A modest acquaintance with modern linguistics was enough to convince me that a revolution had taken place in the study and learning of language no less than in the study and learning of mathematics.

I have endeavored to indicate the implications of linguistics for the study of Greek in the Introduction (§§001–020). There the reader will find some of the basic insights afforded by linguistics as I see them in relation to Greek. I have endeavored to express them without the use of technical language and probably inadequately, by the rigorous standards of leading contemporary linguists. For those who wish to see linguistics in action, a few of the many books which may be consulted are listed in the Table of Abbreviations under modern literature. I should like to emphasize the importance of reading actual grammars rather than, or in addition to, linguistic theory.

These brief remarks invite some further practical advice about the character and organization of the grammar itself.

The first admonition concerns frame of mind. Students who have learned the grammar of some language in a traditional mode will be tempted, in the earlier stages, to assume that they are not learning grammar. They will feel uneasy that they cannot reproduce third declension paradigms or the principal parts of irregular verbs, probably because they think they know what grammar is. They have to be convinced that they can learn a language and learn it well, without first having learned traditional grammar by rote memorization. The watershed comes after the first weeks: on the other side of the divide, the skeptics become fresh converts with all the passion normally attaching thereto. By this time they have discovered that they do indeed know the system of morphological variables, and know it with an assurance not normally attained after months, if not years, of study. They will also have discovered that they can read Greek, an achievement they did not anticipate until months later.

The first admonition, therefore, is: *have faith.*

The grammar is constructed, in broad outline, as follows:

1. Students are introduced to the sight and sound of the language by reading actual texts (they are urged to have a Greek text open before them as they proceed). They are urged to make as much of the sight and sound of the language as their instincts allow, e.g. the meanings of cognate words, the structure of sentences.
2. Student are then taught the system of morphological variables systematically, with a minimum amount of rote memorization. They

learn to recognize the forms of nouns, pronouns, verbs and the like in actual texts. They are not asked to reproduce paradigms, except for the few models they must fix in mind for reference.

3. After approximately twelve weeks (31 lessons),[1] students begin to read actual but selected texts for content.[2] They learn the commonly recurring structures of the language and acquire vocabulary in context. By the time they have completed the Short Syntax (lessons 31–62), they will have sufficient facility to read Greek texts of moderate difficulty at sight. There will be blanks, of course, but they will have learned to fill them in by analogy (grammatical blanks) or context (lexical blanks), or by turning to the grammar and lexicon for help. The aim of the program is to achieve moderate reading proficiency at sight in one year of study or less. This aim is based on the assumption that most students, especially theological students, begin the study of Greek relatively late in their academic programs.

While the grammar is programmed to be completed in slightly more than one semester (24 weeks, 3 hours per week),[3] it is conceived as a beginning-intermediate grammar. An explanation of this conception is in order, since the actual text of the grammar may create some confusion in view of the stated purpose.

Most beginning lesson grammars are used for a year, at most two, and then discarded in favor of an intermediate or advanced grammar. The inefficiency involved in learning to use second and third grammars can be avoided, in part, by incorporating a second level grammar into the first. The present grammar serves as a beginning lesson grammar, but the material is treated exhaustively

---

1. The rate at which lessons are assigned will of course vary. The important thing is to keep the pace and not be deterred by the temptation to master every morphological detail.

2. The selected texts on which this grammar is based are recommended for reading purposes: The Syntax is illustrated with words and sentences drawn from this body of material. Of course, other selections of moderate difficulty would serve equally well.

3. The recommended rate of progress is optional. The teacher and student may find a slightly slower (or even quicker) pace more comfortable.

at many points, especially in connection with morphology, so that the text may also be used subsequently for reference. The difference between the two types of material is indicated in the text by marking the intermediate (and advanced) material, in the Nominal and Verbal Systems, with a background screen to indicate which sections may be skipped by the beginner. Several rather lengthy systematic discussions are included but clearly marked: for reading and reference only. Such sections, e.g. Introduction to the Nominal System (§§100–115), are designed to provide adequate background and rationale for what students are learning. Students are not asked, however, to learn the content of these sections. In addition, the grammar is supplied with several appendices which both teacher and student will find useful at all levels of study. These, too, are included only for reference.

Exercises and directions for practice will appear separately as a workbook. The exercises belong integrally to the program of study represented by the lesson grammar. With a little experience, the teacher will be able to devise his own exercises, making use of those texts with which he/she wishes the student to become acquainted.

This personal note might well conclude with the axioms that the author has endeavored (sometimes vainly!) to keep constantly before him in both teaching Greek and writing this grammar:

1. Since the object of the study of Greek is the use of the language rather than its mortification, students are advised to devote their time to a mastery of the language rather than to a mastery of the grammar.
2. Students (and the teacher!) should keep a Greek text before them at all times. All learning should take place with an actual text in view.
3. The grammar and lexicon are reference works to be consulted repeatedly rather than memorized. Keep them constantly at hand, but always above or to the right and left of the Greek text.
4. Few things need be learned by rote memorization; where memorization is necessary, the data must be absolutely mastered.
5. Students are advised to take every conceivable shortcut reading the signals of the language: explicit, full grammatical knowledge is no substitute for native response where reading ability and comprehension are concerned.

6. Students are urged to believe in the linguistic "signposts," like those on a complicated Interstate, and to trust their own reading of the markers. There will be fewer traffic jams and slowups if students allow themselves to be guided by the markers they see and leave a blank here, make a guess there.

7. A wrong turn is no disgrace: if students misread a sign, the teacher will direct the way back to the highway, provided the students have not already discovered their error. A wrong turn is better than an idle wait on the shoulder studying the map.

Some indication of how this grammar was constructed may be helpful to the user. This work, like most others, has its strengths and weaknesses, and it does no harm to have some notion of them in advance.

The lexical stock represented in Bauer served as the basis for the morphology (the treatment of the nominal and verbal systems). A complete and exhaustive compilation of the data was made for this purpose. Part of the raw results of that compilation may be found in Appendices II and III (posted online at www.westarinstitute.org/store/a-beginning-intermediate-grammar-of-hellenistic-greek/), which may prove of some benefit to both student and instructor. The morphology attempts to be exhaustive wherever possible. However, there appeared to be no good reason to duplicate the advanced materials found in Blass-Debrunner. Frequency counts in the New Testament are derived from Bruce Metzger's *Lexical Aids*.

The Syntax rests, to a large degree, on a fresh analysis of a selected body of texts. In defining a body of texts for the purpose of the Syntax, it seemed wise to make a selection that would introduce students to the contours of the New Testament as well as to the rudiments of Greek. This double function accounts for the character of the selection (the list may be found on pp. xxiif). In accordance with the aims of descriptive analysis, it was determined to proceed empirically insofar as possible. Although the body of selected texts was relatively small, the hand manipulation of 2,000 sentences, although parsed on cards, proved to be slow and highly inefficient. Nevertheless, segments of the Syntax reflect the effort to read the grammatical signals occurring in a specific compendium of actual Greek sentences without prejudice. When time and strength ran out, it was necessary to fall back on the more conventional use of lexicon and concordance. As a consequence, the grammatical tradition reasserts itself at certain points in the Syntax. The user will doubtless be able to discern which sections represent original analysis, and which traditional categories. In my own defense, I can only say that I finally decided it is the better part of wisdom to publish the fruit of ten years of labor rather than wait upon additional years of work. Such a compromise, now that the first complete edition is appearing, seems fairly modest in retrospect. The present sense of relief at having come to a preliminary conclusion does not relieve the necessity of pushing on to further editions, based on further compilations of data.

It had been my original intention to draw far more on texts outside the New Testament and Apostolic Fathers than has in fact been the case. If it proves possible to reduce a significant number of Greek sentences to a code that can be manipulated by a computer, it will be easily possible to work with a much larger body of data. In that case, the promise of the title (hellenistic Greek) will come to fulfillment; as it stands, it is more promise than achievement. There is, of course, a great risk in attempting a new organization of Greek grammar, based on a fresh collection of data. Those who are gracious enough to share the risk will hopefully make suggestions for improvement, note errors of all proportions, and contribute materially to the further editions which will hopefully follow.

The numbering system devised for this Grammar requires comment. It is basically a three digit system (§§001–999) with the possibility of infinite expansion: each major section has been assigned unused numbers, and indefinite subdivision is possible. In addition to the convenience in numbering the first edition, the system will permit subsequent editions to retain the same span of numbers for the same sections (e.g. Nominal Word Clusters will always be treated in §§680–779). Sections may be added or deleted without having to renumber the entire Grammar.

The rationale underlying the system is simple. Introductory paragraphs are indicated by 0 prefixed to a three digit number (e.g. §0335). Paragraphs that are subsidiary to a preceding paragraph or paragraphs, or which constitute notes or advanced materials, are indicated by numbers suffixed to the three basic digits before the point (e.g. §§3360, 3371). In addition, sections may be further divided by numbers following the point (e.g. §409.1, §4080.3). A note to a subsection is indicated by a second number following the point (e.g. §929.70).

A Fellowship awarded by the American Council of Learned Societies made it possible to bring this first complete edition to a conclusion prior to taking up the next stage of the work; computer and parsing code will occupy me during the balance of the Fellowship period as I collect data for a further edition.

To Lola LaRue, Carol Durant, and Joann Armour, who typed dauntlessly through one version after another, go my undying thanks. Joann Armour produced the final copy for the camera with unusual skill.

Robert W. Funk

Missoula, Montana

18 July 1973

Corrected Edition

For courteous and substantial help with the corrections in this printing, I am especially indebted to Rod Whitacre (Gordon-Conwell Theological Seminary), Clarence B. Hale (International Linguistic Center, Dallas), William G. Doty (University of Massachusetts), Marrilla Hasseries (University of Montana), Judy Hubbard (University of Waterloo), and my colleague, Lane C. McGaughy. Without the help of these and other persons, many a deceptive and deceiving mistake would have been overlooked.

Many promising suggestions have been made for a revised edition. While it was not possible to undertake a revision at this time, eventually a thoroughly revised and augmented edition will be issued, together with an abbreviated student edition. Meanwhile, the patrons of this grammar are invited to share further in its improvement.

Robert W. Funk

Missoula, Montana

24 May 1977

Selected Texts

The following is a list of texts on which this grammar is based.
§§ refer to A. Huck, *Synopsis of the First Three Gospels and Gospel Parallels*

I.   Johannine Literature

    1. 8:12–59
    2. 1 John 1:5–2:17
    3. 1:19–51
    4. 3:1–21
    5. 4:43–54
    6. 5:31–47

II.   Synoptics

Narrative

    7. §6 (Baptism) Mk 1:9–11//Mt 3:13–17//Lk 3:21–22
    8. §11 (Call of Disciples) Mk 1:16–20//Mt 4:18–22

Pronouncement Stories

    9. §206 (Question Concerning Tribute) Mk 12:13–17//Mt 22:15–22//
       Lk 20:20–26
    10. §69 (Plucking Corn) Mk 2:23–28//Mt 12:1–8// Lk 6:1–5

Miracle Stories

    11. §12 (Demoniac) Mk 1:21–28//Mt 7:28–29//Lk 4:31–37
    12. §45 (Leper) Mk 1:40–45//Mt 8:1–4//Lk 5:12–16

Great Sermon

    13. §§18–19 (Intro., Beatitudes) Mt 5:1–12//Lk 6:12, 20–23
    14. §30 (Lord's Prayer) Mt 6:9–15//Lk 11:2–4
    15. §27 (Love of Enemies) Mt 5:43–48//Lk 6:27–28, 32–36
    16. §39 (Golden Rule) Mt 7:12//Lk 6:31
    17. §42 (Self-deception) Mt 7:21–23//Lk 6:46, 13:26–27

Parables

    18. §90 (Sower) Mk 4:1–9//Mt 13:1–9//Lk 8:4–8
    19. §170 (Great Supper) Mt 22:1–10//Lk 14:15–24
    20. §186 (Pharisee and Publican) Lk 18:9–14

Abbreviations

New Testament

Mt	Matthew	2 Thess	2 Thessalonians
Mk	Mark	1 Tim	1 Timothy
Lk	Luke	2 Tim	2 Timothy
Jn	John		Titus
	Acts		Philemon
Rom	Romans	Heb	Hebrews
1 Cor	1 Corinthians	Ja	James
2 Cor	2 Corinthians	2 Pet	2 Peter
Gal	Galatians	1 Jn	1 John
Eph	Ephesians	2 Jn	2 John
Phil	Philippians	3 Jn	3 John
Col	Colossians		Jude
1 Thess	1 Thessalonians	Rev	Revelation

Apostolic Fathers

Barn	Barnabas	Ign	Ignatius
1 Clem	1 Clement	Eph	Ephesians
2 Clem	2 Clement	Mag	Magnesians
Did	Didache	Phld	Philadelphians
Diogn	Diognetus	Pol	Polycarp
Herm	Hermas	Rom	Romans
Man	Mandates	Sm	Smyrnaeans
Sim	Similitudes	Tr	Trallians
Vis	Visions	MPol	Martyrdom of Polycarp
		PolPhil	Polycarp to the Philippians

Septuagint

Gen	Genesis
Exod	Exodus
Deut	Deuteronomy

Symbols

zero form (e.g. of a stem vowel)

>   becomes, changes into

<   is derived from

λ   sonant (vocalic) consonant (§906)

ṷ   semivowel or consonantal vowel (§§150, 905)

*   hypothetical form not actually attested

ˣ   grammatically unacceptable or nonsensical

A background screen marks sections which may be skipped by beginners.

For symbols belonging to the parsing code, s. Appendix IV.

Modern Literature

Bauer:

> W. Bauer, *A Greek-English Lexicon of the New Testament and Other Early Christian Literature*, trans, and adaptation by W. F. Arndt and F. W. Gingrich (Chicago: The University of Chicago Press, 1957)

Bl-D:

> F. Blass and A. Debrunner, *A Greek Grammar of the New Testament and Other Early Christian Literature*, trans, and revised by Robert W. Funk (Chicago: The University of Chicago Press, 1961)

Burton:

> E. de Witt Burton, *Syntax of the Moods and Tenses in New Testament Greek* (Chicago: The University of Chicago Press, 1893)

Fries:

> Charles Carpenter Fries, *The Structure of English* (New York: Harcourt, Brace and World, Inc., 1952)

Gleason:

> H. A. Gleason, Jr., *Linguistics and English Grammar* (New York: Holt, Rinehart and Winston, Inc., 1965)

Jespersen:

> Otto Jespersen, *Growth and Structure of the English Language* (Garden City, New York: Doubleday and Company, Inc., 1956)

Liddell-Scott:

    A Greek-English Lexicon compiled by H. G. Liddell and R. Scott. A new edition rev. by H. S. Jones (Oxford, 1925–40)

Metzger:

    Bruce M. Metzger, *Lexical Aids for Students of New Testament Greek*, New Edition (Princeton, New Jersey: 1969)

Moule:

    C.F.D. Moule, *An Idiom Book of New Testament Greek* (Cambridge, 1953)

Moulton-Howard:

    James Hope Moulton, *A Grammar of New Testament Greek*, Volume II, *Accidence and Word-Formation,* edited by W. F. Howard (Edinburgh: T. & T. Clark, 1919)

Roberts, 1954:

    Paul Roberts, *Understanding Grammar* (New York: Harper & Row, 1954)

Roberts, 1958:

    Paul Roberts, *Understanding English* (New York: Harper & Row, 1958)

Roberts, 1962:

    Paul Roberts, *English Sentences* (New York: Harcourt, Brace and World, Inc., 1962)

Robertson-Davis:

    A. T. Robertson and W. Hersey Davis, *A New Short Grammar of the Greek Testament* (New York: Harper & Brothers Publishers, 1933)

Schwab:

    William Schwab, *Guide to Modern Grammar and Exposition* (New York: Harper & Row, 1967)

Smyth:

    H. W. Smyth, *Greek Grammar*, rev. by Gordon M. Messing (Cambridge: Harvard University Press, 1956)

Strang:

    Barbara M. H. Strang, *Modern English Structure* (London: Edward Arnold Ltd., 1962)

Turner:

    James Hope Moulton, *A Grammar of New Testament Greek*, Volume III, Syntax, by Nigel Turner (Edinburgh: T. & T. Clark, 1963)

Introduction

Learning a Language

How We Understand Sentences

001.   We understand sentences because we know (in the sense of, are able to respond to) (1) *structure signals* and the way they function, and (2) *the meaning of words*. Words fall for the most part into these two categories: (1) structure-signaling words, (2) major vocabulary.

A sharp division cannot be drawn between structure-signaling words and major vocabulary. Words in the lexical stock fall on a spectrum, some veering more towards mere signaling function and therefore lexically empty, and some specializing in meaning.

A look at the Greek lexicon is instructive in this regard. Bauer's entry s.v. ἄγγελος indicates that this word is lexically full. ἄγγελος means *messenger*, of which there are two types: (1) human, (2) supernatural (= *angels*, an English loan-word). There is virtually no discussion of the grammar of ἄγγελος. By contrast, ἵνα is primarily a structure-signaling word. Bauer stipulates that ἵνα has two "meanings": (1) to denote purpose, aim, or goal, (2) to indicate something other than purpose. The vagueness of the word definition is a clue to the lexical problem. Bauer is forced to organize the long entry as a grammar of ἵνα, in relation to the two "meanings" mentioned above. Under the first he treats ἵνα as a conjunction used to introduce purpose (final) clauses; these are divided up in accordance with the tense and mood of the verb which precedes and follows. Under the second "meaning" he treats other constructions for which a ἵνα-clause may substitute. It is thus clear that ἵνα does not "mean" in the lexical sense, but in the grammatical sense. What it "means" are the structures in Greek that it signals. In some cases it may rightly be translated that, in order that, but it "means"—in those same cases—a grammatical structure (a final clause), the corresponding form of which in English is introduced by *in order that*.

Every word participates in structure in some way, and most structure—signaling words have some minimal lexical meaning. For practical purposes, however, vocabulary can be thought of in terms of the two basic categories (Gleason: 97 and n. 8).

002.   It must not be supposed that structure signals are confined to words. Some structure signals are less than words (in English the plural ending *-s* [*-es*], for example, is a structure signal), some are greater than a single word (e.g. *either . . . or*). Only in the case of function words is the structure signal coextensive with the word, and even then there are composite function words and there is often correlation with some other signal (e.g. *both . . . and*; cf. the discussion of ἵνα in §001).

The structure signals or *grammatical devices* of English and Greek may be conveniently divided into five categories (Schwab: 3):

(1) *function words*, such as *the, may, and,* which signal word classes, phrase structure, sentence structure;

(2) *inflections (morphological variables)*, such as the plural ending *-s* and the verbal suffix *-ed*, which signal number, tense, etc.;

(3) *derivational forms*, such as *-ly, -ness,* which often, but not always, signal word classes (e.g. *glad, gladly, gladness*);

(4) *word order* (word constellation), which serves to mark off the limits and internal relations of word groups;

(5) *intonation* (e.g. a falling pitch contour marks *You don't believe me.* ↘ as an assertion in spoken English, as distinguished from a rising pitch contour, *You don't believe me?* ↗ which signals a question). Intonation is represented in the written language partially and imperfectly as *punctuation* (cf. the period and question mark).

It should not be supposed, either, that major vocabulary is confined to words. *Put up,* for example, is a different lexical item than simple *put*, as the sentence, *She put up preserves,* indicates. *Put up with* is still another lexical item, as Winston Churchill observed when he protested: 'The rule, a preposition should not be used to end a sentence, is a piece of nonsense, up with which I will not put.'

Learning the Structure Signals

003.   It is commonly supposed that the major task in learning a new language is learning the lexical meanings of words. This is not in fact the case. The more important as well as the more difficult task is learning the grammatical structures and structure signals (Gleason: 98).

The basic significance of grammatical structures and structure signals in relation to major vocabulary is illustrated by the following text, which has been stripped of all major vocabulary.

In his _____ _____, [Socrates] was _____-ed in the _____ _____ of his
_____ and was _____-ed with _____ the _____. _____ he _____-ed the
_____ _____ of _____ and _____-ing. He _____-ed the _____
with whom he _____ in _____ about the _____ _____ of _____. He was a
5   _____ of _____ _____ and _____ _____ of _____. He was _____ _____
to _____ and _____. In _____ he was _____-ed by a _____ _____ on the
_____ of _____-ing _____ _____ and of _____-ing the _____. He was
_____-ed _____ to _____. He _____-ed to _____. _____ _____ after his
_____ he _____ the _____.

The structure of sentences and word groups is clearly discernible, although the major lexical items have been omitted, with the exception of the subject of the paragraph, Socrates. For example, the sentence beginning in line 3 *He* _____ *-ed the* _____ is evidently composed of the "subject" *he*, a verb in the past tense (indicated by the morpheme -ed), and an "object" (*the* _____); the object is then expanded by a relative clause, *with whom . . . .* Similarly, the native speaker of English knows that the sentence beginning in line 4 is that type of sentence in which the "subject" is identified. Taking *He was a* _____ as a sentence frame, any number of predicate nouns might be found to fit:

> *He was a philosopher*
> *He was a Greek*
> *He was a father*

The predicate, however, is expanded by a prepositional phrase initiated by *of*. We therefore have this frame: *He was a* _____ *of* _____ _____. One might also fill in this frame at random:

> *He was a philosopher of great wisdom*
> *He was a Greek of great renown*

The choice of vocabulary is of course limited by the frame, i.e. by the grammatical structure. Given the frame, the speaker of English knows that certain possibilities are "ungrammatical":

> *He was a good*
>
> *He was a very*
>
> *He was a philosopher of extremely wisdom*

This is to say that the native user of English instinctively knows which vocabulary items are possible choices for each slot.

The grammatical frame of reference is the system within which major vocabulary can be distributed in accordance with rules governing the filling of particular slots or the structure of phrases and the structure of the sentence. Violation of these rules produces phrases and sentences that are grammatically unacceptable or nonsensical.

The prior requirement for the use of a language is knowledge of the grammatical system, i.e. of the grammatical structures and structure signals. This means, with reference to the emasculated text given above, that one must be able to "read" the grammatical frame of reference before he can make any intelligent use of major vocabulary. This appears to be proved by the way in which we actually learn to read and understand languages. We know that a reader can make some sense of a text even when he doesn't know all the major vocabulary, but that he can make no sense of a text for which the structure signals are missing or jumbled. *He was a _____ of great wisdom* makes some sense, even when the reader does not know the meaning of the word *philosopher*, represented here by a blank. But the reader can do little with a sentence like *ˣWas philosopher of Socrates great a wisdom* because the structure signals are jumbled. He might put a question mark at the end because he knows questions are often introduced by the verb (in contrast to assertions).

In reading a language we already know, we are often compelled by limited vocabulary to leave certain blanks in the text. We either fill them in by the general sense of the text, or by looking them up in a dictionary. Suppose one wishes to read the paragraph about Socrates but does not know all the words. Twenty-two vocabulary items are omitted in this version:

In his __(1)__ life Socrates was __(2)__ -ed in the __(3)__ philosophy of his time and was __(4)__ -ed with Archelaus the __(5)__ . Later he developed the __(6)__ Socratic method of inquiry and __(7)__ -ing He __(8)__ -ed the people with whom he came in __(9)__ about the right __(10)__ of life. He was a man of __(11)__ physique and great powers of __(12)__ . He was __(13)__ *indifferent to comfort and* __(14)__ . In 399 BCE he was tried by a popular __(15)__ on the charge of introducing strange (16) and of (17) -ing the youth. He was (18) -ed to death. He (19) -ed to escape. (20) days after his (21) he drank the (22) .

Although many of the words are missing, it is still possible to gain certain information from the text and guess at still more. If, however, twenty-two words like *in, was, and, the, a, he* were omitted instead of major vocabulary, how much more difficult it would be to make sense of the whole! Consequently, while we can get along in a language with a limited vocabulary, we cannot get along without knowledge of grammatical structure.

The complete text from which the two versions above were drawn reads as follows (it should be noted that not all the lexical choices are necessarily the best ones; an authority on Socrates might well prefer other major vocabulary than the words supplied):

> In his early life Socrates was interested in the scientific philosophy of his time and was associated with Archelaus the physicist. Later he developed the famous Socratic method of inquiry and teaching. He questioned the people with whom he came in contact about the right conduct of life.
> He was a man of strong physique and great powers of endurance. He was completely indifferent to comfort and luxury. In 399 B.C. he was tried by a popular jury on the charge of introducing strange gods and of corrupting the youth. He was condemned to death. He refused to escape. Thirty days after his condemnation he drank the hemlock.

004.   The role played by structure signals in the grammatical system of a language can be exemplifed in yet another way, namely by means of nonsense language. Nonsense language is created by employing lexically empty major vocabulary within the framework of the grammatical devices or structure signals of the language. In the often cited English nonsense sentence (Fries: 71)

(i)   *Woggles ugged diggles*

the signals *-s, -ed, -s*, in that sequence, indicate that the first and third words are "thing" words and plural, that the middle term is an "action" word referring to past time. The syntactical relations among the three are also indicated by the sequence: *Woggles* must be the "subject" of the verb, *ugged*, and *diggles* the "object." On the basis of the structure signals of English and without knowledge of the lexical meaning of a single word, it is possible to construct other "grammatically correct" sentences with these same terms:

(ii)   *Woggles ugg diggles*
(iii)   *A woggle uggs a diggle*
(iv)   *Woggles will ugg diggles*
(v)   *Diggles have been ugged by woggles*
(vi)   *The woggles which ugged diggles were ugging woggles*

In our nonsense language use has been made of only two "thing" words and one "action" word, plus the structural items of standard English. We could enlarge the scope of our language by creating one new word:

(vii)   *Woggles are fabothful*

Our knowledge of English tells us that the morpheme *-ful* identifies the new word as a descriptive word; this is confirmed by its position after *are* in the sentence. On this basis we can now create an additional sentence:

(viii) *Woggles ugg fabothfully*

and then expand it:

(ix)   *The fabothful woggles ugged diggles fabothfully.*

(ix) shows that *fabothful* may "modify" a "thing" word, and *fabothfully* an "action" word.

If we add the English structure word *and* to our repertoire, it is possible to introduce other structures, e.g.

(x)   *Woggles and diggles have been ugged*

in which two "subjects" are linked to a single verb. And may also link two sentences:

(xi)   *Woggles ugg diggles and diggles ugg woggles*

Nonsense sentences (i)–(xi) contain at least four sentence structures basic to English:

(a)   *Woggles ugg fabothfully*   (viii)

which may be transformed into a sentence with English lexical items:

Altos sing beautifully

(b) *Woggles are fabothful* (vii)

Sunsets are beautiful

(c) *Woggles ugged diggles* (i)

Teachers harassed students

(d) *Diggles have been ugged by waggles* (v)

Students have been harassed by teachers

English nonsense sentences demonstrate that grammatical structure in some important respects is independent of the lexical meaning of major vocabulary items. One does not learn the meaningful arrangement of words by learning major vocabulary. *Teacher the students harassed the* contains standard English vocabulary but is only a jumble of words. It is this important fact that justifies the assertion that in learning a language the prior and more important task is learning the structures and structure signals.

005.1 In the nonsense sentence, *Woggles ugged diggles*, *-s, -ed,* and *-s* are *morphological variables* providing clues to the structure of the sentence. They are called morphological variables because they have to do with the change in the form of words in contrast to some other possible form (*woggles* is shown by *-s* to be plural, in contrast to the singular form *woggle*, without *-s*).

005.2 In the modern printed Greek text the discrete items on the page are (for the most part) words, e.g. πάλιν, αὐτοῖς, ἐλάλησεν. Some of these never vary in form, e.g. πάλιν, οὖν, ἐν. Others vary in form in accordance with their function within the structure of the word cluster or sentence, e.g. αὐτοῖς, ἐλάλησεν. Morphological variables occurring in words therefore indicate word relationships and participate, along with other features of the language, in the larger structure or system known as grammar.

005.3 The signals ἐ- - - -σεν (ἐλάλησεν, Jn 8:12) indicate that the word in question is a verb, that it refers to past time, that the "subject" is singular and acting rather than being acted upon. On this basis one can readily identify the following: ἐ-πία-σεν (Jn 8:20), ἐ-ποίη-σεν (Jn 8:40), ἐ-τύφλω-σεν (1 Jn 2:11). The signals τοῦ- - - -ου (τοῦ κόσμου, Jn 8:12) suggest that the word in question is a "thing" word, that it is singular in number, and that it stands in a "genitive" (i.e. "of," see §112.1) relation to some other word or word group in the sentence. Cf. τοῦ ἀνθρώπου (Jn 8:28), τοῦ θεοῦ (Jn 8:40), τοῦ ἱεροῦ (Jn 8:59).

005.4 The Greek sentence, like the English sentence, exhibits certain structure signals in the form of morphological variables that the competent reader of Greek is able to "read" at a glance. In the sentence

(1) ἡ σκοτία ἐτύφλωσεν τοὺς ὀφθαλμοὺς αὐτοῦ   1 Jn 2:11

the signals ἡ- - - -α and τοὺς- - - -οὺς indicate that the items in question are "thing" words, in the first instance singular, in the second plural. The signals ἐ- - - -σεν indicate the word in question is a verb, with reference to past time. ἡ- - - -α indicates, furthermore, that the first word group is "subject," τοὺς - - - -οὺς that the third word group is "object," of the verb. The signal -ου, as part of the last word, indicates that this word stands in a "genitive" relation to some other item in the sentence.

005.5 Readers will grasp (1) as a whole consisting of three parts, probably of this order:

ἡ σκοτία / ἐτύφλωσεν / τοὺς ὀφθαλμοὺς αὐτοῦ.

They will be led to grasp the first and third word clusters as units because of the sequence of morphological variables, ἡ -α go together as feminine article (*the*) and feminine noun, nominative singular. τοὺς -οὺς go together as masculine article and masculine noun, accusative plural. They also knows that nominal word clusters commonly embrace a "modifying genitive," so that αὐτοῦ is taken with the preceding cluster.

005.6 *Position* (*word order*) also plays a role in seizing word groups, e.g. the words in the first and third clusters occur together and in some acceptable order: the position of article (ἡ, τούς) and noun (σκοτία, ὀφθαλμούς) in relation to each other is fixed—the article always precedes; the genitive αὐτοῦ (pronoun), however, may also come between or before article and noun (and occasionally may be separated from its word group). Word order plays a significant but quite different role in Greek sentence structure than in English.

006.1 There are other structure signals in Greek, as in English, in addition to the morphological variable and word order. Another group of signals consists of words, some of which are fixed in form (indeclinables), and some of which vary in form (inflected). This category is called *function words* (cf. §002). In the case of inflected function words, the morphological variable(s) and the word as a whole, as signals of different orders, converge.

006.2 Questions in Greek are often signaled by interrogative words. In the sentence

(2) ποῦ ἐστιν ὁ πατήρ σου;   Jn 8:19
Where is your father?

ποῦ is an interrogative adverb corresponding to English *where?*. It is fixed in form. On the other hand, τίς is an interrogative pronominal adjective that is inflected. In the sentence

(3) τίς ἐστιν ἡ μήτηρ μου;   Mk 3:33
Who is my mother?

τίς not only signals a question, but its role in the structure of the sentence is indicated by its case form (nominative); it is "subject" of the verb ἐστιν.

006.3 Some function words typically signal subordinate clauses (included dependent sentences).

(4) ταῦτα λέγω ἵνα ὑμεῖς σωθῆτε   Jn 5:34
I say these things in order that you may be saved

In (4) ἵνα indicates that a final (purpose) clause is being joined to the main sentence. Similarly, εἰ regularly introduces a subordinate clause which serves as the protasis (if-clause) of a conditional sentence:

(5) εἰ ἐμὲ ᾔδειτε, καὶ τὸν πατέρα μου ἂν ᾔδειτε   Jn 8:19
If you had known me, you would have known my father also

Such function words as ἵνα and εἰ are known as subordinators.

006.4 Another subclass of function words is known as conjunctions. They are employed to connect or relate sentence elements of the same or similar order. They may be single words, as in

(6) ἐπίστευσεν αὐτὸς καὶ ἡ οἰκία ὅλη   Jn 4:53
He and his whole house believed

where καί links two subjects with a single verb; its grammatical function therefore corresponds to and in the translation, καί is thus an essential clue in the structure of (6). Two such conjunctions may be correlated:

(7) οὔτε ἐμὲ οἴδατε οὔτε τὸν πατέρα μου   Jn 8:19
You know neither me nor my father

οὔτε . . . οὔτε links two objects to a single verb and thus corresponds to *neither . . . nor* in the translation.

006.5 ἵνα, εἰ, καί, οὔτε are fixed in form, but not all function words in these subclasses are indeclinable.

007.1 *Derivational forms* are of assistance in assigning words to word classes. The word *sad* in English is an adjective, as illustrated by the sentence, *that face is sad*, to which the phrase, *that sad face*, is related. By adding the suffix *-ly*, *sad* is turned into an adverb: *sadly*. The suffix *-ness* transforms the same word into a noun: *sadness*. The class membership of derivational forms is grammatically significant. The native user of English knows that the sentence *ˣthat face is sadly*, or the phrase *ˣthat sadly face*, is grammatically unacceptable. The matter can be rectified by adding or inserting an adjective:

> *That face is sadly wrinkled*
> *That sadly wrinkled face.*

Or again, sadness fits certain sentence frames that sad and sadly do not. For example, we may say

> *He had a profound sense of sadness*

but not:

> *ˣHe had a profound sense of sad*
> *ˣHe had a profound sense of sadly*
> *ˣThat sadness face.*

The derivational pattern of *sad*, *sadly*, *sadness* is sufficiently common in English as to suggest other analogous sets:

> *glad, gladly, gladness*
> *mad, madly, madness*
> *bad, badly, badness*

On the basis of the derivational forms the class membership of these terms is immediately evident to the speaker of English, in practice if not formally.

007.2 Derivational forms are also of use in identifying the class membership of words in Greek. A pattern not unlike that illustrated in §007.1 is exemplified by

δίκαιος	*righteous* (adjective)
δικαιοσύνη	*righteousness* (noun)
δικαίως	*justly* (adverb)

Other nouns may be developed from the same stem:

δικαίωμα	*righteous act*
δικαίωσις	*justification*

-συνη, -μα, -σις are noun suffixes, just as -ως is an adverb suffix.

007.3   On the basis of these derivational suffixes, the following words can be identified as nouns:

ἐλεημοσύνη	*charity*
ὄνομα	*name*
πνεύμα	*spirit*
γνῶσις	*knowledge*

And the following can be identified as adverbs:

ἀληθῶς	*truly*
ταχέως	*quickly*

The examples of nouns and adverbs listed above do not necessarily follow the pattern of δίκαιος in other respects.

008.   The structure-signaling devices of Greek form a *coherent* and *finite* system. Because the system is coherent, the structure signals of any phrase, sentence or series of sentences are to be read as a constellation of signals pointing to one grammatical structure or set of structures, in distinction from other possible structures or set of structures. If the structure is "grammatical," the signals will converge in pointing to that structure. That is only to say that "grammaticality" and coherence of the structure-signaling system are one and the same thing. It goes without saying that no grammatical system is perfect, i.e. free of ambiguity.

Because the grammatical system is finite it can be learned without having to learn all possible Greek sentences. The potential output of Greek sentences is infinite, but the grammatical system is sufficiently restricted so that many men, women, and children—not all of whom were bright or linguistically gifted—were able to learn to read and speak Greek.

The Aims of Descriptive Grammar

009.   A descriptive grammar must achieve two things: 1) it must develop a classification of words and other elements; 2) it must state the grammatical relations that obtain among these elements (Gleason: 138).

   The two aims of descriptive grammar may be modestly elaborated, with particular reference to the shape of the present grammar. The balance of the introduction will thus be an immediate introduction to and sketch of the content of the grammar.

The Classification of Words and Other Elements

010.1   The classification of words and other elements must be based on structural, i.e. grammatical, features. Meaning-based classification is not very helpful for two reasons: a) definitions of parts of speech based on meaning tend to be ambiguous; b) such definitions do not conform to the grammatical features of a language (Gleason: 115ff.; Fries: 65–86, 87f., 202ff.). If classification is derived from structure, however, there are two sets of criteria which may be used, and these do not always coincide: 1) One set of criteria may be derived from the words themselves, i.e. from morphological criteria; 2) Another may be derived from the ways a word may be used in a sentence. The ideal would be to achieve a classification that would integrate these two sets as fully as possible.

010.2   Classification by definition may not be feasible in any case. It is difficult to achieve definitions that account for all the phenomena. One may circumvent definition by making use of a set of characteristics that circumscribes a category or class of words (the method of C. C. Fries). In the case of extremely small classes, like negatives, personal pronouns, and the like, one may classify by listing all, or nearly all, the examples. In the case of large classes, one may classify by comparison, i.e. by inquiring, presumably of someone with native response, whether a certain item belongs to one class or another. Native users of a language undoubtedly learn to classify words in just this way. Such a method would only approximate the requirements of a grammar, but it may well have considerable pedagogical value (Gleason: 118ff.).

011.1   Words and other elements in Greek have been customarily classified in relation to traditional "parts of speech," e.g. noun, adjective, verb, etc. One of the respects in which this grammar remains conventional is in its use of "parts of speech." The road to a purely descriptive analysis of the "parts of speech" in Greek appears to be long. Yet some preliminary steps can be taken in that direction. While conventional terminology is retained, some significant modifications have been introduced. It is therefore necessary to state at the outset what is meant by "parts of speech," to indicate how the labels are used in this grammar. It is also necessary to stipulate that there are points at which strict usage breaks down; this failure poses problems for the theoretician, but it does not constitute a major impediment for the beginner, nor, for that matter, for the first stages of descriptive analysis.

011.2 The "parts of speech" as employed in this grammar are based in the first instance on purely morphological considerations. The basic groups are distinguished by means of criteria relative to an inflectional system. This procedure yields three fundamental divisions:

I. Words belonging to the nominal system
II. Words belonging to the verbal system
III.Words fixed in form, i.e. uninflected

The breakdown of these larger categories has proceeded, moreover, along morphological lines, insofar as possible. Certain inflectional patterns are readily isolable within the first and second categories, while other subgroups are more or less arbitrary. In division III, it will be necessary to invoke other than morphological criteria. As a consequence, "parts of speech" refer first of all to morphological distinctions, and secondly to grammatical distinctions. It will be necessary finally to integrate these two sets of data (§010.1).

Where, for example, the term "noun" is used, it is to be understood as denoting a word that belongs to a particular inflectional system, in this case the nominal system. "Adjectives" and "pronouns" also belong to the nominal system, but they can be distinguished from each other and from nouns on purely morphological grounds. That is not to say that each is distinguishable in a given sentence on this basis; distinctions depend upon referring specific items to the inflectional system as a whole.

"Parts of speech" are particularly useful, as a consequence, in helping the student to come to terms with the morphological aspects of the language. This aspect constitutes a serious hurdle for most beginners. Once the inflectional systems and patterns have been grasped, it is then possible to employ "parts of speech" in grammatical descriptions. For example, to say that a "noun" characteristically appears as the head term in word clusters occurring as the "subject" in sentences, is to say that a word belonging to a certain inflectional system and pattern commonly occurs as the head term in such clusters. It is not to say that "nouns" are normally "subjects," or that "nouns" are the names of persons, places, or things.

011.3 Even so, the lines among these major divisions and among the subdivisions are by no means entirely clear. There is a certain amount of duplication and many areas of gray. It will be helpful, consequently, to set out the categories and define them as closely as possible, while maintaining a certain reservation with respect to their precision.

I. Words Belonging to the Nominal System

012.1 *Nouns.* Formally, nouns have one gender (though they may be used in more than one gender, or fluctuate in gender), and are inflected for four cases, and normally two numbers (singular and plural). A noun is a word that belongs to one of three declensions presented in §§130–203. Unfortunately, there is a group of so-called nouns that are only partially declined or indeclinable (consisting largely of foreign proper names taken into Greek). Here we fall back, in part, on the traditional definition of a noun: these words are taken to be nouns because they are "like" Greek nouns, i.e. they name something. But they are "like" nouns in a more important respect: they occur in those structures in which nouns appear.

012.2 *Pronouns.* While pronouns also belong to the nominal system, they are restricted in person and/or number and/or gender and/or case. As a consequence, they manifest declension patterns that are comparable to those of adjectives, only restricted (§§256–2580).

012.3 *Adjectives.* Adjectives differ formally from nouns in that they are inflected for *three* genders (masculine and feminine may be identical in form) rather than one. This makes it possible for the relation of adjective as "modifier" to any noun as head term to be signaled by agreement in gender, number and case. In other respects adjectives follow the inflectional patterns of nouns (§§220–2451).

012.4 *Pronominal adjectives.* Pronominal adjectives are declined like adjectives, but appear exclusively or also in structures in which adjectives do not appear. Since this group belongs morphologically with adjectives, its isolation depends entirely on syntactical criteria (§§259–274).

II. Words Belonging to the Verbal System

013.1   *Verbs.* Finite verbs are formally distinguished by personal endings. They are also marked by morphological variables that specify tense, mood, voice. They have tense and voice in common with infinitives and participles, but not mood and personal endings, which the latter lack. Verbs follow the inflectional patterns treated in §§300–496.

013.2   *Infinitives.* The infinitive is a "verbal noun" in a fixed case, yet it exhibits "tense" (§§0309ff.) and voice like finite verbs (§§464–4662).

013.3   *Participles.* The participle is a "verbal adjective." It is declined like an adjective, yet it also manifests the morphological markers of "tense" (§§0309ff.) and voice like finite verbs (§§246–250; 0467–469). Though participles must be considered under both the nominal and the verbal systems, for convenience they are listed here only under the verbal system.

013.4   The assumption here, as in the case of the nominal system, is that words belonging to these groups can be identified formally, on morphological grounds, without recourse to function in the sentence or lexical meaning. The sole exception thus far is pronominal adjectives (§012.4), which belong formally to the category of adjectives.

III. Words Fixed in Form (Uninflected)

014.1   Words fixed in form are sometimes collected together under the general rubric of "adverbs" or "particles." Distinctions cannot easily be made on a formal basis. Yet there are some natural groups which can be isolated on the basis of form in combination with the structures in which they characteristically appear.

014.2   *Adverbs.* The adverb is characterized by a fixed case form (often obscured) and/or certain suffixes (also fixed in form). Some adverbs are also subject to comparison (positive, comparative, superlative), in which case they are not, strictly speaking, uninflected. The adverb is further distinguishable from the preposition (to which it is closely related) in that the adverb does not "govern a case."

014.3   *Prepositions.* The preposition is an adverb which has come to "govern a case," i.e. it is used with a case that is thought to depend upon the preposition. Prepositions are conventionally divided into "proper" and "improper" prepositions, depending upon whether or not they can also be joined with a verb to form a compound word. The proper preposition can be so employed, the "improper" preposition cannot.

014.4 *Particles.* The remaining words fixed in form may be termed particles for want of a better term. Particles include negatives, sequence words (conjunctions, sentence connectors, subordinators), modalizers and nuance words.

014.5 It is obvious that the breakdown of division III depends more on grammatical than on morphological criteria. Subdivisions will therefore require justification in the syntax (Part III).

Syntactic Relations

015.1 The second step in a descriptive grammar is to state the grammatical relations that obtain between and among words and other elements in the language (§009), as classified on a morphological or other basis (§§010–014).

As illustrated in §003, the native user of a language knows what possibilties are open to him in filling an empty slot in a given sentence frame. This knowledge suggests that word classes coincide in some important respect with other grammatical features. It appears, for example, that sentences in Greek, as in English, most often consist of "subject" and "predicate," and that the "subject" is correlated to a greater or lesser degree with the word class nouns, while the "predicate" is closely related to the word class verbs. An extensive statement of the relations between these features proves to be a very complicated matter. It is made no less complicated by the fact that various word classes require subdivision into smaller classes, and many words belong to more than one class.

015.2 For the purposes of this grammar a less than exhaustive statement of the relations between and among word classes and other grammatical devices is quite satisfactory. Some restriction is, in fact, necessary. Preoccupation with the marginal features of Greek, which would be required in an exhaustive grammar, only misleads where the beginner is struggling to form something like native responses to the bread-and-butter features of the language.

016.1 *Open and restricted word classes.* The simplest sentence pattern consists of noun and finite verb (qualification in §504):

<pre>
        1   2   1   2
(1) γυνὴ / ἀπέθανεν   a woman / died
</pre>

We may use a slash (/) to mark off the noun from the verb and thus the "subject" from the "predicate," and designate the former 1 and the latter 2 (a kind of shorthand to enable us to speak more efficiently of the sentence parts, without having to give a full description each time).

If it is now asked what may stand as element 1 in a sentence of this type, a tentative reply would be: only a noun or some other item in the nominal system. This implies that a finite verb cannot function as "subject." The reverse is also true: only a finite verb or some other item from the verbal system may appear as item 2. Such a generalization does not tell us much specifically about the grammar of Greek, but it does indicate that the "subject" [1] and "predicate" [2] of the sentence are correlated, in some important respects, with the two major word classes represented by the nominal and verbal systems, respectively.

016.2 The generalization that some item from the nominal system must stand as element 1 in the sentence appears to be confirmed by substituting grammatically acceptable words for γυνὴ in sentence (1):

	1	2		1	2
(2)	ἀνὴρ / ἀπέθανεν			a man / died	
	τὸ παιδίον / ἀπέθανεν			the child / died	
	ἡ θυγάτηρ σου / ἀπέθανεν			your daughter / died	
	Ἀβραάμ / ἀπέθανεν			Abraham / died	
	ἀπέθανον / οἱ προφῆται			the prophets / died	

Element 1 in every case is a noun or a word group "headed" by a noun. Words like ἀνήρ, παιδίον, Ἀβραάμ belong to the word class, nouns, which is virtually numberless. It is therefore an open or unrestricted word class.

016.3 One might go so far as to say that any noun may substitute for γυνή in sentence (1):

	1	2		1	2
(3)	δένδρον / ἀπέθανεν			a tree / died	
(4)	βιβλίον / ἀπέθανε			a scroll / died	
(5)	οἶκος / ἀπέθανεν			a house / died	

So long as we are concerned solely with grammar, sentences (4) and (5) are quite acceptable. It may be difficult to imagine the circumstances under which they might be spoken or written, but they belong, nevertheless, to the potential of the language since they conform to the grammatical system.

016.4 For the verb in sentence (1) various acceptable substitutions are likewise easily possible:

	1	2		1	2
(6)	γυνὴ /	μένει		*a woman /*	*abides*
	2	1		1	2
	μένουσιν /	οἱ προφῆται		*the prophets /*	*endure*
	1	2		1	2
(7)	ὁ παῖς /	ζῇ		*the child /*	*lives*
	2	1		1	2
	ζῇ /	ἡ θυγάτηρ σου		*your daughter /*	*lives*

Words like ἀπέθανεν, μένει, ζῇ belong to the word class, verbs, which is also virtually numberless. Verbs and nouns therefore comprise open or unrestricted word classes.

016.5 Verbs and nouns (together with adjectives, adverbs, and infinitives and participles, which are made from verbs) constitute the bulk of the major vocabulary in Greek. Words belonging to these classes may be freely created, change meaning, and die in the history of the language. It is therefore impossible to specify by listing what nouns may appear as element 1 in the sentence, or what verb may appear as element 2. We must be satisfied to say that a sentence like (1) is comprised of a nominal element as "subject" and a verbal element as "predicate."

016.6 These large open or unrestricted word classes are quite distinct from other smaller word classes, the items of which function primarily as structure signals and can be specified by listing.

017.1 The Greek negative adverbs are illustrative of a very small, closed word class.

	1	N> 2		1	2
(8)	γυνὴ /	οὐκ ἀπέθανεν		*a woman /*	*did not die*

A second negative adverb is μή. To this word class we may arbitrarily give the designation *N.* οὐκ and μή may be distinguished from all other adverbs by virtue of the grammatical constructions into which they may enter that other adverbs may not. Cf. §§613–617.

017.2 It was stipulated in §016.1 that the "subject" of a sentence like (1) must be a nominal item. The personal pronouns belong to the nominal system and so may appear as element 1 in the sentence. Yet they constitute a closed or restricted word class, the members of which can be listed.

    1   2   1   2

(9) αὐτὴ / ἀπέθνῃσκεν   *she / was dying*

In (9) αὐτή is a pronoun specifying that the "subject" of the verb is feminine and singular (= *she*). Apart from some context in which this sentence appears, it would be impossible to specify further what is meant by αὐτή. It is for this reason that pronouns are sometimes defined as substitutes for nouns. In one context (Lk 8:42), the antecedent of αὐτή is θυγάτηρ, *daughter*. αὐτή is therefore also a sequence word in that it indicates the continuity of subject matter in contexts where it is inappropriate to express the noun in each sentence or phrase where it is called for. As a consequence, the personal pronouns belong more to the structure-signaling elements of the language than to its major vocabulary.

017.3 On the basis of §017.1–2 one may generalize: closed or restricted word classes belong more intimately to that class of words called function words (§§001, 002, 006) than to major vocabulary, since they participate more directly in the grammatical system. Conversely, the major vocabulary of the language is made up primarily of open-ended word classes.

018. It is impossible to speak of the grammar of Greek without speaking of more than morphology and words. A morphological variable or a word belongs to a grammatical system that transcends the isolated morpheme or word. The reach of the system is stratified. For example, one may speak of the grammar of the phrase

(10) ἡ θυγάτηρ σου   *your daughter*

in which the head term, θυγάτηρ, is "modified" by the article ἡ and the genitive of the personal pronoun, σου (lit. *the daughter of you*).

The phrase (10) also belongs, of course, to a sentence such as

    1   2   1   2

(11) ἡ θυγάτηρ σου / ζῇ   *your daughter / lives*

in which the phrase (10) appears as the "subject" of the verb, ζῇ. We then have a "complete" sentence with "subject" and "predicate."

The reach of the system extends even beyond the sentence. If we take a sequence of sentences, such as

$$
\begin{array}{cccc}
1 & \text{N>} \ 2 & 1 & 2 \\
\text{(12)} \ \ \dot{\eta} \ \vartheta \upsilon \gamma \acute{\alpha} \tau \eta \rho \ \sigma \upsilon \ / \ \upsilon \dot{\upsilon} \kappa \ \dot{\alpha} \pi \acute{\epsilon} \vartheta \alpha \nu \epsilon \nu. & & \alpha \dot{\upsilon} \tau \dot{\eta} \ / \ \zeta \widehat{\eta}. \\
1 & 2 & 1 & 2 \\
\textit{Your daughter} \ / \ \textit{did not die.} & & \textit{She} \ / \ \textit{lives.}
\end{array}
$$

it can be observed that the "subject" of the second sentence, αὐτή, functions to link the "subject" of the second sentence with the "subject" of the first.

In speaking of a grammatical system it is thus necessary to speak of it with respect to overlapping and interrelated levels: the structure of the phrase can be learned in isolation but it must also be learned in the context of the sentence; sentence structure can be learned in isolation, but it, too, must ultimately be referred to sequences of sentences and the construction of such larger units as the paragraph.

019.1 The question confronted by learners of a language, and antecedently the grammarian who teaches them, is how best to take hold of a new language. Aside from becoming initially acquainted with a system of morphological variables that may vary considerably from that employed in their own native languages (e.g. Greek in relation to English), beginners are advised—according to most modern linguists—to endeavor to seize the language at its most immediately workable level, namely the sentence. One learns to use a language (beyond the halting use of single words coupled with sign language) by comprehending sentences. With a few model sentences in hand, novices are in a position to make some use of a language, however pressed they may be to make themselves articulate. A knowledge of morphology, major vocabulary and even phrase structure does not necessarily make a language usable apart from some acquaintance with sentence structure.

019.2 If the sentence is assigned a certain priority for practical, pedagogical reasons, that priority is supported to a large degee by the requirements of descriptive grammar. Word classes, for example, can finally be sorted out only in the context of the sentence. And it is necessary to work with the sentence (and the sequence of sentences) in mapping out the complex network of relationships between and among constructions. In short, the sentence provides a more vi-able focus for descriptive grammar than the word or phrase, and yet primary attention to the sentence does not require that attention to the sentence be diverted from word classification and phrase structure. The sentence is the point of departure, moreover, for the consideration of sentence-transcending structures and devices.

020.1 The Greek language, like English, functions largely with a set of commonly recurring sentence structures. These structures are used over and over again, with modification and expansion, of course. The constituent elements of the sentence consist largely of commonly recurring phrase structures. The structure of sentences and phrases is surprisingly monotonous. It would be even more monotonous were it not possible to include some sentences within the framework of other sentences (subordination) , and to link and connect sentences and parts of sentences by various devices (coordination). Nevertheless, subordinated or included sentences reflect the same basic sentence patterns, modified or transformed in accordance with regular rules so as to make grammatical inclusion possible. Greek thus makes highly repetitious use of a relatively small set of grammatical structures, which are modified and varied within the limits of these structures.

020.2 A commonly recurring sentence pattern in Greek consists of subject, transitive verb, and direct object.

$$\begin{matrix} 2 & 1 & 4 & & 1 & 2 & 4 \end{matrix}$$
(13) οἶδεν / ὁ Πέτρος / τὸν ἄνθρωπον   *Peter / knows / the man*

The subject is set off by slashes and designated 1, the verb is designated 2, as above (§016.1); a slash (/) may also be used to mark off other elements in the sentence, and 4 designates the direct object.

(13) is identical in structure with

$$\begin{matrix} 2 & 1 & 4 & & 1 & 2 & 4 \end{matrix}$$
(14) εἶδεν / ὁ λαὸς / τὸν ἄνθρωπον   *The people / saw / the man*

in that it also consists of subject, transitive verb, and direct object.

020.3 Sentences may be said to be *enate* (Gleason: 199ff.) if they have identical structures. Sentences (13) and (14) are fully enate, i.e. they correspond grammatically item for item as well as in structure. If enation is restricted to structure, sentences may be enate even though they do not correspond item for item. For example,

$$\begin{array}{cccc} 2 & 1 & 4 & 1 \; 2 \qquad 4 \end{array}$$
(15) οἶδα / ἐγὼ / τὸν ἄνθρωπον   *I / know / the man*

is enate to (13) and (14) in structure, although a noun phrase has been replaced by a personal pronoun (ἐγώ). However, the personal pronoun subject does not normally appear in Greek:

$$\begin{array}{ccc} 2\text{-}1 & 4 & 1 \; 2 \qquad 4 \end{array}$$
(16) οἶδα / τὸν ἄνθρωπον   *I / know / the man*

In (16) the subject is signaled solely by the personal ending attached to the verb. Yet (16) remains structurally enate to (15). Further, the object may be represented by a personal pronoun rather than by a noun phrase:

$$\begin{array}{ccc} 2\text{-}1 & 4 & 1 \; 2 \qquad 4 \end{array}$$
(17) οἶδα / αὐτόν   *I / know / him*

The structure of (17) remains identical with that of (13)–(16) although all items but one have been modified.

020.4   The direct object (4) in sentences (13)–(17) is either a word or a noun phrase. For this type of object may be substituted an included sentence or clause without altering the structure:

$$\begin{array}{ccc} 2\text{-}1 & S^4 & 1 \; 2 \qquad S^4 \end{array}$$
(18) οἶδα / τὶ λέγεις   *I / know / what you mean*

Let *S* stand for an included sentence, to which is attached a raised [4] to indicate that the included sentence appears in the structure of object. (18) may be resolved into two sentences:

$$\begin{array}{cc} 2\text{-}1 & 1 \; 2 \end{array}$$
(18a) οἶδα / (4)   *I / know / (4)*

$$\begin{array}{cccc} 4 & 2\text{-}1 & 4 \quad 2 \; 1 & 2 \end{array}$$
(18b) τί / λέγεις;   *what / do / you / mean?*

The sentence (18b) is included in (18a) without internal modification, although in (18) the direct question of (18b) has become an indirect question.

020.5   The included sentence, however, may be incorporated into the larger structure by means of some modification. In that case it becomes an included *dependent* sentence:

$$\overset{\text{1} \qquad \text{2} \qquad \text{s}^4}{}$$

(19) οἱ ὄχλοι / εἶδον / ὃ ἐποίησεν Παῦλος

$$\overset{\text{1} \qquad \text{2} \qquad \text{s}^4}{}$$

The crowd / saw / what Paul did

The capital S is changed to small s to indicate that the included sentence is dependent. Unlike S^4 in (18), s^4 in (19) may not stand as an independent sentence when divorced from its larger context. Rather, (19) is composed of two sentences, one of which has been modified:

$$\overset{\text{1} \qquad \text{2}}{} \qquad\qquad\qquad \overset{\text{1} \qquad \text{2}}{}$$

(19a) οἱ ὄχλοι / εἶδον / (4)   *The crowd / saw / (4)*

$$\overset{\text{1} \qquad \text{2}}{} \qquad\qquad\qquad \overset{\text{1} \quad\, \text{2}}{}$$

(19b) Παῦλος / ἐποίησεν / (4)   *Paul / did / (4)*

The object of (19b), in independent form, would be a noun phrase, pronoun, or other included sentence; when incorporated into (19a) as the object, the object of ἐποίησεν becomes a *relative* pronoun, which is a grammatical device for joining two sentences.

020.6 The structure of (19) is identical with the structures of (13)–(18), i.e. subject, transitive verb, direct object. It may also be observed that the structures of S^4 in (18) and s^4 in (19) are also identical: in (18) τί is the object of λέγεις, so that the structure may be schematically represented as 4/2-1—the same elements as found in (13)–(17). s^4 in (19) may be analyzed as:

$$\overset{\text{4} \quad \text{2} \qquad\quad \text{1}}{}$$

(19b) ὃ / ἐποίησεν / Παῦλος

Once again, the structural elements are identical.

020.7 The sentence structure of (13) is thus utilized in a variety of other sentences, including the included sentences of (18) and (19). All these sentences are enate because they reflect the same basic grammatical structure. Among the commonly recurring sentence patterns in Greek, this type of sentence appears most often. A good grasp of its structure and varieties will go a long way towards the ability to read the structure signals in Greek.

Part One

The Sight & Sound of Greek

Lesson I

The Alphabet

050. The Greek alphabet (ἄλφα-βῆτ[α]) in the Koine or hellenistic period had twenty-four letters.

Form		Name		Sound	
				English	Greek
Capital	Small			Approximations	Examples
Α	α	ἄλφα	alpha	drama	δρᾱ-μᾰ
Β	β	βῆτα	bēta	bible	βι-βλί-ον
Γ	γ	γάμμα	gamma	glucose	γλεῦκος
Δ	δ	δέλτα	delta	decalogue	δε-κά-λο-γος
Ε	ε	ἒ ψιλόν	epsīlon	ego	ἐ-γώ
Ζ	ζ	ζῆτα	zēta	Zeus	Ζεύς
Η	η	ἦτα	ēta	they	μή
Θ	ϑ	ϑῆτα	thēta	theist	ϑε-ός
Ι	ι	ἰῶτα	iōta	intrigue	ἴ-δι-ος, ὑ-μῖν
Κ	κ	κάππα	kappa	crisis	κρί-σις
Λ	λ	λάμβδα	lambda	logic	λό-γος
Μ	μ	μῦ	mu	mother	μή-τηρ
Ν	ν	νῦ	nu	anti	ἀν-τί
Ξ	ξ	ξῖ	xī	axiom	ἀ-ξί-ω-μα
Ο	ο	ὂ μικρόν	omīcron	apology	ἀ-πο-λο-γί-α
Π	π	πῖ	pi	poet	ποι-η-τής
Ρ	ρ	ῥῶ	rhō	catarrh	κα-τάρ-ρο-ος
Σ	σ	σίγμα	sigma	syntax	σύν-τα-ξις
Τ	τ	ταῦ	tau	topic	τό-πος
Υ	υ	ὖ ψιλόν	üpsīlon	French: tu	τύ-πος
				German: Tür	ἰ-χϑύς
Φ	φ	φῖ	phī	phonetic	φω-νή
Χ	χ	χῖ	chī	chasm	χά-σμα
Ψ	ψ	ψῖ	psī	apse	ἀ-ψίς
Ω	ω	ὦ μέγα	ōmega	ode	ὠ-δή

0500.   Notes:

0500.1   The large (capital) letters are called *majuscules* or *uncials* (majuscules are square: E, uncials are rounded: ε). In general, majuscules are older (in imitation of epigraphic writing) than uncials, and both are older than minuscules.

0500.2   The small letters, called *minuscules*, are imitations of forms used in cursive (connected) writing. Handwritten manuscripts are divided into two categories on this basis: majuscules or uncials and minuscules.

0500.3   Modern texts are generally printed in minuscules.

0500.4   At the end of a word sigma is written ς, elsewhere σ, e.g. σεισμός.

0500.5   Two other letters were used in the earlier period: F / ϝ, ϝαῦ, *vau*, called *digamma* (i.e. double-gamma, suggested by its form), which once followed ε in the alphabet. ϝ was pronounced *w* (work). The second was ϙ κόππα *koppa*, which originally followed π. ϙ and another symbol, ϡ sampi, are used as letter-numerals.

051.1   The beginning student should concentrate on the form of the small letters. Each letter should be written many times, and its name pronounced each time (by learning the names of the letters one learns most of the sounds in Greek).

051.2   Hints for writing: α is written like a figure 8 turned on its side and open on the right. Begin β with an upward stroke below the line. γ is written as a small *y* with a tail below the line. δ, ζ, ξ may be learned by imitation: start δ below and ζ, ξ above, completing each in a single stroke. ε may be written as one stroke for the body (C) and the tooth added (as in manuscripts). μ may be written in one stroke (starting below the line) or in two (| from the top, with u added on). Sufficient tail on μ helps distinguish it from υ. ν and υ are often confused: write ν pointed at the bottom and turn the right upward stroke in at the top; υ is written rounded at the bottom with the right upward stroke turned outward. ρ is written as one stroke from the bottom. φ is also written as one stroke.

052.   *Transliteration* of Greek into English, i.e. representing the sound of Greek in English, may be helpful in learning the pronunciation of Greek. It is also of assistance in learning to recognize English words that are derived from Greek words. Transliteration is sometimes used in printing Greek when a Greek font is not available.

052.1   The common equivalencies used in transliteration are as follows:

α = a	η = ē[2]	ν = n	τ = t
β = b	ϑ = th[3]	ξ = x	υ = u, y[4]
γ = g[1]	ι = i	ο = o	φ = ph[3]

δ = d	κ = k, c	π = p	χ = ch[3]
ε = e	λ = l	ρ = r	ψ = ps[3]
ζ = z	μ = m	σ(ς) = s	ω = ō[2]

(1) γ is transliterated as *n* when it is combined with κ, γ, χ, ξ: γκ = *nk*, γγ = *ng*, γχ = *nch*, γξ = *nx*.

(2) ē and ō, when representing η and ω, must be marked long to distinguish them from e and o, which represent ε and o, respectively.

(3) ϑ, φ, χ, and ψ are represented in English by *two* letters.

(4) υ is transliterated as *u* in diphthongs (combined with other vowels, §058), otherwise as *y*.

052.2   A few examples will illustrate the connection between transliteration and English derivatives (Metzger: 1ff., Appendix I).

Greek	Transliteration	Meaning	Derivative
δέρμα	*derma*	*skin*	*dermatology*
διδαχή	*didachē*	*teaching*	*didactic*
πνεῦμα	*pneuma*	*spirit, breath*	*pneumatic*
ὕδωρ	*hydōr*	*water*	*hydroplane*
φωνή	*phōnē*	*sound*	*phonetic, telephone*
ψυχή	*psychē*	*soul, life*	*psychology*

Lesson 2

Sounds, Breathing, Syllables

055. The English approximations to the sounds of Greek given in §050 are more or less arbitrary and designed only to provide a reasonably consistent method of pronunciation. The student should learn to distinguish the *sound* as well as the *sight* of the language. The former can be achieved by pronouncing each word encountered and by regularly reading the text in Greek before, or instead of, translation. Reading a text not yet understood may seem like an empty gesture, but it will pay dividends in the long run.

056. *Consonants* require little special attention as their English equivalents are generally adequate.

056.1 γ is usually hard (as in *go*); before κ, γ, χ or ξ it has the nasal sound of *ng*, as in *sing*: ἄγγελλος = Latin *angelus* = English *angel* (in Greek and Latin, unlike English, the sound approximates the *ng* in *finger*, i.e. the *g* is hard).

056.2 ζ had the *dz* sound earlier (as in *adze*), but in the hellenistic period had been reduced to simple *z* (*zone*).

056.3 ξ is sounded with a slight explosion of the breath; a close English approximation is the *x* in *hex*.

056.4 ρ has both the simple *r* and the *rh* sound (cf. ῥητωρική = *rhetoric*). ρ was in the process of losing its aspirated sound (=*rh*) in the hellenistic period (Bl-D §11).

056.5 σ is voiceless or 'sharp' *s* (as in *sit*). There is evidence that σ also had a soft (voiced) sound before certain voiced consonants (e.g. β, μ), as in *is* (Bl-D §10).

056.6 χ is closely approximated by German *ch* in *ich*, *machen* (certain dialects), or Scottish *ch* in *loch*.

057. There are seven *vowels*: α, ε, η, ι, ο, υ, ω. ω is the long form of ο; ε and ο are always short, η and ω always long. This list, omitting η and ω, corresponds to the English a, e, i, o, u. α, ι, υ are sometimes long and sometimes short; the long and short forms are not distinguished by separate characters. The sounds are indicated in §062.

058.1 A *diphthong* (δίφθογγος, two sounds) is two vowel sounds fused into one. The second is always ι or υ. The diphthongs are:

Form	Sound	Examples	
αι	*ai* in *aisle*	ἀρχαῖος	cf. archaeology or archeology
ει	*ei* in *freight*	εἰκών	cf. *icon* or *eikon*
οι	*oi* in *oil*	οἰκουμενικός	cf. *ecumenical* or *oecumenical*
υι	*we* or *ui* in *colloquial*	υἱός	
αυ	*ow* in *cow*	ναῦς	cf. *nautical*
ευ/ ηυ	*eu* in *eulogy*	εὑρίσκω/ηὕρηκα	cf. *eureka*
ου	*ou* in *group*	οὐρανός	cf. *uranium*

The Greek sound of the diphthong is rarely preserved in the related word in English (last column). The Greek sounds are indicated in §063.

058.2 A long vowel combined with ι forms an improper diphthong: ᾳ, ῃ, ῳ. The iota is written subscript (called iota subscript) and no longer affects the sound. When α, η, ω are written as capitals, the iota must be written on the line (called iota adscript): Αι , Ηι, Ωι.

058.3 All diphthongs are theoretically long, but final αι, οι are considered short for the purposes of accent, except in the optative.

059.1 Every initial vowel or diphthong is marked for *breathing*. Rough breathing (*spiritus asper*) is marked with ('), smooth breathing with ('). (') has the value of *h* pronounced before the vowel: Ἕλλην = *Hellene*; ἕν (henotheism). Initial υ always has rough breathing: ὑπό (cf. *hypodrome*). (') has no effect on the sound: ἄνθρωπος (cf. *anthropology*).

059.2 The signs for breathings are derived from H, which originally had the value of *h*. H came to be used for *ēta*, with the result that new marks were created out of the old sign by dividing it into two parts, ⊢ and ⊣ , one to indicate smooth, the other rough, breathing. These marks were printed as ' and ' respectively.

059.3 Initial ρ is also given rough breathing and is pronounced *rh*: ῥέω (cf. *rheostat*).

059.4 Medial double ρ (ρρ within a word) is sometimes written -ῤῥ- to indicate that the first lacks, the second has, breathing. Cf. Bl-D §11(1).

060. Every Greek word has as many syllables as it has separate vowels or diphthongs: τε-θέ-α-μαι.

060.1 A single consonant goes with the following vowel: λό-γος.

060.2   A cluster of consonants which can begin a word, or a consonant with μ or ν, goes with the following vowel: ἐ-σκη-νω-σεν; τέ-κνον.

060.3   A cluster of consonants which cannot begin a word is divided: ἄν-θρω-πος. Doubled consonants are divided: ἐ-γεν-νή-θη-σαν.

060.4   Compounds are divided where they are joined: κατ-έ-λα-βεν, ἔμ-προσ-θεν.

061.   Familiarity with the sight and sound of Greek can best be achieved by constant use of a Greek text. Especially at the beginning it is important to read and pronounce aloud, preferably with the instructor or a fellow student at hand to correct. The sounds of vowels and consonants are more readily learned, of course, in the context of the common phonetic patterns in Greek. For this purpose the words in any Greek text are suitable for practice.

062.   *The Vowels*

062.1   α is pronounced like the *a* in *father*.

   πάλιν (Jn 8:12), σάρκα (Jn 8:15), κατὰ (Jn 8:15)

062.2   ε is pronounced like the *e* in *bet*.

   ἔλεγεν (Jn 8:31), ἐστε (Jn 8:31), γνώσεσθε (Jn 8:32)

062.3   η is pronounced like the *a* in *hate*.

   μὴ (Jn 8:12), τῆς ζωῆς (Jn 8:12), τὴν ἀρχὴν (Jn 8:25)

062.4   ι is pronounced like either *i* in *ĭntrīgue*. When ι has the circumflex accent (~), it is long, i.e. pronounced like the second *i* in *intrigue*.

   ὅτι (Jn 8:33), ὑμῖν (Jn 8:34), ἐστιν (Jn 8:34)

062.5   ο is pronounced like *aw* in *awful, awl*.

   ὁ (Jn 8:12), τὸ (Jn 8:12), ὅτι (Jn 8:14), πόθεν (Jn 8:14)

062.6   υ is pronounced like German *ü* or French *u* (with lips rounded attempt the *ee* sound in *beet*).

   μαρτυρία (Jn 8:13), ὑπάγω (Jn 8:14), δύο (Jn 8:7)

062.7   ω is pronounced like the *o* in *ode*.

   λέγων (Jn 8:12), ἐγώ (Jn 8:12), φῶς (Jn 8:12)

0620.　Observe the following distinctions:

0620.1　Between ε and η

  ἐλάλησεν (Jn 8:12), ζητήσετέ (Jn 8:21)

0620.2　Between α and o

  αἰῶνας (Rom 1:25) / αἰῶνος (Jn 9:32)

0620.3　Between o and ω

  λόγον (Jn 8:43) / λόγων (Jn 7:40)

0620.4　Among α, o, ω in:

  ὑποκάτω (Jn 1:51), ἄνθρωπον (Jn 8:40)

063.　*The Diphthongs*

063.1　αι is pronounced like *ai* in *aisle*.

  μαθηταί (Jn 8:32), αἰῶνα (Jn 8:35), δαιμόνιον (Jn 8:52)

063.2　ει is pronounced like *ei* in *freight* or *a* in *hate*.

  εἶπον (Jn 8:13), μαρτυρεῖς (Jn 8:13), ἕξει (Jn 8:12)

063.3　οι is pronounced like *oi* in *oil*.

  αὐτοῖς (Jn 8:12), οἱ (Jn 8:13), οἶδα (Jn 8:14)

063.4　υι is pronounced like *ui* in *colloquial*.

  υἱὸν (Jn 8:25)

063.5　αυ is pronounced like *ow* in *sow*.

  αὐτοῖς (Jn 8:12), ἐμαυτοῦ (Jn 8:14), ταῦτα (Jn 8:28)

063.6　ευ and ηυ are pronounced like *eu* in *eulogy*.

  πιστεύσητε (Jn 8:24), εὐαγγέλιον (Rom 1:1), ηὐχόμην (Rom 9:3)

063.7　ου is pronounced like *ou* in *group*.

  κόσμου (Jn 8:12), οὐ (Jn 8:12), οὖν (Jn 8:13)

0630. Observe the following similarities and distinctions:

0630.1 The pronunciations suggested for η and ει (§§062.3, 063.2) are identical. The first and second vowels in μείνητε (Jn 8:31) will therefore sound alike. In such cases, the eye must distinguish what the ear does not.

0630.2 The pronunciation suggested for ευ and ηυ (§063.6) means that these two diphthongs are indistinguishable. There will be a tendency, moreover, to confuse ευ and ηυ with simple υ (§062.6), especially as French *u* and German *ü* is an unfamiliar sound in English. This difficulty may be avoided by giving a true diphthongal sound to ευ and ηυ: ευ may be pronounced like *ew* in *Edward* without the intervening d, and ηυ may be pronounced like *ayw* in *wayward*.

0630.3 The difficulty of maintaining an un-English pronunciation of υ may produce confusion with ου: υ will tend to take on the sound of ου.

0630.4 The possibility of confusing υ, ευ, ου (§063.2–3) may be lessened by keeping the following catchwords in mind and exaggerating the distinctions between and among the vowels and diphthongs:

υ/ευ	εὐθύς	(Mk 1:10)
	κυριεύει	(Rom 6:9)
υ/ου	νῦν	(Jn 8:40) / νοῦν (Rom 1:28)
υ/ευ/ου	κυριεύουσιν	(Lk 22:25)

0630.5 The following words may also be helpful in fixing distinctions:

α/ο/ου/ω	ἀκολουθῶν	(Jn 8:12)
ε/η/υ/ει	ἐληλύθει	(Jn 8:20)
ευ/η/αι	γεύσηται	(Jn 8:52)

064. *Consonants.* The Greek consonants offer little difficulty and the approximations suggested in §§050, 056 are generally adequate to distinguish them from each other.

064.1 κ and χ. χ can be confused with κ unless it is remembered that the breath is not entirely cut off with χ; the emission of breath should produce only a strong *h*.

Contrast χρῆσιν (Rom 1:26) with κρίσιν (Jn 7:24)
Observe the distinction in καύχησις (Rom 3:27)

064.2 γ before γ, κ, χ, ξ is called γ-nasal (§056.1).

> γγ is pronounced like *ng* in *finger*: ἄγγελος (Mt 1:20)
> γκ is pronounced like *nk* in *think*: συγκαλεῖ (Lk 15:6)
> γξ is pronounced like *nx* in *Sphinx* (σφίγξ): ἐλέγξει (Jn 16:8)
> γχ is pronounced like γκ only with more breath: ἐλέγχει (Jn 8:46)

064.3 Other consonants in combination retain the sound they have separately; no consonants in Greek are silent. Note the following:

pn	πνεῦμα	(Jn 1:32); cf. *pneumatic*
pt	πτωχοί	(Mt 5:3)
phth	φθόγγος	(Rom 10:18); cf. δί-φθογγος (*diphthong*)
mn	μνημονεύετε	(Jn 15:20)
chth	ἐχθρόν	(Mt 5:43); cf. χθόνιος (*chthonic*)

065. The eye should be trained to observe rough breathing (initial υ always has rough breathing, §059.1) and thus the vowel preceded by an *h*-sound, e.g. ὁ (Jn 8:12), ἕξει (Jn 8:12), οἱ (Jn 8:13), ἡ (Jn 8:13), ὅτι (Jn 8:14), ὑπάγω (Jn 8:14), ὑμεῖς (Jn 8:14).

Lesson 3

Accents & Punctuation

070. *Elision* is the dropping of a short final vowel before a word beginning with a vowel; an apostrophe marks the omission: ἀλλ᾽ ἕξει, (Jn 8:12, for ἀλλὰ ἕξει); ἀπ᾽ ἐμαυτοῦ (Jn 8:28, for ἀπό ἐμαυτοῦ).

    Elision is common in prepositions, conjunctions, adverbs. The prepositions περί and πρό are not elided. Cf. §918.

071. *Crasis* is the contraction of a final vowel or diphthong with an initial vowel or diphthong; a coronis (᾽ = apostrophe in form) is placed over the contracted syllable: κἄν (Jn 8:14, for καὶ ἄν); κἀγώ (Jn 1:31, 33, for καὶ ἐγώ). Cf. *you're* (for *you are*).

    Crasis is not common in the New Testament. Other examples: τοὔνομα (for τὸ ὄνομα); κἀκεῖ (for καὶ ἐκεῖ). Cf. §919.

072. *Accent.* Most Greek words are written with accents. The accents are the acute (´), the grave (`), and the circumflex (ˆ). Thus, λαμβάνει τὸν δοῦλον; ἀκούω τῆς φωνῆς. The accent stands over the vowel of the accented syllable, and in a diphthong over the second vowel.

072.1 In English accent means a stress of the voice. Also to the native Greeks of today it means simply stress of voice. Originally, however, accents indicated the tone or pitch of the voice in pronouncing syllables.

072.2 The last syllable of a word is called the *ultima;* the next to the last, the *penult;* and the one before the penult, the *antepenult.* Only the last three syllables of a word may take an accent.

0720. Accentuation is governed by certain rules:

0720.1 The acute (´) may stand on any one of the last three syllables of a word; the circumflex (ˆ) on either of the last two syllables; the grave (`) only on the ultima.

0720.2 The circumflex may stand only on a long vowel or diphthong.

0720.3 An accented antepenult must therefore take the acute: ἄνθρωπος. But the antepenult may not be accented if the ultima is long.

0720.4 An accented penult takes the circumflex if it is long *and the ultima is short:* ἦλθεν. Otherwise it takes the acute: κόσμῳ.

0720.5 An accented ultima must take the acute if it is short; if it is long it may take either the acute or the circumflex: θεός; ἀρχῇ; ζωή.

0720.6 The grave (`) may stand only on the ultima. An acute accent falling on the ultima, when an enclitic (s. §074) or mark of punctuation does not follow, is changed to grave: πρὸς τὸν θεόν.

073. *Proclitics* are monosyllabic words which are linked with the *following* word in pronunciation, with the result that they have no accent of their own.

074. *Enclitics* are words (dissyllabic at most) which are joined with the *preceding* word in pronunciation, with the result that they *may* lose their own accent. If permitted, the accent is thrown back on the preceding word; some words, consequently, may have two accents.

075. As indicated in §072.1, accents no longer assist in pronunciation (except in the arbitrary indication of stress), so that the chief function of the accent in modern texts is to assist in distinguishing between words (e.g. τίς *who?*, τὶς *anyone*). Accents, of course, are determined by modern editors (accents were not regularly employed in texts until after the fifth century ce). The proficient student of Greek will want to learn to handle accent correctly, but beginners need not concern themselves beyond the observation of accent in placing stress and in those instances where accent is a clue to identification. Accent will be treated where relevant in the lessons.

076. *Punctuation.* Greek manuscripts of the New Testament books were written for the most part without benefit of punctuation or even separation of words (s. Bl-D §16). The system of punctuation (along with accents and breathing) is provided by modern editors. However, some peculiarities of punctuation are old. The period, comma, dash and parenthesis are employed as in English. The semicolon and colon are indicated by a point above the line (·), the mark of interrogation by (;) (= our semicolon).

077. In reading Greek, the attempt should be made to connect words in phrases. Accent and punctuation may serve as guides. Examples of shorter phrases:

(Jn 8:12)	ἐγώ εἰμι
	τὸ φῶς τοῦ κόσμου
	ὁ ἀκολουθῶν μοι
	οὐ μὴ περιπατήσῃ
	ἐν τῇ σκοτίᾳ
(8:13)	ἡ μαρτυρία σου
	οὐκ ἔστιν
(8:14)	κἂν ἐγὼ μαρτυρῶ
	περὶ ἐμαυτοῦ

(8:15) κατὰ τὴν σάρκα
        ἐγὼ οὐ κρίνω

When some facility with shorter phrasing has been achieved, shorter word groups may be linked together in longer phrases or clauses (utilizing the punctuation marks):

(8:12) ἐγὼ εἰμι τὸ φῶς τοῦ κόσμου·
        ὁ ἀκολουθῶν μοι οὐ μὴ περιπατήσῃ ἐν τῇ
            σκοτίᾳ, αλλ' ἔξει τὸ φῶς τῆς ζωῆς.
(8:13) σὺ περὶ σεαυτοῦ μαρτυρεῖς.
        ἡ μαρτυρία σου οὐκ ἔστιν ἀληθής·

The 'Lord's Prayer' divides up readily:

(Matt 6:9) Πάτερ ἡμῶν ὁ ἐν τοῖς οὐρανοῖς
            Ἁγιασθήτω τὸ ὄνομά σου·
(6:10)   ἐλθάτω ἡ βασιλεία σου·
            γενηθήτω τὸ θέλημά σου,
                ὡς ἐν οὐρανῷ καὶ ἐπὶ γῆς.
            κτλ. (=καὶ τὰ λοιπά)

Lesson 4

Vowel & Consonant Change

080. In mastering the inflectional patterns in Greek and in recognizing derivational forms, it is extremely helpful to know how vowels and consonants in Greek behave. An elementary knowledge of phonology will relieve the tedium of rote memorization of patterns that are otherwise inexplicable and will create a range of expectancy within which phonetic changes will fall. At the early stages of learning, especially, a modest acquaintance with phonology is valuable in identifying words and forms.

Appendix I, §§900–933, is devoted to a schematic presentation of phonetic changes in Greek. The material there is to be used primarily for reference.

081. English is rich in words borrowed from or related to Greek. A number of important New Testament words have been taken over directly by theologians, e.g. *agape* (ἀγάπη), *kerygma* (κήρυγμα), *somatic* (σῶμα, base σωματ-), *eucharist* (εὐχαριστία). The Greek counterparts of such words are the more readily identified if the student is aware of transliteration equivalencies (§052). Many other English words, especially from technical and scientific language, afford means of recognizing Greek ancestors. *Phone*, for example, comes from φωνή, *sound*; *phonology*, the science which treats sounds, is derived from φωνή + λογία. An *ophthalmologist* is an eye doctor: ὀφθαλμός, *eye*. Note the phonetic relationship between the following Greek words and English derivatives (care must be taken, however, in relating meanings; English derivatives do not always mean the same thing as their Greek counterparts): μάρτυς (base μαρτυρ-), *martyr*; ῥήτωρ, *rhetor-ic*; ἡγεμών, *hegemony*; ἔθνος, *ethnic*; πόλις, *Indianapolis*; ἐγώ, *ego*; εἷς (neut. ἕν) and θεός, *henotheism*, cf. *theology*.

The student can begin with a considerable working vocabulary if close attention is given to the sounds of Greek words (rather than their written form) in relation to English. In this connection it should be remembered that consonants are more persistent and hence critical than vowels.

Metzger (Part I) provides the student with English derivatives for approximately 45 per cent of the words appearing in the Greek New Testament ten times or more.

082.   In addition to Greek words taken over virtually unchanged, even the untrained
eye and ear will sense some relation between such phonetically differentiated words as πατήρ (*father*) and English *father* (cf. German *vater*). If the two
words are related, Greek π corresponds to English *f*, and Greek τ corresponds to
English *th*. On the basis of the first (π/f), one might recognize πυρ as a distant
cousin of English *fire*; on the basis of the second (τ/th), τρεις bears some similarity to *three*.

The regularity of correspondences among consonants was formulated as a
phonetic law (or set of laws) by Jacob Grimm (1785–1863) and became known as
Grimm's law (Cf. Metzger: 73–78). In addition to the relationships π/*f* and τ/*th*,
κ appeared to correspond to *h*, δ/*t*, and γ/*k*. Thus, καρδία is related to English
heart (κ/h, δ/t), ὀδούς (stem, ὀδοντ-) to *dental*, but also *tooth* (δ/t, τ/th), γένος to
kin (γ/k) . Also compare δύο with *two*, γινώσκω (stem, γνω-) with *know*, πληγή
with *flog*.

083.   *Consonant changes* within the Greek language itself sometimes obscure the relationship between words and forms to the untrained eye. The trained eye is
one that anticipates, or at least is not surprised by, changes that take place
when certain consonants are juxtaposed. Such eye training may here be only
exemplified.

083.1   ξ and ψ stand for κσ, γσ, χσ and πσ, βσ, φσ, respectively (§§903.5, 9030.3). This
fact makes it readily understandable that κῆρυξ is the nom. sing. of κήρυκος
(gen. sing.), base κηρυκ-: the nom. sing. takes the ending -ς (§160). Similarly, ἕξω
is the future tense of ἔχω, since the tense formative of the future is σ (§346.2):
ἐχ-σ-ω > ἕξω. Analogously, ἔπεμψα (first aorist, tense formative σ, §346.1) has
a base πεμπ-, to be observed in the present tense, πέμπω (ε-πεμπ-σα > ἔπεμψα).
Cf. γράφω, ἔγραψα (base, γραφ-).

083.2   *The lexical form of nouns.* One difficulty common to beginners in Greek is as-
certaining the dictionary form (nom. sg.) of certain nouns, particularly of the
third declension, when they occur in the text in an oblique case (gen., dat.,
acc.). Suppose one does not know the meaning of σαρκί and wishes to look the
word up in a lexicon. We will have to assume that the student knows the declension patterns sufficiently well to identify σαρκί as a dative singular (dative
singulars in the third declension regularly end in -ι, §154). The student will also
know that the nom. sg., or dictionary form, also often ends in -ς (masc. and fem.
nouns, §154). Omitting the dative ending (-ι), the base would be σαρκ-. To this
we might add ς: σαρκ-ς > σαρξ (§083.1), and thus arrive at the correct nomina-

tive form. It is sometimes necessary, to be sure, to arrive at the correct form by trial and error.

083.3   The problem presented in §083.2 can be further illustrated with reference to other types of phonetic change.

The dative form χάριτι (cf. §083.2) has the base χαριτ-. If we assume this noun is masc. or fem. and add σ to form the nom. sg., the result is χαριτ-ς. However, a dental (τ, δ, ϑ) disappears before σ (§927.2): χαριτ-ς > χάρις. Cf. ἐλπίς, dat. sg. ἐλπίδι.

083.4   Only certain consonants in Greek can stand at the end of a word: ν, ρ, ς (χ, ψ) (§923). The dative form ὀνόματι would therefore have the base, ὀνοματ-. If this noun were masc. or fem., the nom. sg. would presumably be ονομας (see above). However, it is neuter, so the nom. sg. has no ending (§154) : ὀνοματ- > ὄνομα.

These examples merely illustrate the way in which a minimal knowledge of phonetic change can be of assistance in locating the dictionary forms of verbs and nouns and in correlating the various forms of the same noun or verb.

084.   *Word families.* The significance of phonetic change can be exemplified in yet another way: the relationship among words belonging to the same word family may not be evident apart from some minimal knowledge of the laws governing phonetic changes.

Observe the family resemblance of the following words:

γράφω — *I write*
γραφή, -ῆς, ἡ — *a writing, scripture*
γραπτός, -ή, -όν — *written*
γράμμα, -ατός, τό — *letter* (of the alphabet), *document, epistle*
γραμματεύς, -έως, ὁ — *secretary, clerk*

The family base is γραφ-, to be observed in γράφω, γραφή. γραπτός (adj.) is comprised of γραφ- plus the adjective suffix -τος; φ before τ is partially assimilated: φτ > πτ (§925.1). γράμμα is made up of γραφ- plus the noun suffix -ματ-; φ before μ is totally assimilated: φμ > μμ (§926.1); since τ cannot stand at the end of a word (§§083.4; 923), and neuter nouns of the third declension have no ending in the nom. sg. (§154) , the dictionary form shows the stem, less τ. γραμματεύς is derived from γράμμα (γραμματ-), plus the noun suffix -ευς (agent).

Compare the English cognates *graph, grapheme, graphic, graphite, graphology.*

Attention to phonetic change will often make it possible to discern family relationships among words that otherwise may appear unrelated.

085.   *The behavior of vowels* is somewhat less predictable and consequently less stable than the behavior of consonants. In the non-literary papyri, for example, the vowels in words are more commonly misspelled than the consonants. Nevertheless, acquaintance with certain categories of vowel changes will prove indispensable.

085.1   *Contraction.* Vowels brought together in inflection and word-formation are often contracted. The verb ποιέω appears in the lexicon but not in any text in that form: -έω always contracts to -ῶ. The final stem vowel ε, however, appears in the future tense of the same verb, ποιήσω, where it is lengthened to η before the tense formative σ (-ω is the personal ending in both cases). Contraction is a common phenomenon in Greek. For a schematic summary of contractions, s. §917.

085.2   *Quantitative vowel gradation.* Vowels in different forms of related words sometimes undergo a change in length (short to long and the reverse). In some first declension nouns, for example, a short final α in the nom. and acc. singulars becomes η in the gen. and dat. singulars: δόξα, δόξαν; δόξης, δόξῃ (s. §132.2). In πατήρ (nom.), the final stem vowel (η) becomes short in the acc. form, πατέρα, and the same vowel disappears altogether in the gen. form, πατρός. In §085.1 it was observed that final ε in ποιέω is lengthened to η before the tense formative σ of the future tense: ποιήσω.

Observe the change from short to long final stem vowel between and among verbs and nouns belonging to the same family:

ποιέω (ποιῶ) — *I do, make*
ποίημα — *doing, working*
ποίησις — *work, creation* (of the artist)
ποιητής — *poet*

νοέω (νοῶ) — *I perceive, apprehend*
νόημα — *thought, mind*

ἀγαπάω (αγαπῶ) — *I love*
ἀγάπη — *love*
ἀγαπητός — *beloved*

Quantitative vowel gradation is summarized in §§908f.

085.3   *Qualitative vowel gradation.* In addition to changes in length, vowels sometimes undergo qualitative change, as, for example, in the English verb, *ring, rang, rung*, and in the noun, *man, men.*

Analogous qualitative vowel change may be observed in a few Greek verbs, e.g. λείπω (present tense), ἔλιπον (aorist), λέλοιπα (perfect). S. §911 for other patterns.

Once again (§085.2), qualitative vowel change may be observed in related verbs and nouns:

ἀποστέλλω — *I send away or out*
ἀπόστολος — *apostle* (someone sent)
ἐπιστολή — *letter* (something sent)

τρέφω — *I nourish, feed, support*
τροφή — *nourishment, food*
τροφός — *nurse*

The relationship among words belonging to the same family may be more readily discerned when there is awareness of the possibilities of quantitative and qualitative vowel change.

086.   The phonetic changes indicated in §§082–085 are illustrative of some of the more common changes to be expected in Greek. A schematic but by no means exhaustive presentation is to be found in Appendix I, §§900–933. Students are well advised not to commit this material to memory in advance, but to study it in a preliminary way, and then let it take shape slowly as they confront the inflectional patterns of the nominal and verbal systems, and build vocabulary by observing relationships among Greek words and between Greek and related English (Latin, etc.) words. Many phonetic changes will appear natural after a brief experience of the language.

Part Two

The Nominal & Verbal Systems

The Nominal System

Introduction

For Reading and Reference

100. Greek, by comparison with English, is a highly inflected language. *Inflection* (also called *accidence*) refers to the changes words undergo in accordance with their grammatical function in the sentence. Inflection in nouns is called *declension;* in verbs *conjugation.* In this respect Greek has more affinity with Latin and German than with French and English. The student who has first learned another inflected language will find Greek easier than the student who must rely solely on English for analogies.

English is by no means uninflected. Yet students to whom English is native will not have noticed inflection in the way in which they will notice it in Greek. They have perhaps struggled with the difference between *who* (subjective) and *whom* (objective), but may not have noticed that *whose* (possessive or genitive) is also a part of the inflection of the relative pronoun. Similarly, *I* and *me, he* and *him, she* and *her* (personal pronouns) show inflectional differences which are related to person (first and third persons), gender (masculine and feminine), and grammatical function (case).

This undergoes an inflectional change in the plural: *these. That* becomes *those.* English normally forms the plural by *adding s* or *es: clock* becomes *clocks, watch* becomes *watches. Child,* on the other hand, becomes *children.*

Inflectional change to represent gender is also not unknown in English. It has already been noted in the personal pronoun of the third person: *he, she, it.* Some nouns show a difference between masculine and feminine, e.g. *prince* and *princess, governor* and *governess.*

Inflectional changes are common in the verbal system as well (cf. §§300–302). The basic forms of the English verb (called principal parts) are formed regularly (*call, called, called*) or irregularly (*speak, spoke, spoken*). In the former (called *weak* verbs), *-ed* (or *-d*) is added to the present to form the past and the past participle; in the latter (*strong* verbs), the verb undergoes some internal change. The verb is also modified to indicate person in the third person singular of the present tense, e.g. *I call,* but *he calls* (add *-s*) . The verb *be* is highly inflected: *am* (*be*), *was*, *been* (principal parts); *am*, *are*, *is* (first, second, third person singular, present tense). The present participle and gerund are formed by adding -*ing* to the present: *being*, *calling*, *speaking*. The infinitive is often formed with *to*: *to be*, *to call*, *to speak*.

Although inflection in English is greatly reduced, there are sufficient inflectional changes in English to provide analogies to many changes in Greek. By noting these analogies, the student will grasp the rationale of the Greek system more readily, clarify his understanding of English, and perhaps come to a new appreciation of the relative simplicity of his own language.

1000. Sections I (The Nominal System) and II (The Verbal System) are designed to help the student grasp the inflectional patterns of the Greek language. These patterns are to be learned, in the sense of habituated, as part of the sight and sound of the language. Learning to respond immediately and without deliberation to these patterns will take place most effectively in the context of the word cluster, in connection with other structure signaling items, e.g. prepositions. Only a few things will require memorization by rote (without context), but those which do must be mastered.

The habituation of the patterns will require the 'reading' of a considerable amount of Greek. Reading means practicing the sound patterns of Greek. Sound patterns are, of course, intertwined with the grammatical structure of phrases, clauses, and sentences. Reading will therefore lead to the ability to seize the structure of word clusters, of longer and shorter compass, in relation to inflectional patterns and other structure signaling elements. Along the way, the reader will acquire some major vocabulary, and will come to understand the meaning of many words and word clusters. One does not have to complete an extensive course in grammar to be able to read Greek any more than one has to study the grammar of his own language to be able to understand and speak it.

The presentations in the lessons will provide only a minimum amount of material for reading practice. For practice any portion of the Greek New Testament or other Greek text is suitable. The *Workbook* provides a reading program and other devised exercises, to go with each of the lessons.

101. *Nouns*, *adjectives*, *pronouns* and *pronominal adjectives* share inflectional characteristics and patterns and so constitute the nominal system. *Participles*, being both verbal adjective (the participle in English) and verbal noun (the gerund in English), are declined like adjectives and thus belong, in this respect, to the nominal system; participles also have certain characteristics of verbs, as a con-

sequence of which they must be treated in the verbal system as well. The verbal system embraces the *finite verb* (i.e. restricted with respect to person and number), the *infinitive* (i.e. unrestricted), and the participle. *Prepositions*, *adverbs* (for the most part), *conjunctions* and *particles* are not inflected. Cf. §§010–014.

For the use of traditional designations for 'parts of speech,' s. §§010–011.

102.   *The inflectional paradigm* for the Greek noun will exhibit the case-forms (§105.1) for each of two numbers. The English relative pronoun may be utilized as an analogy to indicate how the paradigm for the noun will look:

		Singular	Plural
Subjective	(nominative)	who	who
Possessive	(genitive)	whose	whose
	(dative) (to, for)	whom (to, for)	whom
Objective	(accusative)	whom	whom

An inflectional paradigm is a model which illustrates the inflectional changes for a specific pattern of declension or conjugation. The inflectional paradigm has been utilized traditionally as a device in learning the inflectional patterns by rote. In this grammar it is used primarily for reference, but there are a few basic paradigms which must be mastered.

The English relative shows three cases (subjective, possessive, objective), while Greek has four (the paradigm above is expanded to make it conform to the Greek pattern). The *stem* who appears in all three cases: *who-se*, *who-m*. Inflectional similarities end here, inasmuch as the inflection of the English relative (by comparison with Greek) is reduced: singular and plural are identical, the dative and accusative cases are identical (= the objective case), and there is no way to distinguish between masculine and feminine. In Greek all these distinctions are possible in form as well as function.

The other relative pronouns *which* and *that* are uninflected (*whose* is sometimes used as the possessive of *which*). *Who* refers to persons (masculine or feminine); *which* may be said to be the neuter relative (Jespersen: 203), although it is used of animals as well as things. *That* has common gender.

The inflectional paradigm for the Greek adjective, including the pronominal adjective, will show the case-forms for each of three genders and two numbers (the masculine and feminine forms in some patterns are identical). This makes it possible for any adjective to agree with the term it modifies in gender, number and case. The adjective is not inflected in English.

The personal pronouns belong to a group apart. In English there is a distinctive form for each person and number, with the possibility of distinguishing three genders in the third person singular. The English personal pronoun shows distinguishable subjective and objective cases for the most part.

	Singular	Plural
1. Person	I, me	We, us
2. Person	You, you	You, you
3. Person	He, him	They, them
	She, her	
	It, it	

In Greek a pronominal adjective is used for the 3. person both singular and plural, which makes it possible to distinguish gender for both numbers. The 1. and 2. persons are inflected in four cases (as in the case of nouns, adjectives, pronominal adjectives) rather than in two. As in English, the 1. and 2. persons do not indicate gender. The 2. person plural is distinguishable from the 2. person singular in Greek, unlike English.

Gender, Number, Case

0103. Inflection in the nominal system has reference to three factors: *gender, number, case.*

103. *Gender.* In English gender may be said to be natural, i.e. males (men and animals) are masculine, females (women and animals) are feminine, and all inanimate things are neuter. There is also a common gender of nouns which denote persons or animals of either sex, e.g. *parent, cousin, friend.* In relation to Greek, two things require noting:

103.1 In Greek, nouns denoting males are indeed masculine, and nouns denoting females are feminine,[1] but a large number of nouns denoting things which are understood to be neuter in English are either masculine or feminine. Gender is thus both natural and grammatical.[2] *House* is neuter in English as in German

---

1. Greek also has nouns of common gender: ὁ θεός, *god,* ἡ θεός, *goddess;* ὁ and ἡ κάμηλος, *camel;* ὁ παῖς, *boy,* ἡ παῖς, *girl.*
2. Gender in Old English (Anglo-Saxon) was also both natural and grammatical. Grammatical gender may be viewed as simply arbitrary.

(*das Haus*), but in Greek it is feminine (ἡ οἰκία). *Day* is feminine in Greek (ἡ ἡμέρα), masculine in German (*der Tag*), but understood to be neuter in English.[3]

103.2 Gender in English does not affect inflection, except in those nouns for which there are distinct forms for masculine and feminine, and in the pronouns. Of the former, there are some which are cognate,[4] e.g. *actor-actress*, *prince-princess*, *aviator-aviatress* (*aviatrix*), and some which utilize different roots, e.g. *husband-wife*, *nephew-niece*, *gander-goose* (*goose* is also common gender). Relative pronouns distinguish between masculine-feminine (*who*) and neuter (*which*); the third person singular of personal pronouns provides for a triple distinction: *he*, *she*, *it*. It is possible, therefore, to avoid the problem of gender in English for the most part, but in Greek as in German it is essential to know the gender for the purposes of inflection, since not only the endings of the noun but also the endings of words modifying and referring to the noun are affected. For example, *the house is worthy* (ἡ οἰκία ἀξία Mt 10:13) requires a feminine article (ἡ), and a feminine ending on the predicate adjective (ἀξία) to indicate that it goes with οἰκία, which is feminine. In English there is no inflectional modification in either article or predicate adjective to indicate that house is *neuter*.

1030. Gender in Greek may be learned by observation or by consulting a lexicon (dictionary). Gender is always given in the lexical entry by means of the article.

Lexical entries for nouns follow this order: the nominative singular, the genitive singular ending (to establish the declension pattern), and the article in the proper gender. Examples: ζωή, -ῆς, ἡ *life*; λόγος, -ου, ὁ *word*.

Gender need not require excessive attention. In a written text one can nearly always deduce the gender of a noun either from the ending of the noun itself, or from the endings of modifying words. Further, nouns should be learned in association with a declension (there are three in Greek: first, second, third) and a declension pattern (e.g., in the first declension nearly all nouns are feminine;

---

3. There are, however, some interesting abberations in English gender. Of a boat or racing car it can be said, '*she* handles or rides beautifully.' The church is felt to be feminine ("The church's one foundation is Jesus Christ *her* Lord"), as are other institutions (personification). God is taken to be masculine (anthropomorphism). The Holy Spirit is neuter in Greek as in English, but students often write '*he*.' What gender are angels? Demons? While gender in Greek and German are often arbitrary, English permits ambiguities at various points.

4. I.e., the two forms have a common root.

masculine nouns of the first declension exhibit a slightly modified declension pattern: §§131–1341).

The problem will inevitably arise, however, that one cannot determine which modifiers go with what noun on the basis of word order (in English one is dependent entirely on word order). In such cases gender is an aid in determining word relationships. While gender is less important than number and case for those interested solely in a reading knowledge of Greek, a certain facility in gender will provide an effective instrument for untangling complicated Greek sentences.

104.   *Number.* Classical Greek had three numbers: singular, dual (two or a pair), and plural. The dual has disappeared in hellenistic Greek, and was never used much. We have therefore to reckon with two numbers in Greek as in English.

1040.   In English one normally makes a plural by adding *-s* (Old English *-as*, later *-es*, *-s*, originally belonging to a limited number of masculines, was subsequently extended to all masculines and finally other genders). There are, however, a few mutation plurals (*tooth, teeth; man, men*), and one remnant of the Old English suffix in *n*: *ox, oxen*.[5] Then there are the plurals with no change: *deer, deer; moose, moose*. And finally, English makes use of a few borrowed plurals, e.g. *criterion, criteria* (from Greek).

The forms of the English plural may be summarized as follows:

1) Plural in *-s* (*-es*):
   a) simple *-s*: *house, houses*
   b) *-es* (following *ch, sh, j, s, x, z*): *church, churches*[6]
   c) nouns in *-o* (*-s* or *-es*): *hero, heroes; piano, pianos*
   d) nouns in *-y* (*-y* preceded by a consonant or consonantal *u* is changed to *i*, followed by *-es*): *city, cities*
   e) nouns in *-f, -fe* (add *-s*, or change *f* to *v* and add *-es*): *belief, beliefs; life, lives*

---

5. Jespersen: 196. Cf. *child, children; brother, brothers* and *brethren* (now with a difference in meaning); and biblical *kine* (plural of *cow*). Cf. German *der Mensch, die Menschen* (*the man, the men*), *die Frau, die Frauen* (*the woman, the women*) .

6. The phonetic rule for *-s* or *-es* is: when the singular ends with a sound with which *s* can be joined without forming a separate syllable, add *-s*; otherwise *-es*. Exception: a final silent *-e* forms a separate syllable with *-s*: *case, cases; maze, mazes.*

2) Mutation plural: *mouse, mice; goose, geese; woman, women*
3) Singular and plural identical: *sheep, sheep; trout, trout*[7]
4) Plural by suffix: *ox, oxen*
5) Borrowed plurals:[8]
    a) *formula, formulae* (also *formulas*): Latin, first declension, feminine[9]
    b) *focus, foci* (also *focuses*): Latin, second declension, masculine-feminine[10]
    c) *datum, data*: Latin, second declension, neuter[11]
    d) *phenomenon, phenomena*: Greek, second declension, neuter[12]
    e) *thesis, theses*: Greek or Latin, third declension, masculine-feminine[13]
    f) *cherub, cherubim* (also *cherubs*) : Hebrew[14]

1041. Greek forms its plurals regularly by the addition of endings:

1) -αι (first declension, feminine and masculine); cf. Latin -*ae* (first declension)
2) -οι (second declension, masculine and feminine)
3) -ες (third declension, masculine and feminine); cf. Latin -*es* (third and fifth declensions) and English -*s*, -*es*
4) -α (all neuters); cf. Latin -*a* (all neuters)

---

7. Most of the words with identical singular and plural were originally neuters: swine, deer, sheep. In some cases a double plural arose, e.g. *hair, hair* and *hairs* making possible a distinction between a mass and an individual plural. 'He has a mop of *hair*' but 'the *hairs* of your head are numbered.' Similarly fish and fowl (Jespersen: 202).

8. Borrowed plurals, of course, are used only with loanwords.

9. Other examples: *alumna, alumnae; vita, vitae.*

10. *locus, loci; radius, radii; alumnus, alumni; octopus, octopi* (most of these words also form an anglicized plural in -*s*).

11. *stratum, strata; memorandum, memoranda; erratum, errata; stadium, stadia* (some of these words also form an anglicized plural in -*s*).

12. *noumenon, noumena.*

13. *hypothesis, hypotheses; crisis, crises; axis, axes; analysis, analyses. Index, indices* (also *indexes*); *appendix, appendices* (also *appendixes*) are also third declension: the final stem consonant *c* unites with the *singular* ending *s* to form the *x* of the singular; *c* reappears in the plural followed by the plural ending (-*es*).

14. *seraph, seraphim* (*seraphs*).

Thus, οἰκία, οἰκίαι (*house, houses*); λόγος, λόγοι (*word, words*); σωτήρ, σωτῆρες (*savior, saviors*); ἔργον, ἔργα (*work, works*). There are also some nouns in Greek which, in addition to the use of the regular ending, undergo an internal change in the formation of the plural, e.g. πάτηρ, πατέρες (*father, fathers*).

On the whole, the formation and use of the plural in Greek will occasion no more difficulty than in English.

105. *Case.* Three cases are distinguished grammatically in English. The morphological variables which once marked the case-function of the word within the word itself, however, have virtually disappeared. They are retained only in the *s* of the possessive and in the pronouns.

With respect to form, nouns in English show only two cases:

	Singular	Plural
Subjective	house	houses
Possessive	house's	houses'
Objective	house	houses

The subjective and objective cases are identical (for each number) in form; the possessive alone is distinctive. In the pronouns, on the other hand, the objective case is sometimes distinctive (cf. §102), and pronominal adjectives are made to do service for the possessive, e.g. *I, my* (*mine*), *me; he, his, him* (but *you, your(s), you* [Old English: *ye, your, you*]). On account of the pronouns, it may be said that English is a three case system in form as well as in function.

105.1 Nouns (including pronouns, adjectives and participles) are inflected in Greek in five (counting the vocative) distinctive case-forms. The five forms (*nominative, genitive, dative, accusative,* and *vocative*) represent the eight cases found in Indo-European tongues: the genitive form includes both genitive and ablative, the dative form includes dative, locative, and instrumental. Since the vocative often takes the same form as the nominative and since it is infrequent in any case, the Greek nominal system can be adequately treated, so far as form is concerned, as a four-case system. In the presentation of the declension patterns, four case-forms will therefore be employed: nominative (abbreviated nom., N), genitive (gen., G), dative (dat., D), and accusative (acc., A).

105.2 The non-subjective cases (possessive, objective) are called *oblique* cases. The problem which presents itself to the student who comes to Greek from English is that there are *three* oblique cases to choose from in Greek (*genitive, dative, accusative*) , whereas in English there are at most two, one of which is severely limited (possessive).

The grammatical function of the cases is *apparently* made more complicated in Greek by virtue of the fact that the three oblique cases are always distinguished from each other in form, and in masculine and feminine nouns are often distinguished from the nominative (subjective) case as well.

In dealing with word-groups and the sentence in Greek, it is necessary to learn to rely more heavily on the signals conveyed by the form of words than it is in English. With respect to the oblique cases, moreover, it is often significant to inquire why this oblique case and not some other is employed.

106.   *Word order and the cases.* In English the grammatical function of words is more or less dependent on position in the sentence. For example, in the sentence

(i)   Philip finds Nathanael

Nathanael, the object of the verb, follows the verb, while the subject precedes. This word order cannot be easily modified:

(ii)   Finds Philip Nathanael
(iii)   Philip Nathanael finds
(iv)   Nathanael finds Philip

The order of (ii) is impossible, while that of (iii) is unusual, perhaps acceptable only in certain contexts. The order of (iv) reverses the function of subject and object.

The word order in Jn 1:45 runs:

(1)   εὑρίσκει Φίλιππος τὸν Ναθαναὴλ

The nom. ending of Φίλιππ-ος and the acc. article (τὸν) make the grammatical function of each name clear, without dependence on word order. The words in the Greek sentence may theoretically come in any order:

(2)   Φίλιππος εὑρίσκει τὸν Ναθαναὴλ
(3)   τὸν Ναθαναὴλ Φίλιππος εὑρίσκει
(4)   τὸν Ναθαναὴλ εὑρίσκει Φίλιππος

and so on.

A little more freedom in order is created by introducing a preposition in English:

(v)   Philip says *to* him

may also run

(vi)   To him Philip says

but

(vii)   Says to him Philip

is unacceptable.

In Greek (Jn 1:46) the order is the last (vii):

(5)   λέγει αὐτῷ ὁ Φίλιππος

But the sequences of (v) and (vi) could also be employed in Greek.

In sum, distinctive case endings make possible a greater freedom in Greek word order than is possible in English. Word relationships in the sentence are determined by the case endings to an extent not possible in English, where word order is the primary factor. English speaking students, consequently, must be prepared to adjust to what will appear to them to be odd sequences in word order, and must be prepared to depend on case endings to indicate word relationships within the sentence.

107.   *Function of the cases.* English cases are subjective, objective and possessive.

    a) The *subjective* case is employed when the noun is the subject of a sentence ('*the world* did not know him'), when it is in apposition to another noun in the subjective case ('Andrew, *the brother* of Simon Peter, was . . .'), when it is the predicate with a copulative verb ('This is *the witness* of John'), and when the noun is used as a mode of address (vocative) ('*Rabbi*, you are the son of God').

    b) The *objective* case is employed when the noun is the object of a verb ('they asked *him*') or a preposition ('they said *to him*'). It is also used when the noun is in apposition to another noun in the objective case ('we have found Jesus, *the son of Joseph*').

    c) Although the *possessive* case is now largely restricted to personal beings and used mostly to show possession, it has a broader usage, which is complicated some by the encroachment of the preposition *of*. One can say 'mind's eye' (Shakespeare) or 'day's journey.' *Mind* and *day* are not personal beings, nor in the second instance is *day's*, strictly speaking, possessive: = a journey of a day (genitive of measure).[15] Possession, moreover, can be taken in a broad way: there is 'the man's house' (strict possession), but also 'Shakespeare's works' (= works written by Shakespeare), Picasso's pictures (= pictures painted by Picasso),[16] the President's death (one could also say, the death of the President; = a death, namely that of the President: here the possessive limits or specifies).[17] The possessive in the phrase 'John's witness' is a subjective genitive (= the witnessing done by John), while in the sentence 'he took his rejection placidly,' *his* is an objective genitive (= the rejection done to him). The possessive case thus has a broader function than mere possession of things by personal beings. When supplemented by the preposition *of* (*of* can often be used for the possessive case, e.g. 'eye *of* the mind,' 'journey *of* a day,' 'witness *of* John'), the genitive in English has many of the functions of the Greek genitive. For example, 'cup of water' (genitive of content), 'dress of cotton' (genitive of material), 'pearl of great price' (genitive of value), city of Rome (= a city, namely Rome; appositive genitive).

Syntax of the Cases

108. Inflection concerns the modification of words in form in accordance with their grammatical function in the sentence (§100). Syntax (σύνταξις, *arranging* or *ordering together*) treats the grouping of words into phrases, clauses, sentences, paragraphs, books, and thus has to do with the *function* of words and word groups in relation to each other and to the whole. Inflection and syntax together are grammar.

Grammar traditionally also includes other elements such as phonology (spelling, phonetics, punctuation, etc.) and word-formation.

---

15. Cf. arm's length, month's wages.
16. Really a genitive of agent.
17. The genitive in Greek, taken in its root sense, is the limiting or specifying case. Possession is merely a subspecies of specification: 'his thongs,' i.e. thongs, namely his.

109. A traditional syntax of the cases attempts to systematize the various relationships between words and word groups signaled by case-forms (cf. the sketch in §107). Syntactical categories thus developed are seldom clearcut and never exhaustive. They can, however, serve as a *guide* to the interpretation of case-function. The specific functions of the cases are best learned in the context of actual word clusters and sentences.

  Some preliminary acquaintance with the grammatical functions of the cases will assist in fixing in mind the declension (inflectional) patterns of the nominal system. The following brief schematic sketch of the Greek cases will serve as a preview.

  A detailed summary will be found in §§885ff.

1090. The native speaker of English will find that most functions of the Greek cases have analogies in English. Indeed, the sketch of the English cases in §107 could serve, with minor modification, as a sketch of the Greek cases. Difficulties will be encountered primarily at two points: 1) some case functions in Greek will be new, and 2) it will be necessary to learn traditional syntactical terminology in order to make use of advanced and reference grammars. The latter is a more formidable obstacle than the former.

110. *The nominative case.* The nominative is the naming case and corresponds to the English subjective case (§107). It is therefore the case of 1) the subject of the verb or sentence. In closely related ways the nominative is also used 2) as predicate with copulative verbs (ἡ ζωὴ ἦν τὸ φῶς, *the life was the light* Jn 1:4); 3) in appositives (adjuncts to the subject, but also loosely to other cases) (ἦν Ἀνδρέας ὁ ἀδελφὸς Σίμωνος Πέτρου, *Andrew, the brother of Simon Peter, was* . . . Jn 1:40); 4) absolutely (in titles, etc.); and 5) as vocative (γεννήματα ἐχιδνῶν, *you brood of vipers!* Mt 3:7).

111. The oblique cases (§105.2) may be used either alone or in conjunction with prepositions. In the sentence,

  (i) *the man whom everybody knows*

whom is the objective case used alone; in

  (ii) *the students to whom we gave the books*

whom is used in conjunction with the preposition *to*. The variation may not indicate any shift in meaning:

(iii)   *we gave the students the books* and

(iv)   *we gave the books to the students*

are identical in meaning.

In hellenistic Greek there are two tendencies at work which affect the oblique cases: 1) there is a growing preference for the preposition over against the simple case (the latter was freely employed in classical Greek, especially in poetry), and 2) there is less precision in the use of both simple case and preposition. The ascendancy of the prepositions led eventually to the reduction of the case-forms (there is no dative in modern Greek), since the distinctive case-form loses its rationale when its function is regularly indicated by a preposition (cf. English) . The lack of precision means that the nice distinctions possible in classical Greek cannot be pressed upon hellenistic texts.[18]

0112.   The *genitive* is a composite case (Smyth §1279), i.e. the same case form embraces both *genitive* and *ablative*. The two are sometimes treated separately in syntax, but their functions cannot always be distinguished. It is common to use genitive, for the sake of simplicity, to refer to both genitival and ablatival functions.[19]

112.1   The *genitive* is the case of genus or kind; it specifies. It most often corresponds to the preposition *of* in English, but it has affinities with the English possessive (§107). The various derived uses of the genitive are not at once apparent from the root idea, but in general the genitive denotes a relationship between two words, one of which further defines or circumscribes the other. E.g. πλῆθος ἰχθύων, *a large quantity of fish* (Lk 5:6), i.e. a large quantity, namely fish.

112.2   The ablative case is the 'whence' case, denoting source, origin, or separation. It is often represented in English by *from: cease from work.*

---

18. There were, of course, Atticizing authors in the hellenistic period who strove to imitate Attic style.

19. Against the correct but unnecessarily complicated tradition created by A. T. Robertson (which prevails in most American grammars), this grammar proposes to simplify matters wherever possible. The *genitive* will be used generally for both Indo-European *genitive* and *ablative*, and the *dative* case will include *dative, locative* and *instrumental* (s. §0113). Only occasionally will these distinctions be made. The syntactical rubrics will thus conform to the inflectional paradigms (as in most European grammars). In Latin, contrary to Greek, 1) the *genitive* and *ablative* are distinct cases in form; 2) the *dative* and *ablative* are often identical in form (in the plural always).

1120.   The genitive is used to denote 1) *possession* or *belonging* (English possessive or *of*): αὐτοῦ τὰ ἔργα, *his works* Jn 3:21; and 2) *relationship* or *origin* (English *of*) ὁ υἱὸς Ἰωάννου, *the son of John* Jn 1:42. The genitive may be 3) *subjective* (ἡ ἀγάπη τοῦ θεοῦ, *the love of God* 1 Jn 3:17 [RSV *God's love*]), or 4) *objective* (ἡ ἀγάπη τοῦ θεοῦ *the love of God* 1 Jn 2:5 [RSV *love for God*[20]]). It may be 5) *partitive*: ἕτερον δὲ τῶν ἀποστόλων, *another of the apostles* Gal 1:19 (with preposition: ἐκ τῶν μαθητῶν αὐτοῦ δύο, *two of his disciples* [ἐκ with partitive genitive, αὐτοῦ = possessive] Jn 1:35). The genitive is also used in 6) *comparisons*: μείζων τούτων *greater things than these* Jn 1:50 (i.e. *these things* are the point *from* which the comparison is made). The genitive may also specify 7) *content* or *material*, 8) *value*, 9) *time* or 10) *place within which* (note Κανᾶ τῆς Γαλιλαίας, *Cana in Galilee* Jn 2:1). It is used with *adjectives* and *verbs*, the meaning of which corresponds to a function of the genitive, e.g. πλήρης χάριτος καὶ ἀληθείας, *full of grace and truth* Jn 1:14; ἐπλήσθησαν πάντες πνεύματος ἁγίου, *they were all filled with the Holy Spirit* Acts 2:4.

1121.   The oblique cases are often aided in their function by means of a *preposition*. Prepositions supplement (i.e. add nothing and are therefore redundant) or further specify the function of the case. The partitive genitive, for example, may be used alone or with ἐκ (s. §1120): the meaning is identical. The genitive is rarely used alone to express *agent* in Greek, but it is common with the prepositions ὑπό (direct agent) and διά (intermediate agent), e.g. δι' αὐτοῦ, *through him* Jn 1:3.

0113.   The *dative* case is also composite, embracing the dative, locative and instrumental cases (cf. §0112). The single syntactical rubric thus conforms to the single case-form.

113.   The *dative*, as distinct from the locative and instrumental, is the case of *personal interest*. It denotes that *to* or *for* which something is or is done. The *instrumental*, as the designation suggests, indicates *means* or *instrument* (English *by* or *with*), but also includes *association* or *accompaniment* (English *with* in a different sense[21]). The root idea expressed by the *locative* (cf. Latin *locus, place*) is *location*

---

20. RSV interprets the genitive in both 1 John 2:5 and 3:17. The genitive may be either subjective or objective. The English translation 'the love of God' is open to the same ambiguity as the Greek genitive.

21. 'to cut down a tree *with* an ax' = instrument; 'to go *with* him' = accompaniment.

in space or time (English *in* or *at*, also *among, beside,* etc.); the locative is also used figuratively.

1130. The dative proper indicates the person more remotely concerned (*to* or *for* someone). 1) The *indirect object* with a transitive verb[22] is therefore put in the dative case: ἔδωκεν αὐτοῖς ἐξουσίαν, *he gave them power* Jn 1:12.[23] The dative of indirect object is the most common use of the dative case. The dative of indirect object with verbs of speaking (λέγει αὐτοῖς, *he says to them* Jn 1:38) is extremely common (15 times in Jn 1: 35–51), but even so, the prepositions have begun to encroach upon this function of the dative case (πρός with the accusative often takes the place of the dative: λέγει ἡ μήτηρ τοῦ Ἰησοῦ πρὸς αὐτόν, *the mother of Jesus says to him* Jn 2:3). Thus, in Greek as in English, the indirect object may be in the simple objective case (Greek dative) or it may be in the objective case governed by a preposition.

In addition to the dative of indirect object, the dative is also used 2) *with certain verbs*, which are usually transitive in English, to denote the sole complement or object (i.e. when no other object is present). For example, verbs of *serving* take the dative: οἱ ἄγγελοι διηκόνουν αὐτῷ, *the angels served him* Mk 1:13.[24] Such verbs normally express strong personal relationship. The corresponding *adjectives* also take the dative. 3) The person *for* whom something is or exists is put in the dative: ὄνομα αὐτῷ Ἰωάννης, *his name was John* Jn 1:16. This is called the *dative of possession*[25] 4) The person *for* whom something is done is also put in the dative, whether the action is to his advantage or disadvantage (*dative of advantage or disadvantage*): ᾧ σὺ μεμαρτύρηκας, *for whom* (i.e. in whose interests) *you bore witness* Jn 3:26.

---

22. In transitive verbs the action denoted by the verb affects something other than the subject of the verb: 'Paul wrote *a letter*' (*a letter* is the object of the verb). The thing *directly* affected is called the *direct object*. Commonly, but not always, the direct object is in the accusative case in Greek (s. §114). 'Paul wrote a letter *to the Romans*': is the *indirect object* of the verb (= dative in Greek).

23. The indirect object or complement in English is commonly indicated by *to*: 'he gave power *to* them.' If *to* is omitted, the indirect object follows immediately upon the verb: 'he gave *them* power.'

24. One could also translate, 'ministered *to him*.'

25. One can also show possession by means of the genitive (§1120). When the dative is used stress is laid upon the thing possessed (Bl-D §189(1)); the genitive puts the emphasis on the possessor.

1131. In biblical Greek 5) the *instrumental dative* is more often than not supplemented by the preposition ἐν in an instrumental sense:[26] βαπτίζω ἐν ὕδατι, *I baptize with water* Jn 1:26; but Acts 1:5 Ἰωάννης μὲν ἐβάπτισεν ὕδατι, with no difference in meaning. In closely related ways, the dative may indicate 6) *cause* (ἵνα τῷ σταυρῷ τοῦ Χριστοῦ μὴ διώκωνται, *in order that they may not be persecuted for* [= because of] *the cross of Christ* Gal 6:12), or 7) the person or thing to which the assertion is limited (*dative of respect*): ὀνόματι Ἰάϊρος, *Jairus by name* Mk 5:22; οἱ καθαροὶ τῇ καρδίᾳ, *the pure in heart* Mt 5:8. 8) The *associative* (*comitative*) dative is employed *with verbs* which stress *association* or *accompaniment*[27]: ἠκολούθησαν τῷ Ἰησοῦ, *they followed Jesus* Jn 1:37.[28] 9) Similarly, the associative dative may denote *accompanying circumstances* (with ἐν) or *manner*: ἐν ῥάβδῳ ἔλθω, *Shall I come to you with a rod?* 1 Cor 4:21; παντὶ τρόπῳ, εἴτε προφάσει εἴτε ἀληθείᾳ, *in every way, whether in pretense or truth* Phil 1:18.

1132. The *locative dative* to express 10) *place where* is rare in the New Testament except with prepositions (ἐν, ἐπί, παρά, πρός): τῇ δεξιᾷ οὖν τοῦ θεοῦ ὑψωθείς, *exalted to the right hand of God* Acts 2:33. 11) To express *time when* it is more common (often also with ἐν): τῇ ἡμέρᾳ τῇ τρίτῃ, *on the third day* Jn 2:1.[29]

0114. The *accusative* is the normal oblique case. It is the oldest case and has once again become the usual oblique case in modern Greek. Since its function in Greek parallels the objective case in English for the most part, the accusative offers little difficulty. Speakers of English will have to give attention rather to the use of the genitive or dative where they might expect the accusative.

114. The root idea expressed by the *accusative* may be broadly characterized as *extension*, but the specific relationship (as with the genitive) is often indeterminate and must be supplied from the context. The accusative is the case 1) of the *direct object* (i.e. it defines the extent to which the action of the verb is effective: ὁ κόσμος αὐτὸν οὐκ ἔγνω, *the world did not know him* Jn 1:10. Accusative objects are of two kinds: a) *internal* object (object *effected*; object is implied by the verb), and b) *external* object (object *affected*; object not implied by the verb, but neces-

---

26. Under the influence of Hebrew בְּ (Bl-D §195) . Ἐν always takes the dative case.

27. Cf. the dative with verbs of strong personal relationship, §1130.

28. Ἀκολουθέω is also used with μετά and ὀπίσω with the genitive (another example of simple case usage being supplemented or supplanted by a preposition and the same or different case).

29. The dative is also used in hellenistic Greek to express duration of time contrary to classical usage, which employed the accusative for this purpose (Bl-D §201).

sary to define the extent of the action). Thus, the accusative may specify 2) the internal object, either a) as a cognate[30] (ἐχάρησαν χαρὰν μεγάλην σφόδρα, *they rejoiced with exceeding great joy* Mt 2:10), or b) as an object of kindred meaning (εἶδον ὅραμα, *I saw a vision* Acts 11:5) A verb may also take 3) two objects (*double accusative*), a) both of which may be external objects (αἴτησόν με ὃ ἐὰν θέλῃς, *Ask me whatever you wish* Mk 6:22), or b) one of which may be external, the other internal (ἡ ἀγάπην ἣν ἠγάπησάς με, *the love with which you loved me* Jn 17:26), or c) one of which may be the external object, the other a predicate accusative (εὐθείας ποιεῖτε τὰς τρίβους αὐτοῦ, *make his paths* [to be] *straight*[31] Mk 1:3). 4) The *terminal* accusative, denoting goal, is used only with prepositions (εἰς, ἐπί, παρά, πρός).

1140.   Extension, the basic idea of the accusative, is also expressed by 5) the accusative of *respect*[32] (specification or general reference): τὸν ἀριθμὸν ὡς πεντακισχίλιοι, *in number about 5,000* Jn 6:10 (i.e. so far as number is concerned), 6) the accusative of the extent of *space*: ἐληλακότες οὖν ὡς σταδίους εἴκοσι πέντε ἢ τριάκοντα, *when they had rowed about 25 or 30 stadia* Jn 6:19, and 7) the accusative of the extent of *time*: ἦν ἐν τῇ ἐρήμῳ τεσσεράκοντα ἡμέρας, *he was in the wilderness for 40 days* Mk 1:13. 8) The accusative of respect may also be used *adverbially*: καὶ προβὰς ὀλίγον, *and going on a little farther* Mk 1:19. 9) The *accusative subject of the infinitive*, strictly speaking, is an accusative of respect (general reference): πρὸ τοῦ Φίλιππον φωνῆσαι, *Before Philip called you* Jn 1:48 (lit., *before the to call you with respect to Philip*).

115.   The attempt to come to terms with the inflectional patterns of the nominal system (declension) will be more successful if the rationale of inflection in general has been grasped. The three factors involved in declension, gender, number and especially case, have been brought into relation to English in an effort to make the rationale apparent. The complexities of Greek syntax do not need to be mastered at this point, only appreciated. Syntax can better be learned in conjunction with actual texts. Coping with actual texts, however, depends upon 'discerning the signs,' and for that the structure of the nominal system is a first and readily taken step.

---

30. The object is etymologically related to the verb.

31. The second accusative in this case is an adjective rather than a noun, but the construction is the same. Cf. εἰ ἐκείνους εἶπεν θεούς, *if he designated them gods* Jn 10:35.

32. Cf. the dative of respect, §1131.

Lesson 5

The Article

120. The Greek article was originally a demonstrative pronoun (it was so used in Homer). It was subsequently weakened to the status of article, then serving merely as a pointer. Cf. the article *der* in German, which serves as article, relative and demonstrative pronoun; in English *that* is both demonstrative and relative and is related to the article. In Greek the article is definite. Greek does not, strictly speaking, have an indefinite article (corresponding to *a*, *an* in English).

For the most part, the article functions in Greek as it does in English. A number of the idiomatic uses of the article in Greek can be learned by observation, and will occasion no difficulty.

0121. The declension of the article serves as the model for the declension of all first and second declension nouns as well as numerous adjectives and pronouns. Since the article provides the basic declension pattern from which so much can be derived, *it must be mastered.* Prompt mastery will assure rapid control of the bulk of the nominal system.

In addition, the article is often the means at hand for the easy identification (gender, number, case) of other items in the nominal system (e.g. nouns, adjectives, participles), especially where the declension pattern in question does not correspond to that of the article. The article, in short, is the friendly resolver of many identification problems.

121. The article ὁ, ἡ, τό, *the*, is declined as follows:

	Singular			Plural		
	Masc.	Fem.	Neut.	Masc.	Fem.	Neut.
Nom.	ὁ	ἡ	τό	οἱ	αἱ	τά
Gen.	τοῦ	τῆς	τοῦ	τῶν	τῶν	τῶν
Dat.	τῷ	τῇ	τῷ	τοῖς	ταῖς	τοῖς
Acc.	τόν	τήν	τό	τούς	τάς	τά

The endings of the article are set off merely to call attention to them. It should be noted that the article shows only τ as its stem (appearing in all but four forms).

1210. Mnemonic hints:

1210.1 Four forms do not have initial τ: masc. and fem. nom. sing. and plur. These forms have *rough breathing* instead.

1210.2 The middle cases (gen. dat.) masc. and neut. are identical in the sing. and plur. respectively.

1210.3 The genitive plural is identical for all genders.

1210.4 The neuter nom. and acc. sing. are identical; the neuter nom. and acc. plur. likewise.

1210.5 The fem. has η in the sing., α in the plur. (except gen. plur.).

122. First and second declension substantives show the endings of the article with three exceptions: masc. nom. sing. adds -ς; neuter nom. and acc. singulars add ν (shown in parenthesis):

	Singular			Plural		
	Masc.	Fem.	Neut.	Masc.	Fem.	Neut.
Nom.	-ο(ς)	-η	-ο(ν)	-οι	-αι	-α
Gen.	-ου	-ης	-ου	-ων	-ων	-ν
Dat.	-ῳ	-ῃ	-ῳ	-οις	-αις	-οις
Acc.	-ον	-ην	-ο(ν)	-ους	-ας	-α

Thus, on the basis of the fem. article it is possible to identify the form of all nouns of the first declension, and on the basis of the masc. and neut. articles to identify the form of all nouns of the second declension.

123. The relative pronoun, ὅς, ἥ, ὅ, *who, which, that*, follows the same pattern as the article. At three points it may easily be confused with the article. Because of its similarity and frequency, it may be learned along with the article.

The relative pronoun is declined as follows:

	Singular			Plural		
	Masc.	Fem.	Neut.	Masc.	Fem.	Neut.
Nom.	ὅς	ἥ	ὅ	οἵ	αἵ	ἅ
Gen.	οὗ	ἧς	οὗ	ὧν	ὧν	ὧν
Dat.	ᾧ	ᾗ	ᾧ	οἷς	αἷς	οἷς
Acc.	ὅν	ἥν	ὅ	οὕς	ἅς	ἅ

1230. Mnemonic hints:

1230.1 The relative pronoun has *rough breathing throughout* (the masc. and fem. nom. sing. and plur. of the article also have rough breathing, but elsewhere τ).

1230.2   Mnemonic hints 2–5 §1210 apply here also.

1230.3   The masc. nom. sing. has final ς, (the corresponding form of the article does not, but second declension masculine nouns do: §122); the neut. nom. and acc. sing., however, do not add final ν as do neuter substantives of the second declension (§122).

1230.4   ἥ (fem. nom. sing.), οἵ, αἵ (masc., fem. nom. plur.) are identical in form with the corresponding forms of the article, except that the forms of the article lack accent: ἡ, οἱ, αἱ. The accent mark is the only means (other than context) of distinguishing these forms. ὅς is distinguishable from ὁ (the corresponding form of the article) by the final ς, as well as by the accent mark.

124.   It is important to master the declension of the article. Mastery means instant identification (gender, number, case) in context. The most effective practice is scanning a Greek text for articles, at first verbally citing gender, number, case (with options). Then pass as quickly as possible to silent recognition.

    Similarly, one may scan a text for relative pronouns. Learn to identify the relative on the basis of the marks that distinguish it from the article.

    The following notes on John 8:12–59 will be of help in avoiding initial confusions:

> Jn 8:12: οὐ is not to be confused with οὗ (relative): accent and breathing are different.
>
> Jn 8:13: οἱ is the article, not the relative: it lacks accent.
>
> Jn 8:38: ἃ has grave (`) rather than acute (´) accent: this difference is not significant for the identification of the relative pronoun. Cf. τὰ in 8:39 and ὃς in 8:40.
>
> Jn 8:42: ἦν is not to be confused with ἥν (ἣν): the former (which is a form of the verb *be*) has *smooth* rather than *rough* breathing, and a circumflex (~) rather than an acute (´) or grave (`) accent.

1240.   Word list:

> ὁ, ἡ, τό — *the* (definite article)
>
> ὅς, ἥ, ὅ — *who, which, that* (relative pronoun)

Lesson 6

The Article as
Structure Signal

125. Sentences are meaningful because they conform to a grammatical system characteristic of the language as a whole. Nonsense sentences are words strung together without reference to system: *hill the the up go boy high.* One may construct a meaningful sentence out of these words (with one modification): *the boy went up the high hill.* The knowledge that makes it possible to order words into a sentence is knowledge of the grammatical system. The native user of a language may be only dimly aware of the rules by which sentences are constructed, and even the grammarian is rarely conscious of them when speaking or writing. But every user of a language has to conform to the system to be understood.

1250. Grammar attempts to expose the system of a language by describing the various structures into which words and word groups enter. Such structures may be simple or they may be very complex. Whatever the degree of complexity, such structures are signaled by devices within the language itself (in spoken language they are also signaled by intonation contour, stress and the like). Some of these devices have no other function than to indicate structure, e.g. the inflectional endings in the nominal system. In order to be able to understand a sentence one must know 1) these structure signals and how they function; and 2) the meaning of the remaining words (§1).

1251. The article serves as a signal in Greek. Since it is nearly lexically empty itself (i.e. one cannot point to or define a *the*), it is employed primarily in conjunction with other lexically full words or word groups. While it may serve to specify a head term (or cluster) in various ways as a determiner (§§710–7160), it may also serve merely to signal structure. It more often does the latter, but it may do both.

1252. As a signaler of structure, the function of the article ranges from specifying case, by which it contributes indirectly to sentence structure, to indicating changes in the speaker in a dialogue or shifts in subject matter (demonstrative function). At the simplest level, the article assists in the identification (gender, number, case) of various elements in the sentence and in the determination of word groups. Some of the simpler functions should be observed from the outset, since they contribute to the ease with which the nominal system can be mastered and the sentence resolved.

126. *The article with a nominal head.* The simple word group, article plus nominal head, is not often separated by other words (intervening words are usually connectives or nuance words which cannot stand first in their own clause, e.g. μέν, δέ). The sequence is always article, nominal head.

(1)	ὁ Ἰησοῦς	Jn 8:12
(2)	τὸν πατέρα	Jn 8:27
(3)	τῆς ἁμαρτίας	Jn 8:34b

The article signals the gender, number and case of the head. Without knowledge of the inflectional patterns of the nominal heads in question, it is thus possible to determine the case relationship of the word group to the sentence (excluding the options indicated in §1210.2–4).

127. *Article, head with qualifier.* There are three possible sequences for a word group comprised of article, head, adjective qualifier:

127.1 Article, adjective qualifier, head:

(4)	τὸν ἐμὸν λόγον	Jn 8:51b
(5)	τοῖς ἀκαθάρτοις πνεύμασιν	Lk 4:36
(6)	οἱ ἀληθινοὶ προσκυνηταί	Jn 4:23

127.2 Article, head, article, adjective qualifier:

(7)	ἡ κρίσις ἡ ἐμή	Jn 8:16
(8)	ἡ ἐντολή ἡ παλαιά	1 Jn 2:7b
(9)	τὸ φῶς τὸ ἀληθινόν	1 Jn 2:8

127.3 Head, article, adjective qualifier:

(10)	εἰρήνην τὴν ἐμήν	Jn 14:27

127.4 It is to be noted that the article in each sequence precedes the adjective qualifier; the nominal head may lack the article as in (10), but it usually does not.

The article contributes to the determination of the word group and again signals gender, number, case (excluding the options in §1210.2–4).

128. *Article, head with other determiner.* The determiners which may appear with a word group comprised of article and noun (or article, adjective qualifier and noun) are drawn from a closed class of words, and always appear in "predicate" position, i.e. without an article preceding them:

(11) ταῦτα τὰ ῥήματα	(οὗτος)	Jn 8:20a
(12) τὴν ἡμέραν ἐκείνην	(ἐκεῖνος)	Jn 1:39
(13) ἡ χήρα αὕτη ἡ πτωχή	(οὗτος)	Mk 12:43

Such determiners may either precede (11) or follow (12) the article-head. In (13) an adjectival modifier is appended (cf. §127.2).

129.1 *The noun phrase with genitive modifier.* In the noun phrases considered so far all the terms have been in the same gender, number and case. Another commonly occurring noun phrase consists of article-head in one case, modified by an article-noun in the genitive case. The genitive word group limits or specifies the head term (§112.1).

(14) τὸ φῶς τοῦ κοσμοῦ	Jn 8:12a
(15) τὸν υἱὸν τοῦ ἀνθρώπου	Jn 8:28a
(16) ἡ ἀγάπη τοῦ θεοῦ	1 Jn 2:5

This is a very commonly occurring word cluster (it occurs more often than those in §§127, 128). The precise sense in which the genitive word group specifies the head is grammatically indeterminate, but the sense is generally drawn from an established range (§§0112–1120).

This type of phrase is subject to other sequences:

129.2 The defining genitive is sandwiched between article and head:

(17) ὁ τοῦ θεοῦ [γὰρ] υἱός	2 Cor 1:19

Cf. §127.1.

129.3 The relation of the defining genitive to the head is signaled by a repetition of the head article:

(18) ὁ λόγος [γὰρ] ὁ τοῦ σταυροῦ	1 Cor 1:18

Cf. §127.2.

129.4 The genitive word group precedes the head:

(19) τοῦ Ἰησοῦ Χριστοῦ ἡ γένεσις   Mt 1:18

(18) and (19) are by no means common, and (17) is literary (Turner 349).

129.5 The sequence, ὁ (in any gender, number, case)- - - -τοῦ (τῆς, τῶν)- - - -, thus signals a noun phrase in which one component in the genitive case modifies the other. The sequence may be varied: ὁ τοῦ- - - - - - - -/ ὁ- - - -ὁ τοῦ- - - -/ τοῦ- - - - ὁ- - - -. Such noun phrases can often be identified and resolved on the basis of the article alone.

Nouns: First Declension

Stems in -α, -ᾱ, -η, -ας, -ης

130. For purely formal reasons the Greek system of nouns is divided into three categories. The major division is between vowel and consonant stems, i.e. between stems ending in a vowel and consonant respectively. A stem is what remains when the inflectional suffix is removed, e.g. ἀρχῆ-ς: ἀρχῆ- stem, -ς, inflectional ending. The first and second declensions are made up of vowel stems; the third declension is the consonant declension. While the vowel stems appear to behave with greater regularity, the consonant declension is just as consistent, except that one has to reckon with certain phonetic changes occasioned by attaching inflectional endings to stems ending in a consonant.

1300. The article serves as the model for both the first and second declensions.

131.1 Nouns of the first declension are predominantly feminine (indicated by ἡ), with some masculines (indicated by ὁ). There are no neuters (τό).

131.2 The inflectional pattern of these nouns will, of course, follow the feminine of the article: ἡ, τῆς, τῇ, τήν; αἱ, τῶν, ταῖς, τάς.

131.3 There are two minor variations which prompt the division of the first declension into three types of declension pattern. The first has to do with the final vowel of the stem, i.e. whether it is α or η, and whether it appears consistently or not. For purposes of identification in a written text the student may ignore the α/η shift (think of η as another form of α) and concentrate on the endings, which are consistent. The second variation concerns a few masculines of this declension which have nom. and gen. sing. endings borrowed from the second declension. *These variations never concern the plural.*

132. The three major declension patterns are:

132.1 Consistent α or η in singular (I.1)

ἡμέρα, -ας, ἡ — *day* φωνή, -ῆς, ἡ — *sound, voice*

	S	P		S	P
N	ἡμέρα	ἡμέραι	N	φωνή	φωναί
G	ἡμέρας	ἡμερῶν	G	φωνῆς	φωνῶν
D	ἡμέρᾳ	ἡμέραις	D	φωνῇ	φωναῖς
A	ἡμέραν	ἡμέρας	A	φωνήν	φωνάς

132.2   α/η shift in singular (α in nom. and acc., η in gen. and dat.) (I.2)

δόξα, -ης, ἡ — *glory*

	S	P
N	δόξα	δόξαι
G	δόξης	δοξῶν
D	δόξῃ	δόξαις
A	δόξαν	δόξας

Note: The variation concerns only the singular, and occasions no difficulty for identification.

132.3   Masculines in -ας, -ης, genitive -ου (I.3)

μεσσίας, -ου, ὁ — *messiah (christ)*   προφήτης, -ου, ὁ — *prophet*

	S	P		S	P
N	μεσσίας	μεσσίαι	N	προφήτης	προφῆται
G	μεσσίου	μεσσιῶν	G	προφήτου	προφητῶν
D	μεσσίᾳ	μεσσίαις	D	προφήτῃ	προφήταις
A	μεσσίαν	μεσσίας	A	προφήτην	προφήτας

1320.   Mnemonic hints:

1320.1   Nouns of the first declension follow the feminine article except for 1) the interchange of α/η in the singular of a few nouns, and 2) the nom. and gen. singular of the masculines (-ας/-ης and -ου).

1320.2   The nom. sing. (-ς) and gen. sing. (-ου) of the masculines are borrowed from the second declension (cf. the article): the gen. -ου became necessary to distinguish gen. from nom. once -ς had been added to the nom. (i.e. the pattern would have been -ας, -ας). -ς and -ου have the additional virtue of indicating that these nouns, which belong to a predominantly feminine declension, are masculine.

1320.3   Masculines in -ας/-ης, -ου have α or η, respectively, throughout the singular (excluding the genitive, of course), i.e. nouns of this class are not subject to the α/η shift in the middle cases. However, nouns in -της (e.g. προφήτης, -ου, ὁ) have a vocative sing. in -ᾰ: προφῆτα (§205.3).

1320.4   In feminine nouns with consistent α in the singular, the gen. sing. and acc. plural are identical in form. In masculine nouns with α in the singular, the nom. sing. and acc. plural are identical in form.

1321. Additional notes:

1321.1 Regarding the α/η shift in the singular, the following rules are helpful (necessary only to inflect nouns of this type; identification is not complicated by the shift): 1) -η in the nom. sing., keep -η throughout the singular; 2) -α in the nom. sing., keep -α throughout the singular after ε, ι, ρ, elsewhere shift to -η in gen. and dat. (a few nouns in -ρα make the shift, however, e.g. μάχαιρα, -ης, ἡ *sword*).

1321.2 The accent of *all* nouns is persistent, i.e. remains on the same syllable throughout if the rules governing accent permit (in verbs the accent is recessive, i.e. falls back on the word as far as it can). The accent of nouns must be learned from a dictionary.

1321.3 The genitive plural of first declension nouns is always accented -ῶν (< -άων).

133.1 A third minor variation necessitates a fourth subdivision of the first declension. This variation, too, concerns only the nom. and gen. sing. (nom. sing. in -ας/-ης, gen. in -α/-η). Nouns of this category are infrequent (38 nouns of this type appear in the New Testament), consisting largely of proper names.

133.2 Masculines in -ας/-ης, gen. -α/-η (I.4)

> σατανᾶς, -ᾶ, ὁ — *Satan*
>
> S
>
> N σατανᾶς
> G σατανᾶ
> D σατανᾷ
> A σατανᾶν

133.3 The plural does not come into consideration. In this pattern -ς has been added to the nom. sing., and the -ς is accordingly dropped from the gen. sing. These nouns have α or η consistently in the singular.

134. Summary. If the variation between α/η is ignored, all nouns of the first declension follow the declension pattern of the feminine article, except the masculines (I.3 and I.4) in nom. and gen. sing.: here is found -ας or -ης (both groups) in the nom., and -ου (I.3) or -α (I.4) in the gen. By learning the declension of the feminine article and the two (or three) variations thereon, one has learned the inflectional variations in all first declension nouns. This amounts to 1053 nouns in the New Testament vocabulary, or over a third of all inflected nouns found in the New Testament (see Appendix II).

1340. The catalogue of first declension nouns in Appendix II is organized in accordance with the three (four) groups given above. Of the 1053 first declension nouns appearing in the New Testament, the vast majority, 784, belong to group I.1 (111 appear ten times or more). The second largest group is I.3 (189, of which 17 appear ten times or more). I.2 is represented by 42 nouns, and I.4 by 38.

The catalogue may be used for reference when practicing noun identification.

1341. A catalogue of first declension nouns appearing in John 8:12–59 follows. Nouns belonging to I.4 are not represented in this passage. The nouns are listed in the order of their appearance. Those marked with an asterisk (*) appear in the New Testament more than 100 times. This catalogue may also be used as a vocabulary list.

I.1. Consistent α or η in the singular

σκοτία, -ας, ἡ — *darkness, gloom*

* ζωή, -ῆς, ἡ — *life*

μαρτυρία, -ας, ἡ — *testimony* [cf. *martyr*]

* ὥρα, -ας, ἡ — *time of day, hour* [cf. *horoscope*]

* ἁμαρτία, -ας, ἡ — *sin*

ἀρχή, -ῆς, ἡ — *beginning; ruler, authority* [cf. *archaic*]

* ἀλήθεια, -ας, ἡ — *truth*

οἰκία, -ας, ἡ — *house; household*

πορνεία, -ας, ἡ — *prostitution, unchastity*

λαλιά, -ᾶς, ἡ — *speech, speaking*

ἐπιθυμία, -ας, ἡ — *desire*

ἡμέρα, -ας, ἡ — *day* [cf. *ephemeral:* ἐφ' (for) ἡμέραν *a day*)]

I.2. α/η shift in singular

* δόξα, -ης, ἡ — *glory* [cf. *doxology*]

I.3. Masculines in -ας/-ης, gen. -ου

* μαθητής, -οῦ, ἡ — *disciple*

ψεύστης, -ου, ὁ — *liar*

Σαμαρίτης, -ου, ὁ — *Samaritan*

* προφήτης, -ου, ὁ — *prophet* [*prophet*]

Nouns: Second Declension

Stems in -o

135.1 Nouns of the second declension are predominantly masculine and neuter (indicated by ὁ and τό), with some feminines (ἡ).

135.2 The inflectional pattern of the masculine and feminine nouns follows the masculine article, that of the neuter nouns the neuter article, with the three exceptions noted (§122): masc. nom. sing. -ος (rather than -o), neut. nom. and acc. sing. -ον (rather than -o).

135.3 The second declension thus consists of two basic patterns, one for masculines and feminines and one for neuters. The two patterns differ only in the nom. and acc. cases (both numbers). Feminine nouns of the second declension are declined exactly like the masculines; their gender is indicated only by the article (ἡ) and other modifiers. For the sake of completeness, the second declension may likewise be divided into three subcategories.

136. The three major declension patterns of the second declension are:

136.1 Masculines in -ος (II.1)

θεός, οῦ, ὁ — *god*

	S	P
N	θεός	θεοί
G	θεοῦ	θεῶν
D	θεῷ	θεοῖς
A	θεόν	θεούς

136.2 Feminines in -ος (II.2)

ὁδός, -οῦ, ἡ — *way, road, journey*

	S	P
N	ὁδός	ὁδοί
G	ὁδοῦ	ὁδῶν
D	ὁδῷ	ὁδοῖς
A	ὁδόν	ὁδούς

Note: Feminines of the second declension are declined exactly like masculines.

136.3 Neuters in -ον (II.3)

ἔργον, -ου, τό — *work*

	S	P
N	ἔργον	ἔργα
G	ἔργου	ἔργων
D	ἔργῳ	ἔργοις
A	ἔργον	ἔργα

1360. Mnemonic hints:

1360.1 Masculines and feminines = masculine article, except: add -ς, to nom. sing.

1360.2 Neuters = neuter article, except: add -ν to nom. and acc. sing.

1360.3 All middle cases (gen., dat.) in each number are identical.

1360.4 Differences between masculine-feminine and neuter are therefore confined to the nominative and accusative.

1360.5 The neuter nominative and accusative singular are identical, as are the nominative and accusative plural.

1360.6 One may confuse the masculine-feminine accusative singular (-ον) with the neuter nominative or accusative singular (-ον), but the article and other modifiers (and the structure in which they occur) often make it possible to distinguish them: masculine-feminine articles, τόν, τήν neuter articles, τό.

1360.7 One may also confuse the neuter nominative and accusative plural with the nominative singular of first declension nouns in -α (§132). But again the article (ἡ for the feminine nominative, τά for the neuter nominative and accusative) and other modifiers may signal the difference.

1360.8 The gen. plurals of all first and second declension nouns (as in the case of the article) will be identical.

137. Contract substantives of the second declension (II.4) will show -ους (masc.) or -ουν (neut.) in the nom. sing., and -ουν (masc. and neut.) in the acc. sing., rather than -ος, -ον. -ους, -ουν are contracted from -οος or -εος. The declension pattern is in other respects identical with that of other second declension nouns. Only four nouns of this type appear in Bauer (see Appendix II, II.4).

138. The Attic second declension (II.5) follows a pattern in the sing. of -ως, -ω, -ῳ, -ω(ν): it has ω throughout, and, like nouns of I.4, the gen. is the nom. less -ς; the acc. varies between -ω and -ων. The plural does not come into consideration. Only three nouns of this type appear in the New Testament (see Appendix II, II.5).

139.   Summary. Masculines and feminines of the second declension are declined like
the masc. article, but add -ς, to the nom. sing. Neuters of the second declension are declined like the neut. article, but add -v to the nom. and acc. sing.
By learning the declension of the masc. and neut. articles and the three variations thereon, one has learned the inflectional patterns of all second declension nouns (save for nouns in categories II.4 and 5, which are exceedingly rare).

There are 912 second declension nouns in the New Testament vocabulary
(Appendix II). It is now possible to identify the inflectional patterns of well over
two-thirds of the nouns represented in Bauer (not necessarily in a given text,
since frequency has to be taken into account).

1390.   Following is a catalogue of second declension nouns appearing in John 8:12–
59. Nouns belonging to II.2, II.4, and II.5 are not represented in this passage.
The nouns are listed in each category in the order of their appearance. Those
marked with an asterisk (*) appear in the New Testament more than 100 times.
This catalogue may also be used as a vocabulary list.

II.1. Masculines in -ος

*	κόσμος, -ου, ὁ	world [cf. cosmic]
	Φαρασαῖος, -ου, ὁ	Pharisee
*	νόμος, ου, ὁ	law [cf. Deuteronomy: second law]
*	ἄνθρωπος, -ου, ὁ	man [cf. anthropology]
*	υἱός, -ου, ὁ	son
*	λόγος, -ου, ὁ	word [cf. logic]
*	δοῦλος, -ου, ὁ	slave
*	θεός, -οῦ, ὁ	God [cf. theology]
	ἀνθρωποκτόνος, -ου, ὁ	murderer
*	θάνατος, -ου, ὁ	death [cf. thanatopsis]
	λίθος, -ου, ὁ	stone [cf. lithography]

II.2. Feminines in -ος

   (no examples in this passage)

II.3. Neuters in -ον

	γαζοφυλακεῖον, -ου, τό	treasury
	ἱερόν, -οῦ, τό	sanctuary, temple [cf. hierarch]
	τέκνον, -ου, τό	child
*	ἔργον, -ου, τό	work, deed
	δαιμόνιον, -ου, τό	divinity, demon [cf. demon]

1391.   Facility with the Greek noun is generated by practice at identification in context, together with vocabulary building and familiarity with the types of word clusters in which the noun normally appears. Meaning is best learned, however, in conjunction with the word group and the sentence.

1392.   There follows a supplementary catalogue of first and second declension nouns found in John 1:1–51. Omitted are the nouns which appeared in the catalogue in §1390. The words are again given in the order of their appearance, and an asterisk (*) means that they appear in the New Testament more than 100 times.

I.1. Consistent α or η in the singular

*	ἐξουσία, -ου, ἡ	*authority, power*
*	φωνή, -ου, ἡ	*sound, voice* [cf. phonetic, phonograph]
	Βηθανία, -ας, ἡ	(also indeclinable) *Bethany*
	περιστερά, -ᾶς, ἡ	*dove, pigeon*
	Γαλιλαία, -ας, ἡ	*Galilee*
	συκῆ, -ῆς, ἡ	*fig tree*

I.2. α/η shift in the singular (no new examples)

I.3. Masculines in -ας/-ης, gen. -ου

Ἰωάννης, -ου, ὁ	*John*
Λευίτης, -ου, ὁ	*Levite*
Ἠλίας, -ου, ὁ	*Elijah*
Ἠσαΐας, -ου, ὁ	*Isaiah*
Ἰορδάνης, -ου, ὁ	*Jordan*
Ἀνδρέας, -ου, ὁ	*Andrew*
Μεσσίας, -ου, ὁ	*Messiah*
Ἰσραηλίτης, -ου, ὁ	*Israelite*

II.1. Masculines in -ος

	κόλπος, -ου, ὁ	*bosom, breast*
	χριστός, -οῦ, ὁ	*christ*
	ἀμνός, -οῦ, ὁ	*lamb*
*	οὐρανός, -οῦ, ὁ	*heaven* [cf. *Uranus* (planet), *uranium* (element)]
*	ἀδελφός, -οῦ, ὁ	*brother* [cf. *Philadelphia*: (city of) brotherly love]
	Πέτρος, -ου, ὁ	*Peter*
	Φίλιππος, -ου, ὁ	*Philip* [*Philip*: lover (φίλος) of horses (ἵππος)]
	δόλος, -ου, ὁ	*deceit, cunning*
*	ἄγγελος, -ου, ὁ	*angel*

II.2. Feminines in -ος

   *   ὁδός, -οῦ, ἡ   *way, road, journey* [cf. *anode, cathode*: electrical terminals]

II.3. Neuters in -ov (no new examples)

Lesson 9

Prepositions as Structure Signals

140. The prepositions, like the article, are commonly occurring structure signals. Unlike the article, they are indeclinables. They occur in pre-position (hence their name) with verbs, with which, in the hellenistic period, they are usually compounded, i.e. the two elements are conceived as a single word (e.g. εἰσέρχομαι); they occur also in pre-position with nominal elements and hence are employed in conjunction with an oblique case (e.g. εἰς τὴν πόλιν). But they may also appear in pre-position with invariables (i.e. indeclinable words), such as adverbs (e.g. ἀπὸ τότε). The adverbial use of the preposition as a discrete element in the sentence, i.e. without a term in relation to which the preposition stands in pre-position, is rare in hellenistic Greek. Since the cluster preposition-verb has coalesced and the isolated preposition as adverb has virtually disappeared, the discrete preposition normally introduces a word group, most often composed of nominal elements.

    For a sketch of the preposition in hellenistic Greek, s. Bl-D §203; Turner 249ff.

1400. The so-called *proper prepositions* are prepositions which are also compounded with verbs; the *improper prepositions* never occur in composition with verbs. The latter border on the adverbs, from which in fact it is difficult to distinguish them in every instance. These distinctions (proper, improper preposition and adverb) are therefore formal and not particularly germane to grammar, except that the proper prepositions comprise a closed class and are of much higher frequency, while the improper prepositions form an ever expanding and thus unstable class, though occurring less frequently.

141. Attention is to be restricted initially to the word group containing a nominal head and initiated by a preposition.

141.1 In the New Testament eight proper prepositions are employed in conjunction with a single case. Ἀνά, εἰς are used only with the accusative; ἐν and σύν only with the dative; ἀντί, ἀπό, ἐκ (ἐξ before vowels), πρό only with the genitive. When initiating word groups, these prepositions will therefore automatically signal the case of the head nominal term (including those instances where an indeclinable is the head term in the group).

141.2 Ἀνά, ἀντί and πρό are not common in the New Testament and appear for the most part in fixed phrases or with a limited range of meaning (s. Bl-D §§204, 208, 213). Εἰς, ἐν, ἀπό and ἐκ (ἐξ) , on the other hand, are very common and are used with a wide range of meaning. Σύν occupies an intermediate position.

142.1 *The 'meanings' of ἐν, εἰς, ἀπό, ἐκ and σύν.* It is virtually impossible to catalogue the 'meanings' of the prepositions (s. the introduction to ἐν in Bauer s.v.). The prepositions, together with the case-forms (inflectional endings), belong to that grammatical system which signals word-relationships in the sentence. The range of their 'meaning' must therefore be determined in relation to that system, and it can be specified in particular instances only in relation to context (the sentence, paragraph, work, period). An introductory sketch of the range of the prepositions must be confined to the predominant senses in which the individual prepositions contribute to the syntactical function of the cases.

142.2 There is an increasing tendency in hellenistic Greek to supplement the simple cases with prepositions (weakening of the inflectional system; cf. §111). There is also a tendency to reduce the number of cases with which a particular preposition may be used (with reference to those prepositions used with more than one case in the classical period). Some prepositions overlap (e.g. ἐκ and ἀπό), some are beginning to be 'confused' in the hellenistic period (e.g. εἰς and ἐν). The finesse with which the prepositions and cases were used in the classical period can no longer be expected of hellenistic authors.

143.1 The characteristic local (spatial) senses of ἐν, εἰς, ἀπό and ἐκ (ἐξ) in conjunction with their respective cases, may be illustrated by the following examples:

(1) ὁ [δε] δοῦλος οὐ μένει ἐν τῇ οἰκίᾳ   Jn 8:35
The servant does not abide in the house

(2) ἦλθεν εἰς τὴν οἰκίαν   Mt 13:36
he went into the house

(3) οὐ μακρὰν ἀπέχοντος ἀπὸ τῆς οἰκίας   Lk 7:6
when he was not far from the house

(4) μηδὲ εἰσελθάτω ἆραί τι ἐκ τῆς οἰκίας αὐτοῦ   Mk 13:15
let him not enter to fetch anything out of his house

143.2   Ἐν with dat. (locative) indicates place where: ⓔⓥ — *in, among*
Εἰς with acc. direction toward, terminal point, entry: εἰς ——⊕ *toward, to, into.*
Ἀπό with gen. direction away from: ἀπό ◯——▸ *from, away from.*
Ἐκ with gen. exit, separation, direction from: ἐκ ◯——▸ *out of, from.*

1430.   The overlapping of the prepositions with each other and with the function of
the simple cases is illustrated by the triple variant in Mt 13:1:

(5)   ἐξελθὼν ὁ Ἰησοῦς τῆς οἰκίας
(6)   . . .   ἐκ τῆς οἰκίας
(7)   . . .   ἀπὸ τῆς οἰκίας
Jesus, going out of the house

The three forms are identical in meaning. A preposition is normally supplied
in hellenistic Greek where verbs of motion are involved. Constructions like (5)
are thus rare.

144.1   The characteristic temporal senses of ἐν, εἰς, ἀπό and ἐκ (ἐξ) are quite comparable to the local functions:

(8)   ἐν ἐκείνῃ τῇ ἡμέρᾳ ὑμεῖς γνώσεσθε   Jn 14:20
       on that day you shall know
(9)   εἰς τὴν ἡμέραν τοῦ ἐνταφιασμοῦ μου   Jn 12:7
       until the day of my burial
(10)   ἀπ’ ἐκείνης [οὖν] τῆς ἡμέρας ἐβουλεύσαντο   Jn 11:53
       from that day on they plotted
(11)   πάτερ, σῶσόν με ἐκ τῆς ὥρας ταύτης   Jn 12:27
       father, save me from this hour

144.2   It may be observed from these examples and those in §143 that it is impossible
to equate the individual prepositions in Greek with particular prepositions in
English.

1440.1   Similar temporal notions may be expressed by the simple cases:

(12)   τῇ ἡμέρᾳ τῇ τρίτῃ   Jn 2:1
       on the third day
(13)   ἐκεῖ ἔμεινεν οὐ πολλὰς ἡμέρας   Jn 2:12
       they did not stay there (for) many days

1440.2 The simple genitive, however, expresses time within which:

> (14) ἦλθεν πρὸς αὐτὸν νυκτὸς Jn 3:2
> *he came to him at night*

1450. Ἐν is also employed with the dative to indicate means, manner or instrument:

> (15) ἐν μαχαίρῃ ἀπολοῦνται Mt 26:52
> *they will perish by the sword*

For the wide variety of other ways in which ἐν specifies the dative (locative, instrumental), see Bauer s.v. Cf. Bl-D §§205, 206, 219, 220.

1451. Σύν is used with the dative to denote accompaniment or association:

> (16) σὺν τοῖς ὄχλοις Acts 14:13
> *together with the crowd*
> (17) εἰ [δὲ] ἀπεθάνομεν σὺν Χριστῷ Rom 6:8
> *if we die with Christ*

1452. Εἰς, like ἐν, is used in a wide variety of ways. In addition to the spatial and temporal uses (§§143, 144), it may denote goal, end, result, purpose:

> (18) οὗτος ἦλθεν εἰς μαρτυρίαν Jn 1:7
> *this one came as a witness (to bear witness)*
> (19) εἰς κενὸν τρέχω Gal 2:2
> *I am running in vain (to no purpose)*
> (20) ἀφωρισμένος εἰς εὐαγγέλιον θεοῦ Rom 1:1
> *set apart for the gospel of God*

For still other senses, consult Bauer s.v.; Bl-D §207.

1453. Ἀπό is in the process of absorbing ἐκ (ἐξ), although the latter is still more frequent than the former in hellenistic Greek. Their main functions have already tended to converge (cf. §§143–144). They are employed further to denote origin, cause, reason:

> (21) ἦν [δὲ] ὁ Φίλιππος ἀπὸ Βηθσαϊδά, Jn 1:44
> ἐκ τῆς πόλεως Ἀνδρέου καὶ Πέτρου
> *Philip was from Bethsaida*
> *from the city of Andrew and Peter*

(22) οὐκ ἠδύνατο ἀπὸ τοῦ ὄχλου   Lk 19:3
he was not able because of the crowd

(23) οὐ δικαιοῦται ἄνθρωπος ἐξ ἔργων νόμου   Gal 2:16
man is not justified on the basis of works of law

1454. Ἐκ is predominant in the partitive sense (to indicate the whole of which something is a part) :

(24) ἐκ τῶν μαθητῶν αὐτοῦ δύο   Jn 1:35
two of his disciples

Further, s. Moule 71–74; Bl-D §§209–211; and the appropriate entries in Bauer.

146. *The preposition as initiator of a word group containing a nominal 'head.'* Prepositions may initiate word groups which correspond to those considered under the article (§§126–129).

146.1 Ἐν :

(25) ἐν τῇ σκοτίᾳ   Jn 8:12
(26) ἐν τῷ νόμῳ [δὲ] τῷ ὑμετέρῳ   Jn 8:17
(27) ἐν [δὲ] ταῖς ἡμέραις ἐκείναις   Mt 3:1
(28) ἐν τῇ ἡμέρᾳ τοῦ κυρίου   1 Cor 5:5

146.2 Σύν :

(29) σὺν τοῖς ὄχλοις   Acts 14:13
(30) σὺν ὅλῃ τῇ ἐκκλησίᾳ   Acts 15:22

146.3 Εἰς :

(31) εἰς τὴν Γαλιλαίαν   Jn 4:3
(32) εἰς τὴν Ἰουδαίαν γῆν   Jn 3:22
(33) εἰς τὴν βασιλείαν τοῦ θεοῦ   Jn 3:5

146.4 Ἀπό, ἐκ (ἐξ) :

(34) ἐκ τοῦ θεοῦ   Jn 8:42
(35) ἐκ τοῦ κόσμου τούτου   Jn 8:23
(36) ἀπ' ἐκείνης τῆς ὥρας   Jn 19:27
(37) ἀπὸ τῆς γενεᾶς τῆς σκολιᾶς ταύτης   Acts 2:40

146.5   Since each of these prepositions is employed with a single case, each signals the appropriate case of the head term; in all examples given above, the article seconds that signal (the article immediately precedes the head term). The article further supplies number and in some instances gender. The case, number and even gender of the head nominal term in word groups such as these are thus advanced to the reader before he or she reaches the inflectional ending of the nominal head.

1460.   The limits of these word groups are signaled in context, in addition to other factors, by the congruence of the procession of inflectional endings, e.g. ἐν -ῇ -ᾷ (25), ἐκ -οῦ -οῦ (34), ἐν -ῳ -ῳ -ῷ -ῳ (26), ἀπό -ῆς -ᾶς -ῆς -ᾶς -ῆς (37). Attention should be constantly directed to such word groups. Learning to grasp them at a single glance will make the inflectional patterns of the nominal system much easier to master, the sentence much easier to resolve, with the consequence that one's reading rate will improve more rapidly.

147.   Since ἐν and σύν are always followed by the dative, one may confidently expect them to be followed only by the following forms of the article: τῷ, τῇ/τοῖς, ταῖς (where the article occurs and where an adjective or pronominal adjective in predicate position [§128] does not intervene, as e.g. in (30)). Εἰς will be followed only by τόν, τήν, τό/τούς, τάς, τά; ἀπό and ἐκ only by τοῦ, τῆς/τῶν.

1470.   Ἐν, σύν occur only with the dat., εἰς only with acc., ἀπό, ἐκ (ἐξ) only with gen. On this basis alone it is possible to extend the possibilities of case identification (but not identification of number and gender) to those instances where the article does not occur.

1470.1   The following are examples of first and second declension nouns, the inflectional endings of which are already familiar:

(38)	ἐν θεῷ	Jn 3:21
(39)	σὺν Χριστῷ	Rom 6:8
(40)	ἀπ' ἀρχῆς	Jn 8:44
(41)	ἐκ θεοῦ	Jn 1:13

1470.2   But the prepositional signal works equally well for third declension nouns and indeclinables:

(42)	ἐν ὕδατι	Jn 1:26
(43)	ἐν Καφαρναοὺμ (indeclinable)	Jn 2:12
(44)	ἐξ αἱμάτων	Jn 1:13
(45)	ἀπὸ βησαϊδά (indeclinable)	Jn 1:44

1470.3   And for pronouns:

(46) ἐν ᾧ (relative)   Jn 1:47
(47) ἀπ' ἐμαυτοῦ (reflexive)   Jn 8:28
(48) ἀπ' ἐμοῦ (personal)   Jn 10:18

1470.4   The case of each noun and pronoun is signaled by the preposition apart from the inflectional ending of the noun. The latter reinforces the former, of course, and indicates number (in (38)–(41), -ᾧ, -ῆς, -οῦ are all singulars), but not necessarily gender (-ῆς is feminine, but -ᾧ and -οῦ may be either masculine or neuter). One can thus specify the case of the nominal heads in (42)–(48), even though one may not know the inflectional patterns of these nouns (or pronouns).

1471.   It should be emphasized that the sentence is a kind of puzzle, the various pieces of which provide clues to the arrangement and hence the meaning of the whole. Most sentences provide a variety of interlocking clues to their structure. One is invited to read these clues by whatever means is at hand. What students now have at their disposal is the inflectional pattern of the article, the inflectional patterns of all first and second declension nouns, and five one-case prepositions, together with some common word clusters in which these and other nominal elements occur. One can go a very long way with the formal analysis of nominal word groups with only so much in hand.

Nouns: Introduction to Third Declension

Stems in a Consonant or Consonantal ι, υ

150.   Nouns of the third declension end in a consonant or in consonantal ι, υ (§§905, 932, 933). There are two basic patterns, one for masculine and feminine nouns, and one for neuters. Variation on the two basic patterns is due largely to phonetic changes occasioned by the juxtaposition of certain consonants, the restriction imposed upon final consonants (only certain consonants can stand at the end of a word), and vowel gradation in certain stems. The third declension in Greek is comparable to the third and fourth declensions in Latin.

ι and υ sometimes represent two older consonants which disappeared before Greek assumed its classical form (when they represent consonants they are written ι̯ and υ̯ in grammars to distinguish the consonantal from the vocalic form, but they are never written as ι̯ and υ̯ in Greek texts).

Consonantal ι sounded like English y in *yet*; consonantal υ like English w in *water*. ι̯ and υ̯ are also called semivowels. No special sign for them has survived in the Greek language, but υ̯ was written as ϝ (digamma, i.e. double-gamma, so called because it had the appearance of one [Γ] gamma written over another).

English knows their counterparts. Consonantal ι appears in English in *opinion*, *union*; consonantal υ in *persuade*, *quick*. The fickle behavior of these semivowels may be illustrated by English w: the w-sound occurs only before vowels (*we*, *wound*; *wh* in *when* is actually pronounced *hw* or *w*). Written but not pronounced: *write*, *wrong* (initial); *know*, *blow* (final); *two*, *who*, *sword* (coalesced with following vowel): *answer*, *toward* (disappeared before vowel of unaccented syllable). Pronounced but not written: *one*, *once*. The w-sound may be written as w (*work*), u (*quote*), or o (*memoir*).

The original presence of ι̯ and υ̯ accounts for the form of certain words in Greek and kindred languages, e.g. εἶδον for ἐ-ϝιδον *saw*; cf. *videre* in Latin and *video* in English (ϝ in this case = v).

Third declension nouns ending in ι̯ and υ̯ are, of course, affected.

151.   As the article serves as the model for first and second declension nouns, τίς, τί *who? which? what?* (interrogative pronoun) serves as the model for the third declension. The full declension must be committed carefully to memory.

	Singular		Plural	
	Masc.-Fem.	Neuter	Masc.-Fem.	Neuter
N	τί ς	τί	τίν ες	τίν α
G	τίν ος	τίν ος	τίν ων	τίν ων
D	τίν ι	τίν ι	τί σι (ν)	τί σι (ν)
A	τίν α	τί	τίν ας	τίν α

1510.   Mnemonic hints:

1510.1   The stem of τίς, τί is τιν- (τι-). Τιν- appears in all forms except a) masc.-fem. nom. sing., dat. plur. of both genders (ν is dropped before -σι, §929.7), and b) neuter nom. and acc. sing. (ν may stand here, but the original stem may have been τι-).

1510.2   The middle cases (gen., dat.):

   a) gen. and dat. singular endings are identical for both genders, i.e. -ος in gen., -ι in dat.

   b) gen. and dat. plural endings are identical for both genders, i.e. -ων in gen., -σι in dat.

   That is to say, the difference in gender affects only the nom. and acc. cases of both numbers; the middle cases are identical for both numbers in all three genders.

1510.3   The gen. plur. in -ων is like the gen. plur. of first and second declension nouns and the article.

1510.4   Neuter:

   a) the nom. and acc. sing. are always identical; the nom. and acc. plur. likewise (cf. second declension neuters).

   b) the nom. and acc. sing. have no ending; the nom. and acc. plur. end in -α, as do neuters of the second declension and the neuter article.

1510.5   The ν given in parenthesis in the dat. plur. forms is called ν-movable. Such a ν is regularly added to any word ending in -σι when the next word begins with a vowel, but it may be added to such words when the next word begins with a consonant.

In the nominal system ν-movable comes into consideration only in the dat. plur. of third declension nouns. For ν-movable in the verbal system, s. §321.

152. Confusion may arise at the following points:

152.1 The gen. sing. of both patterns (-ος) looks like the nom. sing. of masc.-fem. nouns of the second declension (also in -ος, e.g. ὁ λόγος).

152.2 The masc.-fem. acc. sing. in -α looks like the neuter nom. and acc. plur. in -α and the corresponding forms of second declension neuters, as well as the nom. sing. of nouns in -α in the first declension (e.g. ἡ ἡμέρα).

1520. Endings which have been utilized at more than one point may be summarized as follows:

1520.1 -ος

   a) masc.-fem. nom. sing., second declension
   b) masc.-fem., neut. gen. sing., third declension

1520.2 -α

   a) fem. nom. sing., first declension
   b) neuter nom. and acc. plur., second declension
   c) neuter nom. and acc. plur., third declension
   d) masc.-fem. acc. sing., third declension

1520.3 -ων: gen. plur. in all declension patterns.

1520.4 -ας

   a) masc. nom. sing., first declension (§132.3)
   b) fem. gen. sing., first declension (§132.1)
   c) masc.-fem. acc. plur., first declension
   d) masc.-fem. acc. plur., third declension

153. The indefinite pronoun τὶς, τὶ *someone, something, anyone, anything* is declined exactly like τίς, τί except for accent. Τίς, τί is *always* written with acute accent in texts to distinguish it from τὶς, τὶ which is an enclitic (i.e. pronounced with the preceding word and accented accordingly, §074).

The grave accent on τὶς, τὶ (or lack of accent) in grammars and lexicons is a device to indicate that the indefinite pronoun is meant. As an enclitic, τὶς, τὶ may lose its accent under certain conditions.

154. On the basis of the model, τίς, τί, one expects the following endings in third declension nouns:

	Singular		Plural	
	Masc.-Fem	Neuter	Masc.-Fem	Neuter
N	-ς	—	-ες	-α
G	-ος	-ος	-ων	-ων
D	-ι	-ι	-σι(ν)	-σι(ν)
A	-α	—	-ας	-α

1540. *Irregularities.* Aside from certain phonetic changes (§155), the endings of neuter nouns remain constant. The masculine-feminine pattern, however, has three important variations that must be noted.

1540.1 The masc.-fem. nom. sing. usually has -ς, but nouns ending in ν, ρ, (σ,) or οντ have no ending in the nom. sing. (like the neuters), with the consequence that a short final stem vowel is lengthened in compensation, e.g. ποιμήν (ὁ) *shepherd*, gen. τοῦ ποιμένος, stem ποιμεν- (ε is lengthened to η).

1540.2 The masc.-fem. acc. sing. usually ends in -α, but nouns ending in ι or υ may have ν instead, e.g. πόλις (ἡ) *city*, acc. τὴν πόλιν. Some stems ending in dentals preceded by ι also have ν, e.g. χάρις (ἡ) *grace*, acc. τὴν χάριν (but τὴν χάριτα also occurs), stem χαριτ-.

> The masc.-fem. acc. sing. ending is ν which, following a consonant, becomes vocalic (ν̥ = α), s. §906. Thus α and ν actually represent the same ending.

1540.3 The masc.-fem. acc. plur. usually ends in -ας, but in some cases the acc. plur. is borrowed from the nom. (i.e., -ες), with the result that nom. and acc. plur. are identical, e.g. βασιλεῖς (οἱ) *kings*, acc. pl. τοὺς βασιλεῖς (εῖς by contraction).

1541. The table given in §154 therefore requires modification at three points:

	Singular		Plural	
	Masc.-Fem.	Neuter	Masc.-Fem.	Neuter
N	-ς or —	—	-ες	-α
G	-ος	-ος	-ων	-ων
D	-ι	-ι	-σι(ν)	-σι(ν)
A	-α or -ν	—	-ας or -ες	-α

Irregularities may be expected in masc.-fem. nouns in the nom. sing., acc. sing. and plur.

155. *Phonetic changes.* Certain phonetic changes occur in third declension nouns as the result of the juxtaposition of certain consonants and vowels, and the restrictions imposed upon final consonants.

155.1 In the masc.-fem. nom. sing. (-ς) and in the dat. plur. (all genders) (-σι), the juxtaposition of σ with certain consonants produces changes (consonants with σ, s. §§927, 929.7–9, 930).

155.2 Since only the consonants ν, ρ and σ (ξ, ψ, which are consonants with σ) can stand at the end of a word (§923), other final consonants are sometimes lost where there is no ending (neuter nom. and acc. sing., and occasionally masc.-fem. nom. sing.).

155.3 Intervocalic σ (i.e. occurring between vowels) is usually lost, and the vowels thus brought together contract (§930.2).

155.4 Certain nominal stems in the third declension show vowel gradation (§912).

1550. There are other explicable and inexplicable irregularities which will be noted. The large majority of third declension nouns, however, are readily identifiable on the basis of the model, τίς, τί (§151) and the additional options noted in §1541 for the masc.-fem. pattern. In the presentation of the third declension, all nouns represented in Bauer that do not conform to the pattern in question in every particular will be noted: §§ 160–203 are thus not only a schematic presentation of the third declension, but also a catalogue of deviations (cf. Appendix II).

156. *Organization of the third declension.* Two factors are utilized in the organization of third declension nouns: 1) the two basic patterns, masculine-feminine and neuter (§§150f.), and 2) the consonant with which the stem ends, since any phonetic changes are determined by the final stem consonant. On the basis of these two factors, the third declension is organized into seven classes, with subclasses in each case. The differences, especially among subclasses, are often minimal and may rest on a single point. The detailed analysis has the virtue of calling attention to every particular, but it should not be allowed to obscure the essential conformity of all third declension nouns to two patterns, the masculine-feminine and the neuter.

The classes and subclasses are as follows (cf. Appendix II):

1. Masculine and feminine nouns ending in a stop (mute)
   a. those ending in a labial (π, β, φ)
   b. those ending in a palatal (κ, γ, χ)
   c. those ending in a dental (τ, δ, ϑ)

2. Masculine nouns in -ντ-
   a. those with no ending in the nom. sing.
   b. those with -ς in the nom. sing.
3. Neuter nouns in -τ-
   a. neuters ending in -μα
   b. other neuters belonging to this class (irregular nom. sing.)
4. Masculine and feminine nouns ending in a liquid (λ, ρ)
   a. stems showing no vowel gradation
   b. stems showing variation between strong and middle grades
   c. stems showing three grades
5. Masculine and feminine nouns ending in -ν- (nasal)
   a. stems showing no vowel gradation
   b. stems showing variation between strong and middle grades
   c. stems showing variation between strong and weak grades
6. Nouns with stems in -σ-, (-εσ-, -οσ-, -ασ-)
   a. neuters: -ος, -ους
   b. masculines: -ης, ους (all proper names)
   c. stems in -οσ-, -ασ-
7. Masculine and feminine nouns ending in consonantal -ι- and -υ- (also
   -ευ-, -αυ-, -ου-)
   a. stems in -υ-
   b. stems in -ι-/-ε-
   c. stems in -ευ-/-ε-
   d. stems in -ου-/-ο-

The largest classes are 1c, 3a, 6a, 7b. Nouns in 4b, while few in number (5), have high frequency. A number of subclasses are represented by fewer than ten nouns. See Appendix II for statistics and a full catalogue of classes less well represented.

157. As in the case of the article (§124), it is important to master the declension of τίς, τί. Master again means instant recognition in context. The most effective practice is scanning a Greek text for examples, at first verbally citing gender, number, case (with options), and then passing as quickly as possible to silent recognition.

1570. Word list.

τίς, τί   *who? which? what?* (interrogative pronoun)

τὶς, τὶ   *someone, something, any one, anything* (indefinite pronoun)

Nouns: Third Declension

Stems Ending in π, β, φ, κ, γ, χ, τ, δ, ϑ

Class 1

160. Masculine and feminine nouns ending in a stop (mute).

Third declension nouns which end in a stop will show phonetic change in the nom. sing. and dat. plur., owing to the σ of the ending. The change is regular and takes place according to the following table:

labials	π,	β,	φ	+	σ	=	ψ
palatals	κ,	γ,	χ	+	σ	=	ξ
dentals	τ,	δ,	ϑ	+	σ	=	σ(σ)

The declension pattern otherwise conforms to the model, τίς.

161. Class 1.a. Nouns in a labial (π, β)

Only nine nouns of this type appear in the literature covered by Bauer (they were never common); see Appendix II for a full catalogue. There are no examples in -φ-.

λαῖλαψ, λαίλαπος, ἡ — *whirlwind*

	S	P
N	λαῖλαψ (< π-ς)	λαίλαπες
G	λαίλαπος	λαιλάπων
D	λαίλαπι	λαίλαψι(ν) (< π-σι)
A	λαίλαπα	λαίλαπας

Note: Phonetic change (π + σ = ψ) in nom. sing. and dat. plur.

162. Class 1.b. Nouns in a palatal (κ, γ, χ)

Nouns of this type are more common (35 in the literature covered by Bauer).

σάρξ, σαρκός, ἡ — *flesh*

	S	P
N	σάρξ (< κ - ς)	σάρκες
G	σαρκός	σαρκῶν
D	σαρκί	σαρξί(ν) (< κ - σι)
A	σάρκα	σάρκας

σάλπιγξ, σάλπιγγος, ἡ — *trumpet*

	S	P
N	σάλπιγξ (< γ-ς)	σάλπιγγες
G	σάλπιγγος	σαλπίγγων
D	σάλπιγγι	σάλπιγξι(ν) (< γ - σι)
A	σάλπιγγα	σάλπιγγας

θρίξ, τριχός, ἡ — *hair*

	S	P
N	θρίξ	τρίχες
G	τριχός	τριχῶν
D	τριχί	θριξί(ν)
A	τρίχα	τρίχας

1620. Notes:

1620.1 The phonetic change, κ, γ, χ + σ = ξ, takes place in the nom. sing. and the dat. plur. In all other respects these nouns conform to the model, τίς.

1620.2 In θρίξ the θ is deaspirated (§928.2) wherever the χ appears so as not to have two aspirates in succeeding syllables (the aspirated form concurs with the appearance of the σ in the ending, which transforms χ into ξ).

1621. *Irregularities.*

1621.1 A commonly occurring noun belonging to this class is γυνή, γυναικός, ἡ, woman. The stem is γυναικ-. The nom. sing. shows a shortened stem and is therefore irregular (the vocative γύναι also appears in the New Testament as well as in Attic [Smyth §285.6]).

γυνή, γυναικός, ἡ — *woman*

	S	P
N	γυνή	γυναῖκες
G	γυναικός	γυναικῶν

D γυναικί   γυναιξί(ν)

A γυναῖκα   γυναῖκας

Note: The nom. sing. is a short form of the stem; the dat. plur. shows the regular phonetic change (κ + σ = ξ).

1621.2 νύξ, νυκτός, ἡ, *night*, another commonly occurring noun belonging to this class, really ends in -κτ- (shown by the genitive), but it behaves in the nom. sing. and dat. plur. as though it ended in -κ-: ἡ νύξ, ταῖς νυξί(ν).

1621.3 ἀλώπηξ, -εκος, ἡ, *fox*, shows a change in stem vowel from strong to middle grade (η to ε); the long vowel is found only in the nom. sing. (cf. nouns of classes 2., §§165f., 4.b. and 5.b., §§183f., 188f.).

163. Class 1.c. Nouns in a dental (τ, δ, θ)

In these nouns the dental disappears before the σ of the nom. sing. and dat. plur. endings (§160).

χάρις, χάριτος, ἡ — *grace*

	S	P
N	χάρις (<τ - ς)	χάριτες
G	χάριτος	χαρίτων
D	χάριτι	χάρισι(ν) (< τ - σι)
A	χάριν (χάριτα)	χάριτας

ἐλπίς, ἐλπίδος, ἡ — *hope*

	S	P
N	ἐλπίς, (< δ - ς)	ἐλπίδες
G	ἐλπίδος	ἐλπίδων
D	ἐλπίδι	ἐλπίσι(ν) (< δ - σι)
A	ἐλπίδα	ἐλπίδας

1630. Notes:

1630.1 The only noun with stem in θ is ὄρνις, ὄρνιθος, ὁ (ἡ), *bird*. It also appears in the form ὄρνιξ, ὄρνιχος, ὁ (ἡ) (III.1.b.). Bl-D §47(4).

1630.2 A commonly occurring type of this class has a nom. sing. in -της, gen. -τητος (e.g. χρηστότης, χρηστότητος, ἡ, *goodness*). Although they follow the pattern of χάρις, the multiplication of τ's tends to be confusing.

1630.3 Some nouns of this class have an acc. sing. in -ιν (substitute ν for ς of the nom. sing.), e.g. ἡ χάρις, τὴν χάριν. In the case of χάρις, τὴν χάριτα also appears. Cf. §1540.2 and nouns of classes III.7.a., 7.b., 7.d. (§§199f., 200f., 202f.).

1630.4 This class is the masc.-fem. counterpart to neuter stems in -τ- (III.3.a. and b.; §§170–1730).

1631. *Irregularity.*

A commonly occurring noun belonging to this class is πούς, ποδός, ὁ, *foot*. Like γυνή (§1621.1), πούς is an irregular nom. sing. The stem is ποδ-, and the other forms are regular:

πούς, ποδός, ὁ — *foot*

	S	P
N	πούς	πόδες
G	ποδός	ποδῶν
D	ποδί	ποσί(ν) (< δ - σι)
A	πόδα	πόδας

With πούς belong the compounds of which it is the second element: Ἀγαθόπους, δασύπους, πολύπους, all ὁ.

164. *Summary.* Class 1 nouns are declined like τίς, but one must reckon a) with the phonetic change occasioned by the juxtaposition of σ with a stop in the nom. sing. and dat. plur., and b) with an occasional acc. sing. in -ιν rather than -ιτα or -ιδα. Γυνή and πούς have odd nom. singulars.

Class 2

165. Masculine nouns with stems in -ντ-

The few nouns of this class are divided between those which have no ending in the nom. sing. and those which have -ς. It is necessary to distinguish them from simple τ-stems (class 1.c) because of the dat. plur. In spite of their infrequency, they are important for the reason that the two subclasses offer analogies for the declension of the masculine participle. Nearly all of these nouns show variation between a long stem vowel (ω, η) in the nom. sing. and a short stem vowel (ο, ε) elsewhere (cf. §1621.3 and nouns of classes 4.b. and 5.b., §§183f., 188f.).

Some of these substantives in -ντ-, in fact, were originally participles. Robertson-Davis §177. Cf. §§247f. for the masculine participle.

166. Class 2.a. Stems in -ντ- with no ending in the nominative singular

ἄρχων, ἄρχοντος, ὁ — *ruler*

	S	P
N	ἄρχων (< -ωντ)	ἄρχοντες
G	ἄρχοντος	ἀρχόντων
D	ἄρχοντι	ἄρχουσι(ν) (< -οντσι)
A	ἄρχοντα	ἄρχοντας

1660. Notes:

1660.1 Since τ cannot stand at the end of a word (§923) , it is dropped in the nom. sing.: ἄρχων.

1660.2 The stem shows vowel gradation: long ω in the nom. sing., short o elsewhere. (One proper name, Σολομῶν, -ῶντος, ὁ, retains the long stem vowel; see Bl-D §55(2) for variation in declension.)

1660.3 In the dat. plur., -ντ- disappears before σ (§929.9), and the preceding vowel is lengthened in compensation (compensatory lengthening, §914): αρχοντσι > αρχο-σι > αρχουσι.

167. Class 2.b. Stems in -ντ- with -ς in the nominative singular.

ἱμάς, ἱμάντος, ὁ *strap — thong*

	S	P
N	ἱμάς (< -αντς)	ἱμάντες
G	ἱμάντος	ἱμάντων
D	ἱμάντι	ἱμᾶσι(ν) (< -αντσι)
A	ἱμάντα	ἱμάντας

1670. Notes:

1670.1 The -ντ- is lost before the σ of the nom. sing. and dat. plur. The compensatory lengthening does not visibly affect α, but in ὀδούς, ὀδόντος, ὀδοῦσι(ν), ὁ, *tooth*, the o of the stem is lengthened to ου. ἱμάς and ὀδούς are the only common nouns of this class.

1670.2 Three proper names, however, follow the same pattern: Κλήμης, -εντος, ὁ; Κρήσκης, -εντος, ὁ; Πούδης, -εντος, ὁ, i.e. stems in -ντ- with -ς in the nom. sing. Note the change from long to short stem vowel; the plural, of course, does not come into consideration.

168. *Summary.* Nouns of Class 2 present problems only in the nom. sing. and dat. plur., and in the variation between long and short stem vowel. The dat. plur.,

ἄρχουσι(ν), in particular, is subject to confusion with the third person plur. present, active, indicative of certain verbs: λύουσι(ν) (see §318). Although few in number in themselves (twelve examples in the literature covered by Bauer, see Appendix II), they will be joined by a host of masculine participles.

1680. *Catalogue* of third declension nouns, classes 1. and 2., appearing in the New Testament ten times or more (for a complete catalogue, see Appendix II).

III.1. Masculine and feminine nouns ending in a stop

    a. stems ending in a labial—no examples

    b. stems ending in a palatal

        γυνή, γυναικός, ἡ — *woman* [cf. *gynecology*]

        σάρξ, σαρκός, ἡ — *flesh* [cf. sarcophagus}

        νύξ, νυκτός, ἡ — *night*

        θρίξ, τριχός, ἡ — *hair* [cf. *trichosis, trichology*]

        σάλπιγξ, σάλπιγγος, ἡ — *trumpet*

    c. stems ending in a dental

        χάρις, χάριτος, ἡ — *grace*

        πούς, ποδός, ὁ — *foot* [cf. *chiropodist; podium; tripod*]

        ἐλπίς, ἐλπίδος, ἡ — *hope*

        παῖς, παιδός, ὁ and ἡ — *boy, girl, servant* [cf. *paediatrics* or *ped-*]

        χιλιάς, χιλίαδος, ἡ — *a thousand* [cf. *chiliasm*]

        σφραγίς, σφραγῖδος, ἡ — *seal, signet* [cf. *spragistics*]

        χρηστότης, χρηστότητος, ἡ — *goodness*

III.2. Masculine nouns with stems in -ντ-

    a. no ending in the nominative singular

        ἄρχων, ἄρχοντος, ὁ — *ruler* [cf. *monarch*]

        δράκων, δράκοντος, ὁ — *dragon* [cf. Latin *draco*; Eng. *dragon*]

    b. -ς in the nominative singular

        ὀδούς, ὀδόντος, ὁ — *tooth* [cf. *odontology*]

Lesson 12

Nouns: Third Declension
Stems Ending in τ

Class 3

170.   Neuter nouns in -τ-

Classes 1. and 2. are composed of masculine and feminine nouns. With class 3. is met the first group of neuter nouns in the third declension (the other large group is class 6.). The fact that these nouns are neuter immediately suggests three characteristics, following the model, τί:

1. The nom. and acc. sing. will be identical;
2. The nom. and acc. plur. will be identical (both characteristics apply also to neuter nouns of II.3., and thus to all neuter nouns).
3. The middle cases (gen., dat.) are identical with the corresponding masc.-fem. forms (this applies also to the masculine-feminine nouns of II.1. and II.2. in relation to the neuter nouns of II.3.).

To be reckoned with, therefore, are only the nom. and acc. of both numbers. Again following τί, it can be said:

1. The nom. and acc. sing. have no ending: the question then becomes, what is the stem, and can the consonants which end it stand at the end of a word?
2. The nom. and acc. plur. end in -α, as do neuter nouns of II.3. and the article (τά).

The first point is the crucial one for identifying nouns of this class, especially in moving from an oblique case or the nom. plur. to the nom. sing. and hence the lexical form.

1700. Class 3. is large and again must be divided into two subclasses: 3.a. neuters in -μα, gen. -ματος, and 3.b. neuters following this declension pattern but having irregular nom. (and therefore acc.) singulars.

171. Class 3.a. Neuter nouns in -μα

ὄνομα, ὀνόματος, τό — *name*

	S	P
N	ὄνομα (< -ματ)	ὀνόματα
G	ὀνόματος	ὀνομάτων
D	ὀνόματι	ὀνόμασι(ν) (< -ματσι)
A	ὄνομα (< -ματ)	ὀνόματα

1710. Notes:

1710.1 The nom. and acc. sing. have no ending. Since τ cannot stand at the end of a word (§923), it is dropped.

1710.2 τ disappears before σ in the dat. plur. (§927).

172. Class 3.b. Other neuter nouns belonging to this class

These nouns exhibit the same declension pattern as do the neuters in class 3.a., except for the nom. and acc. sing. Several of these nouns originally belonged to other classes but were subsequently assimilated to the pattern of neuter stems in -τ-. This accounts in part for the irregular nom. (and hence acc.) sing.

Nouns in this group may be further subdivided in relation to the form of the nom. and acc. sing.:

172.1 stems which have short nom. (and acc.) sing. but not -μα

μέλι, μέλιτος, τό — *honey*
οἰνόμελι, οἰνομέλιτος, τό — *honeyed wine* (IgnTr 6:2)
γάλα, γάλακτος, τό — *milk*
γόνυ, γόνατος, τό — *knee*
δόρυ, δόρατος, τό — *spear* (IgnPol 16:2)

172.2 stems with nom. (and acc.) sing. in -ρ

ὕδωρ, ὕδατος, τό — *water*
στέαρ, στέατος, τό — *fat* (1 Clem 4:1, Barn 2:5)
φρέαρ, φρέατος, τό — *well*

172.3   stems with nom. (and acc.) sing. in -ας

        κέρας, κέρατος, τό — *horn*
        πέρας, πέρατος, τό — *end, limit*
        τέρας, τέρατος, τό — *portent*
        ἅλας, ἅλατος, τό — *salt*

172.4   stems with nom. (and acc.) sing. in -ς

        φῶς, φωτός, τό — *light*
        οὖς, ὠτός, τό — *ear*

1720.   Notes:

1720.1   Group (1): -τ and -κτ cannot stand at the end of a word (§923). γόνυ, δόρυ are really old υ-stems which have been assimilated to the pattern of τ-stems.

1720.2   Groups (2), (3), (4) have parallel stems in -ρ, -ας, -ς, respectively, and in -τ.

1720.3   For ἅλας, ἅλατος, τό cf. §1821.4.

1720.4   σάββατον, σαββάτου, τό (II.3.) has a dat. plur. σάββασιν on the analogy of neuter nouns in -τ- (Bl-D §52).

173.   The nom. sing. (lexical form) of neuter nouns in -τ- may be discovered by the following process of elimination:

173.1   acc. sing. = nom. sing.

173.2   drop τ (κτ) plus the ending (dat. plur.: drop -σι[ν])(all class 3.a. nouns and group (1) in class 3.b.).

173.3   drop τ plus the ending (dat. plur.: drop -σι[ν]) and add ρ or σ (Group (2)–(4) of class 3.b.).

173.4   γόνυ, δόρυ and ὕδωρ remain special cases.

1730.   A catalogue of class 3.a. nouns appearing in the New Testament ten times or more may be found in Appendix II. A complete catalogue of class 3.b. may be found in §172 and Appendix II.

174.   *Nominal word clusters with genitive modifiers.* The article was considered as structure signal in §§125–129. Additional word groups initiated by prepositions were considered in §§140–147. Another common minimal word cluster consists of one noun (in any case) qualified by another in the genitive case (the relation of the latter to the former is often represented by the preposition *of* in English: §112.1). One or both nouns may be accompanied by the article. For example,

    (1)   τὸ φῶς τοῦ κόσμου
           the light of the world   Jn 8:12

contains two subclusters, τὸ φῶς and τοῦ κόσμου the second of which (in the genitive case) further specifies the first. The following clusters are identical in structure:

(2) τὸ φῶς τῆς ζωῆς
     the light of life   Jn 8:12

(3) τὸν υἱὸν τοῦ ἀνθρώπου
     the son of man   Jn 8:28

(4) τὰ ῥήματα τοῦ θεοῦ
     the words of God   Jn 8:47

175. These clusters appear with and without the article(s). The word order may vary. The following examples illustrate the various possibilities.

(5)   τὸ φῶς τῶν ἀνθρώπων   Jn 1:4
(6)   υἱοὶ φωτός   Jn 12:26
(7)   ἄγγελον φωτός   2 Cor 11:14
(8)   τέκνα φωτός   Eph 5:8
(9)   ὁ υἱὸς τοῦ θεοῦ   Jn 1:34
(10) Σίμων, ὁ υἱὸς Ἰωάννου   jn 1:42
(11) Ἰησοῦν, υἱὸν τοῦ Ἰωσήφ   Jn 1:45
(12) ὁ υἱὸς τῆς Μαρίας   Mk 6:3
(13) Φαρισαῖος, υἱὸς Φαρισαίων   Acts 23:6
(14) τὴν σάρκα τοῦ υἱοῦ τοῦ ἀνθρώπου   Jn 6:53
(15) ὁ τοῦ θεοῦ υἱός, Χριστὸς Ἰησοῦς   2 Cor 1:19
(16) ῥήματα ζωῆς   Jn 6:68
(17) ὁ λόγος τοῦ θεοῦ   Jn 10:35
(18) ὁ λόγος τοῦ Ἰησοῦ   Jn 18:32
(19) ὁ λόγος τοῦ κυρίου   Acts 12:24
(20) ὁ λόγος τῆς σωτηρίας   Acts 13:26
(21) ὁ λόγος ὁ τοῦ σταυροῦ   1 Cor 1:18

Further treatment of this type of cluster is to be found in §§695ff.

1750. Notes:

1750.1 ῥῆμα = λόγος (in these contexts)

1750.2 Word order may vary:

      a) ὁ -ος τοῦ -ου

      b) ὁ τοῦ -ου -ος

      c) ὁ -ος ὁ τοῦ -ου (article of the initial term repeated)

176. In noun identification, attention should be diverted from the single word to the cluster wherever possible. Identification of the noun in context means seizing the noun in relation to the grammatical structure in which it appears. Early facility with nouns depends on the ability to read all the signals, not just the case ending of the nouns.

Nouns: Third Declension

Stems Ending in λ, ρ, ν

180. Third declension nouns in class 4. end in a liquid (λ, ρ), those in class 5. in a nasal (ν). The chief distinction between the two classes is the dative plural: the ν in nouns of class 5. is lost before the ending, -σι. Nouns in both classes are characterized by varying degrees of vowel gradation in the stem. Division into subgroups is based upon this feature:

  Class 4. Stems in λ, ρ
  4.a. Stems showing strong grade only
  4.b. Stems showing variation between strong/middle grades
  4.c. Stems showing three grades

  Class 5. Stems in ν
  5.a. Stems showing strong grade only
  5.b. Stems showing variation between strong/middle grades
  5.c. Stems showing variation between strong/weak grades

  Nouns in these classes are not numerous, but those in 4.c. are of high frequency.

Class 4

181. Masculine and feminine nouns ending in a liquid.

  Stems in -ηρ, ωρ originally showed three grades of the final stem vowel: strong -ηρ, -ωρ middle -ερ, -ορ, and weak -ρ. These grades were subsequently leveled out, i.e. generalized, in many instances in the interest of simplicity, some in the strong grade, some in the middle grade, and one example, ἀνήρ, ἀνδρός, ὁ, in the weak grade. Those leveled out in the strong grade show the strong grade throughout (4.a., cf. 5.a.); those leveled out in the middle grade show the strong grade in the nom. sing. and the middle grade elsewhere (4.b., cf. 5.b.). The nouns of class 4.c. (mostly relationship nouns, e.g. father, mother, daughter), however, have preserved vowel gradation to a considerable degree.

182.   Class 4.a. Liquid stems showing the strong grade only

σωτήρ, σωτῆρος, ὁ — *savior*

	S	P
N	σωτήρ	σωτῆρες
G	σωτῆρος	σωτήρων
D	σωτῆρι	σωτῆρσι(ν)
A	σωτῆρα	σωτῆρας

1820.   Mnemonic hints:

1820.1 Except for the nom. sing., which has no ending, these nouns follow the pattern of τίς precisely.

1820.2 These nouns have the strong grade throughout: -ηρ, -ωρ.

1821.   A full catalogue of 4.a. nouns may be found in Appendix II. There are a few nouns listed there which exhibit some peculiarity or other:

1821.1 Καῖσαρ, Καίσαρος, ὁ, *Caesar*, is, of course, a Latin word which has been adapted to this pattern in Greek; its only peculiarity is that its stem ends in -αρ rather than -ηρ or -ωρ.

1821.2 χείρ, χειρός, ἡ, *hand*, a commonly occurring noun, is regular except for the dative plur. which is χερσί(ν): χείρ, χειρός, χειρί, χεῖρα; χεῖρες, χειρῶν, χερσί(ν), χεῖρας. Cf. αὐτόχειρ, -ος, ὁ or ἡ.

1821.3 μάρτυς, μάρτυρος, ὁ, *witness*, forms a nom. sing. in -ς (the ρ disappears); the dat. plur. μάρτυσι(ν) follows the nom. sing. in dropping the ρ. The other forms are regular with -ρ-. Cf. πρωτόμαρτυς, -υρος, ὁ; ψευδόμαρτυς, -υρος, ὁ.

1821.4 ἅλς, ἁλός, ὁ, *salt*, is the only noun with stem in λ. In Attic it was declined: ἅλς, ἁλός, ἁλί, ἅλα; ἅλες, ἁλῶν, ἁλσί(ν), ἅλας (i.e. regularly), but this form is rare in hellenistic Greek (ἁλί Mk 9:49 v.l.; στήλη ἁλός, *pillar of salt*, 1 Clem 11:2 [Gen 19:26]). A new form ἅλας, ἅλατος, τό, has been assimilated to stems in -τ- (§172).

1821.5 One *neuter*, πῦρ, πυρός, τό, *fire* belongs to this class. It appears only in the sing. and is regular (nom. and acc. are identical): πῦρ, πυρός, πυρί, πῦρ.

183.   Class 4.b. Liquid stems showing variation between strong/middle grades.

ἀστήρ, ἀστέρος, ὁ — *star*

	S	P
N	ἀστήρ	ἀστέρες
G	ἀστέρος	ἀστέρων
D	ἀστέρι	[ἀστράσι(ν)]
A	ἀστέρα	ἀστέρας

ἀλέκτωρ, ἀλέκτορος, ὁ — *cock*

	S	P
N	ἀλέκτωρ	ἀλέκτορες
G	ἀλέκτορος	ἀλεκτόρων
D	ἀλέκτορι	ἀλέκτορσι(ν)
A	ἀλέκτορα	ἀλέκτορας

Note: a hellenistic dat. plur. is not attested for stems in -ηρ; ἀστράσι(ν) is the Attic form and shows the weak grade (-τρ-). Stems in -ωρ, however, show the middle grade (-ορ-) in the dat. plur.

1830. Mnemonic hints:

1830.1 Except for the nom. sing., which has no ending, these nouns follow the pattern of τίς precisely.

1830.2 These nouns have the strong grade (-ηρ, -ωρ) in the nom. sing., and the middle grade (-ερ, -ορ) elsewhere.

A full catalogue of 4.b. nouns may be found in Appendix II.

184. Class 4.c. Liquid stems showing three grades

This is a small group, mostly relationship nouns, but several are of high frequency.

πατήρ, πατρός, ὁ — *father*

	S	P
N	πατήρ	πατέρες
G	πατρός	πατέρων
D	πατρί	πατράσι(ν)
A	πατέρα	πατέρας

μήτηρ, μητρός, ἡ — *mother*

	S	P
N	μήτηρ	μητέρες
G	μητρός	μητέρων
D	μητρί	μητράσι(ν)
A	μητέρα	μητέρας

θυγάτηρ, θυγατρός, ἡ — *daughter*

	S	P
N	θυγάτηρ	θυγατέρες
G	θυγατρός	θυγατέρων
D	θυγατρί	θυγατράσι(ν)
A	θυγατέρα	θυγατέρας

1840. Mnemonic hints:

1840.1 The pattern is identical for all three nouns (and γαστήρ, γαστρός, ἡ, *belly*).

1840.2 The strong grade appears only in the nom. sing.; there is no ending.

1840.3 The weak grade (-τρ-) appears in the gen. and dat. sing., and dat. plur.; the middle grade (-τερ-) elsewhere.

1840.4 The endings are regular, i.e. like τίς.

1841. Note: The dat. plur. shows the weak grade (-τρ-). When ρ comes between two consonants, it becomes vocalic, i.e. develops a vowel, in order to assist pronunciation (§913). Vocalic or sonant ρ is written ρ̥. The dat. plur. developed thus: πατρ̥σι > πατράσι.

185. Another noun showing vowel gradation is

ἀνήρ, ἀνδρός, ὁ — *man, husband*

	S	P
N	ἀνήρ	ἄνδρες
G	ἀνδρός	ἀνδρῶν
D	ἀνδρί	ἀνδράσι(ν)
A	ἄνδρα	ἄνδρας

While ἀνήρ shows only the strong grade (-ηρ) in the nom. sing. and the weak grade (-ρ) elsewhere, it is closely related to the relationship nouns. Wherever the weak grade appears, δ is developed between ν and ρ to assist in pronunciation (Smyth §130). The dat. plur. is like πατράσι(ν); see. §1841.

Class 5

186. Masculine and feminine nouns ending in ν

Nouns of class 5. also conform to the model, τίς, except for the nom. sing., which has no ending (like class 4.). Only two other features require noting: a) class 5. nouns have either the strong grade of final stem vowel throughout (5.a.), or the strong grade in the nom. sing. and the middle grade elsewhere (5.b.), or the strong grade in the nom. sing. and the weak grade elsewhere (5.c.); b) the ν regularly disappears in the dat. plur. leaving no apparent trace.

187. Class 5.a. Stems in ν showing the strong grade only

αἰών, αἰῶνος, ὁ — *age*

	S	P
N	αἰών	αἰῶνες
G	αἰῶνος	αἰώνων
D	αἰῶνι	αἰῶσι(ν)
A	αἰῶνα	αἰῶνας

Ἕλλην, Ἕλληνος, ὁ — *Greek*

	S	P
N	Ἕλλην	Ἕλληνες
G	Ἕλληνος	Ἑλλήνων
D	Ἕλληνι	Ἕλλησι(ν)
A	Ἕλληνα	Ἕλληνας

Note: The ν disappears in the dat. plur. without leaving any apparent trace (See Smyth §250 N.).

1870. Most nouns in 5. a. are in -ων, -ωνος (only two in -ην, -ηνος). A few stems in -ιν and -αν follow the same pattern:

1870.1 ὠδίν, ὠδῖνος, ἡ, *birth-pain:* ὠδίν (Attic nom. ὠδίς), ὠδῖνος, ὠδῖνι, ὠδῖνα, ὠδῖνες, ὠδίνων, ὠδῖσι(ν), ὠδῖνας.

1870.2 μεγιστάν, μεγιστᾶνος, ὁ, *great man:* μεγιστᾶνες, μεγιστάνων, μεγιστᾶσι(ν), μεγιστάνας (plur. only).

1870.3 μέλαν, μέλανος, τό, *ink:* μέλαν, μέλανος, μέλανι, μέλαν (sing. only; neuter: nom. and acc. alike), though a neuter, belongs to this class.

Like the foregoing but with nom. sing. in -ς:

1870.4 ἀκτίς, ἀκτῖνος, ἡ, *ray, beam* (of the sun)

1870.5 ῥίς, ῥινός, ἡ, *nose;* plur. *nostrils* (Papias 3*: ῥίνας): Attic—LXX—ῥίς, ῥινός, ῥινί, ῥῖνα; ῥῖνες, ῥινῶν, ῥισί(ν), ῥῖνας.

1870.6 Σαλαμίς, Σαλαμῖνος, ἡ, *Salamis:* Acts 13:5 Σαλαμῖνι, v.l. ίνη (Bl-D §57).

A complete catalogue of 5.a. nouns may be found in Appendix II.

188. Class 5.b. Stems in ν showing variation between the strong/middle grades.

εἰκών, εἰκόνος, ἡ — *image form*

	S	P
N	εἰκών	εἰκόνες
G	εἰκόνος	εἰκόνων
D	εἰκόνι	εἰκόσι(ν)
A	εἰκόνα	εἰκόνας

ποιμήν, ποιμένες, ὁ — *shepherd*

	S	P
N	ποιμήν	ποιμένες
G	ποιμένος	ποιμένων
D	ποιμένι	ποιμέσι(ν)
A	ποιμένα	ποιμένας

1880. Notes:

1880.1 The strong grade (-ων, -ην) appears in the nom. sing., the middle grade (-ον, -εν) elsewhere.

1880.2 The ν disappears in the dat. plur. without leaving any apparent trace (see Smyth §250 N.).

A complete catalogue of 5.b. nouns may be found in Appendix II.

189. Class 5.c. Stems in ν showing variation between strong/weak grades.

κύων, κυνός, ὁ — *dog*

	S	P
N	κύων	κυνός
G	κυνός	κυνῶν
D	κυνί	κυσί(ν)
A	κύνα	κύνας

1890. Notes:

1890.1 The strong grade (-ων) appears in the nom. sing., the weak grade (-ν) elsewhere.

1890.2 The ν disappears in the dat. plur. as in nouns of classes 5.a. and 5.b.

1890.3 The only other noun of this type is ἀρήν, ἀρνός, ὁ, *lamb*: ἀρήν (rare nom. sing.), ἀρνός, ἀρνί, ἄρνα; ἄρνες, ἀρνῶν, ἀρνάσι(ν), ἄρνας. Only ἄρνας is found in literature represented in Bauer (Lk 10:3, Barn 2:5). ἀμνός, -οῦ, ὁ, ἀρνίον, -ου, τό, and πρόβατον, -ου, τό (all second declension), *sheep, lamb,* are more common than ἀρήν.

190. Summary of classes 4. and 5.

190.1 The nouns in these classes are masculine or feminine

exceptions: πῦρ, πυρός, τό *fire*   (§1821.5)
             μέλαν, μελάνος, τό *ink*   (§1870.3)

190.2 The nom. sing. regularly has no ending

exceptions: μάρτυς, μάρτυρος, ὁ *witness*   (§1821.3)
             ἅλς, ἁλός, ὁ *salt*   (§1821.4)
             ἀκτίς, ἀκτῖνος, ἡ *ray, beam*   (§1870.4)
             ῥίς, ῥινός, ἡ *nose*   (§1870.5)
             Σαλαμίς, Σαλαμῖνος, ἡ *Salamis*   (§1870.6)

190.3 The dat. plur.:

a) Nouns in 4.c. develop an α following ρ (vocalic ρ): -ρασι(ν);

b) Nouns in 5 (all subgroups) lose ν before -σι without leaving any apparent trace.

190.4 Vowel gradation:

a) Nouns in 4.a. and 5.a. show no vowel gradation, the strong grade appearing throughout;

b) Nouns in 4.b. and 5.b. show variation between the strong grade in the nom. sing., and the middle grade elsewhere;

c) Nouns in 4.c. show three grades, except ἀνήρ, ἀνδρός, ὁ, *man*, which shows only strong and weak grades; the latter is thus comparable to the two nouns in 5.c.

1900. Notes:

1900.1 For vowel gradation in the stem cf. ἀλώπηξ, ἀλώπεκος, ἡ, *fox*, (§1621.3) and the nouns in III.2.a. (§§165ff.).

1900.2 The nom. sing. of 5.a. and 5.b. nouns in -ων will be identical with the nom. sing. of nouns of 2.a., but the stems will be different elsewhere, and the dat. plur. of the latter will be -ουσι(ν) rather than -ωσι(ν) or -οσι(ν).

Lesson 14

Nouns: Third Declension

Stems Ending in σ & Consonantal ι, υ

195. Class 6 comprises the second large group of neuter nouns in the third declension (first group: III.3., §§170–173). They have the same general characteristics as the first group (§170). Nouns in class 6 have stems in -οσ, -εσ. They exhibit contraction, as a result, in the gen. and dat. sing. and in all cases of the plur. Nouns in this class are fairly numerous (a full catalogue may be found in Appendix II).

Class 6

196. Neuter nouns with stems in -ος, -εσ

ἔθνος, ἔθνους, τό — *nation, people*

	S	P
N	ἔθνος	ἔθνη (< εθνεσα)
G	ἔθνους (< εθνεσος)	ἐθνῶν (< εθνεσων)
D	ἔθνει (< εθνεσι)	ἔθνεσι(ν) (< εθνεσσι)
A	ἔθνος	ἔθνη (< εθνεσα)

1960. Mnemonic hints:

1960.1 The nom. and acc. sing. are identical; the nom. and acc. plur. likewise (as in all neuter nouns).

1960.2 The nom. and acc. sing. show the bare stem (in -ος), i.e. have no ending.

1960.3 The gen. and dat. plur. exhibit the regular endings -ων and -σι(ν); cf. the model, τί.

1960.4 All the forms presuppose the regular endings (found on τί), but in some cases contraction has obscured them.

1961. Notes:

1961.1 The stem -εσ appears everywhere but in the nom. and acc. sing.

1961.2 The σ of the stem disappears between two vowels (§930.2), and the vowels thus brought together contract according to regular rules (§917). The relevant contractions may be summarized here:

$$\varepsilon + o = ou$$
$$\varepsilon + \iota = \varepsilon\iota$$
$$\varepsilon + \alpha = \eta$$
$$\varepsilon + \omega = \omega$$

The uncontracted forms are shown in parentheses in the paradigm.

1961.3 The double -σσ- of the dat. plur. is simplified to -σ-.

1962. Additional notes:

1962.1 The gen. plur. of ὄρος, ὄρους, τό, *mountain*, and χείλος, χείλους, τό, *lip*, sometimes remain uncontracted, i.e. ὀρέων (Rev 6:15) and χειλέων (Heb 13:15) (Bl-D §48: ὀρέων uncontracted in Hermas and 1 Clement also; Bauer s.v.: ὀρῶν some 600 times in Josephus).

1962.2 ἔλεος, ἔλεους, τό, *mercy*, is regular (sing. only) despite the fact that its stem is ἐλεεσ-; the remaining ε, which looks as if it should contract, tends to be confusing: ἔλεος, ἔλεους, (< ἐλεεσος), ἐλέει (< ἐλεεσι), ἔλεος. Also note δέος, δέους, τό, *fear, awe* and κλέος, κλέους, τό, *fame, glory*.

197. Confusions

Because the nom. and acc. sing. end in -ος (which in this case is not ending but stem), these cases in nouns of class 6. may be confused with the gen. sing. in -ος of most other third declension nouns; ambiguity may be resolved by referring to the article or other 'qualifiers,' or by consulting the catalogue (Appendix II). These same forms may also be confused with the nom. masc. and fem. sing. of nouns in classes II.1. and II.2. Where the nom. is involved the confusion is not crucial, and the acc. may be identified as neuter (but not as acc.) by the article and other 'qualifiers'. Cf. §§208–214.

1970. Nouns in -ης, -ους (mostly masc. proper names) and those in -ας, -ως, which follow the pattern of neuter nouns of class 6., have largely disappeared from hellenistic Greek (Bl-D §47(1)) and were never common in Attic Greek. The surviving remnants may be noted:

1970.1 Masculine proper names in -ης, -ους, e.g. Σωσθένης, Σωσθένους, ὁ, *Sosthenes*, have nom. in -ης, gen. -ους, dat. -ει, and acc. in -η or -ην (the latter is borrowed from the first declension [Bl-D §46(1)]; -η arises from -εσα). The stem is -εσ- which accounts for the similarity to neuters of class 6. These nouns are catalogued as III.6.b. in Appendix II.

1970.2 There is one noun with stem in -ος-: αἰδώς, αἰδοῦς, ἡ, *modesty*: αἰδώς, αἰδούς (< αἰδοσος), αἰδοῖ (< αἰδοσι), αἰδῶ (< αἰδοσα) (sing. only). While fem., the pattern of contraction makes it analogous to neuter nouns of this class. αἰδώς appears once in the New Testament (1 Tim 2:9; also as v.l. at Heb 12:28).

1970.3 There are also remnants of a few neuter nouns in -ασ-. In Attic γέρας, γέρως, τό, *gift*, was declined: γέρας, γέρως (< γερασος), γέραι (< γερασι), γέρας; γέρα (< γερασα), γερῶν (< γερασων), γέρασι(ν) (< γερασσι), γέρα (cf. nom.), i.e. in accordance with the pattern of class 6. γέρας conforms to the pattern to the extent that it is attested in hellenistic Greek; γῆρας, γήρως or γήρους, τό, *old age*, is being assimilated to the pattern of stems in -εσ-: γήρους (1 Clem 63:3) = ἔθνους; γήρει (Lk 1:36) = ἔθνει; γήρᾳ (iota written subscript, 1 Clem 10:7) is also found; κρέας, κρέως (κρέατος is a later gen.) τό, *meat*, is represented by the plur. τὰ κρέα (Rom 14:21, 1 Cor 8:13). Neuters in -ασ- were being transposed to neuters in -τ- (III.3.b., §172.3).

Nouns in §1970.2. and 3. are catalogued under III.6.c. in Appendix II.

Class 7

198. Masculine and Feminine Nouns with stems ending in consonantal ι and υ

The final group of third declension nouns are masculines and feminines ending in ι and υ (also ευ, αυ, ου, οι). Where they deviate from the model, τίς, it owes to vowel gradation in the stem and irregularity of contraction. They may be divided into four subclasses.

199. Class 7.a. Stems in υ

ἰχθύς, ἰχθύος, ὁ — *fish*

	S	P
N	ἰχθύς	ἰχθύες
G	ἰχθύος	ἰχθύων
D	ἰχθύϊ	ἰχθύσι(ν)
A	ἰχθύν	ἰχθύας

Mnemonic hint:
The endings learned with τίς are added directly to the stem with no changes; the acc. sing., however, has -ν rather than -α (§§1540f.).

1990. Peculiarities:

1990.1 μῆνις, μήνιος (also μήνιδος = III.1.c.), ἡ, *implacable anger*, is a stem in ι belonging to this class (only Herm. Man. S.2.4); νῆστις, νήστιος (also νήστιδος = III.1.e.), ὁ or ἡ, *hungry*, is comparable.

1990.2 δάκρυσιν, a dat. plur. apparently preserved from old δάκρυ, δάκρυος, τό, *tear*, is found at Lk 7:38, 44. The customary form in hellenistic is δάκρυον, -ου, τό (II.3.).

A complete catalogue of 7.a. nouns will be found in Appendix II.

200. Class 7.b. Stems in ι / ε

This is the largest single group in the third declension (245 examples in Bauer; a catalogue of 7.b. nouns appearing ten times or more in the New Testament will be found in Appendix II). With few exceptions, nouns in this group are feminine. A large number have nom. sing. in -σις.

πόλις, πόλεως, ἡ — *city*

	S	P
N	πόλις	πόλεις
G	πόλεως	πόλεων
D	πόλει	πόλεσι(ν)
A	πόλιν	πόλεις

2000. Mnemonic hints:

2000.1 The nom. sing. has -ς

2000.2 The acc. sing. has -ν (cf. 7.a., §199, and §§1540f.).

2000.3 Unlike most masculine and feminine nouns, the nom. and acc. plur. are identical (cf. §1540.3).

2001. Notes:

2001.1 ι appears before consonants (nom. and acc. sing.), ε before vowels and in the dat. plur. by analogy (leveling). The strong grade was originally ει, but ι was subsequently lost.

2001.2 Contraction: dat. sing. πολει < πολε-ι; nom. and acc. plur. πόλεις < πολε-ες (ε + ε = ει, §917.2).

2001.3 The gen. sing. involves an interesting phonetic phenomenon: πόλεως comes from πολήος (a different stem, found in Homer); by transfer of quantity (quantitative metathesis, §909), the length of the vowels -ηο- was interchanged: -εω-. That this is so is demonstrated by the accent (πόλεως), which contradicts the rule (§0720.3) but is suitable for πόληος. However, πόλεως may be thought of as a gen. sing. comparable to those rare forms mentioned in §1970.3.

2001.4 The accent of the gen. plur. (also against the rule, §0720.3), is by analogy with the gen. sing.

2002. Peculiarities:

2002.1 One neuter, σίναπι, σινάπεως, τό, *mustard*, belongs to class 7.a.: σίναπι, σινάπεως, σινάπει, σίναπι (nom. and acc. identical—no ending; sing. only).

2002.2 The masculines, μάντις, μάντεως, ὁ, *soothsayer*, and ὄφις, ὄφεως, ὁ, *serpent*, are declined exactly like the fem. forms.

2003. πῆχυς, πήχεως, ὁ, *forearm, cubit*, actually has a stem in υ/ε (originally υ/ευ; cf. §2001.1), but it follows the pattern of πόλις precisely: merely substitute υ for ι in nom. and acc. sing. (all other forms are identical). πῆχυς is the only noun of its type in the literature covered by Bauer (but in Attic, e.g. πέλεκυς, πελέκεως, ὁ, *axe*, ἄστυ, ἄστεως, τό, *town*).

201. Class 7.c. Stems in ευ/ε

This group follows the pattern of πόλις (7.b.) in most respects. All nouns in this group are masculine.

ἀρχιερεύς, ἀρχιερέως, ὁ — *high priest*

	S	P
N	ἀρχιερεύς	ἀρχιερεῖς
G	ἀρχιερέως	ἀρχιερέων
D	ἀρχιερεῖ	ἀρχιερεῦσι(ν)
A	ἀρχιερέα	ἀρχιερεῖς

2010. Mnemonic hints:

2010.1 ευ is preserved in nom. sing. and dat. plur.; elsewhere ε appears (cf. πόλις, where ι is found in nom. and acc. sing., ε elsewhere: §2001.1).

2010.2 Unlike nouns of 7.a. and 7.b. (with acc. sing. in -ν), nouns in 7.c. have acc. sing. in -έα (cf. τίς -τίνα).

2010.3 The nom. and acc. plur. are identical (cf. πόλις, §2000.3).

2010.4 The pattern conforms to that of πόλις, except for nom. sing. (ευ for ι), acc. sing. (-έα for ιν), and dat. plur. (ευ for ε).

A full catalogue of 7.c. nouns will be found in Appendix II.

202. Class 7.d. Stems in ου/ο

In nouns of this type the variation is between ου and ο: ου appears in the nom. and acc. sing., and dat. plur., ο elsewhere. There are few nouns in this group and none of high frequency (see Appendix II).

βοῦς, βοός, ὁ (or ἡ) — *ox*

	S	P
N	βοῦς	βόες
G	βοός	βοῶν
D	βοΐ	βουσί(ν)
A	βοῦν	βόας

2020. Mnemonic hints:

2020.1 Nom. sing. in -ς, acc. sing. in -ν (like τὸν ἰχθύν [7. a.], τὴν πόλιν [7.b.]).

2020.2 Nom. and acc. plur. have regular ending, i.e. like τίνες-τίνας (unlike τὰς πολεῖς [7.b.], τοὺς βασιλεῖς [7.c.]).

2020.3 ου appears in nom. and acc. sing., and dat. plur., ο elsewhere.

2021. Remnants of other class 7. nouns.

There are only remnants of class 7. nouns with stems in αυ, οι.

2021.1 ναῦς, νεώς, ἡ, *ship*, occurs once in the New Testament at Acts 27:41: acc. sing. τὴν ναῦν. For Attic Greek the final test of one's mastery of the noun is the declension of ναῦς: ναῦς, νεώς, νηΐ, ναῦν; νῆες, νεῶν, ναυσί(ν), ναῦς. It has been replaced in hellenistic by πλοῖον, -ου, τό (II.3.).

2021.2 From stems in οι there are only two problematic instances in the New Testament. πειθοῖ Cor 2:4 (v.l. πειθοις may be a dat. sing. from πειθώ, πειθοῦς, ἡ, *persuasiveness* (Bl-D §7(4)). ἠχοῦς Lk 21:25 (Westcott-Hort) is from ἠχώ, ἠχοῦς, ἡ, *sound*, if it is properly accented (cf. IgnRom 2:1, Bauer s.v.); this noun appears also as ἦχος, ἤχους, τό (III.6.a.) and as ἦχος, ἤχου, ὁ (II.1.) (Bl-D §50). Nouns with stems in οι, for which the plural was lacking even in classical, were declined: ἠχώ (or -ωι), ἠχοῦς (ἠχοιος), ἠχοῖ (< ηχοιι), ἠχώ (ηχοια). Other examples in classical: εὐεστώ *well-being*, φειδώ *sparing*, Σαπφώ, Λητώ, Καλυψώ (proper names).

203. Summary of class 7. Leaving aside the marginal cases, the following generalizations apply to class 7. nouns:

203.1 The nom. sing. is always in -ς.

203.2 The gen. sing.:

    a) in -ος: 7.a., 7.d.

    b) in -ως: 7.b., 7.c.

203.3 The acc. sing.:

    a) in -ν: 7.a., 7.b., 7.d.

    b) in -α: 7.c.

203.4   The nom. and acc. plur.:

     a) in -ες, -ας: 7.a., 7.d.
     b) identical (-εῖς): 7.b., 7.c.

203.5   The dat. plur.:

     a) Nouns in 7.a. and 7.b. show a reduced vowel (υ/ε) before the ending -σι.
     b) Nouns in 7.c. and 7.d. show a diphthong (ευ, ου) [nouns in 7.c. show a diphthong also in the nom. sing., those in 7.d. also in the nom. and acc. sing.].

The only other irregularities concern vowel gradation and contraction, which are difficult to summarize without merely repeating.

Nouns: Vocative, Partial Declension, Noun in Context

Vocative

205. The form of the vocative does not, as a rule, occasion difficulties. It is sometimes (less often in hellenistic than in classical) introduced with ὦ: ὦ Θεόφιλε (Acts 1:1); cf. *0 Theophilus* in English. It is often identical in form with the nominative; there is a tendency in hellenistic Greek to use the nominative form in place of the vocative. Cf. Bl-D §§146f.

The forms which the vocative may take can be summarized schematically as follows:

205.1 The nominative, accusative and vocative are identical for each number of all *neuter* nouns.

205.2 In masculine and feminine nouns the vocative is always identical with the nominative in the plural, and often identical with the nominative in the singular.

205.3 Where the vocative singular is not identical with the nominative it may take the following forms:

a) Masculines in -ας, -ης, gen. -ου (I.3.).
   1) Stems in -της have vocative in short α, e.g. ὑποκριτά (Mt 7:5), δέσποτα (Lk 2:29).
   2) Other stems of this class in -ας, -ης have vocatives in -α or -η (i.e. the nom. less -ς), e.g. Ἀνανία (Acts 5:2).

b) Masculines in -ας, -ης, gen. -α, -η (I.4.) have vocatives which are identical in form with the genitive (i.e. the nom. less -ς), e.g. Σατανᾶ (Mk 8:33).

c) Masculines and feminines in -ος (II.1., II.2.) form a vocative in -ε, e.g. ὦ ἄνθρωπε (Rom 2:3), κύριε (Lk 5:12), Διδάσκαλε (Jn 1:39).

d) Masculines and feminines of the third declension: the vocative is the bare stem (consonants that cannot stand at the end of a word are lost; in stems with vowel gradation, the vocative is often the middle grade). Examples:
   1) ὦ γύναι (Mt 15:28) (< γυναικ-, III.1.b.).
   2) πάτερ (Jn 17:1), θύγατερ (Mt 9:22), ἄνερ (1 Cor 7:16) (III.4.C.).
   3) βασιλεῦ (Acts 26:2) (III.7.c.).

Irregular and Partial Declension

206.   Irregularity of declension has been treated for the most part under the several classes; peculiarities noted there provide a fairly comprehensive index to nouns customarily included in the category 'irregular.' Isolated problems are discussed in Bl-D §§43–58. There are, however, a few remaining examples of irregular and partial declension, having to do with proper names, which may be presented in summary form here.

206.1 Ζεύς, Διός, ὁ *Zeus*, is declined: Ζεύς, Διός, Διΐ, Δία, Ζεῦ (vocative). It appears in the New Testament at Acts 14:12, 13.

206.2 Some Semitic proper names are partially declined in that -ς is added to the stem to form the nom. and -ν is added to signal the acc. (i.e. indeclinable and third declension). E.g.:

   a) Ἰησοῦς, -οῦ, -οῦ, -οῦν, -οῦ (vocative)
   b) Λευίς, -ί, -ί, -ίν

206.3 Μωυσῆς is variable: gen. always Μωυσέως (as if from -εος, III.7.c.); dat. Μωυσεῖ and -η (-ηι); acc. Μωυσέα (III.7.c.) and -ῆν; voc. -ῆ. In the LXX the pattern Μωυσῆς, -η, -ῆ, -ῆν, ῆ predominates (I.4.). Cf. the classical pattern of Ἄρης (ὁ), -εως, -ει, -η, or -ην (Smyth §285.1).

206.4 A few proper names in -ας or -α have an acc. in -αν, but are otherwise indeclinable, e.g. Ἀκύλας, -αν, ὁ; Γολγοθᾶ, -ᾶν, ἡ; Ζηνᾶς, -ᾶν, ὁ.

206.5 Θυάτιρα and Λύστρα are apparently declined -α, -ων, -οις, -αν (ἡ and τά? s. Bl-D §57); cf. Μύρα, Μύρων, τά. Λύδδα has gen. Λύδδας or -ης, acc. Λύδδα or -αν (Bl-D §56(2)).

206.6 Χερούβ, τό and ὁ (כְּרוּב) is indeclinable except that the Hebrew plural is imitated in Greek as Χερουβείν, -βίν, -βείμ, or -βίμ (some of the latter are also taken as singular).

   Bl-D §§53–58 treats the declension of foreign words in detail.

207.   *Indeclinable nouns.* There is also a host of foreign names and loanwords which are wholly indeclinable, e.g. Ἀβραάμ (ὁ), Ἀδάμ, Ἰακώβ (ὁ), Ἰσραήλ (ὁ); μάννα (τό), πάσχα (τό). The case of these words is usually made clear in context by the article, other 'qualifiers,' or by the structure in which they appear.

The Noun in Context

208.   It was once the practice to require the student to master the full paradigms for all three declensions before approaching the text. The paradigms can be

memorized. They can also be forgotten—and usually are. However much virtue there is in being able to reel off paradigms for the various declension patterns, it is a virtue one can manage very well without, provided one's primary interest is in the ability to read Greek with facility. It is appropriate at this juncture, therefore, to stipulate what is important and what is not.

208.1   It is *not* important to be able to assign a noun to its proper class, and hence to be able to cite its paradigm in full (unless, of course, one regards *that* exercise as important).

208.2   It is *not* important to memorize endless paradigms, although it is unfortunately necessary initially to master the models, ὁ, ἡ, τό and τίς, τί.

208.3   It *is* important to be able to grasp a noun in its relationship to the word group in which it occurs. To do this one often needs to know its case, number, gender. However, as already observed (§§125–129; 146–1471; 174–176), the form of the noun is only one clue. In the vast majority of cases other signals (e.g. article, preposition) will tell the reader what he or she needs to know about the noun in question, i.e. what relation it bears to the word group.

208.4   It *is* important to learn to rely on a *constellation of signals in identifying the noun in context.* One of these signals is, of course, the particular form (case ending) of the noun, and it cannot be ignored. For that reason, the formal aspects of the noun have been set out schematically in relation to the two models; this presentation provides an overview and a convenient summary *for reference.* Knowledge of the models (the article and τίς, τί), together with a fairly firm grasp of the organization of the nominal system, will make it possible to identify the noun even in isolation. Nevertheless, the form of the noun should be seized, wherever possible, in conjunction with other signals.

208.5   It *is* important to gain facility in 'reading' word groups, i.e. in determining word relationships within the group, even when one does not know the meanings of individual words. The reason is twofold: a) Without immediate and nearly automatic response to grammatical signals, the reading of a text will remain a laborious and frustrating process; b) the ability to 'read' grammatical signals often makes it possible to fill in lexical blanks (the meaning of words one does not know). Since grammar represents the structure of a language, without it the language remains mute, no matter how many words one knows. Grammatical signals, however, are relatively few in number, highly repetitious, and systematic; they can therefore be learned more readily than vocabulary. Moreover, with a firm grammatical basis, it is easier to expand lexical competence.

209. *Grammatical signals.* The morphological variables indicating gender, number, case are rudimentary grammatical signals. They function in both noun and article, the combination of which often makes the resolution of word groups materially easier (§§125–129). Prepositions add further clues to the grammatical structure of the word group (§§146–1471). These signals were considered in relation to the structure of nominal word clusters with genitive modifier (§§174–176). This constellation of signals may now be expanded.

2090. It should be noted that grammatical signals which are ambiguous in isolation (some possible confusions are noted in §§1210.2–4, 1320.4, 1360.3–8, 152.2, 168, 170, 197) are often resolved in relation to the constellation in which they appear.

210. *Other modifiers as grammatical signals.* Other modifiers, either in conjunction with article and/or preposition, or alone, may assist in identifying noun phrases.

210.1 Adjective in conjunction with article:

(1) ἡ κρίσις ἡ ἐμὴ	(fem. nom. sing.)	Jn 8:16
(2) ὁ λόγος ὁ ἐμὸς	(masc. nom. sing.)	Jn 8:37
(3) τὴν λαλιὰν τὴν ἐμὴν	(fem. acc. sing.)	Jn 8:43
(4) τὸν λόγον τὸν ἐμόν	(masc. acc. sing.)	Jn 8:43

With (4) cf.

(5) τὸν ἐμὸν λόγον	(masc. acc. sing.)	Jn 8:51
(6) ἡ ἐπιστολὴ ἡ παλαιά	(fem. nom. sing.)	1 Jn 2:7
(7) τὸ φῶς τὸ ἀληθινὸν	(neut. nom. or acc. sing.)	1 Jn 2:8
(8) ταῦτα τὰ σημεῖα	(neut. nom. or acc. plur.)	Jn 3:2

Note (1) and (7) where third declension nouns do not follow the declension pattern of the article.

210.2 Adjective in conjunction with article and preposition:

(9) ἐν τῷ νόμῳ (δὲ) τῷ ὑμετέρῳ	(masc. or neut. dat. sing.)	Jn 8:17
(10) ἐκ τοῦ κόσμου τούτου	(masc. or neut. gen. sing.)	Jn 8:23

210.3 Adjective in conjunction with preposition:

(11) ἀπὸ πάσης ἁμαρτίας	(fem. gen. sing.)	1 Jn 1:7
(12) ἀπὸ πάσης ἀδικίας	(fem. gen. sing.)	1 Jn 1:9

210.4 Adjective alone:

(13) ἐντολὴν καινὴν	(fem. acc. sing.)	1 Jn 2:7
(14) ἐντολὴν παλαιὰν	(fem. acc. sing.)	1 Jn 2:7

In most instances the modifier merely reinforces the clues provided by other elements in the phrase. However, the repetition of clues makes it possible to seize the phrase as a whole more easily.

211. Other items in the phrase are of more assistance where, e.g., a third declension noun like πόλις, city (III.7.b., §200) is involved.

(15) εἰς τὴν ἁγίαν πόλιν	Mt 4:5
(16) πᾶσα ἡ πόλις	Mt 8:34
(17) τὰς πόλεις πάσας	Mt 9:35
(18) εἰς πόλιν	Mt 10:5
(19) ἐν ταῖς πόλεσιν	Mt 11:1
(20) ἀπὸ πόλεως εἰς πόλιν	Mt 23:34

Gender, number and case are signaled in (15), (16), (17) and (19) by items other than the noun, i.e. one does not need to know the declension pattern of the noun to be able to identify it. Case is signaled by the prepositions in (18) and (20). There are relatively few appearances of πόλις in the New Testament where at least the case is not signaled by some other item in the phrase.

212. *Parallel structures as grammatical signals.* In addition to the article, preposition, and other modifiers, parallel structures often provide handy clues to noun identification. Parallel structures vary from the simple and obvious, e.g. two nouns as objects of the same verb, to the more oblique and complex, e.g. the repetition of the same basic sentence structure. When the full range is taken into account, parallelisms will be found to abound in any text since the grammar of a language is highly repetitious. Attention is confined initially to a few relatively obvious types of parallel structures.

213. *Nominal items as objects of the same verb.*

(21) εἶδεν / Σίμωνα (καὶ) Ἀνδρέαν // τὸν ἀδελφὸν Σίμωνος   Mk 1:16
    he saw Simon and Andrew the brother of Simon

In (21) Σίμωνα and Ἀνδρέαν are objects of the same verb, εἶδεν; they are linked together by the conjunction of καί. τὸν ἀδελφὸν Σίμωνος stands in apposition to Ἀνδρέαν (indicated by //). There are thus three items which stand in the relationship of object to εἶδεν. The identification of any one of these items is also the identification of the other two—so far as *case* is concerned (case is the primary signal of grammatical function). In this instance, τὸν ἀδελφὸν provides an easy resolution: τὸν = masc. sing. acc. of the article; the ending -ον confirms the identification (ἀδελφός = II.1., §136.1). With this clue there is no need to labor over Σίμωνα and Ἀνδρέαν: they must be accusative as well. Ἀνδρέαν looks first declension (it is, in fact, a noun of I.3., §132.3). The acc. Σίμωνα, when compared with Σίμωνος, which must be genitive, is almost certainly third declension (acc. in -α, gen. in -ος, stem ending in ν, long vowel, -ω-, in both instances: III.5.a., §187, with nom. Σίμων).

(21) is followed in the text shortly by
(22) εἶδεν / Ἰάκωβον // τὸν τοῦ Ζεβεδαίου (καὶ) Ἰωάννην //
　　　τὸν ἀδελφὸν αὐτοῦ　　　　　　　　　　　　　　Mk 1:19
　　　he saw James the son of Zebedee and John his brother

Καί again connects the two objects of εἶδεν, both of which have a phrase in apposition (καί comes between the two complete items). Since τὸν ἀδελφὸν is acc., Ἰάκωβον and Ἰωάννην must also be accusatives, and probably second and first declensions, respectively. In the appositional phrase τὸν τοῦ Ζεβεδαίου, τὸν is masc. acc. sing., but τοῦ Ζεβεδαίου is gen. The whole phrase must therefore run: *James, the something or other of Zebedee* (supply *son*; cf. Bl-D §162(1)).

Compare the parallel sentences in Matthew:

(23) εἶδεν / δύο ἀδελφούς, // Σίμωνα // τὸν
　　　λεγόμενον Πέτρον (καὶ) Ἀνδρέαν // τὸν ἀδελφὸν αὐτοῦ　　Mt 4:18
　　　he saw two brothers, Simon the one called Peter and Andrew
　　　his brother
(24) εἶδεν ἄλλους δύο ἀδελφούς, // Ἰάκωβον // τὸν
　　　τοῦ Ζεβεδαίου (καὶ) Ἰωάννην // τὸν ἀδελφὸν αὐτοῦ　　Mt 4:21
　　　he saw two other brothers, James the son of Zebedee and John
　　　his brother

Note the position of καί in each case. In the Matthean form, the names of the two men in each case stand in apposition to ἀδελφούς (masc. acc. plur.), in addition to having appositional phrases of their own.

214. Apposition and καί frame an even more elaborate example of parallel structures in 1 Jn 2:16:

(25a) πᾶν τὸ ἐν τῷ κόσμῳ //

(25b) ἡ ἐπιθυμία τῆς σαρκὸς (καὶ)

(25c) ἡ ἐπιθυμία τῶν ὀφθαλμῶν (καὶ)

(25d) ἡ ἀλαζονεία τοῦ βίου /

(25e) οὐκ ἔστιν ἐκ τοῦ πατρός ἀλλὰ ἐκ τοῦ κόσμου ἐστίν

Three phrases, identical in structure and connected by καί (25b-d), stand in apposition to the first phrase, which is the subject of the sentence (the head terms are all therefore nom.). In (25e), moreover, οὐκ . . . ἀλλά, *not . . . but* frame negative and positive contrasting statements involving two parallel phrases: ἐκ τοῦ πατρός, ἐκ τοῦ κόσμου. For another example of the latter, cf.

(26) οὐκ ἐξ αἱμάτων / οὐδὲ ἐκ θελήματος σαρκὸς /
    οὐδὲ θελήματος ἀνδρὸς / ἀλλ᾽ ἐκ θεοῦ   Jn 1:13

where three negative phrases introduced by οὐκ (οὐδέ) and ἐκ are contrasted with a positive phrase introduced by ἀλλά and ἐκ.

Parallel grammatical structures may thus be connected by καί *and*, or framed by οὐκ . . . ἀλλά, *not . . . but*. Such structures may involve the object, the subject, or some other grammatical item in the sentence. There are other types of grammatical parallelism, to be introduced subsequently, which will also assist in noun identification.

Lesson 16

Adjectives: Groups I–II

220. An adjective is a word that is subject to inflection in *three genders,* as well as in all cases and both numbers. An adjective may thus be made to agree with any term it qualifies in gender, number and case. Nouns, on the other hand, are inflected in only one gender (although some nouns fluctuate in gender).

All adjectives are declined in conformity with patterns already observed in nouns. A combination of patterns is employed in some instances in effecting a distinction between the masculine and feminine forms. The masculine and feminine forms are identical in other instances. There is always a distinctive pattern for the neuter. Adjectives are grouped according to the pattern or combination of patterns utilized in elaborating the declension:

I. Second Declension: masculine and feminine identical
II. Second and First Declensions: masculine and neuter second declension; feminine first declension
   1. Three endings
   2. Three endings, but contracted
III. Third and First Declensions: masculine and neuter third declension; feminine first declension
   1. Stems in -αντ- (πᾶς is the only example)
   2. Stems in υ/ε
IV. Third Declension: masculine and feminine identical
   1. Stems in -εσ-
   2. Stems in -ον- (including comparatives)
V. Mixed Patterns

Group I: Second Declension

221. Many adjectives in this group are compounds (many with α-privative [negative prefix; cf. *a-theist*]). The number found in Bauer is large, but there are few of high frequency (for a catalogue of those appearing in the New Testament ten times or more see Appendix II).

The masculine and feminine forms are identical (therefore adjectives of two endings). The masculine-feminine is declined precisely like masculine and feminine nouns in -ος (II.1 and II.2); the neuter like neuter nouns in -ον (II.3). For this reason they are called second declension adjectives.

αἰώνιος, αἰώνιον — *eternal*

	Singular		Plural	
	M/F	N	M/F	N
N	αἰώνιος	αἰώνιον	αἰώνιοι	αἰώνια
G	αἰωνίου	αἰωνίου	αἰωνίων	αἰωνίων
D	αἰωνίῳ	αἰωνίῳ	αἰωνίοις	αἰωνίοις
A	αἰώνιον	αἰώνιον	αἰωνίους	αἰώνια

2210.   Mnemonic hints:

2210.1   The middle cases (gen., dat., respectively) of each number are identical in all three genders (like the article).

2210.2   The neuter nom. and acc. of each number are identical (like the article); the masc. acc. sing. is identical with the neut. nom. and acc. sing. (unlike the article, but like second declension nouns: §1360.6).

2211.   Some adjectives in this group fluctuate between two (group I) and three endings (group II. 1): αἰώνιος, (-ία) -ον; ἑδραῖος, (-αία) -ον; ἕτοιμος, (-η) -ον; οἰκεῖος, (-α) -ον; κόσμιος, (-α) -ον; παρόμοιος, (-α) -ον; πτερωτός, (-ή) -ον; πτηνός, (-ή) -ον; σκυθρωπός, (-ή) -όν; ὑπερῷος, (-α) -ον; ὑποχθόνιος, (-α) -ον. Bl-D §59.

222.   Any adjective may be used as a 'substantive,' i.e. utilized in the same structures in which a noun is used. ἔρημος, -ον and περίχωρος, -ον are predominantly so used: ἡ ἔρημος *wilderness*; ἡ περίχωρος *neighborhood* (γῆ may be 'understood': *the wilderness land*; *the surrounding territory*; see Bl-D §241 for other examples).

Group II: Second-First Declension

223.   Adjectives in this group have three endings: masc. and neuter follow the second declension, the fem. follows the first (nouns of class I.1). The masc. and neut. will therefore be identical with adjectives of group I, but there will be a separate fem. form. The fem. sg. form has α after ε, ι, ρ, elsewhere η (the α/η shift is not involved: §132.2, class I.2).

Adjectives in group II.1 do not contract, those in II.2 do. A number of adjectives in II.1 are of high frequency; those in II.2 are rare.

224. Adjectives of group II.1.

ἀγαθός, ἀγαθή, ἀγαθόν — *good*

	Singular			Plural		
	M	F	N	M	F	N
N	ἀγαθός	ἀγαθή	ἀγαθόν	ἀγαθοί	ἀγαθαί	ἀγαθά
G	ἀγαθοῦ	ἀγαθῆς	ἀγαθοῦ	ἀγαθῶν	ἀγαθῶν	ἀγαθῶν
D	ἀγαθῷ	ἀγαθῇ	ἀγαθῷ	ἀγαθοῖς	ἀγαθαῖς	ἀγαθοῖς
A	ἀγαθόν	ἀγαθήν	ἀγαθόν	ἀγαθούς	ἀγαθάς	ἀγαθά

ἅγιος, ἁγία, ἅγιον *holy* is declined precisely like ἀγαθός except that it has α in the fem. sing. rather than η.

2240. Mnemonic hints:

2240.1 The inflection of the article, ὁ, ἡ, τό (§121), may serve as the immediate model for adjectives of class II.1, with the modifications for second declension nouns noted in §1210 (masc. nom. sing. -ος instead of ὁ; neut. nom. and acc. sing. -ον instead of -ο).

2240.2 Whether α or η occurs in the sing. forms is a matter of indifference so far as identification is concerned (§§131.3, 132.2).

2240.3 For the masc. and neut. hints 1. and 2. in §2210 are applicable here also.

225. Adjectives of group II.2.

χρυσοῦς, χρυσῆ, χρυσοῦν — *golden*

	Singular		
	M	F	N
N	χρυσοῦς (< εος)	χρυσῆ	χρυσοῦν (< εον)
G	χρυσοῦ	χρυσῆς	χρυσοῦ
D	χρυσῷ	χρυσῇ	χρυσῷ
A	χρυσοῦν (< εον)	χρυσῆν	χρυσοῦν (< εον)

	Plural		
	M	F	N
N	χρυσοῖ	χρυσαῖ	χρυσᾶ
G	χρυσῶν	χρυσῶν	χρυσῶν
D	χρυσοῖς	χρυσαῖς	χρυσοῖς
A	χρυσοῦς	χρυσᾶς	χρυσᾶ

2250.   Notes:

2250.1   Except for accent only four forms (masc. and neut. nom. and acc. singulars) deviate from the pattern of adjectives in II.1; in each case the contraction is ε + o = ου (§917.4).

2250.2   II.2 adjectives with stems in -ρε have α in the fem. sing. forms (following the rule for first declension nouns: α after ε, ι, ρ, §1321.1).

2250.3   Contract adjectives of this class are occasionally found in an uncontracted form (Bl-D §45).

        A complete catalogue of II.2 adjectives appearing in Bauer will be found in Appendix II.

2251.   A catalogue of adjectives of groups I and II that appear in John 8:12–59, 1 John 1:5–2:17, John 1:19–51 follows. Entries are arranged in the order of first appearance.

ἀληθινός, -ή, -όν	*true* (Jn 8:16; 1 Jn 2:8)
μόνος, -η, -ον	*only, alone* [cf. *monograph*] (Jn 8:16, 29; 1 Jn 2:2)
Ἰουδαῖος, -αία, -αῖον	*Jewish* (Jn 8:22, 31, 48, 52, 57; Jn 1:19)
ἀρεστός, -ή, -όν	*pleasing* (Jn 8:29)
ἐλεύθερος, -α, -ον	*free* (Jn 8:33, 36)
διάβολος, -ον	*slanderous* [cf. *diabolic*] (Jn 8:44)
ἴδιος, -α, -ον	*one's own* [cf. *idiot*] (Jn 8:44; Jn 1:41)
ὅμοιος, -α, -ον	*like, similar* [cf. *homoeopathy*] (Jn 8:55)
πιστός, -ή, -όν	*faithful* (1 Jn 1:9)
δίκαιος, -α, -ον	*just, righteous* (1 Jn 1:9, 2:1, 29)
ὅλος, -η, -ον	*whole* (1 Jn 2:2)
ἀγαπητός, -ή, -όν	*beloved* (1 Jn 2:7)
καινός, -ή, - όν	*new* (1 Jn 2:7, 8)
παλαιός, -ά, - όν	*old* [cf. *palaeolithic*] (1 Jn 2:7, 7)
πονηρός, -ά, - όν	*sick; evil* (1 Jn 2:13 14)
ἰσχυρός, -ά, - όν	*strong* (1 Jn 2:14)
ἔρημος, -ον	*desolate* (Jn 1:23)
μέσος, -η, -ον	*middle, in the middle* (Jn 1:26)
ἄξιος, -α, -ον	*worthy* [cf. *axiology*] (Jn 1:27)
πρῶτος, -α, -ον	*first* [cf. *prototype*] (Jn 1:30, 41)
ἅγιος, -α, -ον	*holy* [cf. *hagiology*] (Jn 1:33)
δέκατος, -η, -ον	*tenth* [cf. *decalogue*] (Jn 1:39)
ἀγαθός, -ή, -όν	*good* (Jn 1:46)

Lesson 17

Adjectives: Groups III–V

Group III: Third-First Declensions

230. Adjectives in this group have three endings: masc. and neut. follow the third declension, the fem. follows the first (nouns of class I.1) as does the fem. of group II adjectives. The masc. and neut. will therefore utilize the endings of the model, τίς, τί. This class is divided into two subgroups: stems in -αντ- (III.1) and stems in υ/ε (III.2).

2300. While the endings attached to the fem. forms in group III adjectives are perfectly regular, the fem. stem is strikingly dissimilar to the masc. and neut. stems. This difference is accounted for by the addition of -ι̯α (consonantal ι, §932) to form the fem. stem.

2300.1 Stems in -αντ-: -αντι̯α (τι̯ becomes σ, §932.5) > -ανσα (ν is lost before σ, and the preceding vowel lengthened to compensate for the loss, §929.8) > -ᾱσα. Cf. the fem. act. participle λυοντ-ι̯α (§2470.1): > λυονσα > λύουσα.

2300.2 Stems in υ/ε: the fem. form derives from a stem in -ευι̯α, from which υ̯ was lost (-εια), and the ε and ι̯ then contracted to -εῖα. Cf. the perfect act. participle λελυκυσ-ι̯α > λελυκυ-ι̯α (the σ is lost) > λελυκυῖα (§2490) .

231. Group III.1. πᾶς, πᾶσα, πᾶν, *every, each, all* [cf. *pandora*], together with compounds with πᾶς as the second element (ἅπας, ἅπασα, ἅπαν; σύμπας, σύμπασα, σύμπαν), is the only example in this category. However, πᾶς itself is of very high frequency, and it serves as the immediate model for the declension of all active participles (except the perfect active) and the aorist passive participle. *It should therefore be committed carefully to memory along with the other models,* ὁ, ἡ, τό *and* τίς, τί. Knowledge of these three models make it easily possible to identify any form in the entire Greek nominal system (personal pronouns excepted).

πᾶς, πᾶσα, πᾶν — *every, each, all*

		Singular			Plural		
		M	F	N	M	F	N
N		πᾶς	πᾶσα	πᾶν	πάντες	πᾶσαι	πάντα
G		παντός	πάσης	παντός	πάντων	πασῶν	πάντων
D		παντί	πάσῃ	παντί	πᾶσι (ν)	πάσαις	πᾶσι (ν)
A		πάντα	πᾶσαν	πᾶν	πάντας	πάσας	πάντα

2310. Mnemonic hints:

2310.1 The first thing to note is that the masc. and neut. are declined like τίς, τί the fem. like the fem. art. (i.e. there are no new endings involved). There is an α/η shift in the singular (α in nom. and acc., η in gen. and dat.), as in the case of nouns of class I.2. (§132.2).

2310.2 Other hints, already familiar, may be repeated:

   a) the middle cases of masc. and neut. are identical for each number;
   b) the neut. nom. and acc. sing. are identical, as are the neut. nom. and acc. plur. (along with the masc. acc. sing.).

2310.3 The neut. nom. and acc. sing., having no ending, loses τ: παντ < πᾶν (τ cannot stand at the end of a word, §923).

2310.4 The masc. nom. sing. loses -ντ- before σ: παντς < πᾶς (§929.9); the masc. and neut. dat. plur. likewise: παντσι < πᾶσι.

232. Group III.2. Adjectives with stems in υ/ε are not common (a complete catalogue from Bauer may be found in Appendix II). For the formation of the fem. stem see §2300.2.

ταχύς, ταχεῖα, ταχύ — *quick, swift*

		Singular			Plural		
		M	F	N	M	F	N
N		ταχύς	ταχεῖα	ταχύ	ταχεῖς	ταχεῖαι	ταχέα
G		ταχέως	ταχείας	ταχέως	ταχέων	ταχειῶν	ταχέων
D		ταχεῖ	ταχείᾳ	ταχεῖ	ταχέσι (ν)	ταχείαις	ταχέσι (ν)
A		ταχύν	ταχεῖαν	ταχύ	ταχεῖς	ταχείας	ταχέα

2320. Mnemonic hints:

2320.1 The general hints apply here also: the middle cases masc. and neut. are identical for each number; the nom. and acc. singulars and plurals are identical, respectively.

2320.2 The masc. is declined like πόλις (§200) or, more precisely, like πῆχυς (§2003): note the -ν in the acc. sing. (cf. §§1540.2, 1630.3, 199, 200, 202 [third declension nouns, III.1.c, III.7.a, b, d]), and the identity of the nom. and acc. plur. (§§2000.3, 2010.3 [nouns of III.7.b and c]).

2320.3 The neut. nom. and acc. sing. have no ending (like all third declension neuters); the nom. and acc. plur. have the regular (τιν-α) ending in -α (uncontracted).

2320.4 The gen. sing., masc. and neut., is by analogy with nouns of III.7.b (πόλις, πόλεως) ; the Attic form, -έος, is occasionally found as a variant (Bl-D §46(3)).

2320.5 The masc. and neut. stem varies between υ and ε (cf. πόλις, πῆχυς); the fem. stem has -ει- throughout.

Group IV: Third Declension

233. Group IV adjectives belong wholly to the third declension. The masc. and fem. forms are therefore identical (as in third declension nouns, §150). Adjectives will then have only two endings (like group I adjectives). They are divided into two subgroups: stems in -εσ- (cf. nouns in III.6, §§195ff.), and stems in -ον- (cf. nouns in III.5.b, §§188f).

234. Group IV.1. Adjectives with stems in -εσ- are fairly numerous (112 examples in Bauer), but none is of high frequency. A complete catalogue will be found in Appendix II.

ἀληθής, ἀληθές — *true*

Singular

M/F		N
N ἀληθής		ἀληθές
G	ἀληθοῦς (< -εσος)	
D	ἀληθεῖ (< -εσι)	
A ἀληθῆ (< -εσα)		ἀληθές

Plural

M/F		N
N ἀληθεῖς (< -εσες)		ἀληθῆ (< -εσα)
G	ἀληθῶν (< εσων)	
D	ἀληθέσι (ν) (< εσσι)	
A ἀληθεῖς		ἀληθῆ

2340.   Mnemonic hints:

2340.1   The middle cases are identical for both numbers, are contracted from the full forms given in parenthesis, and are identical with the corresponding forms of neuter nouns in class III.6 (neuter stems in -oσ, -εσ §196).

2340.2   The neut. nom. and acc. singulars and plurals are identical for each number (as always): the sing. shows the bare stem, the plur. the regular neuter ending (a) contracted with ε (σ is lost between two vowels, §930.2) and is therefore identical with nom. and acc. plur. of III.6 nouns (§196).

2340.3   The masc. nom. sing. has a lengthened stem vowel (-ες < -ης).

2340.4   The masc. nom. and acc. plural are identical (see §2320.2).

2340.5   Note that the masc. acc. sing. is identical in this case with the neut. nom. and acc. plur. (a confusion that is also possible between many third declension masc. and fem. acc. singulars in -α and the neut. nom. and acc. plur. in -α of nouns of class III.3, §§170ff.).

235.   Group IV.2. Adjectives in this class include a number of comparatives in -(ι)ων (§262). Neither number or frequency are high. A complete catalogue will be found in Appendix II.

ἄφρων, ἄφρον — *foolish*

	Singular		Plural	
	M/F	N	M/F	N
N	ἄφρων	ἄφρον	ἄφρονες	ἄφρονα
G	ἄφρονος		ἀφρόνων	
D	ἄφρονι		ἄφροσι (ν)	
A	ἄφρονα	ἄφρον	ἄφρονας	ἄφρονα

2350.   Mnemonic hints:

2350.1   The masc.-fem. is declined exactly like εἰκών, εἰκόνος (III.5.b, §188): -ων in nom. masc.-fem. sing., -ον- elsewhere; loss of ν in dat. plur. without apparent trace (-οσι).

2350.2   The neut. conforms to the neut. pattern: no ending in nom. and acc. sing.; -α in nom. and acc. plur.

2351.1   Comparatives in -(ι)ων (§245) follow the pattern of ἄφρων, ἄφρον . They exhibit an occasional by-form, however, as a result of contraction (loss of σ between vowels [§930.2], based on a different stem in -οσ- [Smyth §293.d]): μείζων, μεῖζον (comparative of μέγας, *great, large*) has masc.-fem. acc. sing. in μείζονα or μείζω (< -οσα); the neut. nom. and acc. plur. present the same options. The masc.-fem. nom. and acc. plur. are μείζονες and μείζονας respectively, with a by-form μείζους (< -οσες); for both (the by-form is identical for both cases). πλείων (or πλέων), πλεῖον (or πλέον) (comparative of πολύς, *much, many*) exhibits some of the same by-forms.

2351.2 One adjective, ἄρσην, ἄρσεν, *male*, has a stem in -ην, -εν rather than -ων, -ον. η appears in the masc.-fem. nom. sing., ε elsewhere.

Group V: Mixed Patterns

236. Two adjectives with mixed patterns are very common; a third is less so.

πολύς, πολλή, πολύ — *much, many*

	Singular			Plural		
	M	F	N	M	F	N
N	πολύς	πολλή	πολύ	πολλοί	πολλαί	πολλά
G	πολλοῦ	πολλῆς	πολλοῦ	πολλῶν	πολλῶν	πολλῶν
D	πολλῷ	πολλῇ	πολλῷ	πολλοῖς	πολλαῖς	πολλοῖς
A	πολύν	πολλήν	πολύ	πολλούς	πολλάς	πολλά

μέγας, μεγάλη, μέγα — *great*

	Singular			Plural		
	M	F	N	M	F	N
N	μέγας	μεγάλη	μέγα	μεγάλοι	μεγάλαι	μεγάλα
G	μεγάλου	μεγάλης	μεγάλου	μεγάλων	μεγάλων	μεγάλων
D	μεγάλῳ	μεγάλη	μεγάλῳ	μεγάλοις	μεγάλαις	μεγάλοις
A	μέγαν	μεγάλην	μέγα	μεγάλους	μεγάλας	μεγάλα

2360. Mnemonic hints:

2360.1 The pattern is regular second and first declension (like adjectives in group II.1, §224) except for the four underlined forms in each case, which appear to be third declension.

2360.2 The masc. and neut. nom. and acc. singulars have abbreviated stems; the endings are like those on ταχύς (III.2, §232, i.e. -ς in masc. nom. sing., -ν in acc., nothing for the neuter forms).

2361. μέλας, μέλαινα, μέλαν, *black*, has a stem μελαν-. The feminine is formed by adding ι (§2300) , which is transposed to the preceding vowel (§932.6). The masc. nom. sing., μέλας, shows the loss of ν before σ (§929.8), as do the masc. and neut. dat. plurals (cf. nouns of III.5.b, §1880.2).

μέλας, μέλαινα, μέλαν — *black*

	Singular			Plural		
	M	F	N	M	F	N
N	μέλας	μέλαινα	μέλαν	μέλανες	μέλαιναι	μέλανα
G	μέλανος	μελαίνης	μέλανος	μελάνων	μελαινῶν	μελάνων
D	μέλανι	μελαίνῃ	μέλανι	μέλασι (ν)	μελαίναις	μέλασι (ν)
A	μέλανα	μέλαιναν	μέλαν	μέλανας	μελαίνας	μέλανα

237. *Summary of Adjectives.* A few observations may be made with respect to adjectives overall.

237.1 Wherever there is a separate fem. form, it is always first declension (II.1, II.2, III.1, III.2, V).

    a) The fem. pattern has consistent α or η in the sing. everywhere except for πᾶς (III.1) and μέλας (V).

237.2 The masc. form of adjectives in III.2 is declined like nouns in III.7.b (πόλις, πῆχυς) ; the neut. declension of adjectives in IV.1 is very nearly identical with the declension of nouns in III.6 (only the stem of the neut. nom. and acc. sing. is different); the masc.-fem, declension of adjectives in IV.2 is identical with nouns in III.5.b.

2370. *Remnants.* A few isolated remnants of other adjective patterns appear in the literature covered by Bauer.

2370.1 Declined like active participles (§2470.1) are ἄκων, ἄκουσα, ἆκον and ἑκών, ἑκοῦσα, ἑκόν (Smyth §305.b).

2370.2 ἵλεως -ων, ἀνίλεως -ων are adjectives of two endings following the pattern of the Attic second declension (§138; cf. Smyth §289, Bl-D §44(1)).

2370.3 A contract adjective, τετράπους -ουν is declined like other contract adjectives of group II.2 (§§225f.), except that it is an adjective of two endings (i.e. masc.-fem. = masc. pattern). Smyth §290.a.

2370.4 ἀμήτωρ, -ορ, gen. -ορος and ἀπάτωρ, -ορ, gen. -ορος belong to group IV (adjectives of the third declension). These and others of the same group were never common. Smyth §291.a.

2370.5 The verbal adjective, βλητέος, -α, -ον, is the only one of its type in the New Testament (Bl-D §65(3)). The declension pattern is regular (group II.1, §224).

Lesson 18

Comparison of Adjectives/Participles

Comparison of Adjectives

240. Adjectives (and adverbs) are subject to comparison in Greek as in other languages. Comparison may be regular, e.g. *long, longer, longest*, or it may be irregular, e.g. *good, better, best*. The three degrees are usually referred to as positive, comparative (strictly speaking, only two items are compared), superlative. The superlative is on the wane in hellenistic Greek with the result that there is a certain amount of confusion: the superlative is often used in an elative sense (e.g. *best = very good*), and the comparative form often does duty for both itself and the superlative (Bl-D §§60–62).

241. The comparative and superlative degrees of adjectives (and adverbs) may be formed in one of two ways: 1) by means of the suffixes -τερος (comparative) and -τατος (superlative) (§§242–245); 2) by means of the suffixes -(ι)ων (comparative) and -ιστος (superlative) (§245). Other ways of expressing comparison belong under syntax; here only the formation and inflection of comparative and superlative forms is to be considered.

242. Comparative in -τερος superlative in -τατος. The comparative is formed from the masculine stem of the adjective.

242.1   ἰσχυρότερος (< ἰσχυρός)
βαρύτερος (< βαρύς)
(-τερος is added to the stem vowel)

242.2   ἀσθενέστερος (< ἀσθενής)
(-τερος is added to a shortened stem vowel)

242.3   μακαριώτερος (< μακάριος)
(-τερος is added to a lengthened stem vowel)

242.4   δεισιδαιμονέστερος (< δεισιδαίμων)
(-εστερος is added to the stem consonant on the analogy of comparison of type 2. above)

242.5 The superlative is also formed from the masculine stem of the adjective:

ἀκριβέστατος (< ἀκριβής) (= type 2. above)
ἁγιώτατος (< ἅγιος) (= type 3. above)
τιμιώτατος (< τίμος) (= type 3. above)

A full list of the comparatives of this type appearing in the New Testament will be found in Moulton-Howard 165; the above list of superlatives of this type is complete for the New Testament.

243. Comparatives in -τερος and superlatives in -τατος are declined exactly like adjectives of group II.1 (§224: comparatives will have α after ρ in the fem. sing., superlatives η after τ in the fem. sing.).

244. A number of comparatives are derived from adverbs.

Positive	Comparative
ἄνω	ἀνώτερον (adv.)
ἔξω	ἐξώτερος
ἔσω	ἐσώτερος
κάτω	κατώτερος
	κατώτερω (adv.)
πέραν	περαιτέρω (adv.)
πόρρω	πορρώτερον (adv.)
πρό (prep.)	πρότερος (superlative: πρῶτος)
—	ὕστερος

The comparative adverbs are not, of course, declined. The adjectival forms are declined like adjectives in class II.1 (s. §243).

245. Comparative in -(ι)ων superlative in -ιστος. Since all adjectives involving irregular comparison (§240) belong to this group, a full catalogue is provided for the New Testament (including adverbs). Where the comparative or superlative is formed from the stem of the positive, the stem vowel is dropped and -ιων, -ιστος added.

Positive	Comparative	Superlative
ἀγαθός	βελτίον (adv. only) (2 Tim 1:18, Acts 10:28D)	
(κρατύς)	κρείσσων (κρείττων)	κράτιστος
(ἄγχι) (adv.)	ἆσσον (adv.) (Acts 27:13)	

ἐγγύς (adv.)	ἐγγύτερον	ἔγγιστα (Mk 6:36D, 1 Clem 5:1)
ἡδύς (ἡδέως adv.)	ἥδιον (adv.) (1 Clem 2:1, 62:3)	ἥδιστα (2 Cor 12:9, 15, Acts 13:8D)
—	ἥσσων	—
(μάλα) (adv.)	μᾶλλον	μάλιστα
μέγας	μείζων	μέγιστος (2 Pet 1:4)
μικρός	μικρότερος	
	ἐλάσσων	ἐλάχιστος
κακός	χείρων	
καλός (καλῶς adv.)	κάλλιον (adv.) (Acts 25:10)	
πολύς	πλείων (πλέον)	πλεῖστος
ταχύς (ταχέως adv.)	τάχιον (adv.) θᾶττον (adv.) (1 Clem 65:1, MPol 13:1)	τάχιστα (Acts 27:15)
(ὕψι) (adv.)		ὕψιστος

2450. Notes:

2450.1 The comparative and superlative forms, κρείσσων, κράτιστος, are from κράτυς, but κρείσσων functions as a comparative of ἀγαθός, *good*.

2450.2 The forms ἐγγύτερον, μικρότερος belong with the comparatives in §242.

2450.3 The weakening of the formal system of comparison led to double comparison upon occasion: μειζότερος, 3 Jn 4 (cf. μείζων); ἐλαχιστότερος, Eph 3:8 (cf. ἐλάχιστος).

2451. Comparatives in -(ι)ων belong to adjective group IV.2 (§235). Superlatives in -ιστος are inflected like adjectives of group II.1 (and superlatives in -τατος, §§224, 243).

Declension of Participles

246. The participle is a verbal adjective. It therefore manifests characteristics of both verb and noun. As a verb it has tense and voice; the formal signals of these aspects will be considered in conjunction with the verbal system (§§0467–469). References to tense and voice may be ignored provisionally; it is only necessary at this juncture to grasp the inflectional patterns of the participle. As an adjec-

tive the participle is subject to full inflection (three genders, two numbers, all cases). *The participle is declined in accordance with patterns already familiar.*

The inflectional patterns of the participle may be divided into three types: 1) those which follow πᾶς, πᾶσα, πᾶν; 2) those which follow πᾶς, πᾶσα, πᾶν but present a unique feminine stem; 3) those which are declined like adjectives of group II.1 (ἀγαθός, -ή, -όν).

247. *Type 1.* All participles in the active voice (except the perfect active) and the aorist passive participle have stems in -ντ- (-οντ-, -εντ-, -αντ-, -υντ-) and are declined like πᾶς, πᾶσα, πᾶν, except for stem vowel (adjective group III.1, §231: third-first declensions).

247.1 Present and second aorist participles with stems in -οντ- form the masc. nom. sing. in -ων (the stem vowel is lengthened; τ is dropped since it cannot stand at the end of a word, §923) without -ς (cf. nouns of class II.2.a, §§165f.).

247.2 Present participles with stems in -αντ-, -εντ-, -υντ- form the nom. masc. sing. with -ς (the -ντ- is lost before the σ and the stem vowel lengthened to compensate for the loss of the ν: α < ᾱ, ε < ει, ο < ου, υ < ῡ, §929.9), e.g. ἱστάς, τιθείς, δεικνύς (cf. nouns of class II.2.b, §167).

All first aorist active and all aorist passive participles follow this pattern, as do present and second aorist participles from μι-verbs with stems in -οντ- (exception to 1. above; e.g. διδούς [present], δούς [aorist]).

2470. Assorted paradigms may be given here for reference:

2470.1 Present and second aorist participles with stems in -οντ- are declined like:

λύων, λύουσα, λῦον — *loosing*

	Singular			Plural		
	M	F	N	M	F	N
N	λύων	λύουσα	λῦον	λύοντες	λύουσαι	λύοντα
G	λύοντος	λυούσης	λύοντος	λυόντων	λυουσῶν	λυόντων
D	λύοντι	λυούσῃ	λύοντι	λύουσι (ν)	λυούσαις	λύουσι (ν)
A	λύοντα	λύουσαν	λῦον	λύοντας	λυούσας	λύοντα

2470.2 The present participle of εἰμί *be* is declined exactly like λύων, λύουσα, λῦον. Indeed, its declension corresponds to the endings attached to all present and second aorist participles with stems in -οντ-.

ὤν, οὖσα, ὄν — *being*

	Singular			Plural		
	M	F	N	M	F	N
N	ὤν	οὖσα	ὄν	ὄντες	οὖσαι	ὄντα
G	ὄντος	οὔσης	ὄντος	ὄντων	οὐσῶν	ὄντων
D	ὄντι	οὔσῃ	ὄντι	οὖσι (ν)	οὔσαις	οὖσι (ν)
A	ὄντα	οὖσαν	ὄν	ὄντας	οὔσας	ὄντα

2470.3 Present participles with stems in -αντ-, -εντ-, -υντ-; first aorist active participles; all aorist passive participles; present and second aorist participles from μι-verbs with stems in -οντ- are declined like:

ἱστάς, ἱστᾶσα, ἱστάν — *putting, placing*, etc.

	Singular			Plural		
	M	F	N	M	F	N
N	ἱστάς	ἱστᾶσα	ἱστάν	ἱστάντες	ἱστᾶσαι	ἱστάντα
G	ἱστάντος	ἱστάσης	ἱστάντος	ἱστάντων	ἱστασῶν	ἱστάντων
D	ἱστάντι	ἱστάσῃ	ἱστάντι	ἱστᾶσι (ν)	ἱστάσαις	ἱστᾶσι (ν)
A	ἱστάντα	ἱστᾶσαν	ἱστάν	ἱστάντας	ἱστάσας	ἱστάντα

Stem in -εντ-: τιθείς, τιθεῖσα, τιθέν; gen. τιθέντος, τιθείσης, τιθέντος; dat. plur. τιθεῖσι (ν), τιθείσαις, τιθεῖσι (ν) (all aorist passive participles have stems in -εντ-).

Stem in -υντ-: δεικνύς, δεικνῦσα, δεικνύν; gen. δεικνύντος, δεικνύσης, δεικνύντος; dat. plur. δεικνῦσι (ν), δεικνύσαις, δεικνῦσι (ν).

First aorist active: λύσας, λύσασα, λῦσαν; gen. λύσαντος, λυσάσης, λύσαντος; dat. plur. λύσασι (ν), λυσάσαις, λύσασι (ν) (identical, except for accent, with πᾶς).

Present and second aorist stems from μι-verbs: διδούς, διδοῦσα, διδόν; gen. διδόντος, διδούσης, διδόντος; dat. plur. διδοῦσι (ν), διδούσαις, διδοῦσι (ν) (aorist: δούς, δοῦσα, δόν, etc.).

2471. Notes:

2471.1 The neut. nom. and acc. sing. show the bare stem (less τ which cannot stand at the end of a word, §293).

2471.2 The dative plur. (masc. and neut.) of all participles with stems in -ντ- lose the -ντ- and lengthen the preceding vowel in compensation, §929.9.

2471.3 The fem. stem (-ουσα, -εισα, -υσα, -ασα) is formed by adding -ια to the stem (s. §2300.1).

2471.4 The present participle of contract verbs (in -άω, -έω, -όω) and the future participle of liquid and nasal futures are contracted according to the regular rules (the thematic vowel is always -o-): -έω and -όω verbs yield -ῶν in the masc. nom. sing., -ου- elsewhere (in the active voice); the middle-passive participle from these verbs (s. §2500.1) has -ου- everywhere; -άω verbs contract to -ω- throughout.

2471.40 Contract participles in -έω: ποιῶν, ποιοῦσα, ποιοῦν; gen. ποιοῦντος, ποιούσης, ποιοῦντος; dat. plur. ποιοῦσι (ν), ποιούσαις, ποιοῦσι (ν).

Contract participles in -όω: πληρῶν, πληροῦσα, πληροῦν; gen. πληροῦντος, πληρούσης, πληροῦντος; dat. plur. πληροῦσι (ν), πληρούσαις, πληροῦσι (ν).

Contract participles in -άω: ἀγαπῶν, ἀγαπῶσα, ἀγαπῶν; gen. ἀγαπῶντος, ἀγαπώσης, ἀγαπῶντος; dat. plur. ἀγαπῶσι (ν), ἀγαπώσαις, ἀγαπῶσι (ν).

248. *Type 2.* The perfect active participle exhibits two stems: -(κ)οτ- (masc. and neut.), -(κ)υς, (fem.). The forms with κ are called first perfect, those without second perfect. The fem. stem is formed by adding -ια: the σ is lost between vowels (§929.8), which then contract into -(κ)υῖα (cf. §2300.1).

249. The perfect active participle is also declined like πᾶς, i.e. third-first declensions.

249.1 The nom. masc. sing. has -(κ)ως (as though the τ were lost and the stem vowel lengthened, as in λύων).

249.2 The neut. nom. and acc. sing., however, have -(κ)ός (indicating an alternate stem in -oσ-).

249.3 The masc. and neut. dat. plur. lost the τ of the stem before σ (§927.2).

2490. First perfect participle:

λελυκώς, λελυκυῖα, λελυκός — having loosed

Singular

	M	F	N
N	λελυκώς	λελυκυῖα	λελυκός
G	λελυκότος	λελυκυίας	λελυκότος
D	λελυκότι	λελυκυίᾳ	λελυκότι
A	λελυκότα	λελυκυῖαν	λελυκός

Plural

	M	F	N
N	λελυκότες	λελυκυῖαι	λελυκότα
G	λελυκότων	λελυκυιῶν	λελυκότων
D	λελυκόσι (ν)	λελυκυίαις	λελυκόσι (ν)
A	λελυκότας	λελυκυίας	λελυκότα

Second perfect participle: εἰδώς, εἰδυῖα, εἰδός; gen. εἰδότος, εἰδυίας, εἰδότος, dat. plur. εἰδόσι (ν), εἰδυίαις, εἰδόσι (ν).

250. *Type 3* . All middle-passive participles in -μεν- (i.e. excepting the aorist passive which has a stem in -εντ-, §247.2) are declined like second-first declension adjectives (group II.1, §224), e.g. λυόμενος, λυομένη, λυόμενον; gen. λυομένου, λυομένης, λυομένου; etc. The suffix -μεν-, moreover, is a handy signal for identifying middle-passive participles.

2500. Notes:

2500.1 Middle-passive participles in -μεν- from contract verbs in -έω and -όω contract to -ου- throughout (the thematic vowel is always o): ποιούμενος, ποιουμένη, ποιούμενον; πληρούμενος, πληρουμένη, πληρούμενον.

2500.2 Middle-passive participles in -μεν- from contract verbs in -άω contract to -ω- throughout (the thematic vowel is always o): ἀγαπώμενος, ἀγαπώμενη, ἀγαπώμενον.

Pronouns & Pronominal Adjectives

255.1 The words commonly called *pronouns* are here separated into two groups on a purely formal basis: I. Pronouns, which, because of the nature of the case, are inflected only in a restricted way (i.e. restricted in person, number or case); II. Pronominal adjectives, which are subject to full inflection. The two major groups are subdivided along conventional lines for the sake of convenience.

255.2 Apart from the personal pronouns (I.1), which must be learned as special cases, pronouns and pronominal adjectives follow models already familiar. Indeed, three of them—the article (ὁ ἡ τό), the interrogative τίς, τί, and the indefinite πᾶς, πᾶσα, πᾶν—have provided the basic models for the whole nominal system. A number of the pronominal adjectives are catalogued with the adjectives (e.g. πᾶς), but are included here to facilitate reference.

Pronouns

256. *Personal pronouns.* The pronouns are personal, reflexive, or reciprocal. There are four distinctive personal pronouns:

	Singular		Plural	
	First Person	Second Person	First Person	Second Person
N	ἐγώ [cf. *ego*]	σύ	ἡμεῖς	ὑμεῖς
G	ἐμοῦ, μου	σοῦ, σου	ἡμῶν	ὑμῶν
D	ἐμοί, μοι	σοί, σοι	ἡμῖν	ὑμῖν
A	ἐμέ, με	σέ, σε	ἡμᾶς	ὑμᾶς

These forms must be committed carefully to memory along with the article, τίς, τί and πᾶς, πᾶσα, πᾶν. These four items comprise all that must be memorized for the nominal system.

2560. Mnemonic hints:

2560.1 Notice that the endings of the oblique cases of the singular forms are identical (-ου, -οι, -ε).

2560.2 The accented forms of the oblique cases in the singular are used for contrast and emphasis and after prepositions (except πρός) ; the unaccented forms are unemphatic and hence enclitic (to be pronounced with the preceding word, §074). Bl-D §279.

2560.3 The plural forms appear to be third declension; the endings are identical for the two persons (-εῖς, -ῶν, -ῖν, -ᾱς).

2561. αὐτός, -ή, -ό is used as the third person pronoun, singular and plural. Since, however, it has other functions and is fully inflected, it is included below (II.1, §260) under pronominal adjectives.

257. *Reflexive and reciprocal pronouns.* The reflexive pronouns are formed from the personal pronouns (§256) and αὐτός (§260) . They appear, by virtue of their function, only in the oblique cases; they do *not* agree with the word they modify in gender, number and case (unlike adjectives, §220).

Singular

	First person	Second Person	Third Person
G	ἐμαυτοῦ, -ῆς	σεαυτοῦ, -ῆς	ἑαυτοῦ, -ῆς, -οῦ
D	ἐμαυτῷ, -ῇ	σεαυτῷ, -ῇ	ἑαυτῷ, -ῇ, -ῷ
A	ἐμαυτόν, -ήν	σεαυτόν, -ήν	ἑαυτόν, -ήν, -ό

Plural

All persons

G	ἑαυτῶν, -ῶν, -ῶν
D	ἑαυτοῖς, -αῖς, -οῖς
A	ἑαυτούς, -άς, -ά

2570. Mnemonic hints:

2570.1 The reflexive pronouns are declined exactly like the article (note the third person neut. acc. sing. in -o).

2570.2 ἐμ- is combined with the oblique cases of αὐτός to form the first person; σε- with αὐτός to form the second person; and ἑ- (the third person sing. personal pronoun in Homer was εἷο [ἕο] [gen.], ἑοῖ [οἷ] [dat.], ἑέ [ἕ] [acc.]) with αὐτός to form the third.

2570.3 ἑαυτῶν does duty for all persons in the plural. The classical forms ἡμῶν αὐτῶν and ὑμῶν αὐτῶν for the first and second persons plural (i.e. ἡμεῖς, ὑμεῖς plus αὐτός, written separately) are occasionally found in hellenistic Greek (Bl-D §288(1)).

258. The reciprocal pronoun, ἀλλήλων, is formed by doubling ἄλλος *other, another* (ἀλλ-αλλο-, with the second element simplified). It appears, like the reflexives, only in the oblique cases, and is restricted, by virtue of its function, to the plural.

ἀλλήλων — *one another, each other*

	M	F	N
G	ἀλλήλων	ἀλλήλων	ἀλλήλων
D	ἀλλήλοις	ἀλλήλαις	ἀλλήλοις
A	ἀλλήλους	ἀλλήλας	ἄλληλα

2580. Mnemonic hints:

2580.1 ἀλλήλων is inflected exactly like the article.

2580.2 ἑαυτῶν is sometimes used in a reciprocal sense (Bl-D §287).

Pronominal Adjectives

259.1 Pronominal adjectives are declined a) like the article, b) like τίς, τί, or c) as third-first declension adjectives of three endings (e.g. πᾶς).

259.2 Most pronominal adjectives come under a); b) is confined to forms of τίς, τί and the numeral adjectives τρεῖς, τέσσαρες; c) includes only πᾶς and the numeral adjective εἷς.

259.3 Pronominal adjectives declined like the article always have -ς, in the nom. masc. sing. (like the relative pronoun, ὅς ἥ ὅ, §123). At only one point is there ever any other variation: the neut. nom. and acc. sing. sometimes have -ν (like neut. nouns of class II.3, §1360.2; adjectives of groups I and II, §§221, 224, 225), sometimes not (like the article and the relative pronoun, §§121, 123).

In the following descriptions, therefore, 'like the relative pronoun' will mean -ς in nom. masc. sing., but without -ν in the neut. nom. and acc. sing.; 'like adjectives of group II.I' will mean -ς in the nom. masc. sing. and with -ν in the two neut. forms.

260. αὐτός, αὐτή, αὐτό. αὐτός is employed a) as a personal pronoun of the third person, both numbers, b) as an intensive pronoun (ὁ λόγος αὐτός *the word itself*), or c) as a pronominal adjective of identity (ὁ αὐτὸς λόγος *the same word*) Cf. §§719–722.

261. It is declined like the relative pronoun:

	Singular			Plural		
	M	F	N	M	F	N
N	αὐτός	αὐτή	αὐτό	αὐτοί	αὐταί	αὐτά
G	αὐτοῦ	αὐτῆς	αὐτοῦ	αὐτῶν	αὐτῶν	αὐτῶν
D	αὐτῷ	αὐτῇ	αὐτῷ	αὐτοῖς	αὐταῖς	αὐτοῖς
A	αὐτόν	αὐτήν	αὐτό	αὐτούς	αὐτάς	αὐτά

262. *Possessive adjectives.* The possessive adjectives are declined like adjectives of group II.1 (§224, e.g. ἀγαθός, ἀγαθή, ἀγαθόν), which in fact they are.

> ἐμός, ἐμή, ἐμόν — *my, mine* [cf. ἐγώ, ἐμοῦ]
>
> σός, σή, σόν — *your (thy, thine)* [cf. σύ]
>
> ἡμέτερος, ἡμετέρα, ἡμέτερον — *our* [cf. ἡμεῖς]
>
> ὑμέτερος, ὑμετέρα, ὑμέτερον — *your* [cf. ὑμεῖς]
>
> ἴδιος, ἰδία, ἴδιον — *one's own* [cf. idiom]
>
> ἀλλότριος, ἀλλοτρία, ἀλλότριον — *belonging to another* [cf. ἄλλος]

263. *Demonstrative pronouns.* The article, ὁ ἡ τό, is a weakened demonstrative pronoun (§§120, 710–7160; cf. Bl-D §§249ff.). The other chief demonstratives are οὗτος *this* and ἐκεῖνος *that*. They are both declined like the relative pronoun.

οὗτος, αὕτη, τοῦτο — *this*

	Singular			Plural		
	M	F	N	M	F	N
N	οὗτος	αὕτη	τοῦτο	οὗτοι	αὗται	ταῦτα
G	τούτου	ταύτης	τούτου	τούτων	τούτων	τούτων
D	τούτῳ	ταύτῃ	τούτῳ	τούτοις	ταύταις	τούτοις
A	τοῦτον	ταύτην	τοῦτο	τούτους	ταύτας	ταῦτα

2630. Mnemonic hints:

2630.1 Rough breathing occurs in place of τ in four forms—precisely where it does in the article.

2630.2 Wherever α/η appears in the ending, the stem vowel is changed to α (assimilation of vowel sounds).

264. ἐκεῖνος, ἐκείνη, ἐκεῖνο conforms to the declension of the relative pronoun.

2640. Some demonstratives are compounds with the article or οὗτος as the head term.

2640.1 ὅδε, ἥδε, τόδε, *this (here)*, is made up of the article (declined as usual) and the indeclinable suffix -δε (cf. the particle δέ).

2640.2 The following are compounds with οὗτος:

τοσοῦτος, τοσαύτη, τοσοῦτο (ν) — *so great, so much*
τοιοῦτος, τοιαύτη, τοιοῦτο (ν) — *such as this*
τηλικοῦτος, τηλικαύτη, τηλικοῦτο (ν) — *so great*

a) These demonstratives are derived from ὅσος *as great, as much*, οἷος *such as*, ἡλίκος *how great* (see below, §272) and οὗτος: the endings of the former are dropped, and the rough breathing replaced by τ (cf. the article and οὗτος).

b) The neut. nom. and acc. sing. vary between -o and -ov.

2640.3 τοιόσδε, τοιάδε, τοιόνδε (from τοῖος, cf. οἷος §272, and -δε), *such as this*, occurs once in the literature represented in Bauer (2 Pet 1:17).

265. *Interrogative pronouns.* The interrogative pronouns are:

265.1 τίς, τί, *who? which? what?*, the declension of which is given in §151 as the model for nouns of the third declension.

265.2 A group declined like adjectives of group II.1 (§224).

πόσος, -η, -ον — *how great? how much?*
ποῖος, -α, -ον — *of what kind? what?*
πηλίκος, -η, -ον — *how large?*
ποταπός, -ή, -όν — *of what sort, kind?*

Note: πηλίκος appears only in exclamations in the New Testament (Gal 6:11, Heb 7:4; Bl-D §304, Bauer s.v.). πότερος, -α, -ον, *which (of two)?* is found only in the fixed form πότερον, indicating a question (Bauer s.v.).

266. *Indefinite pronouns.* The chief indefinite pronoun is τις τι, *someone, something, any one, anything*. It is of course declined like τίς τί except for accent (§153).

267. A group of pronominal adjectives, which function also as indefinite pronouns, are declined for the most part like adjectives of group II.1 (§224):

ἄλλος, -η, -o — *other, another*
ἕτερος, -α, -ον — *other, another*
ἕκαστος, -η, -ον — *each, every*
ἑκάτερος, -α, -ον — *each (of two), both*
ἀμφότεροι, -αι, -α — *both, all*
πολύς, πολλή, πολύ — *much, many*

2670.   Notes:

2670.1   ἄλλος is declined like the relative pronoun, i.e. without ν in the neut. nom. and acc. sing. πολύς belongs to adjective group V (§236), which, except for four forms, is declined like adjectives of group II.1.

2670.2   Strictly speaking, ἄλλος means *other* (of several), ἕτερος *other* (of two), but they are not always correctly used (§§755–760).

2670.3   ἀμφότεροι, *both* (of two), has come to be used like οἱ πάντες, *all* (Bl-D §275(8)).

268.   Following the pattern of third-first and third declension adjectives are the following:

268.1   πᾶς, πᾶσα, πᾶν *every, each, all* (group III.1., §231)

268.2   εἷς, μία, ἕν, *one* (numeral adjective and indefinite pronoun), *someone, anyone*; the one (-the other) is declined:

	M	F	N
N	εἷς	μία	ἕν
G	ἑνός	μιᾶς	ἑνός
D	ἑνί	μιᾷ	ἑνί
A	ἕνα	μίαν	ἕν

2680.   Notes:

2680.1   εἷς is from ἑν-ς (ν is lost and the preceding vowel lengthened); the masc. and neut. forms are therefore regular third declension.

2680.2   μία is from the original stem σμ-, from which the σ was lost (indicated in the masc. and neut. by rough breathing; cf. Smyth §119); the feminine is regular first declension.

269.1   Declined like εἷς, μία, ἕν are: οὐδείς, οὐδεμία, οὐδέν and μηδείς, μηδεμία, μηδέν, *no one, nobody, nothing* (οὐδέ and μηδέ compounded with εἷς) .

269.2   The numeral adjective and pronoun δύο, *two* [cf. *dual*], is only partially inflected: δύο (nom. and gen.), δυσί (ν) (dat.), δύο (acc.).

269.3   The numeral adjectives and pronouns, τρεῖς, τρία, *three* [cf. *trio*] and τέσσαρες τέσσαρα, *four* [cf. *tessara*, a square piece of marble or glass used in mosaics] are declined:

	M/F	N	M/F	N
N	τρεῖς	τρία	τέσσαρες	τέσσαρα
G		τριῶν		τεσσάρων
D		τρισί (ν)		τέσσαρσι (ν)
A	τρεῖς	τρία	τέσσαρας	τέσσαρα

2690. Notes:

2690.1 τρεῖς and τέσσαρες do not have distinctive fem. forms (like adjectives of group IV).

2690.2 The masc.-fem. nom. and acc. forms of τρεῖς are identical (cf. πόλις, III.7.b, §200); τέσσαρας (masc.-fem. acc.) is occasionally found in the form τέσσαρες (like the nom.; Bl-D §46(2)).

2691. The classical indefinite pronoun, ὁ δεῖνα, *such a one*, is found only at Mt 26:18 (Bauer); it is declined δεῖνα, δεῖνος, δεῖνι, δεῖνα.

270. *Relative pronouns.* The definite relative pronoun is ὅς ἥ ὅ, *who, which, what.* For its inflectional relation to the article see §123; on its use as a paradigmatic reference for other pronouns §259.3. ὅσπερ is a combination of ὅς and περ, an intensive and extensive particle; ὅσπερ is inflected like ὅς.

271. The indefinite relative is ὅστις, ἥτις, ὅ τι, *whoever, whatever.* It is compounded from ὅς and τις, both of which are declined. It appears, however, only in the following forms:

	Singular			Plural		
	M	F	N	M	F	N
N	ὅστις	ἥτις	ὅ τι	οἵτινες	αἵτινες	ἅτινα
A			ὅ τι			

2710. Notes:

2710.1 ὅ τι is written as separate words by some modern authors to distinguish it from the conjunction ὅτι.

2710.2 ὅτου (genitive) is found rarely in fixed expressions: ἀφ᾽ ὅτου, ἕως ὅτου, μέχρι ὅτου.

2710.3 ὅς and ὅστις are no longer clearly distinguished (Bl-D §293).

272. Other relatives are declined like adjectives of group II.1 (§224):

ὅσος, -η, -ον — *as great as*
οἷος, -α, -ον — *of what sort, such as*
ὁποῖος, -α, -ον — *of what sort, as*
ἡλίκος, -η, -ον — *how great*

Note: ὁπόσος, -η, -ον, *how great, how much*, appears in the Gospel of Peter 8:28 (Bauer).

273. Certain pronouns appearing under the headings of demonstrative (§2640.2), interrogative (§265.2) and relative (§272) are strikingly similar in form. They may be arranged in a table as follows:

	Demonstrative	Interrogative	Relative
Quantity	τοσοῦτος	πόσος	ὅσος
	so great	*how great?*	*as great as*
	so much	*how much?*	*as much as*
Quality	τοιοῦτος	ποῖος	οἷος
	such as this	*of what kind?*	*of what sort,*
		what?	*such as*
			ὁποῖος
			of what sort,
			such as
Size	τηλικοῦτος	πηλίκος	ἡλικός
	so great	*how large?*	*how great*

It may be noted that the demonstratives begin in τ-, the interrogatives in π- (cf. the interrogative adverbs ποῦ *where?* πόθεν *whence?* πῶς *how?* πότε *when*), the relatives with rough breathing (cf. ὅς, the relative adverbs ὅπου *where*, ὅθεν *whence*, and the temporal conjunctions ὅτε *when*, ὅταν *whenever*).

274. The numeral adjectives from one to four were considered in §§268.2–2690. The numerals (cardinals) from five to one hundred are indeclinable; those from two hundred up are declined like adjectives of group II.1 (§224). The ordinals (πρῶτος *first*, δεύτερος *second*, τρίτος *third*, etc.) are also declined like adjectives of group II.1. The numeral adverbs (ἅπαξ, πρῶτως *once, first time*, δίς *twice*, τρίς *three times*, etc.) are, of course, not declined.

The Verbal System

Introduction

For Reading and Reference

300.1 The verbal system includes *finite verbs*, *infinitives*, and certain features of the *participle* (§§101, 246ff.).

300.2 The full inflectional paradigm (§102 for definition) for the *verb* will exhibit distinctive forms for each of three *persons* (first, second, third) in two *numbers* (singular, plural), a paradigm of six forms that is theoretically repeated with variations for each of three *voices* (active, middle, passive), in seven *tenses* (present, imperfect, future, aorist, perfect, pluperfect, future perfect) for the *indicative mood*, in five tenses for the *optative mood* (present, future, aorist, perfect, future perfect), in three tenses for the *subjunctive and imperative moods* (present, aorist, perfect), in addition to which there are active, middle and passive *infinitives* for each of five tenses (present, future, aorist, perfect, future perfect), and active, middle and passive *participles* for each of the same five tenses.

300.3 The verbal system is thus more complex than the nominal system (cf. §102). However, the morphemes which indicate person are used over and over again in consistent patterns; the middle and passive voices are often identical (in the present, imperfect, perfect, and pluperfect); the future perfect need not be considered for hellenistic Greek, the pluperfect is infrequent, and there is an increasing tendency to form tenses periphrastically, i.e. with a form of the verb *be* (εἶναι) and the participle; the optative is fast disappearing; and the tenses are arranged in systems built on a basic tense stem that is formed in a reasonably consistent manner from the verb stem or base. When all these reductions are taken into account, the verbal system remains more complex than the nominal system, but not nearly so formidable as might appear at first glance.

0301. It is more difficult to illustrate the verbal paradigm from English than it is for the noun (cf. §102). Yet the two verbal systems have much in common. English also exhibits three persons for each of two numbers: I, you, he/she/it; we, you, they. However, except for the verb *be*, only the present tense in English retains form distinctions for person and number, and even then only in the third person, whereas in Greek form distinctions for person and number run through the whole verbal system. English has no middle voice as such, but the active and passive voices do approximate Greek categories. Formally, i.e. traditionally, there are six tenses in English: past, present, future, past perfect, present perfect, future perfect. The Greek tenses correspond roughly to these, except that Greek has two past tenses, the imperfect to indicate continuous or linear action in past time, and the aorist to indicate punctiliar action in past time. The non-indicative moods have virtually vanished from English—so far as form is concerned—with the exception of remnants of the subjunctive, e.g. *If I were you* . . . ; *be he king or pauper*. . . . English, of course, also has participles and infinitives, the former having a present, past and perfect form, the latter only a present and present perfect. Only three tenses of the infinitive and participle are in common use in Greek (present, aorist, perfect).

301.1 The English verb (the verb *be* excepted) has six forms, three finite and three non-finite forms, although there is often overlapping among them. (1) The verb base or lexical form serves for the so-called present tense, the imperative mood, and the infinitive (*I go*; *Go!*; *He wants to go*); (2) the third person singular of the present indicative is differentiated from the base by the addition of *-s* (*-es*): *He goes*. (3) The third finite form is the past, which shows no variation for person or number (*I, you, he, we, you, they went*). The non-finite forms include (4) the infinitive (identical with the base), (5) the past, and (6) the present participles (*go, gone, going*). The infinitive may occur in simple form, i.e. without the function-word *to* (e.g. *I heard the car go down the drive*), or with *to* (e.g. *He hates to go*).

301.2 The paradigm of the English verb is said to derive from three forms: base, past, past participle (e.g. *go, went, gone*). These are consequently called *principal parts*. A principal part is a verb form from which a part of the paradigm or conjugational system (§100) of the verb is derived.

301.3 In English there are two types of conjugation: simple and complex (Strang: 127). In the simple type variation in form is confined to the verb itself; in complex it reaches beyond the limits of the word.

301.4 The present and past tenses are mostly simple conjugations (e.g. leaving aside progressive forms, which are complex); the future and perfective tenses are complex.

301.5 Reduced to schematic form and truncated, the English verb system can be represented thus:

	I. Base		II. Past		III. Past Participle
	go		*went*		*gone*
Present	*I go*	Past	*I went*	Present Perfect	*I have gone*
Future	*I will go*			Past Perfect	*I had gone*
				Future Perfect	*I will have gone*

The future tense is placed in column I because it utilizes the base form of the verb. The perfective tenses all employ the past participle and so are listed in column III.

301.6   The verb system in English is actually much more complicated than indicated in §301.5. In addition to the contrast between non-perfective and perfective aspects (*I go / I have gone*, both considered present in time but differing in the way the action is viewed), there is a contrast between non-durative and durative aspects (*I go / I am going*: the first is indefinite; the latter marks the action as continuous, as a rule [Roberts: 132]). If the contrasts between non-interrogative / interrogative (*I go / do I go*), non-negative / negative (*I go / I don't go*), and active / passive (*I hit / I am hit*) are added, the total number of differentiated forms comes to 32. The same set of contrasts transposed to the past tense brings the number to 64. Verb phrases constructed with the nine common modal auxiliaries (*will*, *shall*, *may*, *might*, *can*, *must*, *would*, *should*, *could*) extends the number to more than 350 possible verb phrases (e.g. *I can go, I can be hit, I will have been hit*). A further contrast between non-emphatic / emphatic forms (*I go / I do go*), and a difference in passive forms (*I was hit / I got hit*) enlarges the paradigm to more than 550 forms. In a full paradigm, moreover, it would be necessary to consider marginal phrases such as *I used to go, I am going to go, I ought to go, I have to go,* etc. (The preceding summary is indebted to Strang: 125ff.) In sum, it is difficult to specify a full paradigm for the English verb since so much variation is inherently possible in the system. By contrast, the full paradigm for the Greek verb exhibits 244 forms, aside from an occasional periphrastic formation (§300.3) and the declension of the participle (which belongs also to the nominal system, §§246ff.).

302.1   As indicated in §301.5, the English verb system is derived from three basic forms: base, past, past participle (e.g. *go, went, gone*). If we add the progressive verb phrases (e.g. *I am going*], it is necessary to expand the basic forms to include the present participle (e.g. *going*). There would then be four principal parts for the English verb system.

302.2   For the Greek verb there are six principal parts. This means that there are six *tense systems*: each system is based on a principal part (a tense stem or base) from which all the forms in that system are derived. *A tense system does not correspond to a tense of the Greek verb*: a system may include more or less than the forms belonging to one tense. The present system, for example, includes both the present and imperfect tenses, whereas the future system, so-called,

Principal Parts	I. Present	II. Future	III. Aorist
Active Voice			
Indicative	λύω	λύσω	ἔλυσα
Subjunctive	λύω	—	λύσω
Optative	λύοιμι	(λύσοιμι)	λύσαιμι
Imperative	λῦε	—	λῦσον
Infinitive	λύειν	λύσειν	λῦσαι
Participle	λύων, -ουσα, -ον	λύσων, -ουσα, -ον	λύσας, -ασα, -αν
Middle Voice			
Indicative	λύομαι	λύσομαι	ἐλυσάμην
Subjunctive	λύωμαι	—	λύσωμαι
Optative	λυοίμην	(λυσοίμην)	λυσαίμην
Imperative	λύου	—	λῦσαι
Infinitive	λύεσθαι	λύσεσθαι	λύσασθαι
Participle	λυόμενος, -η, -ον	λυσόμενος, -η, -ον	λυσάμενος, -η, -ον
Passive Voice			
Indicative	Same as Middle	See Sixth	See Sixth
Subjunctive		Principal Part	Principal Part
Optative			
Imperative			
Infinitive			
Participle			

includes only the future active and future middle (the future passive is built on another principal part).

302.3   A schematic representation of the Greek verb will thus have six columns, each headed by a principal part or tense stem (in full form the 1st person singular indicative). By reading down the columns one discovers all the tenses, moods and voices derived from that tense stem. Such a schematic summary is presented in §303.

303.   Structure of the Verb System

IV. Perfect Active	V. Perfect Middle and Passive	VI. Aorist Passive
λέλυκα		
λελυκὼς ὦ		
(λελυκὼς εἴην)		
(λέλυκε, λελυκὼς ἴσθι)		
λελυκέναι		
λελυκώς, -υῖα, -ός		
See Fifth Principal Part	λέλυμαι	
	λελυμένος ὦ	
	(λελυμένος εἴην)	
	λέλυσο	
	λελύσθαι	
	λελυμένος, -η, -ον	
See Fifth Principal Part	Same as Middle	ἐλύθην
		λυθῶ
		λυθείην
		λύθητι
		λυθῆναι
		λυθείς, -εῖσα, -έν

Tenses formed on the same stem

Principal Parts	I. Present	IV. Perfect Active	V. Perfect Middle and Passive	VI. Aorist Passive
Indicative	Imperfect Active ἔλυον	Pluperfect (ἐ)λελύκειν	Pluperfect (ἐ)λελύμην	Future Passive λυθήσομαι
	Middle and Passive ἐλυόμην			
Infinitive		——	——	(λυθήσεσθαι)
Participle		——	——	λυθησόμενος, -η, -ον

Future Perfect
λελυκὼς ἔσομαι (active)
λελύσομαι (passive)

3030. The tense systems as represented in §303 may be summarized as follows:

3030.1 On the present tense stem is built: the present and imperfect tenses.

3030.2 On the future tense stem: future, active and middle voices.

3030.3 On the aorist tense stem: aorist, active and middle voices.

3030.4 On the perfect active tense stem: perfect and pluperfect, active voice (and future perfect).

3030.5 On the perfect middle-passive tense stem: perfect and pluperfect, middle and passive voices.

3030.6 On the aorist passive tense stem: aorist and future, passive voice.

3031. Notes:

3031.1 The middle and passive voices are identical in form in the present and imperfect (I. Present system), and in the perfect and pluperfect (V. Perfect middle system).

3031.2 The middle and passive voices are distinct in form in the aorist and future (cf. VI. Aorist passive system, with II and III) ; as a consequence, the aorist and future tenses have distinctive forms for each of the three voices.

3031.3 The active voice is never identical in form with either the middle or the passive.

3031.4 All three voices are built on the same tense stem in the present and imperfect (I), whereas in the future and aorist, the active and middle voices are built on one tense stem (II, III), the passive on another (VI), and in the perfect and pluperfect, the active voice is built on one tense stem (IV), the middle and passive voices on another (V).

3031.5 Systems V and VI are thus added to accommodate the distinctive tense stems and forms of the perfect and pluperfect middle-passive (voices are hyphenated where they are identical in form), and the aorist and future passive. (Systems I-IV are commonly called present, future, aorist and perfect systems, although II-IV are not complete without V and VI.)

3031.6 The imperfect tense exhibits only an indicative mood, which is built on the present tense stem (I); the pluperfect exhibits only an indicative mood, which is built on the perfect tense stems (IV, V).

3031.7 The future tense exhibits a defective paradigm with respect to the moods, i.e. there is no future subjunctive or imperative, and the future optative, which is rare in hellenistic Greek, serves only one function (indirect discourse after secondary tenses). For all practical purposes there is only a future indicative, infinitive and participle.

3031.8 The perfect subjunctive, optative and imperative (often formed periphrastically, §300.3) are likewise rare.

3031.9 It may therefore be said, for reasons to be indicated subsequently (§§3100.2, 311) that only the present, aorist (and perfect) show the full range of moods.

Person, Number, Voice

0304. Conjugation (inflection) in the verbal system has reference to five factors: *person*, *number*, *voice*, *mood* and *tense*, as indicated (§305.2).

304. *Person.* Person in the Greek verb is the same as it is in English: *first* (I, we), *second* (you [thou], you [ye]), and *third* (he, she, it; they) persons.

305. *Number.* Number is also identical with the English system: *singular* and *plural*.

3050. Greek had a *dual* number which fell into disuse at an early date and does not appear in the Greek vernacular (Smyth §999; Bl-D §§2, 65).

306.1 *Voice.* Greek has an active voice (*I write, you read, he sends*) and a passive voice (*the book is written, read; the man has been sent*), as in English. But Greek, unlike English, also has a *middle* voice: in the middle voice the subject acts on, for, or with reference to itself (e.g. *they submitted to baptism* would be expressed by the middle voice in Greek). The middle voice is on the decline in hellenistic Greek, with the result that there is some confusion and much overlapping of the active-middle on the one hand, and the middle-passive on the other. The dissolution of the middle into active and passive is understandable for the reason that the middle stands somewhere between active and passive, and its nuances can be expressed for the most part by other linguistic devices.

306.2 The middle voice is formally identical with the passive in all tenses except the future and the aorist, and even here the distinctive middle forms are on the wane (Bl-D §§77–79).

Mood

0307. *Mood* refers to the form of the verb that signals mode or manner of affirmation, e.g. whether the sentence is an assertion, a doubtful statement, a wish, a command, or the like. While there are characteristic uses of the moods, particularly in main clauses, which are appropriate to the traditional definitions, it should be noted that the use of the moods often appears arbitrary, i.e. the connection with the mode of affirmation is not obvious. The syntactical distribution of the moods is therefore best learned in connection with the syntax of the sentence. Some generalizations can, however, be offered as starting points.

307. There are four moods in Greek: indicative, subjunctive, optative, imperative, not counting the infinitive and participle, which, strictly speaking, are not moods since they signal nothing about affirmation (a sentence without a finite verb in a mood is therefore said to be an incomplete sentence). Nevertheless, the infinitive and participle are customarily listed under moods in the paradigm of the Greek verb in order not to have to specify categories for them.

307.1 The *indicative* mood is the mood of assertion, e.g. *Jesus said to them: I am the light of the world.* The indicative is indeed customarily employed in definite statements, but it is also used in other ways.

307.2 The *subjunctive* mood is the mood of dubious assertion, expressing probability. It may also be described as the *shall* and *will* mood since its reference is usually to the future and often expresses aim, purpose, or resolution.

307.3 The *optative* mood is the mood of the wish (from Latin *opto, wish*). It is also used in a potential sense and may therefore be described as the *may* or *might* mood. It, too, is employed to express a dubious assertion but of a greater degree of doubtfulness than the subjunctive; it therefore indicates what is possible.

307.4 The *imperative* mood is the mood of the command and exhortation. Like the indicative, it corresponds to its English counterpart.

3070. Since the indicative and imperative correspond to their English counterparts and the optative is little used in hellenistic Greek, one has to reckon primarily with the subjunctive.

308.1   Verb forms representing any one of the four moods are called *finite* forms because they are limited by personal endings, i.e. each form is restricted to a particular person and number. The infinitive and participle are included in the verbal system although they are hybrids (verb and noun, verb and adjective, respectively) and do not take personal endings. They are thus *infinite* or *nonfinite* 'moods'.

308.2   The *infinitive* is a verbal noun; it has only one ending for each voice of each tense, but is not declined like a noun (though it may have case, which is signaled by some other device, e.g. article, preposition).

308.3   The *participle* is a verbal adjective (or noun); it thus has only one form for each voice of each tense, but these forms are declined like adjectives (§§246ff.).

Tense

0309.   *Tense* refers to the time an 'action' is viewed as occurring or existing; *aspect* refers to the kind of action (*Aktionsart*) or the manner in which an 'action' is conceived as transpiring. Both tense and aspect are customarily embraced under the rubric, tense. This produces a certain amount of confusion since time (tense) is integral only to the indicative mood; aspect (*Aktionsart*) applies to a greater or lesser degree to all the moods and is the sole consideration in the non-indicative moods.

309.   Three kinds of action or aspects are expressed by the Greek verb:

309.1   Punctiliar or point action (.);

309.2   Iterative or linear action (. . . . . . or _____);

309.3   Action conceived as completed or having a lasting effect (_____. or ._____).

310.   In the moods other than the indicative, the aspects as aspects are represented by:

310.1   The aorist: punctiliar action;

310.2   The present: durative or iterative action;

310.3   The perfect: completed action.

3100.   Remarks.

3100.1   Originally verb roots denoted a specific kind of action, but as the language developed other kinds of action were superimposed on the root in order to make the verb more flexible.

3100.2   The form of the verb to which the name 'tense' is given fundamentally denotes aspect or kind of action. The original function of the verb root (§3100.1) was thus taken over largely by 'tense'. This can best be observed in the non-indicative moods where time is not primarily related to tense. Since there are three kinds of action or aspects denoted by the Greek verb (§309), there is need for only three 'tenses' in the non-indicative moods, corresponding to these aspects (§310). Cf. §3031.7–9. (The future and future perfect optative were developed for special syntactical functions.)

311. Tense as *time* is superimposed upon tense as aspect *in the indicative mood*. This is achieved formally by the addition of formants not found in the non-indicative moods, and, in the absence of such formants, by contrast. E.g., if the present indicative tense denotes (among other things) durative or progressive action in present time, the imperfect (formed on the present stem) denotes durative action in past time: the tense stem remains constant (λυ-), but to the imperfect is added a prefix (augment) which denotes past time (ἐ-λυ-). Since tense as time affects only the indicative mood in principle, the imperfect, pluperfect and future (exception noted, §3031.7) tenses will exhibit only an indicative mood (a present and an imperfect subjunctive, for example, would both denote the same thing, durative action in the subjunctive mood, the temporal element being irrelevant).

312. Summary.

312.1 Summarized under the heading of aspect, the Greek verb exhibits three 'tenses': aorist (punctiliar action), present (durative action), and perfect (perfective action). These more or less apply to all the moods, including the indicative, but are alone relevant to the non-indicative moods.

312.2 When tense as time is added to 'tense' as aspect, the picture becomes more complicated; the complications will, of course, affect only the indicative mood.

a) The present stem, although durative as regards aspect, will have to do duty for punctiliar action in present time *in the indicative mood*, the punctiliar stem (aorist) having been relegated to past time *in the indicative mood*.

b) The future indicative functions to express both punctiliar and durative action (the punctiliar and durative stems having been assigned to past and present, respectively).

c) Perfective stems, however, have been developed for all times: past, present, future, just as a distinctive durative form has been developed for past time (imperfect).

312.3　Summarized graphically, the relation of tense as time and 'tense' as aspect *in the indicative mood* may be represented thus:

Aspect

		Punctiliar	Durative	Perfective
E	Present	Present	Present	Perfect
M	Past	Aorist	Imperfect	Pluperfect
T	Future	Future	Future	Future Perfect

3120.　Remarks. Tense as aspect and even as time in the indicative mood should be taken lightly, i.e. not forced. As in English (*He comes tomorrow*), so in Greek, the present tense can refer to future time. The present tense is also used historically (i.e. aoristically, to refer to past time), and there are examples of a perfective present (see Bl-D §§321–323). Similar remarks could be made regarding other tenses.

Verbs: Personal Endings

0315. It was stipulated in §§300.2, 0304 that the Greek verb is inflected (conjugated) with reference to five factors: *person, number, voice, mood,* and *tense* (time, aspect). It must now be indicated in a schematic way what inflectional variables are involved in the verb system, and what these variables signal with respect to the five factors indicated.

315.1 The finite verb in Greek, unlike the English verb, is regularly inflected to show *person* and *number.* This is achieved by suffixing personal endings directly to the verb (called bound morphemes). For the most part personal endings are unambiguous, i.e. the distinctive forms signal one person and number only. Thus, ἔρχομαι, *I come,* is first person singular since the personal ending -μαι is so restricted. Similarly, κρίνετε, *you judge,* can only be second person plural since the personal ending -τε never signals anything else.

If one meets the contrasting forms, κρίνω/κρίνετε, one knows that -ω signals first singular in contrast to -τε , which signals second person plural. The form, μαρτυρεῖς, *you bear witness,* is second singular (personal ending, -ς) in contrast, for example, to μαρτυρεῖτε, which is second plural. Where English does not contrast second singular and plural, Greek does.

The personal endings attached to the Greek verb thus regularly indicate the specific person and number.

315.2 This feature of the Greek verb (personal ending attached to the verb) makes it possible to construct a 'complete' one-word sentence in Greek (i.e. complete with subject and verb): λαλῶ, *I speak;* μένει, *he abides;* ἀκούετε, *you hear* are theoretically complete sentences. Of course, such simple sentences are rare, but they do occur.

316.1 Personal endings serve another signaling function: they regularly indicate *voice.* γράφω, *I write;* γράφομεν, *we write* are active (the subject of the verb does the acting); γέγραπται, *it is written,* on the other hand, is middle-passive (middle and passive are not here distinguished): -ω and -μεν are thus active endings, -ται is middle-passive. Similarly, δώσω, *I shall give* (-ω = active, first singular), but δοθήσεται, *it shall be given* (-ται = middle-passive, third singular), δέδοται, *it has been given* (again, passive). The tense may vary, as in the examples given, but the voice is still indicated by the ending.

316.2   True middles and passives are relatively rare in Greek (i.e. in relation to the preponderance of active forms), but one peculiarity of the Greek verb makes the middle and/or passive forms less rare than they might otherwise be. A number of so-called 'deponent' verbs have only middle and/or passive forms, at least in certain tense-systems, but are actually active in sense. The common verb ἔρχομαι, *I come*, for example, has no active *forms* in the present and future tenses though it is always active in *meaning*. The assertion that personal endings signal voice must therefore be qualified to the extent that 'deponent' verbs are excluded. In such cases, other signals in the sentence will indicate whether the verb is active, middle, or passive, if one's knowledge of the particular verb fails.

316.3   There is a second respect in which the general rule must be qualified: the aorist passive (but not the future passive) tense employs *active* endings even though it is passive in voice. There are historical reasons for the hybrid character of this tense. Nevertheless, voice is sufficiently often signaled by the personal ending to make it worthwhile to notice the contrasting forms.

317.   Personal endings are divided into two categories: *primary* and *secondary*. Primary endings are used in conjunction with primary indicative tenses (present and future in time) and the subjunctive mood; secondary endings are employed with secondary indicative tenses (past in time) and the optative mood. The primary indicative tenses are, of course, the present, future and perfect; the secondary indicative tenses include imperfect, aorist, pluperfect. It may therefore be stated as a general rule that primary endings signal a primary indicative tense (or the subjunctive), secondary endings signal a secondary indicative tense (or the optative). Naturally there are other signals which indicate tense and mood in addition to the personal endings, and it is necessary to take these into account in achieving precision. But it is helpful to know, for example, that -μαι (first singular) is the primary middle-passive ending, while -μην (also first singular) is the contrasting secondary middle-passive form. The contrast serves to narrow the choice even before other signals are considered.

3170.   *Summary.* Among the various inflectional variables, the personal endings signal *person* and *number* in the first instance, but they also provide contrasting forms which assist in the identification of *voice* (active / middle-passive), and they provide a broad distinction between primary and secondary *tenses* in the indicative, as well as that between subjunctive and optative *moods*. In descending order of discrimination, they touch all five factors of the Greek verb: person and number, voice, tense and mood.

Primary Personal Endings

318.   As indicated in §317, there are two sets of personal endings, primary and secondary. Each set is further divided into two voices, active and middle-passive. And, of course, there are endings for each of three persons in two numbers.

The *primary personal endings* are:

		Active Voice	Middle-Passive Voice
Singular	1.	-ω, -μι or #	1. -μαι
	2.	-ς	2. -η : σαι
	3.	-# (ν) or -σι (ν)	3. -ται
Plural	1.	-μεν	1. -μεθα
	2.	-τε	2. -σθε
	3.	-ουσι (ν) or -ασι (ν)	3. -νται

N.1. # indicates no ending, called a *zero* form

N.2. (ν) indicates ν-movable: §321

3180.   Notes:

3180.1   First singular active -ω is really the thematic vowel o (§322) lengthened. The ending -μι occurs with a very restricted class of verbs (§327).

3180.2   The second singular active has an old alternate ending -θα (-σθα), which is rare.

3180.3   The third singular active -σι (ν) occurs with μι-verbs. An alternate form is -τι (ν).

3180.4   The third plural active ending is theoretically *-νσι. The present and future ending -ουσι (ν) derives from -ο-νσι; ν disappears before σ (§929.7), and the preceding vowel lengthened in compensation (§914). The form -ασι (ν), which appears in the present indicative of μι-verbs and in the perfect, is the same ending, except that the long form -ᾱσι is apparently derived from -ανσι > -ᾱσι (compensatory lengthening).

3180.5   The second singular middle-passive -σαι appears in the perfect and present indicative of μι-verbs. Elsewhere it is contracted: e.g. λυ-ε-σαι > λυ-ε-αι (intervocalic σ is lost, §930.21) > λυ-η (contraction). Other contractions (-ᾳ, -οι, -ῳ) occur where thematic vowel is lacking and/or the stem vowel is α or o. Further exception to contraction: §3680.1.

Secondary Personal Endings

319. The secondary verb endings are:

	Active Voice	Middle-Passive Voice
Singular	1. -ν or #	1. -μην
	2. -ς	2. -ου : σο
	3. -# (ν)	3. -το
Plural	1. -μεν	1. -μεθα
	2. -τε	2. -σθε
	3. -ν or -σαν	3. -ντο

N.1. # indicates no ending, called a *zero* form

N.2. (ν) indicates ν-movable: §321

3190. Notes:

3190.1 The original first singular ending was μ which became ν when preceded by a vowel (Smyth §133.c).

3190.2 There is an alternate second singular active ending -σθα, which is rare (originally a perfect ending, it spread to the imperfect by analogy; cf. §§3180.2, 405f.).

3190.3 Like the third singular of the primary active set (§318), the third singular of the secondary active set shows no personal ending (*zero* form). However, where the stem formative vowel in ε, ν-movable may be added (§321).

3190.4 The third plural active ending -ν, when added to tense stems such as the first aorist ελυσα-ν, gave rise to an ending -σαν, which was then employed elsewhere.

3190.5 The second singular middle-passive ending -σο appears in the imperfect indicative of μι-verbs and in the pluperfect indicative (cf. §3180.5 on -σαι). Elsewhere it is contracted, e.g. ελυ-ε-σο > λυ-ε-ο (intervocalic σ is lost) > λυ-ου (contraction). Another contraction -ω occurs when the thematic vowel is lacking and/or the stem vowel is -α.

320. Mnemonic hints:

320.1 It will have been noticed that a certain amount of duplication occurs between the two sets, but which is restricted to the same voice (i.e. active overlaps only with active, middle-passive only with middle-passive). A summary of overlapping forms will facilitate learning:

Active second singular usually -ς

Active third singular always -# (ν)

Active first plural always –μεν

Active second plural always –τε
Middle-Passive first plural always –μεθα
Middle-Passive second plural always -σθε

320.2 In addition, it may be noted that primary middle-passive endings, except for first and second plural, end in -αι: -μαι, -σαι, -ται, -νται. Secondary middle-passive endings, except for the same two forms and the first singular, end in -ο: -σο, -το, -ντο.

320.3 Persistent trouble spots occur at the same points: Active, first singular and third plural; middle-passive, second singular.

3200. *The two sets (primary and secondary) of personal endings must be committed carefully to memory.* Nothing short of mastery will suffice. The sets should be learned in the forms in which they are given in §§318, 319.

321. ν-movable. A final ν may be added to words ending in -σι (§920), and to the third singular of verbs ending with the (thematic) vowel ε, i.e. where there is no personal ending. It may also be added to the verb ἐστί (ν) (the third singular of εἰμί, §371). ν-movable, as it is called, is always added when the next word begins with a vowel (to assist in pronunciation), but it may be added when the next word begins with a consonant (in the latter case, it is sometimes referred to as irrational ν).

In the verb system ν-movable appears only in conjunction with third singular and third plural forms. In the tables of endings in §§318, 319, ν-movable is indicated by parentheses.

On ν-movable in the nominal system, s. §1510.5.

322. *Thematic vowel.* The personal endings are often but not always joined to the verb stem by means of a vowel, called the theme, thematic or variable vowel: λυ-ο-μεν. In the indicative and optative moods, the vowel is -ο- before μ or ν, -ε- elsewhere. In the subjunctive mood, it varies between ω and η (the long forms of ο and ε). Since it varies between ο and ε (ω and η), it is often written ο/ε (ω/η) in grammars, e.g. λυ ο/ε +, i.e. λυ, plus appropriate thematic vowel, plus personal ending.

This vowel may also be regarded as a stem formative. In the perfect and aorist tenses (some forms), α is a stem formative. It appears consistently except in the third singular, where ε is substituted. In these cases, consequently, α/ε, though not properly a thematic vowel, serves the same function (cf. §3663).

Lesson 21

Identifying the Verb: Person & Number

325. The tables of personal endings introduced in §§318, 319 may occasion some bewilderment unless it is realized that the common forms appear repeatedly; that some forms occur rarely or are joined only to specific verbs; that the context often provides clues to person and number that reinforce the personal endings. Identifying the verb in context is easier than identifying it in isolation.

326.1 The second plural active ending -τε is identical for both primary and secondary sets of personal endings. In the context in Jn 8:31ff. it occurs frequently:

μείνητε	8:31
ἐστε	
ἐστε	8:37
ζητεῖτε	
ἠκούσατε	8:38
ποιεῖτε	
ἐστε	8:39
ἐποιεῖτε	
ζητεῖτε	8:40
ποιεῖτε	8:41
ἠγαπᾶτε	8:42
γινώσκετε	8:43
ἐστε	8:44
πιστεύετε	8:45
πιστεύετε	8:46
ἀκούετε	8:47
ἐστε	

326.2 The second plural middle-passive ending -σθε is also identical for both primary and secondary sets of personal endings. In the same context, Jn 8:31ff., it occurs less often:

γνώσεσθε	8:32	ἔσεσθε	8:36
γενήσεσθε	8:33	δύνασθε	8:43

326.3 The second plural endings -τε and -σθε are easily recognizable although attached to a variety of verb forms. They occur with sufficient frequency to be fixed in mind with minimum practice. The same can be said of most of the other personal endings.

327. The first personal singular ending -μι (active, primary) will be found attached only to μι-verbs (so called because the first singular is conjugated with -μι rather than -ω). There are very few μι-verbs compared with ω-verbs, but some μι-verbs are of high frequency. One such verb is εἰμί, *I am*. The only appearances of the ending -μι in the long passage Jn 8:12–59 occur in conjunction with εἰμί (8:12, 23, 24, 28, 58). In comparison with -ω, -μι will not appear often and it will always be joined to a very restricted group of verbs.

328. Person and/or number are sometimes signaled by other elements in the sentence than the personal ending. The sequence

(1) ἐγώ εἰμι   Jn 8:12

can scarcely be mistaken as first person singular: The personal pronoun (cf. §256) ἐγώ concurs in person and number with -μι. In Jn 8:12ff. the following sequences occur in which personal pronoun and personal ending reinforce each other:

(2) σὺ . . . μαρτυρεῖς   Jn 8:13
(3) ἐγώ μαρτυρῶ   Jn 8:14
(4) ὑμεῖς . . . οἴδατε   Jn 8:14
(5) οὐδεὶς ἐπίασεν
    For οὐδείς see §269.1   Jn 8:20
(6) πολλοὶ ἐπίστευσαν
    For πολλοί see §236   Jn 8:30

329. The person and number of the personal endings in §328 are confirmed by personal pronouns or pronominal adjectives. Number (and person) is also indicated in some cases by the noun subject. For example, in the sequence

(7) εἶπον . . . οἱ Φαρισαῖοι   Jn 8:13

εἶπον is clearly plural (third person) because οἱ φαρασαῖοι is plural, although in other contexts εἶπον may be singular. Compare the following sequences:

(8) ἡ μαρτυρία σου οὐκ ἔστιν   Jn 8:13
(9) ἔλεγον οὖν οἱ Ἰουδαῖοι   Jn 8:22

(10)	εἶπεν . . . ὁ Ἰησοῦς	Jn 8:25
(11)	ἐδίδαξέν . . . ὁ πατήρ	Jn 8:28
(12)	ὁ δὲ δοῦλος οὐ μένει	Jn 8:35
(13)	ὁ υἱὸς μένει	Jn 8:35

Whether the verb in each case is singular or plural is also indicated by the number of the noun subject.

330. Signals provided by personal endings are not always confirmed by other elements in the sentence, except perhaps negatively (leaving genuinely ambiguous constructions out of account). In the sentence,

(14) καὶ γνώσεσθε τὴν ἀλήθειαν,
καὶ ἡ ἀλήθεια ἐλευθερώσει ὑμᾶς
And you shall know the truth,
and the truth shall make you free   Jn 8:32

the personal ending (-σθε) of the first verb (γνώσεσθε) is not reinforced by the noun phrase: the verb ending is second plural, the noun singular. But the noun is also in the accusative case; it is therefore the object of the verb and not the subject. In the second line, the verb has no ending (i.e. it is third singular); this is confirmed by the noun phrase (ἡ ἀλήθεια) in the nominative singular, which stands in contrast to ὑμᾶς (accusative plural). The shape of the whole is also a clue, of course, to the structure of the sentence; it is marked by chiastic structure, i.e. *you—the truth / the truth—you* (the shape may be represented by an X).

The sequence in Jn 8:33

(15) ἐλεύθεροι γενήσεσθε   Jn 8:33

is initially misleading: the ending -οι is plural so that one expects a third plural ending on the verb. However, the personal ending is second plural (-σθε). The experienced reader would not have been misled because (a) ἐλεύθεροι would have been recognized as an adjective, and (b) γενήσεσθε is often used with predicate nominatives.

Like the noun, the verb is to be read in context. The first contextual clues for the verb are the personal endings—always to be taken in conjunction with other clues.

Verbs: Augment, Reduplication, Tense Suffixes

Augment

0335. In §317 the distinction between *primary* and *secondary tenses* was introduced: primary *indicative* tenses (the other moods are not involved) are present and future in time and employ primary personal endings; secondary *indicative* tenses refer to the past and employ secondary personal endings. A second inflectional variable marks secondary tenses in the indicative: *augment*.

335. Secondary tenses of the *indicative* receive an augment prefixed to the verb stem. Augment is of two types, *syllabic* and *temporal*.

336. *Syllabic* augment: Verbs beginning with a consonant prefix ε to the tense stem, e.g. ἐ-λάλησεν (Jn 8:12), ἔ-λεγον (Jn 8:19), ἐ-γένετο (Jn 1:3). The augment adds a syllable to the word, hence its name.

3360. Notes:

3360.1 Verbs beginning with ρ sometimes double the ρ when augmented, e.g. ῥίπτω (present), but ἔρριψα (aorist). For a full list of verbs with initial ρ, see §3430.1.

3360.2 Syllabic augment is occasionally made with η instead of ε, e.g. θέλω (present), ἤθελον (imperfect), ἠθέλησα (aorist).

3360.21 The original form of θέλω was ἐθέλω, hence its *temporal* (s. §337) augment ἠ-; ἠ- was retained after the spelling was simplified to θέλω. Δύναμαι and μέλλω also occasionally take augment with ἠ-. Bl-D §66(3).

337. *Temporal* augment: Verbs beginning with a short vowel lengthen the initial vowel to form the augment:

$$\alpha = \eta$$
$$\varepsilon = \eta$$
$$o = \omega$$

Examples: ἤκουσα (Jn 8:26) (for α-), ἠρνήσατο (Jn 1:20) (for ἐ-), ὡμολόγησεν (Jn 1:20) (for ὁ-). Temporal augment allegedly gets its name from the increase in duration of the lengthened vowel.

3370. Notes:

3370.1 Initial ῐ and ῠ are of course merely lengthened to ῑ and ῡ without visible alteration: ἰσχύω (present), but ἴσχυσα (aorist); ὑψόω (present), but ὕψωσα (aorist).

3370.2 The first vowel of an initial diphthong is lengthened in accordance with the rules indicated in §337: αἰσχύνω, ᾐσχυνόμην (imperfect); αὐξάνω, ηὔξησα (aorist); οἰκοδομέω, ᾠκοδόμουν (imperfect). An iota regularly becomes subscript.

3370.3 Initial diphthongs, however, frequently go unaugmented: εὑρίσκω, εὕρισκον (imperfect), εὗρον (aorist). As one might expect under the circumstances, there is also variation in practice: εὔχομαι, imperfect εὐχόμην or ηὐχόμην. ει- is rarely augmented: εἴκω, εἶξα (aorist); οὐ- never is: (ἐξ)-ουθενέω, -ουθένησα.

3370.4 Verbs beginning with a long vowel do not, of course, show augment: ἥκω, ἧκον (imperfect), ἧξα (aorist).

3371. A *few verbs* beginning with a vowel augment in such a way as to indicate the presence at one time of an initial consonant now lost: ει- appears where η- is expected (an unusual form of temporal augment), or ε- is prefixed to a vowel stem (syllabic augment where temporal is expected). The following is a complete catalogue of verbs exhibiting such 'irregular' augment, as represented in Bauer (the hypothetical stem(s) is (are) indicated in parentheses; forms marked with † are 'regular' and are included only for comparison).

Present	Aorist Act.	Aorist Pass.
ἕλκω (<*σέλκω, *σελκύω)	εἵλκυσα	
imperf. εἷλκον		
ἐάω (*σεϝάω)	εἴασα	
imperf. εἴων		
ὠθέω (*ϝωθέω)	-ῶσα† (-έωσα)	
imperf. ὤθουν†		
ἀν-οίγω (*ϝοίγνυμι)	ἀν-έῳξα	ἀνεῴχθην
imperf. ἤνοιγον		
συν-έπομαι (*σέπομαι)		
imperf. συν-ειπόμην		
ἔχω (*σέχω, σχ-)	ἔσχον†	
imperf. εἶχον		
ἐργάζομαι (*ϝεργάζομαι)	ἠργασάμην† (εἰργασάμην)	
imperf. ἠργαζόμην†		

(κατ-)ἄγνυμι (*ϝ άγνυμι)	-έαξα	-εάγην
αἱρέω (αἱρέω, ἑλ-)	-εῖλον	-ηρέθην†
λέγω (λεγ-, ἐρ-, ῥη-, *ϝεπ-)	εἶπον	ἐρρέθην
ὁράω (*ϝοράω, *ϝιδ-)	εἶδον	
imperf. ἑώρων		
ἵστημι, (στη-, στα-)		Pluperf. εἱστήκειν
		(for ἑ-σεστήκειν)
		(also ἱστήκειν†)

3372.   Notes:

3372.1   Intervocalic ϝ and σ regularly disappeared, permitting syllabic augment ἐ- to contract with a following ε, ι (= ει), or to remain uncontracted before a long vowel (ω).

3372.2   The imperfect ἑώρων (from ὁράω) and the aorist ἀν-έῳξα (from ἀν-οίγω) appear to have double augment: ἐ- plus temporal augment. It is assumed, however, that the augment of these verbs is ἠ- (cf. §3360.2), and that 'quantitative metathesis' (interchange of vowel quantity) has taken place:

ἑώρων   < *ἠόρων
ἀν-έῳξα   < *ἀν-ήοιξα

3372.3   For imperf. ἤνοιγον (from ἀν-οίγω), s. §339.3. For ἐρρέθην (from λέγω [ῥη-]), s. §3360.1. Ἀνοίγω sometimes has an aorist passive infinitive ἀνεῳχθῆναι, with misplaced (i.e. incorrect) augment. A future (κατ-)εάξω from (κατ-)άγνυμι is augmented (wrongly). Because misunderstood, the augment has intruded, in these instances, into a primary tense and the infinitive. Cf. Bl-D §66(2).

3373.   A few verbs appear to augment in a peculiar fashion:

3373.1   Αἴρω, aorist ἦρα, aorist passive ἤρθην. The verb stem is ἀρ-, supplemented in the present tense by ι̯ = ἀρι̯ > αἴρ (§484.4 and Appendix III, Class III.4). The augment is regular from the standpoint of the verb stem. Cf. §3430.5.

3373.2   (Ὑπ-)ισχνέομαι, aorist ὑπ-εσχόμην. The stems are ισχ- (supplemented in the present by νε = ίσχνε-; §485.3 and Appendix III, Class IV.3), and σχ- (aorist).

3373.3   Ἵστημι, aorist ἔστησα (or ἔστην), aorist passive ἐστάθην. The verb stems are στη- and στα-. The present stem is reduplicated: *σίστημι > ἵστημι (§345.2).

3373.4   -ἵημι, aorist -ἧκα, aorist passive -ἔθην. The verb stems are ἡ- and ἑ-. The present stem is reduplicated: *σίσημι > ἵημι (§345.2) . The aorist passive tense stem in -έθην lacks augment.

3374. Unusual augment often means unusual reduplication: see §3430.4.

338. Augment of verbs compounded with preposition or adverb.

338.1 Verbs compounded with a preposition or adverb (prefixed to the verb) take augment *between* preposition or adverb and verb: ἀπο-στέλλω, ἀπέστειλα (aorist); κατα-βαίνω, κατέβαινον (imperfect); ὑπο-στρέφω, ὑπέστρεφον (imperfect); ἀπ-αγγέλλω, ἀπήγγελλον (imperfect); εὐ-αγγελίζω, εὐηγγέλισα (aorist).

338.2 Prepositions (except περί and πρό) drop their final vowel when followed by augment (ἀπέστειλα), if they have not already lost it before an initial stem vowel (ἀπαγγέλλω, ἀπήγγελλον) The preposition ἐκ will of course be affected by a following vowel: ἐκβάλλω, but ἐξέβαλλον (§921).

339. Absence and doubling of augment.

339.1 In the New Testament the pluperfect lacks augment as a rule, especially in compounds (Bl-D §66(1)). This is also often the case in hellenistic Greek generally.

339.2 Other than diphthongs, which often go unaugmented (§3370.3), augment is omitted only occasionally in verbs compounded with a preposition. See Bl-D §67(2) for a list.

339.3 Augment is occasionally doubled. The most notorious example is ἀν-οίγω, where the peculiar nature of the stem (-ϝοιγνυμι), plus the fact that the verb never appears without prepositional prefix (ἀν-), led to general confusion: ἀνοίγω, imperfect ἤνοιγον (preposition augmented; cf. §338.1; classical ἀνέῳγον); aorist active ἀνέῳξα (§3372.2), but also ἤνοιξα (preposition augmented) and ἠνέῳξα (both augmented); aorist passive ἀνεῴχθην, but also ἠνοίχθην (ἠνοίγην) (preposition augmented) and ἠνεῴχθην (both augmented). For the few other examples, see Moulton-Howard II: 189.

340. *Summary.*

340.1 Augment indicates that the verb form in question refers to past time and it thus signals a basic contrast between secondary (except for the pluperfect, which often omits augment) and primary tenses in the indicative. An augmented verb will then be either imperfect or aorist indicative (or pluperfect on occasion).

340.2 Since augment is employed only with secondary tenses of the *indicative*, it will never appear with non-indicative moods (subjunctive, optative, infinitive, and participle), even of the secondary tenses. It thus also signals that the verb in question is indicative.

340.3 Given a common verb like γράφω, the secondary tense forms will be readily distinguishable from the primary tense forms by virtue of the augment: ἔγραφον (imperf.), ἐγράψατε (aorist act.), ἐγράφη (aorist pass.), but γράφω (present), γράψω (future). In verbs beginning with a vowel or diphthong, a preposition or an adverb, secondary tenses are less readily identified apart from attention to the personal endings. The imperfect ἦγον contrasts with the present ἄγω in two respects: augment (α > η) and personal endings, whereas the imperfect εὕρισκον contrasts with the present εὑρίσκω only with respect to endings, since εὑ- is left unaugmented. The beginner might fail to notice the augment sandwiched between preposition and verb in κατέλαβον, but the secondary ending will help call it to attention.

It will not be possible, however, to distinguish between present subjunctive γράφωμεν and aorist subjunctive γράψωμεν on the basis of augment (there being none in either case), or even to identify γράψωμεν as aorist. The same applies to the optative and imperative moods, the infinitive, and the participle, e.g. γράφειν (present inf.), γράψαι (aorist inf.), γράψον (aorist impera.).

3400. *Personal endings* and *augment* are inflectional variables that signal *person, number, voice* and the distinction between *primary* and *secondary tenses* (personal endings also obliquely touch the identification of the moods [§3170], the augment only negatively, i.e. an augmented form will be indicative). The ability to discriminate more finely depends upon knowledge of *tense formatives* (prefixes and suffixes), *tense base*, and *mood sign*. However, the next inflectional variable to be considered is the reduplicated prefix, which is commonly associated with the perfect system.

Reduplication

341. The perfect system (perfect, pluperfect, future perfect, i.e. everything appearing under principal parts four and five in the graph, §303) is marked by reduplication. Reduplication is the doubling of the initial consonant or syllable of the verb stem, e.g. πιστευ-/πεπιστευ-. Reduplicated stems appear in the present and aorist tenses also, but generally speaking reduplication signals a form in the perfect system.

3410. Reduplication was probably employed originally to express iterative or intensive action (cf. διδάσκω, *I teach*, where reduplication belongs to the verb stem as such). It later came to be associated with completed action and so is employed as a tense-aspect formant of the perfect system.

342. There are three types of reduplication and one substitute for reduplication: 1)

reduplication of an initial consonant with ε; 2) reduplication of an initial consonant with ι; 3) reduplication of an initial syllable; 4) reduplication that takes the same form as augment (§§0335–3400). Type 2) is confined to the present tense and appears in only a few verbs (to be noted subsequently). Type 3) is rare in any case, but appears in both the aorist and perfect. Types 1) and 4) are characteristic of the perfect.

343.   Reduplication by doubling an initial consonant with ε, and by augment.

343.1   A *single* initial consonant is doubled with ε to form a prefixed syllable:

πιστεύω — I believe	πεπίστευκα	πεπίστευμαι
ποιέω — I do, make	πεποίηκα	πεποίημαι
λαλέω — I say, speak	λελάληκα	λελάλημαι

343.2   An initial consonant (always a stop) followed by λ or ρ is also doubled with ε:

γράφω — I write	γέγραφα	γέγραμμαι
κρίνω — I judge	κέκρικα	κέκριμαι
πληρόω — I fill	πεπλήρωκα	πεπλήρωμαι

343.3   If the stop to be doubled is aspirated (pronounced with a strong emission of breath), the corresponding smooth stop (aspiration absent) is employed in forming the reduplicated syllable: τ for θ, π for φ, κ for χ (the reason being that one would begin to lisp if not to list had he to pronounce θεθ- or φεφ- very often):

φανερόω — I show	πεφανέρωκα	πεφανέρωμαι
θεάομαι — I see		τεθέαμαι
χράομαι — I make use of		κέχρημαι

343.4   If, however, the verb stem begins with a double consonant (ζ, ξ, ψ) , or with two (three) consonants other than a stop with λ or ρ, or with a vowel, the stem is augmented for reduplication, in accordance with the rules set out in §§336ff.

ἀγαπάω — I love	ἠγάπηκα	ἠγάπημαι
ἐλπίζω — I hope	ἤλπικα	
εὐλογέω — I praise	εὐλόγηκα	εὐλόγημαι
ξηραίνω — I dry up		ἐξήραμμαι
(ἀπο)-στέλλω — I send away	-έσταλκα	-έσταλμαι

3430.   Notes:

3430.1 Initial ρ is sometimes reduplicated in accordance with §343.1, i.e. ρερ-, some-
        times augmented (for reduplication) as indicated in §3360.1, i.e. ἐ(ρ)ρ-. A full
        list of verbs with initial ρ showing augment or reduplication is appended. Cf.
        Bl-D §11(1).

Present	Aorist Act. -Mid.	Perfect Act. / Mid.-Pass.	Aorist Pass.
ῥύομαι	ἐ(ρ)ρυσάμην		ἐ(ρ)ρύσθην
ῥᾳθυμέω	ἐρᾳσθύμησα		
ῥιζόω	-ερίζωσα	ἐρριζομένος	-εριζώθην
ῥίπτω	ἔ(ρ)ριψα	ἐ(ρ)ριμμένος	-ε(ρ)ρίθην
Imperf. ἐ(ρ)ρίπτουν			
ῥαβδίζω			ἐραβδίσθην
ῥαντίζω	ἐράντισα	ῥεραντισμένος	
ῥαπίζω	ἐράπισα		
ῥαίνω	ἔρρανα	--ρεραμμένος	
ῥυπαίνω			ἐ(ρ)ρυπάνθην
ῥήγνυμι	ἔ(ρ)ρηξα	-έρρηγα	-ε(ρ)ράγη
ῥωννυμι		ἔρρωμαι	
[εἴρω] (λέγω)	εἶπον	εἴρηκα, εἴρηται	ἐρρέθην

3430.2 There are some exceptions to the rules formulated in §§343.2, 343.4, i.e. stop +
        λ (ρ), double initial consonant with ε; otherwise augment:

μνηστεύω	ἐμνηστευμένην, but μεμνηστευμένη also appears
κτάομαι	κέκτημαι
πίπτω (stem: πτω-)	πέπτωκα
βδελύσσομαι	ἐβδελυγμένος
κάμνω (stem: κμη-)	κέκμηκα
τέμνω (stem: τμη-)	-τέτμηκα / -τετμημένος
θνήσκω	τέθνηκα
μιμνήσκω (stem: μνη-)	μέμνημαι

3430.3 A cluster of three consonants, even where the last two are stop plus λ or ρ, is
        augmented for reduplication:

σφραγίζω	ἐσφραγισμένος
στρωννύω	ἐστρωμένος

3430.4 A few verbs show an odd form of augment for reduplication:

Base	Perfect
ἐθίζω	εἰθισμένος
εἶπον (aorist)	εἴρηκα
ἑλκόω	εἱλκωμένος
ἐργάζομαι	εἰργασμένος
-ίημι	-έωνται
ἵστημι	ἕστηκα / -εσταμένος
λαμβάνω (stem: λαβ-, ληβ-)	εἴληφα
ὁράω	ἑόρακα ἑώρακα

Most of these forms are to be accounted for by the original presence of an initial consonant now lost, e.g. εἰργασμένος < ἐϝεργάζομαι: the ϝ was lost and ε-ε contracted to εἱ-. Ἕστηκα derives from *σέστηκα: initial sigma was lost and rough breathing introduced to mark the loss (Smyth §119; cf. ἵστημι [present base] for *σίστημι). Cf. §§3371f. for the augment of these and similar verbs.

3430.5 What appears to be an odd form of augment for reduplication in some verbs owes to the formation of the present tense stem, e.g. αἴρω, aorist ἦρα, perfect ἦρκα/ἦρμαι: stem ἀρ-, in present tense supplemented by ι̯ = ἀρι̯ < αἰρ- (§484.4 and Appendix III, Class III.4); the aorist and perfect forms are thus 'regular' when regarded from the standpoint of the verb base rather than the present base.

344. Reduplication by doubling an initial syllable. Some verbs reduplicate by doubling an initial syllable (α, ε, ο plus a single consonant) and lengthening the second vowel (α, ε < η, ο < ω):

ἀκούω	ἀκήκοα (> ακ-ακο-)
ἐγείρω (stem: ἐγερ-)	ἐγήγερμαι (> εγ-εγερ-)
ἐλαύνω (stem: ἐλα-)	ἐλήλακα (> ελ-ελα-)
ἔρχομαι (aorist: ἦλθον, stem: ἐλυθ-)	ἐλήλυθα (> ελ-ελυθ-)
ὄλλυμι (stem: ὀλε-)	-ολώλεκα (> ολ-ολε-)
φέρω (aorist, perfect stem: ενενεκ-)	ἐνήνοχα (> εν-ενοχ-)

This form is called 'Attic' reduplication.

3440.   Notes:

3440.1 Ἔρχομαι and φέρω are 'irregular' verbs, i.e. they employ more than one root in the constitution of a single set of principal parts (§487).

3440.2 φέρω has a reduplicated aorist (§§345.1, 487.10): ἤνεγκα (> εν-ενεκ > εν-ενκ [loss of vowel, called syncope, Smyth §44] > ενεγκ- [assimilation, §929.2J]). The aorist and perfect must therefore be distinguished on the basis of stem: ἐνεγκ-/ἐνηνοχ-.

345.   Reduplication in tense systems other than the perfect.

345.1   Aorist system. Two verbs show a reduplicated aorist (active) stem, in both cases by doubling the initial syllable:

ἄγω   ἤγαγον   (< αγ-αγ)
φέρω   ἤνεγκα   (s. §3440.2)

345.2   Present system. A larger number of verbs have reduplicated present bases. Reduplication in the present consists of doubling the initial consonant with ι. The aorist stem is given in the tables below so that the unreduplicated base may be observed.

a) Reduplicated -σκω verbs (Appendix III, Class V.3). The present base = the reduplicated verb base, supplemented by -σκω:

Present	Aorist
βιβρώσκω	ἐβρώθην (passive)
γινώσκω (for classical γιγνώσκω)	ἔγνων
-διδράσκω	-έδραν
μιμνήσκομαι	-έμνησα
πιπράσκω	ἐπράθην (passive)
τιτρώσκω	-έτρωσα

b) Reduplicated μι-verbs (Appendix III, Class I.7b).

Present	Aorist
δίδωμι (stems δω-, δο-)	ἔδωκα
-ἵημι (> *σι-σημι, stems ἡ-, ἑ-)	-ἧκα
ἵστημι (> *σι-στημι, stems στη-, στα-)	ἔστησα
κίχρημαι (stem χρη-)	ἔχρησα
ὀνίνημι (> *ὀν-ονημι, stems ὀνη-, ὀνα-)	ὀνάμην
πίμπλημι (> *πι-πλημι, stems πλη-, πλα-)	ἔπλησα

πίμπρημι (> *πι-πρημι, stems πρη-, πρα-)   ἔπρησα
τίθημι (> *θι-θημι, stems θη-, θε-)   ἔθηκα

c) Reduplicated regular ω-verbs (Appendix III, Class I.7a)

Present	Aorist
γίνομαι (for classical γίγομαι stems γν-, γεν-, γον-, γενε-)	ἐγενόμην
πίπτω (stems πτ-, πετ-, πτω-)	ἔπεσον
τίκτω (> *τι-τεκω, stem τεκ-)	ἔτεκον

3450.   Notes:

3450.1   τίκτω derives from *τιτκ- by metathesis (interchange of consonants).

3450.2   ὀνίνημι by rights is a doubling of the initial syllable (ον-ον-), but the second vowel is ι in conformity with reduplication in the present system; the initial ο appears therefore to have been ignored and the ν reduplicated with ι.

3450.3   πίμπλημι and πίμπρημι develop a nasal, μ, after the reduplicated syllable; this μ is sometimes omitted when the verbs are compounded with ἐν (ἐμ-πί(μ)πλημι, ἐμ-πί(μ)πρημι): dissimilation (Smyth §129).

Tense Suffixes

0346.1   Most native speakers of English manage a very complex verb system with only an occasional slip. The reason they are able to do so is that the English verb is inflected largely in accordance with regular patterns which can be generalized (consciously or unconsciously) and then applied by analogy to other verbs. The child learns early in the game for example, that the past tense of the English verb is often formed by adding -ed to the present tense: *I walk* / *I walked*. This pattern is applied, often with amusing results, to other verbs: *you hurt me* / *you hurted me*; *I eat this* / *I eated this*. What has not yet been mastered, of course, are the exceptions to the so-called 'weak' patterning of the verb.

0346.2   In gaining effective control over the verb system two things are thus necessary: 1) familiarity with the regular pattern; 2) explicit knowledge of the exceptions. The former constitutes an open class of verbs, i.e. it comprises the largest group of verbs and so cannot be learned as a list of individual items; the second constitutes a closed class and so must be learned as individual items, or groups of items. Non-regular (i.e. not conforming to the 'weak' pattern) verbs tend to fall into subgroups which follow identical or comparable patterns; they can therefore be divided into more or less distinct classes and learned as subgroups.

A few verbs are inflected so irregularly as to defy grouping; the term 'irregular' is reserved in this grammar for this very small class of verbs.

346.1 *The regular verb.* Just as the speaker of English learns that -*ed* forms the past tense of most English verbs, so the speaker or writer of Greek learned that -σα formed the past tense of a large class of verbs in Greek. Taking the 'regular' verb πιστεύω, *I believe*, as model, the past tense of the indicative (normally = aorist rather than imperfect) is formed by prefixing ἐ- (augment, added to all secondary tenses in the indicative) to the present base, and suffixing -σα: πιστεύω/ἐπίστευσα, *I believed*. This pattern may be applied to many other verbs whose stems end in a vowel:

> ἀκούω — *I hear* / ἤκουσα — *I heard*
> κωλύω — *I hinder* / ἐκώλυσα — *I hindered*
> παύω — *I stop* / ἔπαυσα — *I stopped*

The first person singular aorist active indicative serves as the *third* principal part of the Greek verb (§§302.2, 303).

346.2 The *second* principal part is the first person singular *future* active indicative. It is formed regularly by inserting σ between the verb stem and personal ending as they are found in the present tense: πιστεύω, I believe / πιστεύσω, I will believe.

> ἀκούω / ἀκούσω — *I will hear*
> παύω / παύσω — *I will stop*

From these few examples it can be learned that -σ- is regularly the tense sign (tense suffix) of the future, and -σα the tense sign (suffix) of the regular or 'weak' aorist (first aorist, as it is called).

346.3 The *fourth* principal part is the first person singular perfect active indicative, the *fifth* the first person singular perfect *middle-passive* indicative. These principal parts are formed by reduplicating the present base (§§341–3450) and adding the tense suffix -κα to form the regular or 'weak' perfect active (first perfect; cf. first aorist): πιστεύω / πεπίστευκα, *I have believed*. The perfect middle-passive is formed by adding primary middle-passive endings directly to the *perfect* base: πεπίστευμαι, *I have been believed*.

The tense sign or suffix of the first perfect active is thus -κα, while the perfect middle-passive has none (the reduplicated stem indicates, of course, that the form is perfect, the endings that the voice is middle-passive).

346.4   The tense sign of the regular or 'weak' aorist *passive* (the sixth principal part) is
         -θη-. Starting out again from πιστεύω, the stem is first augmented (ἐ-πιστευ-),
         and the tense sign then suffixed: ἐπιστευθη-. The secondary ending is -ν (§319):
         ἐπιστεύθην, *I was believed.*

347.   Tense suffixes of the regular verb.

347.1   The tense suffixes together with the first person singular endings may be rep-
         resented schematically (as the six principal parts).

Present	Future	Aorist Active/Middle	Perfect Active	Perfect Middle-Passive	Aorist Passive
πιστεύω	-σω	-σα	-κα	-μαι	-θην

347.2   It should be kept in mind that the aorist forms will be augmented, the perfect
         bases reduplicated. These may be added to the schematic representation:

Present	Future	Aorist Active/Middle	Perfect Active	Perfect Middle-Passive	Aorist Passive
πιστεύω	-σω	ἐ- - - -σα	πε- - - -κα	πε- - -μαι	ἐ- - - -θην

347.3   Since few verbs exhibit a full complement of tenses, further illustrations may
         be drawn from the principal parts of regular verbs in actual use, as represented
         in Bauer:

Present	Future	Aorist Active/Middle	Perfect Active	Perfect Middle-Passive	Aorist Passive
δουλεύω *I serve*	δουλεύσω	ἐδούλευσα	δεδούλευκα		
ἰσχύω *I am strong*	ἰσχύσω	ἴσχυσα			ἰσχύθην
λύω *I loose*	λύσω	ἔλυσα		λέλυμαι	ἐλύθην
παίω *I strike*		ἔπαισα			

For a complete list see Appendix III, Class I.1a.

348.   *The 'strong' verb.* Some English verbs form their past tense by a change in the
         stem vowel (called *ablaut*): *sing / sang; drive / drove; know / knew.* These verbs are

traditionally called 'strong' verbs. Greek also has 'strong' verbs in this sense: λείπω, *I leave*, forms an aorist ἔλιπον, *I left*, and a perfect active, λέλοιπα; the perfect middle reverts to the stem vowel of the present tense: λέλειμμαι (the final π of the stem is assimilated to the μ of the ending -μαι). φεύγω, *I flee*, similarly, has an aorist, ἔφυγον (stem vowel is shortened); the perfect active, however, reverts to the stem vowel of the present: πέφυγα. Πείθω, *I persuade*, retains the present stem vowel in the aorist, ἔπεισα, but modifies it in the perfect active: πέποιθα. There are relatively few verbs showing vowel graduation in Greek, but, unfortunately, some of those that do are of relatively high frequency.

349. There is a second sense in which Greek has a 'strong' verb: three principal parts exhibit alternative modes of formation, and these modes are known as 'strong' formations, by comparison with the 'regular' or 'weak' formations. The 'regular' tense suffixes -σα, -κα, and -θην (aorist active/middle, perfect active, and aorist passive, respectively) may be replaced by 'strong' forms.

349.1 Some verbs exhibit no tense suffix for the aorist active/middle (third principal part): ἔλιπον, ἔφυγον. These are called 'second' or 'strong' aorists. They are indistinguishable from the imperfect except for stem: ἔλειπον / ἔλιπον; ἔφευγον / ἔφυγον. The second or strong aorist (active/middle) will therefore always show a verb base modified in some respect by comparison with the present base (on which the imperfect is formed). Just as one must learn that *sang* is the past of *sing*, so one must become acquainted with the tense stems of verbs showing a second or strong aorist.

349.2 The regular suffix -κα of the perfect active is sometimes simplified to -α: λείπω / λέλοιπα; γράφω / γέγραφα. The forms without -κ- are again known as 'second' or 'strong' perfects. As γράφω / γέγραφα indicates, however, the 'strong' perfect does not necessarily involve a modification of the present base (contrast λείπω / λέλοιπα).

349.3 The regular suffix -θην of the aorist passive is sometimes simplified to -ην: τρέπω / ἐτράπην; γράφω / ἐγράφην. The forms without -θ- are once again called 'second' or 'strong' aorists passive. As in the case with the perfect active, the 'strong' aorist passive does not necessarily involve a modification of the present base (γράφω / ἐγράφην; but contrast τρέπω / ἐτράπην).

350. The alternative ways of forming the third (aorist active/middle), fourth (perfect active), and sixth (aorist passive) principal parts, as indicated in §349, *never*, in the verbs represented in Bauer, converge in one verb, i.e. there is no example of

a consistently 'strong' verb in Greek (in this second sense). And only nine verbs in Bauer exhibit *two* 'strong' principal parts. A much larger number show *one* 'strong' principal part. The 'strong' formations should therefore be regarded as alternative ways of forming particular tense stems, and not as characteristic of the full paradigm of any one verb. With this qualification in mind, the alternative formations may be joined to the schematic representation of the 'regular' verb (πε- represents any reduplicated syllable):

Present	Future	Aorist Active/Middle	Perfect Active	Perfect Middle-Passive	Aorist Passive
-ω	-σω	ἐ- - - -σα	πε- - - -κα	πε- - - -μαι	ἐ- - - -θην
		ἐ- - - -ον	πε- - - -α		ἐ- - - -ην

3500. Remarks.

3500.1 The 'strong' verb in the sense of a modification of the stem vowel in the formation of principal parts (§348) will be taken up in connection with the patterns of forming the tense bases from the verb base (§§489, 907–911).

3500.2 The composite schema given in §350 covers the vast majority of Greek verbs. The rare aberrations of these patterns will be noted in conjunction with the inflection of the various tenses.

3500.3 The table in §350 does not cover the imperfect (built on the first principal part), the pluperfect (built on the fourth and fifth principal parts), the future passive (built on the sixth principal part), or the rare future perfect (built on the fifth principal part). These forms are best considered in conjunction with the inflection of the tenses also.

Verbs: Introduction to Tense Stems

355. *The tense stem.* The tense stem is that form of the verb from which all the forms of a tense-system are presumably derived (there are some incongruities in the traditional system). The tense stem corresponds to the principal part less the first person singular active ending, e.g. present active indicative, first singular πιστεύω, tense stem πιστευ- (present system). A verb with a full paradigm will have six principal parts or tense stems (§§302f.).

3550. Tense stems are formed from the verb base (the actual or hypothetical base form) by one or more of the following modifications:

3550.1 Prefixes: augment (§§335ff.), reduplication (§§341ff.)

3550.2 Suffixes: tense suffixes (§§346ff.), thematic vowel (§322)

3550.3 Internal changes: vowel gradation (*ablaut*) (cf. §§348, 910f.), other stem vowel changes (§§914ff.).

3551. The verb base may be identical with one of the tense stems (less tense formants) or it may be a hypothetical base (conceived as the base form from which all actual forms are derived in accordance with the laws of phonetic change). There is a large class of verbs, for example, in which the verb base and the present tense stem (less any tense formants) are identical, e.g. πιστεύω (verb base and present tense stem, πιστευ-). The verb base may appear in one of the other tense stems (usually aorist), e.g. δίδωμι (present), ἔδωκα (aorist), verb base δω-. However, the hypothetical verb base may not appear at all, e.g. βαπτίζω, βαπτίσω, ἐβάπτισα, βεβαπτισμένος, ἐβαπτίσθην, verb base βαπτιδ-.

3552. Mastery of the Greek verb depends upon automatic recognition of the tense stem and instant identification of the personal endings. The latter must be carefully committed to memory (§§318, 319). With regard to the former, the inflectional variables, i.e. personal endings, augment, reduplication, tense suffixes, provide valuable clues to recognition. However, there is considerable variety in the development of tense stems that includes but goes beyond the variables already considered. The problem is to discover the patterns that underlie this variety and thus to form a well defined range of expectation.

356. The patterning of the formation of tense stems may most conveniently be considered from the standpoint of the formation of the present tense stem. There are two compelling reasons for this procedure:

356.1 The largest single group of Greek verbs is comprised of those verbs whose present tense stem (less thematic vowel) is identical with the verb base.

356.2 The lexical form of the verb is the present tense stem (customarily first person singular active indicative). It is therefore necessary, in looking up a verb, to be able to predict the form of the present tense.

The full range of possibilities in forming the present tense stem will be considered subsequently (§§479ff.; cf. Appendix III). Here may be considered a few of the larger and more important classes.

Class I: The Present Stem = The Verb Stem

357. Class I.1a. Vowel stems (uncontracted). Vowel stems in ι, υ, αυ, ευ, (ει, ου) do not contract and thus form a 'regular' pattern: -ω, -σω, -σα, -κα, -μαι, -θην (§347). It should be recalled that the aorist stems (third and sixth principal parts) are augmented, the perfect stems (fourth and fifth principal parts) reduplicated. The model for this class is πιστεύω: πιστεύω, πιστεύσω, ἐπίστευσα, πεπίστευκα, πεπίστευμαι, ἐπιστεύθην.

There are 86 verbs (not counting compound verbs) in this subclass (Appendix III, I.1a).

The count in all cases to follow is exclusive of compound verbs, i.e. stems compounded with preposition, adverb or the like. Compound verbs follow the pattern of the simple verb. Compounds would, of course, significantly increase the number.

358. Classes I.1b, I.2. Vowel stems (contracted). Vowel stems in α, ε, ο normally contract in the present tense system (§§368–369). They are consequently called contract verbs. In developing the other tense stems, however, these verbs follow regular patterns.

358.1 Contract verbs in -α which retain -α in the formation of the remaining tense stems: -άω, -άσω, -ασα, -ακα, -αμαι, -άθην.

θεάομαι, _____, ἐθεασάμην, _____, τεθέαμαι, ἐθεάθην

There are 23 verbs in this subclass (Appendix III, I.1b).

358.2 Some contract verbs in -α and -ε lengthen the stem vowel to -η in forming the remaining tense stems: -άω / -έω, -ήσω, -ησα, -ηκα, -ημαι, -ήθην

ἀγαπάω, ἀγαπήσω, ἠγάπησα, ἠγάπηκα, ἠγαπημένος, ἀγαπηθήσομαι
λαλέω, λαλήσω, ἐλάλησα, λελάληκα, λελάλημαι, ἐλαλήθην

There are 52 and 164 verbs, respectively, in these groups (Appendix III, 1.2a and 2b).

358.3 Contract verbs in -o lengthen the stem vowel to -ω in forming the remaining tense stems: -όω, ώσω, -ωσα, -ωκα, -ωμαι, -ώθην.

πληρόω, πληρώσω, ἐπλήρωσα, πεπλήρωκα, πεπλήρωμαι, ἐπληρώθην.

There are 93 verbs in this category (Appendix III, I.2c).

Class III: Iota Class

359. Class III constitutes a large group of verbs which add ι to the verb stem to form the present tense stem. ι here is a semi-vowel and occasions certain phonetic changes. A rather large subclass consists of verbs with stems ending in δ: -δι between vowels becomes ζ: the present stem will therefore end in a vowel followed by ζ, the variable vowel and personal ending joined to that, e.g. ἑτοιμάζω; verb stem ἑτοιμαδ-. In the other tense stems, δ before σ (future, aorist) and κ (perfect) disappears, δ before μ (perfect middle) and θ (aorist passive) becomes σ. The pattern of these verbs is therefore

ἑτοιμάζω, ἑτοιμάσω, ἡτοίμασα, ἡτοίμακα, ἡτοίμασμαι, ἡτοιμάσθην.

There are 168 verbs in this group (Appendix III, Class III.1a).

360. The five patterns representing six subclasses of verbs (I.2a and 2b, §358.2 have identical patterns) just presented account for approximately 587 of the 841 verbs listed in Bauer (excluding compounds) or nearly 70%. Familiarity with these patterns will go a long way toward tense identification.

361. It has been assumed that all the verbs in these subclasses are 'weak', i.e. form the tense stems by adding -σω, -σα, -κα, -μαι, -θην (§347) to the verb stem and do not otherwise vary from the 'regular' pattern in each case, e.g. by showing a 'strong' aorist or perfect. This assumption is of course in error, but it is not much in error. Surprisingly few of the 587 verbs exhibit any irregularities at all and these are mostly minor. Such irregularities as do appear will be taken up subsequently, in connection with the inflection of the verb in various moods.

Lesson 24

Indicative Mood: Primary Tenses
Present/Future Active & Middle

Form-sets and Sub-sets

365. The verbal system is comprised of contrasting form-sets with respect to tense-aspect and mood, of contrasting subsets with respect to voice, and of contrasting forms with regard to person and number. That is to say, the system represents contrasting features at three different levels, though these levels are not entirely discrete.

365.1 At the broadest level, the present active indicative and present middle-passive indicative represent a form-set that contrasts, for example, with the future active, middle, and passive indicative. The same set contrasts, of course, with other form-sets representing different tense-aspects and moods.

    In sum, form-sets reflect the contrastive features of the tense systems and the contrastive features of the moods within those systems.

365.2 A number of the form-sets have contrasting sub-sets to reflect a difference in voice. The present indicative, for example, has two sub-sets, one an active, the other a middle-passive sub-set.

365.3 Each form-set and sub-set, in turn, exhibits contrasting features that distinguish each individual form from all other forms in that set. Such contrastive features within a set and sub-set enable one to distinguish person and number.

3650. The verbal system consists not of one but of a number of interlocking systems. Thus far we have attempted to generalize the contrastive features of the verbal system as a whole. These generalizations do, in fact, cover the majority of verb forms appearing in a given text, but it is necessary to take account of a number of sub-systems in order to be able to identify *all* the verb forms in common use. It will be our aim next to lay out the verb system in sufficient detail to gain some experience not only of how the 'regular' system works, but also of how various sub-systems feed into the more 'regular' patterns.

3651. It should be observed that form-sets, sub-sets and individual forms do not always fully contrast with every other possible form or set at the same level. For example, ἐπίστευον can be either first singular or third plural, imperfect active indicative. There is thus 'ambiguity' in the system (in this instance, as regards person and number). πιστεύω can be either indicative or subjunctive (ambiguity in mood). Again, ἐπίστευον is imperfect, but ἔλιπον is aorist: ambiguity arises here only because of false generalization, since ἔλιπον contrasts with its imperfect, ἔλειπον, and ἐπίστευον contrasts with its aorist, ἐπίστευσα. In this case one must know the contours of the system to which the verb in question belongs.

Verb forms are not considered in isolation, of course, except in grammars. The kinds of 'ambiguities' indicated may be resolved by other signals in the context in which they occur. Yet a residue of irresoluble ambiguities will always remain since no language is perfect as it is spoken and written.

The Present Indicative

366. Verbs are conjugated in three ways in the present indicative. The names given to the three conjugations are (1) ω-verbs uncontracted, (2) ω-verbs contracted, (3) μι-verbs. The names are derived from the ending attached to the first person singular active (-ω or -μι), and from whether or not contraction takes place. *Difference in inflectional pattern carries no grammatical significance.*

3660. The two sub-classes of ω-verbs are conjugated alike, except for contraction. The conjugation of the two groups of ω-verbs differs in two particulars from the conjugation of μι-verbs: (1) μι-verbs employ the second alternatives in the table of primary personal endings given in §318 (i.e. -μι, -σι, -ασι in the active, but -σαι [uncontracted] in the middle-passive); (2) ω-verbs are conjugated with a theme or thematic vowel, μι-verbs are not.

3661. A theme (also called thematic or variable) vowel is employed in some inflection patterns to join the personal endings to the stem (§322), e.g. πιστεύ-ο-μεν, πιστεύ-ε-τε. It varies between ο and ε in the indicative mood; ο appears before μ or ν, ε elsewhere. It is not, however, always apparent in forms belonging to the thematic pattern, e.g. πιστεύω, πιστεύουσι (but see §3180.1, 4). Other inflectional patterns do not employ this vowel, e.g. τίθη-μι, ἔγνω-ν. Inflection with such a vowel is called *thematic*, without such a vowel, *athematic*.

3662. Thematic inflections in the indicative, with variable vowel (o/ε) include: some present and imperfect patterns, all futures, some second (strong) aorists (active/middle). Athematic inflections include: some present and imperfect patterns, some second (strong) aorists (active/middle), all perfect and pluperfect middles, all aorists passive, and a very few second (strong) perfects (pluperfects) active.

3663. The first (weak) aorist in -σα, the first (weak) perfect in -κα, and the second (strong) perfect in -α show α before the personal endings in every instance, except third singulars, where ε is used. These stem formatives correspond to the thematic vowel in other patterns. The pluperfect active, which is built on the perfect active base, shows the vowel ει (-κει-, -ει-, i.e. with and without κ).

3664. The thematic conjugation is the more common, athematic the older. There is a number of very common verbs with athematic form-sets, e.g. in the present tense, εἰμί *I am*, ἵστημι *I stand*, τίθημι *I take*; in the aorist, ἔγνων *I knew*.

3665. Verbs will be consistently thematic or athematic within tense systems, but not necessarily across tense systems where options are available, e.g. a verb may have a thematic present conjugation but an athematic aorist conjugation, and conversely.

367. *ω-verbs uncontracted.* To the present base is added theme vowel o/ε and primary personal endings. The contrast between active and middle-passive voices produces two sub-sets:

	Active	Middle-Passive
Sg. 1.	πιστεύω	πιστεύομαι
2.	πιστεύεις	πιστεύῃ
3.	πιστεύει	πιστεύεται
Pl. 1.	πιστεύομεν	πιστευόμεθα
2.	πιστεύετε	πιστεύεσθε
3.	πιστεύουσι (ν)	πιστεύονται

3670. Notes:

3670.1 For -ω in first singular active see §3180.1; -ουσι in third plural active §3180.4; -ῃ in second singular middle-passive §3180.5.

3670.2 -ει- in second and third singular active is inexplicable.

3670.3 Note that the endings given first in,the table, §318, are employed in the thematic conjugation.

368. *ω-verbs contracted.* The present base of contract verbs ends in a short vowel (α, ε, ο), which contracts with the thematic vowel o/ε in accordance with regular rules of contraction (§917). Differences among the form-sets of contract verbs and between contracted and uncontracted ω-verbs are the result of contraction. Since three stem vowels are involved (α, ε, ο), there will be a form-set for each type of stem; the paradigm of the uncontracted ω-verb (§367) may be set alongside for comparison.

Active

Sg. 1. πιστεύω

    2. πιστεύεις

    3. πιστεύει

Pl. 1. πιστεύομεν

    2. πιστεύετε

    3. πιστεύουσι (ν)

	Alpha-contract		Epsilon-contract		Omega-contract	
Sg. 1.	ἀγαπῶ	(α+ω)	ποιῶ	(ε+ω)	πληρῶ	(ο+ω)
2.	ἀγαπᾷς	(α+ει)	ποιεῖς	(ε+ει)	πληροῖς	(ο+ει)
3.	ἀγαπᾷ	(α+ει)	ποιεῖ	(ε+ει)	πληροῖ	(ο+ει)
Pl. 1.	ἀγαπῶμεν	(α+ο)	ποιοῦμεν	(ε+ο)	πληροῦμεν	(ο+ε)
2.	ἀγαπᾶτε	(α+ε)	ποιεῖτε	(ε+ε)	πληροῦτε	(ο+ε)
3.	ἀγαπῶσι (ν)	(α+ου)	ποιοῦσι (ν)	(ε+ου)	πληροῦσι (ν)	(ο+ου)

Middle-Passive

Sg. 1. πιστεύομαι

    2. πιστεύῃ

    3. πιστεύεται

Pl. 1. πιστευόμεθα

    2. πιστεύεσθε

    3. πιστεύονται

Sg. 1.	ἀγαπῶμαι	(α+ο)	ποιοῦμαι	(ε+ο)	πληροῦμαι	(ο+ο)
2.	ἀγαπᾶσαι	(α+ε)	ποιῇ	(ε+η)	πληροῖ	(ο+η)
3.	ἀγαπᾶται	(α+ε)	ποιεῖται	(ε+ε)	πληροῦται	(ο+ε)
Pl. 1.	ἀγαπώμεθα	(α+ο)	ποιούμεθα	(ε+ο)	πληρούμεθα	(ο+ο)
2.	ἀγαπᾶσθε	(α+ε)	ποιεῖσθε	(ε+ε)	πληροῦσθε	(ο+ε)
3.	ἀγαπῶνται	(α+ο)	ποιοῦνται	(ε+ο)	πληροῦνται	(ο+ο)

3680. Notes:

3680.1 The second singular middle-passive of verbs in -άω has the uncontracted personal ending -σαι (often = η < ε + σαι; §3180.5).

3680.2 The accent in the present tense of contract verbs is always on the contracted syllable, a characteristic sometimes helpful in identifying them.

3680.3 The contractions in -άω verbs yield either ω or α (ᾳ); in -έω verbs either ει or ου (except -ῶ and -ῇ); in -όω verbs either οι or ου (except -ῶ).

369. The rules of vowel contraction may be reduced to four formulas (cf. §917):

369.1 Like vowels produce a common long vowel (or diphthong):

$$\varepsilon + \varepsilon = \varepsilon\iota \qquad o + o = o\upsilon$$
$$\varepsilon + \varepsilon\iota = \varepsilon\iota \qquad o + \omega = \omega$$
$$\varepsilon + \eta = \eta$$

369.2 When unlike vowels contract, o or ω prevails over other vowels:

$$\alpha + o = \omega \qquad \varepsilon + o = o\upsilon \qquad o + \varepsilon\iota = o\iota$$
$$\alpha + \omega = \omega \qquad \varepsilon + \omega = \omega \qquad o + \eta = o\iota$$
$$\alpha + o\upsilon = \omega$$

369.3 α prevails when it precedes ε or η:

$$\alpha + \varepsilon = \alpha$$
$$\alpha + \varepsilon\iota = \bar{\alpha}$$
$$\alpha + \eta = \bar{\alpha}$$

369.4 Iota is always retained.

3690. *Uncontracted verbs in -έω.* A few verbs with present bases in -έω show uncontracted forms in the present indicative. The present indicative form-set may be a mixture of contracted and uncontracted forms. None of the verbs exhibiting any uncontracted forms in any mood or tense (δέομαι, δεῖ, ζέω, θέω, πλέω, πνέω, ῥέω, -χέω) shows a complete form-set for the present indicative. A hypothetical form-set for the active voice is derived from the classical model of πλέω, *sail:* πλέω (the actual, not dictionary, form of the first singular), πλεῖς, πλεῖ, πλέομεν, πλεῖτε, πλέουσι (ν). Only πλεῖ is attested in the New Testament. A hypothetical form-set for the middle-passive voice is derived from δέομαι, *request:* δέομαι, δέῃ, δεῖται, δεόμεθα, δεῖσθε, δέονται. The first and third singular and the first plural are attested for the New Testament. Cf. Moulton-Howard:193–201.

3691.   *Contract verbs in -ήω.* Of the contract verbs with long final vowel in classical Greek, e.g. ζήω, *live*, only two have resisted complete assimilation to verbs in -άω. The present indicative active of ζήω (ζάω) is: ζῶ, ζῇς, ζῇ, ζῶμεν, ζῆτε, ζῶσι (ν). In the present indicative middle-passive χρήομαι has apparently been assimilated to verbs in -άω: χρῶμαι, χρᾶσαι, χρᾶται, χρώμεθα, χρᾶσθε, χρῶνται (cf. ἀγαπῶμαι, §368).

370.   *Athematic conjugation.* In athematic conjugations personal endings are added directly to the tense base (without thematic vowel). Some generalizations can be made with respect to the athematic conjugation in the present tense:

370.1   The second alternatives are employed in the table of primary personal endings given in §318, i.e. -μι instead of -ω, -σι instead of -#, -ασι instead of -ουσι.

370.2   The second singular middle-passive ending -σαι does not contract as it customarily does in the thematic conjugation (§3180.5; cf. §3680.1).

370.3   The final stem vowel of -μι, verbs in the present tense varies between long (active singular) and short (active plural, all middle-passive forms) vowel, e.g. ἰστη- / ἰστα-; τιθη- / τιθε-; διδω- / διδο-, except for verbs with stems ending in -υ (e.g. δείκνυμι).

3700.   Paradigms for athematic (μι) conjugations in the present tense.

Active

Sg. 1. ἵστημι	τίθημι	δίδωμι	δείκνυμι
2. ἵστης	τίθης	δίδως	δείκνυς
3. ἵστησι (ν)	τίθησι (ν)	δίδωσι (ν)	δείκνυσι (ν)
Pl. 1. ἵσταμεν	τίθεμεν	δίδομεν	δείκνυμεν
2. ἵστατε	τίθετε	δίδοτε	δείκνυτε
3. ἱστᾶσι (ν)	τιθέασι (ν)	διδόασι (ν)	δεικνύασι (ν)

Middle-Passive

Sg. 1. ἵσταμαι	τίθεμαι	δίδομαι	δείκνυμαι
2. ἵστασαι	τίθεσαι	δίδοσαι	δείκνυσαι
3. ἵσταται	τίθεται	δίδοται	δείκνυται
Pl. 1. ἱστάμεθα	τιθέμεθα	διδόμεθα	δεικνύμεθα
2. ἵστασθε	τίθεσθε	δίδοσθε	δείκνυσθε
3. ἵστανται	τίθενται	δίδονται	δείκνυνται

3701. Notes:

3701.1 The third plural active ἱστᾶσι (ν) is a contraction of ἱστάασι (ν). The corresponding forms elsewhere do not contract.

3701.2 The μι-verbs are on the decline in hellenistic Greek (they have disappeared in modern Greek). There is a tendency for them to pass over to the thematic conjugation, e.g. δείκνυς is replaced by δεικνύεις, ἵστημι has formed a new present stem in ἱστάνω, etc. See Bl-D §§92–94 for particulars.

3702. *Μι-verbs following the paradigms in §370.*

3702.1 Like the middle-passive of ἵσταμαι are conjugated: δύναμαι, ἐπίσταμαι, κρέμαμαι (I.6), πίμπραμαι, ὀνίναμαι (I.7b).

3702.2 More or less like τίθημι is conjugated -ίημι (ἱη- / ἱε-), which occurs only in compound form (s. Appendix III, I.7b): active: -ίημι, -εῖς, -ίησι (ν), -ίεμεν, -ίετε, -ιᾶσι (ν) and -ιοῦσι (ν); middle-passive only -ίεται (3. sg.), -ίενται and -ίονται (3. pl.). Some forms have gone over to the thematic conjugation.

3702.3 Like δείκνυμι are conjugated the verbs in -νυμι and -ννυμι given in Appendix III, IV.4. Note that some of the verbs in this category were or have become ω-verbs.

371. *Εἰμί.* The common verb εἰμί, *I am,* is irregular. The present tense (active; there is, of course, no middle-passive) is conjugated as follows:

Sg. 1.	εἰμί	Pl. 1.	ἐσμέν
2.	εἶ	2.	ἐστέ
3.	ἐστί (ν)	3.	εἰσί (ν)

3710. Notes:

3710.1 The stem of εἰμί is ἐσ-, to which are added personal endings (athematic conjugation). The forms ἐστί (ν) (with old third singular ending, see §3180.3). ἐσμέν, ἐστέ are thus 'regular.'

3710.2 Εἰμί is from *ἐσμι (σ before μ or ν is often dropped and the preceding vowel lengthened in compensation), εἶ from *ἐσι < ἐσ-σι (intervocalic σ disappears, followed by contraction), εἰσί (ν) shows the third plural ending -σι but without α (Homer has ἔασι).

3710.3 Because of the high frequency of this verb and its modest irregularities, *the conjugation must be committed to memory.*

3711. *Other irregular μι-verbs in the present indicative.*

3711.1 φημί, *say* (φη-/φα-): φημί, φησί (3. sg.), φασί (third plural). No middle-passive.

3711.2 *εἶμι, go* (ει-/ι-): only third plural -ίασι (ν). No middle-passive.

3711.3 *κάθημαι, sit* (καθη-) : κάθημαι, κάθη, κάθηται, third plural κάθηνται.

3711.4 *κεῖμαι, lie, recline* (κει-): κεῖμαι, third singular κεῖται, first plural κείμεθα, third plural κεῖνται.

3712. *Catalogue of μι-verbs.* A complete catalogue of verbs (in Bauer) showing any athematic inflection in the present (and imperfect) tense may be found in Appendix III: I.6 and I.7b (the latter is comprised of μι-verbs that reduplicate the present stem [§§342, 345.2]), together with the verbs in -νυμι and -ννυμι in IV.4. Note the large number, especially in IV.4, for which alternative present bases of a thematic type are given. For the athematic imperfect conjugation, see §§404–4050. For the athematic aorist, §§411–4121.

The Future Indicative (Active & Middle)

0372. The future passive is built on the sixth principal part (§303) and so may be reserved for subsequent consideration (§§393–395).

372. The future system is headed by the second principal part (§303). The tense formant is σ (§346.2). Primary endings are employed. All futures are conjugated thematically (i.e. with variable vowel o/ε, §§3661f.).

373. *Vowel stem futures.* Verbs having vowel stems that do not contract in the present tense (Class I.1a, §357) simply join σ to the present base to form the future base. Except for this difference, the future is inflected exactly like the present.

		Active	Middle
Sg.	1.	πιστεύσω	πιστεύσομαι
	2.	πιστεύσεις	πιστεύσῃ
	3.	πιστεύσει	πιστεύσεται
Pl.	1.	πιστεύσομεν	πιστευσόμεθα
	2.	πιστεύσετε	πιστεύσεσθε
	3.	πιστεύσουσι (ν)	πιστεύσονται

374. Contract verbs ending in a short vowel (α, ε, ο) (Class I.2, §358) generally lengthen that vowel before the tense suffix: ἀγαπάω, ἀγαπήσω; λαλέω, λαλήσω; πληρόω, πληρώσω (subclasses I.2a, b, c). Some verbs in -α retain -α in forming the remaining tense stems (§358.1), e.g. γελάω, γελάσω. There is also a small group of verbs in -έω that retain short ε in the future (see Appendix III, I.5d, for a list).

375. *Stop stem futures.* Verbs with stems ending in a stop undergo regular transformation when σ is joined to the stem (Class I.3, Appendix III):

labials	π, β, φ + σ = ψ	(ψ is pronounced πσ)
palatals	κ, γ, χ + σ = ξ	(ξ is pronounced κσ)
dentals	τ, δ, ϑ, + σ = σ	(a dental is lost before σ)

E.g. βλέπω, βλέψω; τρίβω, τρίψω; γράφω, γράψω
διώκω, διώξω; ἄγω, ἄξω; ἄρχω, ἄρξομαι
φείδομαι, φείσομαι; πείθω, πείσω
(no examples in Bauer of τ)

3750. Once the tense stem is formed, the verbs in §§373–375, are inflected exactly like πιστεύσω (§373). The only difference between the present and future form-sets lies in the tense stem (suffix σ, with any consequent modifications).

376. *Liquid futures.* As indicated in §§3750, 346.2, the contrastive feature in present and future form-sets is customarily the obvious presence of the tense formant σ in the latter. The presence of the σ is not always apparent, however. Verbs whose base ends in a liquid (λ, ρ) or nasal (μ, ν) form the future base by adding -εσ ο/ε to the base: the σ disappears (intervocalic σ is often lost, §930.2), and ε contracts with the thematic vowel in accordance with the regular pattern (§917). Since the stem vowel is always ε, future form-sets of verbs of this type will look exactly like contract verbs in -έω in the present (§368, ποιέω). These futures are called 'liquid futures' for short.

	Active	Middle
Sg. 1.	μενῶ (< μενεσω)	μενοῦμαι
2.	μενεῖς etc.	μενῇ
3.	μενεῖ	μενεῖται
Pl. 1.	μενοῦμεν	μενούμεθα
2.	μενεῖτε	μενεῖσθε
3.	μενοῦσι (ν)	μενοῦνται

3760. Another group of verbs having a present tense in -ίζω, e.g. ἐγγίζω, also exhibit a 'contract' future. These verbs have stems ending in a dental (τ, δ or ϑ), which is lost before the σ (tense formant; cf. §359). In the Attic dialect, verbs of more than two syllables of this type added -(σ)ε- to the base to form the future base: ἐγγι-(σ)ε-ω > ἐγγιῶ. The σ disappeared, and the ε contracted with the thematic vowel, yielding a form-set identical with that of liquid verbs (μενῶ, §376). Because the pattern was common only in Attic, it is called the 'Attic future.' In other dialects, however, the customary pattern was followed, i.e. the dental of the base is simply lost before the tense formant: βαπτίζω (base: βαπτιδ-), βαπτίσω. As might be expected, hellenistic Greek utilizes both form-sets, sometimes showing alternative form-sets for the same verb, e.g. καθίζω, καθίσω or καθιῶ. These verbs belong to Class III.1a (Appendix III), but only verbs in -ίζω are involved (verbs in -άζω all have futures on the model, -άσω). Sixteen verbs of the 168 in Class III.1a show contract futures either as the only or the alternative form.

3761. One verb, πίπτω, has a 'Doric future,' πεσοῦμαι (aorist, ἔπεσον), which is also a 'contract' future, but the contraction in this case follows after the σ.

3762. The verbs χέω and πάσχω also show 'contract' futures: χέω, -χεῶ (χῶ is present, -χεῶ future); πάσχω, παθεῖται (only third singular appears in Bauer; the aorist is ἔπαθον).

3763. A few verbs form futures without the tense formant at all. These are verbs employing more than one root in the elaboration of principal parts (Class VI, Appendix III). There are only two listed in Bauer:

πίνω, I drink — πίομαι
ἐσθίω, I eat — φάγομαι or ἔδομαι

These futures are conjugated exactly like the present tense of ω-verbs (§367).

377. The 'liquid futures' referred to in §376 occur with verbs drawn from a number of classes (Appendix III). All, of course, have liquid or nasal stems. There are two major groups:

(1) verbs having ostensibly identical present and future bases;
(2) verbs having an 'expanded' present base (in contrast to other principal parts).

377.1 Verbs of the first type come from Class I.4. A complete list is given below, §3791.4. The list is exhaustive for verbs of this class, except for οἰκτίρω (I.4), which shows a future, οἰκτιρήσω (a sigmatic, i.e. 'regular,' future).

377.2 Verbs of the second type belong to Classes III.3, 4; IV.4; V; VI. The following is a complete catalogue based on Bauer.

III.3 ἀγγέλλω, ἀγγελῶ
      βάλλω, βαλῶ
      στέλλομαι, -στελῶ
      -τέλλω, -τελῶ
      ψάλλω, ψαλῶ

III.4 αἴρω, ἀρῶ
      ἐγείρω, ἐγερῶ
      -κτείνω, -κτενῶ
      μιαίνω, μιανῶ
      πικραίνω, πικρανῶ
      ποιμαίνω, ποιμανῶ
      -τείνω, -τενῶ
      φαίνω, φανοῦμαι
      φθείρω, φθερῶ
      χαίρω, -χαροῦμαι (more commonly, χαρήσομαι)

IV.4 ὄλλυμι, ὀλῶ (more commonly, -ολέσω)

V. θνῄσκω, -θανοῦμαι

VI. αἱρέω, αἱρήσομαι but also -ελῶ
      λέγω, ἐρῶ

378.   *The future of* εἰμί. The common verb εἰμί, *I am*, is irregular in the future tense, but only modestly so. It is deponent in the future, i.e. it takes primary middle-passive endings (§318) but is active in meaning. Except for the third singular, it is conjugated thematically.

Sg. 1. ἔσομαι   Pl. 1. ἐσόμεθα
   2. ἔσῃ   2. ἔσεσθε
   3. ἔσται   3. ἔσονται

The future conjugation, like the present (§371) and imperfect (§405), *must be committed carefully to memory.*

379.   *Contrastive features of the future.* Aside from the two 'irregular' verbs in §3763, the future tense is marked by two form-sets, one showing the tense formant σ attached to the present base (with appropriate phonetic modification where the base ends in a stop consonant, §375), the other exhibiting a contract pattern without the tense formant (the 'Doric future,' §3761, excepted). In both cases the personal endings are identical with those employed in the present tense. The first type of form-set is by far the more common.

3790. In the former, the presence of the tense formant σ in contrast to the present base is a clear signal:

πιστεύω	πιστεύσω
ἀγαπῶ	ἀγαπήσω
πέμπω	πέμψω
ἄγω	ἄξω
πείθω	πείσω
ἵστημι	στήσω

It is often the case, of course, that the future base differs from the present base in other respects as well, e.g. δίδωμι, δώσω.

3791. In the latter, the situation is more complex. The contract pattern of conjugation (§§368f., 376) is confined to the present (including the imperfect, §§402–4031) and future tense systems. And a verb showing a contract pattern in the present system will not show one in the future and conversely (χέω, §3762, excepted; unlike Attic, there are no verbs with identical present and future form-sets; cf. Bl-D §74(1), Smyth §§535, 538f., 540). Since there are other clues to the imperfect (augment, secondary endings), identification of a future contract form depends again on contrastive features in relation to the present forms of the same verbs. The most general rule that applies would be:

3791.1 *A contract form in contrast to an uncontrasted present form of the same verb will be future.*

This general rule should be particularized and the possible confusions pointed out:

3791.2 A contract form ending in -ιῶ, in contrast to a present form in -ζω, is future. Possible confusion: a number of contract verbs in -άω and -όω in the present tense have present bases ending in ι (in their contracted form), e.g. κοπιάω = κοπιῶ, etc.; ἀξιόω = ἀξιῶ, etc. These present forms might be confused, at a few points in the form set, with futures in -ιῶ from verbs in -ζω.

3791.3 A contract form with a base ending in a liquid (λ, ρ) or nasal (μ, ν), in contrast to an uncontracted present form with an 'expanded' base, will be future. That is to say, most verbs with liquid or nasal bases show a contrast also in base as between present and future, e.g.:

βάλλω,	βαλῶ
αἴρω,	ἀρῶ
ἐγείρω,	ἐγερῶ

ὄλλυμι,	ὀλῶ (-ολέσω)
θνήσκω,	θανοῦμαι

Note that the present base is 'expanded' by comparison with the future base.

3791.4 There is, nevertheless, a very small class of liquid verbs with present and future bases ostensibly identical, e.g. μένω / μενῶ. Verbs comprising this small group come from Class I.4, Appendix III:

μεγαλύνω,	μεγαλυνῶ
μένω,	μενῶ
πληθύνω,	πληθυνῶ
πλύνω,	πλυνῶ
σκληρύνω,	σκληρυνῶ
κλίνω,	κλινῶ
κρίνω,	κρινῶ

The contrast turns, in the first singular, solely on the accent, but this possibility of confusion does not extend to the whole set, since other forms in the sets show contrasts involving vowel or diphthong joining base to ending. The full paradigms are given for comparison; forms identical save for accent are underlined.

	Present	Future
Active		
Sg. 1.	μένω	μενῶ
2.	μένεις	μενεῖς
3.	μένει	μενεῖ
Pl. 1.	μένομεν	μενοῦμεν
2.	μένετε	μενεῖτε
3.	μένουσι (ν)	μενοῦσι (ν)
Middle-Passive		
Sg. 1.	μένομαι	μενοῦμαι
2.	μένῃ	μενῇ
3.	μένεται	μενεῖται
Pl. 1.	μενόμεθα	μενούμεθα
2.	μένεσθε	μενεῖσθε
3.	μένονται	μενοῦνται

Easy confusions are thus confined to five forms in the set.

3791.5 It is necessary to bear in mind that not all *contract* forms with liquid or nasal bases are future: there are many verbs with liquid or nasal stems that are conjugated on the contract pattern *in the present tense*, e.g. (λαλέω) λαλῶ, (μαρτυρέω) μαρτυρῶ; these verbs will not, of course, have liquid (=contract) futures, e.g. λαλήσω, μαρτυρήσω. The contrasts set out in §§3791.1–4 therefore refer to the present tense of the same verb.

380. *Summary*. The vast majority of Greek verbs will show the tense formant σ as the sign of the future. Those that do not will have 'contract' futures, and these have to be identified as futures by contrast with present forms of the same verbs. Special attention should therefore be given to the first and second principal parts of these verbs (§§377, 3791.4).

Lesson 25

Indicative Mood: Primary Tenses, cont.
Perfect/Future Passive

The Perfect Active

0385. The perfect middle-passive is built on the fifth principal part (§303) and so may be reserved for the subsequent section (§§389–3922).

385. The perfect active system is headed by the fourth principal part (§303). Since the pluperfect active, which belongs to the system, is a secondary tense, attention is confined here to the perfect active. The perfect active is formed on a re-duplicated base (§§341–3440), to which is added the tense suffix -κα- (§§346.3, 347, 3663), and primary endings (§318).

3850. The perfect active described in §385 is the so-called first perfect. There is also a less common second perfect, which is formed in exactly the same way, except that the tense suffix is -α- rather than -κα-. *There is no grammatical significance in the difference between the two formations.*

386. The first perfect active
Verb base: πιστεύω, perfect active base: πε-πιστευ-κ-α

Sg. 1.	πεπίστευκα	Pl. 1.	πεπιστεύκαμεν
2.	πεπίστευκας	2.	πεπιστεύκατε
3.	πεπίστευκε (ν)	3.	πεπιστεύκασι (ν)

3860. Notes:

3860.1 The 1. sg. has no personal ending, nor does the 3. sg. The sole contrasting feature is the difference between α and ε (to the latter ν-movable may be added).

3860.2 On the 3. pl. ending -σι (ν), s. §3180.4. In place of this ending -αν is occasionally found (borrowed from first aorist active—a secondary ending), s. Bl-D §83 for particulars.

387. The second perfect active
Verb base: γράφω, perfect active base: γε-γραφ-α

Sg. 1.	γέγραφα	Pl. 1.	γεγράφαμεν
2.	γέγραφας	2.	γεγράφατε
3.	γέγραφε (ν)	3.	γεγράφασι (ν)

387. There are twenty-one verbs showing second perfects in the literature covered by Bauer. Arranged in the order of the categories in Appendix III, they are:

I.1a	ἀκούω	ἀκήκοα
I.3a	γράφω	γέγραφα
	λείπω	-λέλοιπα
	πέμπω	πέπομφα
	σήπω	σέσηπα
I.3b	ἀνοίγω	ἀνέῳγα
	φεύγω	-πέφευγα
I.3c	πείθω	πέποιθα
I.7b	γίνομαι	γέγονα
III.1b	κράζω	κέκραγα
III.2	πράσσω	πέπραχα
	τάσσω	τέταχα
	φύλασσω	πεφύλαχα
IV.2	λαμβάνω	εἴληφα
	τυγχάνω	τέτευχα
IV.4	δείκνυμι	δέδειχα
	ὄλλυμι	(-όλωλα)
	ῥήγνυμι	-έρρηγα
VI.	ἔρχομαι	ἐλήλυθα
	πάσχω	πέπονθα
	φέρω	-ενήνοχα

3871. Occasionally second perfects from verbs with stems ending in π, β or κ, γ show an aspirated tense stem on the analogy of the correlative aspirated stops, φ and χ: γράφω / γέγραφα, then λαμβάνω / εἴληφα (stem: λαβ-). There are seven examples in the list in §3870: πέμπω / πέπομφα; πράσσω / πέπραχα; τάσσω / τέταχα; φυλάσσω / πεφύλαχα; λαμβάνω / εἴληφα; δείκνυμι / δέδειχα; φέρω / -ενήνοχα (perfect stem: ενηνοχ-).

388. *Οἶδα*. οἶδα, *I know*, is a second or strong perfect used as a present (i.e. there are no 'tenses' other than perfect and pluperfect [§§418, 487.5]). It does not show reduplication, but its inflection is perfectly regular:

Sg. 1.	οἶδα	Pl. 1.	οἴδαμεν
2.	οἶδας	2.	οἴδατε
3.	οἶδε (ν)	3.	οἴδασι (ν)

Note: A third plural ἴσασι (ν) appears once in the New Testament (Acts 26:4); it is a survival of the old Attic conjugation.

3880. *Perfects without present stem.* Two other verbs have perfect (and pluperfect) forms only: εἴωθα, *I am accustomed*, from an obsolete present ἔθω; ἔοικα, *seem*, used only impersonally, *it seems*, ἔοικεν, from an obsolete present εἴκω.

The Perfect Middle-Passive

389. The perfect middle-passive system is headed by the fifth principal part (§303). Since the pluperfect middle-passive, which belongs to the system, is a secondary tense, attention is confined here to the perfect middle-passive forms. The perfect middle-passive base is formed on a reduplicated base (§§341–3440) , which is regularly identical with this part of the perfect active base. To the reduplicated base primary middle-passive endings (§318) are joined directly, i.e. there is no tense suffix and no other stem formative (cf. the perfect active, §385).

390. In the case of verbs with perfect middle-passive stems ending in a vowel, the personal endings are joined to the stem without phonetic change.

Verb base: πιστεύω, Perfect middle-passive base: πε-πιστευ-μαι

Sg. 1.	πεπίστευμαι	Pl. 1.	πεπιστεύμεθα
2.	πεπίστευσαι	2.	πεπίστευσθε
3.	πεπίστευται	3.	πεπίστευνται

391. Verbs with perfect middle-passive stems ending in a liquid (λ, ρ) or nasal (μ, ν) are also largely free of phonetic change.

391.1 In both cases, however, the σ of the 2. pl. ending (-σθε) drops out between two consonants, e.g. ἔσταλθε (< εσταλσθε), ἐξήρανθε (< εξηρανσθε).

391.2 In the case of stems ending in ν, the ν is of course assimilated to a following μ (§929.5), in the 1. sg. and 1. pl., and in the participle used to form the 3. pl.

	στέλλω, ἔσταλ-	ξηραίνω, ἐξήραν-
Sg. 1.	ἔσταλμαι	ἐξήραμμαι (< -νμαι)
2.	ἔσταλσαι	ἐξήρανσαι
3.	ἔσταλται	ἐξήρανται
Pl. 1.	ἐστάλμεθα	ἐξηράμμεθα (< -νμεθα)
2.	ἔσταλθε (< -λσθε)	ἐξήρανθε (< -νσθε)
3.	ἐσταλμένοι εἰσί (ν)	ἐξηραμμένοι εἰσί (ν) (< -νμένοι)

3910. Note: Perfect middle-passive stems ending in a *consonant* regularly form the 3. pl. periphrastically, i.e. with participle and the 3. pl. of the verb *be*. This applies also to verbs with stems ending in a stop, §392.

392. Verbs with perfect middle-passive stems ending in a stop undergo phonetic change,when joined to the personal endings, in accordance with regular patterns. The pattern depends on whether the stop in question is a labial (π, β, φ), a palatal (κ, γ, χ), or a dental (τ, δ, ϑ). The patterns may be summarized in relation to the endings:

392.1 Before μ (1. sg. -μαι, 1. pl. -μεϑα, and 3. pl. in the participle),

> a labial becomes μ
> a palatal becomes γ
> a dental becomes σ

392.2 Before σ (2. sg. -σαι),

> a labial becomes ψ
> a palatal becomes ξ
> a dental becomes σ (the double σσ is then simplified to σ)

Cf. the formation of the future tense base, §375.

392.3 Before a dental (3. sg. -ται, 2. pl. -(σ)ϑε [the σ drops out]),

> a labial becomes coordinate, i.e. before τ, π, before ϑ, φ
> a palatal becomes coordinate, i.e. before τ, κ, before ϑ, χ
> a dental becomes σ

See §§925, 926, 927 for a fuller account of these phonetic changes.

There are thus three patterns for the perfect middle-passive of verbs ending in a stop, one for labials, one for palatals, and one for dentals.

3920. Ordered as form-sets, the patterns may be exemplified as follows:

	Labial Stems	Palatal Stems	Dental Stems
	γράφω, γεγραφ-	δέχομαι, δεδεχ-	πείϑω, πεπειϑ-
Sg. 1.	γέγραμμαι	δέδεγμαι	πέπεισμαι
2.	γέγραψαι	δέδεξαι	πέπεισαι
3.	γέγραπται	δέδεκται	πέπεισται
Pl. 1.	γεγράμμεϑα	δεδέγμεϑα	πεπείσμεϑα
2.	γέγραφϑε	δέδεχϑε	πέπεισϑε
3.	γεγραμμένοι εἰσί (ν)	δεδεγμένοι εἰσί (ν)	πεπεισμένοι εἰσί (ν)

3921. Notes:

3921.1 Dentals stems show σ throughout.

3921.2 The 3. pl. forms are periphrastic; cf. §3910.

3922. Verbs of classes I.3c and III.1a, Appendix III, will show σ as the final stem consonant in the perfect middle-passive since these verbs all have dental stems. Verbs of class III.1a, especially, are numerous. On the analogy of these verbs and others whose stems end in σ, a number of other verbs show a final stem σ in the perfect middle-passive and/or first aorist passive (on which see §422). This is characteristically the case where the final stem vowel in the perfect middle-passive is short, but it appears also in other cases.

A catalogue of verbs showing an inserted σ in the perfect middle-passive and/or aorist passive is given in §422.

The Future Passive

0393. The future passive is built on the sixth principal part, which is the 1. sg. indicative of the aorist passive (§303). Although the aorist passive is a secondary tense, it will be necessary to give a preliminary account of the formation of the aorist passive base in order to be able to treat the future passive, which is, of course, a primary tense.

393. The aorist passive base of the 'regular' verb will show an augment prefixed to the verb base, and a tense formative in -θη- suffixed to the verb base (§§346.4, 347), e.g. ἐ-πιστεύ-θη-. Secondary *active* endings are employed, which, in the 1. sg., is -ν, giving the full form ἐ-πιστεύ-θη-ν. Analogous to the perfect active, there is a first and second aorist passive: one form with -θη- as the tense suffix, and one form with only -η- (the perfect has forms with and without -κ-, §3850). The second aorist passive is exemplified by φύω: ἐ-φύ-η-ν. *There is normally no grammatical significance in the difference between first and second aorist passive forms.*

394. The future passive base is the aorist passive base, (1) less augment (primary tenses are not augmented, §0335), (2) plus the tense suffix of the future, σ §§346.2, 347), e.g. ἐ-πιστευ-θη: πιστευ-θη-σ-. Primary middle-passive endings are employed (§318), and are joined to the base by means of variable vowel o/ε (§§322, 372): e.g. πιστευ-θή-σ-ο-μαι. The second future passive is formed in precisely the same way from verbs showing a second aorist passive (the tense formant will, of course, be -η- rather than -θη-): ἐ-φύ-η-ν: φυ-ή-σ-ο-μαι.

πιστεύω, ἐπιστεύθην (πιστευθήσομαι)   φύω, ἐφύην (φυήσομαι)

Sg. 1.	πιστευθήσομαι	φυήσομαι
2.	πιστευθήσῃ	φυήσῃ
3.	πιστευθήσεται	φυήσεται
Pl. 1.	πιστευθησόμεθα	φυησόμεθα
2.	πιστευθήσεσθε	φυήσεσθε
3.	πιστευθήσονται	φυήσονται

3940. Mnemonic hints:

3940.1 The 2. sg. ending -σαι contracts to -ῃ as it does in the present middle-passive of ω-verbs and in the future middle (§3180.5).

3940.2 The tense formant -θη- (or -η-) is the only means of distinguishing the future passive from the future middle in 'regular' verbs, e.g. πιστεύσομαι / πιστευθήσομαι. In many verbs, however, there will also be a difference in the verb stem, e.g. πέμπω, future middle πέμψομαι, future passive πεμφθήσομαι; cf. στρέφω, -στρέψομαι, στραφήσομαι.

395. *Summary.* The perfect active, middle-passive and future passive will occur relatively infrequently in texts, in comparison with the frequency of the present, future active and future middle. Forms of the former should be readily identifiable, nevertheless, by virtue of their characteristic markers:

395.1 Perfect active: reduplicated base, plus stem formative α(ε), with or without tense formative κ.

395.2 Perfect middle-passive: reduplicated base, with mid.-pass. primary personal endings joined directly to the stem.

395.3 Future passive: tense formative -θη- or -η-, plus tense sign of the future σ, with variable vowel ο/ε and primary personal endings.

It will naturally be easier to spot these forms after gaining some familiarity with the ways the tense stems of various classes of verbs are normally developed.

Indicative Mood: Secondary Tenses
Imperfect/Aorist Active & Middle

0400. In §§365–395 (Lessons 24–25), the form-sets comprising the primary tenses (present, future, perfect) in the indicative mood were considered. In §§0400–4241 (Lessons 26–27), the corresponding form-sets for the secondary tenses (imperfect, aorist, pluperfect) are to be elaborated.

The Imperfect Indicative

400. As in the present indicative (§366), verbs are conjugated in three ways in the imperfect indicative: (1) ω-verbs uncontracted, (2) ω-verbs contracted, and (3) μι-verbs. Since the present and imperfect form a tense system (§303), the parallel formation of form-sets is to be expected. Differences in inflectional pattern, in the imperfect as in the present, *carry no grammatical significance.*

4000. The two sub-sets of ω-verbs, in the imperfect as in the present, are conjugated alike, except for contraction. The conjugation of μι-verbs differs from that of ω-verbs in three particulars: (1) μι-verbs in the imperfect, as elsewhere, are conjugated without thematic vowel (§§3661f.), whereas ω-verbs are conjugated with thematic vowel. (2) The act. 3. pl. personal ending for μι-verbs is -σαν (the second alternative in §319); for ω-verbs it is -ν. The act. 1. sg. and 3. pl. of ω-verbs will thus be identical (-ν, -ν), while the two forms are distinguished in μι-verbs (-ν, -σαν). (3) The 2. sg. mid.-pass. personal ending (-σο) in ω-verbs contracts: ἐλύου < ἐλυεσο (the σ disappears and the vowels contract, §3190.5; cf. the primary 2. sg. mid.-pass. ending -σαι, §§3180.5, 370.2); in μι-verbs the uncontracted form is retained. With §4000 as a whole cf. §3660.

401. *ω-verbs uncontracted.* The present base is augmented (§§0335–3400), and theme vowel ο/ε and secondary personal endings (the first alternatives given in §319) suffixed, to form the imperfect indicative, e.g. ἐ-πιστευ-ο-ν. The contrast between active and middle-passive voices produces two sub-sets:

	Active	Middle-Passive
Sg. 1.	ἐπίστευον	ἐπιστευόμην
2.	ἐπίστευες	ἐπιστεύου
3.	ἐπίστευε (ν)	ἐπιστεύετο
Pl. 1.	ἐπιστεύομεν	ἐπιστευόμεθα
2.	ἐπιστεύετε	ἐπιστεύεσθε
3.	ἐπίστευον	ἐπιστεύοντο

4010.   Notes:

4010.1   The 1. sg. and 3. pl. act. are identical in form.

4010.2   The 2. sg. mid.-pass. ending -ου constitutes the only aberration in the use of regular secondary endings (§319).

402.   Ω-*verbs contracted.* Since the imperfect tense is built on the present base, verbs whose present bases end in short final vowels (α, ε, ο) will contract in the imperfect as in the present tense (§§368–369). There will be three form-sets, as in the present, corresponding to the three final vowels. The paradigm of the uncontracted ω-verb (§401) may be set alongside the contracted forms for comparison.

Active

Sg. 1.	ἐπίστευον
2.	ἐπίστευες
3.	ἐπίστευε (ν)
Pl. 1.	ἐπιστεύομεν
2.	ἐπιστεύετε
3.	ἐπίστευον

	Alpha-contract		Epsilon-contract		Omega-contract	
Sg. 1.	ἠγάπων	(α+ο)	ἐποίουν	(ε+ο)	ἐπλήρουν	(ο+ο)
2.	ἠγάπας	(α+ε)	ἐποίεις	(ε+ε)	ἐπλήρους	(ο+ε)
3.	ἠγάπα	(α+ε)	ἐποίει	(ε+ε)	ἐπλήρου	(ο+ε)
Pl. 1.	ἠγαπῶμεν	(α+ο)	ἐποιοῦμεν	(ε+ο)	ἐπληροῦμεν	(ο+ο)
2.	ἠγαπᾶτε	(α+ε)	ἐποιεῖτε	(ε+ε)	ἐπληροῦτε	(ο+ε)
3.	ἠγάπων	(α+ο)	ἐποίουν	(ε+ο)	ἐπλήρουν	(ο+ο)

Middle-Passive

Sg. 1. ἐπιστευόμην
2. ἐπιστεύου
3. ἐπιστεύετο

Pl. 1. ἐπιστευόμεθα
2. ἐπιστεύεσθε
3. ἐπιστεύοντο

	Alpha-contract		Epsilon-contract		Omega-contract	
Sg. 1.	ἠγαπώμην	(α+ο)	ἐποιούμην	(ε+ο)	ἐπληρούμην	(ο+ο)
2.	ἠγαπῶ	(α+ου)	ἐποιοῦ	(ο+ου)	ἐπληροῦ	(ο+ου)
3.	ἠγαπᾶτο	(α+ε)	ἐποιεῖτο	(ε+ε)	ἐπληροῦτο	(ο+ε)
Pl. 1.	ἠγαπώμεθα	(α+ο)	ἐποιούμεθα	(ε+ο)	ἐπληρούμεθα	(ο+ο)
2.	ἠγαπᾶσθε	(α+ε)	ἐποιεῖσθε	(ε+ε)	ἐπληροῦσθε	(ο+ε)
3.	ἠγαπῶντο	(α+ο)	ἐποιοῦντο	(ε+ο)	ἐπληροῦντο	(ο+ο)

4020. Notes:

4020.1 The 1. sg. and 3. pl. act. are identical in form.

4020.2 The 2. sg. mid.-pass. is again the result of contraction (§§4000, 4010.2): α, ε, ο + εσο = α, ε, ο + ου = -ω, -ου, -ου.

4021. Mnemonic hints:

4021.1 The contractions in -όω verbs yield ου throughout.

4021.2 The contractions in -άω verbs yield ω or α, those in -έω verbs ου or ει.

403. The rules of contraction for the imperfect form-sets are the same as those for the present (§369, cf. §917):

403.1 Like vowels produce a common long vowel (or diphthong):

$$\varepsilon + \varepsilon = \varepsilon\iota \qquad o + o = ov$$
$$o + ov = ov$$

403.2 When unlike vowels contract, o or ω prevails over other vowels:

$$\alpha + o = \omega \qquad \varepsilon + o = ov \qquad o + \varepsilon = ov$$
$$\alpha + ov = \omega \qquad \varepsilon + ov = ov$$

403.3 α prevails when it precedes ε or η:

$$\alpha + \varepsilon = \alpha$$
$$\alpha + \eta = \alpha$$

403.4 Iota is always retained. (No examples)

4030. A few verbs with present bases in -έω show uncontracted forms in the imperfect, as in the present (§3690). The imperfect indicative form-set may be a mixture of contracted and uncontracted forms. None of the verbs involved (δέομαι, δεῖ, ζέω, πλέω, πνέω, ῥέω, -χέω) exhibits a complete form-set in New Testament Greek. Cf. Moulton-Howard:193–201.

4031. There are two contract verbs with possible *long* final vowel in the imperfect, as in the present (§3691): = ζήω, χρήομαι. The imperfect of ζήω, *live*, is apparently ἔζων, ἔζης, ἔζη, ἐζῶμεν, ἐζῆτε, ἔζων. Only 1. sg. and 2. pl. are attested in the New Testament. There is no middle-passive. The imperfect of χρήομαι, *use*, is apparently ἐχρώμην, ἐχρῶ, ἐχρᾶτο, ἐχρώμεθα, ἐχρᾶσθε, ἐχρῶντο, in which case the form-set has been assimilated to that of verbs in -άω (the paradigm was somewhat different in classical Greek). Only the 3. pl. is attested in the New Testament. Bauer enters the two verbs as [ζάω] and χράομαι.

404. *Athematic conjugation.* The athematic or μι-conjugation is not well represented in the imperfect. Many particular forms are unattested in the literature covered by Bauer, and there is a general tendency for μι-verbs to pass over to the ω-conjugation (cf. §3701.2). Nevertheless, it is necessary to observe the shape of the form-sets in order to be able to cope with forms that do occur. A few generalizations may be made with respect to the group as a whole:

404.1 In athematic conjugations the personal endings are attached directly to the tense base (without thematic vowel).

404.2 The tense base of the imperfect is, of course, the present base plus augment, e.g. τιθη- / ἐτιθη-, δεικνυ- / ἐδεικνυ-.

404.3 The personal endings employed with μι-verbs in the imperfect are the secondary endings found on ω-verbs (§401), except that the 3. pl. act. -ν is replaced by -σαν , and the 2. sg. mid.-pass. -σο is left uncontracted (§4000).

404.4 The same observation regarding the final stem vowel in the present tense (§370.3) applies to the imperfect as well: the long vowel occurs in the act. sing., the short vowel elsewhere (act. plur. and mid.-pass. forms). The long/short variation is illustrated by ἰστη-/ἰστα-, ἐτιθη-/ἐτιθε-.

4040. Paradigms for athematic (μι) conjugation in the imperfect tense.

Active

Sg. 1.	ἵστην	ἐτίθην	ἐδίδουν	ἔδεικνυν
2.	ἵστης	ἐτίθεις	ἐδίδους	ἔδεικνυς
3.	ἵστη	ἐτίθει	ἐδίδου	ἔδεικνυ
Pl. 1.	ἵσταμεν	ἐτίθεμεν	ἐδίδομεν	ἐδείκνυμεν
2.	ἵστατε	ἐτίθετε	ἐδίδοτε	ἐδείκνυτε
3.	ἵστασαν	ἐτίθεσαν	ἐδίδοσαν	ἐδείκνυσαν

Middle-Passive

Sg. 1.	ἱστάμην	ἐτιθέμην	ἐδιδόμην	ἐδεικνύμην
2.	ἵστασο	ἐτίθεσο	ἐδίδοσο	ἐδείκνυσο
3.	ἵστατο	ἐτίθετο	ἐδίδοτο	ἐδείκνυτο
Pl. 1.	ἱστάμεθα	ἐτιθέμεθα	ἐδιδόμεθα	ἐδεικνύμεθα
2.	ἵστασθε	ἐτίθεσθε	ἐδίδοσθε	ἐδείκνυσθε
3.	ἵσταντο	ἐτίθεντο	ἐδίδοντο	ἐδείκνυντο

4041. Notes:

4041.1 Only a few of these forms are attested in the New Testament, principally the 3. sg. and pl. of both voices.

4041.2 The forms ἐτίθεις, ἐτίθει, ἐδίδουν, ἐδίδους, ἐδίδου (underlined in the paradigms) represent the transition to the ω-conjugation, i.e. they reflect the contraction of stem and *thematic* vowel (ἐτίθεις < ἐτιθε-ες; ἐδίδουν < ἐδιδο-ον).

4041.3 The imperfect act. 2. sg., 1. pl. and 2. pl. of ἵστημι are identical in form with the corresponding present forms, owing to the fact that the augment is not visible. The same observation applies to the 1. and 2. pl. mid. -pass. forms. For the augment of ἵστημι s. §3370.1.

405. The common verb εἰμί, *I am*, is also irregular in the imperfect tense (present tense: §371).

Sg. 1.	ἤμην	Pl. 1.	ἦμεν, ἤμεθα
2.	ἦς, ἦσθα	2.	ἦτε
3.	ἦν	3.	ἦσαν

4050. Notes:

4050.1 ἦσθα exhibits an old 2. sg. personal ending -σθα (§3190.2) .

4050.2 The paradigm shows vacillation between act. (-ς. -ν, -μεν, -τε, -σαν) and mid. -pass. (-μην, -μεθα) endings.

4050.3 The long stem vowel η occurs throughout (contrast §404.4) .

4050.4 Because of its high frequency and modest irregularities, *this conjugation must be committed carefully to memory.*

The Aorist Active & Middle

0406. The *aorist active* and *middle* form two sub-sets built on the third principal part (§303) , and so shall be considered together. The *aorist passive* represents a discrete form-set built on the sixth principal part, and so may be reserved for subsequent consideration.

406. *First and second aorist.* The tense base (third principal part) of the aorist active and middle is formed, in general, in one of two ways: (1) the 'first' or 'weak' aorist is formed by augmenting the verb base and suffixing the tense formative -σα, e.g. πιστευ- / ἐπίστευσα (§§346.1, 347). (2) The 'second' or 'strong' aorist is formed by some modification of the verb base (as contrasted with the present base), augment, and thematic vowel plus secondary endings (§349 and 349.1). The 'first' aorist is usually readily distinguishable because of its tense formative. The 'second' aorist will look, except for stem, like the imperfect.

407. *Second aorist active and middle.* The form-sets for the second aorist active and middle, except for stem, are *identical* with the imperfect indicative of uncontracted ω-verbs (augmented stem, thematic vowel o/ε, plus secondary endings):

Second Aorist
λείπω, ἔλιπον

		Active	Middle
Sg.	1.	ἔλιπον	ἐλιπόμην
	2.	ἔλιπες	ἐλίπου (<-εσο)
	3.	ἔλιπε (ν)	ἐλίπετο
Pl.	1.	ἐλίπομεν	ἐλιπόμεθα
	2.	ἐλίπετε	ἐλίπεσθε
	3.	ἔλιπον	ἐλίποντο

Cf. The imperfect form-sets of ἐπίστευον in §401, and the remarks in §4010.

4070. In order to maintain the contrast between aorist and imperfect indicative, the second or strong aorist will therefore *always* show a verb base modified in some respect by comparison with the present base on which the imperfect is built. Conversely, the first or weak aorist need not, *but may*, have a modified aorist base. The second aorist active/middle will thus contrast with an imperfect indicative of the verb in question and not with the imperfect generally, while the first aorist will contrast with the imperfect generally (i.e. with respect to tense formative). It is necessary, as a consequence, to pay special attention to the first and third principal parts of verbs showing second or strong aorists.

The following is a full list of verbs showing a second aorist derived from Appendix III (Bauer):

		Present	Imperfect	Second (Strong) Aorist
I.3a		λείπω	-έλειπον	ἔλιπον
I.3b		ἄγω	ἦγον	ἤγαγον
	→	ἔχω	εἶχον	ἔσχον
		φεύγω		ἔφυγον
I.7a	→	γίνομαι	ἐγινόμην	ἐγενόμην
		πίπτω	ἔπιπτον	ἔπεσον
		τίκτω		ἔτεκον
III.3		ἅλλομαι		ἡλόμην
		βάλλω	-έβαλλον	ἔβαλον
		θάλλω		-έθαλον
IV.1		κάμνω		ἔκαμον
		τέμνω		-έτεμον
IV.2		αἰσθάνομαι		ἠσθόμην
		ἁμαρτάνω		ἥμαρτον (ἡμάρτησα)
		θιγγάνω		ἔθιγον
		λαγχάνω		ἔλαχον
	→	λαμβάνω	ἐλάμβανον	ἔλαβον
		λανθάνω		ἔλαθον
		μανθάνω		ἔμαθον
		πυνθάνομαι	ἐπυνθανόμην	ἐπυθόμην
		τυγχάνω		ἔτυχον
IV.3		-ικνέομαι		-ικόμην
		-ισχνέομαι		-εσχόμην
V.		θνῄσκω	-έθνησκον	-έθανον
		εὑρίσκω	ηὕρισκον	εὗρον (-εὗρα[1])
		-διδράσκω		-έδραν[1]
VI.		αἱρέω	-ἡρούμην	-εἶλον
	→	λέγω	ἔλεγον	εἶπον

→ ἔρχομαι	ἠρχόμην	ἦλθον (ἦλθα[1])
ἐσθίω	ἤσθιον	ἔφαγον
→ ὁράω	ἑώρων	εἶδον (ὠψάμην)
πάσχω		ἔπαθον
πίνω	ἔπινον	ἔπιον
τρέχω	ἔτρεχον	ἔδραμον

→ indicates that the verb appears in the New Testament 200 times or more.

[1]These forms reflect the intrusion of weak aorist endings into the second aorist (§4122).

Roman numerals in the left hand margin refer to the divisions of Appendix III.

Thirty-four verbs out of a total of 844 represented in Bauer thus exhibit a second or strong aorist.

408.　*First aorist active and middle.* The first or weak aorist is formed by augmenting the aorist base and adding the tense formative σα plus secondary endings. The contrast between active and middle voices again yields two sub-sets:

πιστεύω, ἐπίστευσα

	Active	Middle
Sg. 1.	ἐπίστευσα	ἐπιστευσάμην
2.	ἐπίστευσας	ἐπιστεύσω (<-ασο)
3.	ἐπίστευσε (ν)	ἐπιστεύσατο
Pl. 1.	ἐπιστεύσαμεν	ἐπιστευσάμεθα
2.	ἐπιστεύσατε	ἐπιστεύσασθε
3.	ἐπίστευσαν	ἐπιστεύσαντο

4080.　Notes:

4080.1　The first singular active shows the zero form (#), §319.

4080.2　The third singular active shows no ending; ε is substituted for α to distinguish the third from the first person.

4080.3　The second singular middle ending is again contracted (-ασο > -ω), as in the imperfect of ω-verbs (§§4000, 4010.2, 4020.2), and in the second aorist (§407).

4080.4　The first aorist personal endings are thus identical with those attached to the imperfect of ω-verbs and second aorists, except for the first singular active (# for -ν).

0409.　The formation of the first aorist stem for six subclasses (as represented in Appendix III) was considered in §§355–361. To those six subclasses may be added other important subclasses in which some ostensible 'irregularity' is involved in the formation of the first aorist tense stem.

409. *Consonant stems ending in a stop* (Appendix III, Class I.3).

409.1 Consonant stems ending in a labial stop (π, β, φ), form the first aorist, as usual, by adding -σα (plus augment) to the present tense. The juxtaposition of a labial plus σ produces ψ:

> βλέπω, βλέψω, ἔβλεψα
> τρίβω, τρίψω, -έτριψα
> γράφω, γράψω, ἔγραψα

409.2 Consonant stems ending in a palatal (κ, γ, χ) accordingly produce ξ:

> διώκω, διώξω, ἐδίωξα
> ἀνοίγω, ἀνοίξω, ἀνέῳξα
> ἄρχω, ἄρξομαι, ἠρξάμην

409.3 Consonant stems ending in a dental (τ, δ, ϑ) naturally lose the dental before σ:

> ψεύδομαι, ψεύσομαι, ἐψευσάμην
> πείθω, πείσω, ἔπεισα

409.4 The phonetic changes involved are identical with those in the corresponding future tense stems (§375; the future is included here for comparison).

410. *'Liquid' first aorists.* Just as there are 'liquid' form-sets in the future tense (§376), there are also 'liquid' first aorists. Verb stems ending in a liquid (λ, ρ) or a nasal (μ, ν) and forming a first aorist tense stem, lose the σ of the tense formative, and, as a rule, lengthen the stem vowel in compensation, e.g. μένω, ἔμεινα (for *εμενσα). The compensatory lengthening of the stem vowel is not always visible, e.g. not in verbs whose stem vowel is ι or υ. Except for the absence of the σ, the first aorist of liquid verbs is conjugated exactly like that of ἐπίστευσα:

	κρίνω, ἔκρινα	ἀγγέλλω, ἠγγειλάμην
	Active	**Middle**
Sg. 1.	ἔκρινα	ἠγγειλάμην
2.	ἔκρινας	ἠγγείλω
3.	ἔκρινε (ν)	ἠγγείλατο
Pl. 1.	ἐκρίναμεν	ἠγγειλάμεθα
2.	ἐκρίνατε	ἠγγείλασθε
3.	ἔκριναν	ἠγγείλαντο

411.   *'Root' aorists.* A second type of 'strong' aorist, in addition to the thematic second aorist (§§406–4070), is the 'root' aorist, so called because personal endings are added directly to the tense base or 'root' (athematic or μι-conjugation). Such verbs are few in number, but some are of high frequency: ἔστην (ἵστημι), -έβην (βαίνω), ἔγνων (γινώσκω).

Active

Sg. 1.	ἔστην	ἀνέβην	ἔγνων
2.	ἔστης	ἀνέβης	ἔγνως
3.	ἔστη	ἀνέβη	ἔγνω
Pl. 1.	ἔστημεν	ἀνέβημεν	ἔγνωμεν
2.	ἔστητε	ἀνέβητε	ἔγνωτε
3.	ἔστησαν	ἀνέβησαν	ἔγωσαν

In addition, ἔδυ and ἔδυσαν from -δύω appear, and ἐπιπέτομαι has a root aorist, ἐπέπτην. There are no middle forms for these verbs (but see §412.1).

412.   *κ-aorists.* A second type of 'weak' aorist, in addition to the regular sigmatic first aorist (§§408–410), is the κ-aorist, so called because κ replaces σ in the formation of the aorist tense stem; the κ-aorist may be called 'weak' because the κ-forms employ 'weak' or first aorist endings.

4120.   Three verbs of the μι-class have κ-aorists in the active voice, but 'root' aorists in the middle voice: ἔθηκα (τίθημι), ἔδωκα (δίδωμι), ἀφῆκα (ἀφίημι):

Active

Sg. 1.	ἔθηκα	ἔδωκα	ἀφῆκα
2.	ἔθηκας	ἔδωκας	ἀφῆκας
3.	ἔθηκε (ν)	ἔδωκε (ν)	ἀφῆκε (ν)
Pl. 1.	ἐθήκαμεν	ἐδώκαμεν	ἀφήκαμεν
2.	ἐθήκατε	ἐδώκατε	ἀφήκατε
3.	ἔθηκαν	ἔδωκαν	ἀφῆκαν

Middle

Sg. 1.	ἐθέμην	ἐδόμην
2.	ἔθου (< εσο)	ἔδου (< οσο)
3.	ἔθετο	ἔδοτο
Pl. 1.	ἐθέμεθα	ἐδόμεθα
2.	ἔθεσθε	ἔδοσθε
3.	ἔθεντο	ἔδοντο

The middle is lacking for ἀφῆκα.

4121. Notes:

4121.1 The κ-forms follow the first aorist pattern precisely, with the substitution of κ for σ.

4121.2 The middle 'root' aorist forms of τίθημι, δίδωμι show the short stem vowel (cf. §§404.4, 4040 for the imperfect, §§370.3, 3700 for the present), and the second singular is contracted (unlike the imperfect forms: §§404.3, 4040).

4122. *Mixture of paradigms.* A few verbs already in the classical period exhibited alternative 'strong' and 'weak' endings, e.g. the aorist of φέρω could be conjugated either as a 'weak' aorist, ἤνεγκα, -ας, -ε (ν), etc., or as a 'strong' aorist, ἤνεγκον, -ες, -ε(ν), etc. The common second aorist εἶπον, I said, could also take 'weak' endings, e.g. εἶπας, εἶπατε. One advantage of the 'weak' paradigm was that active third plural -αν could be distinguished from active first singular -α, while in the 'strong' paradigm they were identical. This convenience led to the intrusion of 'weak' endings more and more into the strong paradigm. In hellenistic Greek second aorists like ἦλθον (ἔρχομαι), -εῖλον (αἱρέω), ἔβαλον (βάλλω), εὗρον (εὑρίσκω) are found occasionally with 'weak' endings, e.g. ἦλθα, -εῖλα, ἔβαλαν, εὕραμεν, etc. Moreover, second aorists like ἔπεσον (πίπτω) were felt to be σ-aorists and so acquired 'weak' endings, e.g. ἔπεσα. At the same time, new first aorist formations began to displace older second aorist forms, e.g. ἡμάρτησα is found alongside ἥμαρτον (ἁμαρτάνω). The intrusion was not, however, all one way. 'Strong' endings also penetrated the 'weak' paradigm: under the influence of the third singular active -ε(ν), common to both paradigms, the active second singular -ες, and the active second plural -ετε began to penetrate the 'weak' paradigm. As a result of this long development from classical to modern times, a single set of personal endings for the imperfect and both aorists has emerged in modern Greek: -α, -ες, -ε(ν), -αμεν, -ετε (-ατε), -αν. The end product is the conflation of the two paradigms, a conflation that is underway already in hellenistic times. Cf. Bl-D §81.

Lesson 27

Indicative Mood: Secondary Tenses, cont.
Pluperfect/Aorist Passive

The Pluperfect Active & Middle-Passive

0415.   Although the pluperfect active and the pluperfect middle-passive are formed on different principal parts (§303), the infrequency of the tense makes it appropriate to consider them together, and in an abbreviated fashion. Only twenty-two verbs in the New Testament exhibit any pluperfect forms at all.

415.   *Pluperfect active.* Like the perfect active (§§385–3880), the pluperfect active may take the form of either a 'first' ('weak') pluperfect, or a 'second' ('strong') pluperfect; the only distinction is that the tense formative κ is omitted in the 'strong' form (§3850). The pluperfect active is formed by augmenting (usually, see §340.1) the perfect stem, and suffixing the tense formative -κει- (or -ει-) plus secondary active endings:

	First Pluperfect Active λύω, (ἐ)λελύκειν	Second Pluperfect Active γράφω, (ἐ)γεγράφειν
Sg. 1.	(ἐ)λελύκειν	(ἐ)γεγράφειν
2.	(ἐ)λελύκεις	(ἐ)γεγράφεις
3.	(ἐ)λελύκει (ν)	(ἐ)γεγράφει (ν)
Pl. 1.	(ἐ)λελύκειμεν	(ἐ)γεγράφειμεν
2.	(ἐ)λελύκειτε	(ἐ)γεγράφειτε
3.	(ἐ)λελύκεισαν	(ἐ)γεγράφεισαν

4150.   Notes:

4150.1   Except for possible augment, the pluperfect active will look like the perfect active, with the substitution of the tense formative -κει- (-ει-) for -κα- (-α-), and -ν for -α in the 1. sg. and -σαν for -σι(ν) in the 3. pl. (cf. §386).

4150.2   The pluperfect active was conjugated differently in Attic Greek: -κη, -κης, -κει (ν), -κεμεν, -κετε, -κεσαν. The -ει- of the third singular spread to the other forms and the paradigm simplified (Smyth §701).

416. *Pluperfect middle-passive.* As in the perfect middle-passive (§389), the pluperfect middle-passive is formed by adding the personal endings directly to the reduplicated base. The perfect (reduplicated) base is, of course, usually (§340.1) augmented, and the personal endings employed are secondary middle-passive endings.

Pluperfect Middle-Passive
λύω, (ἐ)λελύμην

Sg.	1. (ἐ)λελύμην	Pl.	1. (ἐ)λελύμεθα
	2. (ἐ)λέλυσο		2. (ἐ)λέλυσθε
	3. (ἐ)λέλυτο		3. (ἐ)λέλυντο

417. *Phonetic changes.* The paradigm in §416 serves for all verbs with perfect stems ending in a vowel. Verbs with perfect stems ending in a liquid (λ, ρ) or nasal (μ, ν) undergo the same phonetic changes as verbs in the perfect middle-passive (§391), and verbs with stems ending in a stop likewise (§§392–3922).

4170. *Third person plural.* The third plural of verbs with stems ending in a consonant is formed periphrastically, i.e. ἦσαν plus the perfect participle, nominative masculine plural; cf. the perfect form (§3910).

4171. Paradigms for the pluperfect middle-passive of verbs with consonant stems may be set down for reference:

Stems in a liquid	Stems in π, β, φ	Stems in κ, γ, χ	Stems in τ, δ, θ
ἐστάλμην	(ἐ)γεγράμμην	(ἐ)τετάγμην	(ἐ)πεπείσμην
ἔσταλσο	(ἐ)γέγραψο	(ἐ)τέταξο	(ἐ)πέπεισο
ἔσταλτο	(ἐ)γέγραπτο	(ἐ)τέτακτο	(ἐ)πέπειστο
ἐστάλμεθα	(ἐ)γεγράμμεθα	(ἐ)τετάγμεθα	(ἐ)πεπείσμεθα
ἔσταλθε	(ἐ)γέγραφθε	(ἐ)τέταχθε	(ἐ)πέπεισθε
ἦσαν ἐσταλμένοι	ἦσαν γεγραμμένοι	ἦσαν τεταγμένοι	ἦσαν πεπεισμένοι

4172. On the insertion of σ in the perfect middle-passive stem, s. §3922.

418. *The pluperfect in the New Testament.* Pluperfect forms for the following verbs occur in the New Testament (listed in alphabetical order). The list is exclusive of periphrastic formations.

ἁρπάζω -ηρπάκειν	γινώσκω ἐγνώκειν
βάλλω βεβλήκειν	δέομαι -εδεδέμην
γίνομαι (ἐ)γεγόνειν	δίδωμι (ἐ)δεδώκειν

[εἴωθα] εἰώθειν	μένω μεμενήκειν
λέγω εἰρήκειν	[οἶδα] ᾔδειν
ἔρχομαι ἐληλύθειν	οἰκοδομέω ᾠκοδομήκειν
θεμελιόω τεθεμελιώμην	ὁράω ἑωράκειν
-θνῄσκω ἐτεθνήκειν	πείθω ἐπεποίθειν
ἵστημι (ἐ)ἱστήκειν	πιστεύω πεπιστεύκειν
καλέω (ἐ)κεκλήμην	ποιέω πεποιήκειν
κρίνω κεκρίκειν	τίθημι ἐτεθείκειν

The middle-passive form is given where the active does not occur. The perfect active is given in [ ] where there is no present form of the verb in use.

The Aorist Passive

0419. A preliminary account of the formation of the aorist passive tense stem was given in §393, in connection with the future passive.

419. There are two types of aorist passive, again called 'first' and 'second.' The difference between them lies solely in the tense formative attached to the aorist passive stem: first aorist passive, add -θη-; second aorist passive, add -η- (this is, of course, also the sole difference between first and second future passives, §393).

420. The aorist passive indicative is formed, consequently, by (1) augmenting the aorist passive base, (2) suffixing the tense formative -θη- (or -η-), and (3) joining *active* secondary endings directly to the resultant stem:

Sg. 1.	ἐ- - - -θην	(-ην)	Pl. 1. ἐ- - - -θημεν	(-ημεν)
2.	ἐ- - - -θης	(-ης)	2. ἐ- - - -θητε	(-ητε)
3.	ἐ- - - -θη	(-η)	3. ἐ- - - -θησαν	(-ησαν)

4200. Notes:

4200.1 Observe that the endings are *active* endings. The aorist passive is a hybrid tense formation, created to distinguish the aorist and future passive from the corresponding middle forms (in the present, imperfect, perfect and pluperfect the middle and passive forms are identical). The second aorist passive, in fact, was originally an active athematic formation, which came to be used to express the passive voice (cf. Smyth §§802ff.).

4200.2 There is no thematic vowel: the endings are joined directly to the tense stem.

4200.3 The endings are identical with those attached to the 'root' aorist active (§411), and those employed in the athematic conjugation of the imperfect active (§4040), i.e. the third plural ending is -σαν rather than -ν (used in thematic conjugations of the imperfect and second aorist).

421. *First aorist passive.* The first aorist passive of verbs having vowel stems is readily created on the basis of the sketch in §§420–4200.

πιστεύω, ἐ-πιστευ-θη-ν

Sg. 1.	ἐπιστεύθην	Pl. 1.	ἐπιστεύθημεν
2.	ἐπιστεύθης	2.	ἐπιστεύθητε
3.	ἐπιστεύθη	3.	ἐπιστεύθησαν

4210. *Phonetic change* occasioned by the juxtaposition of certain final stem consonants and the θ of the first aorist passive tense formative is readily explicable:

4210.1 π or β before θ is aspirated (§928.1), i.e. becomes φ:

λείπω, -ελείφθην
λαμβάνω, ἐλήμφθην

4210.2 κ or γ before θ is also aspirated (§928.1), i.e. becomes χ:

ἄγω, ἤχθην
διώκω, ἐδιώχθην

This change applies to all verbs of Class III.1b, -ζω verbs with stems ending in γ (Appendix III).

4210.3 A dental (τ, δ, θ) before θ (a dental) becomes σ:

πείθω, ἐπείσθην

This change applies to all verbs of Class III.1a, -ζω verbs with stems ending in δ (Appendix III).

4210.4 In the verb θύω, the θ of the stem is deaspirated, i.e. changed to τ, before the tense formative in -θη-: ἐτύθην (cf. deaspiration in reduplication, §343.3).

422. *The insertion* of σ before the tense formative takes place in a large number of verbs (cf. §3922 for general discussion and the same phenomenon in the perfect middle):

ἀκούω, ἠκούσθην
τελέω, ἐτελέσθην

Catalogue of verbs showing an inserted σ. The following verbs show a σ inserted in the perfect middle-passive tense stem and/or in the aorist passive tense stem. Excluded are verbs which have σ in one or both of these tense stems by virtue of an original verb stem ending in σ, or by virtue of phonetic change (cf. §3922). The catalogue covers all verbs represented in Bauer. The catalogue is arranged in accordance with the categories of Appendix III; the participle or other form is given where the indicative does not occur.

	Present	Perfect Mid.-Pass.	Aorist Passive
I.1a	ἀκούω		ἠκούσθην
	θραύω	τεθραυσμένος	ἐθραύσθην
	κλείω	κέκλεισμαι	ἐκλείσθην
	κυλίω	-κεκύλισμαι	ἐκυλίσθην
	λούω	λελουμένος	
		λελουσμένος	
	πτύω		-πτυσθήσομαι
	ῥύομαι		ἐ(ρ)ρύσθην
	σείω		ἐσείσθην
	χρίω		ἐχρίσθην
I.1b	ἀγαλλιάω		ἠγαλλιάθην
			(ἠγαλλιάσθην)
	ἐράω		ἠράσθην
	θλάω		-θλασθήσομαι
	κλάω		-εκλάσθην
	σπάω	-εσπάσθαι (inf.)	-εσπάσθην
	χαλάω		ἐχαλάσθην
I.2a	μνάομαι	μεμνησμένη	
I.5d	αἰδέομαι		ἠδέσθην
	ἀρκέω		ἀρκεσθήσομαι
	τελέω	τετέλεσμαι	ἐτελέσθην
I.6	δύναμαι		ἠδυνήθην
			(ἠδυνάσθην)
I.7b	πίμπλημι	-πέπλησμαι	ἐπλήσθην
	πίμπρημι		πρησθείς
IV.4	ἀμφιέννυμι	ἠμφιεσμένος	
	ζώννυμι	-εσζωσμένος	

	κεράννυμι	κεκερασμένος	
	κορέννυμι	κεκερασμένος	ἐκορέσθην
	κρεμάννυμι		ἐκρεμάσθην
	σβέννυμι		σβεσθήσομαι
V.	ἱλάσκομαι		ἱλάσθητι (impera.)
	μεθύσκω		ἐμεθύσθην
	γινώσκω	ἔγνωσμαι	ἐγνώσθην
	μιμνήσκομαι		ἐμνήσθην

423. *Second aorist passive.* The second aorist passive is also readily constructed from the sketch given in §§420–4200, where the aorist passive base is known:

γράφω, ἐ-γράφ-η-ν

Sg. 1. ἐγράφην	Pl. 1. ἐγράφημεν
2. ἐγράφης	2. ἐγράφητε
3. ἐγράφη	3. ἐγράφησαν

424. It was noted that the second aorist passive was originally an athematic active formation (§4200.1). This accounts for the similarities in the form-sets:

	'Root' Aorist Active (§411)	Second Aorist Passive
Sg. 1.	ἀνέβην	ἐκρύβην
2.	ἀνέβης	ἐκρύβης
3.	ἀνέβη	ἐκρύβη
Pl. 1.	ἀνέβημεν	ἐκρύβημεν
2.	ἀνέβητε	ἐκρύβητε
3.	ἀνέβησαν	ἐκρύβησαν

Fortunately, the number of 'root' aorists is very small (a complete list is given in §411). Moreover, as a general rule, *verbs which show second (§4070) or 'root' aorists will not show a second aorist passive*. Confusion is possible, consequently, on the basis of individual forms, but not in relation to the elaboration of a particular verb, e.g. ἔστην might be identified as a second aorist passive on the basis of form, but not if the *first* aorist passive of the same verb is known: ἐστάθην. Conversely, ἐκρύβην has a *first* aorist active: ἔκρυψα (present: κρύπτω).

4240. *Confusion* is also possible among the first-second aorist passive, the 'root' aorist and the athematic conjugation of the imperfect (§4040), e.g. ἐτίθην is imperfect, ἐτέθην aorist passive; ἵστην is imperfect, ἔστην aorist active (these examples are both μι-verbs); ἐλύθην (λύω) is first aorist passive, but its form parallels that of ἐτίθην (imperfect). Such forms and form-sets in isolation may be confusing, but modest familiarity with the principal parts of verbs exhibiting 'root' aorists, second aorist passives and the like, together with a grammatical context, make identification less difficult.

4241. *Catalogue of second aorist passives.* The following is a complete catalogue of verbs showing a second aorist passive as represented in the literature covered by Bauer. Verbs are given in the order in which they appear in Appendix III. Where the aorist passive indicative does not occur, the future passive or other form built on the sixth principal part is given. The first aorist active, where it exists, is given for comparison:

I.1	-δύω	ἔδυσα	ἐδύην*
		ἔδυν	
	παύω	ἔπαυσα	-επαύθην
			(-επάην)
	φύω		ἐφύην
I.5a	ῥέω		-ῥυήσομαι
I.3	γράφω	ἔγραψα	ἐγράφην
	θλίβω		ἐθλίβην
	στρέφω	ἔστρεψα	ἐστράπην
	τρέπω	ἔτρεψα	-ἐτράπην
	τρέφω	ἔθρεψα	-ετράφην
	-τρίβω	-ἔτριψα	-ετρίβην
	ἀνοίγω	ἀνέῳξα	ἀνεῴχθην
			ἠνοίγην
	πλέκω	ἔπλεξα	-επλάκην
	πνίγω	ἔπνιξα	ἐπνίγην
	τήκω		τακήσομαι
	ψύχω	-ἔψυχα	ψυγήσομαι
I.4	δέρω	ἔδειρα	δαρήσομαι
	φύρω		-εφύρην
II.	θάπτω	ἔθαψα	ἐτάφην
	κλέπτω	ἔκλεψα	ἐκλάπην
	κόπτω	ἔκοψα	ἐκόπην
	κρύπτω	ἔκρυψα	ἐκρύβην

	ῥίπτω	ἔ(ρ)ριψα	-ε(ρ)ρίφην
	σκάπτω	ἔσκαψα	ἐσκάφην
III.1a	ἁρπάζω	ἥρπασα	ἡρπάσθην
			(ἡρπάγην)
III.1b	σφάζω	ἔσφαξα	ἐσφάγην
III.2	ἀλλάσσω	ἤλλαξα	-ηλλάγην
	νύσσω	ἔνυξα	-ενύγην
	ὀρύσσω	ὤρυξα	ὠρύγην
			(-ωρύχθην)
	πλήσσω	-έπληξα	ἐπλήγην
	τάσσω	ἔταξα	-ετάχθην
			(-ετάγην)
	φράσσω	ἔφραξα	ἐφράγην
III.3	ἀγγέλλω	ἤγγειλα	~ηγγέλην
	στέλλομαι	-έστειλα	-εστάλην
	σφάλλω		σφαλήσομαι
III.4	σπείρω	ἔσπειρα	ἐσπάρην
	φαίνω	ἔφανα	ἐφάνην
	φθείρω	ἔφθειρα	ἐφθάρην
	χαίρω		ἐχάρην
III.5	καίω	ἔκαυσα	ἐκαύθην
			(ἐκάην)
	-άγνυμι	-έαξα	-εάγην
	μείγνυμι	ἔμειξα	ἐμίγην
	ῥήγνυμι	ἔ(ρ)ρηξα	-ε(ρ)ράγη
			(-ραγήσομαι)

*The appearance of a second aorist passive alongside a 'root' aorist active is an exception to the rule given in §424. But ἐδύην is a new formation in the process of replacing ἔδυν (Bl-D §76(2)); the classical aor. pass. was ἐδύθην.

Identifying the Verb: Tense & Lexical Form

0430. Suggestions for identifying the person and number of finite forms of the verb were made in Lesson 21, §§325–330. Clues were confined to personal endings attached to the verb and to hints gathered from the context. Additional clues to the identification of verbs have been provided in intervening lessons: augment (§§0335–3400), reduplication (§§341–3450), tense suffixes (§§0346–3500), the development of tense stems (§§355–361), and the conjugation of the indicative mood in all primary and secondary tenses (§§365–4241). These additional clues should now be reviewed, systematized, and put to the test.

430.1 Verbs are conjugated, and must therefore be identified, in relation to five factors (§0304): person, number, voice, mood, and tense. Since the non-indicative moods have not yet been explored, and person, number, voice have already been considered, attention may be focused on tense. However, other factors cannot and need not be ignored.

430.2 The beginning student is faced with the problem of identifying the *lexical forms* of verbs: one must be able to get repeatedly and efficiently from particular verb forms in the text to the proper entry in the lexicon. For this purpose, a working knowledge of tense base formation, to be considered subsequently, will prove especially helpful. Meanwhile, the lexical forms of most regular verbs and many less regular verbs can be located with the clues in hand.

430.3 Verb identification may be regarded as a puzzle of interest in and for itself. For those whose primary interest is reading Greek, however, the identification of the verb should be viewed from the perspective of the particular verb form in context: single clues and constellations of clues are to be read as quickly and easily as possible for what they tell the reader about the verb form in question. These clues should be approached in the most practical ways: 1) highly repetitious features of the verbal system may be schematized and reduced to a working key; 2) coping with irregular verbs, especially those of high frequency, is largely a matter of experience; 3) difficulties with actual verb forms will expose gaps in one's knowledge of the verbal system; these gaps may then be corrected by appropriate review.

These suggestions correspond, in a general way, to the proposals made in §0346.2 for control over the verb system: 1) familiarity with the regular patterns; 2) explicit knowledge of the exceptions.

431. The following keys for verb identification cover the subjunctive, optative, infinitive, and participle, as well as the indicative mood.

Prefixes

431.1 *Augment*: if the verb shows augment, it must be aorist, imperfect, or pluperfect (in the order of frequency; the augment is usually omitted with the pluperfect in the New Testament). §§0335–3400.

431.11 Present tense stem augmented and secondary endings: imperfect

431.12 Aorist tense stem augmented: second aorist indicative

431.121 First will have -σα as suffix

431.13 Pluperfect will have reduplicated stem

431.2 *Reduplication*: if the verb stem is reduplicated, the form will most often be perfect (or pluperfect). §§341–3450.

431.20 There are reduplicated stems in the present and aorist tenses also (§345)

Suffixes

431.3 *Tense suffixes*

431.31 σ added to present stem: future

431.32 σα added to aorist stem: first aorist

431.33 κα added to verb stem, either first perfect or aorist of μι-verbs

431.34 θη (η) added to aorist passive stem: aorist passive

431.35 θησ (ησ) added to aorist passive stem: future passive

431.4 *Mood suffixes*

431.41 Lengthened thematic vowel (ω/η): subjunctive

431.42 ιη in place of thematic vowel: optative

431.43 Thematic vowel plus ι: optative

431.5 *Other suffixes*

431.51 -ειν or -αι attached to the tense stem: infinitive

431.52 -ντ-, -οτ-, -μενο- as part of the suffix: participle

Note: The nominative singulars of participles are the exception.

432.   In Jn 8:12–20 there are 41 verb forms (including participles), as follows:

8:12	(1)	ἐλάλησεν	8:16	(22)	κρίνω
	(2)	λέγων		(23)	ἐστιν
	(3)	εἰμι		(24)	εἰμί
	(4)	ἀκολουθῶν		(25)	πέμψας
	(5)	περιπατήσῃ	8:17	(26)	γέγραπται
	(6)	ἕξει		(27)	ἐστιν
8:13	(7)	εἶπον	8:18	(28)	εἰμι
	(8)	μαρτυρεῖς		(29)	μαρτυρῶν
	(9)	ἔστιν		(30)	μαρτυρεῖ
8:14	(10)	ἀπεκρίθη		(31)	πέμψας
	(11)	εἶπεν	8:19	(32)	ἔλεγον
	(12)	μαρτυρῶ		(33)	ἐστιν
	(13)	ἐστιν		(34)	ἀπεκρίθη
	(14)	οἶδα		(35)	οἴδατε
	(15)	ἦλθον		(36)	ἤδειτε
	(16)	ὑπάγω		(37)	ἤδειτε
	(17)	οἴδατε	8:20	(38)	ἐλάλησεν
	(18)	ἔρχομαι		(39)	διδάσκων
	(19)	ὑπάγω		(40)	ἐπίασεν
8:15	(20)	κρίνετε		(41)	ἐληλύθει
	(21)	κρίνω			

432.1   Identification should begin with the obvious: forms of the present tense of ω-verbs uncontracted (§367) and contracted (§368). We may include all forms which appear at first glance to fit the paradigms: (6) ἕξει, (8) μαρτυρεῖς, (12) μαρτυρῶ, (16) ὑπάγω, (18) ἔρχομαι, (19) ὑπάγω, (20) κρίνετε, (21) κρίνω, (22) κρίνω, (30) μαρτυρεῖ.

432.11   (6) ἕξει is a bit misleading: the ξ conceals a σ, the tense sign of the future (§431.31), lexical form ἔχω (see §375 and Appendix III, I.3b).

432.12   (8) μαρτυρεῖς, (12) μαρτυρῶ, (30) μαρτυρεῖ are regular contract forms. (12) μαρτυρῶ is actually a subjunctive (indicative and subjunctive forms in this case are identical; κἀν in the context signals a subjunctive).

432.13   The remaining forms represent uncontracted ω-verbs, ἔρχομαι is of course deponent, i.e. it has only middle-passive forms in the present tense, with active meaning.

432.14 A preliminary survey netted ten forms, eight of which proved to be present indicative forms of ω-verbs.

432.2 The next obvious step is to pick out the forms of εἰμί, which tend to proliferate in any Greek text (see §§371, 405 for paradigms): (3) εἰμι, (9) ἔστιν, (13) ἔστιν, (23) ἔστιν, (24) εἰμί, (27) ἔστιν, (28) εἰμι, (33) ἔστιν. All eight forms are present indicative.

432.3 The next step might be to look for first aorist forms in the list. There will always be more aorist and present forms than all other forms combined in any text of length.

432.31 First aorist forms will have augment and σα (σε) as a tense suffix (§431.121): (1) ἐλάλησεν, (38) ἐλάλησεν, (40) ἐπίασεν qualify and are, in fact, first aorists.

432.32 Rejected were (25), (31) πέμψας: it has a correct ending perhaps, but the form lacks augment. The form is actually an aorist participle. (32) ἔλεγον has augment, but lacks the first aorist tense suffix.

432.4 In §432.2 were collected the forms of the irregular verb εἰμί, which is a verb of high frequency. Other irregular verbs of high frequency should now be added to the list, particularly those of the mixed class, Appendix III, class VI.

432.41 (7) εἶπον is the second aorist form going with λέγω. Another form of εἶπον: (11) εἶπεν.

432.42 (14) οἶδα is a perfect form with present meaning (§§388, 418). Other forms of οἶδα: (17), (35) οἴδατε, and two pluperfect forms: (36), (37) ᾔδειτε.

432.43 (15) ἦλθον is a second aorist form going with present (18) ἔρχομαι. (41) ἐληλύθει is a pluperfect form of the same verb.

432.44 εἶπον, οἶδα, ἔρχομαι are irregular verbs of very high frequency. Familiarity with their principle parts (Appendix III, class VI) will greatly facilitate identification.

432.5 The list of unidentified verbs in Jn 8:12–20 has now been reduced to twelve.

432.51 (26) γέγραπται shows reduplication and a primary middle-passive ending, 3. sg.: γε/γραπ/ται. It must therefore be a perfect middle-passive of a verb with a labial stem (§§392.3, 3920).

432.52 (32) ἔλεγον has augment and secondary active endings (§431.11). It could be second aorist, but a glance at the principle parts of λέγω (Appendix III, class VI) prove it to be imperfect.

432.53 (5) περιπατήσῃ appears to have the tense sign of the future (σ) suffixed: -ση future middle, 2. person sg. (§373). But the preceding οὐ μή indicates that a subjunctive is coming (§818). In this case, the two forms, future indicative and aorist subjunctive, are identical in form.

432.54 For (6) ἕξει, see §432.11.

432.55 (10), (34) ἀπεκρίθη exhibits the tense suffix of the aorist passive (θη, §431.34). It shows augment between prepositional prefix and tense base: ἀπ/ε/κρι/θη. The verb base must therefore be κρι-; in that case, the lexical form would be ἀπο/κρίω. In Bauer only three words begin with ἀποκρι-, and only one of these is a verb: ἀποκρίνομαι, the aorist pass. of which is ἀπεκρίθην. This verb belongs to a very small class of verbs that lose ν in principal parts four through six (§482.30).

432.56 There now remain the following forms, which fall into two distinct groups: (2) λέγων, (4) ἀκολουθῶν, (29) μαρτυρῶν, (39) διδάσκων; and (25), (31) πέμψας. The first group looks to belong to the nominal system, either as a genitive plural (all declensions), or as a nominative masculine singular (third declension nouns ending in -ντ-, §§165f.). In context, ὁ ἀκολουθῶν ἐμοί (Jn 8:12) and ὁ μαρτυρῶν (8:18) look very much like nominal word clusters headed by the article. Indeed, they are. They are nominative masc. sing. forms of the present participle (§247.1). On the other hand, πέμψας looks like it might belong to the first aorist system: -ψας = π/σας, but the form lacks augment. The cluster, ὁ πέμψας με πατήρ, once again suggests a nominal word cluster, in which case πέμψας is a first aorist participle, nom. masc. sing. (§2470.3). The verb base is πεμπ-, lexical form, accordingly, πέμπω.

It is perhaps unusual that all participles in this passage are nominative singulars, in relation to which the key provided in §431.52 is useless.

432.57 There are no infinitives in this passage.

433. The exercise in §432 presupposes that the reader is willing to examine the nearer and more remote contexts of a given form for clues to its identification. One does not normally make a list of verbs when reading a text, of course, although the beginner would profit from such an exercise in the early stages of reading. In any case, the beginner should cultivate the habit of *reading* a paragraph or significant group of sentences before attempting word identifications or translation. This practice will often relieve the blank stare before it hardens into perplexity.

In the following exercise, we shall take up verb forms one at a time, as they occur in Jn 8:21–30, rather than compiling a list first. Nevertheless, we shall constantly lift the eyes to what precedes and what follows the form under examination, as a means of renewing the first, preliminary reading we shall presuppose. We shall skip some forms, particularly those already met (including those met in Jn 8:12–20, §432) and those that are more or less obvious.

433.1　8:21 εἶπεν (irregular, §487.2) is the second aorist going with present λέγω, *say, speak*. This passage is largely dialogue, so forms of this verb should occur frequently: 8:22 ἔλεγον, λέγει, 23 ἔλεγεν, 24 εἶπον, 25 ἔλεγον, εἶπεν 27, ἔλεγεν, 28 εἶπεν. Tenses include present, imperfect, second aorist.

433.2　8:21 ζητήσετε: ζητη/σ/ε/τε, future active indicative, 2. plur. If ζητη/ω does not appear in the lexicon, try ζητα/ω or ζητε/ω (§374).

433.3　8:21 ἀποθανεῖσθε: ἀπο/θανεῖ/σθε could only be present or future (not second aorist: no augment). It could be a contract form: θανεῖ- < θανε-ε. The lexicon does not list a verb *ἀποθανέω, but it does give the entry: ἀποθανοῦμαι, s. ἀποθνήσκω. The beginner should thus have no major difficulty in locating the lexical form, provided the clues are followed up unswervingly. ἀποθνήσκω belongs to the -σκω class of verbs (Appendix III, class V), and it exhibits a liquid future (§376).

433.4　8:21 δύνασθε: δυνα/σθε, where the ending appears to be joined directly to the verb stem (no thematic vowel): a μι-verb (§§370.2, Appendix III, class I.6).

433.5　8:21 ἐλθεῖν: δύναμαι is regularly followed by an infinitive (§571.1), and ἐλθεῖν contains the clue to an infinitive form (-ειν, §431.51).

433.6　8:22 ἀποκτενεῖ looks like a contract verb (a circumflex accent often signals a contracted syllable). The lexicon shows only one verb beginning ἀπο/κτε-: ἀποκτείνω. The future is ἀποκτενῶ, the aorist ἀπέκτεινα. The form in 8:22 must therefore be a liquid future (§376), active, 3. sg.

433.7　8:24 πιστεύσητε: πιστευ/σ/η/τε has a long thematic vowel (η rather than ε), a signal of the subjunctive (§431.41). The preceding ἐάν is also a sure signal that a subjunctive is coming (cf. §432.12: κἄν = καὶ ἐάν). The tense suffix σ indicates that the form is aorist subjunctive.

433.8　8:25 εἶ: from εἰμί, present indicative, 2. sg. (§371). Note that the personal pronoun σύ indicates the person and number: σὺ . . . εἶ (§256).

433.9　8:25 λαλῶ: a present contract form; look for a contract verb in -έω, άω or -όω in the lexicon.

433.10　8:26 λαλεῖν, κρίνειν: infinitives (§431.51).

433.11　8:26 ἤκουσα: η/κου/σα appears to have the first aorist tense suffix, -σα (1. sg.), and η could be the augmented form of α or ε (§337). Look in the lexicon for ακου/ω or εκου/ω.

433.12　8:27 ἔγνωσαν: ε/γνω/σαν, with augment and tense suffix of the first aorist -σα, plus 3. plur. active personal ending (-ν). The particular form is thus easy to identify. The special problem in this case is to locate the lexical form. Bauer does not show a verb beginning γνω- that would yield the form in 8:27. A related form in 8:28 γνώσεσθε (looking ahead for clues) does not help materially, except to indicate that there is perhaps a future form with tense stem γνωσ-.

Without explicit knowledge of the verb, the beginner has two choices. First, one may use the lexicon to assist, provided the form does not really contain its own clues. Bauer does indeed enter ἔγνωκα, ἔγνων, ἔγνωσμαι and asks the reader to see γινώσκω. The lexicon will regularly provide help of this kind for forms which do not lead systematically to their own lexical forms, i.e. present indicative.

The beginner may elect, however, to do a little sleuthing on his own. Since γνω- represents the aorist base, the chances are that the present base will be an expanded version of the aorist base (§480.1) (a check has already been made to determine that the verb is not irregular, i.e. does not belong to the ten verbs in class VI). The options for expanding the verb base to produce the present tense stem include: modification of the stem vowel, reduplication, addition of suffixes ι, ν, or σκω (s. §496 for a summary). A quick check reveals that modifications of ω in γνω- does not help (i.e. try γνο-, γνα-, etc. in the lexicon: the possibilities are found on a single page). A second possibility is that γνω- represents the zero form of a second stem vowel: γανω-, γενω-, γινω-, etc. The first two yield no likely prospects, but the third, γινω-, produces γινώσκω, with second aorist ἔγνων, the 3. plural of which would be ἔγνωσαν (§411, a 'root' aorist). The fact that the hellenistic form γινώσκω is actually an abbreviation of a classical reduplicated present in -σκω (class V), γιγνώσκω, does not matter. The important thing is to be able to locate lexical forms quickly by means of educated guesses. Whatever works is 'right.'

433.13   8:28 ὑψώσητε: ὑψω/σ/η/τε, with long thematic vowel (η: subjunctive, §431.41), therefore tense suffix of the aorist (not future: no future subjunctive). Look for lexical form ὑψόω because *ὑψωω would make no sense.

433.14   8:28 γνώσεσθε: see §433.12.

433.15   8:28 ἐδίδαξέν: obviously a first aorist active, 3. sing. (ξ = κσ, γσ, χσ). The lexicon does not show a verb in διδακ-, διδαγ-, or διδαχ-, but notice the noun διδαχή, *teaching*, and the preceding verb, διδάσκω, *teach*, which has an aorist ἐδίδαξα. διδάσκω loses a stop before -σκω in forming the present tense (§486.2). Observe the new form of help here invoked: in the same lexical context, nouns with similar bases and related meaning are sometimes of assistance in locating the lexical forms of verbs (e.g. the noun base διδαχ- indicates that the related verb may also have a base in διδαχ-).

433.16 8:29 ἀφῆκεν: looks like it is from ἀπο/ηκω or something similar. There is a verb ἀφήκω, but it has no imperfect or aorist (Bauer). Right above ἀφήκω is entered ἀφῆκα, s. ἀφίημι. ἀφῆκεν is actually a κ-aorist of ἀφίημι. (§4120): of ἀφ-ιη/μι only -η- is left of the verb base ιη- (Appendix III, class I.7b). Forms of ἀφίημι are about as tough as they come.

433.17 8:30 λαλοῦντος: The partial suffix -ντ- indicates the form is a participle (§431.52). The model for active participles is πᾶς (§231), gen. masc. and neut. sing. παντός. The form in 8:30 has the identical ending.

433.18 8:30 ἐπίστευσαν: ε/πιστευ/σα/ν is clearly a first aorist form, active 3. plural, from πιστεύω.

434. *Summary.* Exercises of the types carried out in §§432, 433 should be repeated often in the early stages of verb identification. Intense practice will achieve two things: 1) it will reinforce recognition of regular forms and forms of high frequency until identification becomes automatic; 2) it will demonstrate that very quickly forms presenting problems are dramatically reduced in number. Repetition is high, even in texts of high complexity. The student should rely on this linguistic fact, and discipline himself or herself to reading the available clues appearing in the text. The less frequently one is forced to consult grammar or lexicon, the more pleasure one will find in reading a text.

Lesson 29

Non-Indicative Moods:
Subjunctive/Optative

0440. In lessons 24–27 (§§365–4241) were treated the form-sets which together comprise the inflection of the Greek verb in the *indicative* mood. The indicative forms of the verb may serve as the basis for elaborating the *non-indicative* moods (subjunctive, optative, imperative, infinitive, participle), i.e. the non-indicative moods are to be presented from the perspective of the way or ways in which they contrast, formally, with the corresponding indicative forms. Knowledge of the fundamental characteristics of the indicative system will make it possible to abbreviate greatly the elaboration of the non-indicative moods.

The subjunctive (lesson 29), the infinitive and the participle (lesson 30) are in common use in hellenistic Greek; the imperative (lesson 30) and especially the optative (lesson 29) are much less common. The optative is so rare, in fact, that it hardly repays learning the inflectional system in any detail.

440. *Generalizations* touching the non-indicative moods may be helpful.

440.1 Since tense as time is not primarily relevant to the non-indicative moods (it would be well to review §§0309–3120 at this point), it can be expected that they will appear only in the present, aorist and perfect 'tenses' ('tense' here means aspect, §§0309ff.).

440.2 The non-indicative forms of the verb are formed, for the most part, on the appropriate tense bases or stems (principal parts), except that the aorist base of the non-indicative moods lacks augment (principal Parts III and VI). Cf. the formation of the future passive on the aorist passive stem, §§393–3940. The augment, of course, signals past time (§§311, 0335).

440.3 It may be expected that a number of paradigms for the non-indicative moods will be defective, and that the tendency to form tenses periphrastically will increase (contraction of the inflective range of the language, simplification of the verbal system).

The Subjunctive Mood

441. *The characteristic feature of the subjunctive* is the long thematic or variable vowels ω/η, which replace the short variable vowels ο/ε used in thematic conjugations in the indicative (§§322, 3661). Since all subjunctives are thematic, this feature is the key to the subjunctive.

442. *The contours of the subjunctive system* may be indicated by the following:

442.1 There are only present, aorist and perfect subjunctives (§303), owing to the fact that only tense as aspect and not tense as time is relevant to the non-indicative moods (§§3031.7–9, 310, 3100.2).

442.2 The perfect subjunctive, other than for the verb οἶδα, is formed periphrastically (§300.3), i.e. with the perfect participle and the present subjunctive of the verb εἰμί (*be*). The perfect subjunctive is rare (§3031.8). One has therefore to reckon only with finite forms of the present and aorist subjunctive.

442.3 All subjunctives are built on their respective tense stems, *less augment* (§340.2): the present on the present stem, the aorist on the aorist stem, less augment (the perfect is formed periphrastically, §442.2).

442.4 Primary personal endings (§318) are employed throughout.

442.5 All subjunctives are conjugated thematically with long variable vowel ω/η (there are no athematic conjugations).

4420. *Summary.* The present and aorist subjunctives are built on the present and aorist tense stems respectively (less augment), and are formed by suffixing a long thematic vowel ω/η, plus primary personal endings; the perfect subjunctive is formed periphrastically.

443. *The subjunctive system.* The simplicity of the subjunctive system may be seen in the following representative paradigms, based on five verbs:

> Present, first aorist, perfect, aorist passive subjunctives of:
>> λύω, λύσω, ἔλυσα, λέλυκα, λέλυμμαι, ἐλύθην
> Second aorist active/middle subjunctive of:
>> λείπω, -λείψω, ἔλιπον, -λέλοιπα, -λέλειμμαι, -ελείφθην
> Second aorist passive subjunctive of:
>> γράφω, γράψω, ἔγραψα, γέγραφα, γέγραμμαι, ἐγράφην
> The subjunctives of:
>> εἰμί and οἶδα

Subjunctive Mood

	Present			Aorist		Perfect
	Present Indic.	Present Subj.	Future Indic.	First Aor. Subj.	Second Aor. Subj.	
	Active	Active	Active	Active	Active	Active
Sg. 1.	λύω	λύω	λύσω	λύσω	λίπω	λελυκώς ῶ
2.	λύεις	λύῃς	λύσεις	λύσῃς	λίπῃς	" ῇς
3.	λύει	λύῃ	λύσει	λύσῃ	λίπῃ	" ῇ
Pl. 1.	λύομεν	λύωμεν	λύσομεν	λύσωμεν	λίπωμεν	λελυκότες ῶμεν
2.	λύετε	λύητε	λύσετε	λύσητε	λίπητε	" ῆτε
3.	λύουσι(ν)	λύωσι(ν)	λύσουσι(ν)	λύσωσι(ν)	λίπωσι(ν)	" ῶσι(ν)

	Mid.-Pass.	Mid.-Pass.	Middle	Middle	Middle	Mid.-Pass.
Sg. 1.	λύομαι	λύωμαι	λύσομαι	λύσωμαι	λίπωμαι	λελυμένος ῶ
2.	λύῃ	λύῃ	λύσῃ	λύσῃ	λίπῃ	etc.
3.	λύεται	λύηται	λύσεται	λύσηται	λίπηται	
Pl. 1.	λυόμεθα	λυώμεθα	λυσόμεθα	λυσώμεθα	λιπώμεθα	
2.	λύεσθε	λύησθε	λύσεσθε	λύσησθε	λίπησθε	
3.	λύονται	λύωνται	λύσονται	λύσωνται	λίπωνται	

	First Aor. Indic. Passive	First Aor. Subj. Passive	Second Aor. Subj. Passive	
	(εἰμί)			(οἶδα)
Sg. 1. ῶ	Sg. 1. ἐλύθην	λυθῶ	γραφῶ	εἰδῶ
2. ῇς	2. ἐλύθης	λυθῇς	γραφῇς	εἰδῇς
3. ῇ	3. ἐλύθη	λυθῇ	γραφῇ	εἰδῇ
Pl. 1. ῶμεν	Pl. 1. ἐλύθημεν	λυθῶμεν	γφαφῶμεν	εἰδῶμεν
2. ῆτε	2. ἐλύθητε	λυθῆτε	γραφῆτε	εἰδῆτε
3. ῶσι	3. ἐλύθησαν	λυθῶσι(ν)	γραφῶσι(ν)	εἰδῶσι(ν)

4430. Mnemonic hints:

4430.1 It may be observed that in all the form-sets of the subjunctive represented, the pattern of theme vowel plus primary ending is identical for each set, including εἰμί and οἶδα, e.g. active second singular is always -ῃς, active third singular always -ῃ, etc.

4430.2 The only forms showing iota subscript with theme vowel are: second and third singular active (-ῃς, -ῃ) and second singular middle (-passive) (-ῃ). In all other forms the theme vowel is ω or η.

4430.3 The theme vowel ω replaces o of thematic conjugations in the indicative; η replaces ε.

4430.4 The future indicative active and middle is included for comparison because the first aorist subjunctive active and middle will look like the future indicative, except for theme vowel.

4430.5 The second aorist subjunctive, active/middle and passive, will look like the present subjunctive, except for difference in stem and accent.

4431. Notes:

4431.1 In the first aorist active/middle, the tense formative -σα is replaced by -σω/-σῃ, i.e. the α is lost. For this reason, and because the augment has also been dropped, the first aorist subjunctive closely resembles the future indicative active/middle.

4431.2 The aorist passive tense formative in the subjunctive is actually -θε- or -ε- (rather than -θη-, -η-): the ε contracts in each case with ω or η, yielding -ῶ- or -ῆ- (the accent falls on the contracted syllable).

4431.3 The difference between first and second perfect does not enter into the perfect subjunctive, except for the presence or absence of -κ- in the participle, since the perfect subjunctive is formed periphrastically.

444. The bulk of the subjunctive system is covered by the representative paradigms given in §443. A few form-sets that do not follow the same consistent pattern necessitate taking a closer look at: 1) contract verbs in the present tense, 2) μι-verbs in the present tense, 3) athematic or 'root' aorists.

444.1 *The subjunctive of contract verbs.* The subjunctive of contract verbs in -έω follows the regular pattern (§443) precisely, i.e. for -ει- of the indicative substitute -η-, and for -ου- of the indicative -ω-. The present subjunctive of contract verbs in -άω is identical with the indicative forms (§368), owing to the rules of contraction. The present subjunctive of verbs in -όω has been assimilated to the indicative (§368), on the analogy of verbs in -άω, although a few 'Attic' forms occur, i.e. -ω- where -ου- occurs in the indicative (the subjunctive of -όω verbs is not well attested).

444.2 *The present subjunctive of μι-verbs.* Μι-verbs with stems ending in η/α, η/ε, and υ (ἵστημι, τίθημι, δείκνυμι, §§370f.) follow the regular pattern (§443) in forming the present subjunctive, i.e. ω and η (or ῃ) throughout. Μι-verbs with stems in ω/ο (δίδωμι, §§370f.), however, show ω (or ῳ) throughout, with by-forms διδοῖς, διδοῖ in the active second and third singular appearing occasionally (but not in the NT).

444.3 *The athematic aorist subjunctive.* Verbs having a 'root' aorist (§§411, 412) form the subjunctive for the most part according to the regular pattern (§443): verbs with stems in η (α, ε) follow the regular alternation of ω and η; verbs with stems in ω (ο), show ω (ῳ) throughout (δίδωμι, γινώσκω), with by-forms in -οις, -οι in the active second and third singular (cf. §444.2).

The Optative Mood

0445. The optative has strongly retreated in hellenistic Greek by comparison with classical Greek. There are only 67 instances in the New Testament, a number of which appear in stereotyped phrases, e.g. μὴ γένοιτο, "God forbid," literally "may it not be" (Paul 14 times, Lk 20:16). The tense is either present or aorist, the person usually third singular.

445. *The characteristic feature of the optative* is the mood sign -ι-, which is joined with thematic or other vowel (-ιη- in athematic inflection). In the optative it never appears as subscript.

446. *The contours of the optative system* may be indicated by the following:

446.1 The optative is confined for all practical purposes, in hellenistic Greek, to the present and aorist tenses (§§300.2, 303, 3031.7–8).

446.2 The optative is built on the appropriate tense stem, *less augment* (§340.2).

446.3 Secondary personal endings are employed, except for the first singular -μι (a primary ending, §318), which is used in place of -ν everywhere but in the athematic aorist inflection.

446.4 The mood formative is -ι- or -ιη-.

447. *The optative in the present, first and second aorist.* The mood sign -ι- is joined to the theme vowel ο (always ο, not variable) in the present and second aorist, and to the σα of the first aorist tense formative; secondary endings (except first singular -μι) are suffixed.

	Present and Second Aorist Active	First Aorist Active
Sg. 1.	-οι-μι	-σαι-μι
2.	-οι-ς	-σαι-ς
3.	-οι	-σαι
Pl. 1.	-οι-μεν	-σαι-μεν
2.	-οι-τε	-σαι-τε
3.	-οιε-ν	-σαιε-ν

	Middle(-Passive)	Middle
Sg. 1.	-οι-μην	-σαι-μην
2.	-οι-ο (-οι-σο)	-σαι-ο (-αι-σο)
3.	-οι-το	-σαι-το
Pl. 1.	-οι-μεθα	-σαι-μεθα
2.	-οι-σθε	-σαι-σθε
3.	-οι-ντο	-σαι-ντο

4470. Notes:

4470.1 The middle (-passive) second singular loses the σ of the personal ending between vowels (§§3190.5, 930.21).

4470.2 The mood sign of the third plural active is actually -ιε- (cf. -ιη- in the athematic inflection).

4471. No forms of the present optative from contract or μι-verbs occur in the New Testament, with the exception of δυναίμην, δύναιτο from δύναμαι, *I am able*, and the third singular εἴη from εἰμί. Such forms, for the most part, are easily identified.

448. *The athematic aorist optative* (*active*). In the athematic inflection of verbs in the aorist tense (active, middle), the mood sign -ιη- is joined to the short stem vowel of the verb, and secondary endings suffixed:

ἵστημι, ἔστην (στα-)
Active

Sg. 1. σταίην	Pl. 1. σταίημεν
2. σταίης	2. σταίητε
3. σταίη	3. σταίησαν

Verbs with other stem vowels would be modified accordingly, e.g. θείην (τίθημι, θε-), ἀφείην (ἀφίημι, ἀφε-), δοίην (δίδωμι, δο-), γνοίην (γινώσκω, γνο-).

4480. Notes:

4480.1 The first singular is the regular secondary ending -ν. (As a general rule: mood formative -ι-, add -μι; mood formative -ιη-, add -ν.)

4480.2 The third plural is the alternate secondary ending of the third plural (§319), employed also with μι-verbs in the imperfect indicative (§404.3), 'root' aorists (§411), the pluperfect (§415), and the aorist passive (§420).

4481. The single athematic aorist middle in the New Testament is ὀναίμην (Philemon 20), from ὀνίνημι. The aorist middle forms, however, are 'regular' in following the inflection pattern of the singular (Smyth §416).

449. *Aorist passive optative.* The aorist passive optative is formed by suffixing the mood formative -ιη- to the tense formative -θε- (-ε-) and adding secondary *active* endings. (On the tense formative -θε-, with short vowel, cf. the subjunctive, §4431.2.) The aorist passive stem is also divested of augment, of course.

Sg. 1. -θείην (-είην) Pl. 1. -θείημεν (-είημεν)
   2. -θείης (-είης)   2. -θείητε (-είητε)
   3. -θείη (-είη)   3. -θείησαν (-είησαν)

Non-Indicative Moods:
Imperative/Infinitive/Participle

The Imperative Mood

0455. *Introduction.* The imperative mood in Greek, unlike English, is used in the third person as well as in the second person. There is no first person imperative in either language. The third person will have to be handled in translation by some linguistic device, e.g. 'Let him go,' 'Let them remain.' This particular device corresponds to the hortatory subjunctive (in Greek) of the first person, 'Let us go.' Thus, in English the linguistic device with 'let' is employed in the first and third persons, the imperative in the second person only; in Greek the first person is handled by the subjunctive, the second and third persons by the imperative.

455. *The contours of the imperative system* are indicated by the following generalizations:

455.1 The imperative mood, like the subjunctive, is confined to the present, aorist and perfect tenses (§§300.2, 442.1).

455.2 The perfect imperative is exceedingly rare in the New Testament, the active voice being represented by a single form from οἴδε, ἴστε, and the middle-passive attested only once (πεφίμωσο, Mk 4:39).

455.3 Like the subjunctive and optative, the imperative is built on the appropriate tense stem, *less augment*.

455.4 The personal endings employed with the imperative are in part distinctive. It will therefore be necessary to treat the personal endings with the imperative as a separate set (§456).

456. *The personal endings* used with the imperative are:

	Active	Middle
Sg. 2.	#, -ς, -θι	-σο : ου
3.	-τω	-σθω
Pl. 2.	-τε	-σθε
3.	-τωσαν	-σθωσαν

4560. Notes and mnemonic hints:

4560.1 The second person endings, -ς in the active singular, -σο, -τε, -σθε are identical with endings already learned: -ς, -τε, -σθε are both primary and secondary endings (the sets overlap at these points); -σο is a secondary ending (cf. §§318, 319).

4560.2 In the third plural the pluralizing ending -σαν has been added to -τω- and -σθω- respectively (in Attic the forms were -των and -σθων).

4560.3 A handy mnemonic device is: except for -θι (second singular active), forms with -τ- are active, forms with -θ- middle.

4560.4 Active forms, except for the second singular (which is highly irregular), begin with τ, middle forms with σ.

457. *The present imperative of ω-verbs (uncontracted and contracted).*

Active

Sg. 2. πίστευε	τίμα (α+ε)	ποίει (ε+ε)	πλήρου (ο+ε)
3. πιστευέτω	τιμάτω	ποιείτω	πληρούτω
Pl. 2. πιστεύετε	τιμᾶτε	ποιεῖτε	πληροῦτε
3. πιστευέτωσαν	τιμάτωσαν	ποιείτωσαν	πληρούτωσαν

Middle-Passive

Sg. 2. πιστεύου	τιμῶ (α+ου)	ποιοῦ (ε+ου)	πληροῦ (ο+ου)
3. πιστευέσθω	τιμάσθω (α+ε)	ποιείσθω (ε+ε)	πληρούσθω (ο+ε)
Pl. 2. πιστεύεσθε	τιμᾶσθε	ποιεῖσθε	πληροῦσθε
3. πιστευέσθωσαν	τιμάσθωσαν	ποιείσθωσαν	πληρούσθωσαν

4570. Notes:

4570.1 In thematic inflections (present imperative of ω-verbs, second aorist imperative), the theme vowel is always ε (cf. the optative where it is always ο, §447).

4570.2 The second singular active has no ending (in contract verbs, the ε contracts with the final stem vowel).

4570.3 The second singular middle-passive is the result of contraction (-εσο > -ου, §930.21).

4570.4 The theme vowel ε contracts with the final stem vowel in all contracted forms (the contractions are given in parentheses in the paradigms). The rules for contraction have been given in connection with the imperfect (§403, cf. §917).

4570.5 The second plurals, both active and middle-passive, are identical with the corresponding indicative forms.

458. *The present imperative of μι-verbs.*

Active

Sg. 2. ἴστη	τίθει	δίδου	δείκνυ
3. ἱστάτω	τιθέτω	διδότω	δεικνύτω
Pl. 2. ἵστατε	τίθετε	δίδοτε	δείκνυτε
3. ἱστάτωσαν	τιθέτωσαν	διδότωσαν	δεικνύτωσαν

Middle-Passive

Sg. 2. ἵστασο	τίθεσο	δίδοσο	δείκνυσο
3. ἱστάσθω	τιθέσθω	διδόσθω	δεικνύσθω
Pl. 2. ἵστασθε	τίθεσθε	δίδοσθε	δείκνυσθε
3. ἱστάσθωσαν	τιθέσθωσαν	διδόσθωσαν	δεικνύσθωσαν

4580. Notes:

4580.1 Second singular active: τίθει (τιθε-ε) and δίδου (διδο-ε) have gone over to the thematic inflection (cf. the imperfect of the same verbs, §4041.2); otherwise the stem vowel is long where there is no ending (ἴστη).

4580.2 Second singular middle-passive: -σο does not lose σ and contract (cf. the indicative, §404.3).

459. *The present imperative of* εἰμί.

Sg. 2. ἴσθι	Pl. 2. (ἔστε)
3. ἔστω, ἤτω	3. ἔστωσαν

4590. Notes:

4590.1 The second singular ἴσθι is identical with the corresponding form of οἶδα: ἴσθι (perfect active). The identity in second singular forms may have led to confusion in the second plural forms ἔστε (εἰμί), ἴστε (οἶδα); Bl-D §353(6).

4590.2 The second plural form, ἔστε, appears to be virtually obsolete by New Testament times (Bl-D §98).

460. *The first and second aorist imperative.*

	Second Aorist	First Aorist
	λαμβάνω, ἔλαβον	πιστεύω, ἐπίστευσα
Active		
Sg. 2.	λάβε	πίστευσον
3.	λαβέτω	πιστευσάτω
Pl. 2.	λάβετε	πιστεύσατε
3.	λαβέτωσαν	πιστευσάτωσαν

Middle

Sg. 2.	λαβοῦ	πίστευσαι
3.	λαβέσθω	πιστευσάσθω
Pl. 2.	λάβεσθε	πιστεύσασθε
3.	λαβέσθωσαν	πιστευσάσθωσαν

4600. Notes:

4600.1 Except for stem, the second aorist follows the thematic inflection of the present tense exactly (§457; the notes in §4570.1–3 apply to the second aorist also).

4600.2 Except for second singulars, the tense formative -σα appears throughout in the first aorist imperative.

4600.3 The endings for the second singulars are irregular (origin unknown); the second singular middle ending -σαι is identical with that of the first aorist active optative third singular (§447) and the active infinitive (§4662).

4600.4 Liquid first aorists (§410), of course, lose the σ of the tense formative, e.g. μεῖνον, μεινάτω, etc. (μένω, ἔμεινα).

461. *Athematic aorist imperative.* The 'root' aorists (§§411, 412) form the imperative as follows:

Active

	ἵστημι, ἔστην	ἀναβαίνω, ἀνέβην	γινώσκω, ἔγνων
Sg. 2.	στῆθι (-στα)	ἀνάβηθι (-βα)	γνῶθι
3.	στήτω	ἀναβάτω	γνώτω
Pl. 2.	στῆτε	ἀνάβατε	γνῶτε
3.	στήτωσαν	ἀναβάτωσαν	γνώτωσαν

	τίθημι, ἔθηκα	ἀφίημι, ἀφῆκα	δίδωμι, ἔδωκα
Sg. 2.	θές	ἄφες	δός
3.	θέτω	ἀφέτω	δότω
Pl. 2.	θέτε	ἄφετε	δότε
3.	θέτωσαν	ἀφέτωσαν	δότωσαν

Middle

τίθημι, ἔθηκα

Sg. 2.	θοῦ
3.	θέσθω
Pl. 2.	θέσθε
3.	θέσθωσαν

4610. Notes:

4610.1 The personal endings are added directly to the stem.

4610.2 The stem vowel is consistently long (στῆθι, γνῶθι) or short, except in βαίνω.

4610.3 The second singular active ending may be either -θι, -ς, or nothing (-στα, -βα).

4610.4 The only middle forms attested in the New Testament are from τίθημι. The second singular middle contracts: θοῦ < θεσο.

462. *The perfect imperative.* The perfect active imperative, even in classical Greek, was formed periphrastically (perfect participle plus the present imperative of εἰμί). The perfect active is not attested in the New Testament. The perfect middle-passive is almost as rare (§455.2). As in the indicative, the perfect middle-passive imperative is formed by adding the appropriate personal endings directly to the perfect stem:

> Sg. 2. πεπίστευσο
> 3. πεπιστεύσθω
> Pl. 2. πεπίστευσθε
> 3. πεπιστεύσθωσαν

463. *The aorist passive imperative.* The aorist passive imperative is formed by joining *active* endings (as elsewhere) to the aorist passive tense base, less augment:

	Second Aorist	First Aorist
	φαίνω, ἐφάνην	πιστεύω, ἐπιστεύθην
Sg. 2.	φάνηθι	πιστεύθητι
3.	φανήτω	πιστευθήτω
Pl. 2.	φάνητε	πιστεύθητε
3.	φανήτωσαν	πιστευθήτωσαν

4630. Note: The second singular personal ending is -θι, which is deaspirated (§928.2) when it follows upon θ of the tense formative: πιστεύθητι.

The Infinitive

464. *Identification of the infinitive.* Like the indicative and the subjunctive, the infinitive is in common use. Instant identification will greatly facilitate reading. Two clues will be helpful in spotting the infinitive:

464.1 All infinitives, except those of contract verbs in the present, will end in -ειν or -αι (-αι is not necessarily the whole ending).

464.2   The middle-passive forms always end in σθαι (excluding the aorist passive, of course, which always takes *active* endings, §§393, 420, 443, 449, 463).

465.   *Endings of the infinitive.* The endings attached to the respective tense bases are as follows:

Active

-εν: present, future, second aorist (thematic inflection)

-αι: first aorist

-ναι: present, 'root' aorist, perfect, and aorist passive

Middle(-Passive)

-σθαι: present middle-passive, future middle-passive, aorist middle, perfect middle-passive.

466.   The infinitive is employed in the present, future, aorist, and perfect forms in the New Testament (the future perfect is lacking, cf. §300.2). The future passive infinitive is also unattested. The infinitive, like the other non-indicative moods, is built on the appropriate tense base, *less augment.*

4660.   *Synopsis of the forms of the infinitive* by tense, voice, and type of inflection.

	Active	Middle(-Passive)
4660.1	**Present** (active, -εν, -ναι / mid.-pass., -σθαι)	

Active	Middle(-Passive)
ω-verbs uncontracted	
πιστεύειν (-ε-εν)	πιστεύεσθαι
ω-verbs contracted	
τιμᾶν (-αε-εν)	τιμᾶσθαι (-αε-σθαι)
ποιεῖν (-εε-εν)	ποιεῖσθαι (-εε-σθαι)
δηλοῦν (-οε-εν)	δηλοῦσθαι (-οε-σθαι)
μι-verbs	
ἱστάναι	ἵστασθαι
τιθέναι	τίθεσθαι
διδόναι	δίδοσθαι
(εἰμί) εἶναι	

4660.2   **Future** (active, -εν / middle, -σθαι)

       regular
           λύσειν (σε-εν)   λύσεσθαι
       liquid future
           μενεῖν (εε-εν)   μενεῖσθαι (εε-σθαι)
           (εἰμί)   ἔσεσθαι

4660.3   **Aorist** (active, -εν, -αι, -εναι / middle, -σθαι)

       first aorist
           πιστεῦσαι   πιστεύσασθαι
       second aorist
           λιπεῖν (-ε-εν)   λιπέσθαι
       'root' aorist
           στῆναι (-η-εναι)   (στῆσθαι)
           θεῖναι (-ε-εναι)   θέσθαι
           δοῦναι (-ο-εναι)   (δόσθαι)
           -βῆναι (-η-εναι)
           γνῶναι (-ω-εναι)

4660.4   **Perfect** (active, -ναι / middle-passive, -σθαι)

       first perfect
           πεπιστευκέναι   πεπιστεύσθαι
       second perfect
           γεγραφέναι   γεγράφθαι (-φσθαι)
                               δεδέχθαι (-χσθαι)
                               πεπεῖσθαι (-σσθαι)
                               ἐστάλθαι (-λσθαι)

4660.5   **Aorist Passive** (-ναι)

       first aorist passive
           πιστευθῆναι
       second aorist passive
           γραφῆναι

4661. Notes:

4661.1 For the contractions involved in §4660, see §369. Cf. §917 for the additional rules and qualifications necessary to cover all forms of contraction in the infinitive.

4661.2 For the loss of σ in liquid futures, §4660.2, s. §376; for the same phenomenon in §4660.4, s. §§391.1, 392.2. Cf. §930.1.

4661.3 The present infinitives of ω-verbs, the future infinitives, the second aorist infinitives, and apparently the perfect active infinitives are formed with thematic vowel (always ε). The 'root' aorist infinitive suffix is apparently -εναι. (giving the appearance of a theme vowel).

4662. *Possible confusions.* The infinitive forms in -ειν, -ναι, and -σθαι are distinctive in the verb system, except for the marginal similarities of the pluperfect active first singular in -ειν. The first aorist infinitive in -σαι, however, is like the second singular middle-passive ending -σαι, which appears (in uncontracted form) in the present middle-passive of μι-verbs (§3700), and in the perfect middle-passive (§390); the former have infinitives in -ναι, the latter has an infinitive in -σθαι. The first aorist active infinitive will also look like the third singular active optative, except for accent. As a consequence, confusions should be rare.

The Participle

0467. Since the participle is a verbal adjective (§§013.3, 101, 247, 300), it manifests characteristics of both verb and noun. It is inflected like a noun since it exhibits *gender, number,* and *case* (§§246–250). But it also has *tense* and *voice,* as a consequence of which the participle is formed on the various tense stems of the verb, and is subject to active/middle-passive and active/middle/passive distinctions like the verb.

467. Four tenses of the participle are in common use (the future perfect participle was very rare even in classical Greek): present, future, aorist, perfect (cf. §300.2). There will thus be participles formed on each of the principal parts or tense bases, in accordance with the pattern of the finite verb: I. present active and middle-passive participles, II. future active and middle, III. aorist active and middle, IV. perfect active, V. perfect middle-passive, and VI. aorist passive and future passive. As in the case of the infinitive (§466) , there is no imperfect or pluperfect participle. Like the other non-indicative moods, the participle is built on the appropriate tense stem, *less augment.*

468. *The formation of the tense stems of the participles.* Three general rules cover the formation of the tense bases of participles: to the tense base of the finite verb, less augment (if any), add:

468.1 Thematic vowel -o- (never ε, because it always comes before μ or ν, §322) if the corresponding finite tense of the verb is inflected with thematic vowel (the participle always follows the finite tense in this respect);

468.2 The participle stem formative -ντ- to all active participles (except the perfect) and to the aorist passive participle (§247), -μεν- to all middle and middle-passive participles and to the future passive participle (§250), -(κ)οτ- or -(κ)υς, (masc.-neut./fem.) to all perfect active participles (§248);

468.3 Case endings in accordance with the rules set out in §§246–250.

4680. *Present, future, and second aorist active participles* with thematic vowel are formed on the respective tense stems (less augment) by suffixing -ο-ντ- (which is visible e.g. in the masc. gen. sg.; on the nom. forms and the formation of the feminine, s. §§247–2471).

4680.1 πιστεύων, πιστεύουσα, πιστεῦον; gen. sg. πιστεύοντος, πιστευούσης, πιστεύοντος; etc. (present active)

4680.2 πιστεύσων, πιστεύσουσα, πιστεῦσον; gen. sg. πιστεύσοντος, πιστευσούσης, πιστεύσοντος; etc. (future active)

4680.3 λαβών, λαβοῦσα, λαβόν; gen. sg. λαβόντος, λαβούσης, λαβόντος; etc. (aorist active, < λαμβάνω)

Present, future, and second aorist participles are inflected exactly alike, the only difference among them being the tense base of the verb, e.g.

λείπων,	λείπουσα,	λεῖπον;	λείποντος,	etc.
λείψων,	λείψουσα,	λεῖψον;	λείψοντος,	etc.
λιπών,	λιποῦσα,	λιπόν;	λιπόντος,	etc.

For the full inflection s. §§247–2471.

4681. *Present, future, and second aorist middle (-passive) participles* are also formed on the appropriate tense stem (less augment), plus thematic vowel and -μεν- with case endings:

ἀκουόμενος,	ἀκουομένη,	ἀκουόμενον	(present middle-passive)
ἀκουσόμενος,	ἀκουσομένη,	ἀκουσόμενον	(future middle)
λαβόμενος,	λαβομένη,	λαβόμενον	(aorist middle)

4682. *Present active/middle-passive participles* of contract verbs follow the patterns indicated in §§4680–4681. For inflection s. §2471.40.

4683. *The future passive participle* is formed on the future passive tense stem by joining -μεν- to the thematic vowel (ο); like the finite forms, it may be either a first or second future passive, i.e. with or without -ϑ- (§394).

> πιστευϑησόμενος, πιστευϑησομένη, πιστευϑησόμενον, etc.
>
> φυησόμενος, φυησομένη, φυησόμενον, etc.

4684. *Present and 'root' aorist active participles of μι-verbs, first aorist active participles, and aorist passive participles* are formed on the respective tense stems (less augment) by joining -ντ- directly to the tense stem, i.e. without thematic vowel.

4684.1

ἵστημι:	nom. sg.	ἱστάς,	ἱστᾶσα,	ἱστάν
	gen. sg.	ἱστάντος,	ἱστάσης,	ἱστάντος etc.
τίθημι:	nom. sg.	τιθείς,	τιθεῖσα,	τιθέν
	gen. sg.	τιθέντος,	τιθείσης,	τιθέντος etc.
δίδωμι:	nom. sg.	διδούς,	διδοῦσα,	διδόν
	gen. sg.	διδόντος,	διδούσης,	διδόντος etc.
δείκνυμι:	nom. sg.	δεικνύς,	δεικνῦσα,	δεικνύν
	gen. sg.	δεικνύντος,	δεικνύσης,	δεικνύντος

4684.2 ἔστην: στάς, στᾶσα, στάν; gen. sg. στάντος, στάσης, στάντος; etc.

4684.3 ἔλυσα: λύσας, λύσασα, λῦσαν; gen. sg. λύσαντος, λυσάσης, λύσαντος; etc.

4684.4 ἐλύϑη: λυϑείς, λυϑεῖσα, λυϑέν; gen. sg. λυϑέντος, λυϑείσης, λυϑέντος; etc. ἐστάϑην: σταϑείς, σταϑεῖσα, σταϑέν; gen. sg. σταϑέντος, σταϑείσης, σταϑέντος; etc.

For the nom. sg. forms, the formation of the feminine, and inflection, s. §§247–2471.

4685. *The middle and middle-passive participles* of the same groups of verbs (§4684) (the aorist passive excluded, of course) are formed by suffixing -μεν- plus case endings directly to the respective tense stems. For inflection, s. §250.

4685.1 ἱστάμενος, ἱσταμένη, ἱστάμενον, etc.

4685.2 ϑέμενος, ϑεμένη, ϑέμενον, etc.

4685.3 λυσάμενος, λυσαμένη, λυσάμενον, etc.

4686. *The perfect active participle* may take the form of either a first or second perfect, with or without -κ-, corresponding to the finite forms (§§3850, 3870).

πεπίστευκα:	πεπιστευκώς,	πεπιστευκυῖα,	πεπιστευκός
	πεπιστευκότος,	πεπιστευκυίας,	πεπιστευκότος
οἶδα (§§338, 443):	εἰδώς,	εἰδυῖα,	εἰδός
	εἰδότος,	εἰδυίας,	εἰδότος

For the nom. sg. forms, the formation of the feminine, and full inflection, s. §§248–2490.

469. 4687. *The perfect middle-passive participle* is formed on the perfect middle-passive tense stem by adding -μεν- plus case endings directly to the stem.

πεπιστευμένος,	-μένη,	-μένον
γεγραμένος,	-μένη,	-μένον
etc.		

For inflection s. §250.

469. *Identification of participles.*

4691. All middle(-passive) participles and future passive participles have the suffix -μεν-. They are therefore readily identified. Tense signals will be the same as those found in the corresponding forms of the finite verb (except for augment).

4692. Active participles (except perfect) and aorist passive participles generally exhibit the suffix -ντ-. But this suffix is not apparent in the masc., neut. nom. sg. forms, in the masc., neut. dat. pl. forms, and in the feminine forms because of phonetic changes (§§247–2471).

469.3 Perfect active participles generally exhibit the suffix -(κ)οτ- (masc.-neut.) or -υι- (fem). But because of phonetic change (§§249–2490), the τ is lost in the masc., neut. nom. singulars and in the masc., neut. dat. plurals.

469.4 The tense signals of active participles will be the same as those associated with the corresponding finite forms, except for augment.

Lesson 31

Verbs: Tense Base Formation

475.   The inflection of the Greek verb has been treated in relation to six tense systems, at the head of each of which stands the principal part of the verb upon which all the forms in that system are built (§303). The tenses were divided into primary and secondary tenses, owing to the distinction between primary and secondary endings (§317), and the association of augment exclusively with the latter (§0335). The primary tenses were presented first in the order in which the principal parts on which they are built are normally listed in grammars and lexica (§§366–395):

I.   Present, active/middle-passive;
II. Future, active/middle;
IV. Perfect, active;
V.   Perfect, middle-passive;
VI. Future, passive.

The secondary tenses were then treated in the same order (§§400–4241):

I.   Imperfect, active/ middle-passive;
III. Aorist, active/middle;
IV. Pluperfect, active;
V.   Pluperfect, middle-passive;
VI. Aorist, passive.

In addition, types of inflection were recognized within several of the tense systems. E.g. there were three inflectional subdivisions in the present system (including the imperfect): ω-verbs that do not contract, ω-verbs that do contract, and μι-verbs (§366). A summary of such inflectional subcategories follows.

4750. Inflectional Categories in the Verb System (Indicative Mood)

I. Present

Present active/middle-passive

    1. ω-verbs uncontracted (§§367–3670)

    2. ω-verbs contracted (§§368–3691)

    3. μι-verbs (§§370–3712)

Imperfect active/middle-passive

    1. ω-verbs uncontracted (§§401–4010)

    2. ω-verbs contracted (§§402–4031)

    3. μι-verbs (§§404–4050)

II. Future

Future active/middle

    1. regular (§§373–3750)

    2. liquid (§§376, 377)

      -ίζω verbs (§3760)

    3. Doric (§3761)

    4. Without tense formant (§3763)

III. Aorist

Aorist active/middle

    1. second aorist (§§407–4070)

    2. first aorist (§§408–409)

    3. liquid aorists (§410)

    4. 'root' aorists (§411)

    5. κ-aorists (§§412–4121)

    6. mixed (§4122)

IV. Perfect

Perfect active

    1. first perfect (§§385, 386–3860)

    2. second perfect (§§3850, 387–3880)

Pluperfect active

    1. first pluperfect (§§415–4150)

    2. second pluperfect (§§415–4150)

V. Perfect Middle-Passive

Perfect middle-passive (§§389–3922)

Pluperfect middle-passive (§§416–418)

VI. Aorist Passive

Aorist passive

    1. first aorist passive (§§421–422)

    2. second aorist passive (§§423–4241)

Future passive

    1. first future passive (§§393–3940)

    2. second future passive (§§393–3940)

0476.   Attention thus far has been devoted primarily to the reading *down* the columns of the graphic sketch of the verb given in §303, aside from §§0346–3500, 355–361, where some preliminary account was given of the formation of the tense bases or principal parts of the verb. The next and final step in the mastery of the Greek verb system is to learn to read *across* the columns in §303, i.e. to learn the patterns by which the tense bases or principle parts are formed. In this exercise, one is only considering the same fundamental set of variables, e.g. augment, reduplication, tense suffix, from a different point of view.

476.   Variety in the formation of principal parts falls under two major headings:

476.1   Phonetic change in the verb base occasioned by the juxtaposition of tense formatives and verb bases ending in certain vowels and consonants: variety of this type can be reduced to patterns, and the patterns cover the great majority of verbs.

476.2   The formation of the present base or tense stem: in a large number of verbs the same verb base is employed in forming all of the principal parts, but there are five additional categories of verbs (some also quite large) in which the present base is significantly different from that employed in forming the other principal parts.

Patterns of Tense Stem Formation

477.   In lesson 23 (§§355–361) some of the more common patterns of tense stem development were noted. These patterns may now be expanded and systematized.

477.1   There are three basic patterns of tense stem development corresponding to the three types of verb stems: pattern A for verbs whose stems end in a vowel; pattern B for verbs whose stems end in a stop consonant; pattern C for verbs whose stems end in a liquid or nasal.

477.2   Pattern A may be divided into two sub-types, the only difference between them being whether the final stem vowel is constant (A_1), or a short stem vowel in the present base is lengthened before the tense formant in the remaining tenses (A$_2$) (§358). Pattern B is divided into three sub-categories in relation to the phonetic changes occasioned by the nature of the final stop consonant: labials (π, β, φ) constitute pattern B$_1$, palatals (κ, γ, χ) pattern B$_2$, dentals (τ, δ, ϑ) pattern B$_3$. The C pattern varies slightly between verb stems ending in a liquid (λ, ρ) (C$_1$), and those ending in a nasal (μ, ν) (C$_2$).

Variety in tense stem development is thus occasioned largely by differences in the way the verb stem ends.

478. *Patterns of tense stem formation.* In accordance with the remarks in §477, seven patterns of tense stem development may be distinguished:

A$_1$:	-ω	-σω	ἐ - - - σα	πε - - - κα	πε - - - μαι	ἐ - - - ϑην
	-άω	-άσω	ἐ - - - ασα	πε - - - ακα	πε - - - αμαι	ἐ - - - άϑην
A$_2$:	-άω, -έω	-ήσω	ἐ - - - ησα	πε - - - ηκα	πε - - - ημαι	ἐ - - - ήϑην
	-όω	-ώσω	ἐ - - - ωσα	πε - - - ωκα	πε - - - ωμαι	ἐ - - - ώϑην
B$_1$:	-πω	-ψω	ἐ - - - ψα	πε - - - πα	πε - - - μμαι	ἐ - - - φϑην
				(πε - - - φα)		
B$_2$:	-κω	-ξω	ἐ - - - ξα	πε - - - κα	πε - - - γμαι	ἐ - - - χϑην
				(πε - - - γα)		
				(πε - - - χα)		
B$_3$:	-δω	-σω	ἐ - - - σα	πε - - - κα	πε - - - σμαι	ἐ - - - σϑην
C$_1$:	-λω	-λῶ	ἐ - - - λα	πε - - - λκα	πε - - - λμαι	ἐ - - - λϑην
C$_2$:	-νω	-νῶ	ἐ - - - να	πε - - - γκα	πε - - - μμαι	ἐ - - - νϑην

In the schematic outline above, ἐ represents any form of augment, πε- any form of reduplication. The final element of the verb base is given in every instance, except in the case of regular vowel verbs (i.e. A$_1$, first line).

4780. *Notes on pattern A.*

4780.1 Regular vowel verbs develop their principal parts in accordance with the model given in §347.2 (πιστεύω is used as the model verb): A$_1$.

4780.2 Some contract verbs in -άω retain α (rather than lengthening it to η: A$_2$) in the formation of the remaining tenses (§358.1). In the stems of these verbs α usually follows ε, ι or ρ (cf. first declension nouns, §1321.1). The pattern of these verbs is thus indistinguishable from that of regular vowel verbs: A$_1$.

4780.3 The majority of contract verbs in -άω, -έω and -όω *lengthen* the final stem vowel to η and ω, respectively, before the tense formatives or suffixes (§358.2–3): A$_2$.

4780.4 A few verbs in -έω irregularly retain the short final ε before the tense suffixes (cf. §4780.2, verbs in -άω). These verbs therefore follow the regular vowel verb pattern: A₁.

4781.   *Notes on pattern B.*

Verbs with stems ending in a stop exhibit three closely related patterns in the development of their principal parts, depending on whether the verb stem ends in a labial (π, β, φ), a palatal (κ, γ, χ), or a dental (τ, δ, θ). These patterns may be designated B₁, B₂, and B₃ respectively.

4781.1 Verbs with stems ending in a labial (π, β, φ) undergo regular phonetic change when the final stem consonant is juxtaposed with the tense suffix: π, β, φ, + σ = ψ (future, aorist); π, β, φ before μ > μ (perf. mid.-pass.); π, β before θ is aspirated, i.e. > φ (aor. pass.): B₁.

4781.2 Verbs with stems ending in a palatal (κ, γ, χ) undergo regular phonetic change when the final stem consonant is juxtaposed with the tense suffix: κ, γ, χ + σ = ξ. (future, aorist); κ, χ before μ > γ (perf. mid.-pass.); κ, γ before θ is aspirated, i.e. > χ (aor. pass.): B₂.

4781.3 Verbs with stems ending in a dental (τ, δ, θ) undergo comparable phonetic changes: τ, δ, θ + σ =σ (future, aorist); τ, δ, θ before κ disappears (perf. act.); τ, δ, θ before μ, θ > σ (perf. mid.-pass., aor. pass.): B₃.

N. B₃ is virtually identical with A, except that the dental is retained as σ in the perfect middle-passive and the aorist passive.

4782.   *Notes on pattern C.*

Verbs with stems ending in a liquid (λ, ρ) or nasal (μ, ν) also undergo certain phonetic changes, some of which primarily affect the tense suffix:

4782.1 Verbs with bases ending in a liquid or nasal regularly have liquid futures (§376), i.e. "contract" futures in -ῶ; they also regularly have liquid aorists (§410), i.e. the σ of the tense formative is lost.

4782.2 Verbs with bases ending in a liquid are subject to no further modification, but verbs with stems in ν (μ does not come into consideration here) show two other modifications: ν before κ > γ (perf. act.); ν before μ > μ (perf. mid.-pass.). Since there is a slight difference between liquids and nasals with respect to the perfect active and perfect middle-passive tense bases, the liquid pattern may be designated C₁, and the nasal pattern C₂. Where this difference is not relevant, the pattern may be designated simply C.

Formation of the Present Tense Stem

479.1 Where an identical verb base persists through all tense systems, any particular form of the verb can be inferred from the general rules governing the formation of principal parts (patterns *A, B, C*). Unfortunately, the verb base is not constant in every case. Where the verb base is modified, *it is usually the present tense base that is modified by expansion.*

479.2 *Verb base and present base.* In §§3550f. and again in §479.1 reference was made to the verb base. The *verb base* is the actual or hypothetical base from which all the actual forms of the verb, including the tense bases or stems, are presumably derived. As an illustration, the base of δίδωμι is δω-/δο- (the base exhibits both long and short vowels), from which the present base is formed by reduplication (§345.2); the remaining tense bases then appear (in view of the verb base) to be perfectly regular: δώ-σω, ἔ-δω-κα (κ-aorist, §412), δέ-δω-κα, δέ-δο-μαι, ἐ-δό-θην. The base of ἑτοιμάζω is ἑτοιμαδ- (§359), from which the present base is formed by the addition of the suffix ι̯ : ἑτοιμαδ-ι̯ω > ἑτοιμάζω. Since ἑτοιμάζω has a base in a dental, the remaining principal parts follow pattern B₃: ἑτοιμάσω, ἡτοίμασα, ἡτοίμακα, ἡτοίμασμαι, ἡτοιμάσθην.

480. The reasons for gaining a clear picture of the ways in which the present tense stem is formed from the verb stem are two:

480.1 Where the base of the verb is basically modified at all (i.e. where it is modified other than by augment, reduplication, phonetic change occasioned by tense suffixes, vowel gradation), it is the present base that is customarily modified by expansion. *Application of the patterns of tense base formation will therefore depend upon knowledge of the verb base rather than of the present tense stem,* which is the one usually given in lexica and grammars.

480.2 In moving from text to lexicon or grammar (to learn the meaning or syntax of a verb), in the case of a form that does not belong to the present tense system, *it will be necessary to be able to estimate the present tense base.*

   Since students need to be able to move with facility in either direction—from lexical to any particular form, and from any particular form to lexical entry—they need to acquire a precise range of expectation regarding the relation of verb base and present base. It is not necessary, indeed not entirely desirable, to learn principal parts by rote if one is thoroughly familiar with the limited range of possibilities. And a modest amount of practice with actual verb forms in the text will turn educated guesses into native responses.

481.   *The formation of the present tense stem from the verb base.* The ways in which the present tense stem is formed from the verb base can be reduced to a highly simplified, yet for most purposes quite adequate, schema consisting of five major divisions:

    I. Present base = verb base

    II. Present base = verb base + τ

    III. Present base = verb base + ι̯

    IV. Present base = verb base + ν, αν, νε, νυ (ννυ), νι̯

    V. Present base = verb base + σκ, ισκ

Reduplication of the present base (§345.2) is not taken into account in this schema, but the phenomenon is found in verbs of classes I and V. In addition, a complete catalogue of verbs will include a class VI consisting of a very small number of "irregular" verbs which require two or more dissimilar verb bases or "roots" to make up a full complement of principal parts.

This schema is elaborated in §§482–487; the discussion may serve as a commentary on the catalogue of verbs to be found as Appendix III.

482.   *Class I: The present base = the verb base.* In this class the present base is identical with the verb base, except for possible vowel gradation and reduplication. Verbs of class I that reduplicate the verb stem to form the present stem have been collected into subclass I.7 to make their presence conspicuous .

482.1   Verbs may be conjugated in the present tense with thematic vowel (ω-verbs) or without thematic vowel (μι-verbs) (§§366–3661). Although few in number, μι-verbs of class I are often of high frequency. For that reason they have been collected into category I.6. Some class I μι-verbs reduplicate the present stem: these are to be found in I.7b. (Other μι-verbs add -νυ-or -ννυ- to the verb base to form the present base and so belong to class IV: ν-class.)

482.2   Subclasses I.1-I.4 refer, insofar as possible, to patterns of tense base formation (§§476–4782): I.1 = A_1; I.2 = A_2; I.3 = B; I.4 = C.

482.3   Verbs with vowel stems (ω-verbs) are divided between I.1. and I.2. Subclass I.2 contains contract verbs that lengthen the final stem vowel before the tense formant or ending in tenses other than the present (pattern A_2) (in the present tense, the stem vowel contracts with the thematic vowel, §§368ff.). Subclass I.1b contains contract verbs in -άω that retain α in the elaboration of principal parts; there is thus no difference in pattern between these contract verbs and regular vowel bases in class I (I.1a) (pattern A_1).

482.30 Verbs requiring special notice in subclasses I.1–4 are rare.

The principal parts of ἕλκω (I.1a) are derived from ἑλκύω so that the only aberration is an alternate spelling of the present base.

The common verb ἔχω (I.3b) is derived from a hypothetical verb base *σεχ-: the second aorist, ἔ-σχ-ον, shows the base with a zero form of the base vowel; initial σ before a vowel often becomes rough breathing, as in the future form ἕξω. The imperfect is εἶχον, indicating the former presence of σ (§3371). The perfect, ἔσχηκα, is from a base, σχη-.

ψύχω (I.3b) has a second future passive, ψυγήσομαι, although the base is ψυχ-. New hellenistic second aorist (future) passives, with bases ending in stops, prefer a voiced stop even where it is not original (Bl-D §76(1)).

κλίνω and κρίνω (I.4) represent a small group of verbs that lose ν from the verb base in the perfect active, perfect middle-passive, and aorist passive (Smyth §491).

482.4 Into subclass I.5 are collected verbs of class I that show some minor variation in forming the present base from the verb base: I.5a, verbs with vowel stems in ευ that lose υ before the thematic vowel in the present tense (= pattern A$_1$); I.5b, verbs with vowel stems in ε that lose ε before the thematic vowel in the present tense (they will thus follow pattern A$_2$ in developing the remaining principal parts); I.5c, verbs with consonant stems that add ε to form the present base (they follow a B pattern in the remaining tense bases); I.5d, verbs in -έω (contract verbs) that retain ε before the tense formant (cf. I.1b), but do so irregularly. The number of verbs in these subcategories is very small.

482.5 ῥέω and χέω (I.5a) are both derived from bases in ευ-: ῥευ-, χευ-. χέω no longer shows the base χευ-, but exhibits only bases with a weak grade of the original base vowel: χε-, χυ- (§911.3) .

4820. The structure of class I may be summarized:

    I.1. Vowel stems (pattern A$_1$)
        I.1a. Vowel stems in ι, υ, αυ, ευ, (ει, ου) (uncontracted)
        I.1b. Vowel stems in α (contract verbs)
    I.2. Vowel stems (pattern A$_2$)
        I.2a. Vowel stems in α (contract verbs)
        I.2b. Vowel stems in ε (contract verbs)
        I.2c. Vowel stems in ο (contract verbs)

I.3. Consonant stems in a stop (pattern B)

I.3a. Consonant stems in a labial (π, β, φ) (B$_1$)

I.3b. Consonant stems in a palatal (κ, γ, χ) (B$_2$)

I.3c. Consonant stems in a dental (τ, δ, ϑ) (B$_3$)

I.4. Consonant stems in a liquid or nasal (λ, ρ; μ, ν) (C)

I.5. Verbs related to classes I.1–4 but showing some irregularity

I.5a. Vowel stems in ευ which lose υ

I.5b. Vowel stems in ε which lose ε

I.5c. Consonant stems which add ε

I.5d. Vowel stems in -έω showing some irregularity (cf. I.2b)

I.6. Μι-verbs

I.7. Verbs of class I which reduplicate the verb base to form the present base

I.7a. Ω-verbs

I.7b. Μι-verbs

483. *Class II: The present base = the verb base + τ.* In this class τ is added to the verb base to form the present base. All class II verbs have labial stems so they will follow pattern B$_1$ in the elaboration of principal parts.

484. *Class III: The present base = the verb base + ι̯.* To form the present base in this class ι̯ (consonantal ι) is added to the verb base, occasioning a variety of phonetic changes. The rather large class is subdivided on the basis of these changes.

484.1 Subclass III.1 is comprised of verbs with present tenses in -ζω. The ζ is produced by the juxtaposition of ι̯ with δ or γ. Since verbs with verb bases ending in δ will follow B$_3$, in distinction from verb bases ending in γ (a palatal), they are collected into III.1a; verb bases ending in γ, with present tenses in -ζω, are entered in III.1b, and follow pattern B$_2$.

484.10 Many of the verbs in III.1a have bases that do not actually end in δ, but these same verbs elaborate their principal parts for the most part as though they did. This class was being enlarged by analogy and the verbal system simplified at the same time. Of the 168 verbs listed in III.1a, only two show any deviation from pattern B$_3$ (the pattern for dentals) : ἁρπάζω has a second aorist passive ἡρπάγην, indicating a verb base in -γ; σῴζω has an aorist passive ἐσώϑην, indicating a verb base σω-. All other verbs in this category have come to conform to the dental pattern. Cf. Bl-D §71.

484.11 As in the case of III.1a, not all the verbs in III.1b have stems ending in γ. However, only one verb shows any deviation from the palatal pattern (B₂): στηρίζω has a by-form of the first aorist, ἐστήρισα (a dental form); the dominant form has become ἐστήριξα (palatal). Cf. Bl-D §71.

484.2 Subclass III.2 is comprised of verbs with present tenses in -σσω. The -σσ- is produced by the juxtaposition of ι with κ or χ and, by analogy, with γ or τ. Since verbs in this class have verb bases ending in a palatal, they will follow pattern B₂ in the elaboration of principal parts.

484.20 The only verb showing any deviation from pattern B₂ in III.2 is πλάσσω. It has a first aorist ἔπλασα, and a first aorist passive ἐπλάσθην (dental pattern).

484.3 Subclass III.3 is comprised of verbs with present tenses in -λλω. The -λλ- is produced by the juxtaposition of ι with λ (assimilation, §932.4). Since these verbs have verb bases in a liquid (λ) , they follow pattern C₁, in the elaboration of principal parts.

484.4 Subclass III.4 is comprised of verbs with verb bases ending in αν, αρ; εν, ερ. When ι is added to the verb base to form the present base, it affects the preceding vowel: αν, αρ > αιν, αιρ; εν, ερ > ειν, ειρ. Since the verb bases end in ρ (a liquid) or ν (a nasal), these verbs follow patterns C₁ or C₂ in the elaboration of principal parts.

484.40 For practical purposes the account of the phonetic change in verbs of III.4 is entirely adequate. To be more exact but no more illuminating, in the case of ανι, αρι, iota is inserted after the preceding vowel (called epenthesis [ἐπένθεσις]) and ι dropped (actually an assimilation of the stem vowel to the following consonantal ι). Whereas in ενι, ερι, the preceding vowel is lengthened in compensation for the loss of ι (compensatory lengthening, §914).

484.5 Subclass III.5 is comprised of two verbs with verb bases ending in αυ, of which υ represents an original ϝ. When ι is added to form the present base, υ (ϝ) is lost, with αι as the result. The υ (ϝ) is retained in the remaining tense bases, so that these verbs follow pattern A₁. Except for the present tense, they look like verbs of class I.1a.

4840.   The structure of class III may be summarized:

III.   Present base = verb base + ι̭
III.1.   -ζω verbs
III.1a.   δ-stems producing -ζω verbs (B₃)
III.1b.   γ-stems producing -ζω verbs (B₂)
III.2.   -σσω verbs (palatal stems in κ, χ) (pattern B₂)
III.3.   -λλω verbs (stems in λ) (pattern C₁)
III.4.   Liquid and nasal stems in which ι is added to the stem vowel (patterns C₁, C₂)
III.5.   Vowel stems in αυ in which ι replaces υ in the present base (pattern A₁)

485.   *Class IV: The present base = the verb base + ν (αν, νε, νυ or ννυ). The subclasses are determined by the type of suffix added to form the present base. Since a variety of verb bases is involved, no pattern of tense formation can be said to predominate.*

485.1   In subclass IV.1 ν is added to the verb base to form the present base.

485.2   In subclass IV.2 αν is added to the verb base to form the present base.

485.20   In IV. 2, if the last vowel of the stem is short, another nasal is inserted after this vowel: μ before a labial, ν before a dental, γ before a palatal. Thus,

λαμβ-αν-ω (λαβ-);
λανθ-αν-ω (λαθ-), μανθ-αν-ω (μαθ-), πυνθ-αν-ομαι (πυθ-);
θιγγ-αν-ω (θιγ-), λαγχ-αν-ω (λαχ-), τυγχ-αν-ω (τυχ-).

485.3   In subclass IV.3 νε is added to the verb base to form the present base, thus producing a contract verb in the present tense.

485.4   In subclass IV.4 νυ or ννυ is added to the verb base to form the present base. This group contains both ω-verbs and μι-verbs (§482.1).

485.40   ἐλαύνω is derived from *ἐλα-νυ-ω by metathesis (Smyth §128).

485.41   ὄλλυμι is derived from *ολ-νυ-μι by assimilation (§929.3).

485.42   ὀμνύω has a verb base ὀμ-, which is augmented in the aorist tense by the addition of o. This phenomenon is analogous to adding ε to verb bases (§439).

485.5   Subclass IV.5 contains two verbs which form the present tense by adding νι̭ to the verb base (combination of class III and class IV). As in III.4 (§484.4), the ι̭ affects the preceding vowel, i.e. ι is added to the preceding vowel and ι̭ is lost.

4850. The structure of class IV may be summarized:

> IV. Present base = verb base + ν (αν, νε, νυ or ννυ)
>> IV.1. Present base = verb base + ν
>> IV.2. Present base = verb base + αν
>> IV.3. Present base = verb base + νε (contract verbs)
>> IV.4. Present base = verb base + νυ or ννυ
>> IV.5. Present base = verb base + νι̩ (combination of classes III and IV)

486. *Class V: The present base = the verb base + σκ (vowel stems) or ισκ (consonant stems).*

486.1 A number of verbs in this class reduplicate the verb base to form the present base (§345). Cf. class I.7.

486.2 The verb base of διδάσκω is διδαχ- (aorist ἐδίδαξα): a stop is lost before -σκω (Smyth §99).

486.3 The iota-subscript in θνῄσκω and μιμνῄσκομαι is the result of adding -ισκω to a vowel base, contrary to the general rule.

486.4 ὀφλισκάνω has a verb base ὀφλ-, to which is added ισκ (class V) and αν (class IV) to form the present base. Cf. the two verbs in class IV.5.

487. *Class VI: mixed class.* This class includes verbs that are irregular in the sense that one set of principal parts is developed from two or more verb bases.

487.1 The tense bases for αἱρέω, *choose*, are developed from two verb bases: αἱρε- and ἑλ-. The principal parts based on αἱρέω follow pattern A₂ (cf. I.2b, verbs in -έω). A by-form of the future, -ελῶ, and the second aorist, -εῖλον (§§3371f.), are derived from ἑλ-.

487.2 Tense bases for the verb meaning, *say*, are derived from three verb bases: λεγ-, εἰπ-, ἐρ- (ῥη-) . λέγω is used for the present system only. εἰπ- provides the second aorist: εἶπον (< *ϝεπ-, §§3371f.). The remaining tenses are built on ἐρ- (ῥε-): ἐρῶ, εἴρηκα, εἴρηται, ἐρρέθην (< *ϝερ, *ϝρη-). For reduplication s. §3430.1; for the augment of the aorist passive, s. §3360.1.

487.3 The principal parts of ἔρχομαι, *come*, are built on two verb bases: ἐρχ-; ἐλευθ-, ἐλυθ-, ἐλθ- (vowel gradation). In the future, ἐλεύσομαι, the dental (θ) is lost before the tense formant (σ) (§375). For reduplication of the perfect base, ἐλήλυθα, s. §344.

487.4 ἐσθίω (or -έσθω), *eat*, has a future, φάγομαι, and a second aorist, ἔφαγον, from the verb base, φαγ-. The future has no tense formant (§3736). A by-form of the future, ἔδομαι, is from ἐδ-, which is also the ultimate base of the present tense base: ἐσ-θι-ω < ἐδ- plus θι or θ (a rare way of forming a present base from the verb base; a dental before another dental often becomes σ).

487.5   οἶδα, *know*, is a second perfect used as a present tense. The subjunctive is εἰδῶ, infinitive εἰδέναι, participle εἰδώς. These forms are derived from bases οιδ- and *ϝιδ-; from the latter is also derived εἶδον (s.v. ὁράω). From ειδ- a future, εἰδήσω, was developed (Attic εἴσομαι).

487.6   ὁράω, *see*, is being replaced in the present tense by βλέπω, θεωρέω (Bl-D §101), and by a new present, ὀπτάνομαι, formed from the aorist passive tense base, ὤφθην. From ὁρα- (*ϝορα-) is derived the perfect active, ἑώρακα (on reduplication, s. §3430.4). ὄψομαι, ὠψάμην, and ὤφθην are derived from a base ὀπ-; these forms follow the pattern B₁. The common second aorist, εἶδον, is derived from *ϝιδ- (§3371); cf. *video*.

487.7   Strictly speaking, πάσχω belongs to class V (σκω-verbs). The present base is derived from παθ-σκω: θ becomes σ before σ (§927.2), and the aspiration is transferred from θ to κ (§928.4): πασ-σχω; σσ is then simplified: πά-σχω. The second aorist, ἔπαθον, is derived from the same base (παθ-). The future παθεῖται (one occurrence in the literature covered by Bauer), is a back formation from the aorist, perhaps on the analogy of βαλῶ, ἔβαλον (Bl-D §74(3)). The perfect active reflects an alternate stem, πονθ-.

487.8   πίνω is derived from the base πι- by the addition of ν (class IV.1). The future, πίομαι (without tense formant, §3763), and aorist, ἔπιον, are built on the same base. πέπωκα reflects a base πω-, and ἐπόθην a base πο-.

487.9   The two principal parts (present, aorist) of τρέχω, *run*, are built on two bases: τρεχ- and δραμ-.

487.10 The principal parts for φέρω are derived from three bases: φερ- (present), οἰ- (future), and ἐνεκ- (the remainder). The aorist, ἤνεγκα, is derived from ἐνκ- (vowel gradation), with reduplication εν-ενκ (§3440.2), assimilation of ν to κ (§929.2), and augment: ἤνεγκα. The perfect active shows vowel gradation (ἐνοκ), reduplication of the first syllable (§344), and aspiration (§491): ἐνένοχα. The aorist passive, ἠνέχθην, is the base, ἐνεκ-, with augment and assimilation of κ to θ (§925.1).

Other Factors Affecting Variety in Tense Base Formation

488.   In addition to patterns of tense base formation (§§477–4782) and the types of present tense base formation (§§479–487), there are other factors affecting va-

riety in tense base formation. Most of these involve minor aberrations of regular patterns, and most of them have already been discussed exhaustively.

Consideration of these additional factors may be continued with comments on the system of notations employed in the Catalogue of Verbs (Appendix III).

489. *Vowel gradation.* The base vowel of a verb may vary from tense base to tense base, as in the English verb, *sing sang sung.* Cf. §§348, 3550.3, and 907–911 (Appendix I); §911 contains a catalogue of patterns of vowel gradation in Greek verbs appearing in Bauer.

Verbs showing any vowel gradation, other than the lengthening or shortening of a final base vowel, or the addition or loss of ε(η) at the end of the base (s. below, §493), are marked with (†) in the left margin in the Catalogue.

490. *Aberrations in augment, reduplication.* Some verbs exhibit aberrations in augment (§§3371–3374, 339) and/or reduplication (§§3430–3440).

4900. Reduplication other than in the perfect tense is found occasionally in the present tense (classes I.7 and V), and in the aorist (two examples) (§345).

491. *Aspirated second perfect.* Verbs with bases ending in π, β or κ, γ sometimes showed the correlative aspirated stop (φ or χ) (§3871).

492. *σ added to the tense base* is to be observed in some tense bases in the perfect middle-passive and/or aorist passive. S. §§3922, 422 for discussion and catalogue.

493. *The addition or deletion of ε(η).* ε(η) may be added to the verb base to form one or more of the tense bases. Class I.5c (Appendix III) contains two verbs which add ε to form the present base; the examples for other tense bases are much more numerous. Final ε may also be deleted from the verb base to form the tense base, e.g. γαμέω, aorist ἔγημα (liquid aorist, §410). Class I.5b contains a number of verbs that delete final ε to form the present base. Some verbs show alternative present bases with and without ε, e.g. ῥίπτω or ῥιπέω (class II).

494. *Deaspiration and transfer of aspiration.* Deaspiration occurs when two aspirates appear in successive syllables (§928.2). Occasionally aspiration is transferred from one stop to another in an adjoining syllable (§928.4).

4940. The aberrations discussed in §§489–494 are noted in the Catalogue (Appendix III) by a raised number placed to the left of the tense base in question. For the notational system s. the introduction to Appendix III.

Organization of the Catalogue of Verbs

495. The patterns of tense base formation (§§477–4782) are suitable only for 'weak' (regular) verbs. In the discussion of the future, aorist active/middle, perfect

active, and aorist passive tense systems, it was noted, however, that there are alternative ways of forming and conjugating these tenses. Unfortunately, 'strong' tense formation and inflection is not confined to verbs that are 'strong' across the board; 'strong' tenses may appear in a set of principal parts that is otherwise regular or 'weak.' Nor can 'strong' tenses be correlated with classes of verbs (i.e. the way they form their present bases from verb bases). Take, for example, the catalogue of second (strong) aorists in §4070: verbs of most classes are represented; in addition, these same verbs may have regular or weak futures, perfects, or aorist passives. It is therefore necessary in the Catalogue to take notice of strong tenses by special means. This has been done by a series of raised numbers that appear to the *right* of the tense base in question (s. the introduction to Appendix III for particulars). In this way it has been possible to specify the predominate pattern of tense base formation in the left-hand margin, while noting that some tenses may constitute exceptions to the pattern.

496. *Recapitulation.* It is now appropriate to recapitulate the predominant features of the organization of the Catalogue of Verbs, and thus to rehearse the factors that affect tense base formation in the Greek verb.

496.1 Patterns of tense base formation (§§477–4782) are correlated with subclasses of class I verbs insofar as possible (§482.2), and noted in the left hand margin for each verb elsewhere (except where a whole class or subclass follows one pattern, e.g. class II = pattern B_1).

496.2 The Catalogue is divided into five major classes, depending on the way the present tense base is formed from the verb base (§§479–487). To these has been added a sixth or mixed class of verbs (§487).

496.3 If the verb manifests vowel gradation in the development of principal parts, that fact is noted by (†) in the left-hand margin (§489).

496.4 Minor aberrations in the elaboration of principal parts, such as unusual augment or reduplication, the addition of σ or ε to the base, etc., are noted by a series of raised numbers to the *left* of the tense base manifesting that aberration. References to the discussion are provided in the key.

496.5 Deviations from regular or 'weak' tense formation and inflection (= the patterns of tense base formation) are noted by a series of raised numbers to the *right* of the tense base. References to the discussion are provided in the key.

Part Three

Short Syntax

Lesson 32

Sentence Types I–IV

500. *The sentence* is the fundamental grammatical unit in Greek, as in English. There appears to be an infinite variety of sentences which have been or can be composed. Such variety is misleading, however, so far as grammatical structure is concerned. Actually, sentence structure conforms largely to a few basic patterns which are used in the language over and over again. These basic patterns are subject, of course, to elaboration: structural elements may be expanded almost indefinitely, and various qualifications may be added at will. The possibilities for expansion and qualification may obscure but they do not obliterate the underlying sentence structure. Every sentence makes sense because it conforms in one way or another to a grammatical structure already established in the language. There can be understanding (of sentences) only where understanding (of grammatical structure) precedes.

501. A sentence may be arbitrarily defined as a *word group consisting of "subject" and "predicate."* This definition is useful only as a point of departure. It is universally applicable only to sentences that are context-free. In language that is context-bound, single elements in either "subject" or "predicate" may constitute a sentence. For example, in response to the question, ὁ προφήτης εἶ σύ ("Are you the prophet?"), Jesus responds: οὔ ("No"). "No" is a sentence only in context. Again, Jesus inquires: τίνος ἡ εἰκὼν αὕτη καὶ ἡ ἐπιγραφή ("Whose likeness and inscription is this?"), to which his listeners reply: Καίσαρος ("Caesar's"). A genitive of possession can stand as a sentence in this context, but it would be meaningless out of context. The definition of the sentence given above thus takes the fully explicit or context-free sentence as its basis.

502. The common form of the sentence, even in context-bound language, comprises a word or word group in the structure of "subject," and a word or word group in the structure of "predicate." The "subject" commonly consists of, or clusters around, a noun or pronoun. By definition, the "predicate" always consists of or clusters around a finite form of the verb.

503. *The predicate*, as indicated in §502, consists of a finite verb plus the other words and word groups in the sentence that do not belong to the "subject" (sentence connectors, vocatives, nuance words and the like are excluded from both subject and predicate). The key to the grammatical structure of sentences lies predominantly, though not exclusively, in the predicate. The reason for this is that the form of the finite verb (tense-aspect, mood, voice), together with the constituent words and word groups going with verb, determine the fundamental grammatical structure of the sentence. In describing sentence structure, therefore, description will have to do primarily with the predicate.

Sentence Type I

504. The simplest form of the sentence consists of "subject" and verb only. In connected texts in Greek, the "subject" of the sentence is most often indicated by the ending attached to the verb (first, second, third persons; singular and plural). Since the "subject" is attached in these cases to the verb (as a bound morpheme), the simplest form of a type I sentence (=S-I) will consist of verb only:

    (1) εἶδεν   Jn 8:56
          he saw

    (2) ἐχάρη   Jn 8:56
          he rejoiced

    (3) ἦλθαν   Jn 1:39
          they came

505. Type I sentences also include sentences in which the "subject" is expressed as a discrete item:

    (4) ἐγὼ ὑπάγω   Jn 8:21
          I go away

    (5) οἱ προφῆται ἀπέθανον   Jn 8:53
          the prophets died

506. Verbs in S-I are usually called "intransitive," by which is meant, negatively, that they do not require an "object" and, positively, that they may form a complete predicate by themselves.

Sentence Type II

507.   In S-I the verb may form a complete predicate by itself, but in type II sentences (=S-II) the verb connects the "subject" with a subjective complement, e.g. "*I am the light of the world*" (Jn 8:12). The verb does not therefore form a complete predicate by itself, but must be supplemented by a predicate noun or adjective. These verbs constitute a very small class, and are called *copulative* or *equative* verbs. The two common equative verbs are εἰμί and γίνομαι. The inflectional mark of S-II is that the subjective complement takes the same case as the "subject" (in independent sentences the nominative).

(6)   ἐγώ εἰμι τὸ φῶς τοῦ κοσμοῦ   Jn 8:12
I am the light of the world

(7)   ἡ μαρτυρία σου οὐκ ἔστιν ἀληθής   Jn 8:13
Your testimony is not true

Sentence Type III

508.   The following are examples of type III sentences (S-III) :

(8)   γνώσεσθε τὴν ἀλήθειαν   Jn 8:32
You shall know the truth

(9)   ὑμεῖς ποιεῖτε τὰ ἔργα τοῦ πατρὸς ὑμῶν   Jn 8:41
You do the works of your father

(10) τιμῶ τὸν πατέρα μου   Jn 8:49
I honor my father

Verbs in S-III likewise do not form complete predicates by themselves. However, instead of being supplemented by a subjective complement, these verbs require an objective complement, or, more precisely a direct object. Consequently, they are called transitive verbs. A direct object may be distinguished from a subjective complement by three criteria:

508.1   A direct object is normally indicated by the accusative case (in contrast to the nominative in independent sentences of S-II).

508.2   The direct object and the "subject" in S-III refer to different persons or things, whereas the subjective complement and the "subject" in S-II refer to the same person or thing.

508.3 The direct object of the active form of S-III may become the "subject" in the passive form of the same sentence:

(10) Active: τιμῶ τὸν πατέρα μου   Jn 8:49
        I honor my father

(11) Passive: ὑπὸ θεοῦ τετίμηται   IgnSm 9:1
        He has been honored by God

This transformation is not possible for S-II : sentences with equative verbs do not have passive forms.

Sentence Type IV

509. Some transitive verbs take an indirect object in addition to a direct object. The indirect object is customarily defined as "that to which or for which the action is performed," i.e. the more remotely concerned person. The dative case is one means of signaling the indirect object in Greek.

(12) ταῦτα γράφω ὑμῖν . . .   1 Jn 2:1
        I write these things to you . . .

(13) οἱ δὲ προσήνεγκαν αὐτῷ δηνάριον   Mt 22:19
        They brought him a denarius

510. Type IV sentences, like S-III, permit the active form to be transformed into a passive form. However, two different passive transformations are possible with some verbs in S-IV:

510.1 The active form of a type IV sentence with πιστεύω, *trust, entrust,* is illustrated by:

(14) τὸ ἀληθινὸν τίς ὑμῖν πιστεύσει;   Lk 16:11
        Who will entrust true riches to you?

In the passive form the indirect object (dat.) becomes the subject of the passive verb, and the direct object (acc.) is retained, e.g.

(15) πεπίστευμαι τὸ εὐαγγέλιον τῆς ἀκροβυστίας   Gal 2:7
        I had been entrusted with the gospel to the uncircumcised

510.2 The active form of S-IV with δίδωμι is structurally identical with (14):

(16) ταῦτά σοι πάντα δώσω   Mt 4:9
     I shall give all these things to you

But the passive form of this S-IV differs from (15) in that, in this case, the direct object becomes the subject of the passive verb, and the indirect object is retained:

(17) σημεῖον οὐ δοθήσεται αὐτῇ   Mt 12:39
     A sign shall not be given to it [this generation]

Type IV sentences are thus subject to two passive transformations, one in which the indirect object becomes subject and the direct object is retained (with verbs like πιστεύω), and one in which the direct object becomes subject and the indirect object is retained (with verbs like δίδωμι). While both forms are passive transformations of S-IV, it appears that only one type is used with a given verb (unlike English).

Analysis of Sentence Types

511. Sentence types I-IV constitute the bread-and-butter sentence structures of Greek. In Jn 8:12–59, for example, among approximately 163 sentences, there is barely a half-dozen sentences the grammatical structures of which do not conform to one of these four types. In 1 Jn 1:5–2:17, there is only one exception among 79 sentences. There are about 18 sentences in Jn 1:19–51 that do not fall into one of the four categories among 114 sentences. The ability to "read" these grammatical structures therefore means the ability to seize the vast majority of sentences in Greek as grammatical wholes, and it is this ability which makes any language grammatically intelligible, quite apart from the lexical meaning of specific words.

512.1 The description of the grammatical structure or syntax of a sentence is called *parsing*. The traditional shorthand method of parsing is diagramming (for a summary and discussion, see Gleason: 142–151). The sentence, *You shall know the truth*, for example, was diagrammed as:

You | shall know | the truth

The vertical line crossing the base line separates subject from predicate, and the vertical line resting on the base line divides direct object from verb. The structure of this sentence could also be represented as: S - V - DO (subject-verb-direct object). Schematic analysis of this type would also appear to be desirable for Greek, since the student needs some practice at reading the grammatical structure of Greek sentences.

512.2 There appear to be at least two requirements for any analytical shorthand used in connection with Greek: (a) the scheme ought to be practically serviceable in that it requires a minimum of rewriting; it would obviously be advantageous if a scheme of notations could be employed on sentences as they stand in the text. (b) The scheme ought to combine morphological description and syntactic analysis insofar as possible, since inflection and syntax belong to the same grammatical system (Gleason: 118). It would also be highly desirable, of course, if such a scheme were kept as simple as possible, yet it must be subject to elaboration in accordance with the complexity of the linguistic phenomena.

513. *Analytic scheme of notation.* In developing a notational scheme that can be used on actual texts without having to rewrite them, and that appears to meet the requirements stated above (§512.2), the following symbols may be proposed.

513.1 The slash (/) may be used to set off the subject from the predicate and to mark the limits of words and word groups in the predicate.

513.2 Arabic 1 may be allowed to stand for any word or word group in the structure of subject, and arabic 2 for the finite verb in the predicate. Thus,

$$\overset{1}{} \quad \overset{2}{}$$

(4) ἐγώ / ὑπάγω   Jn 8:21

513.3 If the subject is contained in the verb and not expressed as a discrete item, the symbols for subject and verb will have to be written in hyphenated form, e.g.

2-1
(1) εἶδεν   Jn 8:56

The order is 2-1 because the morpheme indicating the subject is in the tail of the verb.

513.4 Arabic 3 may stand for any word or word group in the predicate, the head term (definition: §541) of which is in the *nominative* case, e.g.

1   2   3
(6) ἐγώ / εἰμι / τὸ φῶς τοῦ κόσμου   Jn 8·12

513.5   Similarly, 4 may stand for any word or word group in the predicate, the head term of which is in the *accusative* case, e.g.

$$\text{2-1} \qquad \text{4}$$
(10) τιμῶ / τὸν πατέρα μου   Jn 8:49

513.6   Again, 5 may stand for any word or word group in the predicate, the head term of which is in the *dative* case, e.g.

$$\text{4} \qquad \text{2-1} \qquad \text{5}$$
(13) ταῦτα / γράφω / ὑμῖν   1 Jn 2:1

513.7   These notations may be written directly in the text (the arabic symbols being placed above the head term [§541]), or they may be written separately as schematic descriptions, e.g.

(6)   1/2/3
(10) 2-1/4

513.8   In anticipation of subsequent needs, it may be indicated that one additional arabic number, 6, will be used to mark the *genitive* case in the predicate.

514.   *Analytic notation and sentence structure.* In sentences in which only the basic grammatical elements appear, the analytic notation amounts to a description of the grammatical structure of the sentence, *in most cases*. Thus, a description 1/2 or 2-1 will normally be S-I. S-II would be represented by 1/2/3 or 2-1/3 (nominative in predicate), S-III by 1/2/4 or 2-1/4, and S-IV by 1/2/4/5 or 2-1/4/5. Description, however, will not always match structure, e.g.

$$\text{4} \qquad \text{2-1}$$
(18) ὀλίγον / ἀγαπᾷ   Lk 7:47
     he loves little

is not S-III but S-I, since ὀλίγον here is an adverbial accusative. It will therefore sometimes be necessary to indicate sentence structure separately. For example, (18) could be described structurally as I.4, i.e. S-I with an adverb signaled by the accusative case. Sentence (10) can be noted as III.4 (S-III, with direct object in the accusative case), (13) as IV.4/5, and (6) as II.3. The roman numerals refer to sentence types, and the arabic numerals to elements other than verb that appear in the predicate.

515.   Three types of notation are thus possible using the same set of symbols: (a) description written in the text; (b) detached description; (c) sentence type, together with elements other than verb appearing in the predicate. These three types may be further illustrated:

		3	2-1	
(a)	(19)	σπέρμα Ἀβραάμ / ἐσμεν		Jn 8:33
		We are seed of Abraham		
(b)		3/2-1		
(c)		II.3		

		1	2	4	
(a)	(20)	οὐδεὶς / ἐπίασεν / αὐτόν			Jn 8:20
		No one seized him			
(b)		1/2/4			
(c)		III.4			

		2-1	5	4	
(a)	(21)	ἄφες / ἡμῖν / τὰ ὀφειλήματα ἡμῶν			Mt 6:12
		Forgive us our debts			
(b)		2-1/5/4			
(c)		IV. 4/5			

516.   The analytic scheme will be subsequently elaborated and refined. Meanwhile it may be employed as a means of aiding the student in seizing words and word groups in the sentence on a morphological basis, and in grasping the structure of sentences. In no case should the notational scheme be emphasized in and of itself. Rather, it should be viewed as a symbolic language that is useful in talking about the structure of Greek sentences. There is no virtue in talking about sentence structure, of course, when sentence structure is "read" readily off the actual sentences—unless one aspires to be a grammarian in addition to becoming a reader of Greek.

Lesson 33

Sentence Types V–VI

While sentence types I–IV comprise the bulk of sentences occurring in the average Greek text, there is a number of other types that require notice.

520.   Some verbs take not one but two objects in the *accusative* case:

2-1 4 4	
(1) ἐδίδαξεν / αὐτοὺς . . . / πολλά	Mk 4:2
he taught them many things	

4 2-1 4	
(2) . . . ψεύστην / ποιοῦμεν / αὐτόν	1 Jn 1:10
we make him a liar	

The pattern of both of these sentences is 1/2/4/4 or 2-1/4/4, where 4 represents a word or word group, the head term of which is in the accusative case.

While the patterns of (1) and (2) are superficially identical, other factors suggest that it is grammatically necessary to distinguish them.

Sentence Type V

521.1   In (2) it will be observed that the two accusatives refer to the same person or thing: *him, liar*. For that reason ψεύστην is called the *object complement*, while *him* is referred to as the direct object. Now it was observed that the identity of reference is also characteristic of S-II, and the predicate of such sentences with an equative verb is called the *subject complement*, e.g.

αὐτὸς . . . ψεύστης ἐστιν   cf. 1 Jn 2:4
he is a liar

The similarity of the two constructions has led grammarians to call the second accusative in sentences like (2) the *predicate accusative*. And there is good justification for this designation when it is observed that an equative verb sometimes actually links the two accusatives. Compare these sentences:

$$\overset{\text{2-1}}{} \qquad \overset{4}{} \qquad \overset{4}{}$$

(3) ποιήσω / ὑμᾶς / ἁλιεῖς ἀνθρώπων   Mt 4:19
I shall make you fishers of men

$$\overset{\text{2-1}}{} \qquad \overset{4}{} \qquad \overset{i}{} \qquad \overset{4}{}$$

(4) ποιήσω / ὑμᾶς / γενέσθαι / ἁλιεῖς ἀνθρώπων   Mk 1:17
I shall make you (to become) fishers of men

The insertion of the infinitive γενέσθαι (designated i) in (4) proves that the second accusative is grammatically a predicate accusative or an object complement, since the two sentences mean the same thing. While (4) must be considered a different grammatical structure because of the infinitive (to be considered subsequently) , the similarity between the two helps to determine the deep grammatical structure of (3) and hence (2) .

521.2   A sentence with two accusatives but with a verb other than ποιέω is

$$\overset{\text{2-1}}{} \qquad \overset{4}{} \qquad \overset{4}{}$$

(5) καλέσεις / τὸ ὄνομα αὐτοῦ / Ἰησοῦν   Lk 1:13
You shall call his name Jesus

This sentence meets the criterion of §521.1, i.e. the two accusatives refer to the same person or thing: *his name, Jesus*. The second accusative is therefore a predicate accusative, and (5) is grammatically comparable to (2) and (3). While ποιέω does not appear in the passive voice, καλέω does. We may inquire what the passive form of a sentence like (5) would be.

$$\overset{2}{} \qquad \overset{1}{} \qquad \overset{3}{}$$

(6) ἐκλήθη / τὸ ὄνομα αὐτοῦ / Ἰησοῦς   Lk 2:21
His name was called Jesus

From (6) we may deduce two generalizations in relation to (5):

(a) In the passive transformation, the *direct object* becomes the "*subject*" of the passive verb;

(b) the *predicate accusative* is retained as a predicate with the passive verb, but is changed to the *nominative case*.

The passive form of a sentence like (5), i.e. (6), will therefore look like S-II (1/2/3), except that the verb will be passive. It will be recalled that there are no passive forms of S-II with equative verbs (§508.3). We should thus distinguish the structure of (6) from S-II by indicating the voice of the verb: 1/2pass/3.

521.3 Let sentences with two accusatives that meet the criteria in §521.1–2 be given the designation S-V.

          1   4   4   2

(7) V. Δαυὶδ [οὖν] / αὐτὸν / Κύριον / καλεῖ   Lk 20:44
David [therefore] calls him Lord

          1   2pass   3

(8) VP. σὺ / κληθήσῃ / Κηφᾶς   Jn 1:42
You shall be called Cephas

VP. stands for the passive transformation of V.

522. Type V sentences are not common, but they do appear occasionally with verbs such as:

ποιέω — *make*
καλέω — *call, name*
ἐπικαλέω — *name*
λέγω — *call, name*
ἔχω — *hold, regard as*
ὀνομάζω — *call, name*
τίθημι — *make*

Bl-D §157.

Sentence Type VI

523.1 In sentences with two accusatives like (1), neither accusative is a predicate accusative (they do not refer to the same person or thing). Rather, both appear to be objects of the verb. Indeed, the accusatives in (1) may appear separately with the verb:

        2-1   4

(9) ἐδίδασκεν [γὰρ] / τοὺς μαθητὰς αὐτοῦ   Mk 9:31
[For] he taught his disciples

       4   2-1

(10) τὴν ὁδὸν τοῦ θεοῦ / διδάσκεις   Mk 12:14
You teach the way of God

Or, as in (1) , they may be combined:

```
      1      4    2        4
```
(11) ἐκεῖνος / ὑμᾶς / διδάξει / πάντα   Jn 14:26
      That one will teach you all things

Double forms like (9) and (10) are not possible with verbs of S-V (§522) (where the verbs have the same meaning with each object as they do with two objects).

523.2   In the passive transformation of S-V, the direct object becomes the "subject" of the passive verb and the predicate accusative is retained but changed to the nominative case (§521.2). The passive form of sentences like (1) and (11) is illustrated by this example:

```
        4             2pass        1
```
(12) [καὶ] τὰ ἀρεστά σου / ἐδιδάχθησαν / ἄνθρωποι   WsdSol 9:18
      [And] men were taught the things that please you

Notice that one object becomes the "subject" of the passive verb, while the second is retained as an *object* and in the *accusative* case. Actually, either object may become "subject" of the passive verb, though examples are exceedingly rare (see Liddell-Scott, s.v. διδάσκω).

523.3   Let the sentences that meet the criteria in §523.1–2 be called S-VI.

```
        2      4       1
```
(13) VI. ἠρώτων / αὐτὸν / οἱ περὶ αὐτὸν σὺν τοῖς δώδεκα / τὰς
```
        4
```
      παραβολάς   Mk 4:10
      Those about him with the twelve asked him [about]
      the parables

```
           4     2-1
```
(14) VIP. . . . τὰς παραδόσεις] ἃς / ἐδιδάχθητε   2 Thess 2:15
      . . . the traditions] which you were taught

VIP. stands for the passive form of S-VI.

524.   Type VI sentences are not at all common, but they occur rarely with such verbs as:

διδάσκω — *teach*
ἐρωτάω — *ask, inquire* (someone about)
αἰτέω — *ask* (someone for)

ὑπομιμνῄσκω — *remind* (someone of something)
ἀναμιμνῄσκω — *remind* (someone of something)

Bl-D §§155–156.

Statements, Questions, Requests

525.　The sentence types examined thus far have been predominantly in the form of statements. So far as grammatical structure is concerned, the same sentence types apply with equal validity to questions and requests (commands). There will normally be some signal in the sentence that will indicate whether the sentence is a question or a request, if it is not a statement. Questions are often signaled by interrogative words, and commands are normally signaled by the imperative mood of the verb. Our immediate concern is to notice that questions and requests conform to the same grammatical structures as do statements.

526.　*Questions* are often, though not always, signaled by an interrogative word. Interrogative words may be interrogative pronouns, which are declined (§265), or interrogative adverbs, which are not. Such interrogative words may belong to the structure of the sentence as a constitutive element, or they may be an optional item. For example,

> 2-1
> (1)　ποῦ / μένεις　　　　　　　　　　Jn 1:38
> 　　　*Where are you staying?*

is S-I with an interrogative adverb, ποῦ *where?* On the other hand, τίς in the question

> 　　1　3　2
> (2)　σὺ / τίς / εἶ　　　　　　　　　　Jn 8:25
> 　　　*Who are you?*

belongs to the grammatical structure of S-II as the predicate (σὺ is tied to εἶ by agreement in number and person, i.e. 2nd person sg. and is therefore the "subject"). The order of words in the interrogative sentence in Greek is not as fixed as it is in English. In edited Greek texts the question mark (?) is (;).
The following questions illustrate the same basic grammatical structures as found in declarative sentences. The symbol Q is used to designate interrogative

words in the analysis; if it is an optional element in the sentence type, it is put in (). Sentence-type is given at left.

<blockquote>
Q   2-1

(3) I.(Q)   τί [οὖν] βαπτίζεις;   Jn 1:25
Then why do you baptize?
</blockquote>

<blockquote>
3   2 1

(4) II.3   ὁ προφήτης / εἶ / σύ;   Jn 1:22
Are you the prophet?
</blockquote>

<blockquote>
Q 4   2-1

(5) III.4   τί / με / πειράζετε;   Mt 12:15
Why do you test me?
</blockquote>

<blockquote>
2   4   5

(6) IV.4/5   ἔξεστιν δοῦναι / κῆνσον / Καίσαρι / ἢ οὔ;   Mt 22:17
Is it lawful to give tribute to Caesar or not?
</blockquote>

<blockquote>
4^Q   4   2-1

(7) V.4/4^Q   τίνα / σεαυτὸν / ποιεῖς;   Jn 8:53
What do you make yourself out to be?
</blockquote>

527.   *Requests and commands* are normally signaled by the imperative mood of the verb. The prohibitive subjunctive with negative μή is also used. Unlike English, the Greek imperative has a 3. sg. and 3. pl., which is represented in English by "Let him . . . ," "Let them . . ." (§0455). Requests and commands reflect the same grammatical structures as do statements and questions.

<blockquote>
2-1

(8) I.   χαίρετε   Mt 5:12
Rejoice!
</blockquote>

<blockquote>
2-1   3

(9) II.3   ἤτω / ἀνάθεμα   1 Cor 16:22
Let him be anathema.
</blockquote>

<blockquote>
2-1   4

(10) III.4   ἀγαπᾶτε / τοὺς ἐχθροὺς ὑμῶν   Mt 5:44
Love your enemies.
</blockquote>

		2pass	1	
(11)	IIIP	Ἁγιασθήτω /	τὸ ὄνομά σου	Mt 6:9

(11) IIIP Ἁγιασθήτω / τὸ ὄνομά σου   Mt 6:9
Let your name be hallowed.

(12) IV.4/5 ἄφες / ἡμῖν / τὰ ὀφειλήματα ἡμῶν   Mt 6:12
Forgive us our debts.

(13) V.4/4 ἐυθείας / ποιεῖτε / τὰς τρίβους αὐτοῦ   Mk 1:3
Make his paths straight.

With prohibitive subjunctive:

(14) III.4 μὴ εἰσενέγκης / ἡμᾶς / εἰς πειρασμόν   Mt 6:13
Do not lead us into temptation.

The "Subject"

530. The term "subject" has regularly been enclosed in quotation marks since a grammatical definition of the "subject" has not yet been offered. Traditionally the "subject" is defined as "the performer of the action." Such a definition indicates the relation of the "subject" to the verb (or whole predicate), and it fits a good many cases, e.g.

(1) τιμῶ τὸν πατέρα μου   Jn 8:48
     I honor my father

It does not, however, fit such a sentence as

(2) ἐκαθερίσθη   Mk 1:42
     He was cleansed

in which the "subject" *undergoes* the action. The grammatical "subject" of the sentence thus sustains more than one relation to the verb (and predicate). In fact, the "subject" sustains a wide variety of relationships to the verb (and predicate), so that the traditional definition is scarcely adequate as a general definition.

Relation of "Subject" to Predicate: Voice

531. The following sentences indicate the range of relationships between "subject" and predicate.

531.1 The "subject" is *performer* of the action.

          2-1   4

(3) I. εἰσπορεύονται / εἰς Καφαρναούμ   Mk 1:21
         They journeyed into Capernaum

          2-1   4

(4) III. εὑρίσκει / Φίλιππον   Jn 1:43
          He finds Philip

        2-1   4   5

(5) IV. ἔδωκεν / αὐτὸν / τῇ μητρὶ αὐτοῦ   Lk 7:15
          He gave him to his mother

531.2   The "subject" *undergoes* the action.

        2pass-1   4   6

(6) IIIP. ἐβαπτίσθη / εἰς τὸν Ἰορδάνην / ὑπὸ Ἰωάννου   Mk 1:9
           He was baptized in the Jordan by John

        2pass   5   1

(7) IVP. ἀφέωνται / ὑμῖν / αἱ ἁμαρτίαι   1 Jn 2:12
           Your sins are forgiven you

        3   2pass-1

(8) VP. υἱοὶ θεοῦ / κληθήσονται   Mt 5:9
           They shall be called sons of God

531.3   The "subject" is that *to* or *for* which the action is undertaken.

        2pass-1   4

(9) IVP. πεπίστευμαι / τὸ εὐαγγέλιον τῆς ἀκροβυστίας   Gal 2:7
           I have been entrusted with the gospel of uncircumcision

531.4   The "subject" is *identified*.

        1   2   3

(10) II. ἐγώ / εἰμι / τὸ φῶς τοῦ κόσμου   Jn 8:12
           I am the light of the world

        2-1   3

(11) II. ἦσαν [γὰρ] ἁλιεῖς   Mk 1:16
           For they were fishermen

531.5   The "subject" is *described*.

        1   2   3

(12) II. ἡ μαρτυρία σου / οὐκ ἔστιν / ἀληθής   Jn 8:13
           Your testimony is not true

3   2-1   3

(13) II.   πιστός / ἐστιν (καὶ) δίκαιος   1 Jn 1:9
           He is faithful and just

531.6   The "subject" acts *on* or *with reference to itself.*

2-1

(14) I.   ἀπήγξατο   Mt 27:5
           He hanged himself

532.1   Of the relationships between "subject" and predicate illustrated in §531, (1) and (3)–(5) fit the traditional definition: the "subject" performs the action. This relationship is found in sentences of types I, III-VI. When the "subject" is the performer of the action, the voice of the verb is said to be *active.*

532.2   If the "subject" undergoes the action, the voice of the verb is normally *passive.* Sentence types which have passive transformations, and whose verbs are thus transitive (§508), manifest this relation between "subject" and verb (IIIP, IVP, VP; (2), (6)–(8)).

532.3   Verbs in S-II *link* the "subject" with a subject complement, which identifies or describes the "subject." The "subjects" in such sentences therefore sustain a different relationship to the predicate than that indicated by either active or passive verbs. (10)–(13) are examples.

532.4   In (9) the "subject" of the sentence in its passive form was the indirect object of the sentence in its active form (§511), i.e.

> *[God] entrusted the gospel of uncircumcision to me*

becomes

> *I was entrusted with the gospel of uncircumcision.*

In (9) the relation between "subject" and predicate is different than in (7), which is also a passive transformation of S-IV. In (7) the direct object of the active form has become the "subject" of the passive. Cf. §511.

532.5   (14) illustrates the middle voice (§306): the "subject" acts on, for, or with reference to itself. This relationship may be expressed entirely by the voice of the verb, although the middle voice is on the decline in hellenistic Greek and true middles are rare. In the hellenistic period, the middle voice is expressed more often by an active verb and a reflexive or personal pronoun as object, as in English:

$$\overset{1}{} \quad \overset{2}{} \quad \overset{4}{}$$

(15) III. (ἐὰν) ἐγὼ / δοξάσω / ἐμαυτόν . . .   Jn 8:54

       (*If*) *I glorify myself*

(15) is another example of S-III, but the relation of the "subject" to the predicate corresponds to the middle voice. (14) and (15) thus express the same "subject"-predicate relationship, but in different grammatical forms.

Formal Signals of the "Subject"

533.   The traditional definition of the "subject" as the performer of the action is inadequate as a means of identifying the grammatical "subjects" of sentences (§§530–532). Nevertheless, the "subject" of the sentence must be identified in relation to the main or finite verb in the predominant sentence form (the full sentence).

533.1   The "subject" may be defined grammatically as that word or word-group that is "tied" to the main or finite verb by virtue of certain agreements. To state it more precisely: *the "subject" is that word or word-group that determines the personal ending* (bound morpheme) *attached to the finite verb.* The tie between "subject" and verb is effected by agreement in *person* and *number*: 1., 2., 3. person singular; 1., 2., 3. person plural (abbreviated: 1. sg., 2. sg., 3. sg.; 1. pl., 2. pl., 3. pl.).

533.2   A second means of identifying the "subject" grammatically is case: *the "subject" is signaled by the nominative ease.* This signal, however, is by no means infallible. Some "subjects" are not marked by case, e.g. an infinitive in the structure of "subject." In some sentences both the "subject" and the subject complement are in the nominative case, e.g. S-II (§532). And in some embedded sentences the "subject" is signaled by a case other than the nominative, e.g. the accusative "subject" with an infinitive. Thus, while the nominative case often signals the "subject," especially in independent and context-free sentences, it is not a universal guide.

The subject has now been defined grammatically as that word or word group which is tied to the main or finite verb by agreement in person and number, and which is often signaled by the nominative case. The subject can thus be identified everywhere on purely grammatical grounds.

It should be emphasized that identification of the subject always takes place in the context of the sentence as a whole: a subject is not a subject without a corresponding predicate, expressed or implied. Formal signals of the subject are operative within a constellation of grammatical clues. The former must contrast with the latter in some way or ways, unless the sentence is gramatically ambiguous.

The formal signals of the subject may be illustrated from sentences with personal pronouns as subjects.

The personal pronouns are listed in §256. Only the nominatives come under consideration here.

The personal endings attached to the verb are given in §§318, 319.

534. *Pronoun subjects, first person singular.* Ἐγώ is the nominative case of the 1. sg. pronoun (§256), which, as subject, will be tied to the 1. sg. personal endings, -ω, -μι, -#, or -ν; -μαι or -μην (§§318, 319). Note: -# stands for the zero form of the 1. sg. secondary ending, active (§319).

1 2 4		

(1) ἐγώ / οὐ κρίνω / οὐδένα   Jn 8:15
I judge no one

   1   2   3
(2) ἐγώ / εἰμι / τὸ φῶς τοῦ κόσμου   Jn 8:12
I am the light of the world

   1   2   5
(3) ἐγώ / ἐλήλυθα / ἐν τῷ ὀνόματι τοῦ πατρός μου   Jn 5:43
I have come In the name of my father

    2   1 i   6   4
(4) οὐ δύναμαι / ἐγώ / ποιεῖν / ἀπ' ἐμαυτοῦ / οὐδέν   Jn 5:30
I am able to do nothing of myself

    4   2   1   5   3
(5) διὰ τοῦτο / ἦλθον / ἐγώ / ἐν ὕδατι / βαπτίζων   Jn 1:31
For this reason I came baptizing in water

   1   2   4
(6) ἐγώ / ἐξελεξάμην / ὑμᾶς   Jn 15:16
I chose you

Observe that in (1) ἐγώ agrees in person and number with -ω (which can be written ἐγώ ↔ -ω), i.e. both are 1. sg., in addition to which ἐγώ is the only nominative in the sentence: agreement plus the nominative case identifies ἐγώ as the subject. The double signal might be written: (nom.) ἐγώ ↔ -ω. Accordingly, in (3) the subject might be indicated thus: (nom.) ἐγώ ↔ -#, in (4) (nom.) ἐγώ ↔ -μαι, and in (6) (nom.) ἐγώ ↔ -μην. In (2), however, the nom. case of ἐγώ competes with the nom. case of the predicate (τὸ φῶς . . .); this ambiguity is resolved by agreement: ἐγώ ↔ -μι (*the light of the world* as subject would be 3. sg., i.e. would require ἐστίν). There is a less acute ambiguity in (5): ἐγώ ↔ -ν is also nom. However, a participle without its own article (ὁ) does not normally appear in the structure of subject.

535. *Pronoun subjects, other than first person singular.* Other persons and numbers may be illustrated out of an abundance of examples. The form of notation is that employed in §534.

	1	6	2	
(7)	σὺ /	περὶ σεαυτοῦ /	μαρτυρεῖς	Jn 8:13

You bear witness concerning yourself
(nom.) σὺ ↔ -ς

	1	4	2	
(8)	ὑμεῖς /	κατὰ τὴν σάρκα /	κρίνετε	Jn 8:15

You judge according to the flesh
(nom.) ὑμεῖς ↔ -τε

	1	6	2	
(9)	ἡμεῖς /	ἐκ πορνείας /	οὐκ ἐγεννήθημεν	Jn 8:41

We were not born of fornication
(nom.) ἡμεῖς ↔ -μεν

	2	1	3	
(10)	ἔσεσθε [οὖν] /	ὑμεῖς /	τέλειοι	Mt 5:48

Therefore, you shall be perfect
ὑμεῖς ↔ -σθε

	1	2	4	
(11)	αὐτὸς /	[γὰρ] σώσει /	τὸν λαὸν αὐτοῦ	Mt 1:21

For he shall save his people
(nom.) αὐτός ↔ -#

N. -# stands for the zero form of the 3. sg. ending, active; cf. §3190.3.

    1   2

(12) αὐτοὶ / παρακληθήσονται   Mt 5:4
     They shall be comforted
     (nom.) αὐτοί ↔ -νται

536.   *Neuter plural subject and singular verb.* The rule that the person and number of the subject determines the person and number of the personal ending attached to the verb (§533.1) is subject to one peculiar exception in Greek: *a neuter plural subject may be tied to a singular verb.*

       1   5   2   6

(13) ταῦτα / ἐν Βηθανίᾳ / ἐγένετο / πέραν τοῦ Ἰορδάνου   Jn 1:28
     These things took place in Bethany beyond the Jordan

The singular verb appears most often when the subject is a pronoun (cf. (13)) or an abstract or non-personal noun.

      2   6   3   1

(14) ἦν [γὰρ] αὐτῶν / πονηρὰ / τὰ ἔργα   Jn 3:19
     For their deeds were evil
Bl-D §133.

537.   *Two or more subjects connected by καί.* In general, where two or more subjects are connected with one verb, the verb agrees in person and number with the first subject if the verb stands before the first or between two subjects.

       4   2   1   1

(15) μετὰ ταῦτα / ἦλθεν / ὁ Ἰησοῦς (καὶ) οἱ μαθηταὶ αὐτοῦ /
                 4

     εἰς τὴν Ἰουδαίαν γῆν   Jn 3:22
     After these things Jesus and his disciples went into Judea

      1   2   1

(16) Ἀβραὰμ / ἀπέθανεν (καὶ) / οἱ προφῆται   Jn 8:52
     Abraham died and the prophets (died)

If the verb stands after two or more subjects it agrees with the subjects taken together:

    3   1   1   2

(17) ἀποκριθεὶς δὲ / Πέτρος (καὶ) οἱ ἀπόστολοι / εἶπαν, . . .   Acts 5:29

     Answering, Peter and the apostles said, . . .

Observe that the participle, ἀποκριθείς, which stands before the two subjects, is singular in agreement with Πέτρος, while the main verb, εἶπαν, is plural in agreement with both subjects. Cf. Bl-D §135 for particulars.

538.   *Constructio ad sensum.* Agreement is occasionally determined by the sense of the subject rather than by its grammatical number (as in English), e.g. a collective noun which embraces a plurality of persons in the singular *may* be tied to a plural verb:

              1   2   5

(18) πολύς (τε) ὄχλος τῶν ἱερῶν / ὑπήκουον / τῇ πίστει   Acts 6:7

     A great crowd of priests (= many priests) *were obedient*
     to the faith.

Bl-D §134.

Lesson 35

The Structure of Subject

540. The consideration of the formal signals pointing to the subject (§§533–538) did not yield systematic information concerning the variety of words and word clusters that actually appear as subject, nor did it indicate anything of the boundaries and structure of such word clusters. The boundaries and structure of subject clusters are crucial for seizing the subject and predicate of sentences as wholes—rather than as conglomerations of words. Knowledge of the variety of subject clusters defines the range of expectation so that the reader is more readily able to "recognize" subjects when he or she meets them in the text. The types of words and word clusters that appear as subject are outlined in §§542–548. The boundaries and structures of some common word clusters are considered in §§549–551.

541. A word group appearing as a grammatical unit in a sentence consists of a *head term* plus a *modifier* or modifiers. In the word group ἡ μαρτυρία σου (Jn 8:13), μαρτυρία is the head term; ἡ and σου are modifiers. ἡ is here the definite article determining μαρτυρία as some particular *testimony*, and σου is a possessive genitive of the personal pronoun indicating that the particular testimony in question was given by *you*: *the testimony of you* (English: *your testimony*). The syntactical relationships which bind these words together are relatively simple. Such relationships can, upon occasion, become very complicated.

The relationships that obtain between a head term and its modifiers is called *modification structure* (Roberts, 1958: 185). Modification structure is the syntax that governs the formation of intelligible word clusters.

Note: In this grammar, nominal word groups initiated by a preposition will be treated as if they were single head-and-modifier units, although the prepositional phrase is a non-headed group of a particular order (Gleason: 153). There seems to be no compelling reason to note each time that the preposition and its "object" constitute separate units. And many prepositional phrases do function as other nominal word clusters do in the sentence. In any case, the nominal word clusters occurring as the objects of prepositions are subject to the same analysis as clusters not initiated by a preposition.

541.1 In classifying the words and word groups that appear as subject, use will be made of "parts of speech" or word classes (§§010–014). The same applies to the descriptions of modification structure.

541.2 The notational scheme (§§511–516) will be employed and expanded for reasons of efficiency.

541.3 The classification of words and word groups and the analysis of modification structure with respect to the subject can subsequently be carried over to words and word clusters appearing as other grammatical elements in the sentence (§§681ff.).

542. *"Subjectless" sentences.* In context-bound Greek the subject is expressed as often as not solely by the personal ending attached to the verb. "Subjectless" with reference to Greek means that the subject of the sentence is not expressed by a discrete word. All Greek sentences containing a finite verb at least have a subject in the form of a personal ending (bound morpheme). It is quite possible occasionally to find full Greek sentences consisting of verb only (examples in §504), although "subjectless" sentences more commonly contain elements in the predicate other than the verb.

Arabic 1 stands for the subject expressed solely by the personal ending attached to the verb. Since a subject in this form is bound to the verb as a suffix, it should be hyphenated with the symbol representing the verb: 2-1 (cf. §513.3).

>   5   2-1
> (1) ἐν τῇ ἁμαρτίᾳ ὑμῶν / ἀποθανεῖσθε   Jn 8:21
>   *You will die in your sin*

>   5   2-1
> (2) (ἀλλ') ἔξω / ἐπ' ἐρήμοις τόποις / ἦν   Mk 1:45
>   *(but) he was out in the wilderness places*

543. *Single words as subject.* The subject is often expressed by single, discrete words. Divided into subgroups on a morphological basis ("parts of speech"), such words include:

> 1b   pronouns
> 1d   pronominal adjectives
> 1n   nouns
> 1a   adjectives
> 1g   participles
> 1i   infinitives

543.1 A pronoun as subject.

         1b   2   4

(3) ὑμεῖς / ποιεῖτε / τὰ ἔργα τοῦ πατρὸς ὑμῶν   Jn 8:41
You do the works of your father

543.2 A pronominal adjective as subject.

        1d   4   2

(4) ἐκεῖνός / με / ἀπέστειλεν   Jn 8:42
That one sent me

543.3 A noun as subject.

       4   1n   2

(5) τοῦτο / Ἀβραὰμ / οὐκ ἐποίησεν   Jn 8:40
This Abraham did not do

543.4 An adjective as subject.

       2   4   1a

(6) (καὶ) ἔρχεται / πρὸς αὐτὸν / λεπρός   Mk 1:40
(And) a leper aame to him

Note: A bare adjective as subject is rare.

543.5 A participle as subject.

       6   2   1g

(7) ἐκ σοῦ [γὰρ] ἐξελεύσεται / ἡγούμενος   Mt 2:6
(For) out of you shall come a leader

Note: A bare participle as subject is extremely rare.

543.6 An infinitive as subject.

       2   1i

(8) δεῖ / γενέσθαι   Mk 13:7
It is necessary [for these things] to take place

Note: Literally: *to take place is necessary* (*these things* is understood from the context). Infinitive subjects of the type *To err is human* appear to be rare in Greek.

5430. Among single word subjects, the pronominal adjective (1d) is the most frequent, with pronouns (1b) running a close second. The solitary noun as subject

(1n) is restricted mostly to instances of proper names. Other single word subjects are not common.

545.   *Word clusters as subject.* Word clusters also commonly appear in the structure of subject. The most common of these is the word cluster with a noun as the head term. Other types of word clusters, while of much lower frequency, also appear as subject. Divided into subgroups in accordance with §543, such word cluster subjects include:

> 1b+   a word cluster with a pronoun as head term
> 1d+   a word cluster with a pronominal adjective as head term
> 1n+   a word cluster with a noun as head term
> 1a+   a word cluster with an adjective as head term
> 1g+   a word cluster with a participle as head term
> 1i+   a word cluster with an infinitive as head term

545.1   A word cluster headed by a pronoun as subject.

> 1b+   6   2
> (9) πάντες ἡμεῖς / ἐνώπιον τοῦ θεοῦ / πάρεσμεν   Acts 10:33
>   *We are all here present in the sight of God*

545.2   A word cluster headed by a pronominal adjective as subject.

> 1d+   2
> (10) τινὲς [δὲ] τῶν Φαρισαίων / εἶπαν / . . .   Lk 6:2
>   *Some of the Pharisees said.*

545.3   A word cluster headed by a noun as subject.

> 1n+   2   4
> (11) καὶ / ἡ ἀλήθεια / ἐλευθερώσει / ὑμᾶς   Jn 8:32
>   *And the truth shall make you free*

545.4   A word cluster headed by an adjective as subject.

> 3   1a+
> (12) μακάριοι / οἱ πτωχοί   Lk 6:20
>   *Blessed are the poor*

545.5 A word cluster headed by a participle as subject.

1g+ 2 5
(13) ὁ ἀκολουθῶν ἐμοὶ / οὐ μὴ περιπατήσῃ / ἐν τῇ σκοτίᾳ   Jn 8:12
The one following me shall not walk in darkness

545.6 A word cluster headed by an infinitive as subject.

2 1i+
(14) ἔξεστιν / τοῖς σάββασιν καλῶς ποιεῖν   Mk 12:12
To do good on the sabbath is lawful

546. *An included sentence as subject.* In addition to the words and word clusters 1b–1i, an included sentence (a sentence with its own subject and predicate) may also appear in the structure of subject. Let s stand for any included sentence; an included sentence as subject would then be marked 1s.

5 2pass 1s
(15) καὶ ἐν τῷ νόμῳ [δὲ] τῷ ὑμετέρῳ / γέγραπται / ὅτι δύο
ἀνθρώπων ἡ μαρτυρία ἀληθής ἐστιν   Jn 8:17
And in your own law it is written that the testimony of two
men is true

547. *Compound and expanded subjects.* There are also compound subjects (subjects consisting of two or more of the above words and / or word clusters) and expanded subjects (a word or word group expanded by an appositional phrase, an adjectival clause, etc.). For example,

2 1d 1n+
(16) ἐπίστευσεν / αὐτὸς (καὶ) ἡ οἰκία αὐτοῦ ὅλη   Jn 4:53
He and his whole house believed

contains a compound subject consisting of 1d + 1n+. On the other hand, in the sentence

1n 1n+ 2
(17) Ἀβραὰμ // ὁ πατὴρ ὑμῶν / ἠγαλλιάσατο . . .   Jn 8:56
Abraham, your father, rejoiced . . .

the subject is expanded: the 1n+ cluster stands in apposition to and elaborates upon 1n (// is placed between appositional elements).

5470.   *Other subject clusters.* Virtually any word or word cluster—other than those already indicated—can be "substantivized" (i.e. used as a head term) by means of the article and used as subject.

5470.1 Articular (i.e. with article) adverbs as subject.

$$\overset{1}{}\qquad\overset{2}{}\qquad\overset{6}{}$$

(18) ἡ [γὰρ] αὔριον / μεριμνήσει / αὐτῆς   Mt 6:34
For the morrow will be anxious for itself

5470.2   A word as word, or a group of words as such, can be subject.

$$\overset{1}{}\quad\overset{3}{}\qquad\overset{1}{}\quad\overset{3}{}$$

(19) τὸ Ναὶ / ναὶ (καὶ) / τὸ Οὔ / οὔ;   2 Cor 1:17
Is not my "Yes" yes and my "No" no?

$$\overset{1}{}\qquad\overset{2}{}$$

(20) τὸ [δὲ] Ἔτι ἅπαξ / δηλοῖ / τὴν τῶν σαλευομένων

$$\overset{4}{}$$

μετάθεσιν . . .   Heb 12:27
The (phrase) "Yet once more" indicates the
removal of what is shaken . . .

These and other marginal subject clusters appear rarely and in special contexts.

548.   *Summary.* All the words and word clusters (including the personal ending attached to the verb) that appear as subject in the Greek sentence have been catalogued in §§542–547. While the categories listed are virtually exhaustive, the variety and structure of the word clusters remain to be explored. The descriptive rubrics listed above, and the mode of notation, may be consolidated for easy reference.

Words and Word Clusters Appearing as Subject
1   Subject signaled by personal ending attached to the verb
1b   Pronoun as subject
1b+ Word cluster with pronoun as head term as subject
        ἐγώ   ἡμεῖς
        σύ   ὑμεῖς
1d   Pronominal adjective as subject

1d+ Word cluster with pronominal adjective as head term as subject

ἐκεῖνος, ἐκείνη, ἐκεῖνο

οὗτος, αὕτη, τοῦτο

τίς, τί

τις, τι

ὁ, ἡ, τό

ὅς, ἥ, ὅ

ὅστις, ἥτις, ὅ τι

αὐτός, αὐτή, αὐτό

ἄλλος, ἄλλη, ἄλλο

ἕτερος, ἕτερα, ἕτερον

ἕκαστος, ἑκάστη, ἕκαστον

πᾶς, πᾶσα, πᾶν

πολύς, πολλή, πολύ

εἷς, μία, ἕν

οὐδείς, οὐδεμία, οὐδέν

μηδείς, μηδεμία, μηδέν

Note: The list of pronominal adjectives is not exhaustive.

1n	Noun as subject
1n+	Word cluster with noun as head term as subject
1a	Adjective as subject
1a+	Word cluster with adjective as head term as subject
1g	Participle as subject
1g+	Word cluster with participle as head term as subject
1i	Infinitive as subject
1i+	Word cluster with infinitive as head term as subject
1s	Included sentence as subject
1x + 1x	(x = any of the above items) as compound subject
1x // 1x	as expanded subject

Note: The designations for these words and word clusters will be employed in the descriptions of words and word clusters appearing elsewhere in the sentence as well.

549.   *Word clusters with a noun as head term.* Among the word clusters appearing as subject, sketched in §545, the most common is that headed by a noun (1n+). What may be expected in such clusters with nominal head, and how are they structured?

549.1   The simplest 1n+ cluster, as might be expected, is the sequence, article/noun:

(1)	ὁ ᾿Ιησοῦς	*Jesus*	Jn 8:12
(2)	οἱ Φαρισαῖοι	*the Pharisees*	Jn 8:13

The article as signaler of grammatical structure was considered briefly in §§125–129; the function of the article was indicated in §120. The syntax of the article is considered in greater detail below, §§710–7160.

549.2   Word clusters are of course built up in a systematic way—otherwise they would not be intelligible. If a nominal head is modified by an article, the most frequent way of expanding the cluster is by the addition of a defining or modifying genitive. This genitive may take the form of a personal pronoun:

(3)	ἡ μαρτία σου	*your testimony*	Jn 8:13

or another word cluster in the genitive:

(4)	ἡ ἀγάπη τοῦ θεοῦ	*the love of God*	1 Jn 2:5

The words in these clusters normally appear in immediate sequence (only particles like μέν, δέ, γάρ may intervene) and in the order indicated. The article always precedes the head it modifies, §126. The modifying genitives, however, may appear in other positions. The genitive (cluster) may precede:

(5)	αὐτοῦ τὰ ἔργα	*his works*	Jn 3:21
(6)	τοῦ ᾿Ιησοῦ Χριστοῦ ἡ γένεσις	*the birth of Jesus Christ*	Mt 1:18

Or it may be sandwiched between:

(7)	ὁ τοῦ θεοῦ (γὰρ) υἱός	*the son of God*	2 Cor 1:19

549.3   A nominal head may be modified by a pronominal adjective other than the article:

(8)	ἄνθρωπός τις	*a certain man*	Lk 14:16
(9)	ἄλλα πλοῖα	*other boats*	Mk 4:36

Some pronominal adjectives, however, never modify a nominal head unless an article is present:

(10) οἱ δοῦλοι ἐκεῖνοι	*those servants*	Mt 22:10
(11) οἱ λίθοι οὗτοι	*these stones*	Mt 4:3

A variety of combinations is possible with pronominal adjectives, with and without article, in attributive and predicate positions. The pronominal adjectives thus require to be separated into subgroups on the basis of the structures into which they may enter (s. below, §§0710ff.).

549.4   A nominal head may be modified by an adjective:

(12) σεισμὸς μέγας	*a great storm*	Mt 8:24

This modification structure is usually made more evident by the use of the article (cf. §127). The adjective may appear in *first attributive* position, i.e. between article and noun:

(13) οἱ ἀληθινοὶ προσκυνηταί	*the true worshippers*	Jn 4:23

Or, in *second attributive*, i.e. after the nominal head with article preceding:

(14) ὁ λόγος ὁ ἐμός	*my word*	Jn 8:37
(15) εἰρήνην τὴν ἐμήν	*my peace*	Jn 14:27

In the New Testament a common phrase of this type is:

(16) τὸ πνεῦμα τὸ ἅγιον	*the holy spirit*	Acts 10:44

549.5   A noun may be modified by a word cluster initiated by a preposition:

(17) οἱ ἱερεῖς ἐν τῷ ἱερῷ	*the priests in the temple*	Mt 12:5

Once again, this modification structure may be made clearer by the use of the article:

(18) ὁ πατὴρ ὑμῶν ὁ ἐν τοῖς οὐρανοῖς	*our father in heaven*	Mk 11:25

550.   *Concord and types of modification structure.* Modifiers that are articles, pronominal adjectives, and adjectives agree with the nominal head they modify in gender, number and case (§549.1, 3, 4). Triple concord thus makes it easily possible, as a rule, to seize these subject clusters as wholes. A modifying genitive word

or cluster represents a different type of modification structure, of course, and the possible differences in gender, number, and case make the relationships less perspicuous (§549.2). The case of the head term in a word cluster that is the object of a preposition is determined by the preposition; the gender and number of the head term is inherent in the term itself (§549.5). There are thus two types of 1n+ clusters: one containing a single head term; the other containing a modifying subcluster with its own head term. The difference has to do with the "part of speech" employed as modifier.

550.1 Genitive modifiers are nouns or pronouns, which constitute a separate cluster at another level.

(4) ἡ ἀγάπη τοῦ θεοῦ

is a word cluster as a whole, appearing as the subject of the sentence. Analyzed as a word cluster, it is made up of two subclusters:

(4) ἡ ἀγάπη / τοῦ θεοῦ

Similarly, (3) can be subdivided:

(3) ἡ μαρτυρία / σου

550.2 Modifiers consisting of a cluster initiated by a preposition also have their own head terms, e.g. in:

(17) οἱ ἱερεῖς / ἐν τῷ ἱερῷ

ἱερῷ is the nominal head of a subcluster, which, in turn, is the object of a preposition.

(18) may be cut into three subclusters:

(18) ὁ πατὴρ / ὑμῶν / (ὁ) ἐν τοῖς οὐρανοῖς

The second (ὁ) is a structure signaling word and as such does not belong to the third subcluster but to the larger cluster as a whole.

550.3 Clusters involving pronominal adjectives and adjectives as modifiers, on the other hand, cannot be cut into subclusters where they are in concord with their nominal head (all the examples in §549.1, 3, 4).

551. The types of modification structures outlined in §§549–550 are represented in the following clusters with the same nominal head.

(19) ὁ πατήρ	Jn 8:28
(20) ὁ πατὴρ / ὑμῶν	Jn 8:39
(21) ὁ πατὴρ / ὑμῶν / (ὁ) οὐράνιος	Mt 6:14
(22) ὁ πατὴρ / ὑμῶν / (ὁ) ἐν τοῖς οὐρανοῖς	Mk 11:25

In every instance πατήρ is modified by the article. (20)–(22) have a second modifier in the form of a genitive (of the personal pronoun). The third modifier in (21) is an adjective, the third modifier in (22) a cluster initiated by a preposition. The second article in both instances is a structure signaling item. (21) and (22), incidentally, are virtually synonymous in meaning.

Lesson 36

The Predicate & Adverbials

The Predicate

555. The predicate consists of the main (finite) verb plus its modifiers. The predicate may be defined as everything that does not belong to the subject (excluding sentence-transcending words, e.g. οὖν, *therefore*).

> 1b   2
> (1) ἐγὼ / ὑπάγω   Jn 8:21
>   *I go away*

> 1b   2   3n+
> (2) ἐγώ / εἰμι / τὸ φῶς τοῦ κόσμου   Jn 8:12
>   *I am the light of the world*

> 2   5d   1n+
> (3) εἶπον [οὖν] αὐτῷ / οἱ Φαρισαῖοι / . . .   Jn 8:13
>   *The Pharisees [therefore] said to him . . .*

In (1) the predicate consists of verb only (S-I). The predicate in (2) includes the equative verb (εἰμί) plus the subjective complement (3n+). Example (3) is S-IV with indirect object (5d) and direct object (what they said); the predicate thus consists of 2 (verb) + 5d + the statements made. οὖν is a sentence transcending word and is consequently put in brackets.

The heart of the predicate is the finite verb or verb chain that serves as the head term of the predicate.

The sentence types enumerated in §§504–510, 520–524 are really types of predicates (§503). In addition to the constituent elements belonging to the basic structure of each of these types, other words and word groups may modify the verb in a variety of ways. Such other modifying words and word groups include verbs, adverbs, a noun or adjective in an oblique case, a word group initiated by a preposition, a participle or a word group headed by a participle, and an included dependent sentence.

A provisional sketch of the predicate will indicate what common adverbials may be expected in the predicate beyond the constituent elements belonging to the basic structure of each sentence type.

5550.   *Analytic scheme of notation.* In view of the new symbols 3n+ and 5d in (2) and (3) (§555), it is necessary to recall the essential features of the notational scheme and expand it somewhat.

5550.1 *Arabic numbers* have been employed as follows (§513–516):

1	= word or word group in the structure of *subject*
2	= *finite verb* or main verb in the *predicate*
3	= in the predicate, a word or word group with the head term in the *nominative* case
4	= in the predicate, a word or word group with the head term in the *accusative* case
5	= in the predicate, a word or word group with the head term in the *dative* case
6	= in the predicate, a word or word group with the head term in the *genitive* case

To supplement the system of arabic numbers, A will be employed (§557) to mark any *adverb* (indeclinable) in the predicate:

A	= in the predicate, any *adverb*

5550.2 *Small letters* were used to describe the various types of words and word groups appearing as subject (§548). It was observed that the same letters could be employed elsewhere to describe words and word groups.

b	= pronoun
b+	= word cluster headed by a pronoun
d	= pronominal adjective
d+	= word cluster headed by a pronominal adjective
n	= noun
n+	= word cluster headed by a noun
a	= adjective
a+	= word cluster headed by an adjective
g	= participle
g+	= word cluster headed by a participle

   i = infinitive

   i+ = word cluster headed by an infinitive

   s = included sentence

5550.3 The symbol 3n+ in (2), §555, thus describes a word group in the predicate, headed by a noun in the nominative case. 5d in (3) describes a pronominal adjective in the predicate, in the dative case. The same arabic numbers and small letters may be variously combined to describe other words and word groups.

5550.4 *Prepositions* are designated p. A word cluster initiated by a preposition would then be described as p, followed by the case of the head term of the nominal cluster (4, 5, or 6), followed in turn by a description of the word or word groups. Examples may be found in §558.

Common Adverbials

556. Consider the adverbials in the following English sentences:

  (i) *He came / silently / to him / at night*

  (ii) *He stayed / there / two days*

  (iii) *I write / this way / customarily*

  (iv) *He went / his way / laughing*

  (v) *You cannot go / where I go*

These examples reveal that the following words and word groups may serve as modifiers of the verb (adverbials) in the English sentence: (a) adverbs (*silently, there, customarily*); (b) word groups initiated by prepositions (p-groups) (*to him, at night*); (c) noun clusters, i.e. groups headed by nouns (*two days, this way, his way*); (d) participles (*laughing*); (e) included dependent sentences (*where I go*).

  Such adverbials may appear singly or in various combinations, and they may be entirely optional in the sentence. Example (i) could be rewritten in a variety of ways:

  (ia) *He came*

  (ib) *He came silently*

  (ic) *He came at night*

  (id) *He came to him*

  (ie) *He came to him at night*

    etc.

  (i) is thus a type I sentence with numerous adverbial options.

557.   In Greek, as in English, adverbs may modify verbs:

          2-1   A

(1) ἔμεινεν / ἐκεῖ   Jn 4:40

He stayed / there

          A   2pass-1

(2) ἤδη / κέκριται   Jn 3:18

He has / already / been judged

          A   2-1

(3) οὕτως / γράφω   2 Thess 3:17

Thus / I write

Note: The designation A appears over the adverb in the illustrations above; it may be used to mark adverbs wherever they appear (§5550.1)

Sentences (1)–(3) illustrate three meaning-based categories of adverbs and adverbials: In (1) ἐκεῖ is an adverb of place or a *locative* adverb; ἤδη in (2) indicates *time* and is therefore a *temporal* adverb; οὕτως (3) is an adverb of *manner*. The three groups may be represented by the catchwords *there, then, thus*; in Greek: ἐκεῖ, τότε, οὕτως. There are other categories of adverbs as well.

558.   Word groups initiated by prepositions (p-groups) may also appear as modifiers of verbs:

          p5d   2-1

(4) παρ' αὐτῷ / ἔμεινεν   Jn 1:39

They stayed with him

          1n+   2   p4n+

(5) ὁ υἱὸς / μένει / εἰς τὸν αἰῶνα   Jn 8:35

The son abides forever

          1d   4d   p5n   2

(6) οὐδεὶς / [γὰρ] τι / ἐν κρυπτῷ / ποιεῖ   Jn 7:4

[For] No one does anything secretly

The three p-groups in (4)–(6) correspond to the three categories of adverbs represented by the catchwords ἐκεῖ, τότε, οὕτως (§557).

559.   Noun clusters may be used as adverbials in Greek as in English (§556). Since all nouns are inflected in Greek, the head term of the cluster will have to appear in a specific case. The head term may appear, for example, in the accusative case:

```
        2-1          4n+
```
(7) ἔμεινεν / τὴν ἡμέραν ἐκείνην   Jn 1:39
They stayed that day

Or in the genitive case:

```
        1d     2     6n
```
(8) οὗτος / ἦλθεν / νυκτός   Jn 3:2
This one came by night

Or in the dative case:

```
        2pass-1   5n+
```
(9) ἐγήγερται / τῇ ἡμέρᾳ τῇ τρίτῃ   1 Cor 15:4
He was raised on the third day

Examples (7)–(9) reveal that the cases express different temporal ideas when used adverbially. Generally speaking, the accusative expresses *duration*, the genitive *time within which*, and the dative *time when*. The cases are not always used in such contexts with great precision, however.

560.   Various types of adverbials may, of course, be combined. Examples (4) and (7) are actually from the same sentence, so that the full sentence contains both a p-group and a noun cluster:

```
        p5d        2-1          4n+
```
(10) παρ' αὐτῷ / ἔμειναν / τὴν ἡμέραν ταύτην   Jn 1:39
They stayed with him that day

The full form of (1) also contains adverbials expressing both place and time, this time an adverb and a noun cluster:

```
        2-1        A      4n+
```
(11) ἔμεινεν / ἐκεῖ / δύο ἡμέρας   Jn 4:40
He stayed there two days

Both ideas may be expressed by p-groups:

```
        1n+        2      p5n+        p5n+
```
(12) ὁ [δὲ] δοῦλος / οὐ μένει / ἐν τῇ οἰκίᾳ / εἰς τὸν αἰῶνα   Jn 8:35
The slave does not abide in the house forever

Or by a p-group and the genitive case (the actual form of (8)) :

1d   2   p4d   6n

(13) οὗτος / ἦλθεν / πρὸς αὐτὸν / νυκτός   Jn 3:2

This one came to him by night

Common adverbials in the forms of adverbs, p-groups and noun clusters may thus be employed in a variety of combinations.

561.   Participles (g) and word groups headed by participles (g+) often appear as adverbials.

2   1n+   3g   3g

(14) ἦλθεν / ὁ υἱὸς τοῦ ἀνθρώπου / ἐσθίων καὶ πίνων   Mt 11:19

The son of man came eating and drinking

The twin participles, ἐσθίων καὶ πίνων, express manner: How did he come? He came eating and drinking.

A word group headed by a participle may be used temporally:

4n+   2   1n+   3g+

(15) τοῦτο . . . δεύτερον σημεῖον / ἐποίησεν / ὁ Ἰησοῦς / ἐλθὼν

ἐκ τῆς Ἰουδαίας εἰς τὴν Γαλιλαίαν   Jn 4:54

This second sign Jesus did after coming out of Judea into Galilee

The participle itself does not specify which adverbial idea is meant. The particular meaning must be inferred from the context in each instance so that more than one meaning is often possible.

5610.   Other uses of the participle as an adverbial and the infinitive as a modifier of the verb are considered under verb chains, §§565–585, the infinitive, §§0830ff., and the participle, §§0845ff.

Lesson 37

Verb Chains: Groups I–II

565. The common adverbials considered in §§556–5610 were exclusive of verbs. Verbs may also be modified by other verbs. The simple statement *I go to town*, may be slightly altered by the insertion of a "modal auxiliary": *I may go to town*. *May* modifies the main verb, *go*: instead of a simple assertion, the sentence may now be interpreted, e.g., as a deliberative statement. Other illustrative examples of verbs modifying verbs are the following:

I	wanted	to go	to town
	kept	going	
	attempted	to go	
	began	to go	
	stopped	going	
	attempted	to stop going	

May go, wanted to go, kept going, etc. may be characterized as verb chains because two or more verbs are linked together in a chain. The first verb is called a *catenative* verb because it is capable of initiating a verb chain. Such chains have their own internal structure, depending on the catenative verb and the other verbs in the chain. For example, one may say, *I kept going*, but not *ˣI kept to go*. *Kept* must be followed by a *participle*, not an *infinitive*. Other catenatives may be followed by either participle or infinitive, with little apparent difference in meaning:

> I began to go
> I began going

The sentences in which still others occur are sharply modified by a change from one to the other:

> I stopped speaking
> I stopped to speak

Verb chains are common in English and are governed by structures peculiar to the several possible combinations (Gleason: 312ff.).

566. Verb chains also appear in Greek. Some found in Greek are quite comparable to some found in English, some common in English are unknown to Greek, and some found in Greek have no counterparts in English. It is therefore important to understand the Greek system of verb chains in terms of its own rationale.

Some definitions and generalizations may be given respecting verb chains in Greek:

566.1 The finite verb or the first verb in a verb chain is called a *catenative* verb because it is able to initiate a verb chain. In a chain of more than two verbs, all but the last must be catenative verbs.

A chain of more than two verbs is apparently rare (unlike English, e.g. *He determined to begin trying to do better*).

μέλλει [γὰρ] Ἡρῴδης ζητεῖν τὸ παιδίον τοῦ ἀπολέσαι αὐτό   Mt 2:13
[For] Herod intends to search for the child to destroy him

566.2 Any verb can occur in final position in a verb chain; only relatively few verbs can initiate a chain (=catenative verb).

566.3 The second (and third) verb in a chain must be either an *infinitive* or *participle*.

566.4 The final verb (infinitive or participle) in a chain may take any of the complements it may take were it the only verb (finite) in the sentence. Sentence (or predicate) types I–VI are thus possible with verb chains as well as with simple verbs. For example, a type III sentence may contain a verb chain:

     2-1   i   4n+
οὐ δύνασθε / ἀκούειν / τὸν λόγον τὸν ἐμόν   Jn 8:43
You are not able to hear my word

566.41 The actual order of verbs and verbals in a chain may be at variance with the grammatical progression in Greek, e.g. the catenative may not actually come first in the sentence, although it is logically first in the chain.

5660.1 The main or finite verb is marked 2 in accordance with §5550. If it is a catenative verb, it may be marked 2c (c for catenative).

5660.2 In the description of words and word groups (§5550.2), i stood for the simple *infinitive*. i may also be used to mark an infinitive in the predicate. Since the infinitive is an indeclinable verbal noun, it will not exhibit case (i will therefore never be preceded by 3, 4, 5, or 6). However, an infinitive with a catenative verb is sometimes preceded by an article, or an article with preposition. In that case it will be marked i+ (a word group headed by an infinitive), with appropriate case designation (arabic number). For example,

6i+

τοῦ σπείρειν   Mt 13:3

p5i+

ἐν τῷ σπείρειν αὐτὸν   Mt 13:4

5660.3 In the description of subjects, g stood for the simple *participle*, and g+ for a word cluster headed by a participle. The participle is a *declinable* verbal adjective and thus will always exhibit case. Accordingly, in the predicate, the participle may be marked 3g, 4g, 5g, 6g, or g+, depending on its case and whether it appears alone or in a word group.

Catenatives: Group I

567. *Auxiliary verbs.* Unlike English, "auxiliary" verbs are by and large foreign to Greek. An "auxiliary" verb may be defined as a catenative verb that is lexically empty, i.e. does not add to the lexical meaning of the verb with which it forms a chain. What "meaning" it adds is therefore grammatical. In English the auxiliaries add tense and/or aspect and/or mood to the main verb, e.g. *had gone*, *was going*, *may go*. What is added to the main verb by *had*, *was*, *may* in English may be expressed in Greek by the form of the simple verb itself.

    A   2   1n+

(1) οὔπω / ἐληλύθει / ἡ ὥρα αὐτοῦ   Jn 8:20
    His hour had not yet come

    2-1   p4d

(2) ἤρχοντο / πρὸς αὐτόν   Jn 4:30
    They were coming to him

      2-1   p4n

(3) ἵνα] μὴ ἔλθητε / εἰς πειρασμόν   Mk 14:38
    That] you may not come into temptation

The meaning supplied by other verbs modifying verbs in English may also be expressed in Greek by the form of the simple verb. For example, *the widow kept coming to him* is expressed in Greek by:

1n   2   p4d

(4) χήρα / . . . ἤρχετο / πρὸς αὐτόν   Lk 18:3

The tense-aspect in (1) is supplied by the pluperfect form of the verb, in (2), (4) by the imperfect, and the mood of (3) is supplied by the subjunctive.

568.   *Periphrasis with εἰμί and the participle.* Some tenses in Greek were regularly formed with an auxiliary verb, e.g. perfect middle-passive 3. pl. of verbs ending in a consonant (§3910), the perfect subjunctive (§442.2). The use of an appropriate form of εἰμί (*be*) with the participle to form tense-aspect/mood is called periphrasis (literally, a circumlocution). Periphrasis for the simple form of the verb is found most frequently, though not often, in the imperfect, perfect and pluperfect tenses, rarely in the present, future and future perfect tenses. For example,

       2c   1n+   3g

(5)   καὶ) ἦσαν / οἱ μαθηταὶ Ἰωάννου / . . . νηστεύοντες   Mk 2:18
      John's disciples used to fast

       A   3g   2c-1

(6)   μόνον [δὲ] ἀκούοντες / ἦσαν [ὅτι . . .   Gal 1:23
      Only they kept hearing [that . . .

(5), (6) are to be compared with (2), (4), i.e. the simple imperfect could have been employed in all cases, or, alternatively, the periphrastic form. The periphrastic form often gives emphasis to continued, repeated or habitual action.

The following are examples of periphrasis for the perfect and pluperfect:

       p5n   2c-1   3g

(7)   αὐτοῦ τὰ ἔργα] ὅτι / ἐν θεῷ / ἐστιν / εἰργασμένα   Jn 3:21
      his works] that they have been wrought in God

Note: Neuter plural subject with a singular verb (§536)

       A   2c   3g   p4n+   1n+

(8)   οὔπω [γὰρ] ἦν / βεβλημένος / εἰς τὴν φυλάκην / ὁ Ἰωάννης   Jn 3:24
      [For] John had not yet been cast into prison

Bl-D §§352–353.

569.   *Periphrasis with μέλλω and the infinitive.* Μέλλω with the infinitive expresses imminence. It is occasionally used as periphrasis for the simple future.

4d 2c-1   5b   i
(9) . . . ἣν / μέλλω / σοι / λέγειν . . .   Herm Sim 5.2.1

    . . . which I will tell you

Since μέλλω with an infinitive expresses the imminence of the action, it may be used to express imminence in past time.

2c-1   i
(10) ἤμελλεν / τελευτᾶν   Lk 7:2

    He was about to die

In both (9) and (10), μέλλω contributes only to the tense-aspect of the verb chain, and thus functions as an "auxiliary." In (10), the tense-aspect expressed by μέλλω is analogous to the ingressive imperfect or aorist (§§792.4, 788.2). Cf. Bl-D §356; Bauer s.v.

570.   *Periphrasis with ἄρχομαι and the infinitive.* The verb chain

(11) ἤρξατο κηρύσσειν   Mk 1:45

    He began to preach

is scarcely distinguishable from ἐκήρυσσεν (Bl-D §392(2)). In that case ἄρχομαι (middle voice only) with an infinitive may often be regarded as periphrasis for the ingressive aorist or imperfect (§§792.4, 788.2), and thus classified as an "auxiliary." Turner: 138.

571.   The uses of εἰμί, μέλλω, and ἄρχομαι described in §§568–570 may be characterized as "auxiliary." Other catenative verbs are not lexically empty and thus cannot be characterized as "auxiliaries." Some form verb chains with an infinitive, some with a participle.

571.1   Common verbs forming a verb chain with an infinitive include:

δύναμαι — *I can, am able*
ἰσχύω — *I am strong, able*

1b   2c   i
(12) ὑμεῖς / οὐ δύνασθε / ἐλθεῖν   Jn 8:21

    You are not able to come

i   2c-1
(13) σκάπτειν / οὐκ ἰσχύω   Lk 16:3

    I am not strong enough to dig

571.2   Common verbs forming a verb chain with a participle include:

παύομαι — *I stop* (myself), *cease*
καλῶς ποιῶ — *I do well*

2c-1	3g	4n+

(14) ἐπαύσαντο / τύπτοντες / τὸν Παῦλον   Acts 21:32
They stopped beating Paul

1b	A	2c	3g

(15) σύ / [τὲ] καλῶς / ἐποίησας / παραγενόμενος   Acts 10:33
[*And*] *you were good enough* [lit., *did well*] *to come*

Bl-D §§392, 414ff.

572.   The infinitive or participle in verb chains such as those described in §§568ff. is often referred to as *supplementary* (or *complementary*) because they supplement the finite or catenative verb in the chain, either grammatically (e.g. εἰμί, §568) or lexically (e.g. δύναμαι, §571.1), or both.

The supplementary infinitive is much more common in hellenistic Greek than the supplementary participle.

573.   The catenative verbs in §571 were characterized as *not* lexically empty, i.e. they contribute to the lexical meaning of the infinitive or participle, by comparison with the "auxiliaries" in §§568–570, which are lexically but not grammatically empty. However, all the sentences with catenative verbs illustrated thus far (examples (5)–(15)), have manifested identical or comparable grammatical structures: catenative verb plus infinitive or participle. This is to disregard the basic sentence type involved—the sentence type depends on the supplementary verb—and to attend only to the verb chain itself. Of the verb chains considered thus far two things can be said:

573.1   The subject of the catenative verb and the subject of the supplementary infinitive or participle has always been identical.

573.2   The catenative verb has taken no immediate complements or modifiers other than the infinitive or participle.

573.3   We may add a third characteristic in anticipation of other types of verb chains: Alternative constructions, such as the substitution of ἵνα and the subjunctive for the infinitive, are not possible.

Given the grammatical similarities, the verb chains represented by(5)–(15) may be designated Group I. In view of the difference in the lexical import of the catenatives themselves, Group I may be subdivided into two Groups:

Ia. Catenative lexically empty
Ib. Catenative not lexically empty

We have now to consider verb chains which differ in one or more of these respects.

Catenatives: Group II

574. *An infinitive of purpose with intransitive verbs.* Intransitive verbs (verbs not normally taking an object) *may* be followed by an infinitive of purpose.

<pre>
      2c-1   i   4b
(16) ἦλθες / ἀπολέσαι / ἡμᾶς;   Mk 1:24
      Have you come to destroy us?
</pre>

The infinitive ἀπολέσαι expresses the purpose of the motion indicated by the finite verb (here in a question). Yet the grammatical structure is identical with the verb chains already considered, i.e. it meets the criteria of §573.1–2. Is there any way to distinguish the type of verb chain represented by (16) from those represented by (5)–(15)?

574.1 One way to make the distinction would be to list the verbs which may be followed by an infinitive of purpose. But the list would be too long to remember easily, and it would include more than intransitive verbs (as we shall see, there is need to isolate intransitive from transitive verbs). One could characterize such a list as all intransitive verbs of motion (cf. Bl-D §390(1)) and this would cover most verbs in the list but not all. It would be more efficient, consequently, to discover simple, universally applicable grammatical criteria as the basis of the distinction.

574.2 The grammatical criteria given in §573.1–2 provide such a basis:

(a) *Like* the verb chains in §§568–571, the subject of an intransitive verb and an infinitive of purpose is always identical.

(b) *Unlike* the verb chains in §§568–571, an intransitive verb followed by an infinitive of purpose *may* take *immediate adverbial modifiers* (other than a negative). By *immediate* is meant adverbials which modify the catenative verb only, not the verb chain as a whole. Taking (16) as an example, one may ask (in Greek):

(i) *Have you come* here
　　　　　　to this place
　　　　　　into the world *to destroy us?*

The adverbials in this sentence intervene, so to speak, between catenative and infinitive and modify the catenative only. In a sentence like (12) (§571.1), additional adverbials are to be interpreted as modifying the verb chain as a whole:

(ii) *You are not able to come* here
(iii) *You are not* quite *able to come* at this time

The distinguishing test, then, is whether an adverbial may be inserted between catenative and infinitive.

575. Intransitive verbs which *may* be followed by an infinitive of purpose include:

ἔρχομαι — *I come, go* (and compounds)
παραγίνομαι — *I come, appear, be present*
πορεύομαι — *I go*
ἀναβαίνω — *I go up, ascend*
πάρειμι — *I am present*

575.1 Examples without intervening adverbial (cf. (16)):

　　　　　　　2c　　　　　　1n+　　　　　　i
(17) καὶ) συνήρχοντο / ὄχλοι πολλοὶ / ἀκούειν (καὶ)
　　　ipass　　　　　　　　　　p6n+
　　　θεραπεύεσθαι / ἀπὸ τῶν ἀσθενειῶν αὐτῶν　　　　　　Lk 5:15
　　　And) great crowds gathered to hear and to be healed
　　　of their infirmities

　　　2c-1　　　　i　　　　　4d
(18) πορεύομαι / δοκιμάσαι / αὐτά　　　　　　Lk 14:19
　　　I go to examine them

575.2 Examples with intervening adverbial:

<pre>
        1n+   2c   p4n+   i
</pre>
(19) ἄνθρωποι δύο / ἀνέβησαν / εἰς τὸ ἱερὸν / προσεύξασθαι   Lk 18:10
Two men went up to the temple to pray

<pre>
        2c-1   p4n   i   4n
</pre>
(20) ἀνῆλθον / εἰς Ἱεροσόλυμα / ἱστορῆσαι / Κηφᾶν
I went up to Jerusalem to visit Peter   Gal 1:18

An infinitive of purpose with an intransitive verb is quite common in hellenistic Greek.

576. Verb chains like those represented by (16)–(20) may be designated Group II. Verb chains of Group II differ from those in Group I in one other important respect: an "analytical" construction with ἵνα and the subjunctive may substitute for the former but not for the latter (§573.3; cf. §580.3):

<pre>
        2-1   p4n+   s
</pre>
(21) ἦλθον / οὐ διὰ τὸν Ἰησοῦν μόνον / ἀλλ᾽ ἵνα καὶ τὸν
Λάζαρον ἴδωσιν   Jn 12:9
They came, not only on account of Jesus, but also to see Lazarus

<pre>
        2c-1   i   p4b   s
</pre>
(22) καὶ) οὐ θέλετε / ἐλθεῖν / πρός με / ἵνα ζωὴν ἔχητε   Jn 5:40
Yet you do not want to come to me that you may have life

The ἵνα-clauses in (21) and (22) are the grammatical equivalent of an infinitive of purpose; like the infinitives in (16)–(20), they follow an intransitive verb of motion (ἔρχομαι).

Lesson 38

Verb Chains: Groups III–VI

Catenatives: Group III

580. *Transitive verbs chaining with an infinitive.*

580.1 In traditional grammars, verb chains like those represented by

2c   4b   1n   i

(23) οὐ [γὰρ] ἀπέστειλέν / με / Χριστὸς / βαπτίζειν   1 Cor 1:17

[For] Christ did not send me to baptize

are customarily grouped with verb chains of Group II on the grounds that in both cases the infinitive expresses purpose. However, the structure of (23) differs from the structure of the verb chains in Group II in one important respect: the subject of the infinitive is different from the subject of the catenative verb, and is normally signaled by the accusative case. The construction with accusative (subject of the infinitive) and infinitive suggests that the catenative verb is transitive. If the catenative is transitive, it should be subject to a passive transformation (§508.3). And the passive form of ἀποστέλλω with infinitive does appear:

2pass-1   i   p4b

(24) καὶ) ἀπεστάλην / λαλῆσαι, / πρὸς σέ   Lk 1:19

And I was sent to speak to you

In the passive transform, the accusative subject of the infinitive becomes the subject of the catenative verb, while the infinitive is retained as a verbal complement.

580.2 Verb chains like that represented by (23) and (24) are further illustrated by:

2c-1   4d   p4n+

(25) καὶ) ἔπεμψεν / αὐτὸν / εἰς τοὺς ἀγροὺς αὐτοῦ /

i   4n

βόσκειν / χοίρους   Lk 15:15

And he sent him into his fields to feed swine

Verb chains of this type with συνάγω appear in the New Testament only in the passive form:

$\qquad\qquad$ 1n+ $\qquad$ 2pass-c

(26) σχεδὸν πᾶσα ἡ πόλις / συνήχθη /

$\qquad$ i $\qquad\qquad$ 4n+

ἀκοῦσαι / τὸν λόγον τοῦ κυρίου $\qquad\qquad\qquad\qquad$ Acts 13:44

Almost the whole city was gathered together
to hear the word of the Lord

$\qquad$ 2pass-c $\qquad\qquad$ 1n+ $\qquad\qquad$ 1n+ $\qquad\qquad$ i

(27) συνήχθησαν [δὲ] οἱ ἀπόστολοὶ (καὶ) οἱ πρεσβύτεροι / ἰδεῖν /

$\qquad\qquad$ p6n+

περὶ τοῦ λόγου τούτου $\qquad\qquad\qquad\qquad\qquad$ Acts 15:6

The apostles and elders were gathered together to consider this
matter

580.3 As is the case with verb chains in Group II, an agnate (§592.2) construction with ἵνα and the subjunctive may substitute for the infinitive in chains like those represented by (23)–(27). We may call the ἵνα-construction the ἵνα-transformation (T-ἵνα, for short), since the relations between the two constructions are regular and systematic. For example, (28) may be regarded as T-ἵνα of a sentence identical in structure with (23):

$\qquad\qquad$ 2 $\qquad\qquad$ 1n+ $\qquad\qquad$ 4n+ $\qquad\qquad$ p4n+

(28) οὐ [γὰρ] ἀπέστειλεν / ὁ θεὸς / τὸν υἱὸν / εἰς τὸν κόσμον /

$\qquad$ s

ἵνα κρίνῃ τὸν κόσμον $\qquad\qquad\qquad\qquad\qquad$ Jn 3:17

For God did not send his son into the world
to condemn the world

And (29) is the corresponding T-ἵνα of (25):

$\qquad$ 2-1 $\qquad$ 4n $\qquad$ s

(29) πέμψον / Λάζαρον / ἵνα βάψῃ τὸ ἄκρον τοῦ δακτύλου αὐτοῦ

$\qquad\qquad$ s

ὕδατος (καὶ) καταψύξῃ τὴν γλῶσσάν μου $\qquad\qquad$ Lk 16:24

Send Lazarus to dip the end of his finger in water and cool
my tongue

580.4 It may be said that transitive verbs like ἀποστέλλω, πέμπω, and ἀνάγω are causatives of motion, and so may be followed by an infinitive expressing purpose in a way quite similar to the catenatives in Group II. Indeed, (25) and (28) show that catenatives of this type may take immediate adverbial modifiers like the catenatives of Group II (§574.2). However, the grammatical difference is critical: The catenatives in Group II are intransitive and thus can have no passive transform; this also means that the subject of catenative and infinitive is always identical (§574.2). In verb chains of the type represented by (23)–(29), the catenative is transitive; consequently, it may have a passive transform (the passive form is not always attested) , and the subject of the catenative and infinitive differ (in the active form). Such verb chains may be designated Group III.

580.5 Verb chains of Group III include more than causatives of motion (§580.4), and the infinitive does not always express purpose, as will be noted below (§§581ff.).

581. *θέλω as Catenative.* A complementary infinitive often appears with θέλω, *wish, want, be willing.* If we take

(30) θέλω δὲ ὑμᾶς ἀμερίμνους εἶναι   1 Cor 7:32
   I want you to be free from anxieties

as the paradigm case, verb chains with θέλω belong to Group III (§580). However, a passive transform of (30) is not attested. On the other hand, θέλω may take a direct object in a type III sentence (e.g. Mt 9:13); it is therefore transitive, in spite of the fact that a passive form was not developed. The limitation of §580 (§508.3), viz. that a transitive verb is subject to a passive transformation, does not apply to θέλω.

Alongside (30) must now be set:

(31) οὐκ ἤθελον ἐλθεῖν   Mt 22:3
   They did not want to come

in which the subject of catenative and infinitive are identical. The structure of (31) is identical with the structure of verb chains in Group I (§573). How is θέλω to be classified as a catenative verb?

It was observed that for verb chains in Group I analytic constructions with ἵνα and the subjunctive are not possible (§573.3). For verb chains in Groups II (§576) and III (§580.3), however, they are possible. In the case of θέλω, an alternative construction with ἵνα and the subjunctive is permitted only in those instances where the subject of the catenative and the subject of the infinitive are different, e.g.

> (32) θέλω δὲ πάντας ὑμᾶς λαλεῖν γλώσσαις, μᾶλλον δὲ ἵνα
> προφητεύητε   1 Cor 14:5
> *[Now] I want you all to speak in tongues, but even more*
> *to prophesy*

In (32) θέλω is followed by both an infinitive and a ἵνα-clause, with a subject different from that of the catenative. T-ἵνα is not possible for (31).

θέλω may thus initiate two types of verb chains: (1) those belonging to Group Ib, in which the subject of catenative and infinitive are identical and an analytic construction is not permitted (§573.3), and (2) those belonging to Group III, in which the subjects are different and an analytic construction is permitted. Neither the infinitive nor ἵνα and the subjunctive with θέλω, strictly speaking, denotes purpose.

Many catenative verbs initiate verb chains of more than one type.

582.   *Verb chains in Group III*, as identified in §§580–581 meet the following criteria:

582.1   The catenative verb is transitive;

582.2   The subject of the infinitive complement (signaled by the accusative case) differs from the subject of the catenative;

582.3   The verb chain is subject to a passive transformation (where the catenative appears in a passive form), in which the accusative subject of the infinitive becomes the subject of the passive catenative and the infinitive is retained as a verbal complement;

582.4   The verb chain is subject to T-ἵνα (cf. §580.3), in which ἵνα and the subjunctive replaces the infinitive.

582.5   Criteria (1) and (2) will isolate a much larger group of verb chains than can be accommodated by (3) and (4). Criterion (3), the T-pass, is not always applicable (cf. θέλω, §581), and, as we shall see, it is not always applicable in the form stated (§§583.3–4, 585.3–5). Criterion (4), moreover, can be used to distinguish two fundamentally different types of verb chains, both of which meet criteria (1) and (2). As defined, then, Group III includes a variety of verb chains, which require further analysis.

Catenatives: Group IV

583.   Sometimes included among infinitives of purpose are constructions like

> (33) ἔδωκαν αὐτῷ πιεῖν οἶνον   Mt 27:34
>   *They gave him wine to drink*

(e.g. Bl-D §390(2)), on the grounds that the original datival function of the infinitive is manifest: wine *for* drinking.

583.1   It should be noted that the peculiar arrangement of complements with this verb chain is occasioned by the nature of the catenative verb, δίδωμι, which takes both a direct and an indirect object:

> (34) ταῦτά σοι πάντα δώσω   Mt 4:9
>   *I shall give you all these things*

The direct and indirect objects are related to the verb in (34) but in different ways (S-IV, §§509f.). The same set of relationships holds in (33) between αὐτῷ, οἶνον and the main verb, in spite of the presence of the infinitive.

583.2   The relationships between αὐτῷ, οἶνον and the infinitive, πιεῖν, are not the same as between αὐτῷ, οἶνον and the main verb: The indirect object of the main verb, αὐτῷ, is the subject of the infinitive, while οἶνον is the direct object of both the infinitive and the main verb. In other words, the deep structure of αὐτῷ πιεῖν οἶνον is: *he drinks wine.*

583.3   The passive transformation of (33) is

> (35) ὑμῖν δέδοται γνῶναι τὰ μυστήρια τῆς βασιλείας τῶν
>   οὐρανῶν   Mt 13:11
>   *The secrets of the kingdom have been given to you to know*

With this may be compared the passive form of (34):

> (36) σημεῖον οὐ δοθήσεται αὐτῇ   Mt 12:39
>   *A sign shall not be given to it [this generation]*

In both cases the direct object of the finite verb becomes the subject in the passive transformation. And this is the only passive form attested for predicates headed by δίδωμι.

583.4   In relation to the verb chains of Group III, the verb chains of Group IV meet the first two criteria given in §582.1–2, but in the T-passive of IV it is the *object of* the infinitive that becomes the subject of the passive form (35), rather than the accusative subject of the infinitive (23). The "subject" of the infinitives in Group IV are in the dative case, because the catenatives may head predicates of S-IV, which take both direct and indirect objects.

583.5 An analytical construction with ἵνα and the subjunctive is attested for (33):

(37) τὰ γὰρ ἔργα ἃ δέδωκέν μοι ὁ πατὴρ ἵνα τελειώσω αὐτά, . . .   Jn 5:36
For the works which the Father has given me to do, . . .

This construction proves that the indirect object in the deep structure of (33) is the "subject" of the infinitive, since μοι and the subject of τελειώσω in (37) refer to the same person. An identical example is to be found in Jn 17:4.

583.6 On the basis of the distinction indicated in §583.4, verb chains like that represented by (33) should be given the designation, Group IV. The catenative verbs in Group IV are related to the verbs of S-IV (§§509f.).

583.7 The structure of verb chains of Group IV is indicated by the following parallel clauses:

(38) ὥσπερ γὰρ ὁ πατὴρ ἔχει ζωὴν ἐν ἑαυτῷ,
οὕτως καὶ τῷ υἱῷ ἔδωκεν ζωὴν ἔχειν ἐν ἑαυτῷ   Jn 5:26
For just as the father has life in himself,
so he has given life to the son to have in himself

The deep structure of τῷ υἱῷ . . . ζωὴν ἔχειν is: *the son has life*, as is indicated by the preceding clause: *the father has life*.

583.8 Constituent elements may of course be deleted with verb chains as with common sentence types (§§604–608). In the following, the direct object is deleted:

(39) καὶ ἐδώκατέ μοι φαγεῖν   Mt 5:35
and you gave me (something) to eat

Catenatives: Group V

584. Catenatives of Group V consist of verbs of perception, i.e. verbs meaning to *hear, see, perceive, find* (= *discover, detect*). These verbs may take a *supplementary participle* when they denote an actual physical act of perception:

(40) καὶ ἤκουσαν οἱ δύο μαθηταὶ αὐτοῦ λαλοῦντος   Jn 1:37
And the two disciples heard him speaking

what they heard is: *him speaking.*

584.1   The structure of (40) is comparable to the structure of verb chains in Group III: The catenative is transitive, and the subject of the participle differs from the subject of the main verb (cf. §582.1–2). The participle and its subject here appear in the genitive case: ἀκούω takes the genitive of the person heard (accusative of the thing, §595).

584.2   Verb chains like that in (40) are also subject to a passive transformation, in which the subject of the supplementary participle (in an oblique case) becomes the subject of the main (passive) verb:

> (41) εὑρέθη ἐν γαστρὶ ἔχουσα ἐκ πνεύματος ἁγίου   Mt 1:18
> *She was found to be with child of the holy spirit*

The active form of (41) would be something like:

> (i)   *They found her to be with child of the holy spirit*

Verb chains in Group V thus meet the T-pass criterion of verb chains in Group III (§582.3).

584.3   The grammatical difference between verb chains of Group V and those of Group III (and IV) is that Group V chains are not subject to T-ἵνα (§582.4). Indeed, for all verb chains like (40) there is no correlative analytical construction at all.

584.4   Verb chains of Group V are also to be distinguished from the supplementary participles appearing in Groups Ia (§568) and Ib (§571). In the Group V, the subject of the participle always differs from the subject of the main verb; the catenative may take complements other than the participle. The reverse of these statements characterizes Groups 1a and Ib (§573).

584.5   Catenatives of perception may take complements in a case other than the genitive. The most frequent case is the accusative:

> (42) εἶδεν Ἰησοῦς τὸν Ναθαναὴλ ἐρχόμενον πρὸς αὐτόν   Jn 1:47
> *Jesus saw Nathaniel coming to him*
> (43) καὶ θεωρεῖ τὸν οὐρανὸν ἀνεῳγμένον καὶ καταβαῖνον
> σκεῦός τι ὡς ὀθόνην μεγάλην   Acts 10:11
> *And he saw the heaven opened, and something descending,*
> *like a great sheet*

A catenative may occasionally require the dative:

(44) καὶ ἐμβλέψας τῷ Ἰησοῦ περιπατοῦντι λέγει, . . .   Jn 1:36

    And he looked at Jesus walking and says, . . .

The case depends, of course, on the nature of the catenative verb.

584.6   Supplementary participles belonging to Group V are relatively common in hellenistic texts. This type is traditionally referred to as a supplementary participle not in indirect discourse, in order to distinguish it from the supplementary participle in indirect discourse (Group VI, §585). The two resemble each other closely, and are sometimes hard to distinguish.

Catenatives: Group VI

585.1   In sentences (45) and (46),

(45) ἤκουσαν τοῦτο αὐτὸν πεποιηκέναι, τὸ σημεῖον   Jn 12:18

    They heard (that) he had done this sign

(46) ἀκούω σχίσματα ἐν ὑμῖν ὑπάρχειν   1 Cor 11:18

    I hear (that) there are divisions among you

the catenative is transitive and the subject of the infinitive, in these instances, differs from the subject of the catenative. In these respects verb chains of Group VI are like those of Groups III–V, but in other respects they differ. Since verb chains in Group VI occur in what is customarily called indirect discourse, it may be helpful to consider what that entails before proceeding.

585.2   Sentence (45) is usually described as *indirect discourse* in the form of the (accusative subject and) infinitive after verbs of perception, believing, saying, showing. Someone makes the assertion,

(i)   *He has done this sign*

which may then be heard:

(ii)   *They heard that he had done this sign*

or believed:

(iii)   *They believed that he had done this sign*

or said:

(iv)   *They said that he had done this sign*

or indicated:

(v) *They indicated that he had done this sign*

Similarly, a group may have observed a certain activity and are reported to have taken note of it mentally:

(vi) *They observed that he had done this sign*

Verbs of perception followed by indirect discourse (vi) denote an intellectual act of perception. This usage is to be distinguished from catenatives of perception denoting a physical act of perception and taking a supplementary participle (§584).

In sentences (ii)–(vi), the original assertion (i) is said to be reported indirectly. That (ii)–(vi) represent indirect speech is indicated by the shift in tense (in English but not necessarily in Greek) between (i) and the other forms. Other examples of indirect discourse may also involve a change in person (e.g. *I saw him do it/He said that he saw him do it*). The assertion in (i) may, of course, be reported directly:

(vii) *They said, "He has done this sign"*

in which (i) is embedded unchanged.

In Greek, (i) is embedded in indirect form either by means of the (accusative and) infinitive, or by means of a ὅτι-clause (§648). Less frequently, indirect discourse is represented by the supplementary participle.

585.3   In the passive form of (45), (46), the infinitive and its complements become the subject of the passive verb, i.e. the indirectly reported statement becomes the subject of the passive verb:

(47) καὶ ἦν αὐτῷ κεχρηματισμένον ὑπὸ τοῦ πνεύματος τοῦ
     ἁγίου μὴ ἰδεῖν θάνατον   Lk 2:26
     And it had been revealed to him by the holy spirit that he
     should not see death

The passive form is not common.

585.4   The use of the infinitive in indirect discourse is on the decline in the hellenistic period (Bl-D §§396, 470). The correlative analytic construction with ὅτι (§648) is more common:

(48) ἠκούσατε ὅτι ἐγὼ εἶπον ὑμῖν,
    ὑπάγω καὶ ἔρχομαι πρὸς ὑμᾶς   Jn 14:28
You heard that I said to you,
"I go away and I will come to you"

This example is cited not only because it illustrates indirect discourse introduced by ὅτι, but also because it contains a direct quotation embedded in the indirect.

The passive form of (48) is:

(49) ἠκούσθη ὅτι ἐν οἴκῳ ἐστίν   Mk 2:1
It was reported that he was at home

As in the form with infinitive (47), the entire indirectly quoted statement becomes the subject of the passive verb.

585.5   Verb chains of Group VI are like those of Groups III–V in that the catenative is transitive and, in the examples given thus far, the subject of the infinitive differs from the subject of the main (catenative) verb. Verb chains in Groups III and IV are subject to T-ἵνα (§§582.4, 583.5); those in Group V have no correlative analytical construction, while those in Group VI are subject to T-ὅτι (§585.4). The T-pass of VI differs from the passive transformations of the preceding groups as well (cf. §585.3 with §§582.3, 583.2, 584.2). Verb chains like those represented by (45) and (46) therefore represent a distinct group.

585.50   It is possible in indirect discourse for the subject of the catenative and the subject of the infinitive (or participle) to be identical:

(50) φάσκοντες εἶναι, σοφοὶ . . .   Rom 1:22
Asserting that they are wise . . .

In this case, the subject of the infinitive has to be supplied from the main verb, and complements of the subject will accordingly be in the nominative case. This construction is not common in the New Testament (Bl-D §405). This form of indirect discourse does not belong, of course, to verb chains in Group VI as defined in §585.5.

585.6   Further examples of the infinitive in indirect discourse:

(51) ἔλεγον αὐτὸν εἶναι θεόν   Acts 28:6
They said that he was a God

(52) τίνα με λέγουσιν οἱ ἄνθρωποι εἶναι;   Mk 8:27
Who do men say that I am?

Another example of T-ὅτι:

(53) ἀλλ᾽ ὅτε εἶδον ὅτι οὐκ ὀρθοποδοῦσιν   Gal 2:14
But when I saw that they were not straightforward

585.7   The participle is also found in verb chains of Group VI:

(54) ἀκούομεν γάρ τινας περιπατοῦντας ἐν ὑμῖν ἀτάκτως   2 Thess 3:11
For we hear that some of you are living in idleness

(55) ὃς οὐ γινώσκει τὴν Ἐφεσίων πόλιν νεωκόρον οὖσαν τῆς
μεγάλης Ἀρτέμιδος . . . ;   Acts 19:35
*Who does not know that the city of the Ephesians is the
guardian of the temple of the great Artemis?*

The supplementary participle in indirect discourse is to be distinguished from the supplementary participle in Group V (§584) in accordance with §585.2. The construction with the participle in Group VI is not common in hellenistic Greek. Cf. Bl-D §416.

Lesson 39

Variations on Sentence Type III

590.   The predicate of a sentence type III was defined (§508) as a transitive verb taking a direct object in the accusative case; the subject and object of the verb refer to different persons or things. A further example is:

	1n+	4d	2	
(1)	ἡ ἀγάπη /	. . . πάντα /	πιστεύει	

(1)   ἡ ἀγάπη / . . . πάντα / πιστεύει   1 Cor 13:7
      Love . . . believes all things

S-III is capable of a passive transformation in which the object of the active form becomes the subject in the passive:

        2pass   1n+
(2)   ὅτι] ἐπιστεύθη / τὸ μαρτύριον ἡμῶν   2 Thess 1:10
      because] our testimony was believed

The direct object in S-III was marked 4 as a symbol for the accusative case (§513.5), although it was noted that not all words and word groups in the predicate with the head term in the accusative case were direct objects in S-III (§514). It may now be asked whether the direct object in S-III is always signaled by the accusative case.

Verbs Taking a Dative Object

591.   πιστεύω, *I believe (in) something; I believe (in), trust someone,* is a common verb in the New Testament manifesting a wide range of constructions. It may be used illustratively to answer the question posed in §590. Consider the following sentences:

(i)   *Many believed him*
(ii)   *The man believed the word*
(iii) *You believe that Jesus is the Christ*

In (i) and (ii) *him* and *the word* are the direct objects of *believe;* in (iii) an included dependent sentence is the direct object of the same verb. We may now consider the forms the object with πιστεύω may take in Greek.

591.1   Example (1) indicates that πιστεύω may take an *accusative* object of the *thing*.

591.2   In the sentence

>   2   1n+   5n+
> (3)   ἐπίστευσεν / ὁ ἄνθρωπος / τῷ λόγῳ   Jn 4:50
>   *The man believed the word*

πιστεύω takes a *dative* object of the *thing*.

591.3   πιστεύω may also be followed by εἰς and the *accusative* object of the *thing*:

>   2-1   p4n+
> (4)   ὅτι] οὐ πεπίστευκεν / εἰς τὴν μαρτυρίαν   1 Jn 5:10
>   *because] he has not believed the testimony*

591.4   And by ἐν and the *dative* object of the *thing*:

>   2-1   p5n+
> (5)   πιστεύετε / ἐν τῷ εὐαγγελίῳ   Mk 1:15
>   *believe in the gospel*

591.5   πιστεύω is never followed by an *accusative* object of the person; when a person is object, the case is *dative*:

>   1n+   1n+   2   5d
> (6)   οἱ [δὲ] τελῶναι (καὶ) αἱ πόρναι / ἐπίστευσαν / αὐτῷ   Mt 21:32
>   *The tax collectors and prostitutes believed him*

591.6   For this personal object may be substituted εἰς and the accusative (cf. §591.3):

>   1d   2   p4d
> (7)   πολλοὶ / ἐπίστευσαν / εἰς αὐτόν   Jn 8:30
>   *Many believed (in, on) him*

That the last two constructions are really grammatically synonymous is proved by variation in the same context. Sentence (7) is followed immediately by

>   2-1   p4n+
> (8)   ἔλεγεν . . . / πρὸς τοὺς πεπιστευκότας αὐτῷ Ἰουδαίους   Jn 8:31
>   *he said . . . to the Jews who believed him*

in which the participles takes a dative object of the person.

591.7 And, of course, πιστεύω may be followed by an included dependent sentence as object:

$$\overset{2-1}{} \quad \overset{s}{}$$

(9) ἵνα] πιστεύσητε / ὅτι Ἰησοῦς ἐστιν ὁ Χριστὸς   Jn 20:31
in order that] you may believe that Jesus is the Christ

The included dependent sentence is introduced by ὅτι (*that*), as in English.

5910. The predominant constructions with πιστεύω have been introduced in sentences (1)–(9). All are common except (5), ἐν with the dative. Other marginal constructions with πιστεύω are illustrated by the variant readings found at Jn 3:15:

ἵνα] πᾶς ὁ πιστεύων   ἐν αὐτῷ   ἔχῃ ζωὴν αἰώιον
                  ἐπ' αὐτῷ
                  εἰς αὐτὸν
                  ἐπ' αὐτὸν

in order that] everyone believing in (on) him may have eternal life

On this passage, however, s. Bl-D §187(6).

For πιστεύω in S-IV, s. §510.1.

592.1 Objects with πιστεύω may thus take the following forms (using the descriptive analytic scheme; omitting the marginal constructions):

1/2/4
1/2/5
1/2/p4n+
1/2/s

i.e. it may be followed by the simple accusative, the simple dative, a preposition with accusative, an included dependent sentence.

592.2 If the difference between person and thing may be ignored (note §591.5), these forms of the object with πιστεύω may be said to be grammatically equivalent. The sentences in which they appear can then be said to be *agnate*, i.e. different grammatical constructions are used to express the same grammatical relation (Gleason: 202ff., 209ff.).

592.3 The analytical scheme employed in this grammar seeks to combine morphological description (the form of words) with syntactic analysis (the relations between and among words) insofar as possible (§512.2). The symbol 4 was used to designate the direct object (accusative case) in S-III (§513.5). However, not all 4's in the predicate, i.e. not all accusatives, signal direct objects. We must therefore distinguish the 4 that is not an object from those which are. In §514, (18) contains a 4 that is not a direct object but an *adverbial* accusative; since this accusative functions as an adverbial, it should be marked in a secondary fashion with the symbol for adverbs, i.e. A:

       $4a^A$ 2-1

(18) ὀλίγον / ἀγαπᾷ   Lk 7:47

     he loves little

Similarly, the objects of πιστεύω not signaled by the simple accusative may be marked in a secondary fashion with a raised 4:

(3) $2/1n+/5n+^4$

(4) $2-1/p4n+^4$

(5) $2-1/p5n+^4$

(6) $1n+/1n+/2/5d^4$

(7) $1d/2/p4d^4$

(8) $2-1/s^4$

Where morphological description and syntactic analysis coincide, no secondary marking is needed:

(1) $1n+ \ldots 4d/2$

Note: This scheme assumes that the direct object in Greek is normally signaled by the accusative case. This assumption is doubtless correct, but it ignores a considerable number of verbs that customarily take objects in other cases. The conflation of symbols as suggested above is in the interests of the parsimony of symbols.

593. *Verbs taking a dative object.* In addition to πιστεύω, which may take an object in either the dative or accusative cases, with and without preposition, other verbs characteristically take an object in the *dative* case.

593.1 ἀκολουθέω, *follow, obey.*

        2              $5d^4$ 1n+

(10) ἠκολούθησαν / αὐτῷ / ὄχλοι πολλοί   Mt 4:25

     Great crowds followed him

593.2 ὑπακούω, *obey.*

         1n+   1n+   5d[4]   2

(11) οἱ ἄνεμοι (καὶ) ἡ θάλασσα / αὐτῷ / ὑπακούουσιν   Mt 8:27
    The winds and the sea obey him

593.3 πέποιθα (2. perf. and pluperf. act.), *trust in, depend on.*

        3g   5n+[4]

(12) πεποιθὼς / τῇ ὑπακουῇ σου . . .   Philemon 21
    Confident of your obedience

Note: πέποιθα is also followed by ἔν τινι, ἐπί τινι or τινα, εἴς τινα (s. Bl-D §187(6)).

Verbs of *following, obeying* comprise only a small sample of verbs taking a dative object, sometimes in addition to an accusative object and/or an object introduced by a preposition. A fuller list and details will be found in Bl-D §§187, 188, 193.

Verbs Taking a Genitive Object

594. Just as some verbs take a dative object in type III sentences, some verbs may take an object in the genitive case. The genitive is often employed where only a part of the whole denoted by the object is involved, e.g. *to touch someone or something* (one touches a part of the whole), or where the object denotes the source, e.g., *to hear someone* (the speaker is the source of the words heard). In refined Greek the difference between an accusative and a genitive object provides the basis for fine nuances, e.g. *to remember something* (as a whole) requires an accusative of the object, but *to remember something* (about someone or something) takes the genitive. Such fine distinctions have been lost to a large extent in colloquial hellenistic Greek and the genitive (and dative) cases with certain verbs are retained to a certain extent as a habit of language.

595. ἀκούω, *hear, listen to,* is a common verb manifesting a wide range of constructions (cf. πιστεύω, §591).

595.1 ἀκούω may appear in a typical S-III with an *accusative* object of the *thing:*

        2-1   4n+

(1) ἀκούσατε / τοὺς λόγους τούτους   Acts 2:22
    hear (imperative) *these words!*

Since ἀκούω is a transitive verb taking a direct object, it is subject to a passive transformation (IIIP; §508.3):

$$\text{1n} \qquad \text{p5n} \qquad \text{2pass}$$
(2) φωνὴ / ἐν ῾Ραμὰ / ἠκούσθη   Mt 2:18
A voice was heard in Ramah

595.2   In accordance with good classical usage, ἀκούω takes a *genitive* object of the *person* (the source of what is heard):

$$\text{1n+} \quad \text{2} \qquad \text{6d}^4 \qquad \text{A}$$
(3) ὁ πολὺς ὄχλος / ἤκουεν / αὐτοῦ / ἡδέως   Mk 12:37
The great throng heard him gladly

595.3   Sentences (1) and (3) indicate that ἀκούω takes an accusative object of the thing but a genitive object of the person. However, ἀκούω—not always in accordance with classical usage (Bl-D §173)—sometimes takes a *genitive* object of the *thing*:

$$\text{1d} \quad \text{6b} \quad \text{2} \qquad\qquad \text{6n+}^4$$
(4) ἐάν] τίς / μου / ἀκούσῃ / τῶν ῥημάτων   Jn 12:47
If] any one hears my words

Note: 6b is a possessive pronoun going with the word group 6n+.

595.4   The accusative object of (1) and the genitive object of (3) may be *combined* in a single sentence:

$$\text{4d} \quad \text{2-1} \qquad\quad \text{6b}$$
(5) τὴν ἐπαγγελίαν . . .] ἣν / ἠκούσατέ / μου   Acts 1:4
The promise . . .] which you heard from me

(5) shows that the gen. of person, when ἀκούω is strictly a verb of perception, is dependent upon a deleted object in the acc. case. For example, (3) may be interpreted to mean:

The great throng heard his (teaching) gladly

i.e. they listened to his words. This is confirmed by agnate (§592.2) constructions with preposition (§595.6). However, ἀκούω may be used in a slightly different sense in which the genitive appears to be the only and immediate object:

595.5 ἀκούω, *listen to, obey*

      2-1   6d⁴

(6) ἀκούετε / αὐτοῦ   Mt 17:5
     Listen to him! (i.e. *obey* him)

In (6) ἀκούω is not a verb of perception.

The gen. obj. of (3) is therefore to be distinguished from the gen. obj. of (6). Strictly speaking, only the latter should be marked with a small, raised ⁴ (§592.3); the former may be so marked (when the acc. obj. is not expressed, cf. (5)), provided the distinction is kept in mind.

595.6 The genitive object of (5)—but not that of (6)—may be introduced by a preposition (παρά, ἀπό).

           4d 2-1   p6n+

(7) τὴν ἀλήθειαν . . .] ἡν / ἠκουσα / παρὰ τοῦ θεοῦ   Jn 8:40
     The truth . . .] which I heard from God

           4d 2-1   p6n+

(8) ἡ ἀγγελία] ἡν / ἀκηκόαμεν / ἀπ' αὐτοῦ   1 Jn 1:15
     The message] which we have heard from him

Note: ἔκ τινος is also found.

595.7 The genitive object of person (3) may be followed by a (genitive) participle of a verb of saying:

      2   1n+   6d   6g

(9) καὶ) ἠκουσαν / οἱ δύο μαθηταὶ / αὐτοῦ ,' λαλοῦντος   Jn 1:37
     And] the two disciples heard him speaking

See §584 for the supplementary participle with verbs of perception.

595.8 ἀκούω, like πιστεύω (§591.7), may take an *included dependent sentence as object*, which does not, of course, show case.

      2   1n   s⁴

(10) ἠκουεν / Ἰησοῦς / ὅτι ἐξέβαλον αὐτόν   Jn 9:35
     Jesus heard that they had cast him out

This form of S-III with ἀκούω is also subject to a passive transformation (cf. §595.1):

2pass   1s

(11) ἠκούσθη / ὅτι ἐν οἴκῳ ἐστίν   Mk 2:1

It was heard that he was at home

(literally, *that he is at home was heard*)

595.9   (10) and (11) are examples of *reported statements*. They may be understood as reported *directly: Jesus heard, "They have expelled him"*, or indirectly: *"Jesus heard that they had expelled him"*. Greek permits the retention of the original tense in indirect statements, where English requires that the tense of the indirect form follow the tense of the introductory verb (cf. the two forms above). If (10) and (11) are taken to be *indirectly* reported statements, then two other *agnate* (§592.2) constructions are possible with ἀκούω, i.e. different grammatical structures expressing the same grammatical relations.

The first is ἀκούω followed by a participle with its own subject in the accusative (§585.7):

3g   1n   4g   4n   p4n

(12) ἀκούσας [δὲ] Ἰακὼβ / ὄντα ;' σιτία / εἰς Αἴγυπτον . . .   Acts 7:12

When Jacob heard that there was grain in Egypt . . .

The second is ἀκούω followed by an infinitive with its own subject in the accusative (s. §585):

2-1   4d   4d   i   4n+

(13) ἤκουσαν / τοῦτο / αὐτὸν / πεποιηκέναι / τὸ σημεῖον   Jn 12:18

They heard that he had done this sign

Note: 4d (τοῦτο) + 4n+ is the object of i; 4d (αὐτόν) is the subject of i.

(12) and (13) are thus ways of reporting statements indirectly that differ structurally from (10) but express the same grammatical relationships.

596.   *The genitive object with verbs of sensation.* Closely related to verbs of perception, like ἀκούω, are verbs of sensation (e.g. *to touch*), and verbs meaning to *eat of, remember, rule.*

596.1 ἅπτομαι, *touch, take hold of*, with gen. object:

<pre>
        3g+   2-1   6d⁴
(14) ἐκτείνας τὴν χεῖρα / ἥψατο / αὐτοῦ   Mt 8:3
     Stretching out his hand he touched him
</pre>

Compare ἐπιλαμβάνομαι, *take hold of, grasp*:

<pre>
       1n+   3g+   2   6d⁴
(15) ὁ Ἰησοῦς / ἐκτείνας τὴν χεῖρα / ἐπελάβετο / αὐτοῦ   Mt 14:31
     Jesus stretched out his hand and caught him
</pre>

Bl-D §170 for a full list and details.

596.2 γεύομαι, *take, partake of*, with gen. object:

<pre>
        1d   2   6n+⁴
(16) οὐδεὶς / . . . γεύσεταί / μου τοῦ δείπνου   Lk 14:24
     No one . . . shall have a taste of my banquet
</pre>

Bl-D §169.

596.3 μιμνήσκομαι, *remember*, also with gen. object:

<pre>
        2-1   6n+⁴
(17) ἐμνήσθην [δὲ] / τοῦ ῥήματος τοῦ κυρίου   Acts 11:16
     I remembered the word of the Lord
</pre>

Bl-D §175.

596.4 κυριεύω, *rule, master* someone, something (gen.):

<pre>
       1n   6d⁴   A   2
(18) θάνατος / αὐτοῦ / οὐκέτι / κυριεύει   Rom 6:9
     Death no longer has dominion over him
</pre>

Bl-D §177.

Verbs taking the genitive are discussed in Bl-D §§169–181, although genitives other than the genitive of object are included indiscriminately.

597. *Summary.* The agnate constructions discussed and illustrated in §§591–596 reveal that the direct object in S-III may be signaled not only by the accusative case, but also by:

> the dative case
> the genitive case
> an oblique case introduced by a preposition

The simple accusative case in the predicate more often than not will signal the direct object. Nevertheless, some verbs permit agnate constructions. The recognition of such agnate constructions depends upon acquaintance with the range of possibilities and specific verbs.

Lesson 40

Variations on Sentence Type IV

600. The predicate of a type IV sentence (S-IV) was defined (§509) as a verb taking both a direct (accusative case) and an indirect (dative case) object. Type IV sentences are common with verbs of *saying, answering,* and related words (λέγω, εἶπον [s. Appendix III, class VI for the principal parts], λαλέω, ἀποκρίνομαι, φημί), e.g.

1b   4n+   2   5b

(1) ἀλλ'] ἐγὼ / τὴν ἀλήθειαν / λέγω / ὑμῖν   Jn 16:7
     But] I tell you the truth

One form of the passive transformation of S-IV (s. §510) is the following:

5n+   2pass   1n+

(2) τῷ [δὲ] Ἀβραὰμ / ἐρρέθησαν / αἱ ἐπαγγελίαι / (καὶ) τῷ
     5n+
     σπέρματι αὐτοῦ   Gal 3:16
     The promises were made (said) to Abraham and to his
     descendants

In this form the direct object of the active becomes the subject in the passive.

The Direct Object in S-IV

601. Compare the following trio of sentences:

   (i)   *I tell you the truth*
   (ii) *I tell you that you can do it*
   (iii) *I tell you, "You can do it"*

(i)–(iii) indicate that the direct object with verbs of *saying* can take the form of (i) a noun cluster (or equivalent), (ii) an indirectly quoted statement, and (iii) a directly quoted statement. In Greek texts like the New Testament, forms (ii) and (iii) are more common than (i). In fact, the preponderance of type IV sentences in the gospels consists of sentences with the structure of (iii).

601.1　An included sentence as object is not, of course, signaled by case. The quoted statement, however, normally comes last in the sentence. This example is typical:

　　　　2　　　　　5d　　　1n+　　　　S⁴
　　(3)　εἶπον [οὖν] αὐτῷ / οἱ Φαρισαῖοι / σὺ περὶ σεαυτοῦ μαρτυρεῖς　　Jn 8:13
　　　　The Pharisees [then] said to him, "You give testimony on your
　　　　own behalf . . . "

Note: s was the symbol adopted for any included sentence (§5550). It is marked s⁴ when the included sentence is object (§592). A convenient convention is to capitalize the symbol (S⁴) when the included statement represents a direct (as opposed to an indirect) quotation.

601.2　A quoted statement as object may also take the indirect form, as in (ii):

　　　　2-1　　　　　5b　　s⁴
　　(4)　εἶπον [οὖν] ὑμῖν / ὅτι ἀποθανεῖσθε ἐν ταῖς ἁμαρτίας ὑμῶν　　Jn 8:24
　　　　I [therefore] told you that you would die in your sins

601.3　The direct object in S-IV with verbs of *saying* may thus commonly take the form of 4n+ (noun cluster with head term in the accusative case), S⁴, and s⁴.

The Indirect Object in S-IV

602.　Compare the following sentences:

　　(i)　*I told him the truth*
　　(ii)　*I told the truth to him*
　　(iii)　*I tell you, "You will die in your sins"*
　　(iv)　*I say to you, "You will die in your sins"*

(i) and (ii) indicate that the indirect object in English is used without preposition if it *precedes* the direct object, but with preposition if it *follows* the direct object. This convention appears to be rigid since a violation produces nonsense or at least awkwardness:

　　　ˣ*I told the truth him*
　　　ˣ*I told to him the truth*

Some verbs of *saying* in English require a preposition with the indirect object, others do not admit it under certain circumstances. We may say, *I tell you, " . . . ",* but not *ˣI tell to you, " . . . ".* Or, *I say to you, " . . . ",* but not, *ˣI say you, ". . . ".*

602.1   The indirect object in Greek, too, may be introduced by a preposition. With

$$\begin{array}{llll} 2 & 5d & 1n & S^4 \end{array}$$

(5)   εἶπεν / αὐτοῖς / Ἰησοῦς / . . .   Jn 8:58
      Jesus said to them, . . .

compare

$$\begin{array}{lll} 2 & 1n+ & p4d^5 \end{array}$$

(6)   εἶπον [οὖν] οἱ Ἰουδαῖοι / πρὸς αὐτόν, . . .   Jn 8:57
      The Jews [then] said to him, . . .

p4d in (6) replaced 5d in (5) with no apparent difference in grammatical relation. (6) may therefore be said to be *agnate* to (5); p4d is thus marked p4d⁵ to indicate that the p-group functions as indirect object.

Note: This use of the symbol 5 assumes that the dative case normally signals the indirect object in the predicate. Statistically this is probably an incorrect assumption. Nevertheless, in order to conserve symbols and to relate morphology and syntax wherever possible, it seems appropriate to utilize the symbol for the form of the dative also as a designation for one of the basic syntactical relations the dative serves to express. Cf. §592.3, Note.

602.2   πρός with the acc. is used to signal the indirect object with all the verbs of *saying* listed in §600. It is the common agnate construction for the simple dative of the indirect object with these verbs. Occasionally one finds still other agnate constructions, e.g.

$$\begin{array}{lll} 4d & 2\text{-}1 & p4n+^5 \end{array}$$

(7)   ταῦτα / λαλῶ / εἰς τὸν κόσμον   Jn 8:26
      These things I declare to the world

And with a slight difference in nuance:

$$\begin{array}{llll} 2 & 4n & 1d & p6A \end{array}$$

(8)   λαλεῖτε / ἀλήθειαν / ἕκαστος / μετὰ τοῦ πλησίον αὐτοῦ   Eph 5:25
      Let every one speak the truth with his neighbor

i.e. reciprocally.

Note: μετὰ τοῦ πλήσιον αὐτοῦ is marked p6A because πλήσιον is an indeclinable adverb, often used as a substantive (ὁ πλήσιον = *the near one*).

602.3   With verbs other than verbs of saying, agnate constructions for the simple dative of the indirect object in S-IV are perhaps less common. Nevertheless, πέμπω, *send*, admits πρός and acc. along with the dative:

$$\begin{array}{ccc} \text{2-1} & \text{5b} & \text{4n} \end{array}$$

(9)   διὰ τοῦτο] ἔπεμψα / ὑμῖν / Τιμόθεον   1 Cor 4:17
       For this reason] I sent Timothy to you

$$\begin{array}{ccc} \text{4n} & \text{2-1} & \text{4n} \end{array}$$

(10)   ἀναγκαῖον [δὲ] ἡγησάμην / Ἐπαφρόδιτον / . . .
        i   p4b5
       πέμψαι / πρὸς ὑμᾶς   Phil 2:25
       I deemed it necessary to send Epaphroditus . . .
       to you

ἀποστέλλω, also meaning *send*, takes πρός and εἰς with the acc. as agnate constructions for the simple dative. δίδωμι, *give*, does not admit πρός, but does admit εἰς and the acc.:

$$\begin{array}{cc} \text{4g+} & \text{4n+} \end{array}$$

(11)   . . . τὸν θεὸν] τὸν διδόντα / τὸ πνεῦμα αὐτοῦ τὸ
                                    p4b5
       ἅγιον / εἰς ὑμᾶς   1 Thess 4:8
       . . . God] the one who gives his holy spirit to you

along with the more common dat.:

$$\begin{array}{cccc} \text{1d} & \text{2} & \text{5b} & \text{4n+} \end{array}$$

(12)   . . . ὃς / ἔδωκεν / ἡμῖν / τὸ φρέαρ   Jn 4:12
       . . . who gave us the well

On the other hand, γράφω, *write*; ἀφίημι, *forgive*; δείκνυμι, *show*, admit no agnate constructions for the simple dative in S-IV.

A full list of agnate constructions for the simple dative of indirect object would require cataloguing the verbs which appear in S-IV.

603. *Summary.* The agnate constructions described in §§601–602 indicate that the direct object in S-IV take the form of:

> a word or word group with head term in the accusative case
> an included sentence (s⁴, S⁴)

The indirect object may be signaled by:

> the simple dative case
> an oblique case introduced by a preposition

There is thus less variation in S-IV than in S-III (cf. §597).

The Deletion of Constituent Elements

604. Some verbs characteristically appear in specific sentence types. For example, many verbs are characteristically transitive and so regularly appear in S-III, while others are characteristically intransitive and so regularly appear in S-I. Some verbs may appear in more than one sentence type, often with a difference in meaning. The type of sentence in which a given verb appears may thus be a significant clue to its meaning in that context. Yet it is not always easy to determine the sentence type owing to what may be called the *deletion of constituent elements.*

In English the verb *forgive* may appear in a type IV sentence:

> (i) *God forgives us our sins*

This same sentence may be written in abbreviated form, without direct object:

> (ii) *God forgives us*

or, without indirect object:

> (iii) *God forgives our sins*

Both objects could conceivably (i.e. in particular contexts) be omitted:

> (iv) *God forgives*

where *us our sins* is to be understood from the context.

If (i) represents the full, context-free form of the sentence, (ii) would then be an example of *object deletion*, (iii) an example of the *deletion of the indirect object*, and (iv) an example of the *deletion of both*.

605. ἀφίημι with the meaning *let, let go, let alone* takes a personal object in the accusative case (S-III):

      2-1   4d

(1) ἄφετε / αὐτούς   Mt 15:14
    Let them alone

With the meaning *cancel, remit, pardon, forgive* it characteristically appears in S-IV:

      2-1   5b   4n+

(2) ἄφες / ἡμῖν / τὰ ὀφειλήματα ἡμῶν   Mt 6:12
    Forgive us our debts

This sentence may be described as IV.4n+/5b (S-IV with 4n+ as direct object and 5b as indirect object).

In the same context of the Lord's Prayer compare the following forms of the same sentence type:

      1b   2   5n+

(3) ἡμεῖς / ἀφήκαμεν / τοῖς ὀφειλέταις ἡμῶν   Mt 6:12
    We have forgiven our debtors

Description: IV.0/5n+

      1n+   2   4n+

(4) οὐδὲ / ὁ πατὴρ ὑμῶν / ἀφήσει / τὰ παραπτώματα ὑμῶν   Mt 6:15
    Neither will your father forgive your trespasses

Description: IV.4n+/0

      1b   2

(5) εἰ δὲ] ὑμεῖς / οὐκ ἀφίετε, . . .   Mk 11:26
    But if] you do not forgive, . . .

Description: IV. 0/0

It thus appears quite permissible, in context, to delete the direct object (3), the indirect object (4), or both (5) with this verb. The symbol 0 represents the deletion of constituent elements in examples (3)–(5).

606. The passive transformation of (2), i.e. the sentence in its full form, is represented by:

> 2pass   5b   1n+
> (6) ἀφέωνταί / σοι / αἱ ἁμαρτίαι σου   Lk 5:20
> *Your sins have been forgiven you*

in which the direct object has become the subject. This form of the sentence may be described as IVP. (4n+>1n+)/5b (P = the passive transformation); (4n+>1n+) means that the direct object, 4n+, of the active form has become the subject, 1n+, in the passive form.

The indirect object may be deleted in a sentence with the basic form of (6):

> 2pass   1n+
> (7) ἀφέωνται / αἱ ἁμαρτίαι αὐτῆς αἱ πολλαί   Lk 7:47
> *Her many sins are forgiven*

Description: IVP. (4n+>1n+)/0

Note: (6) and (7) are the only passive forms of the sentence that appear in the New Testament, i.e. the indirect object never becomes subject. Cf. §510.

607. The direct object may also occasionally be deleted with transitive verbs that characteristically appear in S-III. The object can normally be supplied from the immediate context.

>   1a+   3g+   2
> (8) οἱ [δὲ] λοιποὶ / κρατήσαντες τοὺς δούλους αὐτοῦ / ὕβρισαν
>   2
> (καὶ) ἀπέκτειναν   Mt 22:6
> *While the others seizing his servants abused and killed [them]*

This sentence may be described as III.0 (i.e. S-III with object deleted). The object is easily supplied from the object of the participle.

608. Constituent elements are deleted in other sentence types as well, e.g. the verb in S-II. Greek also permits the ellipsis of non-constituent items, sometimes on the basis of convention, sometimes out of the individual author's whim. Cf. Bl-D §§479–481. Object deletion in S-III and S-IV can be pursued by studying the verb entries in Bauer, although not all the articles are so arranged as to permit analysis of this type without the use of a concordance.

Lesson 41

Negatives

Introduction to Function Words

610. On the basis of the morphological description of the Greek language, words may be divided into three broad categories: (1) those belonging to the nominal system; (2) those belonging to the verbal system; and (3) those not inflected (§011). Two major components of the third group (§014) are (3a) *adverbs*, and (3b) *prepositions*. These two subgroups have already been tentatively considered in various connections. Aside from adverbs and prepositions, the remaining words in the third, uninflected category were termed (3c) *particles* (§014.4). The term *particle* is only a convenient designation for a highly diversified group of words which requires precise and manifold subclassification. In this and the following lessons we shall deal with: (1) *negatives*, (2) *conjunctions*, (3) *sentence connectors*, and (4) *subordinators*.

611. Negatives, conjunctions, sentence connectors, and subordinators may be termed *function words* (Fries: 87–109) or *structure signaling words* (Roberts, 1958: 151f., 224ff.). The point of these labels is that such words are nearly lexically empty, i.e. they have little or no dictionary meaning of their own. However, they are grammatically significant in indicating the structure of sentences and parts of sentences (cf. §§001ff.). Some of them are so common as to require acquaintance at the grossest level of the language. This simply means that one must learn how they function early in the process. One may guess at the meaning of lexically full words, or leave them blank when reading (cf. §003), but one must know the grammatical "meaning" of function words to be able to proceed at all. It is the case, of course, that some function words are more pervasive and significant than others.

612. In the analysis of sentences thus far function words have either been put in brackets or parentheses and ignored. It will be recalled that adverbs and prepositions, which also belong to the third, uninflected category, have been marked:

A   adverbs

p   prepositions (followed by the designation for the case and type of word group)

For the remainder of the particles capital letters may be employed:

- N   Negative particles
- B   Subordinators
- C   Conjunctions
- D   Sentence connectors

Adverbs are lexically full words, so they have been given a separate designation. The choice of p for prepositions was self-evident. Among the remaining function words (other than prepositions, which are also function words), N was suggested by the English word *negative*, C by the name *conjunction*, D by the name *determiner*; B is arbitrary.

Negatives

613.   *Negatives* are a pervasive feature of every language. Here we shall consider only negative adverbs. Negatives that are bound morphemes (e.g. α-*privative* in such words as ἄ-καρπος, -ον *un-fruitful*; ἀ-θάνατος, -ον *im-mortal*), and negative pronominal adjectives will be considered in other connections.

   Negatives do have lexical meaning, but they are also often important structure signaling devices. We shall consider the whole range of negative usage, in broadest outline.

614.   *The common negatives* are οὐ (οὐκ, οὐχ) and μή. Combinations of these two and compounds of which one or the other is a part are also frequent.

614.1   οὐ appears before a following consonant. When a vowel with smooth breathing follows, οὐκ is employed. Before rough breathing οὐχ is used. μή is not affected by the following sound.

614.2   A common combination of negatives is οὐ μή, which is a more definite and for the most part more emphatic form of negation than a simple negative. The two negatives in this case do not cancel each other out. Bl-D §365.

614.3   Examples of compounds with οὐ:

οὐδέ	(οὐ + δέ)	*and not, nor*
οὐδέποτε	(οὐ + δέ + ποτέ)	*never*
οὐκέτι	(οὐκ + ἔτι)	*no more, no longer*
οὔπω	(οὐ + πω)	*not yet*

Cf. the pronominal adjective οὐδείς (οὐ + δέ + εἷς) *no one*.

Examples of compounds with μή:

μηδέ	(μή + δέ)	*and not, nor*
μηδέποτε	(μή + δέ + ποτε)	*never*
μηκέτι	(μή + ἔτι)	*no longer*

N. -κ- is by analogy with οὐκέτι

| μήτε | (μή + τε) | *and not* |

Cf. the pronominal adjective μηδείς (μή + δέ + εἷς) *no one.*

615.   οὐ and μή most often negate the finite verb in a sentence or clause.

615.1   As a general rule, οὐ negates the indicative mood, μή the other moods, including the infinitive and participle. Bl-D §426.

615.2   Where οὐ or μή negates the finite verb, the negative appears regularly just before the verb. The group consisting of negative and verb may be marked N → 2.

> 1n+   N→2   p5b
> (1) ὁ λόγος ὁ ἐμὸς / οὐ χωρεῖ / ἐν ὑμῖν   Jn 8:37
>   *My word has no place in you*

> N→2-1
> (2) οὐχ ἡμαρτήκαμεν   1 Jn 1:10
>   *We have not sinned*

A postpositive particle (a particle that may not stand first in its clause or word group), however, may intervene between negative and verb:

> N→D   2-1   p4n+
> (3) οὐ [γὰρ] βλέπεις / εἰς πρόσωπον ἀνθρώπων   Mk 12:14
>   *[For] you do not regard the appearance of man*

The particle ἄν (§§6740, 857) may also intervene:

> 3n+   N→H   2-1
> (4) Χριστοῦ δοῦλος / οὐκ ἄν ἤμην   Gal 1:10
>   *I would not (in that case, then) be a servant of Christ*

Note: H is used to mark nuance words and sentence modalizers.

615.3 The rule regarding the position of the simple negative (§615.1) applies also to the emphatic double negative, οὐ μή:

      4n   NN→2-1   p4n+

(5) θάνατον / οὐ μὴ θεωρήσῃ / εἰς τὸν αἰῶνα   Jn 8:51

He shall certainly not see death forever

615.4 Compound negatives also regularly immediately precede the verb:

      N→   2   1n+

(6) οὔπω ἐληλύθει / ἡ ὥρα αὐτοῦ   Jn 8:20

His hour had not yet come

      1a   C 1a   N→   2

(7) κοινὸν (ἢ) ἀκάθαρτον / οὐδέποτε εἰσῆλθεν / εἰς τὸ

p4n+

στόμα μου   Acts 11:8

A common or unclean thing has never gone into my mouth

616. οὐ and μή may negate elements in the sentence other than the verb. When they do, they immediately precede the element they negate.

      C   4n+   N→3g

(8) καὶ) τὰς ἐντολὰς αὐτοῦ / μὴ τηρῶν . . .   1 Jn 2:4

and not keeping his commandments . . .

Note: μή negates the participle (§615.1).

      1a+ (N→1a) 3a   p4n

(9) οὐ πολλοὶ / σοφοὶ / κατὰ σάρκα,

    1a+ (N→1a) 3a

οὐ πολλοὶ / δυνατοί,

    1a+ (N→1a) 3a

οὐ πολλοὶ / εὐγενεῖς   1 Cor 1:26

Not many (were) wise by human standards,

Not many (were) powerful,

Not many (were) well-born

617. Negatives participate in a variety of *structure signaling devices*. Cf. §§212–214.

617.1 οὐ (οὐ μή) may be followed by ἀλλά: *not . . . but . . .* (negative statement followed by a contrary positive statement; cf. German *nicht . . . sondern . . .*).

1b   4n   N^c→2   C   2-1   4n+

(10) ἐγὼ / δαιμόνιον / οὐκ ἔχω (ἀλλὰ) τιμῶ / τὸν πατέρα μου   Jn 8:49

I do not have a demon, but I honor my father

Note: When N is conjunctive, it may be marked N^c.

1g+   NN^c→2   p5n+   C

(11) ὁ ἀκολουθῶν ἐμοὶ / οὐ μὴ περιπατήσῃ / ἐν τῇ σκοτίᾳ, (ἀλλ')

2-1   4n+

ἕξει / τὸ φῶς τῆς ζωῆς   Jn 8:12

The one following me shall certainly not walk in darkness, but
shall have the light of life

Bl-D §448(1).

617.2 οὐ . . . ἀλλά . . . is sometimes expanded as οὐ (μόνον) . . . ἀλλὰ (καί), . . . *not*
only . . . but also (but even) . . .

N→   p6b+   D   4a^A   C   A

(12) . . . οὐ περὶ τῶν ἡμετέρων [δὲ] μόνον / (ἀλλὰ) καὶ /

p6n+

περὶ ὅλου τοῦ κόσμου   1 Jn 2:2

. . . and not only for ours, but also for [the sins] of the whole world

617.3 οὔτε . . . οὔτε . . . (μήτε . . . μήτε . . .) correlate comparable grammatical elements within the sentence, e.g.

N^c→4b   2-1   N^c→   4n+

(13) οὔτε ἐμὲ / οἴδατε / οὔτε τὸν πατέρα μου   Jn 8:19

You know neither me nor my father

In (13) οὔτε . . . οὔτε . . . joins two objects to a single verb. Similarly, οὔτε . . .
οὔτε . . . may correlate two or more subjects (Rom 8:39), two verbs (Lk 12:24),
two adverbial phrases initiated by prepositions (Mt 12:32). μήτε is used where
μή is appropriate (§615.1), e.g. with participles:

2   D   1n   N^c→ 3g   N^c→ 3g

(14) ἦλθεν [γὰρ] / Ἰωάννης / μήτε ἐσθίων / μήτε πίνων   Mt 11:18

For John came neither eating nor drinking

These uses of οὔτε and μήτε correspond to some uses of the conjunctions καί and τε (§§622, 625).

617.4 οὐδέ and μηδέ are negative conjunctions which, in strict usage (Attic prose), join clauses (included sentences) and sentences (independent sentences) of the same kind. This means that οὐδέ and μηδέ, *when conjunctive*, regularly follow another negative (when not conjunctive, οὐδέ and μηδέ mean *not even*).

$$N^C {\rightarrow} 2\text{-}1 \qquad N^C {\rightarrow} 2\text{-}1 \qquad N^C {\rightarrow} 2\text{-}1 \qquad p4n$$

(15) οὐ σπείρουσιν οὐδέ θερίζουσιν οὐδέ συναγούσιν / εἰς ἀποθήκας

They neither sow nor reap nor gather into barns

But strict usage is not uniformly observed, so that οὐδέ (μηδέ) are also used to join other grammatical elements (cf. οὔτε, §617.3):

$$N^C {\rightarrow} 2\text{-}1 \qquad 4n+ \quad N^C {\rightarrow} 4d+$$

(16) μὴ ἀγαπᾶτε / τὸν κόσμον μηδὲ τὰ ἐν τῷ κόσμῳ   1 Jn 2:15

Do not love the world nor the things in the world

In (16) μηδέ connects a second object with the verb negated by μή.

617.5 Various other combinations of negatives (and conjunctions) are possible, of which the following are merely illustrative.

$$A \qquad N^C {\rightarrow} 2\text{-}1 \qquad\qquad 5n+ \quad C \quad 5n+$$

(17) εὐθέως / οὐ προσανεθέμην / σαρκὶ (καὶ) αἵματι, /

$$N^C {\rightarrow} 2\text{-}1 \qquad\qquad p4n$$

οὐδὲ ἀνῆλθον / εἰς Ἱεροσόλυμα / πρὸς τοὺς πρὸ ἐμοῦ

$$p4η+$$

ἀποστόλους, /

$$C \qquad 2\text{-}1 \qquad p4n$$

(ἀλλὰ) ἀπῆλθον / εἰς Ἀραβίαν   Gal 1:16f.

I did not immediately confer with flesh and blood (= anyone),
nor did I go up to Jerusalem to those who were apostles before me,
but I went away into Arabia

The combination οὐκ . . . οὐδὲ . . . ἀλλὰ . . . appears also in Gal 1:1. In Gal 1:11f. the sequence is οὐκ . . . οὐδὲ . . . οὔτε . . . ἀλλὰ . . . . In stricter usage the third item, οὔτε, would be replaced by οὐδέ (§617.4).

A negative pronominal adjective may be followed by a series of negatives:

```
        C    1d      2c              p5n+
(18) καὶ) οὐδεὶς / ἐδύνατο / ἐν τῷ οὐρανῷ
                    Nᶜ→              p6n+
                    οὐδὲ     ἐπὶ τῆς γῆς
                    Nᶜ→                  p6n+
                    οὐδὲ     ὑποκάτω τῆς γῆς
        i        4n+
        ἀνοῖξαι / τὸ βιβλίον
        Nᶜ→ i       4d
        οὔτε βλέπειν / αὐτό                      Rev 5:3
```

And no one in heaven
    or on earth
    or under the earth
was able to open the scroll
or to look into it

617.6   Rom 6:12–14 contains a number of negatives and conjunctions illustrative of some common usages:

(19) μὴ οὖν βασιλευέτω, . . . μηδὲ παριστάνετε
    . . . ἀλλὰ παραστήσατε . . . .
    . . . οὐ κυριεύσει, οὐ γὰρ . . . ἀλλὰ . . .

Let not . . . therefore reign, . . . do not
    yield . . . but yield . . . will not
    have dominion, since not . . . but . . .

The overall structure of the five sentences involved is made evident by the sequence of negatives together with the conjunction ἀλλά.

617.7   οὐ and μή, and the strengthened forms, οὐχί and μήτι, are employed as question signaling devices. The choice of negative indicates the answer expected: οὐ (οὐχί) anticipates a positive answer (whether or not it is forthcoming), μή (μήτι) expects a negative answer. As signals of questions, these negatives stand regularly at the head of their sentence or clause. μή is followed in this case by the indicative (cf. §615.1).

    N^Q   1n   2pass   p6b

(20) μὴ / Παῦλος / ἐσταυρώθη / ὑπὲρ ὑμῶν;   1 Cor 1:13

      Paul was not crucified for you, was he?

The question expects a negative answer: *certainly not*. Notice that in English the kind of answer expected is indicated by the placement of the negative.

    Paul was not crucified for you, was he? (No)
    Paul was crucified for you, was he not? (Yes)

The same nuance is achieved in Greek by the negative chosen. With (20) compare

    N^Q A   2   1b   s⁴

(21) οὐ / καλῶς / λέγομεν / ἡμεῖς / ὅτι Σαμαρίτης εἶ σύ;   Jn 8:48

      Did we not rightly say that you are a Samaritan?

where the answer, *Yes, we did*, is assumed.

    The same nuances are expressed by μήτι and οὐχί, respectively:

    N^Q   2-1   4b

(22) μήτι / ἀποκτενεῖ / ἑαυτόν;   Jn 8:22

      He won't kill himself, will he? (No, probably not)

    N^Q   2   1n+   4n+

(23) οὐχὶ / ἐμώρανεν / ὁ θεὸς / τὴν σοφίαν τοῦ κόσμου;   1 Cor 1:20

      Did not God make foolish the wisdom of the world? (Yes, he did)

Q is the designation for question signaling words (§526). When N also signals a question, it may be marked N^Q as in (20)–(23).

Lesson 42

Conjunctions

620.   *A conjunction is a word that may connect or link one grammatical element of any order with another of the same order.* In considering negatives (§§610–617), we have already encroached upon conjunctions, since the simple negatives (οὐ, μή) sometimes have conjunctive force (§617.1-2), and there are, of course, negative conjunctions, e.g. οὔτε, οὐδέ (§617.3–5). But the negatives can be isolated as a special class of function words since they function in ways other particles do not. *Sentence connectors*, like conjunctions, connect grammatical elements of the same type, but the type of element they may connect is limited to *sentences* (independent) and *clauses* (included sentences). Conjunctions may thus function as sentence connectors, but also in ways sentence connectors do not; they may therefore be identified as a special group (Roberts, 1958: 233f.).

The common conjunctions include:

καί
καὶ . . . καὶ . . .
τέ
τε καί
τε . . . καί
ἤ
ἤ . . . ἤ
ἀλλά (οὐ . . . ἀλλά)

And the negative conjunctions:

οὔτε (μήτε)
οὐδέ (μηδέ)

621.   καί is the most common of the conjunctions. It links elements of the same grammatical order and stands between them.

621.1 καί is often used, especially in narrative portions of the New Testament, in a monotonous and colloquial way to string sentences together (a colloquial running style).

In Mk 1:12f., for example, καί is used to string four relatively brief sentences together. In the short narrative, Mk 1:16–20, the sequence of conjunctions and sentence connectors is as follows: (16) καί . . . γάρ . . . (17) καί . . . καί . . . (18) καί . . . (19) καί . . . (20) καί . . . καί . . . The uses of καί to connect other than full sentences are omitted. Thus, only γάρ appears among 7 examples of καί linking sentences. Cf. Bl-D §§442, 458.

621.2   καί may also be used to link included sentences of both dependent and independent types.

> 2-1   s⁴   C   s⁴
> (1) οἶδα / πόθεν ἦλθον (καὶ) ποῦ ὑπάγω   Jn 8:14
> *I know whence I come and where I go*

> N^Q A   2   1b
> (2) οὐ / καλῶς / λέγομεν / ἡμεῖς / ὅτι
>   S⁴   C
>   Σαμαρίτης εἶ σὺ (καὶ)
>   S⁴
>   δαιμόνιον ἔχεις;   Jn 8:48
> *Did we not rightly say,*
>   *"You are a Samaritan" and*
>   *"You have a demon"?*

Note: (2) is here interpreted as direct discourse, although it could just as well be taken as indirect discourse.

In some instances of linked included dependent sentences, one or more elements may be omitted from the second sentence. For example, in

> B4d   2-1   p6d   C
> (3) . . . ἣν / ἀκηκόαμεν / ἀπ' αὐτοῦ (καὶ)
>   2-1   5b
>   ἀναγγέλομεν / ὑμῖν   1 Jn 1:5
>   *. . . which we heard from him and*
>   *[which] we proclaim to you*

the relative pronoun is not repeated in the second sentence. This is an example of a deleted object in S-IV (§§604ff.).

621.3 Among grammatical elements of lesser compass than the sentence, καί links two subjects with one verb:

$$\begin{array}{cccccc} C & 2 & & 1d & C & 1n+ \end{array}$$

(4) καὶ) ἐπίστευσεν / αὐτὸς / καὶ / ἡ οἰκία αὐτοῦ ὅλη   Jn 4:53
And he and his whole house believed

Note: The elements linked may be different types of word groups (d and n+) so long as they are of the same grammatical order (1). On the singular verb with two subjects, s. §537.

While καί stands between the elements it links, it is not the only item which may come between:

$$\begin{array}{cccc} 1n & 2 & C & 1n+ \end{array}$$

(5) Ἀβραὰμ / ἀπέθανεν (καὶ) / οἱ προφῆται   Jn 8:52
Abraham and the prophets died

Note: The descriptive analysis of (5) indicates what two items must be linked by καί: 1n and 1n+ are the only two grammatical elements of the *same* order.

621.4 καί may link two verbs with a single subject:

$$\begin{array}{ccccc} 2 & 1n & C & 2 & 5d \end{array}$$

(6) ἀπεκρίθη / Ἰησοῦς / (καὶ) εἶπεν / αὐτοῖς . . .   Jn 8:13
Jesus answered and said to them . . .

621.5 καί may link two predicate adjectives with verb and subject in S-II:

$$\begin{array}{cccc} 3a & 2\text{-}1 & C & 3a \end{array}$$

(7) πιστός / ἐστιν (καὶ) δίκαιος   1 Jn 1:9
he is faithful and just

621.6 καί may link two objects in S-III:

$$\begin{array}{cccc} 4n & 2\text{-}1 & C & N{\rightarrow}4n \end{array}$$

(8) ἔλεος / θέλω (καὶ) οὐ θυσίαν   Mt 12:7
I desire mercy and not sacrifice

621.7 In S-IV καί may connect two indirect and two direct objects with a single verb:

$$\begin{array}{cccc} 2\text{-}1 & D & 4d+ & 5n \end{array}$$

(9) ἀποδότε [οὖν] τὰ Καίσαρος / Καίσαρι

```
C      4d+          5n+
```
(καὶ) τὰ τοῦ θεοῦ / τῷ θεῷ   Mt 22:21

Therefore render the things of Caesar to Caesar,
and the things of God to God

Or two indirect objects to a single verb and single object:

```
       B      i          4d        5n+  C    5n+
```
(10) . . . ὥστε / παραδοῦναι / αὐτὸν / τῇ ἀρχῇ (καὶ) τῇ ἐξουσίᾳ
τοῦ ἡγεμόνος   Lk 20:20

. . . so as to deliver him to the authority and jurisdiction of
the governor

621.8 καί is used to link two infinitives to a single catenative verb (§566.1):

```
      C    2-1      i        4n       C    i
```
(11) καὶ) ἤρξαντο / τίλλειν / στάχυας (καὶ) ἐσθίειν   Mt 12:1

And they began to pluck ears of grain and to eat

621.9 καί may link two participles:

```
      3d        p6d+                           C
```
(12) . . . εἷς / ἐκ τῶν δύο ἀκουσάντων παρὰ Ἰωάννου (καὶ)
```
      6d+
```
ἀκολουθησάντων αὐτῷ   Jn 1:40

. . . one of the two who heard John and followed him

Note: (12) is a single word group within the structure of the whole sentence,
but it is composed of 3d + p6d+ (C) 6d+.

621.10 καί may link two nouns governed by a single preposition (cf. (12) above):

```
      B      1d    2pass       p6n   C    6n
```
(13) ἐὰν μή / τις / γεννηθῇ / ἐξ ὕδατος (καὶ) πνεύματος   Jn 3:5

Unless one is born of water and spirit

In sum, καί may link any two grammatical items of the same order. It is
therefore an exceedingly common signal of sentence structure.

622. καὶ . . . καὶ, . . . *both . . . and.* . . . In linking two grammatical elements of the
same order, καί may be doubled. In that case, the first καί precedes the first
element and the second καί comes between them.

<blockquote>

C   2-1   C   A   2-1

(14) (καὶ) ἐδόξασα (καὶ) πάλιν / δοξάσω   Jn 12:28

I have both glorified [it] and I shall glorify [it] again.

</blockquote>

Bl-D §444(3).

623.   Although καί is used predominantly as a conjunction, it is also employed in a variety of other ways.

623.1   It often means *also, too, likewise* (adverbial), and with this meaning καί often contrasts two elements of the same order.

<blockquote>

(15) εἰ ἐμὲ ᾔδειτε, καὶ τὸν πατέρα μου ἂν ᾔδειτε   Jn 8:19

If you knew me, you would know my father also

</blockquote>

Here καί stands between a subordinate and a main clause, in which ἐμέ and πατέρα are contrasted.

623.2   Ascensive καί means *even:*

<blockquote>

(16) οὐχὶ καὶ οἱ τελῶναι τὸ αὐτὸ ποιοῦσιν;   Mt 5:46

Do not even the tax collectors do the same?

</blockquote>

Ascensive καί does not connect or contrast elements.

On the variety of uses of καί, s. Bl-D §442.

624.   τέ is a much less common conjunction. It has the range but not the frequency of καί. Unlike καί, τέ is post-positive (it cannot stand first in its word group) and cannot, therefore, stand between the elements it connects; it must take second or later position in the word group constituting the second element.

<blockquote>

1b   C   A   2   3g

(17) σύ (τε) καλῶς / ἐποίησας / παραγενόμενος   Acts 10:33

And you did well to come

</blockquote>

Cf. Acts 11:21.

<blockquote>

p5n   5n+   C

(18) ἐν ἀγάπῃ / πνεύματί (τε) πραΰτητος   1 Cor 4:21

in love and a spirit of gentleness

</blockquote>

Cf. Acts 10:22.

625.   τέ and καί appear in various combinations (in addition to καί . . . καί, §622).

625.1 τε . . . τε, . . . *both . . . and, . . . as . . . so, . . . not only . . . but also. . . .*

          p4n   C   3g

(19) καθ' ἡμέραν (τε) προσκαρτεροῦντες ὁμοθυμαδὸν ἐν τῷ

         3g   C

ἱερῷ κλῶντές (τε) κατ' οἶκον ἄρτον, . . .   Acts 2:46

Daily both spending time in the temple and breaking bread from
house to house, . . .

Bl-D §444(1).

625.2 . . . τε καί . . . and τε . . . καί are used in a similar way.

         B6d 2   1n+   i   CC   i

(20) ὧν / ἤρξατο / ὁ Ἰησοῦς / ποιεῖν (τε καί) διδάσκειν   Acts 1:1

which Jesus began both to do and to teach

      B   D 2   4n+   C 1n+

(21) ὡς (δὲ) ἤκουσαν / τοὺς λόγους τούτους / ὅ (τε) στρατηγὸς

                  C

τοῦ ἱεροῦ (καὶ) οἱ ἀρχιερεῖς, . . .   Acts 5:24

Now when both the captain of the temple and the chief priests
heard these words, . . .

625.3 τέ may be followed by more than one καί:

       C   2-1   3n+   C p5n   C

(22) καὶ) ἔσεσθέ / μου μάρτυρες / ἐν (τε) Ἰερουσαλὴμ (καὶ) ἐν

        p5n   C   5n   C   p6a+

πάσῃ τῇ Ἰουδαίᾳ (καὶ) Σαμαρείᾳ (καὶ) ἕως ἐσχάτου

τῆς γῆς   Acts 1:8

And you will be my witnesses in Jerusalem and in all Judea and
in Samaria and to the end of the earth

Word groups headed by participles (3g) are connected by τε . . . τε in (19);
infinitives (i) are joined by . . . τε καί . . . in (20); in (21) subject groups are
linked by τε . . . καί . . .; and in (22) adverbial phrases headed by prepositions
are joined by τε . . . καί . . . καί . . . καί. . . .

625.4 τέ is not only post-positive (§624) but *enclitic* (§074) as well: it is pronounced
with the preceding word and so loses its accent to that word.

626. ἤ is a particile that serves (a) as a disjunctive conjunction (i.e. it joins alternatives), (b) to denote comparison. In sense (b) it also joins elements: *more this* than *that*.

626.1 ἤ as a disjunctive conjunction links elements of the same order grammatically, although in meaning they may be opposites:

> N→2c-1   4n+   4a   i   C 4a
> (23) οὐ δύνασαι / μίαν τρίχα / λευκὴν / ποιῆσαι (ἢ) μέλαιναν   Mt 5:36
> *You are not able to make one hair white or black*

(23) is a type V sentence (§521).

626.2 Like καί and τέ, ἤ may be doubled, in which case it means *either . . . or*.

> C D   4d+   2-1   C   4d+   2-1
> (24) ἢ (γὰρ) τὸν ἕνα / μισήσει (καὶ) τὸν ἕτερον / ἀγαπήσει,
> C 6d   2-1   C   6d+   2-1
> (ἢ) ἑνὸς / ἀνθέξεται (καὶ) τοῦ ἑτέρου / καταφρονήσει   Mt 6:24
> *For either he will hate the one and love the other,*
> *or he will be devoted to one and despise the other.*

ἢ . . . ἢ links the two compound sentences, each of which, in turn, is composed of two sentences linked by καί.

626.3 In comparisons ἤ is often preceded by a comparative:

> 2   1n+   Aᶜ   4n+   C   4n+
> (25) ἠγάπησαν / οἱ ἄνθρωποι / μᾶλλον / τὸ σκότος (ἢ) τὸ φῶς   Jn 3:19
> *Men loved the darkness rather than the light*

μᾶλλον is a comparative adverb and hence has conjunctive force.

627. ἀλλά, *but, yet, nevertheless, however,* is commonly preceded by a negative (*not . . . but . . .*, cf. §617), although it is also used in other ways (§628). In combination with a negative, ἀλλά is employed to join grammatical elements of the same order, as is the case with other conjunctions.

627.1 οὐ . . . ἀλλά . . . may link two subjects:

> 5g+   2-1
> (26) τοῖς (δὲ) γεγαμηκόσιν / παραγγέλλω //
> Nᶜ→1b C   1n+
> οὐκ ἐγὼ ἀλλὰ ὁ κύριος . . .   1 Cor 7:10

To the married I give charge,
not I but the Lord . . .

627.2   Two predicates in S-II:

          1n+   N^C→2   3n+   C   3d

(27) καὶ γὰρ] τὸ σῶμα / οὐκ ἔστιν / ἓν μέλος ἀλλὰ πολλά   1 Cor 12:14

For the body is not one member but many

627.3   Two objects:

        N^C→2-1   4n+

(28) οὐ ζητῶ / τὸ θέλημα τὸ ἐμὸν

        C   4n+

ἀλλὰ τὸ θέλημα τοῦ πέμψαντός με   Jn 5:30

I seek not my will
but the will of the one who sent me

Cf. Jn 6:38; Mt 9:13 // Lk 5:32.

627.4   Two p-phrases:

        N^C→   p4a+

(29) οὐκ εἰς τὸ κρεῖσσον

        C   p4a+   2-1

ἀλλὰ εἰς τὸ ἧσσον / συνέρχεσθε   1 Cor 11:17

You come together not for the better
but for the worse

627.5   Two predicate datives:

         1n+   N^C→ 5n+

(30) τὸ [δέ] σῶμα / οὐ τῇ πορνείᾳ

        C   5n+

ἀλλὰ τῷ κυρίῳ   1 Cor 6:13

The body belongs not to fornication
but to the Lord

For examples of οὐ . . . ἀλλά . . . joining sentences, s. §617.1–2, 5.

628.   ἀλλά not preceded by a negative may mark a transition to something contrasted or different:

>   2-1   s4
> (31) οἶδα / ὅτι σπέρμα Ἀβραάμ ἐστε //
>   C   2-1   4b i
> ἀλλὰ ζητεῖτέ / με / ἀποκτεῖναι   Jn 8:37
> *I know that you are seed of Abraham;*
> *nevertheless you seek to kill me*

For other nuances of ἀλλά, s. Bauer s.v. 3–6.

Lesson 43

Sentence Connectors

630. Sentence connectors join sentences and clauses (cf. §620). As a rule, they are less crucial than conjunctions at the gross level of language. That is only to say that one can more easily put brackets around them and read on without losing the sense. Nevertheless, it is important to have some notion of the connective function of some common sentence connectors fairly early in the learning process, since such words carry the weight of intersentence grammar.

630.1 It should be recalled that some conjunctions also function as sentence connectors, e.g. καί (§§621, 622), ἤ (§626), ἀλλά (§§617, 628).

630.2 The common sentence connectors include:

> δέ
> γάρ
> οὖν
> ὁ δέ
> μὲν . . . δέ . . .

631. δέ, γάρ, and οὖν are the most common of the sentence connectors. The beginning student can get along very well with just these three in hand, plus the conjunctions treated above (§§620–628). All three are post-positive, i.e. cannot stand first in their own word group; they normally come second, but may appear as the third or even the fourth element.

632. δέ is a mildly adversative connector: it indicates the general contrast of a clause or sentence with one preceding. Its English counterparts are *but, however, yet*. But δέ is so commonly used that the contrastive nuance in the majority of instances is nearly or wholly absent. In that case, it has merely copulative force, like καί, *and*. In some instances it is merely transitional: *now, then*.

The strong adversative mate to δέ is ἀλλά. In its adversative role, δέ corresponds roughly to German *aber* (general contrast), ἀλλά to *sondern* (directly contrary).

632.1   δέ indicating contrast:

       C   N^c→2-1   4d

(1) καὶ οὐκ ἐγνώκατε / αὐτόν,

       1b   D 2   4d

      ἐγὼ / [δὲ] οἶδα / αὐτόν   Jn 8:55

      And you have not known him,

      but I know him

Cf. οὐ . . . ἀλλά, §617.

632.2   δέ without contrastive force:

       A   D 3g   2-1   p4n+

(2) ἐκεῖθεν [δὲ] ἀναστὰς / ἀπῆλθεν / εἰς τὸ ὅρια Τύρου   Mk 7:24

      And *from there he arose and went away to the regions of Tyre*

For other nuances of δέ, s. Bauer s.v. On these and other minor adversative connectors, s. Bl-D §§447–450.

633.   γάρ is a causal connector, indicating that its sentence states the cause or reason for something stated previously. In this sense its English counterpart is *for*. But, like δέ, γάρ has a wider range of functions: it can also indicate inference (like οὖν), continuation (like δέ), or explanation.

633.1   γάρ indicating cause or reason:

       2-1   s^4

(3) οἴδαμεν / ὅτι ἀπὸ θεοῦ ἐλήλυθας διδάσκαλος·

       1b   D 2c   4n+   i   s

      οὐδεὶς [γὰρ] δύναται / ταῦτα τὰ σημεῖα / ποιεῖν / ἃ σὺ

            s

      ποιεῖς, / ἐὰν μὴ ᾖ ὁ θεὸς μετ' αὐτοῦ.   Jn 3:2

      We know that you, a teacher, have come from God;

      for no one can do these signs that you do, unless God is with him

633.2   To questions γάρ often adds a nuance not easily translated into English, but for which words like *then, pray, what!, why!* come close. γάρ introduces the reason for the skeptical tone in (4):

       1d   2   S^4

(4) ἄλλοι / ἔλεγον / οὗτός ἐστιν ὁ Χριστός·

1d D   2   S⁴

οἱ [δὲ] ἔλεγον, / μὴ γὰρ ἐκ τῆς Γαλιλαίας ὁ Χριστὸς ἔρχεται; Jn 7:41
Others said, "This is the Christ."
Still others replied, "What! The Christ is not to come from Galilee,
is he?"

Bl-D §452.

634.1 οὖν is a consecutive (inferential) connector, indicating that the sentence in
which it appears is a result of or inference from something preceding. English
counterparts are: *so, therefore, consequently, accordingly, then*. Once again, like δέ
and γάρ, οὖν also has a wider range of functions. In historical narrative particularly, οὖν may be used to continue a subject (continuative), resume a subject
(resumptive), or mark a transition to something new (transitional).

634.2 Other inferential particles are ἄρα (not to be confused with interrogative ἆρα),
and the strengthened forms ἄραγε and ἄρα οὖν. These connectors are not necessarily postpositive, i.e. may stand first in the sentence, contrary to classical
usage.

634.3 οὖν indicating inference:

2-1   4n+
(5) ἀγαπᾶτε / τοὺς ἐχθροὺς ὑμῶν . . .
2   D   1b   3a
ἔσεσθε [οὖν] ὑμεῖς / τέλειοι   Mt 5:44–48
Love your enemies . . .
Then you shall be perfect

634.4 οὖν indicating transition:

2   D   5d   1n+
(6) εἶπον [οὖν] αὐτῷ / οἱ Φαρισαῖοι, . . .   Jn 8:13
Then the Pharisees said to him, . . .

Bl-D §451.

635. The functions of δέ were considered in a general way in §632 (with and without
contrastive force). A few more specialized functions of δέ are worth noting.

635.1 In narrative and especially in dialogue, δέ is used with the article (without other substantive) to indicate a change in subject or speaker. In (7) such a shift is twice indicated by this device:

(7) [Ἰησοῦς] φέρετέ μοι δηνάριον ἵνα ἴδω.
οἱ δὲ ἤνεγκαν.
καὶ λέγει αὐτοῖς, τίνος ἡ εἰκὼν αὕτη καὶ ἡ ἐπιγραφή;
οἱ δὲ εἶπαν αὐτῷ, Καίσαρος.
ὁ δὲ Ἰησοῦς εἶπεν αὐτοῖς, . . .   Mk 12:15b–17a
[Jesus:] "Bring me a denarius that I may see."
They brought [one]
And he says to them, "Whose likeness and inscription is this?"
They said to him, "Caesar's."
Then Jesus said to them, . . .

οἱ δέ twice signals the change in subject or speaker. Both times no other substantive occurs. In the third instance, Ἰησοῦς stands in apposition to ὁ δέ to relieve the strain on the reader's memory.

635.2 Just as ἀλλά may be correlated with a preceding οὐ (§617), δέ may be correlated with a preceding μέν (an affirmative particle with no single or near English equivalent). μέν . . . δέ . . . generally implies something like *on the one hand . . . on the other, . . .* though this way of putting it in English is sometimes too strong. In (8) μέν . . . δέ . . . point to the two things set over against each other:

(8) οὕτως καὶ ὑμεῖς λογίζεσθε ἑαυτοὺς εἶναι
νεκροὺς μὲν τῇ ἁμαρτίᾳ
ζῶντας δὲ τῷ θεῷ   Rom 6:11
So you also must consider yourselves to be
dead to sin
but living to God

Bl-D §447(2).

635.3 μέν sometimes appears by itself, without correlative δέ; in that case the contrast may be supplied from the context, or it may actually be expressed but not signaled by δέ. Bl-D §447(3)–(5).

635.4 The combination μὲν οὖν, however, is merely continuative: *then, so* (common in Acts). Bl-D §451(1).

Lesson 44

Subordinators & Subordination

640. The subject of subordinators and subordination cannot be taken up without going beyond the simple sentence and thus raising all the grammatical questions involved in subordination. These questions are too complex to be presented and digested in brief compass. Nevertheless, one cannot read any Greek text for very long without meeting some form of subordination. It is therefore necessary to broach the subject generally and to introduce certain exceedingly common forms of subordination at the gross level of grammar. Subordinators like ἵνα, ὅτι, ὅς play too vital and too pervasive a role in Greek to be ignored beyond the most elementary stage.

641. Language without subordination would be dreary reading indeed. We might take as an example,

> *You seek to kill me. I have spoken the truth to you.*
> *I heard the truth from God.*

To produce a less staccato style, the second sentence can quite easily be subordinated to the first, and the third to the second, as in Jn 8:40:

(1) νῦν δὲ ζητεῖτέ με ἀποκτεῖναι,
     ἄνθρωπον ὃς τὴν ἀλήθειαν ὑμῖν λελάληκα
     ἣν ἤκουσα παρὰ τοῦ θεοῦ   Jn 8:40
     But now you seek to kill me,
     a man who has spoken the truth to you
     which I heard from God

The means by which subordination is accomplished in these instances are the two relative pronouns ὅς and ἥν.

As another example, the two sentences

> *No one arrested him. His hour had not yet come.*

can be joined, the second subordinated to the first, as in Jn 8:20.

(2) καὶ οὐδεὶς ἐπίασεν αὐτόν,
     ὅτι οὔπω ἐληλύθει ἡ ὥρα αὐτοῦ   Jn 8:20
     And no one arrested him,
     because *his hour had not yet come*

In this instance ὅτι is the means by which the second sentence is subordinated to the first.

Subordination is one means of lending variety to language and thus rendering style more interesting. The two examples given above are taken from a text not particularly rich in stylistic variation, but they represent common forms that appear over and over again in texts of any length. Subordination, like other aspects of structure, are repetitious when isolated. It is the infinite possibility of combination that gives language its potential for variety.

642. *Subordinators* are the means by which one sentence is inserted into or subordinated to another. The sentence

(1) τὴν ἀλήθειαν ὑμῖν λελάληκα
     ἥν ἤκουσα παρὰ τοῦ θεοῦ

may be thought of as deriving from two simple sentences:

(1a) τὴν ἀλήθειαν ὑμῖν λελάληκα
(1b) τὴν ἀλήθειαν ἤκουσα παρὰ τοῦ θεοῦ

What these sentences have in common is the direct object τὴν ἀλήθειαν. The second may be transformed into a subordinate relative clause by replacing the direct object with a relative pronoun in the appropriate (accusative) case:

τὴν ἀλήθειαν → ἥν

This form of subordination is one of two broad types involving subordinators, namely that form in which the subordinator has a grammatical function of its own in the subordinated or inserted sentence. ἥν functions in this instance as the direct object of ἤκουσα. All relative pronouns (listed in §§270ff.) are subordinators of this type.

The second broad type of subordination involves subordinators that merely connect, i.e. that do not have a grammatical function of their own in the clause. Example (2) is of this second type: ὅτι can be bracketed out, leaving a complete sentence:

καὶ οὐδεὶς ἐπίασεν αὐτόν, [ὅτι] οὔπω ἐληλύθει ἡ ὥρα αὐτοῦ

There is also a form of subordination that does not require a subordinator at all:

(3) εἶπεν οὖν αὐτοῖς Ἐγὼ ὑπάγω   Jn 8:21
Then he said to them, "I go away."

ἐγὼ ὑπάγω is a quoted sentence inserted into the larger structure as an object clause (a clause that is the object of the verb εἶπεν), but without benefit of a subordinator.

These, then, are the three general categories of subordination.

643.1   Subordinated sentences or subordinate clauses, as they are traditionally called, *may modify a constituent element* in a sentence, e.g.

(4) καὶ ἔστιν αὕτη ἡ ἀγγελία
ἣν ἀκηκόαμεν ἀπ' αὐτοῦ   1 Jn 1:5
And this is the message
that we heard from him

In (4) the relative clause introduced by ἣν modifies the predicate nominative of an S-II, ἡ ἀγγελία. As another example, in (5) the relative clause introduced by ἅ modifies the direct object, ταῦτα τὰ σημεῖα, in an S-III:

(5) οὐδεὶς γὰρ δύναται ταῦτα τὰ σημεῖα ποιεῖν ἃ σὺ ποιεῖς   Jn 3:2
For no one can do these signs that you do

In (4) and (5) the relative subordinator has an antecedent in the main clause to which it refers: *message* ← *which*; *signs* ← *that*. For this reason the relative subordinate clause is said to modify that antecedent.

643.2   In Greek it is not necessary that a relative subordinator have an expressed antecedent. In cases where an antecedent is not expressed, *the relative clause may itself serve as the constituent element* in the sentence (rather than modify one). For example, a relative clause may appear as subject:

(6) καὶ ὃς οὐ λαμβάνει τὸν σταυρὸν αὐτοῦ
καὶ ἀκολουθεῖ ὀπίσω μου οὐκ ἔστιν μου ἄξιος   Mt 10:38
And [he] who does not take his cross
and follow me is not worthy of me

The relative clause introduced by ὅς is the subject of the main verb ἔστιν. English usage requires that an antecedent be supplied where it is missing in Greek (*he* in the translation).

Similarly a relative clause may serve as the direct object:

(7) ἀπαγγείλατε Ἰωάννῃ ἃ ἀκούετε καὶ βλέπετε   Mt 11:4
Tell John what you hear and see

Or, if we reproduce the relative pronoun in English, we must supply the antecedent:

Tell John [the things] that you hear and see

In English the relative *that* may be omitted but not the antecedent.

643.3   In addition to modifying constituent elements in sentences or serving as constituent elements, subordinate clauses may sustain a more or less loose relation to the main clause as a whole. In this relation subordinate clauses generally function as adverbials.

(8) καὶ ἐὰν κρίνω δὲ ἐγώ
ἡ κρίσις ἡ ἐμὴ ἀληθινή ἐστιν   Jn 8:16
Yet even if I do judge,
my judgment is true

(9) ὅτε οὖν ἦλθεν εἰς τὴν Γαλιλαίαν
ἐδέξαντο αὐτὸν οἱ Γαλιλαῖοι   Jn 4:45
So when he came to Galilee,
the Galileans welcomed him

The subordinate clauses in (8) and (9) are introduced by καὶ ἐάν *even if*, and ὅτε *when*, respectively. Subordinate adverbial clauses of this type exhibit a wide range and great variety.

644.   The grammar of subordinate clauses may be ordered in a variety of ways. Some traditional grammars divide subordinate clauses into three groups: (1) those which function as a constituent element in the larger sentence (called nominal or substantive clause); (2) those which modify a nominal element in the larger sentence (adjective clause); and (3) those which function as an adverbial (adverbial clause). This three-fold division was the basis of the discussion in §643. Other grammars treat the internal structure of the subordinate clause, i.e. whether and how its internal structure (mood, tense, word order, etc.) is

affected by subordination and/or subordinator (cf. §642). Still other grammars employ subordinating words as the index to subordinate clauses.

Some grammars combine or mix the categories, with a certain amount of confusion as the result.

An exhaustive treatment of subordinate clauses would, of course, require a full treatment of all aspects of the subordinate clause. For the purposes of this grammar, however, it is sufficient to concentrate on certain aspects. These aspects are arranged in the order of ascending complexity:

644.1 Subordinate clauses will be treated, first of all, from the standpoint of the syntax of some very common subordinators, in relation to the role the subordinate clauses introduced by them play in the larger sentence (subordinators as function words).

644.2 The internal structure of the subordinate clause will be examined in relation to other analogous constructions not qualifying as subordinate clauses (transformations).

Subordinators ὅτι & ἵνα

645.   ὅτι is an exceedingly common subordinator. Like English *that*, it is often employed to introduce so-called substantive clauses (§643.2), which may appear as the subject or object of the sentence, or stand in apposition (a modifying structure) to some element in the sentence. Functionally speaking, the last might be more accurately described as an adjective clause. In addition, ὅτι is often a causal subordinator in either a strong (*because*) or a weak (*for*) sense. In this sense ὅτι introduces an adverbial clause.

    English equivalents of ὅτι are therefore *that*; *because, since, for.*

646.   ὅτι occasionally initiates a clause that functions as the subject of the sentence (1s):

<pre>
         C   p5n+   D   2pass
(1)   καὶ) ἐν τῷ νόμῳ [δὲ] τῷ ὑμετέρῳ / γέγραπται /
      1s
      ὅτι δύο ἀνθρώπων ἡ μαρτυρία ἀληθής ἐστιν   Jn 8:17
      And in your own law it is written
      that the testimony of two men is true
</pre>

The English It-transformation makes the sentence read more smoothly, but it would be quite possible to translate literally:

> *that the testimony of two men is true has been*
> *written in your own law*

In either case the ὅτι-clause is the subject of the sentence.

647.   ὅτι is much more commonly used to introduce object clauses. One form of the object clause is that in which ὅτι serves to introduce the content, in the form of statements, of what is said, thought, etc., after verbs denoting mental or sense perception or the transmission of what is said or thought. This form is commonly known as *indirect discourse* (discourse in the broad sense, including sense perceptions, observations, thoughts, reflections, etc., as well as what is spoken). Another form of the object clause is that in which ὅτι serves to introduce speech reported directly. This form is called *direct discourse*, and ὅτι serves

merely as the initial pair of quotation marks. In this function ὅτι is known as ὅτι-*recitativum*. Direct speech in the structure of an object clause after a verb of saying, however, may not be signaled by a subordinator at all, as noted earlier (§642, (3)). A variety of examples will serve to indicate the range of ὅτι.

648.   ὅτι used to introduce object clauses after verbs of perception, saying, etc. (indirect discourse):

2-1   s⁴
(2)   οἶδα / ὅτι σπέρμα Ἀβραάμ ἐστε   Jn 8:37
I know that you are descendants of Abraham

2-1   s⁴
(3)   θεωρῶ / ὅτι προφήτης εἶ   Jn 4:19
I perceive that you are a prophet

2-1   D   5b   s⁴
(4)   εἶπον [οὖν] ὑμῖν / ὅτι ἀποθανεῖσθε ἐν ταῖς ἁμαρτίαις ὑμῶν   Jn 8:24
I told you that you would die in your sins

Bl-D §§396, 397.

649.   ὅτι used to introduce direct speech (object clauses after verbs of saying).
With (4) may be compared

2-1   D   A   5d
(5)   εἶπεν [οὖν] πάλιν / αὐτοῖς / . . .
S⁴
ἐν τῇ ἁμαρτίᾳ ὑμῶν ἀποθανεῖσθε   Jn 8:21
Again he said to them, . . .
"You will die in your sin"

where the reported statement, though an object clause, is *not* introduced by ὅτι. However, ὅτι may be used to introduce directly reported speech of just this type:

(6)   ὡμολόγησεν ὅτι ἐγὼ οὐκ εἰμὶ ὁ Χριστός   Jn 1:20
He confessed, "I am not the Christ"

650.   In summary, ὅτι is never omitted with indirect discourse (in the form in which ὅτι may appear), but it may be used or not, at the discretion of the author, with direct discourse. The line between indirect and direct discourse with ὅτι

is consequently difficult or impossible to draw where the indirect form has not undergone modification of person or tense after verbs of saying. However, direct discourse purports to give the exact words of the original, while indirect discourse is obligated to report only the sense. For the infinitive and participle in indirect discourse, s. §585.

651.   What type of subordination ὅτι signals is further complicated by the fact that ὅτι also serves as a causal subordinator (cf. γάρ as a causal sentence connector, §633).

651.1   ὅτι as a strong causal subordinator:

> C   2c-1   4b   i
> (7) ἀλλὰ) ζητεῖτέ / με / ἀποκτεῖναι,
>   sᴬ
>   ὅτι ὁ λόγος ὁ ἐμὸς οὐ χωρεῖ ἐν ὑμῖν   Jn 8:37
>   *Yet you seek to kill me,*
>   *because my word finds no place in you*

Cf. §641(2).

651.2   ὅτι as a weak causal subordinator:

> 3a   2   1n+
> (8) ἀληθής / ἐστιν / ἡ μαρτυρία μου,
>   sᴬ
>   ὅτι οἶδα πόθεν ἦλθον καὶ ποῦ ὑπάγω   Jn 8:14
>   *My witness is true,*
>   *for I know whence I come and whither I go*

Weak and strong causal ὅτι cannot everywhere be distinguished with certainty, since the difference depends on a reading of the context.

652.1   ὅτι may also introduce clauses that stand in apposition to some other element in the sentence, usually with a demonstrative pronoun (οὗτος) preceding.

> 1d   D   2   1n+
> (9) αὕτη [δέ] ἐστιν / ἡ κρίσις,//
>   s
>   ὅτι τὸ φῶς ἐλήλυθεν εἰς τὸν κόσμον   Jn 3:19
>   *And this is the judgment,*
>   *that light has come into the world*

The ὅτι-clause here modifies αὕτη: *The judgment is this, namely that . . .*

652.2 Such appositional ὅτι-clauses may approximate direct discourse, as can be seen by the translation of the following example:

    C   2   1d   1n+
(10) καὶ) ἔστιν / αὕτη / ἡ ἀγγελία / . . . //
     s
     ὅτι ὁ θεὸς φῶς ἐστιν   1 John 1:5
     and this is the message . . . :
     "God is light"

652.3 Appositional words, word groups and clauses are separated from that to which they refer by // in order to indicate that they are parallel to and qualify their antecedent. Although usually interpreted as substantive clauses, they might equally well be taken as adjective (modifying) clauses (s. further, §§668–669).

653. Summary of the functions of ὅτι:

653.1 Used to introduce substantive clauses in the structure of subject (§646).

653.2 Used to introduce object clauses in the form of indirect discourse after verbs of perception, saying, etc. (§648).

653.3 Used to introduce object clauses in the form of directly quoted speech (§649).

653.4 Used as a causal subordinator (§651).

653.5 Used to introduce clauses in apposition to a demonstrative pronoun.

654. ἵνα exhibits the same broad range of usage as does ὅτι, and is also exceedingly common. Like ὅτι, it may be used to introduce substantive clauses, of which the most common is the object clause after certain categories of transitive verbs. The ἵνα-clause may also stand in apposition to another element in the sentence. Perhaps the most characteristic use of the ἵνα-clause is as an adverbial clause denoting purpose (traditionally called a final clause).

English equivalents for ἵνα are *in order that, that.*

655. ἵνα customarily signals that the subjunctive mood is coming in the subordinate clause. Since a subordinate clause introduced by ἵνα usually expresses something contemplated, desired, intended, the appropriate mood is subjunctive, as the mood appropriate to statements that are not yet fact. The subjunctive is the mood of dubious assertion, the *shall* and *will* mood, with reference to the future (§307.2).

656. ἵνα introducing adverbial clauses of purpose (final clauses):

> 4d   2-1   s^A
> (1) ταῦτα / λέγω / ἵνα ὑμεῖς σωθῆτε   Jn 5:34
> *I say these things in order that you might be saved*

> 2-1   5b   4n   s^A
> (2) φέρετέ / μοι / δηνάριον / ἵνα ἴδω   Mk 12:15
> *Bring me a denarius that I may see*

The following example has two contrasting final clauses introduced by ἵνα:

> N^c→D   2   1n+   4n+   p4n+
> (3) οὐ [γὰρ] ἀπέστειλεν / ὁ θεὸς / τὸν υἱὸν / εἰς τὸν κόσμον /
> s^A
> ἵνα κρίνῃ τὸν κόσμον /
> C   s^A
> ἀλλ') ἵνα σωθῇ ὁ κόσμος δι' αὐτοῦ   Jn 3:17
> *For God did not send his son into the world*
> *in order that he might condemn the world,*
> *but in order that the world might be saved through him*

The verb in the first of these clauses might just as well be translated by an infinitive, in which case *in order that* is to be omitted:

> *For God did not send his son into the world to condemn the world . . .*

With the same main verb compare

> N^c→D   2c   4b 1n   i
> (4) οὐ [γὰρ] ἀπέστειλεν / με / Χριστὸς / βαπτίζειν
> C   i
> (ἀλλὰ) εὐαγγελίζεσθαι   1 Cor 1:17
> *For Christ did not send me to baptize,*
> *but to preach the gospel.*

where the two contrasting infinitives are the equivalent of two ἵνα-clauses. The final ἵνα-clause is thus *agnate* (§592.2) to an infinitive of purpose (cf. §§574–575, 833). Bl-D §390.

657. A final ἵνα-clause may also stand in apposition to another phrase expressing purpose:

> p4d   2pass   1n+
> (5) εἰς τοῦτο / ἐφανερώθη / ὁ υἱὸς τοῦ θεοῦ,
>
>   s
> ἵνα λύσῃ τὰ ἔργα τοῦ διαβόλου   1 Jn 3:8
> *For this reason the son of God was made manifest,*
> *namely that he might destroy the works of the devil*

The ἵνα-clause stands in apposition to and explains εἰς τοῦτο. Observe that ἵνα and the subjunctive in this example may also be translated by an infinitive:

> *. . . namely to destroy the works of the devil*

Bl-D §394.

658. A ἵνα-clause may be used as a complement of certain adjectives and nouns; the latter appear for the most part with generalized verbs εἰμί, ἔχω, e.g. εἰμὶ ἱκανός, *I am fit;* ἔχω χρείαν, *I have need.*

> (6) οὐκ εἰμὶ ἱκανὸς ἵνα μου ὑπὸ τὴν στέγην εἰσέλθῃς   Mt 8:8
> *I am not worthy that you should come under my roof*
> (7) καὶ οὐ χρείαν ἔχετε ἵνα τις διδάσκῃ ὑμᾶς   1 Jn 2:27
> *And you have no need that any one should teach you*

These constructions are again agnate to constructions with the infinitive (§835). Bl-D §393.

659. ἵνα may be used to introduce an object clause after certain transitive verbs. In the sentence

>   2-1   s⁴
> (8) ἠρώτα / ἵνα καταβῇ καὶ ἰάσηται αὐτοῦ τὸν υἱόν   Jn 4:47
> *He begged that he come down and heal his son*

the ἵνα-clause is the object of the verb *begged* (ἐρωτάω). The following example with θέλω is comparable:

> N→ 2-1   s⁴
> (9) οὐκ ἤθελεν / ἵνα τις γνοῖ   Mk 9:30
> *He did not wish that any one know [it]*

The translation of such sentences with a *that*-clause in English is sometimes felt to be awkward. An alternative is to use the infinitive:

(8) *He begged him to come down and heal his son*

(9) *He did not wish any one to know [it]*

The same option is open in Greek, e.g.

	A	2-1	4d	i	4n+

(10) τότε / ἠρώτησαν / αὐτὸν / ἐπιμεῖναι / ἡμέρας τινάς   Acts 10:48

Then they asked him to remain for some days

Object clauses with ἵνα after certain verbs appear to be agnate (§592.2) to imperatives, e.g. in (8), the ἵνα-clause = *Come down and heal my son.*

660.   In addition to its use in object clauses (§659), ἵνα appears in substantive clauses of other types, though less often than ὅτι (§646) . For example, a ἵνα-clause may appear as the predicate in S-II:

	1n+	2	s

(11) ἐμὸν βρῶμά / ἐστιν / ἵνα ποιήσω τὸ θέλημα τοῦ
     πέμψαντός με   Jn 4:34

My food is to do the will of the one sending me

Note that an infinitive is used to translate this ἵνα-clause. One might translate:

My food is that I do the will of the one sending me

The translation indicates that the two constructions are agnate in English; they are also agnate in Greek, but the construction with an infinitive is less common in Greek.

661.   A ἵνα-clause rarely appears as subject:

	C	Q	2pass		p4n+

(12) καὶ) πῶς / γέγραπται / ἐπὶ τὸν υἱὸν τοῦ ἀνθρώπου /
     1s
     ἵνα πολλὰ πάθῃ καὶ ἐξουδενηθῇ;   Mk 9:12
     And how is it written of the son of man
     that he should suffer many things and be treated with contempt?

This construction is agnate to a ὅτι-clause as exemplified in (1), §646: both are subjects of a passive verb.

662. Like ὅτι (§652), ἵνα may introduce clauses that stand in apposition to some other element in a sentence, usually with a demonstrative pronoun (οὗτος) preceding. (5) in §657 exhibits the same construction but with a purposive nuance. In the following example, this nuance is missing; the ἵνα-clause is merely explanatory.

> D   1d   2   3n+
> (13) ὅτι] αὕτη / ἐστιν / ἡ ἀγγελία . . . //
>   s
>   ἵνα ἀγαπῶμεν ἀλλήλους   1 Jn 3:11
>   *For this is the message . . .*
>   *namely that we should love one another*

s modifies 3n+, i.e. stands in apposition to it (indicated by //). Bl-D §394.

Lesson 46

Relative Clauses

665.   *Relative subordinators* (relative pronouns, pronominal adjectives, adverbs) differ from subordinators of the type of ὅτι and ἵνα in that the former have a grammatical function of their own in the subordinate sentence; the latter merely connect the subordinate clause with the main clause. In the case of relative pronouns, the grammatical function in the subordinate sentence is always that of a constituent element (subject, object, etc.).

666.   *Relative pronouns* link an included or inserted sentence to the main or matrix sentence by replacing, in the inserted sentence, the item the two sentences have in common when taken as separate sentences. An illustration will make this point clear.

   The sentence

       1n+   3   3n+   s

(1)   ἡ ἐντολὴ ἡ παλαιά / ἐστιν / ὁ λόγος / ὃν ἠκούσατε   1 Jn 2:7
     The old commandment is the word which you heard

contains a matrix sentence, *The old commandment is the word*, and an included sentence, *which you heard*, introduced by a relative pronoun. This complex sentence may be thought of as deriving from two independent sentences:

(1a) ἡ ἐντολὴ ἡ παλαιά ἐστιν ὁ λόγος
(1b) τὸν λόγον ἠκούσατε

The two sentences have the item ὁ λόγος in common (in (1b) in the accusative case). To include (1b) in (1a), the common item, ὁ λόγος, is replaced in the second sentence by a relative pronoun: τὸν λόγον → ὅν. The relative pronoun ὅν therefore has ὁ λόγος in the matrix sentence as its *antecedent*. Cf. the example given in §642.

667.   The rules for transforming a sentence to be inserted into a relative clause are simple:

667.1   The relative pronoun *agrees* with the item in the inserted sentence which it replaces and the item in the matrix sentence to which it refers (they are the same item) in *gender* and *number*.

667.2   The relative pronoun takes its *case* from its use in its own clause (the inserted sentence), i.e. it takes the case the item it replaces had in the independent sentence.

667.3   In (1) ὅν is masculine and singular because that is the gender and number of λόγος; it is accusative because τὸν λόγον is the object of the verb ἠκούσατε in (1b), just as ὅν is in (1).

There are important exceptions to the second rule, which will be noted subsequently (§670).

668.   Relative clauses introduced by relative pronouns are commonly adjective clauses, i.e. they modify some (nominal) item in the matrix sentence.

668.1   The relative clause may modify the subject:

       3a   2   1n+   s

(2)   ἀληθής / ἐστιν / ἡ μαρτυρία // ἣν μαρτυρεῖ περὶ ἐμοῦ   Jn 5:32
      The testimony which he bears on my behalf is true

s expands the subject, 1n+.

668.2   It may modify the object:

        2-1   4d   s

(3)   . . . συνήγαγον / πάντας // οὓς εὗρον   Mt 22:10
      . . . they gathered all whom they found

s expands the object, 4d.

668.3   It may modify the predicate nominative in S-II:

      C   2   1d   3n+

(4)   καὶ ἔστιν / αὕτη / ἡ ἀγγελία //
      s
      ἣν ἀκηκόαμεν ἀπ᾽ αὐτοῦ   1 Jn 1:5
      And this is the message
      which we heard from him

s expands the predicate nominative, 3n+.

668.4   Or an item in a prepositional phrase:

       p4n+   s

(5)   . . . μετὰ τὸ βάπτισμα // ὃ ἐκήρυξεν Ἰωάννης   Acts 10:37
      . . . after the baptism which John preached

s expands the noun in the p-phrase.

668.5 A relative clause may modify or expand any nominal element in the matrix sentence, of which examples (2)–(5) are merely illustrative.

669. In sentences (1)–(5) the antecedent immediately precedes the relative pronoun. This need not be the case, e.g.

    1d   D   2   4n+   i

(6) οὐδεὶς / [γὰρ] δύναται / ταῦτα τὰ σημεῖα / ποιεῖν //

    s

    ἃ σὺ ποιεῖς   Jn 3:2

    For no one is able to do these signs

    which you do

s is separated from its antecedent (4n+ in this instance) by an infinitive (i).

670. It was stipulated in §667 that a relative pronoun agrees with its antecedent in gender and number but takes its case from its use in its own clause. This is in fact not always the case. The relative is commonly *attracted* or *assimilated* to the case of its antecedent, especially where the relative ought to be accusative (by the rule) and the antecedent is genitive or dative. Attraction is understandably more common where other items do not intervene between antecedent and relative.

670.1 Attraction from accusative to genitive:

    1d+   D   2   p6n+

(7) ὃς [δ’] ἂν / πίῃ / ἐκ τοῦ ὕδατος //

    s

    οὗ ἐγὼ δώσω αὐτῷ   Jn 4:14

    Whoever drinks from the water

    which I shall give him . . .

οὗ is by attraction to ὕδατος; cf. a comparable construction in the same verse:

    C   1n+   s

(8) ἀλλὰ) τὸ ὕδωρ // ὃ δώσω αὐτῷ . . .   Jn 4:14

    But the water which I shall give him . . .

In (8) the antecedent (ὕδωρ) is nominative; ὃ may be taken as accusative (the nom. and acc. are identical in form).

670.2 Attraction from accusative to dative:

(9) . . . αἰνοῦντες / τὸν θεὸν / ἐπὶ πᾶσιν /

       s

    οἷς ἤκουσαν καὶ εἶδον   Lk 2:20

    . . . praising God for everything

    that they had heard and seen

The labels above example (9): 3g, 4n+, p5d.

οἷς (instead of ἅ) is by attraction to πᾶσιν. Bl-D §294.

671.   In classical Greek ὅς was the definite relative pronoun (*who, which, that*), ὅστις (ὅς + τις, both parts of which are declined, §259) the indefinite relative (*whoever, whichever*). This distinction has been largely obscured in hellenistic Greek (Bl-D §293). For most purposes the student may ignore the difference. ὅστις is used in the New Testament only in the nom. sing. and plur. (ὅστις, ἥτις, ὅ τι [written divided in order to distinguish it from the other subordinator ὅτι, to which it is related]; οἵτινες, αἵτινες, ἅτινα (ὅ τι also appears as an acc.) (§271; Bl-D §64(3)).

672.   As an adjective clause, the relative clause is often agnate to an articular participle. Observe the sequence in Lk 12:8f.:

(10) πᾶς ὃς ἂν ὁμολογήσῃ ἐν ἐμοὶ . . .

     ὁ δὲ ἀρνησάμενός με . . .   Lk 12:8f.

     Everyone who acknowledges me . . .

     But he who denies me . . .

The relative clause is here agnate to the participial phrase. This relationship is confirmed by the form of the second word group in the parallel passage in Matthew:

(11) ὅστις δ' ἂν ἀρνήσηταί με . . .   Mt 10:33

     Whoever denies me . . .

The kinship is also evident in the following two word groups:

(12) . . . Ἰησοῦ Χριστοῦ, ὃς ἔδωκεν ἑαυτὸν ὑπὲρ ἡμῶν   Titus 2:14

     . . . Jesus Christ, who gave himself for us

(13) . . . Ἰησοῦ Χριστοῦ, τοῦ δόντος ἑαυτὸν ὑπὲρ τῶν ἁμαρτιῶν

     ἡμῶν   Gal 1:4

     . . . Jesus Christ, the one giving himself for our sins

The articular participal in (13) may just as well be translated by a relative clause in English:

> . . . Jesus Christ, who gave himself for our sins

Further, cf. Mt. 7:24 with Lk 6:47.

673. Relative clauses may also function as substantive clauses, i.e. as an element in the matrix sentence. When they do so, their antecedent is "omitted" (from, the standpoint of English).

673.1 A relative clause may appear as subject:

C   1s

(14) καὶ) ὃς οὐ λαμβάνει τὸν σταυρὸν αὐτοῦ
καὶ ἀκολουθεῖ ὀπίσω μου /

N→ 2   6b   3a

οὐκ ἔστιν / μου / ἄξιος   Mt 10:38

And [he] who does not take his cross
and follow me
is not worthy of me

The relative clause is subject (1s) of the verb ἔστιν (2). In English it is customary to supply an antecedent (put in brackets in the translation).

673.2 As object:

C   N→2-1   s⁴

(15) καὶ) οὐ ποιεῖτε / ἃ λέγω   Lk 6:46

And you do not do what I say

The relative clause is the object of the verb ποιεῖτε.

673.3 As the predicate in S-II:

1b   2   s³

(16) Ἰδοὺ / ἐγώ / εἰμι / ὃν ζητεῖτε   Acts 10:21

Look, I am [he] whom you seek

The relative clause functions as the predicate nominative (designated 3).

674. Relative clauses may function as adverbial clauses although they retain the structure of adjective or substantive clauses.

(17) ἔπεμψα ὑμῖν Τιμόθεον . . .

  ὃς ὑμᾶς ἀναμνήσει τὰς ὁδούς μου   1 Cor 4:17

  I sent Timothy to you . . .

  who will remind you of my ways

The relative clause in (17) is the equivalent of a purpose clause (*in order to remind you*) with ἵνα or an infinitive (s. §§656, 574–575, 833). Structurally, the relative clause is an adjective clause modifying Τιμόθεον.

Similarly, a relative clause may be the equivalent of a conditional clause (if-clause):

(18) ὃς ἂν γὰρ ἔχῃ, δοθήσεται αὐτῷ   Lk 8:18

  For it shall be given to him who has

ὃς ἂν ἔχῃ is the equivalent of ἐάν τις ἔχῃ, *if anyone has*. For the variety of relative clauses in the New Testament, s. Bl-D §§377–380.

6740.   With the relative pronoun the particle ἄν has a generalizing force, ὃς ἄν = *whoever*. With ὅστις, ἄν merely heightens the indefiniteness. In hellenistic Greek this ἄν is often written ἐάν (εἰ, -*if*, plus ἄν), as though ἐάν did not contain εἰ, *if*.

Other subordinators are given an indefinite nuance by the addition of ἄν: ἐάν (= εἰ + ἄν), *if ever*; ὅταν (= ὅτε + ἄν), *whenever*; ὅπου ἄν, *wherever*. Cf. §§858 and 870.

ἄν is also taken to modify the meaning of the moods. Rather than as a means of marking indefiniteness, it is understood to limit the verb to particular conditions or circumstances: in that case, under the circumstances. Smyth §1762.

Lesson 47

Simple Nominal Word Clusters

680. The syntax presented in Lessons 32–46 has had to do for the most part with the sentence and hence with the gross features of the Greek language. The discussion of sentence types, subjects, adverbials, verb chains, constituent elements, and function words has been aimed at the structure of the sentence as a whole. Grammar at the grossest level is grammar of the sentence.

A second level of grammar still at the gross or elementary level is concerned with the structure of elements within and smaller than the sentence. The sentence is now to be held under a magnifying glass, so to speak, and its parts, and the parts of those parts, examined in greater detail.

Whether one is examining the sentence as a whole or the constituent elements of the sentence, at the gross or elementary level the student is preoccupied with the highly repetitive features of the language—the "regular" features. Advanced grammar tends to be interested in the "irregular" or aberrant features of the language. Advanced grammars are therefore of little help to those who do not already know the language well. Since this is an elementary (and intermediate) grammar, in this phase, as in the earlier phase, only the highly repetitive aspects of the language will be considered.

681. *Word clusters* appearing as the subject of a sentence were enumerated in §§545–5470 (Summary, §548). Some subject clusters with a noun as head term were described in §§549–551. It was observed (§541.3) that word clusters appearing as subject may also serve other grammatical functions in the sentence, *without their internal structure being affected*. The internal structure of word clusters may thus be described systematically since their structure is uniform throughout the sentence.

A few word clusters initiated by prepositions and others headed by nouns were given in §§558–559. These clusters functioned as adverbials. Whether appearing as subject or as adverbial, the word clusters so far encountered belong to that part of the grammatical system which governs the organization of word clusters of smaller scope than the sentence.

Introduction to Nominal Word Clusters

682. A word group appearing as a grammatical unit in a sentence consists of a *head term* plus a *modifier* or modifiers (cf. §541). A nominal word cluster is a word group that has a word from the nominal system as head term: a noun, a pronoun, a pronominal adjective, or an adjective. (For participles in nominal word clusters, see §§770–779.) The grammatical relationships that obtain between a head term and its modifiers is called *modification structure* (§541). The purpose of this lesson is to describe the modification structure of nominal word clusters, and to illustrate the fact that the same modification structure governs nominal word clusters regardless of grammatical function.

683. *Glossary.* In describing the modification structure of nominal word clusters a number of conventional grammatical terms will be useful.

683.1 The designations *head term* and *modifier* have already been introduced (§§541, 682). In the word cluster

 (i) *cold water*

water is the head term and *cold* the modifier. To this cluster may be added an article:

 (ii) *the cold water*

In English (in Greek, too, but with differences), some words can substitute for *the* and others for *cold*. The former are called determiners and the latter adjectives. For example, we may say

 (iii) *some cold water*
 (iv) *much cold water*

but not

 (v) *ˣmany cold water*

Similarly, we may say

 (vi) *the hot water*
 (vii) *the green water*

but not

 (viii) *ˣthe some water*

Paradigms of this type are used to sort out word classes and to determine what modifiers can be used with what heads and in what order.

683.2 The modifiers *the* and *cold* in (ii) are said to be *attributive* because they ascribe some quality to the water or in some other way specify the head term.

683.3 Determiners and adjectives are not the only modifiers or attributives in use in English. A prepositional phrase may be employed, for example, to specify what water is meant:

(ix) *the water in the river*

Again, an included sentence (relative clause) may be employed as a modifier or attributive:

(x) *the water that flowed down from the mountains*

In Greek also a variety of attributives or modifiers are in common use.

683.4 Any word or word group that is modified is called a *head* (term, cluster), and any word or word group that qualifies, describes, limits, or identifies is called an *attributive* or *modifier*.

683.5 A word cluster appearing as a grammatical unit in a sentence may be *simple* or it may be *complex*. The group (i) *the cold water* is said to be simple because it consists of a single head and two ordered modifiers. However, the cluster (ix) *the water in the river* is said to be complex because it consists of two subclusters, *the water* and *in the river*. The second subcluster has its own head, *river*, which in turn is qualified by the article, *the*. The division between subclusters in a complex cluster is called a *cut*. A complex cluster may consist of two or more subclusters, but one or more subclusters may consist of single words. The term cluster is used, imprecisely, of subclusters consisting of a single word since the whole remains a cluster.

683.6 A noun that is determined by the article (*the water, the river*) is said to be *articular*. If the noun is not determined by an article, it is said to be *anarthrous*.

683.7 The adjective *cold* in (ii) *the cold water* is said to be in *attributive position*; the same holds for *cold* in (i), (iii), etc. But in the sentence

(xi) *the water is cold*

cold is said to be in *predicate* position, i.e. it forms the predicate of the sentence.

683.8 Word clusters from which the head term is omitted are said to be 'headless.' In the sentence

(xii) *He turned off the hot water and then the cold*

the hot water is a full subcluster, while *the cold* is a headless subcluster with the head, *water*, understood from the context.

683.9 The designations *cluster* (group), *subcluster*, *head* (term), *headless*, *modifier*, *attributive*, *simple*, *complex*, *cut*, *articular*, and *anarthrous* will be used in describing the modification structure of nominal clusters in Greek as they are illustrated and defined above. However, the designations *attributive position* and *predicate position* require further elaboration when applied to Greek.

684.1 When the article is present, three *attributive positions* are possible in Greek:

(1) τοὺς ἀναγκαίους φίλους   Acts 10:24
the close friends

(2) ἡ ἐντολὴ ἡ παλαιά   1 Jn 2:7
the ancient commandment

(3) εἰρήνην τὴν ἐμήν   Jn 14:27
my peace

These positions are called *first*, *second*, and *third attributive positions*, respectively. In each case the article appears immediately before the adjective, thus signaling that the adjective in question modifies the noun.

684.2 The position of attributives other than adjectives may be designated similarly. For example, a prepositional phrase may occur in first attributive position:

(4) πρὸς τοὺς πρὸ ἐμοῦ ἀποστόλους   Gal 1:17
to those who were apostles before me
(literally, "to the before me apostles")

In second attributive position:

(5) τοὺς προφήτας τοὺς πρὸ ὑμῶν   Mt 5:12
the prophets before you

In third attributive position:

(6) Ἰησοῦν τὸν ἀπὸ Ναζαρέθ   Acts 10:38
Jesus of Nazareth
(literally, "Jesus, the from Nazareth")

684.3   When the article is present, modifiers in other positions are said to be in *predicate* position. This is a loose way of speaking since such attributives do not always form the predicate of S-II. For example, the demonstrative pronouns ἐκεῖνος, οὗτος always take *predicate* position:

(7)   οἱ δοῦλοι ἐκεῖνοι   Mt 22:10
      those servants

(8)   ταῦτα τὰ ῥήματα   Jn 8:20
      these words

Prepositional clusters commonly take *predicate* position:

(9)   οἱ ἱερεῖς ἐν τῷ ἱερῷ   Mt 12:5
      the priests in the temple

684.4   An adjective in predicate position customarily forms the predicate of the sentence, even where an equative verb is not present:

(10) ὁ ἄνθρωπος οὗτος δίκαιος καὶ εὐλαβής   Lk 2:25
      This man [was] just and righteous

684.5   When an article is *not* present, attributives may come before or after the head, with no difference in modification structure:

(11) πιστὸς ἀρχιερεύς   Heb 2:17
      a faithful high priest

(12) ζωὴν αἰώνιον   Jn 3:15
      life eternal

6840.   The parsing code used to describe subject word clusters (§548) was expanded and refined in §5550. The same basic notations are employed here.

6840.1 The designations for single words in the nominal system were:

b = pronoun
d = pronominal adjective (determiner)
n = noun
a = adjective

Word clusters headed by each of these parts of speech were indicated by attaching a plus sign (+) to the basic designation.

6840.2   Because of its pervasive and special function in the structure of nominal word clusters, the article is singled out from other determiners and given the code *t* (suggested by the oblique case forms; used regardless of gender, number, or case). Consequently,

> *t* = any form of the article

6840.3   Although qualifying as word clusters, word groups consisting of preposition and single nominal are omitted from consideration as such. Complex nominal word clusters initiated by a preposition are, of course, included.

685.   *Types of modification structure in nominal word clusters.* Generally speaking, there are two types or categories of modification structure in nominal word groups (excluding groups involving the infinitive or participle):

685.1   That type of structure in which all the nominal words in the group agree in gender, number, and case, e.g.

> (1)   ἡ ἀλήθεια   Jn 8:32
>   *the truth*

Such a cluster is said to be *simple* (§683.5).

685.2   That type of structure incorporating two or more subclusters, in which some relationship(s) is (are) usually indicated by differences in case (also gender and number), e.g.

> (2)   τινὲς / τῶν Φαρισαίων   Lk 6:2
>   *Some of the Pharisees*

In (2) τινὲς is nominative, τῶν Φαρισαίων gen. plur. In this instance, the genitive is partitive: it specifies the whole of which that indicated by the head term is a part.

These two types of modification structure may of course be combined. In (2), for example, τῶν Φαρυσαίων is a word cluster of the first type within a larger word cluster of the second type.

Simple Nominal Word Clusters

686.   It will be helpful to describe the patterns characteristic of nominal word clusters with all terms in agreement before turning to an analysis of the syntactical functions of various types of modifiers. For the purposes of description, the notational scheme will serve more efficiently than words.

687.   *Nominal clusters with a noun as head term* are, not surprisingly, by far the most common. The patterns that obtain in such n-clusters are few in number and relatively simple.

687.1   Among n-clusters with all terms in agreement, the bread-and-butter cluster consists of article and noun: t-n. Such clusters appear in virtually every grammatical function in the sentence.

      (3) ὁ πατήρ   Jn 8:28
          the father (subject)

      (4) ἡ ἀγγελία   1 Jn 1:5
          the promise (predicate nominative)

      (5) τὸν λόγον   Mk 1:45
          the report (direct object)

      (6) τῷ ἱερεῖ   Mk 1:44
          to the priest (indirect object)

      (7) τοῖς σάββασιν   Mt 12:1
          on the sabbath (adverbial)

This type of word group appears frequently in clusters initiated by prepositions:

      (8) ἐπὶ τὸ δῶμα   Acts 10:9
          up to the housetop (adverbial)

      (9) εἰς τὸν αἰῶνα   Jn 8:35
          forever (adverbial)

687.2   Much less common is the n-cluster consisting of t-n plus a d-word, most often one of the demonstratives, οὗτος (*this*) or ἐκεῖνος (*that*). Cf. §684.3.

      (10) ταῦτα τὰ ῥήματα   Jn 8:20
          these words

      (11) ἐν ἐκείναις ταῖς ἡμέραις   Mk 1:9
          in those days

(10) and (11) may be described as (p-) d-t-n. However, the word order is not invariable: d may follow t-n.

      (12) ὁ λόγος οὗτος   Lk 4:36
          this word

687.3   Some d-words (but ordinarily not the demonstratives οὗτος and ἐκεῖνος) may modify an anarthrous noun (i.e. one without t):

> (13) ἡμέρας τινάς   Acts 10:48
> *some days*
> (14) εἰς ἕτερον εὐαγγέλιον   Gal 1:6
> *to a different gospel*

Notice that the order may be either n-d or d-n.

687.4   An adjective (a) may of course modify a noun. It may appear in a cluster, t-a-n, e.g.

> (15) τοὺς ἀναγκαίους φίλους   Acts 10:24
> *the close friends*

687.5   Syntactically synonymous with the structure t-a-n is the structure t-n-t-a:

> (16) ἡ ἐντολὴ ἡ παλαιά   1 Jn 2:7
> *the ancient commandment*

687.6   An adjective may modify an anarthrous noun (a noun without article). In that case, too, it may come either before or after the noun:

> (17) πιστὸς ἀρχιερεύς   Heb 2:17
> *a faithful high priest*
> (18) ἐν πνεύματι ἁγίῳ   Jn 1:33
> *with the holy spirit*

687.7   Where the article is present, the pattern with adjectives is customarily t-a-n (§687.4) or t-n-t-a (§687.5). However, the adjective μόνος, *only, alone*, appears in the pattern a-t-n or t-n-a (cf. the d-words in §687.2):

> (19) τοῖς ἱερεῦσιν μόνοις   Mt 12:4
> *for the priests alone*

687.8   A d-word may appear in combination with an adjective (a):

> (20) ἄλλον ἄγγελον ἰσχυρόν   Rev 10:1
> *another mighty angel*

6870. The patterns described in §687.1–8, while not exhaustive, represent the basic patterns of n-clusters with all terms in agreement. The patterns may be conveniently summarized here:

t-n
d-t-n (t-n-d)
d-n (n-d)
t-a-n
t-n-t-a
n-a (a-n)
t-n-a
d-n-a

688. *Nominal clusters with an adjective or a pronominal adjective as head term*, in which all forms are in agreement, are much less common.

688.1 Clusters consisting of article and adjective head (t-a) correspond to the n-cluster, t-n (§687.1). It is customary to say that the adjective is "substantivized" in such cases. One may prefer to think that a noun is to be "understood," though it is not always easily possible to specify the noun.

(21) οἱ πτωχοί	Lk 6:20
the poor (people)	
(22) ἐν ταῖς ἐρήμοις	Lk 5:16
in the wilderness (places)	

688.2 A second type of a-cluster consists of a d-word plus an adjective (d-a), once again corresponding to the n-cluster, d-n (§687.3).

(23) πᾶν πονηρόν	Mt 5:11
every evil (thing)	
(24) τις βασιλικός	Jn 4:46
a certain royal (person)	

689. The same patterns appear in d-clusters (pronominal adjective as head term).

689.1 Article plus pronominal adjective (t-d):

(25) τὰ πάντα	Col 3:8
all things	
(26) τὸν ἕτερον	Lk 16:13
the other (one)	

689.2 Pronominal adjective and pronominal adjective (d-d):

    (27) τινα ἄλλον   1 Cor 1:16
        any other (person)

    (28) οὐδεὶς ἄλλος   Jn 15:24
        no one else

6890. To the n-clusters listed in §6870 should be added a+:

    t-a
    d-a

and d+:

    t-d
    d-d

690. *Simple nominal clusters with a pronoun as head term* are few in number. Such clusters consist, for the most part, of a personal pronoun modified by a determiner.

690.1 With intensifying αὐτός (§721):

    (1) ἐγὼ αὐτός   Acts 10:26
       I myself

    (2) ὑμεῖς αὐτοί   Mk 6:31
       You yourselves

    (3) ἐξ ὑμῶν αὐτῶν   1 Cor 5:13
       from among yourselves

690.2 With πάντες (§743) :

    (4) πάντες ἡμεῖς   Acts 10:33
       we all

    (5) πάντες [γὰρ] ὑμεῖς   Gal 3:28
       you all

    (6) αὐτοὺς πάντας   Mt 12:15
       them all

690.3 With ὅλος:

            →   ←

    (7) ἐν ἁμαρτίαις /σὺ /ἐγεννήθης /ὅλος   Jn 9:34
       You were born wholly in sin

Note: ὅλος, though separated from σύ, clearly modifies it. This modification structure cannot be represented smoothly in English; ὅλος is most conveniently translated in this context as an adverb.

690.4   With μόνος (cf. §687.7):

(8) ὑμεῖς μόνοι   Phil 4:15
       You only

(9) αὐτῷ μόνῳ   Mt 4:10
       him only

690.5   With ἕκαστος (§§750ff.), in a structure in which ἕκαστος stands in apposition to a plural personal pronoun:

(10) ἡμεῖς ἀκούομεν ἕκαστος   Acts 2:8
       We hear, each one

(11) δώσω ὑμῖν ἑκάστῳ   Rev 2:23
       I will give to you, to each one

Lesson 48

Complex Nominal Word Clusters

Complex Clusters with a Noun as Head Term

695.1 The second type of nominal word cluster (§685.2) incorporates at least two sub-clusters, the syntactical relationship between or among which is usually signaled by a difference in case (gender, number).

695.2 The predominant type of modification structure consists of a nominal word or cluster (with all terms in agreement), to which the syntactical relationship of a second nominal word or cluster is signaled by the genitive case. For example,

> (1) ἡ μαρτυρία / τοῦ Ἰωάννου   Jn 1:19
>   *the testimony of John*

contains two subclusters, ἡ μαρτυρία and τοῦ Ἰωάννου. The first is the head cluster. The second "modifies" or "qualifies" the first (in grammatical parlance, an *attributive*). The way in which the second modifies the first is indicated by the genitive case. Broadly speaking, the genitive is the *of* case: *The testimony of John*, in this instance, the testimony that John gave. The range of meanings signaled by the genitive case is indicated in §§0888–890.

The terms of each subcluster are in agreement. Each subcluster therefore represents the first type of nominal cluster (§§686ff.). This means that, theoretically, any cluster of the first type may appear in either first or second position.

695.3 The nominal cluster given as (1) may be represented schematically as t-n/t-n^6, where t-n stands for any article and noun in agreement, and t-n^6 represents any article and noun in the genitive case; the slash (/) represents a cut between the head cluster and the attributive genitive cluster.

695.4 A head cluster t-n may be modified by a word group initiated by a preposition:

> (2) οἱ ἱερεῖς / ἐν τῷ ἱερῷ   Mt 12:5
>   *the priests in the temple*

A difference in case between the head and attributive cluster is also involved here. In this instance a locative dative is specified by the preposition ἐν. This cluster may be schematically represented as t-n/p-t-n^5.

695.5   Another type of modification structure involves the simple dative:

   (3) εἰς μαρτύριον / αὐτοῖς   Mk 1:44
        for a witness to them

The dative with the noun corresponds to the dative with the verb: μαρτυρέω τινι, *bear witness to someone*. This structure may be schematically represented as p-n⁴/d⁵.

695.6   Examples (1)–(3) are n-clusters: The head term (3) or the head term of the head cluster (1), (2) is a noun (n). In each case, in addition, there is a modifying word or word group, the modification structure of which is signaled by a difference in case.

There are thus at least three types of modification structure involving n+ clusters:

   (a) With an attributive genitive
   (b) With an attributive p-cluster
   (c) With an attributive dative

695.7   The (a) type of modification structure calls for further subdivision. The attributive genitive in example (1) is a cluster headed by a noun (n), and is therefore also an n+ group. The attributive genitive, however, is more commonly the genitive of a personal pronoun (b). In addition, there is a small category combining a genitive n-cluster and a genitive personal pronoun. The last contains three subclusters rather than two, of which the third (syntactically, not necessarily the third in order) modifies the second, and the second modifies the first. The three categories may be schematically sketched as follows:

   (a.1) t-n/b⁶
   (a.2) t-n/t-n⁶
   (a.3) t-n <- t-n⁶ <- b⁶

The patterns of modification structure involving n+ clusters or nouns as heads and a difference in case may now be illustrated in detail.

696.   *Noun Clusters with an Attributive Genitive.* The cluster t-n/b⁶ is illustrated by:

   (2) ὁ πατὴρ / ἡμῶν   Jn 8:39
        our father

where it appears as the subject of S-II. The head subcluster is therefore in the nominative case. The head subcluster may, however, appear in other cases:

(3) τὸν πατέρα / μου   Jn 8:19
     my father
(4) τοῖς ὀφειλέταις / ἡμῶν   Mt 6:12
     our debtors

Including those governed by a preposition:

(5) εἰς τὸν οἶκον / αὐτοῦ   Lk 18:14
     into his house
(6) ἐν τῇ ἁμαρτίᾳ / ὑμῶν   Jn 8:21
     in your sin
(7) περὶ τοῦ καθαρισμοῦ / σου   Lk 5:14
     for your cleansing

696.1 Notice that in (7) the case of the head cluster is genitive also. The identical cases need not lead to confusion, however, since σου is a pronoun (not an adjective), and thus not designed to agree with a nominal head in gender, number, and case (§§012.2, 255.1). Of more immediate significance is the structural model offered by examples (1)–(6): The reader will seize (7) as a cluster with the same structure as the preceding examples, in spite of the identity in case. The cluster t-n/b[6] is exceedingly common.

696.2 One may alter the composition of the head subcluster without affecting the structure of the whole cluster:

(8) μαθηταί / μου   Jn 8:31
     my disciples
(9) σὺν παντὶ τῷ οἴκῳ / αὐτοῦ   Acts 10:2
     with all his household

696.3 One may alter the order of the subclusters (and the composition of the head subcluster) without affecting the structure of the whole:

(10) αὐτοῦ / τὸν λόγον   1 Jn 2:5
      his word
(11) τοῖς / ἐκείνου / γράμμασιν   Jn 5:47
      his writings

(12) αὐτοῦ / λόγου   Lk 20:20
     his word

(13) ὁ πατὴρ / ὑμῶν / ὁ οὐράνιος   Mt 6:14
     your heavenly father

(14) ἐν τῷ θνητῷ / ὑμῶν / σώματι   Rom 6:12
     in your mortal body

696.4   Examples (10)–(14) show that the genitive pronoun may come before or appear in the midst of the head subcluster. The alteration in word order does not alter the structure, except that, perhaps, in certain instances, a modest shift in emphasis is indicated (Bl-D §284).

697.   What was sketched in §696 regarding the cluster t-n/b^6 can be virtually repeated for the cluster t-n/t-n^6, except that one must also reckon with the modification of the second (dependent) subcluster also.

697.1   The cluster t-n/t-n^6 is illustrated by:

(15) ὁ λόγος / τοῦ θεοῦ   1 Jn 2:14
     the word of God

(16) τὸν υἱὸν / τοῦ ἀνθρώπου   Jn 8:28
     the son of man

(17) τοῦ ῥήματος / τοῦ κυρίου   Acts 11:16
     the word of the lord

(18) ἐν τῇ σοφίᾳ / τοῦ θεοῦ   1 Cor 1:21
     in the wisdom of God

697.2   One may modify the composition of the first and/or second subcluster without affecting the structure of the whole:

(19) τέκνα / τοῦ Ἀβραάμ   Jn 8:39
     children of Abraham

Note: Ἀβραάμ is indeclinable, but its case is signaled by τοῦ.

(20) ἐκ τῆς πόλεως / Ἀνδρέου καὶ Πέτρου   Jn 1:44
     out of the city of Andrew and Peter

(21) ἐν καινότητι / ζωῆς   Rom 6:4
     in newness of life

697.3 One may alter the order of the subclusters (and their composition) without affecting the structure of the whole:

> (22) τὸν / Στεφανᾶ / οἶκον   1 Cor 1:16
> *the household of Stephanas*

Note: For the declension of Στεφανᾶς, s. §133.

> (23) Χριστοῦ / δοῦλος   Gal 1:10
> *a servant of Christ*

697.4 That the second subcluster (in the genitive) stands in an attributive relation to the first may be indicated by the repetition of the article, on the analogy of t-n-t-a (§687.5):

> (24) ὁ λόγος [γὰρ] / ὁ τοῦ σταυροῦ   1 Cor 1:18
> *the word of the cross*

697.5 The order t-n/t-n^6 (with variations in the composition of the component parts) is by far the most common. The order t-/t-n^6/n appears occasionally. The other variations on order are rare. Cf. Bl-D §271.

698. A nominal word cluster with two attributive genitives, one of the personal pronoun (b^6), the other of the type t-n^6, is found occasionally:

> (25) τὰ ἔργα / τοῦ πατρὸς / ὑμῶν   Jn 8:41
> *the works of your father*
> (26) ἐκ κοιλίας / μητρός / μου   Gal 1:15
> *out of the womb of my mother*

The order may of course be varied:

> (27) αὐτοῦ / τὸν ἱμάντα / τοῦ ὑποδήματος   Jn 1:27
> *the thong of his sandal*
> (28) τὸν / τῆς παροικίας / ὑμῶν / χρόνον   1 Pt 1:17
> *the time of your exile*

In these clusters, b^6 modifies t-n^6, while t-n^6 modifies the head cluster.

6980. The complex cluster with an attributive p-cluster, referred to in §695.4 and analyzed in §699, will be frequently represented in any Greek text of length, and in a variety of grammatical functions in the sentence. As indicated, the stock structures are t-n/b⁶ and t-n/t-n⁶, with variations in composition and occasionally in order. The student should learn to seize clusters such as those represented by (1) and (2) as wholes and at a glance. The ability to "read off" such structures without deliberate analysis will greatly increase reading speed and comprehension.

699.1 *Noun Clusters with an Attributive p-Cluster.* Attributive p-clusters often appear in predicate position (§684.3):

    (1) οἱ ἱερεῖς / ἐν τῷ ἱερῷ   Mt 12:5
        the priests in the temple

    (2) ὁ λόγος / περὶ αὐτοῦ   Lk 5:15
        the report concerning him

699.2 The head may of course be anarthrous:

    (3) ἀνὴρ / πλήρης λέπρας   Lk 5:12
        a man full of leprosy

    (4) ἦχος / περὶ αὐτοῦ   Lk 4:37
        news about him

699.3 Attributive p-clusters also appear, though less often, in second attributive position (§684.2):

    (5) τοὺς προφήτας / τοὺς πρὸ ὑμῶν   Mt 5:12
        the prophets before you

699.4 Attributive p-clusters appear occasionally in first attributive position (§684.2):

    (6) πρὸς τοὺς / πρὸ ἐμοῦ / ἀποστόλους   Gal 1:17
        to the apostles before me

699.5 And occasionally in third attributive position (§684.2)

    (7) Ἰησοῦν / τὸν ἀπὸ Ναζαρέθ   Acts 10:38
        Jesus, the (one) from Nazareth

699.6 Slightly more complex nominal word groups (n+ clusters) incorporating an attributive p-cluster are not unknown. The following illustrate the range of possibilities.

(8) τὴν δόξαν / τὴν παρὰ τοῦ μόνου θεοῦ   Jn 5:44
the glory from the only God

(9) τὴν ἐμὴν ἀναστροφήν / ποτε / ἐν τῷ Ἰουδαϊσμῷ   Gal 1:13
my former conduct in Judaism

(10) ὁ πατὴρ / ὑμῶν / ὁ ἐν τοῖς οὐρανοῖς   Mk 11:25
your heavenly father

(11) ταῖς ἐκκλησίαις / τῆς Ἰουδαίας / ταῖς ἐν Χριστῷ   Gal 1:22
to the churches of Judea in Christ

(12) τὸ θέλημα / τοῦ πατρός / μου / τοῦ ἐν τοῖς οὐρανοῖς   Mt 7:21
the will of my father in heaven

Examples (8), (10), (11), (12) have attributive p-clusters in second attributive position. The modifying cluster in (8) follows the pattern (p-) t-a-n (§687.4). (10) and (11) have attributive genitives intervening between the head subcluster and the p-cluster (cf. §§696, 697); (12) has two attributive genitives intervening (cf. §698). (9) is comprised of a head subcluster with the pattern t-a-n, an attributive adverb, and a p-cluster in predicate position.

With three items (attributive adverb, p-cluster, genitive) in first attributive position, note:

(13) ταῖς / πρότερον / ἐν τῇ ἀγνοίᾳ / ὑμῶν / ἐπιθυμίαις   1 Pet 1:14
to the passions of your former ignorance

Structures like (13) are rare.

6990.   *Noun clusters with an attributive dative* (§695.5) are relatively rare. They may be considered along with adjective clusters (a+) with an attributive dative (§703), which are more common.

Complex Clusters with an Adjective as Head Term

700.   Complex adjective clusters may be considered next, owing to their overall similarity to noun clusters. To describe adjective clusters in full would be to repeat the description of noun clusters (§§695–6990), for the most part. We may therefore confine ourselves to illustration, elaborating only where adjective clusters call for special notice.

701.   *Adjective clusters with an attributive genitive* follow the patterns of noun clusters.

701.1   With an attributive genitive of a personal pronoun:

       (1)   αὐτοῦ / ἡ λέπρα   Mt 8:3
            his leprosy

701.2   With an attributive genitive of an n+ group or single noun:

       (2)   τὰ τετράποδα / τῆς γῆς   Acts 11:6
            the fourfooted (animals) of the earth
       (3)   ἐν δεξιᾷ / τοῦ θεοῦ   Col 3:1
            at the right (hand) of God
       (4)   τὴν ὁδὸν / κυρίου   Jn 1:23
            the way of the lord
       (5)   ἐν μέσῳ / ἐκκλησίας   Heb 2:12
            in the midst of the congregation

701.3   With an attributive p-cluster in predicate position:

       (6)   σοφοὶ / κατὰ σάρκα   1 Cor 1:26
            wise according to the flesh (i.e. worldly standards)

In first attributive position:

       (7)   οἱ / ἐκ περιτομῆς / πιστοί   Acts 10:45
            The faithful among the circumcised

With both:

       (8)   τοὺς / δι' αὐτοῦ / πιστοὺς / εἰς θεόν   1 Pet 1:21
            the faithful to God on his account

702.   The comparative degree of adjectives (§§240–2451) is sometimes followed by the genitive, which indicates the object of comparison:

       (9)   σοφώτερον / τῶν ἀνθρώπων
            ἰσχυρότερον / τῶν ἀνθρώπων   1 Cor 1:25
            (is) wiser than men
            (is) stronger than men
      (10) τοῦ ἱεροῦ / μεῖζον   Mt 12:6
            greater than the temple

Complex Nominal Word Clusters

To distinguish these genitives from the attributive genitives discussed in §701, the structure may be designated a^c/t-n^6 (the raised (^{c}) indicates the comparative degree).

703.   *Adjective clusters with an attributive dative* fall into a number of categories, depending on what the dative specifies. For convenience, noun clusters are also included here (§6990).

703.1   The dative may be a dative of respect (denoting the respect in which the attribution applies):

(11) οἱ πτωχοὶ / τῷ πνεύματι   Mt 5:3
     The poor in spirit (i.e. poor with respect to spirit)
(12) νεκροὺς [μὲν] / τῇ ἁμαρτίᾳ   Rom 6:11
     dead to sin (i.e. dead with respect to sin)

703.2   The dative may be analogous to the dative used with the corresponding verbs:

(13) εἰς μαρτύριον / αὐτοῖς (μαρτυρέω τινί)   Mk 1:44
     for a witness to them
(14) τὰ ἀρεστὰ / αὐτῷ (ἀρέσκω τινί)   Jn 8:29
     the (things) pleasing to him
(15) ὅμοιος / ὑμῖν (ὁμοιόω τινί)   Jn 8:55
     like you

Complex Clusters with a Pronominal Adjective as Head Term

704.   Clusters with a pronominal adjective (determiner) as the head term of the head subcluster may be divided into two categories: the article functions as the grammatical head of a variety of clusters, some of which are peculiar to the article; other pronominal adjectives serve as heads of related clusters.

705.   *Clusters with the article as head.*

705.1   The article with an attributive genitive:

(1) τὰ / τοῦ θεοῦ   Mk 12:17
    the (things) of God
(2) τὰ / Καίσαρος   Mk 12:17
    the (things) of Caesar

Note: It is often necessary to supply a generalized noun (e.g. *thing*) with a solitary article head when translating into English. In some cases a more particularized noun can be supplied.

705.2 The article with an attributive p-cluster:

(3) τὰ / ἐν τῷ κόσμῳ 1 Jn 2:15
the (things) in the world

(4) τοῖς / μετ' αὐτοῦ Lk 6:4
to the (ones) with him

(5) οἱ / ἐκ περιτομῆς Acts 11:2
the (ones) out of the circumcision

(6) τὰ / ἐν αὐτῷ Rev 10:6
the (things) in it

705.3 The article with an attributive adverb:

(7) τοῖς / ἐκεῖ Mt 26:71
to the (ones) there

(8) τῇ / ἐπαύριον Jn 1:29
on the morrow

(9) ἐκ τῶν / κάτω Jn 8:23
from the nether (regions)

Note: Cf. §699 (9), (13) for clusters with attributive adverbs.

705.4 Some adverbs approach the status of an indeclinable noun when used with the article:

(10) εἰς τὸ πέραν Mk 4:35
to the other side
πέραν is an adv. of place: *beyond, on the other side*

(11) τὸν πλησίον σου Mt 5:43
your neighbor (lit., *the one near you*)

705.5 The article may itself be modified by another d-word:

(12) πᾶν τὸ / ἐν τῷ κόσμῳ 1 Jn 2:16
everything in the world

706. *Clusters with a d-word other than the article as head.*

706.1 Determiners with an attributive genitive, usually a partitive genitive (§888.3):

> (13) ἕκαστος / ὑμῶν 1 Cor 1:12
> *each of you*
>
> (14) ἕτερον [δὲ] / τῶν ἀποστόλων Gal 1:19
> *another of the apostles*
>
> (15) ἐν μιᾷ / τῶν πόλεων Lk 5:12
> *in one of the cities*

Cf. §685.2 (2) for an example with τινές.

706.2 Determiners with an attributive p-cluster often correspond to d-words with a partitive genitive (§706.1):

> (16) τίς / ἐξ ὑμῶν Jn 8:46
> *Who among you*

Lesson 49

Determiners: The Definite Article

0710. The consideration of the structure of nominal word clusters as wholes (§§680–706) did not permit closer examination of the function of certain high frequency words belonging to the closed classes (i.e. the members of which are fixed and can be listed §§016.6, 017) or of the relationships between subclusters signaled by cases, particularly the genitive. In this and following lessons the function of a closed class usually given the designation "determiners" will be analyzed. For the function of the cases in nominal word clusters see §§0885–894.

Determiners are like adjectives in some respects (e.g. declension patterns, attributive relation to nominal heads), but differ from adjectives in other important respects (cf. §683.1).

The Article

710 Foremost among the determiners is the article (§§120–1240). Its function as a signaler of grammatical structure was considered briefly in §§125–129. It figured prominently in the description of nominal word clusters in §§680–706. It remains to consider the "meaning" and function of the article systematically.

711. As a modifier of a noun (or nominal head) the article determines the noun in one of two ways:

711.1 *Individual:* ὁ πατήρ, the known, particular *father*, whom both reader and writer know is meant.

    (1) ἐδίδαξεν με ὁ πατήρ   Jn 8:28
        the father (viz. God) taught me

711.2 *Generic:* ὁ δοῦλος, the slave as a genus, as opposed say, to the child, peer, king, etc.

    (2) ὁ δὲ δοῦλος οὐ μένει ἐν τῇ οἰκίᾳ εἰς τὸν αἰῶνα   Jn 8:35
        the slave does not abide in the house forever

In content, the slave as opposed to the son.

711.3   The individualizing article also determines *the thing par excellence*

> (3)   ὁ προφήτης εἶ σύ;   Jn 1:21
>   *Are you the prophet?*

I.e. the forerunner of the messiah, whom everybody expects.

711.4   When the individualizing article determines a "subject" previously introduced into the discussion, its use is known as *anaphoric* (*anaphora*: reference back [to something under discussion]) :

> (4)   καὶ ἤκουσαν οἱ δύο μαθηταὶ αὐτοῦ . . .   Jn 1:37
>   *and his two disciples heard . . .*

The two disciples were introduced in 1:35.

711.5   The "meanings" illustrated in 711.1–4 indicate why ὁ, ἡ, τό is often called the *definite* article: it determines nouns and nominal clusters as definite. But anarthrous nouns and nominal clusters may also be definite, i.e. the article is not indispensable to definite determination. And the article also serves other, more purely grammatical functions.

712.   The article sometimes functions as a *pronoun*: it marks the continuation or change of subject in a narrative or dialogue, or contrasts two items. It is always joined to μέν or δέ.

712.1   The article marking a change in speaker (cf. §635.1):

> (5)   οἱ δὲ εἶπαν αὐτῷ . . .   Jn 1:38
>   *They said to him . . .*

Jesus had just been speaking. Cf. Mt 3:14: 4:20, 22: 12:3. Bl-D §251.

712.2   ὁ μὲν . . . ὁ δὲ . . . contrasting two items is no longer common (in contrast to classical usage) (cf. §635.2):

> (6)   ὁ μὲν . . . ὁ δὲ . . .   Heb 7:20f.
>   *that one . . . but this one . . .*

Cf. Gal 4:23, Acts 17:32. Bl-D §250.

712.3   The correlation of other determiners with the article is also possible, e.g. οἱ μὲν . . . ἄλλοι δὲ . . . ἕτεροι δὲ (Mt 16:14). Bl-D §306(2).

713.   *The article as a grammatical device.* Where the article functions more or less exclusively as a grammatical device, i.e. where it is lexically entirely empty, it can

rarely be represented in translation. It is impossible, for example, to represent, in English translation, the second article in the nominal cluster

(7)	ὁ λόγος ὁ ἐμός	Jn 8:37
	my word	

simply because the structure of English does not correspond at this point to the structure of Greek. Even where the article has some "meaning," it is not always possible or desirable to represent it in translation. The anaphoric article (§711.4), for example, is often used with proper names in narrative:

(8)	ἔλεγεν οὖν ὁ Ἰησοῦς	Jn 8:31
	Jesus then said	

The writer reminds the reader that it is that Jesus speaking who is the main figure of his narrative (Jesus was then a common name like John).

The article in Greek is often a purely grammatical device and should be assigned only grammatical "meaning" in such instances.

714. *The article as a signaler of case (gender, number).* In §§125–129 it was observed that the article often serves to signal the case (gender, number) of the head and attributives in nominal clusters. In addition to its utilitarian function when used with fully inflected items, it is especially helpful in the case of indeclinables:

(9)	εὑρίσκει Φίλιππος τὸν Ναθαναήλ	Jn 1:45
	Philip finds Nathaniel	

In (9) the article marks the indeclinable name Ναθαναήλ as accusative and therefore as the object of the verb. Although Φίλιππος is declinable, the article makes the structure of this sentence immediately clear. In signaling case the article contributes to grammatical lucidity. Bl-D §260(2).

715. *The article as a "substantivizer."* The article may signal that words other than nouns are being used in noun position in the formation of nominal clusters. Since nouns are more precisely designated substantives, the article is said to "substantivize" non-substantive words. This means only that the article alerts the reader to the fact that something other than a substantive is coming where a substantive is expected. The article is so used:

715.1 With adjectives:

(10)	οἱ λοιποί	Mt 22:6
	the rest (the others)	

Cf. §688.1 for other examples. The article is by no means necessary to "substantivize" adjectives, any more than it is necessary to make nouns definite. Bl-D §264.

715.2 With adverbs:

(11) ἐκ τῶν ἄνω   Jn 8:23
out of the above (heavenly regions)

Cf. §§5470.1, 705.3 for further examples. Bl-D §266.

715.3 With p-clusters:

(12) οἱ περὶ αὐτόν   Mk 4:10
the ones around him

Cf. §705.2 for other examples.

715.4 The article also "substantivizes" quotations, phrases and words as such:

(13) ἐν τῷ Ἀγαπήσεις τὸν πλησίον σου ὡς σεαυτόν   Gal 5:14
in the (saying), You shall love your neighbor as yourself

Other examples in §5470.2. Bl-D §267.

715.5 The article is used with numerals to indicate that some fraction of a previously stated or well-known sum is being introduced:

(14) μετὰ τῶν ἔνδεκα   Acts 1:26
with the eleven

The twelve was presumably the larger group of disciples. This use of the article converges on the anaphoric use, §711.4. Bl-D §265.

716. *The article signals modification structure* in nominal clusters, as indicated frequently in §§680–706. In general the article identifies the immediate attributives of a nominal head and distinguishes them from attributives that belong to the predicate of the sentence. Note, in the following, how a preceding article signals the attributive relationship of a modifier to a head:

(15) τὸν παλαιὸν ἄνθρωπον   Col 3:9
the old man
(16) εἰς τὴν γῆν τὴν καλήν   Mk 4:8
into the good earth
(17) ὁ πέμψας με πατήρ   Jn 8:18
the father who sent me

(18) τὸ εὐαγγέλιον <u>τὸ</u> εὐαγγελισθὲν ὑπ᾽ ἐμοῦ   Gal 1:11
    the gospel preached by me

Examples (15)–(18) involve adjectives and participles. Many other examples may be found in §§685ff.

7160.   *The article with pronominal adjectives.* Variation between attributive and predicate order with the article is the means of distinguishing among the meanings of αὐτός (§§719–722), πᾶς (§740.1), ὅλος (Bauer s.v.). The article is an essential component in nominal clusters with the demonstratives οὗτος and ἐκεῖνος (§§684.3, 729–730).

Αὐτός

719.   Among the determiners, αὐτός, like the article (§§710–716), belongs in a class by itself because of its range and peculiarities of function. Its uses include:

719.1   A pronominal adjective of identity:

(1)   τὸν αὐτὸν λόγον   Mt 26:44
     the same word

719.2   An intensifying pronominal adjective:

(2)   αὐτὸ τὸ πνεῦμα   Rom 8:16
     the spirit itself

719.3   A personal pronoun of the third person, mainly in the oblique cases:

(3)   οὐδεὶς ἐπίασεν αὐτόν   Jn 8:20
     no one arrested him

These three uses can be distinguished by the structure of the word clusters (or sentences) in which αὐτός appears.

720.   As a *pronominal adjective of identity* αὐτός appears in simple nominal word clusters (all terms in agreement) in *attributive position* (§684.1).

720.1   With other nominal head:

(4)   ὁ [γὰρ] αὐτὸς Κύριος   Rom 10:12
     the same lord

(5)   ἐν τῇ χώρᾳ τῇ αὐτῇ   Lk 2:8
     in the same region

Note: Either first or second attributive position is acceptable.
Another modifier may also appear in the cluster:

(6) τὸ αὐτὸ πνευματικὸν βρῶμα   1 Cor 10:3
the same spiritual food

720.2 As nominal head:

(7) οὐχὶ καὶ οἱ τελῶναι τὸ αὐτὸ ποιοῦσιν;   Mt 5:46
Do not even the tax collectors do the same?

A number of set phrases like τὸ αὐτό in (7) are in common use:

(8) τὸ αὐτό or τὰ αὐτά   Mt 5:47
the same thing(s)

(9) ἐπὶ τὸ αυτό   Acts 1:15
at the same place, together

(10) κατὰ τὸ αὐτό or κατὰ τὰ αὐτά   Lk 6:26
in the same way

(11) ἕν καὶ τὸ αὐτό   1 Cor 11:5
one and the same

The clues to the use of αὐτός as a pronominal adjective of identity are: (1) it must appear in a nominal word cluster; (2) it must appear in attributive position (i.e. the article must precede).

721. *As an intensifying pronominal adjective* αὐτός appears in simple nominal word clusters (all terms in agreement), but in *predicate position* (§684.3; contrast §720).

721.1 With a noun as head term:

(12) αὐτὸς [δὲ] ὁ θεὸς καὶ πατὴρ ἡμῶν   1 Thess 3:11
our God and Father himself

The translation *-self* is not always satisfactory. The English words *even, very* are sometimes more apt since αὐτός often directs attention to a person or thing in a way that borders on demonstrative force (*even this man, this very man*).

(13) αὐτὸς [δὲ] ὁ Ἰωάννης   Mt 3:4
this very John

(14) αὐτὸς [γὰρ] ὁ Σατανᾶς   2 Cor 11:14
even Satan

(15) αὐτὰ τὰ ἔργα   Jn 5:36
     these very works

Two set phrases are in common use:

(16) ἐν αὐτῇ τῇ ἡμέρᾳ   Lk 24:13
     on that very day
(17) αὐτῇ τῇ ὥρᾳ   Lk 24:33
     that very hour

English *same* can be used in an intensifying sense in some of these contexts. For example, (13) could be translated *this same John*, and (16) could be translated *on that same day* or, heightened, *on that very same day*, depending on the degree of intensity.

721.2   Αὐτός is used in an intensifying sense with some nominal heads that do not permit or do not require the article. In the absence of the article αὐτός is said to be in predicate position (contrast adjectives with anarthrous nouns, §687.6), i.e. it is intensifying.

721.3   With a pronoun as head term:

(18) ἐγὼ αὐτός   Acts 10:26
     I myself
(19) αὐτοὶ ὑμεῖς   Jn 3:28
     You yourselves

721.4   With a demonstrative pronoun as head term:

(20) αὐτοὶ οὗτοι   Acts 24:15
     these themselves
(21) αὐτὸ τοῦτο   Phil 1:6
     just this
(22) εἰς αὐτὸ τοῦτο   Rom 9:17
     for this very purpose

αὐτὸ τοῦτο in (21) and (22) is a crystallized phrase used in a variety of contexts and therefore subject to a variety of translations in English.

722.   *As a personal pronoun of the third person* αὐτός appears *alone*, so to speak. In the nominative case it may agree with the personal ending attached to a finite verb.

In the oblique cases it may serve as a grammatical item in the sentence (direct object, indirect object, etc.), or it may appear as a subcluster in a nominal word cluster, most often as a genitive of possession.

722.1 As a personal pronoun αὐτός serves all the grammatical functions served by the personal pronouns of the first and second persons (ἐγώ, σύ, ἡμεῖς, ὑμεῖς).

722.2 In the nom. case αὐτός may serve as the subject of a verb:

> (23) αὐτὸς γὰρ σώσει τὸν λαὸν αὐτοῦ   Mt 1:21
> *For he will save his people*

722.3 As the subject of a verb, αὐτός, like the other personal pronouns, is sometimes used for emphasis, contrast, or grammatical clarity.

> (24) ἐγὼ ἐβάπτισα ὑμᾶς ὕδατι
> αὐτὸς δὲ βαπτίσει ὑμᾶς ἐν πνεύματι ἁγίῳ   Mk 1:8
> *I baptized you with water,*
> *but he will baptize you with the holy spirit*

Since the subject of the verb is already expressed by the personal ending attached to the verb (§542), αὐτός in this structure was traditionally taken as intensifying. However, the emphasis or contrast produced in classical Greek is often minimal or lacking in hellenistic Greek, so that αὐτός may often be taken as a personal pronoun in the nominative as well as in the oblique cases.

In (24), nevertheless, ἐγώ and αὐτός are contrasted, a nuance that is made certain by the use of δέ (§632.1). Cf. Bl-D §277; Bauer s.v. 2.

722.4 In the oblique cases, αὐτός may function as a grammatical element in the sentence, e.g. as the object of a verb:

> (25) ὁ κόσμος αὐτὸν οὐκ ἔγνω   Jn 1:10
> *the world did not know him*

Or as the "object" of a preposition:

> (26) παρ' αὐτῷ ἔμειναν   Jn 1:39
> *They stayed with him*

It may appear in any other syntactical position in the sentence common to nouns and pronouns.

722.5 Αὐτός may also form a subcluster in a nominal word cluster:

> (27) ἡ ὥρα / αὐτοῦ   Jn 8:20
> *his hour*
>
> (28) τὸν πατέρα / αὐτῶν   Mk 1:20
> *their father*

See §696 (5), (9), (10) and (12) for other examples.

Determiners: Demonstratives

Οὗτος & Ἐκεῖνος

0725. The demonstrative pronominal adjectives οὗτος (*this*, referring to something relatively nearer at hand) and ἐκεῖνος (*that*, referring to something relatively more remote) appear in both simple and complex nominal word clusters, and alone as a grammatical item in the sentence (like the pronouns). Their uses are so nearly identical that they may be conveniently considered together.

725. The contrast between the demonstratives as pointers can be observed in the following two common clusters:

> (1) ἐν τούτῳ τῷ αἰῶνι   Mt 12:32
> *in this (present) age*

> (2) ἐν ἐκείνῃ τῇ ἡμέρᾳ   Mt 7:22
> *on that (last) day*

Οὗτος generally points to something present, proximate, or under discussion, while ἐκεῖνος refers to persons absent or to the more remote, although the two demonstratives are not often contrasted in the same context.

726.1 <u>Οὗτος</u> may point to someone (or something) present:

> (3) οὐχ οὗτός ἐστιν Ἰησοῦς ὁ υἱὸς Ἰωσήφ;   Jn 6:42
> *Is this man not Jesus the son of Joseph?*
> (in the presence of Jesus)

726.2 To a subject just introduced:

> (4) οὗτός ἐστιν ὑπὲρ οὗ ἐγὼ εἶπον . . .   Jn 1:30
> *This is (he) concerning whom I said . . .*
> (The subject was introduced in 1:29.)

726.3   Or to a series of preceding events (items, words) collectively:

(5) ταῦτα ἐν βηθανίᾳ ἐγένετο   Jn 1:28
These things happened in Bethany
(referring to what is narrated Jn 1:19–27)

Cf. comparable uses in Jn 3:22, 8:20.

726.4   Οὗτος may also be used to refer to what follows:

(6) καὶ αὕτη ἐστιν ἡ μαρτυρία τοῦ ᾽Ιωάννου   Jn 1:19
And this is the testimony of John
(which is then narrated)

727.1   <u>᾽Εκεῖνος</u> may point to someone (or something) absent or assumed to be absent:

(7) οἶδα ὅτι Μεσσίας ἔρχεται . . .
ὅταν ἔλθῃ ἐκεῖνος . . .   Jn 4:25
I know that the messiah is coming . . .
when he (that one) comes . . .

Note: ἐκεῖνος (and οὗτος) are sometimes best translated in English by the simple personal pronoun where the antecedent is unambiguous.

727.2   To contrast someone present or speaking with someone else:

(8) ἐκεῖνον δεῖ αὐξάνειν,
ἐμὲ δὲ ἐλαττοῦσθαι   Jn 3:30
He (that one) must increase,
but I must decrease

727.3   ᾽Εκεῖνος may refer to the more remote item in a dialogue or narrative:

(9) ἐκεῖνος δὲ ἔλεγεν περὶ τοῦ ναοῦ τοῦ σώματος αὐτοῦ   Jn 2:21
But he (that one) spoke of the temple of his body

(referring to Jesus' remark in 2:19; the Jews, meanwhile, had interposed a question).

(10) ἐκ δὲ τῆς πόλεως ἐκείνης πολλοί   Jn 4:39
Many out of that city

(referring to the city last mentioned in 4:30; another conversation had meanwhile taken place).

727.4 Or to what is temporally more remote (from the standpoint of the narrative):

> (11) καὶ παρ' αὐτῷ ἔμειναν τὴν ἡμέραν ἐκείνην   Jn 1:39
> *and they stayed with him that day*
> (*that day* is referred to the past by the tense of the verb.)

728. Οὗτος and ἐκεῖνος may be used in combination in order to distinguish antecedents:

> (12) κἀγὼ οὐκ ᾔδειν αὐτόν
> *and I myself did not know him (him = Jesus)*
> ἀλλ' ὁ πέμψας με βαπτίζειν ἐν ὕδατι ἐκεῖνός μου εἶπεν . . .
> *but the one who sent me to baptize in water (he, that one) said to me . . .*
> (a new subject is introduced, identified by εκεῖνος)
> ἐφ' ὃν ἂν ἴδῃς . . . οὗτός ἐστιν . . .   Jn 1:33
> *upon whomever you see . . . this one is . . .*
> (referring once again to Jesus; cf. οὗτος in 1:34 as well.)

Cf. the use of οὗτος and ἐκεῖνος in Jn 1:6–8, where both demonstratives have the same antecedent, but a new subject intervenes between them.

729. *Demonstratives appear in simple word clusters*, both with a noun as head term and with themselves as head terms. In simple clusters with a noun as head term, *the noun is nearly always articular and the demonstrative always takes predicate position.* This means that the demonstratives do not modify anarthrous nouns as a rule (exceptions, Bl-D §292) and that they never occur in attributive position.

729.1 The demonstratives may appear in either predicate position:

> (13) ὁ λόγος οὗτος   Jn 7:36
> *this word*
> (14) οὗτος ὁ λαός   Mk 7:6
> *this people*
> (15) οἱ δοῦλοι ἐκεῖνοι   Mt 22:10
> *those servants*
> (16) ἐν ἐκείνῃ τῇ ἡμέρᾳ   Jn 5:9
> *on that day*

Other modifiers may appear in the cluster:

> (17) αὕτη [οὖν] ἡ χαρὰ ἡ ἐμή   Jn 3:29
> *this joy of mine*

(18) ἡ χήρα αὕτη ἡ πτωχή   Lk 21:3
this poor widow

(19) Ἰησοῦς ὁ Ναζωραῖος οὗτος   Acts 6:14
this Jesus the Nazarene

Even two modifiers in predicate position:

(20) ὅλην τὴν χώραν ἐκείνην   Mk 6:55
that whole region

729.2   The simple cluster in which the demonstrative appears may, of course, be a subcluster within a complex word cluster:

(21) συζητητὴς / τοῦ αἰῶνος τούτου   1 Cor 1:20
debater of this age

(22) τὸ φῶς / τοῦ κόσμου τούτου   Jn 11:9
the light of this world

(23) οὗτος ὁ υἱὸς τοῦ ἀνθρώπου   Jn 12:34
this son of man

730.1   Since the demonstratives always appear in predicate position, careful attention must be given to the structure of word clusters, especially in S-II (§507; sentences with a copulative verb). In (24) what is subject and what is predicate is readily discernible:

(24) οὗτός ἐστιν ὁ υἱὸς ὑμῶν   Jn 9:19
This is your son

Even when the copula is lacking the subject and predicate can be readily isolated:

(25) ὁ βασιλεὺς τῶν Ἰουδαίων οὗτος   Mk 3:35
this is the king of the Jews

Assuming (25) to be a complete sentence, no other division of words is possible. If (25) were a sentence fragment, it would of course read:

this king of the Jews

730.2   When, however, οὗτος appears with an *anarthrous* noun or adjective, one must stand in predicate relation to the other, since the demonstratives rarely modify anarthrous nouns or adjectives. In (26) the equative verb is present:

     (26) οὗτος ἀδελφός μου καὶ ἀδελφὴ καὶ μήτηρ ἐστίν   Mk 3:35
         this is my brother and sister and mother

In (27) an equative verb is lacking:

     (27) οὗτος τέλειος ἀνήρ   Ja 3:2
         this is a perfect man

     Example (27) is more readily identified as a complete sentence than (25), since (25) is a possible nominal word cluster, whereas (27) is ordinarily not grammatically acceptable as a word cluster.

730.3   Predicate adjectives are recognizable by the same rules of structure applying to nominal word clusters:

     (28) οὗτος ὁ ἄνθρωπος ἁμαρτωλός ἐστιν   Jn 9:24
         this man is a sinner

ἁμαρτωλός (an adjective) does not stand in attributive relation to ἄνθρωπος and so must belong to the predicate. Similarly, ἐκεῖνος ἁγνός cannot be a word cluster in

     (29) ἐκεῖνος ἁγνός ἐστίν   1 Jn 3:3
         that one is pure

but must be subject and predicate.

731.   The few simple word clusters with demonstratives as head terms (s. §729) are illustrated by the following:

731.1   With πᾶς (ἅπας) as a modifier (cf. §§741.3, 744):

     (30) οὗτοι πάντες   Acts 1:14
         all these
     (31) ἅπαντες οὗτοι   Acts 2:7
         all these

731.2   With ὅλος as a modifier:

     (32) τοῦτο [δὲ] ὅλον   Mt 1:22
         all this

731.3   With μόνος as a modifier (cf. §690.4):

> (33) τοῦτο μόνον   Gal 3:2
> *only this*

731.4   For examples with αὐτός as a modifier, s. §721.4.

732.1   Demonstratives also appear as a subcluster in *complex word clusters*, most often as a modifying genitive.

$$\rightarrow \qquad \leftarrow$$

> (34) σὺ μαθητὴς / εἶ / ἐκείνου   Jn 9:28
> *You are a disciple of that man*

Note: The complex cluster is here separated by the verb.

> (35) ἵνα ὑμεῖς τῇ / ἐκείνου / πτωχείᾳ πλουτήσητε   2 Cor 8:9
> *in order that you, by the poverty of that one, might become rich*

> (36) ὡς ἓν / τούτων   Mt 6:29
> *as one of these*

With a genitive of comparison (§702):

> (37) μείζονα / τούτων ποιήσει.   Jn 14:12
> *Greater things than these shall he do*

On the order of subclusters with a modifying genitive, s. §696.3.

732.2   A demonstrative occasionally appears in a complex cluster with an attributive adverb (cf. §705.3).

> (38) ἐκείνοις [δὲ] τοῖς ἔξω   Mk 4:11
> *to those outside*

733.   As an independent grammatical item in the sentence, the demonstratives may serve all the functions served by pronouns. The following are merely illustrative.

733.1   The demonstrative may serve as subject:

> (39) ἐκεῖνός με ἀπέστειλεν   Jn 8:42
> *That one sent me*
> (40) οὗτοι δέ εἰσιν οἱ παρὰ τὴν ὁδόν   Mk 4:15
> *These are the ones along the path*

Cf. §726 (3), (4), (5), (6), (7), etc.

733.2   As object:

> (41) ἄρατε ταῦτα ἐντεῦθεν   Jn 2:16
>   *take these things away*
> (42) ἐκεῖνο δὲ γινώσκετε   Mt 24:43
>   *but know this*

733.3   As indirect object:

> (43) καὶ ἐκείνοις εἶπεν . . .   Mt 20:4
>   *and to them he said . . .*

733.4   As a genitive object:

> (44) τούτου ἀκούει   Jn 9:31
>   *he listens to him*

733.5   With a preposition:

> (45) μετὰ ταῦτα   Jn 3:22
>   *after these things*
> (46) ἐν ταύταις   Jn 5:3
>   *in these* (porticoes = αἱ στοαί)

734.   Οὗτος is used with prepositions in a number of crystallized phrases.

> (47) διὰ τοῦτο   Jn 8:47
>   *for this reason*
> (48) ἐκ τούτου   Jn 19:12
>   *for this reason, therefore*
> (49) ἐν τούτῳ   1 Jn 3:19
>   *for this reason, by this*

Cf. Bauer s.v. 1.b.

Lesson 51

Determiner: Πᾶς

740.1 Πᾶς (ἅπας) appears in both simple and complex nominal word clusters, and alone as a grammatical item in the sentence. Like the demonstratives (§730), πᾶς (ἅπας) appears predominantly in predicate position in relation to arthrous nouns (§684.3), but it may also appear in attributive position (§684.1) as a means of expressing contrast.

Πᾶς serves the declension model for all active participles (§§231, 246). The Attic use of ἅπας after consonants and πᾶς after vowels is no longer observed; ἅπας is consequently on the decline.

740.2 Πᾶς (ἅπας) means *every, any, all (the), the whole,* depending on context and whether it is singular or plural. It is therefore a high frequency word with a variety of English counterparts.

741. Πᾶς *appears in simple nominal word clusters,* with nouns and adjectives as head terms, with a pronoun as head term, with other pronominal adjectives as head term, and with itself as head term.

741.1 With a noun or adjective as head term, πᾶς most often takes predicate position when the head is articular:

(1) πᾶς [γὰρ] ὁ ὄχλος
    the whole multitude   Mk 11:8

(2) πάντες οἱ προφῆται.
    all the prophets   Acts 10:43

(3) πάσῃ τῇ περιχώρῳ
    in all the surrounding country   Lk 7:17

(4) τὴν κρίσιν πᾶσαν
    all judgment   Jn 5:22

(5) τὰ ἴδια πάντα
    all his own (sheep)   Jn 10:4

Note: When πᾶς is in second predicate position ((4) and (5) above), the nominal head receives special emphasis: Bl-D §275(5).

741.2 The head may be anarthrous, especially when singular:

(6) πάντα ἄνθρωπον   Jn 1:9
every man

(7) πᾶσα σάρξ   1 Cor 1:29
all flesh (= everyone)

741.3 The cluster may include a demonstrative, which is also in predicate position (§729):

(8) πάντα τὰ ῥήματα ταῦτα   Lk 1:65
all these things

(9) πᾶσαν τὴν ὀφείλην ἐκείνην   Mt 18:32
all that debt

742.1 Πᾶς occasionally appears in *attributive position* (with an articular noun), in which case it denotes the whole regarded as a sum of its parts:

(10) ἤμεθα δὲ αἱ πᾶσαι ψυχαὶ ἐν τῷ πλοίῳ διακόσιαι
ἑβδομήκοντα ἕξ   Acts 27:37
*We were in all two hundred and seventy-six souls in
the boat*

(11) ἦσαν δὲ οἱ πάντες ἄνδρες ὡσεὶ δώδεκα   Acts 19:7
There were about twelve men in all

742.2 The whole (as a sum of its parts) may be contrasted with its individual parts:

(12) ὁ γὰρ πᾶς νόμος ἐν ἑνὶ λόγῳ   Gal 5:14
For the whole law is fulfilled in one word

743.1 Πᾶς appears in simple nominal word clusters with a *pronoun* as head term, and comes either before or after the pronoun:

(13) πάντες ἡμεῖς   Acts 10:33
we all

(14) ἡμεῖς πάντες   Jn 1:16
we all

(15) ἐπὶ πάντας αὐτούς   Acts 4:33
upon them all

743.2 Though such clusters with pronoun as head term are normally anarthrous, the article may be used for emphasis (cf. §742):

    (16) τοὺς γὰρ πάντας ἡμᾶς φανερωθῆναι δεῖ   2 Cor 5:10
         For all of us must appear

744. Πᾶς is also used with a *demonstrative* as head term, and again in either order (§743.1):

    (17) ταῦτα [γὰρ] πάντα   Lk 12:30
         all these things
    (18) πάντες [γὰρ] οὗτοι   Lk 21:4
         they all
    (19) τούτων ἁπάντων   Mt 6:32
         of all those things
    (20) καὶ ἐν πᾶσι τούτοις   Lk 16:26
         and besides all these things

745.1 *Simple nominal clusters with πᾶς as head term* consist of the article plus πᾶς. The most common cluster is τὰ πάντα, either in an absolute sense:

    (21) ἐξ οὗ τὰ πάντα   1 Cor 8:6
         from whom are all things (= the whole creation)

or in a relative (restricted) sense:

    (22) ἐν παραβολαῖς τὰ πάντα γίνεται   Mk 4:11
         everything (= all teaching) is in parables

The reference may also be to persons:

    (23) οἱ γὰρ πάντες ἐκ τοῦ ἑνὸς ἄρτου μετέχομεν   1 Cor 10:17
         For we all partake of the one bread
    (24) τοῖς πᾶσιν γέγονα πάντα   1 Cor 9:22
          I have become all things to all men

745.2 The function of the article in these clusters (§745.1) is comparable to the use of πᾶς in attributive position (§742). Bl-D §275(7).

746. Πᾶς *may be used alone* as a grammatical item in the sentence (note πάντα in (24), §745).

(25) ἵνα πάντες πιστεύσωσιν   Jn 1:7

    in order that all (everyone) might believe (subject)

(26) πάντα σὺ οἶδας   Jn 21:17

    You know all things (object)

(27) διεμέριζον αὐτὰ πᾶσιν   Acts 2:45

    They distributed them to all (indirect object)

(28) ἔσεσθε μισούμενοι ὑπὸ πάντων   Lk 21:17

    (with preposition) *You shall be hated by all*

Like the demonstratives (§733), πᾶς may serve any of the grammatical functions served by pronouns.

747.1   *Πᾶς is frequently used with an articular participle*, in first predicate position:

(29) πᾶς ὁ πιστεύων   Jn 3:15

    everyone who (whoever) believes

(30) πᾶν τὸ ὀφειλόμενον   Mt 18:34

    everything that is owed

(31) πάντας τοὺς κακῶς ἔχοντας   Mt 18:16

    all those who were sick (lit., *all those having it badly*)

(32) πάντα τὰ γεγραμμένα   Lk 21:22

    all that is written

747.2   *Πᾶς is also frequently followed by a relative clause*, which is the equivalent of an articular participle (§773):

(33) πάντα ἃ ἐποίησα   Jn 4:29

    everything that I did

(34) πᾶς ὃς ἐρεῖ λόγον   Lk 12:10

    everyone who speaks a word

(35) παντὶ [δὲ] ᾧ ἐδόθη πολύ   Lk 12:48

    of everyone to whom much is given

Note: παντί is here attracted to the case of the relative (inverse attraction, cf. §670).

The relative pronoun may be an indefinite or quantitative relative:

(36) καὶ πᾶς ὅστις ἀφῆκεν οἰκίας   Mt 19:29

    and everyone who has forsaken houses

> (37) πάντες ὅσοι ἦλθον πρὸ ἐμοῦ   Jn 10:8
> *all who came before me*

748. *In complex nominal word clusters,* πᾶς *appears alone as a subcluster, as an element in a simple subcluster, and in complex clusters with the article as head term. These clusters utilize, within a more complex structure, simpler uses of* πᾶς.

748.1 Πᾶς alone (cf. §746) as a subcluster, most often as a modifying genitive:

> (38) οὗτός ἐστιν πάντων / κύριος   Acts 10:36
> *He is lord of all*
>
> (39) ἄχρι χρόνων / ἀποκαταστάσεως / πάντων   Acts 3:21
> *until the time of the restoration of all things*
>
> (40) ἔσχατον [δὲ] / πάντων   1 Cor 15:8
> *last of all*

748.2 Πᾶς as an element in a simple subcluster (cf. §§741–745) that is itself a part of a complex cluster:

> (41) διὰ στόματος / πάντων τῶν προφητῶν   Acts 3:18
> *through the mouth of all the prophets*
>
> (42) πάντα τὰ ῥήματα / αὐτοῦ   Lk 7:1
> *all his sayings*

With the modifying genitive subcluster in first attributive position:

> (43) τὴν / πάντων ὑμῶν / ὑπακοήν   2 Cor 7:15
> *the obedience of you all*

With two modifying genitives separating πᾶς from its head:

> (44) αἱ τρίχες / τῆς κεφαλῆς / ὑμῶν / πᾶσαι,   Lk 12:7
> *all the hairs of your head*

748.3 Πᾶς in complex clusters with the article as head term (cf. §§705.2, 715.3):

> (45) σὺν πᾶσιν τοῖς / ἐν τῇ οἰκίᾳ / αὐτοῦ   Acts 16:32
> *with all those in his house*

With the attributive p-phrase in first attributive position:

> (46) οἱ / σὺν ἐμοὶ / πάντες ἀδελφοί   Gal 1:2
> *all the brethren with me*

With an attributive p-phrase, followed by a relative (cf. §749.2 (37)):

> (47) καὶ πᾶσιν τοῖς / εἰς μακράν, / ὅσους . . .   Acts 2:39
> *and to all that are far off, as many as . . .*

749.   Πᾶς *may be negated* by οὐ which normally precedes:

> (48) οὐ πᾶς ὁ λέγων μοι, κύριε κύριε   Mt 7:21
> *not everyone who says to me, 'lord, lord'*
>
> (49) οὐ πάντες ὑπήκουσαν τῷ εὐαγγελίῳ   Rom 10:16
> *They have not all heeded the gospel*

Lesson 52

Other Determiners

Ἕκαστος, Ἄλλος & Ἕτερος, Τις

750.   *Ἕκαστος, each, every,* appears in simple nominal word clusters, in complex clusters, and by itself as a grammatical item in the sentence.

750.1   In classical Greek ἕκαστος took predicate position in simple clusters, but the article was often omitted (Smyth §1179). In hellenistic Greek the article rarely appears in simple clusters, in the New Testament never. Ἕκαστος is therefore regularly used with anarthrous nominal heads in simple clusters. Cf. Bl-D §275.

750.2   The plural of ἕκαστος (e.g. ἕκαστοι) is rare. One reason for this is that the singular is used with the plural of pronouns and verbs (s. §751.2–4 below).

751.   *In simple word clusters* ἕκαστος appears with nouns, pronouns, and with εἷς.

751.1   Modifying a noun:

    (1) ἕκαστον γὰρ δένδρον ἐκ τοῦ ἰδίου καρποῦ γινώσκεται   Lk 6:44
        For each tree is known by its own fruit

    (2) ἑκάστῳ στρατιώτῳ μέρος   Jn 19:23
        to each soldier a part

751.2   Ἕκαστος occasionally appears with the plural of a personal pronoun, e.g.

    (3) ἡμεῖς ἀκούομεν ἕκαστος τῇ ἰδίᾳ διαλέκτῳ ἡμῶν   Acts 2:8
        we each hear in our own dialect

In (3) pronoun and adjective are separated by the verb; in (4) the two appear together:

    (4) δώσω ὑμῖν ἑκάστῳ κατὰ τὰ ἔργα ὑμῶν   Rev 2:23
        I shall give to each of you according to your deeds

751.3   Ἕκαστος may also appear *alone* with a plural verb:

    (5) ἐὰν μὴ ἀφῆτε ἕκαστος τῷ ἀδελφῷ αὐτοῦ   Mt 18:35
        unless each of you forgives his brother

Note: The number of the verb in English depends on which is made head term, the plural pronoun or *each*: *we each hear*, but *each of us hears*.

751.4 Ἕκαστος may appear with πάντες (plural):

(6) καὶ ἐπορεύοντο πάντες ἀπογράφεσθαι, ἕκαστος
εἰς τὴν ἑαυτοῦ πόλιν   Lk 2:3
And all went to be enrolled, each to his own city

751.5 *Εἷς ἕκαστος.* The uses of ἕκαστος in §751.2–4 involve the juxtaposition of singular and plural. A more common cluster is the use of ἕκαστος with the singular pronominal adjective εἷς, *one* (a cardinal numeral; declension in §268.2). Εἷς ἕκαστος is a slightly strengthened form of ἕκαστος (or εἷς), corresponding roughly to the difference between English *each* and *each one*.

(7) ἤκουσεν εἷς ἕκαστος τῇ ἰδίᾳ διαλέκτῳ   Acts 2:6
each one heard in his own dialect

The pair also appears in the p-cluster, καθ᾽ ἓν ἕκαστον, *one by one*, i.e. *in detail*:

(8) ἐξηγεῖτο καθ᾽ ἓν ἕκαστον ὧν ἐποίησεν ὁ θεός   Acts 21:19
He related one by one the things God had done

752.1 *In complex word clusters, ἕκαστος appears most often with a modifying partitive genitive:*

(9) ἕκαστος ὑμῶν λέγει   1 Cor 1:12
each of you says
(10) βαπτισθήτω ἕκαστος ὑμῶν   Acts 2:38
let each of you be baptized

752.2 Ἕκαστος may itself serve as a modifying genitive:

(11) κατὰ τὸ ἑκάστου ἔργον   1 Pet 1:17
according to the work of each

752.3 Ἕκαστος may appear as an element in a simple subcluster that is part of a complex cluster.

(12) ἑνὶ δὲ ἑκάστῳ ἡμῶν ἐδόθη ἡ χάρις   Eph 4:7
But grace was given to each one of us

(13) πλεονάζει ἡ ἀγάπη ἑνὸς ἑκάστου πάντων ὑμῶν εἰς
    ἀλλήλους   2 Thess 1:3
    The love of each one of you all for one another is increasing

753.   Ἕκαστος, *alone*, may serve any of the grammatical functions served by pronouns, like the demonstratives (§733) and πᾶς (§746).

As subject:

(14) ἕκαστος δὲ τὸν ἴδιον μισθὸν λήμψεται   1 Cor 3:8
    And each shall receive his wages

As indirect object:

(15) τότε ἀποδώσει ἑκάστῳ κατὰ τὴν πρᾶξιν αὐτοῦ   Mt 16:27
    Then he will repay every man for what he has done

S. §751.3 for ἕκαστος alone with a plural verb.

Ἄλλος & Ἕτερος

0755.   Ἄλλος and Ἕτερος, *another, other*, are virtually synonymous in hellenistic Greek. Ἕτερος was originally a dual pronominal adjective, referring to the *other* of two parts, but it is no longer used with precision. Ἄλλος, moreover, has encroached upon the domain of ἕτερος. Cf. Bl-D §306. As a consequence, the two pronominal adjectives may conveniently be considered together.

    The patterns characteristic of determiners have now been firmly established (§§710–753). For the most part they need only to be illustrated for ἄλλος and ἕτερος.

755.   Ἄλλος and ἕτερος may be used attributively in *simple nominal word clusters*, with a noun or adjective as head, with or without the article, with or without another modifier. When the article is present in the cluster, ἄλλος and ἕτερος always take *attributive position* (§684), in contrast to the demonstratives (§729) and some uses of πᾶς (§740).

(1) πρὸς τὸν ἄλλον μαθητήν   Jn 20:2
      to the other disciple
(2) ἐν τῷ ἑτέρῳ πλοίῳ   Lk 5:7
      in the other boat
(3) ἄλλην παραβολήν   Mt 13:33
      another parable

(4) ἐν ἑτέρῳ σαββάτῳ	Lk 6:6
on another sabbath	
(5) ἄλλα πέντε τάλαντα ἐκέρδησα	Mt 20:20
I have made another five talents (= five talents more)	
(6) ἑπτὰ ἕτερα πνεύματα	Mt 12:45
seven other spirits	

756. Ἄλλος and ἕτερος may be used *with other pronominal adjectives* in simple clusters, with or without a noun as head:

(7) ἄλλον τινὰ ὅρκον	Ja 5:12
any other oath	
(8) τις ἑτέρα ἐντολή	Rom 13:9
any other commandment	
(9) οὐκ οἶδα εἴ τινα ἄλλον ἐβάπτισα	1 Cor 1:16
I do not know whether I baptized any one else	
(10) καὶ εἴ τι ἕτερον τῇ ὑγιαινούσῃ διδασκαλίᾳ ἀντίκειται	1 Tim 1:10
and whatever else is contrary to sound doctrine	
(11) οὐδεὶς ἄλλος	Jn 15:24
no one else	
(12) εἰς οὐδὲν ἕτερον . . . ἢ	Acts 17:21
at nothing other than	

757. Ἄλλος and ἕτερος are used as *heads of simple clusters* (with the article).

(13) στρέψον αὐτῷ καὶ τὴν ἄλλην	Mt 5:39
turn to him the other [cheek] also	
(14) οἱ ἄλλοι διακρινέτωσαν	1 Cor 14:29
let the others judge	
(15) φεύγετε εἰς τὴν ἑτέραν	Mt 10:23
flee to the next [town]	

Note: A variant reading for this text is εἰς τὴν ἄλλην, indicating that the two terms are virtually interchangeable.

(16) ἐν ᾧ γὰρ κρίνεις τὸν ἕτερον	Rom 2:1
for when you judge another	

758.   Ἄλλος and ἕτερος also appear in a variety of complex clusters, occasionally alone as a subcluster, but more often as an item in a simple cluster that belongs to a complex cluster.

758.1   Alone as a subcluster:

(17) ἀλλὰ διὰ τῆς ἑτέρων σπουδῆς   2 Cor 8:8
     but through the earnestness of others

(18) ἕτερον δὲ τῶν ἀποστόλων οὐκ εἶδον   Gal 1:19
     but another of the apostles I did not see

758.2   As an item in a simple subcluster belonging to a complex cluster:

(19) καὶ ἄλλοι ἐκ τῶν μαθητῶν αὐτοῦ δύο   Jn 21:2
     and two others of his disciples

Note: The p-cluster with modifying genitive separates ἄλλος and δύο.

(20) καὶ τινας ἄλλους ἐξ αὐτῶν   Acts 15:2
     and some of the others (some others of them)

(21) μηδεὶς τὸ ἑαυτοῦ ζητείτω ἀλλὰ τὸ τοῦ ἑτέρου   1 Cor 10:24
     Let no one seek his own [good], but the [good] of the other

759.   *Alone* ἄλλος and ἕτερος may serve any of the grammatical functions served by pronouns, as can either with the article (§757). Once again, this is a characteristic shared with other determiners (cf. §§733, 746, 753).

759.1   Subject:

(22) ἄλλοι, δὲ ἔλεγον, οὔ   Jn 7:12
     Others said, "No"

(23) εἶπεν δὲ καὶ ἕτερος, ἀκολουθήσω σοι   Lk 9:61
     And another said, "I will follow you"

759.2   Object:

(24) ἄλλους ἔσωσεν   Mt 27:42
     He saved others

(25) ἢ ἕτερον προσδοκῶμεν;   Mt 11:3
     Or shall we look for another?

759.3   Indirect object:

> (26) καὶ δώσει τὸν ἀμπελῶνα ἄλλοις   Mk 12:9
> *And he will give the vineyard to others*
> (27) ἔπειτα ἑτέρῳ εἶπεν . . .   Lk 16:7
> *Then he said to another . . .*

As a variation on the indirect object in S-IV compare

> (28) εἶπεν δὲ πρός ἕτερον . . .   Lk 9:59
> *And he said to another . . .*

where πρός with the accusative functions as indirect object (§602).

760.   Ἄλλος and ἕτερος are sometimes used correlatively, but without fixed pattern. For example, in the sequence

> (29) οἱ μὲν . . . ἄλλοι δὲ . . . ἕτεροι δὲ . . .   Mt 16:14

ἄλλοι and ἕτεροι are alternated, it seems, only for the sake of variety. Similar alternation is found in a longer sequence:

> (30) ᾧ μὲν . . . ἄλλῳ δὲ . . . ἑτέρῳ . . . ἄλλῳ δὲ . . .
>   ἄλλῳ δὲ . . . ἄλλῳ δὲ . . . ἄλλῳ δὲ . . . ἑτέρῳ . . .
>   ἄλλῳ δὲ . . .   1 Cor 12:8–10

Note: μέν followed by δέ is a further clue to the correlation (§635.2).

An established correlation appears to be:

> (31) ὁ εἷς . . . ὁ δὲ ἕτερος . . .   Lk 7:41

Cf. Mt. 6:24 (two examples). But in Rev 17:10 we find:

> (32) ὁ εἷς . . . ὁ ἄλλος . . .   Rev 17:10

Ἄλλος or ἕτερος may also be used consistently, apart from the first item, in a series:

> (33) οἱ δὲ . . . καὶ ἄλλοι . . . ἄλλοι δὲ . . .   Mk 8:28
> (34) ὃ μὲν . . . καὶ ἕτερον . . . καὶ ἕτερον . . . καὶ ἕτερον   Lk 8:5–8

Τις

0765.1 *The indefinite pronominal adjective* τις, τι *is identical in form to the interrogative pronominal adjective* τίς, τί, *except for accent* (§§151, 153: τίς, τί *serves as the inflectional model for the third declension*). The interrogative *always* has an *acute* accent; the indefinite form either has no accent (as an enclitic, §074) , or it is accented on the ultima in the case of dissyllabic forms, e.g. τινός, τινές, τινῶν, whereas the dissyllabic forms of the interrogative receive an acute accent on the penult, e.g. τίνος, τίνες, τίνων.

0765.2 Τις, τι corresponds to a number of expressions in English: *a, any, anyone, anything, some, someone, somebody, something, one, certain, a certain one, person, man, or thing, many a, several.* Since it embraces a wide range of indefinite terms and phrases in English, it is often subject to more than one translation in a given context.

765. Τις appears in a variety of simple and complex word clusters:

(1)	ἄνθρωπός τις ἐποίει δεῖπνον μέγα	Lk 14:16
	A certain man gave a great banquet	
(2)	μετάπεμψαι Σίμωνά τινα	Acts 10:5
	Bring one Simon	
(3)	ἠρώτησαν αὐτὸν ἐπιμεῖναι ἡμέρας τινάς	Acts 10:48
	They asked him to remain for some days	
(4)	ἤλπιζέν τι σημεῖον ἰδεῖν	Lk 23:8
	He was hoping to see some sign	
(5)	τυφλός τις ἐκάθητο παρὰ τὴν ὁδόν	Lk 18:35
	A blind man was sitting beside the road	
(6)	εἶδεν δὲ τινα χήραν πενιχράν	Lk 21:2
	And he saw a poor widow	
(7)	περὶ ἑαυτοῦ ἢ περὶ ἑτέρου τινός;	Acts 8:34
	Concerning himself or concerning someone else?	
(8)	ἐάν τινος ἀδελφός ἀποθανῇ . . .	Mk 12:19
	If the brother of someone dies . . .	
(9)	τινὲς δὲ τῶν Φαρισαίων εἶπαν . . .	Lk 6:2
	But some of the Pharisees said . . .	
(10)	ἔλεγον οὖν ἐκ τῶν Φαρισαίων τινές . . .	Jn 9:16
	Then some of the Pharisees said . . .	

(11) ἀνέστησαν δέ τινες τῶν ἐκ τῆς συναγωγῆς τῆς λεγομένης
Λιβερτίνων   Acts 6:9
Then some of those from the synagogue called Libertine stood up

766.1   Examples (1)–(7) illustrate the use of τις in simple word clusters: (1)–(4) and
(6) have nouns as heads, (5) has an adjective as head term, and (7) another pronominal adjective as head term. (6) includes an adjective modifier along with
τις.

766.2   Examples (8)–(11) exhibit complex word clusters with τις. Note that the simple
partitive genitive in (9) is agnate to the p-phrase with ἐκ in (10). The partitive
genitive in (11) is signaled only by the article τῶν, which is followed by a long
attributive p-phrase.

766.3   For other examples of τις modifying another pronominal adjective (d-words)
in simple clusters, s. §756 (9), (10); for simple clusters with noun head and two
attributive d-words, one of which is τις, s. §756 (7), (8).

767.   *Alone* τις may serve any of the grammatical functions served by pronouns (cf.
§§733, 746, 753, 759).

(12) ἐὰν μή τις γεννηθῇ ἄνωθεν . . .   Jn 3:3
Unless one is born anew . . .
(13) εἴ τι ἔχετε κατά τινος . . .   Mk 11:25
If you have anything against anyone . . .
(14) ὁρᾶτε μή τις κακὸν ἀντὶ κακοῦ τινι ἀποδῷ   1 Thess 5:15
See that no one repays anyone evil for evil
(15) εἴδομέν τινα ἐν τῷ ὀνόματί σου ἐκβάλλοντα δαιμόνια   Mk 9:38
We saw a man casting out demons in your name

Τις appears as subject in (12) and (14) (first occurrence), as direct object in (13),
and as indirect object in (14) (second occurrence). In (15) τινα is an object (going with the participle, ἐκβάλλοντα).

The Participle

Functions of Participles

0770. Nominal word clusters incorporating participles were excluded from consideration thus far (§§680–767) because the modification structure of such clusters is sometimes affected by the dual nature of the participle: it belongs to both the verbal and the nominal systems (§0467). As a verbal *adjective*, the participle may function adjectivally in nominal word clusters just like any other adjective (cf. §§687.4–8; 688). But because the participle is also a *verbal*, it may take complements characteristic of verbs, e.g. an object. It is the verbal properties of the participle that make it necessary to distinguish the participle from ordinary adjectives.

770. *Range of functions.* Before considering the modification structure of nominal word groups incorporating participles, it will be prudent to survey the range of functions exhibited by the participle. It will thus be possible to hold in view the larger reach of the participle while considering one function in detail.

The following sentences illustrate the three major functions of the participle:

(1) ἐκεῖνος ἦν ὁ λύχνος ὁ καιόμενος καὶ φαίνων   Jn 5:35
He was the burning and shining lamp

(2) ἐπαύσαντο τύπτοντες τὸν Παῦλον   Acts 21:32
They stopped beating Paul

(3) καὶ ἀκούσαντες ἐθαύμασαν   Mt 22:22
And when they heard, they marveled

770.1 In (1) the two participles (καιόμενος καὶ φαίνων) are employed adjectivally to modify λύχνος, as the repetition of the article indicates (ὁ . . . ὁ . . .) (§684). This use of the participle in nominal word clusters is said to be *attributive* (to be considered in detail below).

770.2 The participle (τύπτοντες) in (2) is said to supplement the main or finite verb (ἐπαύσαντο) in forming a verb chain. This use of the participle is conventionally called *supplementary*. It is treated in this grammar under *verb chains* (§§568, 571f.; see §§584, 585 for additional uses of the supplementary participle).

770.3 In example (3), ἀκούσαντες functions adverbially, in that it depicts the circumstances under which the action denoted by the main verb takes place. Here it is the equivalent of a temporal clause. This use of the participle is termed *circumstantial* because the participle (and its complements) depicts the circumstances, e.g. time, cause, means, manner, condition, under which the action denoted by the main verb takes place. The circumstantial participle will be treated under adverbial clauses (§§0845–849).

It is the modification structure of nominal word groups incorporating an *attributive* participle that is to be sketched in the balance of this lesson.

The Attributive Participle in Nominal Word Clusters

771. All participles are verbal *adjectives* and therefore must, as a rule, agree with some noun or pronoun (present or understood) in gender, number, and case (§§246–2500). The participle is often used as the head term (§§541, 682) in a nominal word cluster, i.e. functions as a substantive (s. §§688–689, 715 for adjectives so used). In this case, the participle may be said to agree with a noun or pronoun 'understood' or to be supplied; descriptively speaking, the participle simply functions as the nominal head.

772. *Types of clusters.* Attributive participles occur in nominal word clusters of both the *simple* and *complex* type (§685), and in clusters both with and without other nominal heads (§771).

772.1 The cluster

(4) ὁ λύχνος ὁ καιόμενος καὶ φαίνων   Jn 5:35
     the burning and shining lamp

is said to be *simple* because all terms agree in gender, number, and case. On the other hand, in the cluster

(5) ὁ πέμψας με πατήρ   Jn 8:18
     the sending me father

με is accusative (it is the object of the participle πέμψας), while the remaining terms are nom. masc. sing. This cluster is therefore *complex*: The participle heads a complex subcluster (πέμψας με), which as a whole modifies πατήρ: *the / sending me / father.*

It is to be noted that the complexity in (5) is occasioned by the syntactic relationships that obtain between verbs and their complements, rather than by syntactic relationships characteristic of nominals and nominal clusters (cf. §695).

772.2 Clusters (4) and (5) both have nominal heads (λύχνος, πατήρ). Attributive participles also occur in clusters which may be said to be 'headless' (the nominal head is not expressed), or in which the participle itself may be regarded as the nominal head. The attributive participle is a verbal *adjective* (§0770), and may be regarded as having the same range of functions as the adjective. Since the adjective may be 'substantivized' (= regarded as nominal head, §688.1), the participle, too, may be said to function as the head term in nominal word clusters lacking another nominal head.

With (4) may be compared

(6) οἱ πενθοῦντες   Mt 5:4
     the mourning (ones)

in which article and participle function as a nominal cluster. Since both terms are in agreement, the cluster is simple. With (5) may be compared

(7) ὁ πέμψας με   Jn 8:26
     the sending me (one)

which is also a complex cluster, but in which the participle serves as nominal head. A literal translation of (6) and (7) does not make sense in English, so one must supply the generalized nominal head, *one* (from the context of (7) *father* could have been supplied).

773. *The attributive participle and the relative clause.* The literalistic translation of (5), *the sending me father*, is unacceptable grammatical structure in English. The attributive participle and object is perhaps best rendered into English by a relative clause: *the father who sent me*. This translation suggests that attributive participles (with complements) and relative clauses are agnate constructions in Greek as well as in English, i.e. they are alternate ways of saying the same thing. This agnate relationship for Greek was demonstrated in §672, in connection with the discussion of relative clauses.

Even when a literal rendering into English is acceptable, as in the case of the translation of (4), *the burning and shining lamp* (only the word order has been modified), a relative clause may still substitute: *the lamp which burns and shines*.

The relative clause is thus a means of transforming a verbal (participle) into a verb. Looked at from the other side, the attributive participle is the means by which a verb can be employed in nominal position: The verb is transformed into a verbal and used as an adjective.

The relative clause is common enough in Greek, but Greek is hospitable to the attributive participle and encourages its lavish use.

774. *n-clusters with a participle.* Examples (4) and (5) (§772.1) are n-clusters (= a word cluster headed by a noun, §6840.1) incorporating an attributive participle. Example (4) is a simple n-cluster, while (5) represents a complex n-cluster.

774.1 Simple n-clusters with an attributive participle follow the patterns of simple n-clusters with an attributive adjective (§687.4–7). The participle may appear in first attributive position (for a summary of attributive positions, s. §684):

> (8) ἀπὸ τῆς μελλούσης ὀργῆς   Mt 3:7
> *from the coming wrath*

Or in second attributive position:

> (9) ὁ λύχνος ὁ καιόμενος καὶ φαίνων   Jn 5:35
> *the burning and shining lamp*

Or in third attributive position:

> (10) θεοῦ σοφίαν . . . τὴν ἀποκεκρυμμένην   1 Cor 2:7
> *the hidden wisdom of God*

An attributive participle may also modify an anarthrous noun, in which case it normally follows the noun:

> (11) Χριστὸν ἐσταυρωμένον   1 Cor 1:23
> *Christ crucified*

These four patterns with attributive adjectives were described in §6870 in accordance with the symbols of the analytic notational scheme, i.e. t = any article, n = a noun, a = an adjective. The descriptions are repeated in the lefthand column below. In the righthand column will be found the corresponding descriptions of n-clusters with an attributive participle: g = a participle.

> (i)   *t-a-n*   *t-g-n* = (8)
> (ii)   *t-n-t-a*   *t-n-t-g* (C) g = (9)
> (iii) *n-t-a*   *n-t-g* = (10)
> (iv) *n-a*   *n-g* = (11)

774.2   Complex n-clusters with an attributive participle and complements may also be described with reference to attributive positions. With participle and complements in first attributive order:

> (12) ὁ πέμψας με πατήρ   Jn 8:18
> *the father who sent me*

In second attributive order:

> (13) τὸν πατέρα τὸν πέμψαντα αὐτόν   Jn 5:23
> *the father who sent him*

And in third attributive order:

> (14) ἔθνη τὰ μὴ νόμον ἔχοντα   Rom 2:14
> *Gentiles who do not have law*

As in the case of simple clusters, complex clusters may be formed without benefit of article:

> (15) πηγὴ ὕδατος ἁλλομένου εἰς ζωὴν αἰώνιον   Jn 4:14
> *a spring of water welling up into life eternal*

First attributive order is not common with complex clusters (example (12)), nor is the anarthrous type (15) met frequently. Structures like (13) and (14), however, are common.

774.3   The attributive participle in complex n-clusters may theoretically take any of the complements or adjuncts the corresponding finite verb may take. The participles in (12), (13), and (14) take direct objects. Were these participles transformed into relative clauses, the relative clauses would be included type III sentences (§508). The participle in (15) is complemented by a p-cluster functioning as an adverb; the transformation of this cluster would thus yield a type I sentence (§§504–505).

    Other types of complements are also found. In (16), for example, the participle takes an indirect object (μοι):

> (16) τὴν χάριν τὴν δοθεῖσάν μοι   Gal 2:9
> *the grace which was given to me*

The participle is passive; its direct object in the active form has become the antecedent (*the grace*), which, in the transformation into a relative clause, would become the relative pronoun subject. The transformation would therefore yield a type IVP sentence (§510).

These examples merely illustrate the wide range of constructions possible with the attributive participle. Further treatment of these possibilities will be found in §776.

0775. *A nominal word cluster with a participle as head term (g-cluster) appears in Greek texts much more frequently than the n-cluster with attributive participle, considered above (§774). Like the latter, the g-cluster appears in both simple and complex forms (§772).*

775. *The simple g-cluster, consisting of article and participle, occasionally with the negative, abounds in both active and passive forms.*

The *active* form is illustrated by the following:

(17) ὁ σπείρων	Mk 4:3
the one sowing	
(18) ὁ καυχώμενος	1 Cor 1:31
the one boasting	

With negative:

| (19) ὁ [δὲ] μὴ πιστεύων | Jn 3:18 |
| *the one not believing* | |

The *passive* form is illustrated by:

| (20) οἱ [δὲ] κεκλημένοι | Mt 22:8 |
| *the ones invited* | |

776. *In the complex g-cluster, as in the complex n-cluster (§774.3), the participle may take any of the complements the corresponding finite verb may take.*

776.1 The complement may consist of a direct object in the accusative case:

| (21) ὁ πέμψας με | Jn 8:26 |
| *the one sending me* | |

The direct object may itself consist of a complex nominal cluster, with the head term in the accusative case:

| (22) ὁ [δὲ] ποιῶν τὸ θέλημα τοῦ θεοῦ | 1 Jn 2:17 |
| *the one doing the will of God* | |

The object may be in the dative case (cf. §§591–593):

(23) ὁ ἀκολουθῶν ἐμοί   Jn 8:12
the one following me

Or in the genitive case (cf. §§594–596):

(24) ὁ κατηγορῶν ὑμῶν   Jn 5:45
the one accusing you

776.2 The complement may consist of a p-cluster:

(25) ὁ πιστεύων εἰς αὐτόν   Jn 3:18
the one believing in him
(26) ὁ ὀπίσω μου ἐρχόμενος   Jn 1:27
the one coming after me
(27) ὁ ὢν ἐκ τοῦ θεοῦ   Jn 8:47
the one who is of God
(28) τὸ γεγεννημένον ἐκ τοῦ πνεύματος   Jn 3:6
that which is born of the spirit

Notice that the p-cluster is in first attributive order in (26). The p-cluster, εἰς αὐτόν, in (25) is agnate to a direct object in the dative case (§591.5–6). The transformation of (26) into a relative clause would yield S-I: *he who comes after me*; the transformation of (27) would yield S-II: *he who is of God*. The participle in (28) is passive (cf. §775 (20)).

776.3 The complement may consist of an adverb:

(29) οἱ κλαίοντες νῦν   Lk 6:21
the ones weeping now
(30) οἱ πεινῶντες νῦν   Lk 6:21
the ones hungering now

Or an adverb and a direct object:

(31) ὁ διώκων ἡμᾶς ποτε   Gal 1:23
the one persecuting us then

776.4 Examples (21)–(31), when transformed into relative clauses, would all yield sentences of types I–III. For an example of a g-cluster that would yield S-IV, note:

(32) ὁ δούς σοι τὴν ἐξουσίαν ταύτην   Lk 20:2
the one giving this authority to you

777.   A high frequency construction is πᾶς with an articular participle, which is agnate to πᾶς with a relative clause (§747).

(33) πᾶς ὁ ποιῶν τὴν ἁμαρτίαν   Jn 8:34
Everyone committing sin

(34) πᾶς ὁ ὑψῶν ἑαυτόν   Lk 18:14
Everyone exalting himself

With a negative:

(35) οὐ πᾶς ὁ λέγων μοι, κύριε, κύριε   Mt 7:21
Not everyone saying to me, 'Lord, Lord'

The affinity between the participial construction and the relative clause can be observed in the following parallel constructions:

(36) πᾶς ὁ πίνων ἐκ τοῦ ὕδατος τούτου   Jn 4:13
Everyone drinking of this water

(37) ὃς [δ'] ἂν πίῃ ἐκ τοῦ ὕδατος   Jn 4:14
Whoever drinks of the water

Cf. §747.2 (36) for an example with ὅστις instead of ὃς ἄν.

778.   *g-clusters as constituent elements in S-types.* The *internal* structure of complex g-clusters was considered in §776; that structure was found to correspond to S-I-IV, i.e. the g-clusters, when transformed into relative clauses, would yield sentences of types I–IV. Another way of looking at g-clusters, of both the simple and complex types, is to consider what role the g-cluster as a whole may play in the larger grammatical structure of the sentence. We may generalize: the g-cluster may play virtually any role in the structure of the sentence that any other nominal or nominal word group may play.

778.1   The g-cluster may function as the *subject* of the sentence:

     1g+   NN→ 2   p5n+

(38) ὁ ἀκολουθῶν ἐμοι / οὐ μὴ περιπατήσῃ / ἐν τῇ σκοτίᾳ   Jn 8:12
the one following me shall not walk in darkness

        1g+   3a   2e

(39) ὁ πέμψας με / ἀληθής / ἐστιν   Jn 8:26

     the one sending me is true

778.2   The g-cluster may function as the *predicate* in S-II:

       1b   2e   3g+

(40) ἐγώ / εἰμι / ὁ μαρτυρῶν περὶ ἐμαυτοῦ   Jn 8:18

     I am the one bearing witness to myself

778.3   The g-cluster may function as the *direct object* in S-III, with the head term in the accusative case:

       1a+   4g+   2

(41) οἱ ἁμαρτωλοὶ / τοὺς ἀγαπῶντας αὐτοὺς / ἀγαπῶσιν   Lk 6:32

     The sinners love the ones loving them

With the head term in the dative case:

       2-1   5g+   i

(42) δύναται / τοῖς περαζομένοις / βοηθῆσαι,   Heb 2:18

     He is able to help the ones being tempted

778.4   The g-cluster may also function as the *indirect object* in S-IV:

       4n   2-1   5g+

(43) ἵνα] ἀπόκρισιν / δῶμεν / τοῖς πέμψασιν ἡμᾶς   Jn 1:22

     in order that] we may give an answer to those who sent us

Examples (38)–(43) are merely illustrative of the possibilities.

779.   *Levels of complexity.* In considering complexity in n-clusters with an attributive participle (§774.2-3), and in g-clusters (§776), attention has thus far been restricted to the relationships that obtain between the participle and its complements. Attention should now be called to other types of complexity to be found in nominal clusters with a participle. Such additional complexities are of course those characteristic of nominal word clusters without a participle (§§685, 695ff.). Although not altogether common in simple Greek prose, one occasionally finds two, three, or even more types of complexity exhibited in word clusters with an attributive participle. The following discussion suggests the range of possibilities.

779.1 As an example of a g-cluster that is doubly complex, we may take (22) given in §776.1:

> (22) ὁ [δὲ] ποιῶν τὸ θέλημα τοῦ θεοῦ   1 Jn 2:17
> *the one doing the will of God*

In the first instance, the cluster as a whole is divided into two parts

> (22) ὁ [δὲ] ποιῶν / τὸ θέλημα τοῦ θεοῦ

since the second word group represents the direct object, with head term in the accusative case, going with the participle. But this subcluster is itself complex:

> τὸ θέλημα / τοῦ θεοῦ

The relationship of the second sub-subcluster to the first subcluster is signaled by the genitive case (s. §695). Cluster (22) is thus doubly complex but at two different levels, and the second level is on the downward scale, i.e. it has to do with the next smaller, constituent grammatical units.

779.2 There are also clusters doubly complex where the second level of complexity (from the point of view of the participle) is on the upward side, i.e. in the next larger grammatical structure. In the cluster

> (44) φωνὴ / βοῶντος ′ ἐν τῇ ἐρήμῳ   Jn 1:23
> *A voice of one crying in the wilderness*

the half slash [′] represents a cut between the participle and its p-phrase complement (cf. §776.2), which together form a subcluster in the larger cluster. The larger cluster is itself complex, in that the second subcluster is headed by a term (participle) in the genitive case, which signals the relationship of the second subcluster to φωνή: *A voice / of one. . . .*

779.3 Complexities on both the upward and downward sides of the participle are not difficult to grasp *if the cluster is taken as a whole* and *allowed to fall apart at the grammatical seams*. For example, observe the complexities on the downward side of both participles, at various levels, in this cluster:

> (45) ὁ ἀφορίσας / με
> ἐκ κοιλίας / μητρός ′ μου
> (καὶ) καλέσας
> διὰ τῆς χάριτος ′ αὐτοῦ   Gal 1:15

The one setting me apart
from the womb of my mother
(and) calling [me]
through his grace

In (46) complexities are to be observed on both sides of the participles:

(46) εἷς / ἐκ τῶν δύο
τῶν ἀκουσάντων ʹ παρὰ Ἰωάννου
(καὶ) ἀκολουθησάντων ʹ αὐτῷ   Jn 1:40
One of the two who
heard from John
(and) followed him

The types of complexity found in (45) and (46) are already familiar from simpler constructions. Here they are merely piled up as a means of packing the sentence with detail.

Lesson 54

The Verb: Tense-Aspect
Present/Aorist Indicative

Tense in English & Greek

0780. Native speakers of English are able, for the most part, to appropriate the tenses in Greek, particularly in the indicative mood, and understand them as they think they are to be understood. This means simply that the present, past, future, present perfect, past perfect, and future perfect tenses in English do in fact correspond roughly to the present, aorist (with imperfect), future, perfect, pluperfect, and future perfect tenses in Greek. What the native speaker of English has by way of native response to the Greek verb should not be impaired. The tense-systems in both Greek and English are much too simple and used with far too much imprecision to be greatly labored at the elementary level. At the same time, both tense-systems, when examined closely, are far too ambiguous and complex to be reduced to a few generalizations. The beginner is therefore well advised to allow his customary responses to guide him initially, and then to build slowly a more refined set of responses to the peculiarities of the Greek system. The treatment of tense-aspect in the Greek verb in what follows is conceived as a modification and adjustment of English responses. Consideration is confined, initially, to the indicative mood.

The remarks on tense in §§0309–3120 are presupposed and should be carefully reviewed in connection with the following discussion.

780. *Present/Past/Perfect.* Notice the tense of the verbs in the following sentences (for the formation of the tenses of ἔρχομαι, s. §487.3):

(1) ὁ δὲ ποιῶν τὴν ἀλήθειαν ἔρχεται πρὸς τὸ φῶς   Jn 3:21
   But the one doing the truth comes to the light

(2) οὗτος ἦλθεν πρὸς αὐτὸν νυκτός   Jn 3:2
   This (man) came to him by night

(3) τὸ φῶς ἐλήλυθεν εἰς τὸν κόσμον   Jn 3:19
   The light has come into the world

The present tense in (1) is accurately represented by the present tense in English, the aorist in (2) by the English past, and the perfect in (3) by the English present perfect. These correspondences are quite functional, and should be allowed to occur naturally to the beginner.

The Present

781.1 Upon closer examination, the tense of the English translation of (1)

(i)   *The one doing the truth comes to the light*

does not necessarily imply that the subject is in the process of coming at the present moment (either from the standpoint of the original speaker or the narrator). The time referred to is thus not necessarily present time. The tense of the verb generalizes the action: *he always comes to the light*. The time is past, present, and future.

With (i) may be compared

(ii)   *I arrive each morning at 8:00 A.M.*

in which the tense is again present although the time is not confined to the present. The verb in (i) generalizes the action, while the verb in (ii) indicates a customary or habitual action.

In a sentence like

(iii) *He is my friend*

the present tense denotes a present state of affairs. However, the state of affairs is rarely thought of as confined strictly to the present moment.

The present tense in English, as examples (i)–(iii) show, is by no means confined to present time. The kind of action (= aspect, §§0309ff.) represented by the English present in these examples is durative or prolonged (———) , or iterative or repeated (. . . . .). Of course, the duration of the state of affairs indicated by (iii) intersects a present moment of time (—x—) , and the generalized or habitual action represented by (i) and (ii) includes present time.

781.2 To examples (i)–(iii) should now be added:

(iv) *Everybody hits the ball*
(v)   *Everybody is hitting the ball*
(vi) *John does hit the ball*
(vii)*John hits the ball now*

Sentence (iv) is comparable to (i) in that the action is generalized. One could imagine that (v) was spoken by someone present on the scene, with reference to full participation in the game. Called the progressive present, this form denotes action in progress at the present moment. We could imagine (vi) as a response to some assertion that John is not participating: the emphatic generalized present. The present tense in (vii) is buttressed by the adverb *now*, by means of which the time of the action is narrowly focused on the present moment.

Example (vii) illustrates how difficult it is to represent an action or state of affairs as confined strictly to the fleeting moment. The present moment, after all, is the hypothetical juncture between past and future; as such, it has minimal duration. Nevertheless, it is possible to concentrate on that moment, or to conceive an action as belonging logically to the present moment. For the most part, however, the English present tense spills over into the past on the one side, and the future on the other. It therefore tends to represent a durative or repeated action or state of affairs (Roberts, 1954: 132f., 136ff.).

781.3   The English present tense in (i)–(vii) pointed to or included present time. The same tense may also point specifically to future time:

(viii) The milkman comes tomorrow
(ix)   Our friends are arriving on Tuesday

The simple present and the progressive present in (viii) and (ix) refer to the future and can scarcely be distinguished from:

(x)   *The milkman will come tomorrow*
(xi)   *Our friends will arrive on Tuesday*

781.4   Similarly, the present tense may be used to refer to past time. This use is customarily called the *historical present*. In vivid historical narrative, for example, one might find sentences like:

(xii) *Socrates then drinks the hemlock*
(xiii) *Then these guys come in, see, and I says to them, 'Where do you think you're going?'*

in which past events are narrated as though the narrator were present.

782.   *The present tense in Greek* represents much the same range of time and aspect as the present tense in English.

782.1   The disciples of John the Baptist come to him and say:

> (4) οὗτος βαπτίζει καὶ πάντες ἔρχονται πρὸς αὐτόν   Jn 3:26
> *This fellow is baptizing and everyone is going to him*

The disciples are reporting an action that is in progress. The Greek present is therefore best represented by the English progressive present. This use of the present tense might best be called the *descriptive present.*

782.2   In the same sentence, the disciples of John recall that John bore favorable witness to Jesus. John replies:

> (5) αὐτοὶ ὑμεῖς μοι μαρτυρεῖτε ὅτι εἶπον . . .   Jn 3:28
> *You yourselves testify that I said . . .*

John thus refers to an event that occurred only seconds earlier, an event that has the duration only of the speaking of a single clause in a single sentence.

A centurion is explaining his authority as a military commander:

> (6) λέγω τούτῳ, Πορεύθητι, καὶ πορεύεται
> καὶ ἄλλῳ, Ἔρχου, καὶ ἔρχεται   Lk 7:8
> *I say to this man, "Go," and off he goes,*
> *and to another, "Come," and here he comes*

The description of the two responses in the present tense indicates instantaneous compliance, which is thought, of as a single, punctiliar event of no particular duration.

Sentences (5) and (6) thus reflect the use of the present tense to refer to punctiliar actions (·) in present or nearly contemporaneous time; this use of the present is sometimes called the *aoristic present* (cf. Bl-D §320).

782.3   The present tense in Greek, as in English (§781.1), may be *generalized:*

> (7) ὑμεῖς ποιεῖτε τὰ ἔργα τοῦ πατρὸς ὑμῶν   Jn 8:41
> *You do the works of your father*

i.e., always, in the past, present, and future.

Or it may refer to a *customary* or *habitual* action:

> (8) νηστεύω δὶς τοῦ σαββάτου   Lk 18:12
> *I fast twice a week*

It may also refer to a *state of affairs* that holds good for the present moment (and usually other, unspecified moments as well):

(9) ὑμεῖς ἐκ τούτου τοῦ κόσμου ἐστέ   Jn 8:23
     You are of this world

The uses of the present tense in (7)–(9) correspond to the English examples cited in §781.1.

782.4 The present tense of a few verbs is *perfective* in character: the action denoted has been completed as of the present moment. The most common of these verbs is ἥκω, *I have come, arrived.*

(10) ὁ ἀδελφός σου ἥκει   Lk 15:27
     Your brother has arrived

Bl-D §322.

782.5 To be distinguished from the perfective present (§782.4), is the present tense referring to an act prolonged or repeated up to and including the present:

(11) ἰδοὺ τρία ἔτη ἀφ' οὗ ἔρχομαι ζητῶν καρπὸν ἐν τῇ συκῇ
     καὶ οὐχ εὑρίσκω   Lk 13:7
     Look, for three years I have come seeking fruit on this fig tree,
     and I have found none

Although both (10) and (11) are translated by the English present perfect, the present tense in (11) includes a present as well as past acts.

782.6 *The conative present* is used to refer to an act attempted but not achieved (in present time). This interpretation must, of course, be suggested by the context.

(12) καὶ σὺ διδάσκεις ἡμᾶς;   Jn 9:34
     And are you now trying to teach us?

The imperfect more commonly has this nuance (§792.3). Bl-D §319.

783. *The historical present,* used commonly in good Greek style but only in English colloquial style (§781.4), may be used in vivid narrative to refer to events in past time, at which the narrator imagines himself to be present.

(13) τῇ ἐπαύριον βλέπει τὸν Ἰησοῦν ἐρχόμενον   Jn 1:29
     On the morrow he sees Jesus coming
(14) καὶ ἔρχεται πρὸς αὐτὸν λεπρός   Mk 1:40
     And a leper comes to him

The aspect of the historical present is usually punctiliar. Had a past tense been used, it would therefore have been aorist (§788). Bl-D §321.

784. *The futuristic present* is used in vivid assertions about future events. It is therefore the futuristic counterpart to the historical present (§783). An indication of the time is often present in the context, e.g.

(15) ἐγὼ ὑπάγω καὶ ζητήσετέ με   Jn 8:21
    I am going away and you will seek me

The present tense is here followed by the future. Compare

(16) πάλιν ἔρχομαι καὶ παραλήμψομαι ὑμᾶς πρὸς ἐμαυτόν   Jn 14:
    I will come again and take you to myself

for the same sequence.

The futuristic present may also refer to the process of coming or going, with arrival time still in the future:

(17) τρίτον τοῦτο ἔρχομαι πρὸς ὑμᾶς   2 Cor 13:1
    This is the third time I am coming to you

Sentence (17) may be translated into English in a variety of ways (as may many of the other examples of the Greek present cited above). In addition to

(i)   *This is the third time I am coming to you*

with the progressive present, one might represent the futuristic present by the future:

(ii)   *This is the third time I will come to you*

Other possibilities include:

(iii) *I am going to come to you for the third time*
(iv) *This will be my third time to come to you*

These translation possibilities illustrate that the simple present tense in Greek may be represented in English in a number of ways. English is a richer (and more complicated) language in this respect than Greek.

785. The present tense is rarely formed periphrastically in Greek, i.e. with the appropriate form of the verb *be* (εἰμί) and the present participle (§568). The

periphrastic present corresponds to the English progressive present (e.g. *I am going*), but it is not in common use. For the few examples in the New Testament, s. Bl-D §353(4).

786.   *Present/Past.* With example (4)

(4) πάντες ἔρχονται πρὸς αὐτόν   Jn 3:26
     Everyone is going to him

(§782.1), in which the present tense is used to denote action in progress in present time, may be contrasted *two* forms of the past tense:

(2) οὗτος ἦλθεν πρὸς αὐτὸν νυκτός   Jn 3:2
     This (man) came to him by night
(18) ἤρχοντο πρὸς αὐτὸν πάντοθεν   Mk 1:45
     They kept coming to him from everywhere

The aorist ἦλθεν in (2) (§780) denotes a simple event in past time; the imperfect ἤρχοντο in (18) refers to repeated (iterative) action in past time.

The present tense (indicative) is used, as indicated in §782.1–2, to express both durative and punctiliar action in present time (cf. §312.3). For past time, however, Greek developed parallel tenses: one, built on its own peculiar stem (§406), is used to express indefinite aspect or punctiliar action; the other, built on the present stem (§303), is used to denote durative or iterative action (cf. §312.3).

7860. The tense stems in Indo-European tongues originally referred to aspects or kinds of action rather than to time. The so-called present stem was in reality the durative or iterative stem, e.g. βάλλειν, *to throw* (repeatedly) while the aorist stem was punctiliar, βαλεῖν, *to throw* (a single act). With the development of tense, however, the augment was added to the aorist stem to indicate past time, and a corresponding past tense was created out of the present stem: the imperfect = the present stem, plus augment, plus secondary endings (§401), to indicate durative or iterative action in past time. The aorist and imperfect indicative contrast with each other as regards *aspect*, and both contrast with the present as regards *time*. The present tense was thus left with the function of indicating both durative and punctiliar action in present time (hence the so-called aoristic present, §802.2). Cf. Bl-D §318.

The Aorist

787. *The Aorist indicative* is the dominant mode of expressing action in past time (the verb *to be* excepted, which has only an imperfect, §405). That is to say, the aorist is the tense normally used, unless special nuances are to be expressed by means of the imperfect. The aorist is therefore of much higher frequency than the imperfect. By the same token, the nuances of the imperfect are more numerous and subtle.

788. The aorist indicative refers to *past time*. The *aspect* or kind of action is *indefinite* or *punctiliar*: whatever its actual duration, the act or series of acts is conceived as a whole, and thus with indefinite aspect. When linear or iterative actions are summed up in this fashion, the aorist is called *complexive* or *constative*, e.g.

> (i) *He taught for thirty-five years* (and then retired)

Occasionally the focal point of the action is its beginning, in which case the aorist is called *ingressive* or *inceptive*, e.g.

> (ii) *He fell silent*

Or, the aorist may point to the effect or result of an act, in which case it is called *effective* or *resultative*, e.g.

> (iii) *Moses led the children of Israel out of Egypt*
> (a whole series of events was involved, but the result is fastened on)

788.1 *The complexive or constative (summary) aorist* may involve a momentary action:

> (19) ἥψατό μού τις   Lk 8:46
> *Some one touched me*

Or an action of modest duration:

> (20) παρ' αὐτῷ ἔμειναν τὴν ἡμέραν ἐκείνην   Jn 1:39
> *They stayed with him that day*

Or a series of acts:

> (21) τρὶς ἐραβδίσθην   2 Cor 11:25
> *Three times I was beaten with rods*

Or an act of considerable duration:

> (22) ἐκάθισεν δὲ ἐνιαυτὸν καὶ μῆνας ἕξ   Acts 18:11
> *And he stayed a year and six months*

These distinctions are not expressed by the aorist; on the contrary, the complexive aorist blurs the distinctions by conceiving the act of greater or shorter duration, or a series of acts, as one act or event of the past. Bl-D §332.

788.2   *The ingressive or inceptive aorist* concentrates on the beginning of an act or event, e.g.

> (23) ἐπύθετο οὖν τὴν ὥραν παρ᾽ αὐτῶν ἐν ᾗ κομψότερον ἔσχεν   Jn 4:52
> *So he inquired of them the hour in which he began to get better*

Bl-D §331.

788.3   *The effective or resultative aorist* views an act primarily from the standpoint of its conclusion, e.g.

> (24) καὶ ἐσώθη ἡ γυνὴ ἀπὸ τῆς ὥρας ἐκείνης   Mt 9:22
> *And the woman was healed at once*

7880.   *The gnomic aorist* is used of acts conceived as valid for all times, but it is relatively rare (Bl-D §333). The *epistolary aorist* is employed by letter writers when they adopt the standpoint of an orally delivered message; it, too, is not common (Bl-D §334).

The Verb: Tense-Aspect, cont.
Imperfect/Perfect/Pluperfect/Future

The Imperfect

0790. *The imperfect* is employed with considerable subtlety. While the present and aorist were stock modes of expression— and used, consequently, with less precision—the imperfect was felt to be a special tense designed for specific purposes. It is always in order to ask why an imperfect was chosen, in a given expression, rather than the aorist; the reverse of this question is not so often applicable. However, the case should not be overstated: with some verbs the difference between aorist and imperfect is not sharply drawn; this is particularly true of verbs of saying (e.g. ἔλεγεν is not consistently used to introduce a lengthy discourse, and εἶπεν does not always introduce a short speech, as might be expected).

790. The nuances of the imperfect may readily be observed in one or two passages in Galatians. In this letter Paul is framing his argument deftly, and we may anticipate that he will choose his tenses with care.

Notice the tenses in Gal 1:13–14:

(24) ἠκούσατε γὰρ τὴν ἐμὴν ἀναστροφήν ποτε ἐν τῷ Ἰουδαϊσμῷ
For you have heard of my former mode of life in Judaism

(25) ὅτι καθ' ὑπερβολὴν ἐδίωκον τὴν ἐκκλησίαν τοῦ θεοῦ
viz., I used to persecute the church of God violently

(26) καὶ ἐπόρθουν αὐτήν
and tried to destroy it

(27) καὶ προέκοπτον ἐν Ἰουδαϊσμῷ ὑπὲρ πολλοὺς συνηλικιώτας
And I kept advancing in Judaism beyond many my own age

790.1 The aorist in (24) is most naturally translated by the English present perfect: the English perfect, unlike the Greek perfect (§794), does not emphasize a result or effect; its use merely means that the speaker does not intend to interpose a distinct interval between the act expressed by the perfect and the moment of speaking. In this context, consequently, the English perfect sounds natural to English ears since what was heard is immediately relevant to the subject under discussion (the simple past interposes an interval, and so sounds odd).

790.2   The imperfect in (25) indicates action in progress in past time, like all imperfects. But in view of the context, it doubtless means an activity *characteristic* of that former way of life in Judaism. *Used to persecute* is therefore a way of representing the *customary* or *habitual* imperfect.

790.3   The activity denoted by the imperfect in (26) was evidently not successful: Paul did not succeed in destroying the church. This imperfect is therefore *conative*: an action attempted but not fulfilled. One may translate: *tried, endeavored, attempted to destroy.*

790.4   At the same time, Paul was making progress as a Jew. The *progressive imperfect* may be translated by the English past progressive, *was advancing*, to indicate the linear character of the activity. Alternately, a helping verb like *kept* serves the same purpose.

791.   Three occurrences of the imperfect in Gal 1:23f. present one new form and one additional nuance:

(28) μόνον δὲ ἀκούοντες ἦσαν
Only they kept hearing

(29) ὅτι, ὁ διώκων ἡμᾶς ποτε νῦν εὐαγγελίζεται τὴν πίστιν ἥν ποτε ἐπόρθει
that the fellow who was persecuting us once now preaches the faith he once tried to destroy

(30) καὶ ἐδόξαζον ἐν ἐμοὶ τὸν θεόν
and they began to glorify God because of me

791.1   The imperfect is occasionally formed *periphrastically*, i.e. with the appropriate form of the imperfect of εἰμί (ἦν, §568) and the present participle (cf. §785 for the present tense). In (28), ἀκούοντες ἦσαν is the formal equivalent of the English past progressive, *they were hearing*. In this case, hearing reports is probably iterative rather than continuous (the periphrastic imperfect may be used to emphasize either continuous or iterative action), hence the translation, *kept hearing.*

791.2   The imperfect in (29), ἐπόρθει (cf. (26), §790), is again *conative: tried to destroy.*

791.3   In (30), the imperfect probably has the *inception* of repeated activity in past time in view. It is therefore called the *inceptive* or *ingressive imperfect* (cf. §788.2 for the ingressive aorist).

792.   *Summary: nuances of the imperfect.* Examples (25)–(30) have served to illustrate the major nuances of the imperfect. Since the imperfect denotes durative (linear) or iterative action in past time, the basic nuances of the imperfect are:

792.1   *The progressive imperfect,* denoting action in progress, either linear or iterative, e.g.

> (31) πολλοὶ πλούσιοι ἔβαλλον πολλά   Mk 12:41
> *Many rich people were putting in large sums*

792.2   *The customary imperfect,* e.g.

> (32) μετὰ τῶν ἐθνῶν συνήσθιεν   Gal 2:12
> *He used to eat with the Gentiles*

(Peter acquired the custom of eating with the Gentiles and then stopped.) Cf. (27), (28) above, and Bl-D §325.

Other nuances include:

792.3   *The conative imperfect* (repeated effort), e.g.

> (33) ὁ δὲ Ἰωάννης διεκώλυεν αὐτόν   Mt 3:14
> *But John wanted to prevent him*

Cf. (26), (29) above, and Bl-D §326.

792.4   *The inceptive imperfect*

> (34) καὶ ἐγόγγυζον οἱ Φαρισαῖοι   Lk 5:30
> *And the Pharisees began to grumble*

Cf. (30) above.

792.5   *The periphrastic imperfect* is usually either durative or iterative, e.g.

> (35) ἀτενίζοντες ἦσαν εἰς τὸν οὐρανόν   Acts 1:10
> *They were gazing into heaven*

Cf. (28) above. On periphrasis generally, see Bl-D §353.

793.   *The perfect tenses* occasion slightly more difficulty for the native speaker of English than the tenses already considered. One reason is that the perfect tenses are used in a slightly different way in Greek. The difference is not large but it is now and then puzzling. Another reason is that the perfect tenses in Greek sustain a different set of relations to the other tenses of the past, the aorist and imperfect, than do the English perfect tenses to the simple and progres-

sive past. Since native English responses are involved, it will be helpful to begin with a few observations on the English perfect tenses.

793.1   There are two forms each of the present perfect and the past perfect:

(ia) *He has gone*
(ib) *He has been going*
(iia) *He had gone*
(iib) *He had been going*

(ib) and (iib) are, of course, the progressive forms (cf. the present progressive, *I am going*, and the past progressive, *I was going*).

793.2   The simple past contrasts with the present perfect as regards the interval of time between the past event mentioned and the moment of speaking:

(iii) *He wrote a book* (a year ago)
(iv) *He has written a book (just now completed)*

The simple past refers to action in past time, and that past is now severed from the present. The past time of the present perfect, however, abuts the present. To sever the present perfect from the present would be felt to be odd:

(v) ˣ*He has written a book a year ago*

It may therefore be said: *The present perfect in English interposes no interval between the past event and the moment of speaking.*

793.3   The same can be said of the progressive form of the present perfect. Contrast, for example,

(vi) *He is writing a book*
(vii) *He has been writing a book*
(viii) *He was writing a book*

The temporal distinctions may be represented graphically: the slash represents the speaker's present, the dots the activity referred to.

(vi) Present progressive: . . . / . .
(vii) Present perfect progressive: . . . . . /
(viii) Past progressive: . . . . .   /

The activity in (viii) ceased some time back; that in (vii) continues up to the present; and that in (vi) crosses the threshold of the present.

793.4 The past time referred to by the past perfect is doubly past, i.e. it is past from the standpoint of another event or point of reference in the past. Contrast the present and past perfects:

(ix) *I have written a book* (completed recently)
(x) *I had written a book* (completed earlier)

And the progressive forms:

(xi) *I have been writing a book* (for the last several weeks)
(xii) *I had been writing a book* (before I left on vacation)

793.5 The English present perfect thus (a) refers to past action but no definite time is indicated and no interval is interposed between the action referred to and the present. In contrast to the Greek perfect, (b) there is no particular reference to continuing effects of that action.

793.6 The English past perfect (a) refers to what is past with reference to a second point also in the past. Like the present perfect, (b) the past perfect does not have continuing effects in view.

The Perfect

794. *The Greek perfect* denotes action having taken place in the past *but with effects reaching to the present*. When the perfect is used with precision, the latter distinguishes it from the aorist (and the English present perfect, §793.5):

(36) ἦχος . . . ἐπλήρωσεν ὅλον τὸν οἶκον   Acts 2:2
     A sound . . . filled the whole house
(37) πεπληρώκατε τὴν Ἰερουσαλὴμ τῆς διδαχῆς ὑμῶν   Acts 5:38
     You have filled Jerusalem with your teaching

The aorist in (36) denotes a punctiliar act, without reference to effect. The perfect in (37) means: *you have spread your teaching around in the city and its effects are everywhere apparent*. One could therefore say: the perfect represents a combination of the aorist (·) and the durative present (———) (cf. §§309ff. and Bl-D §340).

795. Unlike the English present perfect, the Greek perfect may be accompanied by a specific temporal reference. The following example also affords a contrast between aorist and perfect.

(38) ὅτι ἐτάφη, καὶ ὅτι ἐγήγερται τῇ ἡμέρᾳ τῇ τρίτῃ   1 Cor 15:4
     that he was buried, and that he was raised on the third day

The aorist ἐτάφη refers to a past event; the perfect ἐγήγερται also refers to a past event (which took place on the third day), but with the added nuance: *is still risen*. The temporal reference requires the simple past (passive) in English, because an interval of time is interposed (§793.2), but the Greek perfect can accommodate such temporal references.

796. The Greek perfect may often be translated by the English present perfect (though with some loss of nuance). However, it is sometimes necessary to translate with a simple past in English, owing to a definite past time indicated in Greek, e.g.

> (39) τεθέαμαι τὸ πνεῦμα καταβαῖνον   Jn 1:32
>   *I beheld the spirit descending*

Cf. (38), §795.

Conversely, a Greek aorist may be properly represented in English by the present perfect:

> (40) ἡ σκοτία ἐτύφλωσεν τοὺς ὀφθαλμοὺς αὐτοῦ   1 Jn 2:11
>   *The darkness has blinded his eyes*

The aorist in (40) is preceded by a series of verbs in the present tense and no particular interval is indicated by the aorist, so that the English present perfect is the natural sequence in English.

797. Observe the characteristic nuance of the perfect (past act with effects reaching to the present) in the following examples:

797.1 With continuing effect on the *subject*:

> (41) ἡμεῖς ἐκ πορνείας οὐ γεγεννήμεθα   Jn 8:41
>   *We were not illicitly conceived* (and so are not illegitimate)
> (42) οὐχὶ Ἰησοῦν τὸν κύριον ἡμῶν ἑώρακα;   1 Cor 9:1
>   *Have I not seen Jesus our Lord?*
>   (of course I have; otherwise I would not be an apostle)

797.2 With continuing effect on the *object*:

> (43) ἡ πίστις σου σέσωκέν σε   Mk 10:52
>   *Your faith has saved you*
> (44) Ἕλληνας εἰσήγαγεν εἰς τὸ ἱερὸν καὶ κεκοίνωκεν τὸν
>   ἅγιον τόπον τοῦτον   Acts 21:28

He brought Greeks into the temple and has profaned this
holy place

797.3   With continuing effect on the *indirect object*:

    (45) ἀφέωνται ὑμῖν αἱ ἁμαρτίαι   1 Jn 2:12
          Your sins have been forgiven you

    (46) καὶ εἴρηκέν μοι, ἀρκεῖ σοι ἡ χάρις μου   2 Cor 12:9
          And he said to me, 'My grace is sufficient for you'
          (What he said put an end to the matter)

Bl-D §342.

798.   The perfect may also be formed periphrastically, i.e. with the appropriate form of εἰμί, *be* and the perfect participle (in addition to the 3. pl. middle-passive of verbs with stems ending in a consonant, §3910). The periphrastic form is scarcely to be distinguished from the regularly inflected form, as the following parallel statements indicate:

    (47) ἡ ἀγάπη αὐτοῦ τετελειωμένη ἐν ἡμῖν ἐστίν   1 Jn 4:12
          His love is perfected in us

    (48) ἀληθῶς ἐν τούτῳ ἡ ἀγάπη τοῦ θεοῦ τετελείωται   1 Jn 4:25
          In this one truly the love of God is perfected

Bl-D §352.

799.   *The present perfect* in Greek is the perfect used to denote a state or condition, or an effect resulting from some previous act (hypothetically, at least). Some of these are perfects without present stem (§§388–3880), e.g.

    οἶδα, *I know* (ᾔδειν, pluperfect = imperfect)

Others have corresponding present forms, but the perfect is used to express state or condition (the lasting effect of some previous activity), e.g.

ἕστηκα	*I stand*	(< ἵστημι)
πέποιθα	*I trust*	(< πείθω)
μέμνημαι	*I remember*	(< μιμνῄσκομαι)
τέθνηκα	*I am dead*	(< θνῄσκω)
πέπεισμαι	*I am persuaded*	(< πείθω)

Bl-D §341.

7990. *The aoristic perfect.* It is sometimes alleged that the perfect had so transgressed on the domain of the aorist, especially in narrative, by the hellenistic period that its special force was spent. In the Byzantine period, the perfect and aorist are indiscriminantly mixed. The perfect eventually disappeared and was replaced wholly by periphrases (modern Greek). There is doubtless point to these allegations. It is difficult, for example, to see the perfective force in:

(49) ἄλλοι ἔλεγον, ἄγγελος αὐτῷ λελάληκεν   Jn 12:29
     Others said, 'An angel spoke to him'

One early manuscript (P66), in fact, reads the aorist here. At all events, the perfect is certainly occasionally used in the hellenistic period without its special nuance, i.e. as an aorist. But pending a full study of the Greek tenses of the period, the student will do well to continue to inquire what, if any, special force a given perfect has.

The Pluperfect

800. *The pluperfect,* like the English past perfect (§793.4, 6), refers to time that is past from the perspective of another, more recent point of reference in the past. Unlike the English past perfect (§793.6), the pluperfect normally points to some continuing effect, or denotes a state or condition, that obtains at the more recent past point of reference. Bl-D §347.

The pluperfect appears with only 22 verbs in the New Testament. It was never in common use. See §§0415–418 for conjugation.

800.1 The use of the pluperfect is simply illustrated by

(50) καὶ οὐδεὶς ἐπίασεν αὐτόν,
    ὅτι οὔπω ἐληλύθει ἡ ὥρα αὐτοῦ   Jn 8:20
    And no one arrested him,
    because his hour had not yet come
(51) παρ' ἧς ἐκβεβλήκει ἑπτὰ δαιμόνια   Mk 16:9
    From whom he had cast out seven demons

800.2 The perfects which denote a present state or condition (§799) in the pluperfect denote a past state or condition, e.g. ᾔδειν (< οἶδα)

(52) κἀγὼ οὐκ ᾔδειν αὐτόν   Jn 1:33
    And I myself did not know him

800.3　The pluperfect may also be formed periphrastically (the appropriate form of ἦν and the perfect participle), e.g.

(53) καὶ ἀπεσταλμένοι ἦσαν ἐκ τῶν Φαρισαίων　　　　　Jn 1:24
　　　Now they had been sent from the Pharisees

Cf. Jn 3:24; Bl-D §352.

800.4　The Greek aorist is frequently used of a past event that precedes another past event in the narrative, where the special nuance of the pluperfect is not required. Consequently, an aorist will sometimes be translated by an English pluperfect.

(54) καὶ ἐπελάθοντο λαβεῖν ἄρτους　　　　　　　　　Mk 8:14
　　　And they had forgotten to bring food

The Future

801.　*The future tense*, in contrast to the other tenses, expresses only *time* (not aspect, cf. §312.2–3). Kind of action may be implied, of course, by a specific context, but the tense stem itself was developed, probably in conjunction with the subjunctive (Bl-D §318), to express future time.

801.1　The future indicative is employed to make assertions about the future:

(55) ἕξει τὸ φῶς τῆς ζωῆς　　　　　　　　　　　　Jn 8:12
　　　He shall have the light of life
(56) ζητήσετέ με　　　　　　　　　　　　　　　Jn 8:21
　　　You will seek me

801.2　The future is occasionally used in injunctions and prohibitions, in the style of the Old Testament.

(57) οὐ φονεύσεις　　　　　　　　　　　　　　　Mt 5:21
　　　You shall not kill
(58) ἀγαπήσεις τὸν πλησίον σου　　　　　　　　　　Mt 5:43
　　　You shall love your neighbor

Bl-D §362. Cf. the imperative, §§808f.

801.3　The future is occasionally formed periphrastically (§568). For μέλλω with an infinitive to express the future, s. §569. On the rare gnomic future, s. Bl-D §349.

The Verb: Mood

Subjunctive/Imperative/Optative

805. *Introduction.* The predicate of a Greek sentence will most often be headed by a verb in the indicative mood (§0780). The verb heading the predicate may also be in the imperative mood, as in English, but it is in the common use of the subjunctive that Greek differs most markedly from English. The imperative and subjunctive are closely related in both English (Roberts, 1954: §156) and Greek, as we shall observe. The imperative and subjunctive are used both in independent sentences (and main clauses of complex sentences), and in included sentences. The use of the subjunctive in included sentences introduced by ἵνα was examined in §§654–662. In this section attention will be devoted primarily to the subjunctive and imperative as employed in independent sentences (and main clauses).

The optative may be given brief consideration subsequently.

806. *The imperative* is the mood in which *commands* and *requests* are normally expressed (§§307.4, 0455ff.):

(i)   Come *here*
(ii)   Keep off *the grass*

The form of the imperative may be compound:

(iii) Be ready
(iv)   Be advised *that the shipment will arrive on Tuesday*
(v)   Keep working *on it*

Commands and requests may, of course, be expressed in other ways (i.e. without a verb in the imperative mood):

(vi)   *You must learn Greek*
(vii) *You will report immediately for induction*
(viii) *Quiet!*
(ix)   *No smoking*

The verb *let*, used as an auxiliary, may express a command or request:

(x) Let's go *home*
(xi) Let *us* concentrate *on the text*

The imperative also functions as the mood of petitions and entreaties:

(xii) Help *me*
(xiii) Forgive *us our sins*

And the imperative may be used to indicate a concession or an hypothesis:

(xiv) Give *him an inch, and he'll take a mile*

Give him an inch might be said to be the equivalent of *If you give him an inch.*

    In sum, the imperative is the normal mood of commands, requests, and petitions, but it is not the only way of expressing these 'moods,' nor is it limited to them (cf. xiv). The imperative in Greek corresponds in most important respects to the imperative in English.

807.1 *The subjunctive* is very nearly obsolete in English. It is distinguished formally from the indicative by the deletion of -s in the 3. sing.:

(xv) *He* plays *the guitar* (indicative)
(xvi) *I asked that he* play *the guitar* (subjunctive)

(xvi) will probably not be heard often in spoken English. An alternative construction with the infinitive is more colloquial:

(xvii) *I asked him to play the guitar*

For comparable alternative constructions in Greek, see §659.

    The only other verb in which the subjunctive is formally distinguished from the indicative, except in the present 3. sg. , is the verb *be*. *Be* is the present subjunctive and *were* is the past subjunctive:

(xviii) *My teacher requests that I* be *prompt.*
(xix)   *His parents insist that he* be *home by midnight*
(xx)   *If it* were *to rain, we would not be able to go*

These forms are also sometimes avoided in colloquial speech by using alternative constructions, e.g. for (xviii) a construction with the infinitive:

(xxi)   *My teacher requests me to be prompt*

Or, e.g. for (xix) a construction with *should*:

(xxii) *His parents insist that he should be home by midnight*

The subjunctive is better preserved in certain set phrases and expressions:

(xxiii) *If I were you*, . . .
(xxiv) *Be it ever so humble, there's no place like home*
(xxv) *Heaven help us*

In extemporaneous formulations, however, there is a tendency to substitute the indicative forms of be for the subjunctive in constructions comparable to (xxiii):

(xxvi) *If she was my daughter*, . . .

807.2   In contrast to present day spoken English, the subjunctive is very much in evidence even in colloquial hellenistic Greek. It is used in a great variety of ways, some of which are quite comparable to those illustrated above for English, others of which are alien to English. One may generalize with respect to the development in Greek: (1) the subjunctive is intermingling with the future indicative (Bl-D §363; cf. §318), and eventually drives the latter out (in modern Greek); (2) the optative, which has affinities with the subjunctive (the two are not distinguished in English), is being replaced by the imperative, subjunctive, and in certain instances by the indicative (Bl-D §§384–386). These generalizations, however, have little bearing on the common uses of the imperative and subjunctive in hellenistic Greek.

The Imperative & Subjunctive: Commands & Petitions

808.   *Tense-aspect.* Theoretically, the present and aorist imperatives differ in the same way as the imperfect and aorist indicatives (§786): the present imperative is durative or linear, the aorist imperative is punctiliar. The same principle applies to the subjunctive of prohibition (which replaces the aorist in negative injunctions, 2. person) and to the hortatory subjunctive (1. sing. and plur.) (cf. Bl-D §335). What this means specifically can best be set out, and exceptions noted, in relation to particular types of expression.

809.   In general, the present imperative is preferred for general injunctions (precepts, attitudes, conduct), the aorist for conduct in specific cases, e.g.

(1) Διὸ προσλαμβάνεσθε ἀλλήλους   Rom 15:7
Therefore welcome one another

(2) ἐξάρατε τὸν πονηρὸν ἐξ ὑμῶν αὐτῶν   1 Cor 5:12
Drive out the wicked person from among you

In considering the force of tense as aspect in the imperative (and subjunctive), this is a good first question to put to the text. Nevertheless, there are notable exceptions to this generalization, e.g. categorical injunctions and prohibitions, and categorical petitions (in prayers) take the aorist (complexive or constative, §788.1; see §813 below). It is difficult, as a consequence, to make any real distinction between a general injunction (present = durative) and a categorical injunction (aorist = summary), although nuances may be detected in particular instances.

8090. Precision regarding tense-aspect in the imperative/subjunctive, as well as in the indicative, is impossible apart from the study of individual verbs. For example, in the sequence of injunctions in Mt. 5:39ff., all injunctive verbs are aorist (five examples), except for ὕπαγε (5:41), which is present imperative. This verb is often used in the imperative in the New Testament and always in the present tense (Bl-D §101, s.v. ἄγειν). In fact, it occurs only in the present (and imperfect) in any mood. It would therefore be a serious error to attach special significance to this present imperative occurring among a series of aorists in Mt 5:39ff.

The data for a study of individual verbs have not yet been collected from a significant body of texts (the use of concordances is a cumbersome and time consuming method). For that matter, the data for an analysis of tense-aspect in general are not yet readily available. Traditional Greek grammar has operated largely on intuitions based on theory and a few random examples.

810. *Prohibitions* are expressed by the present imperative or the aorist subjunctive (2. person sing. and plur.). It is the general pattern in Indo-European languages that negative commands are expressed by the present imperative (not subjunctive) and the aorist subjunctive (not imperative). The negative is μή. There are a few examples of the 3. person aorist subjunctive with μή, and rare occurrences of the aorist imperative with μή.

810.1 Categorical prohibitions take the aorist (complexive) subjunctive (Bl-D §337(3)):

(3) μὴ δῶτε τὸ ἅγιον τοῖς κυσίν   Mt 7:6
Do not give what is holy to the dogs

(4) μὴ φονεύσῃς   Mk 10:19
Do not kill

810.2   The present imperative is employed in negative injunctions to stop doing something (Bl-D §336(3)), e.g.

(5) μὴ οὖν βασιλευέτω ἡ ἁμαρτία ἐν τῷ θνητῷ ὑμῶν σώματι   Rom 6:12
Therefore let sin no longer reign in your mortal bodies

(6) μὴ γογγύζετε μετ' ἀλλήλων   Jn 6:43
Stop murmuring among yourselves

811.   *The present imperative*, in accordance with the principle laid down in §810.2, is employed in positive injunctions to continue doing something (Bl-D §336(3)):

(7) φεύγετε τὴν πορνείαν   1 Cor 6:18
Shun immorality (i.e. Keep on shunning immorality)

(8) ἀδιαλείπτως προσεύχεσθε   1 Thess 5:17
Pray constantly

812.   It is difficult in practice to distinguish between a general injunction (§809, (1)) and an injunction in which the present imperative is specifically durative (= continue to do something: §811, (7)). Compare, for example, the parallel sentences in Mt. 6:19f.:

(9) μὴ θησαυρίζετε ὑμῖν θησαυροὺς ἐπὶ τῆς γῆς   Mt 6:19
Do not lay up for yourselves treasures upon earth

(10) θησαυρίζετε δὲ ὑμῖν θησαυροὺς ἐν οὐρανῷ   Mt 6:20
But lay up for yourselves treasures in heaven

In accordance with §810.2, (9) means *stop laying up*. However, (10) cannot then mean *continue laying up*, but must be read as a general injunction, in which case it is indistinguishable from the categorical aorist command (cf. §§809 and 813.1).

A similar pair is found in Mk 10:14:

(11) ἄφετε τὰ παιδία ἔρχεσθαι πρός με,
μὴ κωλύετε αὐτά   Mk 10:14
Permit the children to come to me,
do not hinder them

in which both positive and negative are again present imperatives. Since the disciples had frowned on the presence of children, the negative is to be taken as *stop hindering*; the positive present preceding must then be understood as a general injunction (§809), rather than in accordance with §811.

When positive and negative injunctions are not paired, the decision is more difficult: in the long list of injunctions in 1 Thess 5:16ff., all of which are present imperative, is Paul enjoining the congregation to continue good practices, or is he admonishing them generally (and thus without particular reference to what they have been doing)?

813.   *The aorist imperative* is characteristically used in other contexts, or may carry other nuances.

813.1   The (complexive) aorist is used in greetings, e.g.

(12) ἀσπάσασθε τοὺς ἀδελφοὺς πάντας   1 Thess 5:26
Greet all the brethren

And in prayers, viz. in requests addressed to the deity:

(13) ἐλθέτω ἡ βασιλεία σου
γενηθήτω τὸ θέλημά σου   Mt 6:10
Let your kingdom come
Let your will be done

Cf. the subjunctive of prohibition (negative request) in the same prayer:

(14) μὴ εἰσενέγκῃς ἡμᾶς εἰς πειρασμόν   Mt 6:13
Do not lead us into temptation

Cf. Bl-D §337(4) and below on the iterative present in prayers.

813.2   The aorist imperative may be *ingressive* or *inceptive* (§788.2: the enjoining of new conduct in contrast to old), e.g.

(15) εἴ τις δοκεῖ σοφὸς εἶναι ἐν ὑμῖν ἐν τῷ αἰῶνι
τούτῳ, μωρὸς γενέσθω   1 Cor 3:18
If anyone among you thinks he is wise in this age, let him
become a fool
(16) δοξάσατε δὴ τὸν θεὸν ἐν τῷ σώματι ὑμῶν   1 Cor 6:20
So glorify God with your body

In the context, the imperative is probably ingressive. Bl-D §337(1).

814. *The present imperative* is used in a specifically *iterative* (or *durative*) sense, sometimes without reference to past conduct. Contrast the Lukan form of the petition,

> (17) τὸν ἄρτον ἡμῶν τὸν ἐπιούσιον δίδου ἡμῖν τὸ καθ᾽ ἡμέραν   Lk 11:3
> *Give us each day our daily bread*

with the form found in Matthew:

> (18) τὸν ἄρτον ἡμῶν τὸν ἐπιούσιον δὸς ἡμῖν σήμερον   Mt 6:11
> *Give us this day our daily bread*

In Luke the imperative (present) is iterative: (continue to give us each day); in Matthew the imperative (aorist) is categorical (§813.1).

There is an interesting contrast in the two forms of another saying:

> (19) τῷ αἰτοῦντί σε δός,
> καὶ τὸν θέλοντα ἀπό σου δανίσασθαι μὴ ἀποστροφῇς   Mt 5:42
> *Give to him who begs you*
> *And do not refuse him who wants to borrow from you*
> (20) παντὶ αἰτοῦντί σε δίδου,
> καὶ ἀπὸ τοῦ αἴροντας τὰ σὰ μὴ ἀπαίτει   Lk 6:30
> *Give to everyone who begs you,*
> *And of him who takes away your things do not ask them back*

The aorist forms in (19) are categorical. In (20), the present imperative δίδου is iterative: give each time someone begs you. This presumably carries no reference to prior conduct (§811), though it might be interpreted as a general (iterative) injunction. The negative present imperative which follows (μὴ ἀπαίτει) might be interpreted in accordance with §810.2 (stop asking), but it could also mean: do not ask them back on any occasion (iterative; no reference to prior conduct).

In line with the last suggestion,

> (21) μὴ πρὸ καιροῦ τι κρίνετε, ἕως ἂν ἔλθη ὁ κύριος   1 Cor 4:5
> *Do not pronounce judgment on anything before the*
> *time, before the Lord comes*

could be taken to mean: do not, in the future, pronounce judgment on any occasion (iterative; no reference to past conduct).

In any case, the present imperatives in (18), (20), and (21) are clearly iterative.

815. *Other ways of expressing commands.* In Greek, as in English, commands, petitions, and the like may be expressed in a variety of ways. The imperative is the predominant commanding and petitioning mood in the 2. and 3. persons sing. and plur. (§§808–814). The prohibitive subjunctive is commonly used for negative commands in the 2. person (rarely the 3.) (§810). And there are still other ways of expressing the injunctive mood:

815.1 *The future indicative* is used in injunctions and prohibitions in the style of the Old Testament (§801.2).

815.2 ἵνα *with the subjunctive* is occasionally used, quite idiomatically, for the imperative:

> (22) ἵνα καὶ ἐν ταύτῃ τῇ χάριτι περισσεύητε 2 Cor 8:7
> *Excel in this gracious work also*

See Turner: 94f. for a list of New Testament exx. and discussion. Cf. Bl-D §387(3).

815.3 *The infinitive* is occasionally employed for the imperative:

> (23) χαίρειν μετὰ χαιρόντων,
> κλαίειν μετὰ κλαιόντων Rom 12:15
> *Rejoice with the ones rejoicing,*
> *Weep with the ones weeping*

The question in examples of this type is whether a verb of saying or bidding is to be understood, viz. *I tell you to rejoice.* Bl-D §389.

815.4 *The participle* is also used with imperatival force if a finite verb with which it is associated is imperative:

> (24) μηδενὶ κακὸν ἀντὶ κακοῦ ἀποδιδόντες Rom 12:17
> *Repay no one evil for evil*

i.e. the participle derives its mood from an associated finite form.

815.5 *The hortatory subjunctive* (§819) is a means of expressing the imperative mood in the 1. person.

816. *Person.* In English the imperative form of the verb is limited to the 2. person (*You,* sg. and pl.). In Greek, by contrast, the imperative has 3. sg. and pl. forms, as well as 2. sg. and pl. forms. These have to be translated by some device, such as *let him . . .* , in English (cf. §0455, and examples (5), (13), (15) above). The hor-

tatory subjunctive (§819) is employed in Greek for what might be called the imperative of the 1. person (= *let me, let us*).

The Subjunctive: Futuristic Uses

817. *Introduction.* In addition to its kinship with the imperative (§§808–816), the subjunctive is also related to the future. The future tense does not have a subjunctive (§3100.2) but aorist subjunctive and future indicative forms were often confused (§807.2). The confusion owes not only to formal similarities but also to similarities of function. The subjunctive is the mood of dubious assertion, expressing probability (§307.2), and therefore refers, commonly, to the future, i.e. to what may be or what may have been (the future from the standpoint of the past).

The uses of the subjunctive to head predicates in independent sentences (or main clauses) are usually divided into three categories: futuristic, volitive (hortatory), and deliberative.

818. *The futuristic subjunctive* is used in more or less emphatic negative assertions with the double negative οὐ μή.

(25) ὁ ἀκολουθῶν ἐμοὶ οὐ μὴ περιπατήσῃ ἐν τῇ σκοτίᾳ   Jn 8:12
The one following me shall certainly not walk in darkness

(26) οὐ μὴ εἰσέλθητε εἰς τὴν βασιλείαν τῶν οὐρανῶν   Mt 5:20
You will never enter the kingdom of heaven
(unless you meet certain conditions)

Such negative assertions with double negative tend to be less emphatic in the hellenistic period than earlier (overuse, weakening of the language).

818.1 The same construction may express a strong negative injunction (cf. the prohibitive subjunctive, §810.1):

(27) ἐπιθυμίαν σαρκὸς οὐ μὴ τελέσητε   Gal 5:16
Do not gratify the desires of the flesh

818.2 *The future indicative* may also be used in strong negative assertions:

(28) οὐ μὴ ἔσται σοι τοῦτο   Mt 16:22
This shall never happen to you

Either the future indicative or the aorist subjunctive were used in classical Greek. (28) is the only certain example with the future indicative in the New

Testament; in other instances the manuscript tradition vacillates between future indicative and aorist subjunctive (Bl-D §365).

819. *The hortatory (volitive) subjunctive* is the use of the subjunctive in the 1. person (plural, rarely singular) to express an admonition: in the 1. plur. the speaker exhorts others to join him in doing something; in the 1. sing. the speaker requests others to *permit* him to do something.

819.1 1. Plural:

(29) ἀγαπητοί, ἀγαπῶμεν ἀλλήλους   1 Jn 4:7
Beloved, let us love one another

(30) μηκέτι οὖν ἀλλήλους κρίνωμεν   Rom 14:13
Then let us no longer pass judgment on one another

819.2 1. Singular:

(31) ἄφες ἐκβάλω τὸ κάρφος ἐκ τοῦ ὀφθαλμοῦ σου   Mt 7:4
Let me cast the mote out of your eye

Cf. §816. Bl-D §364.

820. *The deliberative subjunctive* is employed in deliberative questions, real or rhetorical, regarding the future (Bl-D §366). In deliberative questions the possibilities are being weighed:

(32) δῶμεν ἢ μὴ δῶμεν;   Mk 12:14
Are we to give (tribute) or not?

In questions of fact, the speaker asks for information:

(33) ποῦ ἐστιν ἐκεῖνος;   Jn 9:12
Where is he?

The yes and no possibilities of a deliberative question may be only implicit (rather than explicit, as in (32)):

(34) ἐν ῥάβδῳ ἔλθω πρὸς ὑμᾶς;   1 Cor 4:21
Shall I come to you with a rod (or not)?

Or, the possibilities may be entirely open:

(35) τί φάγωμεν; ἤ, τί πίωμεν;   Mt 6:31
What shall we eat? or What shall we drink?

820.1 *The future indicative* may also be used in deliberative questions:

    (36) πρὸς τίνα ἀπελευσόμεθα;   Jn 6:68
       To whom shall we go?

820.2 *The present indicative* rarely appears in such questions:

    (37) τί ποιοῦμεν;   Jn 11:47
       What are we to do?

820.3 *Certain analytical constructions* also have the force of deliberative questions (with δεῖ, δύναμαι, etc.; Bl-D §366(4)), e.g.

    (38) πῶς δύναται ταῦτα γενέσθαι;   Jn 3:9
       How can these things be?

821. *Introductory words* with volitive and deliberative subjunctives add a note of politeness or function as attention getters.

821.1 ὅρα, ὅρατε, βλέπετε (*look! take care! watch out!*) sometimes introduce the prohibitive subjunctive (§810.1):

    (39) ὅρα μηδενὶ εἴπης   Mt 8:4
       See that you tell no one
    (40) βλέπετε μὴ πλανηθῆτε   Lk 21:8
       Take heed! Do not be led astray

821.2 ἄφες, ἄφετε; δεῦρο, δεῦτε sometimes introduce the hortatory subjunctive.

    (41) ἄφετε ἴδωμεν εἰ ἔρχεται Ἡλίας καθελεῖν αὐτόν   Mk 15:36
       Let's see if Elijah will come to take him down
    (42) δεῦτε ἀποκτείνωμεν αὐτόν   Mt 21:38
       Come, let's kill him!

ἄφες means *let, permit*; δεῦρο *come*, but translation should suit the context and English idiom.

821.3 θέλεις, θέλετε, βούλεσθε (*do you wish*) may introduce a deliberative question:

    (43) βούλεσθε οὖν ἀπολύσω ὑμῖν τὸν βασιλέα τῶν Ἰουδαίων;   Jn 18:39
       Do you want me to release the king of the Jews to you?

821.4 These introductory expressions are grammatically independent of the sentence, i.e. they do not affect the following construction.

The Optative

822.   *Introduction.* The optative is the mood of wish (from Latin *opto, wish*). The optative is used to express what could or might happen, under certain hypothetical conditions. It is therefore sometimes called the *may* or *might* mood. Cf. §307.3. In classical idiom, the optative was also employed in certain types of conditional sentences (§859), and in indirect discourse after secondary tenses (Smyth §2599).

The use of the optative has greatly diminished in hellenistic Greek, by comparison with classical usage (cf. §0445). Its two principal uses in main clauses need only be briefly illustrated; its use in conditional sentences and indirect speech may be noted.

See §§445–449 for the conjugation of the optative.

822.1   The optative is used to express a *wish* or a *prayer*:

> (44) μὴ γένοιτο   Rom 3:4
> *May it not be! (God forbid)*

Fifteen of the 38 exx. of the optative in wishes in the New Testament are the strong deprecatory formula represented by (44).

This same optative may appear in a prayer:

> (45) χάρις ὑμῖν καὶ εἰρήνη πληθυνθείη   1 Pet 1:2
> *May grace and peace be multiplied to you*

And in an imprecation:

> (46) τὸ ἀργύριόν σου σὺν σοὶ εἴη εἰς ἀπώλειαν Acts 8:20
> *May your silver perish with you!*

Bl-D §384.

822.2   *The potential optative* is used with and without ἄν to express what could or might happen under some hypothetical condition. This optative is therefore the apodosis of a truncated conditional sentence: The if-clause or protasis is suppressed. Cf. the English sentence:

(i)   *I could eat a horse (if one were available)*

The Greek counterpart is:

> (47) τί ἂν θέλοι ὁ σπερμολόγος οὗτος λέγειν;   Acts 17:18
> *What would this babbler wish to say?*

In (48) the condition is actually expressed:

> (48) πῶς γὰρ ἂν δυναίμην
> ἐὰν μή τις ὁδηγήσει με;   Acts 8:31
> *How could I,*
> *unless someone guides me?*

For the potential optative of something only thought, see Acts 26:29 and Bl-D §385.

822.3   For the optative in conditional sentences, see §859. Example (48) above exhibits the apodosis of a fourth class condition, but the protasis is from another type of condition.

822.4   The optative appears rarely in indirect discourse in the New Testament, if only for the reason that direct discourse is much preferred (cf. Bl-D §386; see §585 for other forms of indirect discourse). Yet there are a few examples in Luke, e.g.

> (49) καὶ διελάλουν πρὸς ἀλλήλους
> τί ἂν ποιήσαιεν τῷ Ἰησοῦ   Lk 6:11
> *And they discussed with one another*
> *what they might do to Jesus*

Lesson 57

The Verb: Mood
The Infinitive

0830. The simple infinitive as subject and a word cluster headed by an infinitive as subject were previously noted (§§543.6, 545.6). The function of the infinitive in forming verb chains was sketched in §§565–576, 580–585. It is now appropriate to outline the full range of functions of the infinitive and to specify some functions in greater detail.

830. The infinitive is a verbal noun. As a substantive it is an indeclinable neuter, although it may be used with the article to show case. As a verbal *noun*, it may appear in structures in which nouns appear: as subject, object, modifier, object of preposition, with the article, and at one place in the New Testament an infinitive is modified by an adjective (διὰ παντὸς τοῦ ζῆν, *through their entire life*, Heb 2:15). As a *verbal* noun, it has tense (present, aorist, perfect, and occasionally future), i.e. aspect (§0309), but not time (except in indirect discourse where it represents a finite verb); voice (active, middle, passive); and may "govern" a case (gen., dat., acc.). It is not strictly speaking a mood, although it may represent a finite verb in some constructions.

8300. All classical usages of the infinitive appear in hellenistic Greek in spite of the fact that constructions with ἵνα and ὅτι have become rivals of the infinitive (Bl-D §388). Only in the case of τοῦ with the infinitive has its use been enlarged. The infinitive is used about half as frequently, relatively speaking, in the Septuagint as it is in the New Testament. The infinitive appears approximately 2,276 times in the New Testament, of which 1,957 are anarthrous (unaccompanied by article), 319 articular (accompanied by article). Of the New Testament authors, Luke has the most varied use; it is used least in the Gospel of John. The articular infinitive is confined chiefly to Luke and Paul.

Except for its use with auxiliary verbs, the infinitive is dying out in late hellenistic Greek (it is being replaced by the finite verb), a trend consummated in modern Greek where the infinitive has virtually disappeared.

831. *Range of functions.* In the following presentation, this outline of the functions of the infinitive will be followed:

831.1 The simple infinitive or word cluster headed by an infinitive as subject (or object). Cf. Nominal Word Clusters, §§680–779.

831.2 The infinitive in verb chains, including the infinitive in p-clusters to express purpose, etc.; the infinitive with nouns and adjectives, where the verb and noun (or adjective) function as a complex verb. Cf. Verb Chains, §§565–585.

831.3 The infinitive (articular, in p-clusters; with πρίν) with complements as adverbial clause. Cf. §§643.3, 674 and the treatment of temporal clauses, §873, and the circumstantial participle, §846.1.

831.4 The infinitive in explanatory (appositional, epexegetical) word clusters.

831.5 The absolute infinitive (no grammatical connection to rest of sentence).

8310. There is no clear line of demarcation between the functions of the anarthrous infinitive and those of the articular infinitive, except that the anarthrous infinitive never occurs in p-clusters as the object of a preposition, and the articular infinitive does not occur in verb chains of Group I (§§567–573).

The Infinitive in Nominal Word Clusters

832. The simple infinitive or a word cluster headed by an infinitive may appear in the structure of subject (cf. §§543.6, 545.6). The infinitive appears most often as subject with impersonal verbs, e.g. δεῖ *it is necessary*, ἔξεστιν *it is lawful*, πρέπει *it is fitting.* Examples may conveniently be divided into groups depending on the complements that appear with the infinitive.

832.1 The simple infinitive as subject:

(1) δεῖ γενέσθαι   Mk 13:7
It is necessary [for these things] to take place
(literally, *to take place is necessary [for these things* is understood])

This usage is rare; normally the infinitive has some complements.

832.2 The infinitive with its own subject accusative as subject:

(2) δεῖ ὑμᾶς γεννηθῆναι ἄνωθεν   Jn 3:7
It is necessary for you to be born from above (or: *again*)

832.3 The infinitive with its own subject in the dative case as subject:

(3) ἐπετράπη τῷ Παύλῳ μένειν καθ’ ἑαυτὸν   Acts 28:16
Paul was permitted to stay by himself

832.4　The infinitive may, of course, take any of the complements in its own predicate that the corresponding finite verb may take. The following are random examples.

(4)　ἔξεστιν δοῦναι κῆνσον Καίσαρι ἢ οὔ;　　　　　Mk 12:14
　　　Is it lawful to give tribute to Caesar or not?

(4) is S-IV with direct and indirect object.

(5)　τὸ δὲ ἀνίπτοις χερσὶν φαγεῖν οὐ κοινοῖ τὸν ἄνθρωπον　　Mt 15:20
　　　But to eat with unwashed hands does not defile a man

(6)　ἀνένδεκτόν ἐστιν τοῦ τὰ σκάνδαλα μὴ ἐλθεῖν　　　Lk 17:1
　　　It is impossible that temptations to sin not come

τοῦ with the infinitive (the function of the case has entirely faded); literally, *the not to come with respect to temptations to sin is impossible.*

(7)　μηδενὶ μηδὲν ὀφείλετε, εἰ μὴ τὸ ἀλλήλους ἀγαπᾶν　　Rom 13:8
　　　Owe nothing to no one, except to love one another

The infinitive with its complements is object of the verb.

The Infinitive in Verb Chains

0833.　The infinitive appears in verb chains as the second (or third) term (§566) in a variety of constructions. The use of the infinitive with catenative verbs of Groups I-IV and VI has already been sketched (§§567–583, 585) and need not be treated here. It remains to note variations on these constructions.

833.　The simple infinitive may be employed in verb chains to express purpose (Group II, §§574–576; Group III, §580). The infinitive may be used to express purpose in correlative constructions in which the infinitive is not simple.

833.1　*The genitive of the articular infinitive* may also be used to express purpose:

(8)　ἰδοὺ ἐξῆλθεν ὁ σπείρων τοῦ σπείρειν　　　　Mt 13:3
　　　Look, a sower went out to sow

(9)　τότε παραγίνεται ὁ Ἰησοῦς ἀπὸ τῆς Γαλιλαίας ἐπὶ τὸν
　　　Ἰορδάνην πρὸς τὸν Ἰωάννην τοῦ βαπτισθῆναι ὑπ' αὐτοῦ　Mt 3:13
　　　Then Jesus came from Galilee to the Jordan, to John, to be baptized by him

There is no distinction in meaning between (8) and (9) above and the examples of the simple infinitive of purpose given in §575.

833.2 *The accusative of the articular infinitive following εἰς or πρός is also a means of expressing purpose.*

> (10) ἔπεμψα εἰς τὸ γνῶναι τὴν πίστιν ὑμῶν   1 Thess 3:5
>   *I sent that I might know your faith*
> (11) πάντα δὲ τὰ ἔργα αὐτῶν ποιοῦσιν πρὸς τὸ θεαθῆναι τοῖς
>   ἀνθρώποις   Mt 23:5
>   *They do all their deeds in order to be seen of men*

These constructions are grammatically synonymous with τοῦ and the infinitive (§833.1) and the simple infinitive of purpose (§575).

833.3 The infinitive is occasionally used with ὥστε or ὡς to express purpose. Examples may be found in Mt 10:1 and Lk 9:52, Cf. §834.1 and Bl-D §391(1).

833.4 All these constructions with the infinitive to express purpose are of course agnate to final clauses with ἵνα (§656).

834. *The infinitive of result* has not been previously noted. In classical idiom ὥστε and the infinitive indicated probable result, ὥστε and the indicative actual result. In the New Testament the infinitive is employed for both; there are only two examples of ὥστε and the indicative (Jn 3:16, Gal 2:13). The line between intended or probable result and purpose is often fine. There is thus some overlapping between consecutive (result) clauses with the infinitive and final (purpose) clauses with the infinitive. Bl-D §391.

834.1 The infinitive of result introduced by ὥστε:

> (12) καὶ ἐθεράπευσεν αὐτοὺς
>   ὥστε τὸν ὄχλον θαυμάσαι.   Mt 15:31
>   *And he healed them,*
>   *so that the crowd marveled*

834.2 Less commonly, τοῦ and the infinitive may express result:

> (13) ὑμεῖς δὲ ἰδόντες οὐδὲ μετεμελήθητε ὕστερον τοῦ πιστεῦσαι
>   αὐτῷ   Mt 21:32
>   *But even when you saw it, you did not subsequently repent and*
>   *believe him (= so that you believed)*

834.3 The simple infinitive is occasionally used to express result:

> (14) διὰ τί ἐπλήρωσεν ὁ Σατανᾶς τὴν καρδίαν σου ψεύσασθαί σε; Acts 5:3
> *Why has Satan filled your heart so that you lie?*

Only in context is it possible to distinguish the simple infinitive of result from the simple infinitive of purpose.

835. *The infinitive with certain nouns and adjectives* meaning ability, fitness, need, etc. is also related to the infinitive in verb chains. Combinations of εἶναι with adjectives like δυνατός (*able*), ἄξιος (*worthy*), ἱκανός (*fit*), ἕτοιμος (*ready*) are actually complex verbs. The same thing can be said of the combinations of verbs and certain nouns, e.g. ἐξουσίαν ἔχειν (*to have authority*), χρείαν ἔχειν (*to have need*).

Both anarthrous and articular infinitives occur in these constructions, without difference in meaning.

835.1 The infinitive with adjectives:

> (15) οὐκέτι εἰμὶ ἄξιος κληθῆναι υἱός σου   Lk 15:19
> *I am no longer worthy to be called your son*
>
> (16) ἕτοιμοί ἐσμεν τοῦ ἀνελεῖν αὐτόν   Acts 23:15
> *We are ready to kill him*
>
> (17) οὐκ εἰμὶ ἱκανὸς καλεῖσθαι ἀπόστολος   1 Cor 15:9
> *I am not fit to be called an apostle*
>
> (18) καὶ ἐκ νεκρῶν ἐγείρειν δυνατὸς ὁ θεός   Heb 11:19
> *God is able to raise even from the dead*

835.2 The infinitive with nouns:

> (19) πάλιν χρείαν ἔχετε τοῦ διδάσκειν ὑμᾶς τινὰ   Heb 5:12
> *You need someone to teach you again*
>
> (20) ἔδωκεν αὐτοῖς ἐξουσίαν τέκνα θεοῦ γενέσθαι   Jn 1:12
> *He gave them the right to become children of God*
>
> (21) ὀφειλέτης ἐστίν ὅλον τὸν νόμον ποιῆσαι   Gal 5:3
> *He is obligated to keep the whole law*

835.3 In most of these cases, an agnate construction with ἵνα and the subjunctive may substitute. The following examples are illustrative:

> (22) οὐκ εἰμὶ ἱκανὸς ἵνα μου ὑπὸ τὴν στέγην εἰσέλθῃς   Mt 8:8
> *I am not worthy for you to come under my roof*

(23) καὶ χρείαν ἔχετε ἵνα τις διδάσκῃ ὑμᾶς   1 Jn 2:27

And you need no one to teach you

The Infinitive in Adverbial Clauses

836.   *The infinitive and its complements may function as an adverbial clause* (temporal, causal) when introduced by a preposition or πρίν (πρὶν ἤ).

836.1   The articular infinitive appears with prepositions in temporal clauses as follows: ἐν τῷ and the infinitive are used of contemporaneous time, μετὰ τό for subsequent time, πρὸ τοῦ for previous time, ἕως τοῦ of future time, all in relation to the time of the main verb. Bl-D §§402–404.

(24) μετὰ δὲ τὸ παραδοθῆναι τὸν Ἰωάννην . . .   Mk 1:14

Now after John was arrested . . .

(25) ἐν τῷ ἐλθεῖν αὐτὸν εἰς οἶκον τινος τῶν
ἀρχόντων . . .   Lk 14:1

When he went into the house of one of the rulers . . .

(26) πρὸ τοῦ ἐγγίσαι αὐτὸν . . .   Acts 23:15

Before he draws near . . .

(27) ἕως τοῦ ἐλθεῖν αὐτὸν εἰς Καισάρειαν . . .   Acts 8:40

Until he came to Caesarea . . .

836.2   The infinitive with διὰ τό may be used in an adverbial clause of cause. Bl-D §402(1).

(28) καὶ διὰ τὸ μὴ ἔχειν ῥίζαν ἐξηράνθη   Mk 4:6

And because it lacked root it withered away

836.3   The articular infinitive in the dative case *without preposition* appears once. It denotes cause. Bl-D §401.

(29) οὐκ ἔσχηκα ἄνεσιν τῷ πνεύματί μου, τῷ μὴ εὑρεῖν με Τίτον   2 Cor 2:13

My spirit had no rest because I did not find Titus

836.4   πρίν (πρὶν ἤ) is used with the infinitive in a temporal clause meaning *before*. Bl-D §395.

(30) κατάβηθι πρὶν ἀποθανεῖν τὸ παιδίον μου   Jn 4:49

Come down before my child dies

(31) πρὶν ἢ συνελθεῖν αὐτούς   Mt 1:18
   Before they came together

The Infinitive in Explanatory Word Clusters

837.   *The explanatory (epexegetical) infinitive* may be appended to a demonstrative pro-
       noun, a noun, a verb, or more loosely to other elements in the sentence. It is
       difficult to draw sharp lines between and among various constructions. Both
       articular and anarthrous infinitives appear. Some of these infinitives are re-
       lated to infinitives in verb chains, infinitives with nouns, etc. For some an ag-
       nate construction with ἵνα and the subjunctive is possible. Cf. Bl-D §394.

       The following examples illustrate the range of the explanatory or epexegeti-
       cal infinitive.

837.1 The simple infinitive appended to a demonstrative pronoun:

       (32) θρησκεία καθαρὰ καὶ ἀμίαντος . . . αὕτη ἐστίν,
            ἐπισκέπτεσθαι ὀρφανοὺς καὶ χήρας
            ἐν τῇ θλίψει αὐτῶν   Ja 1:27
            Pure and undefiled religion is this,
            to visit the orphans and widows
            in their affliction

837.10 A ἵνα-clause may be substituted for this infinitive:

       (33) αὕτη γάρ ἐστιν ἡ ἀγάπη τοῦ θεοῦ,
            ἵνα τὰς ἐντολὰς αὐτοῦ τηρῶμεν   1 Jn 5:3
            For this is the love of God,
            that we keep his commandments

837.2 An articular infinitive appended to a demonstrative pronoun:

       (34) ἔκρινα γὰρ ἐμαυτῷ τοῦτο,
            τὸ μὴ πάλιν ἐν λύπῃ πρὸς ὑμᾶς ἐλθεῖν   2 Cor 2:1
            For I made up my mind to this,
            not to pay you another painful visit

837.3 An infinitive (anarthrous or articular) appended to a noun:

       (35) ἐξῆλθεν δόγμα παρὰ Καίσαρος Αὐγούστου ἀπογράφεσθαι
            πᾶσαν τὴν οἰκουμένην   Lk 2:1

A decree went out from Augustus Caesar to enroll the whole world

(36) ἐπλήσθη ὁ χρόνος τοῦ τεκεῖν αὐτήν   Lk 1:57

The time for her to give birth came

837.4 An infinitive (anarthrous or articular) appended to a verb:

(37) παρέδωκεν αὐτοὺς ὁ θεὸς εἰς ἀδόκιμον νοῦν,
ποιεῖν τὰ μὴ καθήκοντα   Rom 1:28

God gave them up to a base mind,
to do what was not proper

(38) ἐπικατάρατος πᾶς ὃς οὐκ ἐμμένει πᾶσιν τοῖς γεγραμμένοις
ἐν τῷ βιβλίῳ τοῦ νόμου τοῦ ποιῆσαι αὐτά   Gal 3:10

Cursed be everyone who does not abide by all things written in
 the book of law, to do them

The Infinitive Absolute

838. *The infinitive absolute* (so called because it sustains no grammatical connection to the sentence in which it appears) occurs once in the New Testament, in a classical idiom with ὡς:

(39) ὡς ἔπος εἰπεῖν   Heb 7:9

so to speak

The Circumstantial Participle

Functions of Circumstantial Participles

0845. The range of participial function is sketched in §770. Of the three principal functions of the participle, the *attributive* use was considered in §§771–779, under the heading, the attributive participle in nominal word clusters, while the *supplementary* participle was presented in the treatment of verb chains, §§565–576, 580–585 (note especially §§568, 571f., 584, 585). The third principal function, circumstantial or adverbial, remains to be considered.

845. The circumstantial participle indicates the circumstances under which the action of the main verb takes place. It thus modifies the verb and so is adverbial. It may be the equivalent of an adverbial clause denoting time, cause, means, manner, purpose, condition, concession or attendant circumstance(s). These ideas are not, of course, expressed by the participle itself (except for the future participle, §846.5) but must be inferred from the context. The circumstantial participle may be illustrated from English in a limited way:

    (i)   *They died fighting* (manner)
    (ii) *They fled by crossing the river* (means)
    (iii) *Although hearing, they did not understand* (concession)
    (iv) *The students prepared their lessons, the teacher assisting* (attendant circumstance)

Words like *by* in (ii) and *although* in (iii) help make the nuance of the participle clear in English. Such helping words, although not unknown in Greek, are less often employed. The Greek circumstantial participle is therefore a less precise form of expression than corresponding subordinate clauses of time, condition, concession, etc. When translating from Greek to English, it is often best to translate a participle with a participle where possible and thus preserve the ambiguity of the Greek participle. For example,

    (v) *They were baptized, confessing their sins*

may be a close approximation of a circumstantial participle in Greek, whereas

> (vi) *After confessing their sins, they were baptized*
> (vii) *Because they confessed their sins, they were baptized*

are more precise and thus interpretive.

845.1 The circumstantial participle refers to a noun (pronoun) in the same sentence and is in agreement with it (gender, number, case), or it is used absolutely. The absolute circumstantial participle, i.e. having no grammatical connection with the rest of the sentence, normally stands in the genitive case along with its subject, if expressed (genitive absolute, §847).

845.2 The 'tenses' of participles do not, strictly speaking, represent time but denote only aspect (*Aktionsart*, §§309f.). The temporal relation of the participle to the main verb is derived from the context. Since, however, the action expressed by the circumstantial participle customarily precedes that represented by the main verb, the aorist participle came to be associated to a certain degree with relative past time. Yet the aorist participle may express present and even future time (Bl-D §339(1)) relative to the main verb. The present participle, likewise, may be used for a variety of times relative to the main verb. Only in the case of the future participle is there a temporal nuance (used to express purpose, §846.5). It is appropriate to hold only the aspect of the various tenses of the participle in view in interpreting the circumstantial participle, unless there is specific indication to the contrary. Bl-D §339.

845.3 The circumstantial participle may take any of the complements the corresponding verb may take, e.g. subject, object or objects, etc.

845.4 In contrast to the attributive participle (§774, cf. §716), the circumstantial participle is regularly anarthrous, i.e. it is not preceded by the article. The supplementary participle is also anarthrous, of course (references in §0845).

846. *The circumstantial participle as the equivalent of an adverbial clause* may be taken (i.e. inferred from the context) to denote time, cause, means, manner, purpose, condition, concession, or attendant circumstance. Distinctions between and among these nuances are sometimes difficult to make in practice, in the absence of helping particles. The circumstantial participle most often denotes the manner in which an action takes place or what precedes and what accompanies it (Bl-D §418). The preponderant usage is thus a more or less vague descriptive function. A temporal clause in English often represents this lack of precision:

> (viii) *He said these things while giving a lecture*

Nevertheless, in some cases the context affords clues to a more precise interpretation of the participle.

846.1   The circumstantial participle may function as a *temporal* clause:

(1) τοῦτο δὲ πάλιν δεύτερον σημεῖον ἐποίησεν ὁ Ἰησοῦς,
     ἐλθὼν ἐκ τῆς Ἰουδαίας εἰς τὴν Γαλιλαίαν   Jn 4:54
     This was now the second sign Jesus did
     after coming from Judea to Galilee

(2) ταῦτα τὰ ῥήματα ἐλάλησεν ἐν τῷ γαζοφυλακείῳ,
     διδάσκων ἐν τῷ ἱερῷ   Jn 8:20
     He spoke these words in the treasury
     while teaching in the temple

The action represented by the participle in (1) is temporally antecedent to the action of the main verb, in (2) it is concurrent.

846.2   The circumstantial participle may serve as a *causal* clause:

(3) καὶ ἐφοβοῦντο αὐτόν,
     μὴ πιστεύοντες ὅτι ἐστὶν μαθητής   Acts 9:26
     And they feared him,
     since they did not believe he was a disciple

There is another example in Mt 1:19: Bl-D §418(1).

846.3   The circumstantial participle may indicate means:

(4) τοῦτο γὰρ ποιῶν
     ἄνθρακας πυρὸς σωρεύεις ἐπὶ τὴν κεφαλὴν αὐτοῦ   Rom 12:20
     For by doing this,
     you will heap coals of fire upon his head

846.4   The circumstantial participle may express *manner*:

(5) ἕτεροι δὲ διαχλευάζοντες ἔλεγον . . .   Acts 2:13
     But others mocking said . . .

The participle of manner may be introduced by the comparative particle, ὡς:

(6) οὕτως πυκτεύω ὡς οὐκ ἀέρα δέρων   1 Cor 9:26
     I do not fight as one beating the air

846.5   The circumstantial participle used to express purpose was put in the future tense in classical idiom. The future participle of purpose is rare in the New Testament (Bl-D §418(4)):

(7) ὃς ἐληλύθει προσκυνήσων εἰς Ἰερουσαλήμ   Acts 8:27
who had come to Jerusalem to worship

The present participle used to express purpose is more common:

(8) ἀπέστειλεν αὐτὸν εὐλογοῦντα ὑμᾶς   Acts 3:26
He sent him to bless you

846.6   The circumstantial participle may be the equivalent of a *conditional* clause.

(9) τί γὰρ ὠφελεῖται ἄνθρωπος
κερδήσας τὸν κόσμον ὅλον
ἑαυτὸν δὲ ἀπολέσας ἢ ζημιωθείς;   Lk 9:25
For what shall it profit a man
if he gain the whole world
but loses or forfeits himself?

The parallel passage in Matthew has a conditional clause with ἐάν and finite verb in place of the circumstantial participle:

(10) . . . ἐὰν τὸν κόσμον ὅλον κερδήσῃ,
τὴν δὲ ψυχὴν αὐτοῦ ζημιωθῇ;   Mt 16:26
. . . if he gain the whole world
but forfeits his own life?

846.7   The circumstantial participle may also serve as a *concessive* clause:

(11) ἀλλ᾽ οὐδὲ Τίτος . . . Ἕλλην ὤν, ἠναγκάσθη περιτμηθῆναι   Gal 2:3
But Titus . . . although a Greek, was not compelled to be circumcised

The concessive circumstantial participle is occasionally introduced by the particle, καίπερ:

(12) καὶ ἔλαβον σωτηρίαν,
καίπερ ἀλλότριοι τοῦ θεοῦ ὄντες   1 Clem 7:7
And they gained salvation,
although they were aliens to God

846.8   The circumstantial participle may indicate *attendant circumstance*:

> (13) καὶ αὐτὸς ἐδίδασκεν ἐν ταῖς συναγωγαῖς αὐτῶν,
>   δοξαζόμενος ὑπὸ πάντων   Lk 4:15
>   *And he taught in their synagogues,*
>   *being glorified by all*

For this construction, two finite verbs connected by καί would serve equally well, since the participle of attendant circumstance does not specify the relation between the action of the main verb and the attendant circumstance.

8460.   *Agreement.* The circumstantial participle may refer to a noun (pronoun) elsewhere in the sentence. If so, it should agree with its referent in gender, number, and case (§845). In examples (1)–(9) and (11)–(13), §846, with one exception, the circumstantial participle refers to the subject of the sentence and so stands in the nominative case. Gender and number vary in accordance with the antecedent. In (8), §846.5, the subject of the action represented by the participle is the object of the main verb and so stands in the accusative case. The participle agrees in case (as well as gender and number).

Circumstantial participles most often refer to the subject of the main verb and so take the nominative case. As (8) indicates, they may refer to some other element in the sentence in another case. The antecedent may be in the dative case:

> (14) καὶ <u>ἐμβάντι αὐτῷ</u> εἰς τὸ πλοῖον,
>   ἠκολούθησαν <u>αὐτῷ</u> οἱ μαθηταὶ αὐτοῦ   Mt 8:23
>   *And when he got into the boat,*
>   *his disciples followed him*

Another example with the antecedent in the accusative case:

> (15) ὥστε <u>αὐτὸν</u> εἰς πλοῖον <u>ἐμβάντα</u>
>   καθῆσθαι ἐν τῇ θαλάσσῃ   Mk 4:1
>   *so that he, getting into a boat,*
>   *sat [in it] on the sea*

In (15), ὥστε is followed by an infinitive of result, καθῆσθαι (§834).

Genitive Absolute

847. If the circumstantial participle does not refer to a noun (pronoun) elsewhere in the sentence, it is put in the genitive case, together with its complements, and called a genitive absolute (§845.1). It is called an absolute construction because it has no formal grammatical connection with the rest of the sentence. In English compare,

(ix) *The professor having finished his lecture, the students departed*

(x) *The passage having been translated, he closed his book*

where the participle and its subject are grammatically independent of the main clause.

The genitive absolute functions as any other circumstantial participle; it therefore has the range indicated in §846, which need only be illustrated here:

(16) καὶ ἐκβληθέντος τοῦ δαιμονίου,
ἐλάλησεν ὁ κωφός   Mt 9:33
And the demon having been cast out,
(= And when the demon had been cast out,)
the dumb man spoke

(17) πάλιν ἀνακάμψω πρὸς ὑμᾶς,
τοῦ θεοῦ θέλοντος   Acts 18:21
I will return to you,
God willing (= if God wills)

(18) οὐ ψεύδομαι,
συμμαρτυρούσης μοι τῆς συνειδήσεώς μου   Rom 9:1
I do not lie,
my conscience bearing witness with me
(= since my conscience bears witness with me)

8470. The rule that the genitive absolute can be employed only when its referent does *not* appear in the main clause is sometimes broken. It is found

8470.1 referring to a following accusative:

(19) ταῦτα αὐτοῦ λαλοῦντος,
πολλοὶ ἐπίστευσαν εἰς αὐτόν   Jn 8:30
Because he said these things,
many believed on him

8470.2 referring to a following dative:

> (20) ἤδη δὲ αὐτοῦ καταβαίνοντος
> οἱ δοῦλοι αὐτοῦ ὑπήντησαν <u>αὐτῷ</u>   Jn 4:51
> *As he was going down,*
> *his servants met him*

8470.3 and referring even to a following nominative:

> (21) μνηστευθείσης τῆς μητρὸς αὐτοῦ Μαρίας τῷ Ἰωσήφ,
> πρὶν ἢ συνελθεῖν αὐτούς,
> <u>εὑρέθη</u> ἐν γαστρὶ ἔχουσα   Mt 1:18
> *His mother Mary having been betrothed to Joseph,*
> *before they came together,*
> *she was found to be pregnant*

Cf. Bl-D §423.

8471.   *Nominative absolute.* Not to be confused with the circumstantial participle, particularly the genitive absolute, is the nominative absolute or hanging nominative with a participle. The real but not the grammatical subject of the sentence is introduced in the nominative case, but the referent of the participle appears in another case in the main clause:

> (22) ὁ πιστεύων εἰς ἐμέ, . . .
> ποταμοὶ ἐκ τῆς κοιλίας <u>αὐτοῦ</u> ῥεύσουσιν ὕδατος ζῶντος   Jn 7:38
> *He who believes in me, . . .*
> *out of his belly shall rivers of living water flow*

Cf. Rev 2:26 and Bl-D §466(4).

848.   *The circumstantial participle with verbs of saying* is often redundant from the perspective of English usage. A finite verb meaning *ask, answer, bear witness,* etc. is often followed by λέγων, which is loosely a circumstantial participle of manner:

> (23) ἐλάλησεν ὁ Ἰησοῦς λέγων . . .   Jn 8:12
> *Jesus spoke, saying . . .*
> (24) καὶ ἐμαρτύρησεν Ἰωάννης λέγων . . .   Jn 1:32
> *And John bore witness, saying . . .*

This participle usually introduces direct discourse. Cf. Bl-D §420.

849. *Present and aorist participles: 'tense.'* The tenses of the participle do not, strictly speaking, represent time. The temporal element is derived from the relation of the participle to the main verb (§846.2).

849.1 Since the action represented by the participle customarily precedes that of the main verb, the aorist participle most often indicates past time relative to the main verb.

849.11 Examples of an aorist participle representing time antecedent to a main verb in the aorist tense may be found in §846 (1), §8460 (14), (15), §847 (16).

849.12 An aorist participle representing action antecedent to a present tense:

  (25) εὐχαριστοῦμεν τῷ θεῷ . . .
       ἀκούσαντες τὴν πίστην ὑμῶν   Col 1:3f
       We give thanks to God . . .
       because we have heard of your faith

849.13 An aorist participle representing action prior to a future tense:

  (26) ἐγὼ ἐλθὼν θεραπεύσω αὐτόν   Mt 8:7
       I will come and heal him

  Cf. Jn 16:8 and Heb 2:3.

849.2 The aorist participle may also represent an action that is concurrent with that of the main verb:

  (27) καὶ προσευξάμενοι εἶπαν, . . .   Acts 1:24
       And praying they said, . . .

  Bl-D §339(1).

849.3 The present participle usually represents action in progress at the same time as the action of the main verb. The simultaneous participial action may thus be in the past, present, or future, depending on the tense of the main verb. Examples of a present participle correlated with an aorist tense are (2) and (13) in §846; (3) exhibits a present participle linked to an imperfect (cf. Lk 6:1). For a present participle representing action concurrent with a present tense, see (18) in §847 and compare Jn 5:44. Example (17) in §847 shows a present participle correlated with a future tense.

849.4 The present participle may occasionally represent an action that is temporally prior to the action of the main verb. In such instances the present participle represents the imperfect tense.

(28) πωλοῦντες ἔφερον τὰς τιμὰς
τῶν πιπρασκομένων   Acts 4:34
And when they had sold [the goods],
they brought the proceeds of what had been sold

Bl-D §339(3).

849.5   The present participle may also represent an action that is subsequent to the action of the main verb:

(29) ἐξῆλθεν,
διερχόμενος καθεξῆς τὴν Γαλατικὴν χώραν καὶ Φρυγίαν,
ἐπιστηρίζων πάντας τοὺς μαθητάς   Acts 18:23
He departed,
going through the regions of Galatia and Phrygia place by place,
strengthening all the disciples

Lesson 59

Conditional Sentences

855.1   Conditional sentences consist of a subordinate clause stating the condition or supposition (the if-clause) and a main clause giving the inference or conclusion. The if-clause is called the *protasis*, the main clause the *apodosis*. The subordinating conjunction in Greek used to introduce the protasis is εἰ or ἐάν (= εἰ + ἄν).

855.2   Conditional sentences are classified fundamentally in accordance with the character of the assumption in the if-clause, i.e. whether the condition is assumed to be true, whether it is assumed to be untrue, or whether its reality or unreality is left undetermined. Accordingly, there are three basic types of conditional sentences.

855.20   Conditional sentences are sometimes divided into as many as nine subtypes (Smyth §2297). These finer distinctions depend upon the correlation of a variety of apodoses with the protasis. This variety can be observed equally well in a simpler scheme.

     The use of the optative mood in the classical period made possible a fourth type of condition related to but distinct from the third type of assumption indicated in §855.2. Since this type of conditional sentence is rare in hellenistic Greek (there is no complete example in the New Testament), it need be noted only in passing.

     The classification scheme adopted in this grammar is basically that of A. T. Robertson (Robertson-David: 349–357; cf. Bl-D §371).

First Class Condition

856.   In a first class condition the protasis is a simple conditional assumption with emphasis on the reality of the assumption (but not on the reality of what is being assumed). It is therefore taken to be a real case, though it may, in fact, be an unreal case.

     The protasis consists of εἰ plus any tense of the indicative; the apodosis has any tense of the indicative (or imperative, or independent use of the subjunctive). Bl-D §§371–372.

856.1 The present tense in the protasis:

(1) τί οὖν βαπτίζεις
εἰ σὺ οὐκ εἶ ὁ Χριστός;   Jn 1:25
Why, then, do you baptize
if you are not the Christ?

856.2 A past tense in the protasis:

(2) εἰ ἐμὲ ἐδίωξαν,
καὶ ὑμᾶς διώξουσιν   Jn 15:20
If they persecuted me,
they will also persecute you

856.3 The future tense in the protasis:

(3) εἰ πάντες σκανδαλισθήσονται ἐν σοι,
ἐγὼ οὐδέποτε σκανδαλισθήσομαι   Mt 26:33
If everyone takes offense at you,
I will never take offense

856.4 The apodosis or conclusion assumes a variety of forms. Examples (1)–(3) all exhibit the indicative mood, although the apodosis in (1) is a question. The apodosis may also take the form of an imperative:

(4) εἰ υἱὸς εἶ τοῦ θεοῦ
εἰπὲ τῷ λιθῷ τούτῳ ἵνα γένηται ἄρτος   Lk 4:3
If you are the son of God,
tell this stone to become bread

Among other possibilities, a hortatory (volitive) subjunctive (§819) may serve as an apodosis.

856.5 The protasis may be initiated by καὶ εἰ *even if*:

(5) καὶ, εἰ ἐγὼ ἐν Βεελζεβοὺλ ἐκβάλλω τὰ δαιμόνια,
οἱ υἱοὶ ὑμῶν ἐν τίνι ἐκβάλλουσιν;   Mt 12:27
Even if I cast out demons by Beelzebub,
by whom do your sons cast them out?

This form of the protasis is sometimes called a concessive clause. The assumption in the protasis is taken to be true for the sake of the argument, but Jesus would deny that he, in fact, cast out demons by the power of Beelzebub. It is therefore important to emphasize that the assumption, not the fact, is assumed to be true.

856.6 For an apodosis introduced by the inferential particle ἄρα *then*, s. Mt. 12:28.

Second Class Condition

857. The assumption is taken to be untrue in the protasis of a second class condition; it is considered an unreal case (whether it is, in fact, is another matter). The conclusion follows from the premise.

The protasis consists of εἰ plus a past (augmented) tense of the indicative; the apodosis also has a past tense of the indicative, usually with ἄν. Bl-D §360.

857.1 Referring to present or past time, with the imperfect in both clauses:

(6) εἰ γὰρ ἐπιστεύετε Μωϋσεῖ,
   ἐπιστεύετε ἂν ἐμοί   Jn 5:46
   If you believed Moses [but you don't],
   you would believe me

Cf. Heb 11:15.

857.2 Referring to past time, with the aorist in both clauses:

(7) εἰ γὰρ ἔγνωσαν,
   οὐκ ἂν τὸν κύριον τῆς δόξης ἐσταύρωσαν   1 Cor 2:8
   If they had known,
   they would not have crucified the lord of glory

Cf. Mt 11:21.

857.3 The tenses in the protasis and apodosis may be different:

(8) εἰ ἠγαπᾶτέ με,
   ἐχάρητε ἄν   Jn 14:28
   If you loved me,
   you would have rejoiced

(imperfect and aorist)

(9) εἰ γὰρ ἐξ ἡμῶν ἦσαν,
   μεμενήκεισαν ἂν μεθ' ἡμῶν   1 Jn 2:19
   For if they had been of us,
   they would have continued with us

857.4   Contrary to classical usage, ἄν is sometimes omitted in the apodosis:

> (10) οὐκ εἶχες ἐξουσίαν κατ' ἐμοῦ οὐδεμίαν,
>   εἰ μὴ ἦν δεδομένον σοι ἄνωθεν   Jn 19:11
>   *You would have no power over me,*
>   *unless it had been given you from above*

Cf. Jn 15:22, 24; Gal 4:15.

Third Class Condition

858.   The assumption in a third class condition is left undetermined. Since it indicates what is expected under general or specific circumstances, ἐάν with the subjunctive appears in the protasis. There is some expectation of realization, so the subjunctive is used in preference to the optative, which would indicate that the prospect of realization is remote. It may therefore be said that a third class condition is undetermined but with the objective possibility of fulfillment.

A first class condition is taken to be a real case; a second class condition is considered an unreal case; a third class condition is a probable case. The third class condition is an expected case or a generalizing case in present time. The examples below will help locate its primary sphere.

The future, present indicative, imperative, gnomic aorist, or independent use of the subjunctive may form the apodosis.

Bl-D §§371, 373.

858.1   A third class condition may have the present indicative in the apodosis:

> (11) ἐὰν εἴπωμεν ὅτι οὐχ ἡμαρτήκαμεν,
>   ψεύστην ποιοῦμεν αὐτόν   1 Jn 1:10
>   *If we (ever) say that we have not sinned,*
>   *we make him a liar*

The present tense in the apodosis often gives the condition a generalizing force (indicated by *ever* in the translation).

Cf. Jn 5:31, 8:31.

858.2   The apodosis may show an imperative:

> (12) ἐὰν ἔλθῃ πρὸς ὑμᾶς,
>   δέξασθε αὐτόν   Col 4:10
>   *If he comes to you,*
>   *welcome him*

858.3 Or a gnomic aorist (= valid for all times, §7880):

(13) ἐὰν δὲ καὶ γαμήσῃς,
    οὐχ ἥμαρτες   1 Cor 7:28
    But if you do marry,
    you do not sin

858.4 A third class condition with the future indicative in the apodosis is called a future more vivid condition by some grammarians (Smyth §§2323ff.): it is a stronger statement of the case:

(14) ἐὰν οὖν ὁ υἱὸς ὑμᾶς ἐλευθερώσῃ,
    ὄντως ἐλεύθεροι ἔσεσθε   Jn 8:36
    If, therefore, the son makes you free,
    you shall be truly free

An even stronger statement of the case, a future most vivid (Smyth §2328), has the future indicative in both clauses; this is a special form of a first class condition, and an example may be found in (3), §856.3.

For additional examples of the future more vivid, see Jn 5:43, 8:24, Mt 6:14, 15.

858.5 Another form of the future more vivid condition has οὐ μή and the subjunctive in the apodosis (futuristic emphatic negative assertion, §818):

(15) ἐάν τις τὸν ἐμὸν λόγον τηρήσῃ,
    θάνατον οὐ μὴ θεωρήσῃ εἰς τὸν αἰῶνα   Jn 8:51
    If anyone keeps my word,
    he will never see death

Cf. Jn 4:48, Mt 10:42.

Fourth Class Condition

859. The *fourth class condition* had εἰ with the optative in the protasis and the optative with ἄν in the apodosis. It represents something as thought of, without regard for the reality or unreality of the assumption, and emphasizes the hypothetical character of the assumption; it is a potential case (the optative is the mood of potentiality, §307.3).

The fourth class condition has virtually disappeared in later colloquial Greek. The past general condition with εἰ and the optative in the protasis and the imperfect or its equivalent in the apodosis (Smyth §2340), has also all but disappeared.

There are some examples of εἰ with the optative in the protasis, but with a conclusion from another class of condition, e.g.

(16) ἀλλ' εἰ καὶ πάσχοιτε διὰ δικαιοσύνην,
μακάριοι   1 Pet 3:14
But even if you suffer for righteousness' sake,
you are blessed

Cf. Acts 20:16, 24:19; 1 Pet 3:17. Bl-D §§371, 385(2).

8590.   *Concessive clauses* introduced by εἰ καί or ἐὰν καί, *although*, are a subspecies of conditional sentences.

(17) ἐὰν καὶ προλημφθῇ ἄνθρωπος ἔν τινι παραπτώματι,
ὑμεῖς οἱ πνευματικοὶ καταρτίζετε τὸν τοιοῦτον   Gal 6:1
Although a man's sin be detected,
you who are spiritual are to restore him

Cf. (5), §856.5.

860.   *Equivalents of the conditional clause.* The protasis of a conditional sentence may take forms other than those introduced by εἰ (ἐάν).

860.1   A circumstantial participle may be the equivalent of an if-clause:

(18) ὁ γὰρ ἐσθίων καὶ πίνων κρίμα ἑαυτῷ ἐσθίει καὶ πίνει,
μὴ διακρίνων τὸ σῶμα   1 Cor 11:29
For the one eating and drinking eats and drinks judgment
to himself,
if he does not discern the body

Cf. §846.6 and the example cited there. Cf. also Heb 2:3.

860.2   An indefinite relative clause with ὅς (ὅστις) ἄν (ἐάν = ἄν, Bl-D §§107, 371) may be the equivalent of a protasis, usually in a third class condition (§858) :

(19) ὃς ἐὰν οὖν λύσῃ μίαν τῶν ἐντολῶν τούτων τῶν ἐλαχίστων, . . .
ἐλάχιστος κληθήσεται ἐν τῇ βασιλείᾳ τῶν οὐρανῶν   Mt 5:19
Whoever then relaxes one of the least of these commandments, . . .
shall be called least in the kingdom of heaven

The relative may also appear in relative conditions of other types:

> (20) ὃς γὰρ οὐκ ἔστιν καθ' ὑμῶν
> ὑπὲρ ὑμῶν ἐστιν   Lk 9:50
> *For he that is not against you*
> *is for you (= if he is not against you)*

Cf. §674, (18). Bl-D §380.

860.3   Indefinite local clauses also exhibit an affinity with conditional clauses:

> (21) ἀκολουθήσω σοι,
> ὅπου ἐὰν ἀπέρχῃ   Lk 9:57
> *I shall follow you*
> *wherever you go*

ἐάν again = ἄν (Bl-D §107) .

860.4   A temporal clause with ὅταν (= ὅτε + ἄν) and the subjunctive corresponds to the protasis of a third class condition:

> (22) μακάριοί ἐστε
> ὅταν ὀνειδίσωσιν ὑμᾶς   Mt 5:11
> *Blessed are you*
> *whenever they revile you*

(22) corresponds to a present general condition (§858.1), with the present indicative (or equivalent) in the apodosis. See Mt 6:5 for an example of ὅταν and the subjunctive in the equivalent of a future more vivid condition (§858.4). For the imperative or a subjunctive of prohibition in the apodosis, see Mt 6:2, 6, 16.

861.   *Key for identifying conditional sentences or equivalents.* Identifying conditional sentences in accordance with the terms set out in §§855–860 depends on identifying the type of protasis (if-clause). For that purpose a simple key may prove useful.

861.1   ἐάν with subjunctive in the protasis: third class (§858)

    1a) present indicative or equivalent in apodosis:
        present general (§858.1)

    1b) future indicative or equivalent in apodosis:
        future more vivid (§858.4)

861.2   Augmented (past) tenses of the indicative in both clauses, with ἄν in the apodosis: second class (§857)

861.3   If the sentence does not have ἐάν and the subjunctive in the protasis or ἐάν in the apodosis, it is: first class (§856)

    3a) future indicative in both clauses:
         future most vivid (§§858.4, 856.3)

861.4   Note: ἄν is sometimes omitted in the apodosis of second class conditions (§857.4).

Lesson 60

Comparative & Temporal Clauses

ὡς as Subordinator

0865.　As a subordinator, ὡς is used in the New Testament chiefly to introduce comparative and temporal clauses. Like its English counterpart, (*just*) *as*, ὡς is an extremely versatile particle. In its full classical powers, ὡς was used as a relative adverb to introduce comparative clauses and comparisons, as well as a subordinator to initiate declarative, final, causal, consecutive, and temporal clauses (Smyth §§2990ff.).

The versatility of *as*, as a means of introducing adverbial clauses of various types, may be illustrated by the following English sentences:

(i)　*He writes as fast as John* (comparative)
(ii)　*He reads as he rides to work* (temporal)
(iii)　*As I have no place to go, I will stay here* (causal)
(iv)　*I breathed heavily as I ran* (attendant circumstance)

Such adverbial clauses may be elliptical, i.e. the adverbial clause may be abbreviated:

(v)　*I used to speak as a child* (*is accustomed to speak*)

Both *as* and ὡς have functions other than that of a subordinator. For the full range of ὡς in the literature covered by Bauer, see the entry in Bauer on ὡς. In this section, only ὡς as a subordinator introducing comparative and temporal clauses will be considered.

865.　*ὡς introducing comparative clauses.* Comparative clauses are included sentences, which may be complete or elliptical (abbreviated). Such clauses may serve as constituent elements in various types of sentences. And ὡς may be correlated with καί and οὕτως.

865.1   Full comparative clauses:

(1) ἔσεσθε οὖν ὑμεῖς τέλειοι
   ὡς ὁ πατὴρ ὑμῶν ὁ οὐράνιος τέλειός ἐστιν   Mt 5:48
   You therefore must be perfect,
   as your heavenly father is perfect

(2) καὶ ἄφες ἡμῖν τὰ ὀφειλήματα ἡμῶν,
   ὡς καὶ ἡμεῖς ἀφήκαμεν τοῖς ὀφειλέταις ἡμῶν   Mt 6:12
   And forgive us our debts,
   as we have forgiven our debtors

Cf. Mt 18:33.

865.2   ὡς is used parenthetically:

(3) οὐ γὰρ ὡς ὑπολαμβάνετε οὗτοι μεθύουσιν   Acts 2:15
   For these men are not drunk, as you suppose

865.3   Comparative clauses introduced by ὡς may serve as constituent elements in various types of sentences.

865.31   As object clause:

(4) ἐποίησεν ὡς προσέταξεν αὐτῷ ὁ ἄγγελος κυρίου   Mt 1:24
   He did as the angel of the Lord commanded him

865.32   As subject:

(5) ὡς ἐπίστευσας γενηθήτω σοι   Mt 8:13
   Let it be done to you as you believe

865.33   As the predicate in S-II (§507)

(6) οὔτε γαμοῦσιν οὔτε γαμίζονται,
   ἀλλ᾽ εἰσὶν ὡς ἄγγελοι ἐν τοῖς οὐρανοῖς   Mk 12:25
   They neither marry nor are given in marriage,
   but are like angels in heaven

865.4   The comparative clause may be abbreviated:

(7) ὅτε ἤμην νήπιος,
   ἐλάλουν ὡς νήπιος,

ἐφρόνουν ὡς νήπιος,

ἐλογιζόμην ὡς νήπιος   1 Cor 13:11

When I was a child,

I spoke as a child (speaks),

I thought as a child (thinks),

I reasoned as a child (reasons)

In English such sentences may be taken as *not* elliptical and *like* substituted for *as* (Roberts, 1954: 239). Cf. Mk 10:15.

865.5   ὡς may be correlated with καί:

(8) ὡς προειρήκαμεν, καὶ ἄρτι πάλιν λέγω   Gal 1:9

As we have said before, so now I say again

Cf. Mt 6:10.

865.6   ὡς is more frequently correlated with οὕτως:

(9) ἕκαστον ὡς κέκληκεν ὁ θεός,

οὕτως περιπατείτω   1 Cor 7:17

As God has called each one,

let him so walk

Note that in (9) ὡς does not initiate the subordinate clause. In Greek, unlike English, subordinators occasionally do not initiate their clauses.

Cf. 2 Cor 7:14. One or the other of the clauses in this correlation may also be elliptical: 1 Thess 5:2, 2 Cor 1:7.

866.   *ὡς introducing temporal clauses.* ὡς initiates temporal clauses with various tenses of the indicative; ὡς ἄν is followed by the subjunctive (cf. §868.2).

866.1   ὡς is most frequently followed by the aorist indicative:

(10) ὡς δὲ ἐγεύσατο ὁ ἀρχιτρίκλινος τὸ ὕδωρ οἶνον γεγενημένον, . . . Jn 2:9

And when the steward of the feast tasted the water now made wine, . . .

Cf. Jn 4:1, etc.

866.2   With the imperfect indicative:

(11) καὶ ὡς ἀτενίζοντες ἦσαν εἰς τὸν οὐρανὸν . . .   Acts 1:10

And while they were gazing into heaven . . .

866.3   With the present indicative:

(12) ὡς ἔτι καιρὸν ἔχομεν εἰς θεὸν μετανοεῖν   IgnSm 9:1
      While we still have time to repent toward God

Cf. Jn 12:35f., Gal 6:10, 2 Clem 8:1, 9:7, IgnRom 2:2.

866.4   With ἄν and the subjunctive:

(13) ὡς ἄν πορεύωμαι εἰς τὴν Σπανίαν   Rom 15:24
      When I go to Spain

Cf. 1 Cor 11:34, Phil 2:23.

Comparative Clauses

0867.   A comparative clause compares an act or state quantitatively or qualitatively
         with the act or state denoted by the verb in the main clause.

         Comparative clauses in the New Testament are most often introduced by ὡς
         (§865). They are introduced less frequently by καθώς, occasionally by ὥσπερ
         and καθάπερ, and rarely by καθό and καθότι.

         Constructions with these subordinators do not require special comment; it is
         sufficient to illustrate them briefly.

867.   *Comparative clauses introduced by* καθώς, ὥσπερ, καθάπερ.

867.1   καθώς:

(14) καὶ τοιαύταις παραβολαῖς πολλαῖς ἐλάλει αὐτοῖς τὸν λόγον,
      καθὼς ἠδύναντο ἀκούειν   Mk 4:33
      With many such parables he used to speak the word to them,
      as they were able to hear

Cf. Jn 8:28.

867.2   καθώς may be correlated with ὁμοίως or οὕτως (cf. ως, §865.5–6):

(15) καὶ καθὼς θέλετε ἵνα ποιῶσιν ὑμῖν οἱ ἄνθρωποι,
      ποιεῖτε αὐτοῖς ὁμοίως   Lk 6:31
      And just as you want men to do to you,
      do to them likewise

(16) καὶ καθὼς Μωϋσῆς ὕψωσεν τὸν ὄφιν ἐν τῇ ἐρήμῳ,
      οὕτως ὑψωθῆναι δεῖ τὸν υἱὸν τοῦ ἀνθρώπου   Jn 3:14

And just as Moses lifted up the serpent in the wilderness
so it is necessary for the son of man to be lifted up

867.3 ὥσπερ:

(17) μὴ σαλπίσῃς ἔμπροσθέν σου,
ὥσπερ οἱ ὑποκριταὶ ποιοῦσιν   Mt 6:2
Sound no trumpet before you,
as the hypocrites do

867.4 καθάπερ:

(18) μηδὲ γογγύζετε,
καθάπερ τινὲς αὐτῶν ἐγόγγυσαν   1 Cor 10:10
But do not grumble,
as some of them did

8670. Comparative clauses are sometimes clauses of *manner*. Note (7), §865.4 and (17), §867.3 above, and cf. the circumstantial participle of manner (§846.4), especially when introduced by ὡς.

Temporal Clauses

0868. A temporal clause refers to an act or state that occurs prior to, at the same time as, or subsequent to the act or state denoted by the verb in the main clause.

Temporal clauses with the indicative or subjunctive are introduced by a variety of subordinators, some of which are simple (ὅτε), some of which are complex (ἐν ᾧ). The principal temporal subordinators in the New Testament are ὅτε, ὅταν, ἕως. The infinitive introduced by πρίν (πρὶν ἤ) may also function as a temporal clause (§836), and the circumstantial participle is often the equivalent of a temporal clause (§846.1).

868.1 Temporal clauses may be either adjectival (rare) or adverbial (common). In adjectival temporal clauses, the time is specified by a noun (or equivalent) in the main clause; this noun is then further specified by an adjective clause:

(19) ἔρχεται ὥρα
ὅτε οὔτε ἐν τῷ ὄρει τούτῳ οὔτε ἐν Ἰεροσολύμοις
προσκυνήσετε τῷ πατρί   Jn 4:21
The hour is coming
when neither on this mountain nor in Jerusalem
will you worship the father

Adverbial temporal clauses modify the verb in the main clause. Compare (i) (adjectival) and (ii) (adverbial) below:

(i)   *He arrived on the day (when) he was due*

(ii) *He arrived when he was due*

(i) has close affinities with a relative clause, as this simple modification makes clear:

(iii) *He arrived on the day on which he was due*

Cf. relative clauses, §§665–674.

Attention in this section will be focused on adverbial temporal clauses.

868.2   Adverbial temporal clauses, like relative clauses (§§671, 6740), are either definite or indefinite, depending on whether they refer to an event or events occurring at a definite time or times, or to an event or events occurring at unspecified times. For example,

(iv) *I heard him when he spoke*

is definite. The following are indefinite:

(v)   *I heard him whenever he spoke*

(vi) *I will hear him whenever he speaks*

(v) and (vi) have affinities with conditional clauses (see §860.4 for discussion).

Definite temporal clauses take the indicative mood, as a rule. One may expect ἄν and the subjunctive to appear most often in indefinite temporal clauses.

869.   *Definite temporal clauses* are initiated by ὅτε or ὡς and are followed by the indicative mood (aorist, imperfect, perfect, present, future, according to the circumstances), e.g.

(20) ὅτε ἐτέλεσεν ὁ Ἰησοῦς τοὺς λόγους τούτους,
      μετῆρεν ἀπὸ τῆς Γαλιλαίας   Mt 19:1
      When Jesus finished these sayings,
      he went away from Galilee

(21) καὶ ὅτε ἐγγίζουσιν εἰς Ἱεροσόλυμα . . .
      ἀποστέλλει δύο τῶν μαθητῶν αὐτοῦ   Mk 11:1
      And when they draw near Jerusalem . . .
      he sends two of his disciples

(22) ἐλεύσονται ἡμέραι
   ὅτε ἐπιθυμήσετε μίαν τῶν ἡμερῶν
   τοῦ υἱοῦ τοῦ ἀνθρώπου   Lk 17:22
   The days are coming
   when you will desire to see one of the days
   of the son of man

The future usually occurs with constructions like ἔρχεται, ὥρα, ἡμέρα, and thus in adjectival temporal clauses (§868.1). Bl-D §382.

For examples with ὡς, see §866.1–3.

870.   *Indefinite temporal clauses* are introduced by ὅταν (= ὅτε + ἄν) or ὡς ἄν (ἐάν: §6740) followed by the subjunctive or an augmented tense of the indicative (repetition in past time, §§Bl-D 367, 382(4)).

870.1   An augmented tense of the indicative with ἄν indicates repetition in past time:

(23) καὶ τὰ πνεύματα τὰ ἀκάθαρτα
   ὅταν αὐτὸν ἐθεώρουν
   προσέπιπτον αὐτῷ   Mk 3:11
   And the unclean spirits,
   whenever they saw him,
   fell down before him

870.2   The subjunctive with ἄν refers to future time:

(24) καὶ ὅταν προσεύχησθε,
   οὐκ ἔσεσθε ὡς οἱ ὑποκριταί   Mt 6:5
   And whenever you pray,
   do not be like the hypocrites

Cf. Jn 4:25, Titus 3:12.

(25) τὰ δὲ λοιπά, ὡς ἂν ἔλθω, διατάξομαι   1 Cor 11:34
   About the other matters, I will give instructions when I come

For other examples of ὡς ἄν with the subjunctive, see §866.4.

870.3   ὅταν is sometimes correlated with τότε, *then*:

(26) ὅταν ὑψώσητε τὸν υἱὸν τοῦ ἀνθρώπου,
   τότε γνώσεσθε ὅτι ἐγώ εἰμι   Jn 8:28
   When you lift up the son of man,
   then you will know that I am he

871. *Temporal clauses introduced by* ἕως. Temporally speaking, ἕως meaning *until* introduces a verb denoting an act or state which marks the termination of an act (or state) denoted by the main verb, e.g.

(vii) *Sit there until you finish your lesson*

i.e. when you have finished your lesson, you need no longer sit there. ἕως meaning *while* introduces a verb denoting an act or state which is more or less coterminous with the act (or state) denoted by the main verb. When the one is precisely coterminous with the other, ἕως means *as long as* (*while* is simply less precise).

The two meanings of ἕως can be distinguished only in context.

Temporal clauses introduced by ἕως, like other temporal clauses, are either definite or indefinite (cf. §870). Definite temporal clauses with ἕως take the indicative (cf. §869); indefinite, iterative, or contingent clauses take the subjunctive with or without (Bl-D §383(2)) ἄν. Cf. Smyth §§2422ff.

871.1 ἕως, *until*, with the indicative (= definite clause):

(27) καὶ οὐκ ἔγνωσαν
ἕως ἦλθεν ὁ κατακλυσμός   Mt 24:39
And they did not know
until the flood came

(28) καὶ χαράκωσον αὐτόν,
ἕως ἔρχομαι   HermSim 5.2.2
And fence it,
until I come

871.2 ἕως, *while*, with the indicative (= definite clause):

(29) ἡμᾶς δεῖ ἐργάζεσθαι τὰ ἔργα τοῦ πέμψαντός με
ἕως ἡμέρα ἐστίν   Jn 9:4
It is necessary for us to do the works of the one sending me
while it is day

Cf. 2 Clem 16:1.

871.3 ἕως, *until*, with ἄν and the subjunctive:

(30) ἕως ἄν παρέλθῃ ὁ οὐρανὸς καὶ ἡ γῆ,
ἰῶτα ἓν ἢ μία κέραια οὐ μὴ παρέλθῃ ἀπὸ τοῦ νόμου
ἕως ἄν πάντα γένηται   Mt 5:18

Till heaven and earth pass away,
not one iota, not one dot, will pass from the law
until all is fulfilled

Both ἕως-clauses are contingent.
Cf. Mt 5:26, Mk 6:10 (indefinite), Mk 9:1.
Without ἄν:

(31) καὶ πορεύεται ἐπὶ τὸ ἀπολωλὸς
ἕως εὕρῃ αὐτό   Lk 15:4
And goes after the lost one,
until he finds it

871.4   ἕως, *while*, with the subjunctive:

(32) καὶ περιζωσάμενος διακόνει μοι
ἕως φάγω καὶ πίω   Lk 17:8
And gird yourself and serve me,
while I eat and drink

Cf. Mk 14:32. Both Lk 17:8 and Mk 14:32 could be interpreted to mean *until* (Burton: 127f.), and there are textual variants in both cases (Bl-D §383(2)).

872.   Clauses introduced by ἕως οὗ, ἕως ὅτου, ἐν ᾧ, ἄχρι(ς), ἄχρις οὗ, μέχρι(ς), μέχρις οὗ in general take the same constructions as simple ἕως, except that they are rarely followed by ἄν (Bl-D §383). The following illustrate constructions with these subordinators.

(33) ἐν ᾧ δὲ ἔρχομαι ἐγὼ
ἄλλος πρὸ ἐμοῦ καταβαίνει   Jn 5:7
But while I am going,
another steps down before me

(34) οὐκ ἐπίστευσαν οὖν οἱ Ἰουδαῖοι . . . ,
ἕως ὅτου ἐφώνησαν τοὺς γονεῖς αὐτοῦ   Jn 9:18
Therefore the Jews did not believe . . . ,
until they called his parents

(35) οὐ μὴ παρέλθῃ ἡ γενεὰ αὕτη
μέχρις οὗ ταῦτα πάντα γένηται   Mk 13:30
This generation will certainly not pass away,
until all these things take place

873.   *Other forms of temporal clauses.*

873.1   Temporal clauses may be introduced by πρίν or πρὶν ἤ, *before*. When the main clause is affirmative, πρίν (ἤ) is followed by the infinitive (§836). When the main clause is negative, πρίν (ἤ) takes the same constructions as ἕως (§871). In hellenistic Greek, however, the construction with the indicative, subjunctive, or optative has virtually disappeared. Cf. Lk 2:26, Acts 25:16, and Bl-D §383(3).

873.2   Certain prepositions may introduce clauses with the infinitive which are the equivalent of temporal clauses (§836).

873.3   The circumstantial participle is often the equivalent of a temporal clause (§846.1).

Lesson 61

Local, Causal, Final & Consecutive Clauses

Local Clauses

0875. An adverbial local clause specifies the place of the action of the main verb.

Local clauses are introduced by οὗ, ὅπου *where*, and ὅθεν *whence*.

875.1 Local clauses may be adjectival or adverbial. In adjectival local clauses, the place is specified by a noun or equivalent in the main clause; this noun is then further specified by an adjective clause, e.g.

(1) καὶ ἦλθεν εἰς Ναζαρά,
οὗ ἦν τεθραμμένος   Lk 4:16
And he came to Nazareth,
where he had been brought up

(2) εἰς τὸν οἶκον μου ἐπιστρέψω,
ὅθεν ἐξῆλθον   Mt 12:44
I will return to my house
from which I came

οὗ and ὅθεν appear predominantly in adjectival local clauses in the New Testament.

Adverbial local clauses modify the verb in the main clause. The first example (i) is adjectival, the second (ii) adverbial:

(i)   *He is going to Chicago, where he lives*
(ii) *He goes wherever he wants*

ὅπου is the subordinator used most often to introduce adverbial local clauses.

875.2 Adverbial local clauses, like temporal clauses (§868.2), are either definite or indefinite. Definite local clauses take the indicative mood, as a rule. Indefinite local clauses take a past tense of the indicative with ἄν in an iterative sense or ἄν and the subjunctive.

876.1 *Definite local clauses.* The following are examples of ὅπου and the indicative in definite local clauses:

> (3) τὸ πνεῦμα ὅπου θέλει, πνεῖ   Jn 3:8
> *The spirit blows where it wills*
>
> (4) οὐχ ὅπου ὠνομάσθη Χριστός   Rom 15:20
> *not where the Christ has been named*
>
> (5) ὅπου ἦν τὸ πρότερον   Jn 6:62
> *where he was earlier*

876.2 *Indefinite local clauses.*

> (6) καὶ ὅπου ἂν εἰσεπορεύετο εἰς κώμας ἢ εἰς πόλεις ἢ εἰς
> ἀγρούς, . . .   Mk 6:56
> *And wherever he would go, into villages, towns, or the country, . . .*
>
> (7) ὅπου ἐὰν εἰσέλθητε εἰς οἰκίαν,
> ἐκεῖ μένετε   Mk 6:10
> *Wherever you enter a house,*
> *stay there*
>
> (8) ὅπου ἐὰν κηρυχθῇ τὸ εὐαγγέλιον τοῦτο . . .   Mt 26:13
> *Wherever this gospel is preached . . .*

In (6) ὅπου is followed by ἄν and the imperfect. ἐάν in (7) and (8) stands for ἄν, as frequently elsewhere (Bl-D §§107, 371).

Causal Clauses

0877. A causal clause states the reason or basis for the action of the main verb.

The principal subordinator used to introduce causal clauses is ὅτι (§651). Other causal subordinators include ἐπεί, ἐπειδή, διότι, καθότι, ὅθεν, listed roughly in the order of their frequency in the New Testament.

διὰ τό and the infinitive also functions as a causal clause (§836.2), and the circumstantial participle may serve as a causal clause (§846.2).

877. Causal clauses regularly take the indicative (in classical the optative also appears). The following is a representative sample of causal clauses:

> (9) πῶς ἔσται τοῦτο,
> ἐπεὶ ἄνδρα οὐ γινώσκω;   Lk 1:34
> *How can this be,*
> *since I have no husband?*

(10) νουθετοῦνται . . .

    διότι εὑρέθη ἐν αὐτοῖς πονηρία   HermVis 3.5.4

    They are being admonished . . .

    because wickedness has been found in them

(11) χρῆσόν μοι τρεῖς ἄρτοις,

    ἐπειδὴ φίλος μου παρεγένετο ἐξ ὁδοῦ   Lk 11:6

    Lend me three loaves,

    because my friend has arrived from a journey

8770.   It should be noted that ἐπεί and ἐπειδή are occasionally used in a temporal sense, and that ὅθεν is also a local subordinator (§0875). καθότι is also used to introduce comparative clauses (§0867).

Final (Purpose) Clauses

0878.   Final (purpose) clauses denote the purpose or aim of the action of the verb in the main clause.

    The principal subordinator used to introduce final clauses in hellenistic Greek is ἵνα (with the subjunctive) (examples and discussion §§656f.). A close rival for expressing purpose is the supplementary infinitive (§§574–576, 580, 833). Relative clauses sometimes have final force (§674), and the circumstantial participle may function as a purpose clause (§846.5). The discussion of these forms of final clauses need not be repeated here.

    The only final subordinators remaining to be treated are ὅπως and μή: The use of ὡς as a final subordinator has been largely discontinued (one example in the New Testament: Acts 20:24, Bl-D §391(1)). Closely related to final clauses are expressions of apprehension (often after verbs of fearing); these are also introduced by μή (μήποτε, μήπως).

878.1   *Final clauses with ὅπως.* As in the case of ἵνα, the subjunctive is normally used with ὅπως (although the future indicative sometimes appears as a variant); ἄν occasionally appears with ὅπως (frequent in Attic).

(12) ἀγαπᾶτε τοὺς ἐχθροὺς ὑμῶν . . . ,

    ὅπως γένησθε υἱοὶ τοῦ πατρός ὑμῶν τοῦ ἐν οὐρανοῖς   Mt 5:45

    Love your enemies . . . ,

    so that you may be sons of your heavenly father

(13) μετανοήσατε . . . ,

    ὅπως ἂν ἔλθωσιν καιροὶ ἀναψύξεως   Acts 3:19f.

> *Repent . . . ,*
> *so that times of refreshing may come*

Bl-D §369.

878.2 *Negative final clauses.* These merely express negative purpose; the negative is μή. μή is also occasionally used alone as a final subordinator.

(14) τὸ πρόσωπόν σου νίψαι,
    ὅπως μὴ φανῇς τοῖς ἀνθρώποις νηστεύων   Mt 6:17f.
    Wash your face,
    so that your fasting not be evident to men

(15) οὐκ ἔρχεται πρὸς τὸ φῶς,
    ἵνα μὴ ἐλεγχθῇ τὰ ἔργα αὐτοῦ   Jn 3:20
    He does not come to the light,
    in order that his deeds not be exposed

(16) γρηγορεῖτε οὖν, . . .
    μὴ ἐλθὼν ἐξαίφνης εὕρῃ ὑμᾶς καθεύδοντας   Mk 13:35f.
    Watch therefore, . . .
    lest he come suddenly and find you sleeping
    (= in order that he not . . .)

879. *Expressions of apprehension with μή (μήπως, μήποτε)* seek to avert an undesired result or express the fear that a desired result may not materialize. Such expressions are therefore closely related to the negative purpose clauses illustrated in §878.2.

(17) φοβοῦμαι,
    μὴ νηπίοις οὖσιν ὑμῖν βλάβην παραθῶ   IgnTr 5:1
    I fear,
    lest I do you harm, since you are babes

Indeed, the translation *lest* is often suitable for ὅπως μή and ἵνα μή, as in (15).

(18) φοβοῦμαι δὲ μή πως, . . .
    φθαρῇ τὰ νοήματα ὑμῶν   2 Cor 11:3
    I fear,
    lest your thoughts be corrupted

Such expressions need not be dependent upon a verb of fearing, e.g. φοβέομαι as in (17), (18), but may be made to depend upon almost any verb:

(19) καὶ ἀνεθέμην αὐτοῖς τὸ εὐαγγέλιον . . . ,

    μή πως εἰς κενὸν τρέχω ἢ ἔδραμον   Gal 2:2

    And I laid the gospel before them . . . ,

    lest I should be running or had run in vain

In (19) τρέχω is subjunctive, ἔδραμον aorist. This sentence illustrates the principle of mood: if the anxiety is directed toward something still dependent on the will, the subjunctive is used; if toward something already accomplished or otherwise independent of the will, the indicative is appropriate. Bl-D §370.

Consecutive (Result) Clauses

0880.   Consecutive clauses denote the result (intended or actual) of the action indicated by the verb in the main clause.

    In classical idiom a distinction was maintained between expressions of intended result (therefore a subspecies of the purpose clause) and actual result. The indicative introduced by ὥστε was reserved for actual result if stated as a fact; the infinitive was used for all other cases, again introduced by ὥστε (or ὡς). The indicative with ὥστε is not native to the New Testament (there are two possible examples). As a consequence, the infinitive has come to express both nuances of the consecutive clause.

    The use of ὥστε and the infinitive, the infinitive with τοῦ, and the simple infinitive, to express result was treated in §834. To these constructions with the consecutive infinitive should now be added εἰς τό and πρὸς τό with the infinitive (Bl-D §402(2), (4)). Because of the affinity of intended result and purpose, a ἵνα-clause may be used in a consecutive sense (Bl-D §391(5)). Relative clauses may also have consecutive force (cf. §674).

880.   *Consecutive clauses with ὥστε.*

880.1   The indicative with ὥστε may be used to express actual result:

    (20) καὶ συνυπεκρίθησαν αὐτῷ καὶ οἱ λοιποὶ Ἰουδαῖοι,

        ὥστε καὶ Βαρναβᾶς συναπήχθη αὐτῶν τῇ ὑποκρίσει   Gal 2:13

        And with him the rest of the Jews acted insincerely,

        so that even Barnabas was carried away by their hypocrisy

See Jn 3:16 for the only other example in the New Testament.

880.2   The infinitive with ὥστε may also express actual result:

> (21) καὶ ἰδοὺ σεισμὸς μέγας ἐγένετο ἐν τῇ θαλάσσῃ,
> ὥστε τὸ πλοῖον καλύπτεσθαι ὑπὸ τῶν κυμάτων   Mt 8:24
> *And behold, a severe storm came up on the sea,*
> *so that the boat was swamped by the waves*

880.3   The infinitive with ὥστε is used in its classical sense to denote intended result:

> (22) ἔδωκεν αὐτοῖς ἐξουσίαν πνευμάτων ἀκαθάρτων
> ὥστε ἐκβάλλειν αὐτά   Mt 10:1
> *He gave them authority over unclean spirits,*
> *to cast them out*

880.4   A ἵνα-clause (with the subjunctive) may be substituted for ὥστε and the infinitive of intended result:

> (23) πιστός ἐστιν καὶ δίκαιος
> ἵνα ἀφῇ ἡμῖν τὰς ἁμαρτίας   1 Jn 1:9
> *He is faithful and just,*
> *to forgive our sins*

880.5   It should be noted that ὥστε also functions as a sentence connector (§§620, 630ff.), meaning *for this reason, therefore*. In this function it is closely related to ὥστε with the indicative, §880.1.

881.   *The infinitive with εἰς τό and πρὸς τό is also a means of expressing result:*

> (24) ἑαυτοὺς ἔδωκαν πρῶτον τῷ κυρίῳ . . . ,
> εἰς τὸ παρακαλέσαι ἡμᾶς Τίτον . . .   2 Cor 8:6
> *They gave themselves first to the Lord . . . ,*
> *so that we urged Titus . . .*
> (25) πᾶς ὁ βλέπων γυναῖκα
> πρὸς τὸ ἐπιθυμῆσαι αὐτήν   Mt 5:28
> *Every one who looks at a woman*
> *to lust for her*

The translation of (25) avoids interpreting the construction one way or the other. The sentence illustrates how closely related intended result and purpose are: it could mean *looking with a view to lusting* (purpose), or *looking with lust as a result*.

Lesson 62

The Cases

0885. The discussion of the cases and summary of their syntactical function, found in the Introduction to the Nominal System, §§105–1140, is presupposed in the following detailed sketch of the function of the cases. The earlier discussion and summary serves as an introduction; the following catalogue is intended primarily for reference.

Nominative

885. *The nominative is the naming case.* It is used most commonly, therefore, as the subject of the sentence. In closely related ways it is used also for predicates, appositives (adjuncts to the subject, but also loosely to other cases), absolutely (in titles and the like), and as vocative.

8850. It is to be remembered that the personal endings attached to the verb constitute the real subject of the verb (§542). Strictly speaking, a subject added in the nominative case is in apposition to the subject contained in the personal ending. Nouns and nominals so used define the subject more closely, so to speak. Originally, personal pronouns used with the finite verb were emphatic, but the extent to which this nuance is retained in hellenistic Greek is uncertain (cf. §722.3 and Bl-D §277).

886. *Functions of the nominative.*

886.1 The nominative signals the subject (§533.2):

    (1) ἐν ἀρχῇ ἦν ὁ λόγος   Jn 1:1
        In the beginning was the word

886.2 The predicate noun or equivalent in S-II takes the nominative case, if it is declinable (§507):

    (2) ἡ ζωὴ ἦν τὸ φῶς τῶν ἀνθρώπων   Jn 1:4
        The life was the light of men

Note: The predicate is nominative if the subject is nominative; the two must agree.

886.3   The nominative is used for words and the head terms of word groups in apposition to a noun or equivalent in the nominative case:

> (3) Ἠσαΐας ὁ προφήτης   Jn 1:23
> *Isaiah the prophet*

886.4   The nominative is used absolutely (i.e. not as a part of a larger grammatical structure) in titles, headings, inside addresses in letters, and the like:

> (4) Παῦλος δοῦλος Χριστοῦ Ἰησοῦ   Rom 1:1
> *Paul, a servant of Christ Jesus*

886.5   The nominative is also used for the vocative (the two case-forms are often identical, §205):

> (5) ἡ παῖς, ἔγειρε   Lk 8:54
> *Child, arise*

886.50   The nominative as vocative is usually preceded by the article (Bl-D §147(3)).

Vocative

0887.   *The vocative is the case of address.* It is not a case in the formal sense, since it signals no relationship to other words and word groups in the sentence and has no real endings. In form it is often identical with the nominative.

887.   The vocative may be used with or without the interjection ὦ:

887.1   With emotion:

> (6) ὦ ἄνθρωπε   Rom 2:1
> *O man*

887.2   Without emotion:

> (7) ὦ Θεόφιλε   Acts 1:1
> *O Theophilus*

887.3   Simple vocative:

> (8) ἄνδρες Ἰουδαῖοι   Acts 2:14
> *Men of Judea*

Note also §§886.5 and 886.50. Bl-D §§146f.

Genitive

0888. *The genitive is the limiting of specifying case* and is used to circumscribe the meaning of substantives, adjectives, adverbs, and less often verbs. The genitive has absorbed the ablative case in Greek (distinct in Latin) and so *embraces the idea of origin or separation as well.*

The precise relation expressed by a genitive has to be determined by the meaning of the words involved and the larger context. English *of* and *from* will most often cover the meaning of the genitive.

The relation of object to verb is normally expressed by the accusative, less often by the genitive (and dative).

The following classifications are in part arbitrary, since the various relationships expressed by the genitive overlap at numerous points. The sketch is intended only as a guide to the major functions of the case.

Adnominal Genitive

888. The adnominal genitive is the genitive with the function of an adjective and hence its use with substantives.

888.1 The genitive is used to denote *possession, origin,* or *relationship*:

> (9) μὴ ποιεῖτε τὸν οἶκον τοῦ πατρός μου οἶκον ἐμπορίου   Jn 2:16
> *Do not make my father's house a house of trade*

The three genitives in this sentence are: possession (*father's*), relationship (*my*), description (*of trade*).

> (10) Σίμων ὁ υἱὸς Ἰωάννου   Jn 1:42
> *Simon the son of John*
> (11) Ἰάκωβον τὸν τοῦ Ζεβεδαίου   Mk 1:19
> *James the son of Zebedee*

Bl-D §162.

888.2 *Subjective and objective genitives.* When the noun in the genitive is the subject of the action, emotion, etc. expressed by the noun to which it is related, it is called the subjective genitive.

> (12) ἡ γὰρ ἀγάπη τοῦ Χριστοῦ συνέχει ἡμᾶς   2 Cor 5:14
> *For the love of Christ controls us*

The context makes it clear that Christ is the subject of the love involved; in another context the same genitive might refer to love directed toward Christ.

When the noun in the genitive is the object of the action, emotion, etc. expressed by the noun to which it is related, it is called the objective genitive.

> (13) διὰ τὸν φόβον τῶν Ἰουδαίων   Jn 7:13
> *on account of the fear of the Jews*

The Jews in (13) are the object of fear. Bl-D §163.

888.3   *The partitive genitive.* The genitive denotes the whole, a part of which is designated by the noun it limits. The partitive genitive is especially common after words denoting a part or fraction, e.g. εἷς, *one;* τις, *someone, some;* ἕκαστος, *each;* οἱ λοιποί, *the rest, the remainder.* The use of the prepositions ἐκ, ἀπό, ἐν in an ablative sense has greatly reduced the use of the simple case in hellenistic Greek. Bl-D §164.

> (14) εἷς τῶν προφητῶν   Mk 6:15
> *one of the prophets*

Compare with preposition:

> (15) εἷς ἐκ τῶν μαθητῶν αὐτοῦ   Jn 6:8
> *one of his disciples*

Without preposition:

> (16) εἰς τοὺς πτωχοὺς τῶν ἁγίων   Rom 15:26
> *to the poor among the saints*

888.31 The land within which a city, etc. lies stands in the genitive (chorographic genitive):

> (17) ἀπὸ Ναζαρὲτ τῆς Γαλιλαίας   Mk 1:9
> *from Nazareth of Galilee*

Bl-D §164.

888.4   The genitive of *quality* or *attributive* genitive:

> (18) ἐκ τοῦ μαμωνᾶ τῆς ἀδικίας   Lk 16:9
> *by means of mammon of unrighteousness*

The genitive in (18) is paralleled by an attributive adjective in the same context:

(19) ἐν τῷ ἀδίκῳ μαμωνᾷ   Lk 16:11
in the unrighteous mammon

The attributive genitive may also be used as a predicate in S-II:

(20) ἦν γὰρ ἐτῶν δώδεκα   Mk 5:42
For she was of twelve years (i.e. twelve years old)

Bl-D §165.

888.5   The *appositive* genitive or genitive of *explanation* in some cases is really a noun in apposition:

(21) καὶ σημεῖον ἔλαβεν περιτομῆς   Rom 4:11
And he received a sign of circumcision
(i.e. he received a sign, namely circumcision)

Bl-D §167.

888.6   The genitive of *material* or *content* indicates the material of which something is made, or that with which it is filled.

(22) ποτήριον ὕδατος   Mk 9:41
cup of water

Cf. Rev 6:6. Bl-D §167.

888.7   The genitive is used to indicate the *price, value,* or *measure* of something.

(23) διακοσίων δηναρίων ἄρτοι οὐκ ἀρκοῦσιν αὐτοῖς   Jn 6:7
two hundred denarii worth of bread would not be enough for them

888.8   The genitive may also be used to express *direction* or *purpose.*

(24) συνεργοί ἐσμεν τῆς χαρᾶς ὑμῶν   2 Cor 1:24
We are co-laborers for your joy
(25) εἰς ὁδὸν ἐθνῶν μὴ ἀπέλθητε   Mt 10:5
Do not go (on the way) to Gentiles

Bl-D §166.

Adverbial Genitive

0889.   The adverbial genitive is used to mark the object of certain verbs (cf. §§594–596) when the object is related to the nominal idea of the verb, e.g.

(26) Ἀρχέλαος βασιλεύει τῆς Ἰουδαίας   Mt 2:22
     Archelaus rules the Jews (= is king of)

or when the verb expresses a relationship to its object which corresponds to a function of the genitive, e.g. partitive, material, context, separation.

0889.1   Prepositions are often used to supplement the simple case in the hellenistic period.

0889.2   The genitive is sometimes dependent to a certain extent on the preposition in compound verbs (Bl-D §181).

0889.3   The distinction between the genitive and accusative with verbs cannot always be pressed owing to the inroads of the accusative on the genitive in the hellenistic period.

889.1   The *partitive* genitive is used with verbs (Bl-D §§169ff.) if only a part of the object is affected; if the object as a whole is involved, the accusative is appropriate.

    (27) ἥψατο τοῦ ἱματίου αὐτοῦ   Mk 5:27
      she touched his garment

    (28) μετελάμβανον τροφῆς   Acts 2:46
      They partook of food

889.2   The genitive is used with some verbs of perception:

    (29) ἀκούετε αὐτοῦ   Mk 9:7
      listen to him

This genitive is perhaps a genitive of *source*.

889.3   The genitive of *content* is used with verbs meaning *fill* (cf. §888.6):

    (30) γεμίσατε τὰς ὑδρίας ὕδατος   Jn 2:7
      Fill the jars with water

This construction takes the genitive of the filler, the accusative of the thing filled.

889.4   The genitive of *price* or *value* is used with verbs meaning *buy* or *sell*:

    (31) ἐγὼ πολλοῦ κεφαλαίου τὴν πολυτείαν ταύτην ἐκτησάμην   Acts 22:28
      I bought this citizenship for a large sum

889.5   The genitive of *separation* is also found with certain verbs.

(32) ὁ παθὼν σαρκὶ πέπαυται ἁμαρτίας   1 Pet 4:1
The one who has suffered in the flesh has ceased from sin

Other Uses of the Genitive

890.1   The genitive is used with adjectives and adverbs which call for a genitive relationship, e.g.

(33) ποιήσατε οὖν καρπὸν ἄξιον τῆς μετανοίας   Mt 3:8
Therefore produce fruit worthy of repentance

Bl-D §182.

890.2   The genitive is used to mark the standard or point of departure from which a *comparison* is made (i.e. a genitive of separation).

(34) μείζω τούτων ὄψῃ   Jn 1:50
You shall see greater (things) than these

(35) τὸ μωρὸν τοῦ θεοῦ σοφώτερον τῶν ἀνθρώπων ἐστίν   1 Cor 1:25
The foolishness of God is wiser than men

Bl-D §185.

890.3   The genitive of *time* expresses the time within which something takes place (the accusative expresses extent of time = time during which, while the dative expresses point of time = time at which, whether a particular moment or a longer period conceived as a unit).

(36) οὗτος ἦλθεν πρὸς αὐτὸν νυκτός   Jn 3:2
That one came to him at night

Bl-D §186.

Dative

0891.   The single case-form (dative) serves for three distinct cases: dative, instrumental, and locative. The relationships expressed by the single case-form may therefore be divided into three subcategories.

The Dative

891.   *The dative is the case of personal interest*; it marks that *to* or *for* which something is done. It will be focused, consequently, on persons (or personifications), to whom something is favorable (advantage) or unfavorable (disadvantage).

891.1 The dative may mark the *indirect object* with a transitive verb (S-IV, §§509–510).

> (37) ταῦτα γράφω ὑμῖν   1 Jn 2:1
> *I write these things to you*

With verb to be supplied:

> (38) Παῦλος ἀπόστολος . . . ταῖς ἐκκλησίαις τῆς Γαλατίας   Gal 1:1f.
> *Paul an apostle . . . to the churches of Galatia*

891.2 The dative signals *the sole object with many verbs denoting a personal relationship* (cf. §§591–593), e.g.

> (39) καὶ οἱ ἄγγελοι διηκόνουν αὐτῷ   Mk 1:13
> *And the angels ministered to him*
>
> (40) ἢ ζητῶ ἀνθρώποις ἀρέσκειν;   Gal 1:10
> *Or do I seek to please men?*

Bl-D §187.

891.3 The dative of *advantage* and *disadvantage*. The dative may denote the person or persons to whose advantage something is done:

> (41) εἴτε γὰρ ἐξέστημεν, θεῷ
> εἴτε σωφρονοῦμεν, ὑμῖν   2 Cor 5:13
> *For if we are beside ourselves, it is for God;*
> *if we are in our right mind, it is for you*

Or, to whose disadvantage something is performed:

> (42) ὥστε μαρτυρεῖτε ἑαυτοῖς   Mt 23:31
> *Thus you witness against yourselves*
> (i.e. *to yourselves, to your disadvantage*)

Bl-D §188.

891.4 *The dative of possession* is closely related to the dative of advantage. Simple possession is expressed by the genitive (§888.1); the one for whom something exists (i.e. in his or her interest) is put in the dative:

> (43) διότι οὐκ ἦν αὐτοῖς τόπος ἐν τῷ καταλύματι   Lk 2:7
> *Because there was no place for them in the inn*

(44) ὄνομα αὐτῷ Ἰωάννης   Jn 1:6
His name was John

Bl-D §189.

891.5   The dative is also used with *adjectives*, many of which are related in meaning to the verbs referred to in §891.2:

(45) ἀρκετὸν τῇ ἡμέρᾳ ἡ κακία αὐτῆς   Mt 6:34
Sufficient for the day is the evil thereof

(46) ἱκανὸν τῷ τοιούτῳ ἡ ἐπιτιμία αὕτη   2 Cor 2:6
For such a one this punishment is sufficient

Bl-D §187.

The Instrumental

0892.   The instrumental denotes that *by* which or *with* which something is done. It may thus express either means or instrument, or association or accompaniment.

892.1   The *associative* instrumental is used with verbs denoting friendly or hostile association or accompaniment (cf. §§591–593).

(47) ἠκολούθησαν αὐτῷ   Mk 1:18
They followed him

(48) ἐπὶ σάββατα τρία διελέξατο αὐτοῖς   Acts 17:2
For three sabbaths he discussed with them

Bl-D §193.

892.2   The *instrumental proper* is often supplemented in the New Testament by ἐν (in imitation of Hebrew, Bl-D §195).

(49) ἀνεῖλεν δὲ Ἰάκωβον τὸν ἀδελφὸν Ἰωάννου μαχαίρῃ   Acts 12:2
He killed James the brother of John with the sword

Cf. with ἐν:

(50) πάντες γὰρ οἱ λαβόντες μάχαιραν ἐν μαχαίρῃ ἀπολοῦνται   Mt 26:52
For all who take the sword shall perish by the sword

892.3   The dative of *means* is closely related to the instrumental dative:

(51) ὥστε καὶ Βαρναβᾶς συναπήχθη αὐτῶν τῇ ὑποκρίσει   Gal 2:13
So that even Barnabas was carried away by their hypocrisy

892.4   The dative of *cause* denotes the occasion or basis:

> (52) μόνον ἵνα τῷ σταυρῷ τοῦ Χριστοῦ μὴ διώκωνται   Gal 6:12
>   *only in order that they not be persecuted for the cross of Christ*
>
> (53) τοιαύταις γὰρ θυσίαις εὐαρεστεῖται ὁ θεός   Heb 13:16
>   *For with such sacrifices God is pleased*

Bl-D §196.

892.5   The dative of *respect* (or *relation*) is used to denote the standard or person to which the assertion is limited (cf. the accusative of specification or respect, which is sometimes the virtual equivalent of the dative of respect, §894.6).

> (54) ἡμεῖς φύσει Ἰουδαῖοι   Gal 2:15
>   *We who are Jews by nature*
>
> (55) ἐὰν μὴ περιτμηθῆτε τῷ ἔθει τῷ Μωϋσέως, . . .   Acts 15:1
>   *Unless you are circumcised according to the custom of Moses, . . .*
>
> (56) ἤμην δὲ ἀγνοούμενος τῷ προσώπῳ ταῖς ἐκκλησίαις
>   τῆς Ἰουδαίας   Gal 1:22
>   *And I was unknown by sight to the churches of Judea*

Example (56) provides the basis for comparing *respect* (τῷ προσώπῳ, *by face*) and *relation* (ταῖς ἐκκλησίαις, *to the churches*): The former refers to that with respect to which the assertion holds, the latter denotes the person with respect to whom the assertion holds. Cf. Bl-D §197, Smyth §§1495, 1512, 1516.

892.6   *The associative dative* is used to indicate accompanying circumstances and manner:

> (57) εἰ ἐγὼ χάριτι μετέχω, . . .   1 Cor 10:30
>   *If I partake with thankfulness, . . .*
>
> (58) εἰ σὺ εἶ ὁ Χριστός,
>   εἰπὲ ἡμῖν παρρησίᾳ   Jn 10:24
>   *If you are the Christ,*
>   *tell us plainly*

The dative of manner may be replaced by a preposition with the genitive:

> (59) καὶ ἐλάλουν τὸν λόγον τοῦ θεοῦ μετὰ παρρησίας   Acts 4:31
>   *And they spoke the word of God with boldness*

The accompanying circumstance is put in the dative:

(60) πᾶσα δὲ γυνὴ προσευχομένη ἢ προφητεύουσα
ἀκατακαλύπτῳ τῇ κεφαλῇ . . .   1 Cor 11:5
But every woman who prays or prophesies with her head
uncovered . . .

Bl-D §198.

The Locative

893.   *The locative indicates location in space or time.* In English the locative is represented by the prepositions *in* and *at*, also by *on, among, beside, upon,* etc.

893.1 The locative of *place* is rare in the New Testament without a preposition (ἐν, ἐπί,
παρά, πρός).

(61) τῇ δεξιᾷ οὖν τοῦ θεοῦ ὑψωθεὶς . . .   Acts 2:33
Being therefore exalted at the right hand of God . . .

is probably locative. Bl-D §199.

893.2 The locative of *time* is fairly common. It is often supplemented by the preposition ἐν.

(62) τῇ τρίτῃ ἡμέρᾳ   Mt 16:21
on the third day

(63) αὐτῇ τῇ ὥρᾳ   Lk 2:38
at that very hour

(64) τῇ ἐπαύριον   Jn 1:29
on the morrow

(65) μὴ . . . χειμῶνος μηδὲ σαββάτῳ   Mt 24:20
not during winter or on the sabbath

In (65) note the genitive of time within which (§890.3) alongside a temporal
locative. Bl-D §200.

Accusative

0894. *The root idea expressed by the accusative is extension:* it answers the question, how
far? (Robertson-Davis: 215). As with the other cases, the relationship expressed
is often indeterminate and must be supplied from the context. It is the case of

the direct object of the verb (the direct object indicates the extent to which the action of the verb is effective). It is used with verbs of motion and specifies the goal (usually accompanied by a preposition). It also denotes extent of space and time.

894.1   The accusative marks the *direct object* (in S-III, §508 and S-IV, §§509–510) or the object affected:

> (66) ἠγάπησεν ὁ θεὸς τὸν κόσμον   Jn 3:16
> *God loved the world*

894.2   The accusative may denote the *content* with transitive verbs or object effected (also called cognate accusative). This accusative may be cognate with the verb (etymologically related) or of kindred meaning.

> (67) ἐχάρησαν χαρὰν μεγάλην σφόδρα   Mt 2:10
> *They rejoiced with exceeding great joy*
> (68) εἶδον ἐν ἐκστάσει ὅραμα   Acts 11:5
> *In a trance I saw a vision*

Bl-D §153.

894.3   A verb may take *two accusatives* in S-V (§521):

> (69) τὴν ψυχὴν λέγει τὸ ἔσω
> τὸ δε ἔξω τὸ σῶμα λέγει   2 Clem 12:4
> *He calls the inside the soul,*
> *and he calls the outside the body*
> (70) ἵνα ἡ ἀγάπη ἣν ἠγάπησάς με ἐν αὐτοῖς ᾖ   Jn 17:26
> *in order that the love with which you loved me may be in them*

Note: (69) contains an accusative of the object affected and an object complement; (70) has an accusative of content and an accusative of the object affected.

894.4   A verb may take *two accusatives* in S-VI (§523):

> (71) πάλιν χρείαν ἔχετε τοῦ διδάσκειν ὑμᾶς τινὰ τὰ στοιχεῖα   Heb 5:12
> *You have need for someone to teach you again the*
> *elementary things*

894.5   An accusative of the thing is sometimes retained in the passive form of S-VI (§523):

(72) τὰς παραδόσεις ἃς ἐδιδάχθητε   2 Thess 2:15
The traditions which you were taught

Bl-D §159.

894.6   The accusative of *specification* or *respect* is used to limit or define:

(73) ἀνέπεσαν οὖν οἱ ἄνδρες τὸν ἀριθμὸν ὡς πεντακισχίλιοι   Jn 6:10
The men then sat down, in number about 5,000

Compare: κάμνω τὴν κεφαλήν, *I have a pain with respect to my head*, i.e. a headache. Bl-D §160.

894.7   The *adverbial accusative* is the adverbial counterpart of the accusative of respect.

(74) καὶ προβὰς ὀλίγον . . .   Mk 1:19
And going on a little farther . . .

Bl-D §160.

894.8   The accusative may denote the *extent of space or time.*

(75) ἐληλακότες οὖν ὡς σταδίους εἴκοσι πέντε ἢ τριάκοντα . . . Jn 6:19
When they had rowed twenty-five or thirty stadia

(76) καὶ ἦν ἐν τῇ ἐρήμῳ τεσσαράκοντα ἡμέρας   Mk 1:13
And he was in the wilderness forty days

Bl-D §161.

894.9   The *terminal accusative*, denoting goal, with verbs of motion is found in the New Testament only with prepositions (εἰς, ἐπί, παρά, πρός).

894.10   The *accusative subject of an infinitive*: since the infinitive does not have personal endings (being an "infinite" form) with which to express a subject, the subject with reference to which the action is predicated is put in the accusative:

(77) μετὰ δὲ τὸ παραδοθῆναι τὸν Ἰωάννην . . .   Mk 1:14
After John was put in prison . . .

This accusative is really an accusative of specification or respect (§894.6), i.e. *After the to be imprisoned with respect to John.*

Appendix I

Phonetic Change

900. Appendix I is a schematic summary of phonetic changes that arise in Greek from the juxtaposition of certain consonants and vowels in inflection, word-formation, and word sequence. For the most part, items presented at relevant points in the grammar are here collected together. This summary is designed to facilitate easy reference. Cf. §§080–085.

The following symbols are employed:

> becomes, changes into
< is derived from
\# zero form (e.g. of a stem vowel)
λ̥ sonant (vocalic) consonant
u̯ semivowel or consonantal vowel

The Classification of Vowels and Consonants

0901. A descriptively accurate classification of vowels and consonants in Greek is beyond the scope of this grammar. Such a full, scientific description would be illuminating, but for an elementary acquaintance with the phonological system of Greek it is unnecessary. A few preliminary remarks with respect to classification will suffice.

Vowels

901. There are seven vowels in Greek: α, ε, η, ι, ο, υ, ω.

901.1 ε and ο are always short; their long counterparts are η and ω, respectively.

901.2 α, ι, υ may be either long or short.

902. A diphthong (δίφθογγος [two sounds]) is the fusion of two vowels into one syllable. The second vowel is always ι or υ.

902.1 The diphthongs may be classified in three groups:

(1)	αι	ει	οι	υι
(2)	ᾳ	η	ῳ	
(3)	αυ	ευ	ηυ	ου

902.2   In group (2) the second vowel (ι) is written under the long vowel and is called *iota-subscript;* in this group the ι is silent. Cf. §058.2.

902.3   All diphthongs are long, except that final αι and οι are considered short everywhere but in the optative.

902.4   When ι or υ do not form a diphthong with a preceding vowel, a diaresis (διαίρεσις, *separation*) is written over them, e.g. προΐστημι.

902.5   ει and ου are either *spurious* or *genuine.* Spurious ει and ου arise from the contraction of ε + ε, ε + ο, ο + ε, ο + ο (§917.2, 4), or from compensatory lengthening (§914). They are otherwise genuine, i.e. arise from the combination of ε + ι and ο + υ.

Consonants

0903.   Consonants may be classified in various ways, e.g. according to the nature of the sound, according to the vocal organs used in producing them, according to whether or not they are syllabic.

A full elaboration of these categories will serve no useful purpose in this context. It is sufficient to note certain categories and characteristics, the significance of which will subsequently become apparent.

903.   The seventeen consonants may be divided into sub-groups as follows:

903.1   *Stops* (also called mutes), so-called because the breath is allowed to collect behind a closure before being released with a slight pop or explosion: π, β, φ; κ, γ, χ; τ, δ, ϑ (cf. English p, t).

903.2   A *spirant* (σ, ς), so-called because the breath is allowed to escape with friction through a narrow passage in the mouth (cf. English f, s).

903.3   *Liquids,* so-called because they are produced by allowing breath to pass through the oral cavity without friction; they get their name from the rippling nature of the sound: λ, ρ (cf. English *l, r*).

903.4   *Nasals* as the name indicates, are produced by allowing part of the breath to escape through the nose: μ, ν (cf. English m, n). γ-nasal (§9030.1) is, of course, also a nasal (note §064.2).

903.5   *Double consonants* are single letters representing combinations of consonants: ζ, ξ, ψ (cf. English x in lax, i.e. = ks).

9030.   Notes:

9030.1   γ before κ, γ, χ, and ξ (= κσ, γσ, χσ) becomes nasal (§056.1).

9030.2   Initial ρ always has rough breathing.

9030.3 ζ is a combination of σδ, δσ, or δι̯ (§932.·1). ξ is written for κσ, γσ, χσ; however, it is not written for κσ when ἐκ (preposition) is compounded with another word, e.g. ἐκ-στασις, *ecstasy*. ψ is written for πσ, βσ, φσ.

9030.4 The term liquid often embraces both liquids and nasals.

904. The nine *stops* are divided into three *orders* and three *classes*. The classes are determined by the part of the oral cavity used in producing them: *labials* (lips), *palatals* (throat), *dentals* (teeth). The orders are determined by whether or not the stop is *voiced* and by whether it is *aspirated*. A consonant is said to be voiced when the vocal chords vibrate as the air passes through; it is said to be voiceless when the vocal chords are slack in pronunciation; aspiration means pronounced with a strong emission of breath.

904.1 Stops belonging to the same class are said to be *cognate*; stops belonging to the same order are said to be *coordinate*. These relationships may be conveniently represented by the "square" of stops.

	Orders		
	Smooth	Middle	Rough
	(Voiceless)	(Voiced)	(Aspirated)
Labials (lips)	π	β	φ
Palatals (throat)	κ	γ	χ
Dentals (teeth)	τ	δ	θ

The kinship between and among stops plays an important role in consonant change.

904.2 Rough breathing is also an aspirate (Note §928).

904.3 μ is a labial nasal and is thus akin to the labial class of stops (note §§926.1, 929.1); it is also voiced and is thus related to the middle order of stops (note §926.2).

905. Semivowels. ι and υ are sometimes called semivowels because, in addition to vowel sounds, they also often represent the consonantal sounds y and w. Consonantal ι and υ are designated thus: ι̯, υ̯. Consonantal υ was represented by the letter ϝ/Ϝ (digamma) in an earlier period (disappeared in Attic; written as late as 200 B.C. in Boeotian). While ι̯ and υ̯ do not appear in Hellenistic Greek as such, their former presence often makes itself felt in various phonetic changes or lack of them.

906.   *Sonants.* Liquids, nasals (and σ) may function as syllables, i.e. when an unpronounceable combination of consonants arises, one of them may develop the force of a vowel. Cf. sonant ḷ in English *battle*, m̥ in English *bottom*, n̥ in *button*, ṣ in *pst*. When they are syllabic they are called sonant or vocalic (designated λ̥, ρ̥, etc.). Sonant λ̥ may become αλ or λα; ρ̥ > αρ or ρα; μ̥ > α; γ̥ > α.

Vowel Change

907.   *Vowel gradation* is the quantitative (short to long and the reverse) and qualitative change in the vocalic elements in related words. It is to be observed in both inflection and word-formation.

908.   *Quantitative vowel gradation.* A short vowel may interchange with its corresponding long vowel: α with η (ᾱ after ε, ι, ρ); ε with η; ι with ῑ; ο with ω; υ with ῡ.

908.1   In the development of principal parts of the verb, e.g., τιμάω (present tense stem) becomes τιμήσω (fut.); ἐάω (pres.) becomes ἐάσω (fut.); ποιέω (pres.) becomes ποιήσω (fut.); δηλόω (pres.) becomes δηλώσω (fut.). S. §§358, 374.

908.2   In the inflection of nouns, e.g., γλῶσσα (nom.) becomes γλώσσης (gen.); ἀλήθειᾱ (nom.) becomes ἀληθείᾱς (gen.); πατήρ (nom.) becomes πατέρα (ace); ἄρχων (nom.) becomes ἄρχοντος (gen.). S. §§132.2, 184, 166.

908.3   In the interchange of long and short α, α becomes ᾱ after ε, ι, and ρ, otherwise η. There are some exceptions. S. §§9140, 1321.1.

909.   *Transfer of quantity.* The combinations ηο and ηα may exchange quantity: πόλεως < πόληος; βασιλέᾱ < βασιλῆα.

910.   *Qualitative vowel gradation.* Vowels and diphthongs may interchange in the same root or suffix in quality as well as in quantity. Cf. English *sing, sang, sung; man, men; goose, geese.*

911.   In the verb system, qualitative and quantitative variations in corresponding vowels are classified as strong and weak grades. The weak grade includes the loss of a vowel altogether (# stands for the zero form) and the loss of one vowel of a diphthong. The following summary of patterns includes all the verbs in Appendix III (Bauer) showing vowel gradation (marked with ↑ in the catalogue).

	Strong Grade(S)	Weak Grade(S)
911.1	ε/ο	α/#
(I.7)	ἐ-γεν-όμην/γέ-γον-α	γί-ν-ομαι (< γί-γν-ομαι)
(VI)	ἠνέχ-θην/ἐν-ήνοχ-α	ἤν-εγκ-α
(I.3)	πέμπ-ω/πέ-πομφ-α	
(I.3)	στρέφ-ω	ἐ-στράφ-ην

(I.3)	τρέπ-ω	ἐ -τράπ-ην
(I.3)	τρέφ-ω	-ε-τράφ-ην
(I.3)	πλέκ-ω	-ε-πλάκ-ην
(I.4)	δέρ-ω	δαρ-ήσομαι
(II)	κλέπ-τω	ἐ-κλάπ-ην
(III.3)	στέλλ-ομαι	-ε-στάλ-ην
(III.3)	τέλλ-ω	τέ-ταλ-κα
(III.4)	-κτεν-ῶ	-ε-κτάν-θην
(III.4)	σπείρ-ω	ἐ-σπάρ-ην
(III.4)	φθερ-ῶ	ἐ-φθάρ-ην
(I.3)	ἔχ-ω (< *σεχ-ω)	ἔ-σχ-ον
(I.3)	πέτ-ομαι	-έ-πτη-ν
(I.7)	ἔ-πεσ-ον	πί-πτ-ω
(I.7)	ἔ-τεκ-ον	τί-κτ-ω (< *τι-τκ-ω)
(IV)	τέμν-ω	-τέ-τμη-κα
(VI)	ἐρ-ῶ (< *ϝερ-)	ἐρ-ρέ-θην

911.2   ει/οι   ι

(I.3)	λείπ-ω/-λέ-λοιπ-α	ἔ-λιπ-ον
(I.3)	πέιθ-ω/πέ-ποιθ-α	
(IV)	μείγ-νυμι	ἐ-μίγ-ην

911.3   ευ   υ/ε/#

(I.3)	φεύγ-ω	ἔ-φυγ-ον
(IV)	τέ-τευχ-α	ἔ-τυχ-ον
(I.5)	ῥεύ-σω	-ρυ-ήσομαι /ῥέ-ω
(I.5)		-ε-χύ-θην/-έ-χε-α
(VI)	ἐλεύ-σομαι	ἐλ-ήλυθ-α/ἦλθ-ον

911.4   η/ει   α/ε

(1.3)	τήκ-ω	τακ-ήσομαι
(1.7)	στή-σω	ἐ-στά-θην
(1.7)	ὀν-ίνη-μι	ὀνα-ίμην
(IV)	ἐ-δήχ-θην	δάκ-νω
(IV)	ἐ-λήμφ-θην	ἔ-λαβ-ον
(IV)	-λέ-λησ-μαι	ἔ-λαθ-ον
(IV)	ῥήγ-νυμι	ἐρ-ράγ-ην

(IV)	-ἔ-βη-ν	-βα-ίνω
(IV)	ἐ-κέρδη-σα	κερδα-ίνω
(I.7)	-ἦ-κα	-ἔ-θην
(I.7)	τί-θη-μι/τέ-θει-κα	ἐ-τέ-θην

911.5   α   #

(I.5)	ἐ-κάλε-σα	ἐ-κλή-θην
(III.3)	ἔ-βαλ-ον	ἐ-βλή-θην
(IV)	ἐ-καμ-ον	κέ-κμη-κα
(V)	-ἔ-θαν-ον	τέ-θνη-κα

911.6   ω   ο

(I.7)	δί-δω-μι	ἐ-δό-θην
(VI)	πέ-πω-κα	-ε-πό-θην

911.7   ου/αυ   ο/α

(I.1a)	ἀκού-ω	ἀκ-ήκο-α
(I.1a)	παύ-ω	(-ε-πά-ην)
(III.5)	ἔ-καυ-σα	(ἐ-κά-ην)

912.   In the noun system, quantitative variations in stem vowels are classified as strong, middle, weak. The following patterns are among those found:

Strong	Middle	Weak
912.1 ω	ο	
ῥήτωρ	ῥήτορ-ος	
912.2 η	ε	#
πατήρ	πατέρ-α	πατρ-ός
ἀστήρ	ἀστέρ-ος	

913.   An unpronounceable combination of consonants arising from the loss of a vowel in the weak grade leads to the production of a vowel from a sonant liquid or nasal (§906).

πατήρ, dat. pl. πατρά-σι(ν)   (< πατ<u>r</u>-σι)
μήτηρ, dat. pl. μητρά-σι (ν)   (< μητ<u>r</u>-σι)

914.   *Compensatory lengthening* is the lengthening of a preceding short vowel to compensate for the loss of a consonant. The rules for lengthening are slightly different than those given in §908: ε > ει, ο > ου (spurious diphthongs); α > ᾱ, ι > ῑ, υ > ῡ.

ἐ-μεν-σα > ἔμεινα	(§930.5)
τι-θεντ-ς > τιθείς	(§929.9)
τονς > τούς	(§930.5)
δι-δοντ-ς > διδούς	(§929.9)
λυ-ο-νσι > λύουσι	(§930.5)
παντ-ς > πᾶς	(§929.9)
ἐ-κλιν-σα > ἔκλῑνα	(§930.5)
δεικνυντ-ς > δεικνῡς	(§929.9)

9140.   In the 1st aorist tense of liquid (and nasal) stems, α > η (contrary to §914), except before ι or ρ (cf. §908.3), e.g. ἔ-φαν-σα > ἔφηνα

915.   *Prothetic vowels.* Occasionally an initial short vowel is developed before λ, μ, ρ (called prothetic, place before)· E.g. ἀ-λείφω, *anoint with oil* (< λίπος, *fat*) ἐ-χθές, *yesterday* (<χθές).

916.   *Euphony of vowels.* The Greek ear, especially that of the Atticist (and later imitators), did not like the immediate succession of vowel sounds, whether they arose from inflection, word-formation, or the ordering of words in the sentence. To avoid hiatus (a slight pause between vowels to allow each to be sounded separately) various devices were employed:

916.1   *Contraction* (§917), the fusion of two vowels (or a vowel and diphthong) within a word;

916.2   *Elision* (§918), the omission of a short final vowel before another word beginning with a vowel;

916.3   *Crasis* (§919), the contraction of final and initial vowels of words, thus joining two words into one;

916.4   *Movable consonants* (ν, ς) (§§920, 921), added at the end of words when the next word begins with a vowel. Hiatus between words was of course allowable, but in varying degrees by different users of the language; within words a succession of vowels is often allowable, especially where contraction would obscure the root or form. Vowels once separated by σ, υ, or ι in particular are contracted.

917.   *Contraction.* Vowels brought together in inflection and word-formation are often contracted in accordance with regular patterns. These patterns may be schematized in the form of rules that are designed to reduce the bewildering variety of combinations to a relatively few principles.

917.1   *Rule 1.* Two vowels which may naturally form a diphthong do so:

$$\alpha + \iota = \alpha\iota \qquad\qquad \varepsilon + \upsilon = \varepsilon\upsilon$$
$$\varepsilon + \iota = \varepsilon\iota$$
$$\eta + \iota = \eta$$
$$o + \iota = o\iota$$

917.2   *Rule 2.* Identical and related vowels (§908) unite in a common long vowel or diphthong:

$$\alpha + \alpha = \bar{\alpha} \qquad\qquad \iota + \iota = \bar{\iota}$$
$$\varepsilon + \eta = \eta \qquad\qquad o + o = o\upsilon \text{ (spurious, §902.5)}$$
$$\varepsilon + \varepsilon = \varepsilon\iota \text{ (spurious, §902.5)} \qquad o + \omega = \omega$$

917.3   Unrelated vowels, which cannot form a genuine diphthong, are assimilated, either the first to the second, or the second to the first:

917.4   *Rule 3.* α and ε are always assimilated to o or ω:

$$\left.\begin{array}{l} \alpha + o \\ o + \alpha \end{array}\right\} = \omega \qquad \left.\begin{array}{l} o + \eta \\ \omega + \eta \end{array}\right\} = \omega$$

$$\left.\begin{array}{l} \alpha + \omega \\ \omega + \alpha \end{array}\right\} = \omega \qquad \left.\begin{array}{l} \varepsilon + o \\ o + \varepsilon \end{array}\right\} = o\upsilon \text{ (spurious, §902.5)}$$

$$\varepsilon + \omega = \omega$$

917.5   *Rule 4.* In the combination α + ε or η, the second is assimilated to the first and yields either α or η:

$$\left.\begin{array}{l} \alpha + \varepsilon \\ \alpha + \eta \end{array}\right\} = \alpha \qquad \begin{array}{l} \varepsilon + \alpha = \eta \\ \eta + \varepsilon = \eta \end{array}$$

917.6   *Rule 5.* A single vowel disappears when united with a diphthong beginning with the same vowel:

$$\left.\begin{array}{l} \alpha + \alpha\iota \\ \alpha + \dot{\alpha} \end{array}\right\} = \alpha\iota \qquad \begin{array}{l} o + o\iota \\ o + o\upsilon = o\upsilon \end{array}$$

$$\varepsilon + \varepsilon\iota = \varepsilon\iota \qquad\qquad o + \dot{\omega} = \dot{\omega}$$

917.7   *Rule 6.* A single vowel, when united with a diphthong beginning with a different vowel, contracts with the first vowel of the diphthong in accordance with the regular patterns; the iota becomes subscript (or adscript):

α + ει = ᾳ   ε + αι = η   η + αι = η

α + η = ᾳ   ε + η = η   η + ει = η

α + οι = ῳ   ε + ου = ου   η + οι = ῳ

ε + ῳ = ῳ

917.8   *Qualifications of Rule 6.* Diphthongs ει and ου, when spurious (§902.5), are regarded as simple ε and o:

α + ει (spurious)   = α

η + ει (spurious)   = η

o + ει (spurious)   = ου

α + ου (spurious)   = ω

i.e. the second vowel of the diphthong (ι, υ) is ignored.

917.9   Contrary to *rule 6 and the qualification in §917.8,*

ε + οι   = οι

o + ει (genuine)   = οι

o + η   = οι

Although the o prevails in each case, the resultant initial vowel of the diphthong does not accord with rule 3 (§917.4).

917.10   In the contraction of three vowels, the last two are contracted first, and the resulting vowel or diphthong then contracted with the first, e.g. ποιε-ε-σαι > ποιε-η (loss of intervocalic σ, §930.21) > ποιῇ.

918.   *Elision* is the omission of a short final vowel before an initial vowel; the omission is marked with an apostrophe ('). Examples: δι' αὐτοῦ (for διὰ αὐτοῦ) (Jn 1:3); ἀλλ' ἵνα (for ἀλλὰ ἵνα) (Jn 1:8).

Elision occurs predominantly in adverbs, prepositions, and conjunctions. It does not affect the prepositions πρό and περί, the conjunction ὅτι (ὅτ' = ὅτε, *when*), and the forms which take ν-movable (§920). Bl-D §17.

919.   *Crasis* is the contraction of the final and initial vowels of successive words so that two words are written as one. A *coronis* (apostrophe in form) marks the contraction.

Crasis is less common in hellenistic Greek than in earlier periods. The common forms in the New Testament are: τοὔνομα (τὸ ὄνομα), τοὐναντίον (τὸ ἐναντίον), ταὐτά (τὰ αὐτά), and in combinations with καί, *and*: κἀγώ (καὶ ἐγώ), κἀμοί (καὶ ἐμοί), κἀκεῖ (καὶ ἐκεῖ), κἀκεῖνος (καὶ ἐκεῖνος), κἄν (καὶ ἄν). B1-D §18.

920. *Movable* ν. A ν may be added to words ending in -σι (dat. pl. 3rd declension nouns, pronouns, adjectives; verbal endings), to the 3rd sg. verbal ending in -ε, and to ἐστί(ν), theoretically to avoid hiatus (§916). ν-movable is regularly put in parentheses in grammars and lexicons. Bl-D §20.

From a later point of view, ν-movable is appropriate only at the end of a clause or sentence, or where the next word begins with a vowel. However, movable- ν was employed in earlier periods before consonants as well. In the hellenistic era ν was sometimes added indiscriminately to forms other than those listed above; this ν is called irrational ν.

921. *Movable* ς. A ς may be added to a few words for the same reason as ν-movable, i.e. to avoid hiatus. Like ν, it is employed inconsistently. It appears with οὕτω(ς), ἄχρι(ς) , and μέχρι(ς). ἐκ also takes a ς before vowels (ἐξ). Bl-D §21.

922. *The negative* οὐ is so written before consonants, but the form ουκ is employed before a vowel with smooth breathing, οὐχ before a vowel with rough breathing (aspiration, §928.1). The strong form, οὐχί, is unaffected.

9220. μηκέτι, *no longer* (μή + ἔτι) derives the κ by analogy from οὐκέτι.

Consonant Change

923. *Final consonants.* Only ν, ρ, and σ (ξ, ψ) may stand at the end of a word in Greek. As a consequence, in inflection it is sometimes necessary to drop other consonants. E.g. σῶμα (nom.), σώματος (gen.), σωματ- (stem).

9230.1 Exceptions are the proclitics ἐκ (preposition) and negative adverb οὐκ.

9230.2 Foreign words taken over into Greek, however, are permitted to violate the rule, e.g. Ἰσραήλ, Ἀβραάμ, Δαυίδ, Ἰακώβ.

924. *Assimilation.* In inflection and word-formation clusters of consonants occasionally arise which are phonetically intolerable, i.e. they are either unpronounceable or difficult to pronounce. The tendency is to conserve movement and thus to assimilate such juxtaposed sounds to each other. Assimilation may be partial, e.g. a palatal (γ, χ) before τ is assimilated to κ so that the two juxtaposed consonants will be coordinate (§904.1). Or, assimilation may be total, e.g. ν before λ becomes λ. If the first consonant in a cluster undergoes change, it is called

regressive assimilation; if the second (or last) changes, it is called progressive assimilation.

Assimilation may be classified in accordance with the types of consonants involved (§903).

925.   *Stops before stops.* The "square" of stops (§904.1) is relevant to the following forms of assimilation.

925.1 A labial or palatal before a dental is assimilated to a labial or palatal of the same order, i.e. it is made coordinate:

βτ, φτ > πτ
γτ, χτ > κτ
πδ, φδ > βδ
κδ> γδ
πϑ, βϑ > φϑ
κϑ, γϑ > χϑ

925.2 A dental before another dental may become σ.
Note: ττ arising from κι and χι (§932.2) is retained from Attic in a few words, e.g. κρείττων, ἐλάττων.

925.3 γ before κ, γ, χ (and ξ) becomes γ-nasal (§9030.1). Its form, however, is unchanged.

926.   *Stops before μ.*

926.1 A labial before μ becomes μ (total assimilation).

πμ, βμ, φμ > μμ

926.2 A palatal before μ becomes γ (partial assimilation).

κμ, χμ > γμ

N. κ, χ are sometimes retained before μ in a noun-suffix and occasionally elsewhere.

926.3 A dental before μ sometimes becomes σ by analogy to a dental before a dental (§925.2) in the perfect middle conjugation (§§392.1, 3920).

927.   *Stops before σ.*

927.1 A preceding labial coalesces with σ to form ψ; a preceding palatal coalesces with σ to form ξ (§9030.3).

πσ, βσ, φσ > ψ

κσ, γσ, χσ > ξ

Exceptions: §9030.3.

927.2 A dental preceding σ is assimilated to σ and one σ is then dropped.

τσ, δσ, θσ > σσ > σ

928. *Aspiration and deaspiration.*

928.1 A stop of the smooth order (π, κ, τ) is aspirated, i.e. assimilated to the corresponding aspirated stop (φ, χ, θ), before rough breathing (also an aspirate, §904.2). A labial or palatal before θ (as aspirate) is also assimilated to the corresponding aspirated stop (§925.1).

928.2 When two successive syllables begin with a rough stop, the first is customarily changed to the corresponding smooth stop (to avoid aspiration in successive syllables).

τεθέαμαι	(for *θεθεαμαι, reduplication, §343.3)
τρίχος	(gen., for *θριχος, nom. sg· θρίξ, hair, §§162, 1620)
ἐτάφην	(for *ἐθάφην, verb base θαπ-)
πιστεύθητι	(for *πιστευθηθι, §463)

928.3 Rough breathing is often lost when the successive syllable contains an aspirated stop:

ἔχω < ἔχω < σέχω (§930.40)

928.4 There is occasionally a transfer of aspiration: πάσχω < παθ-σκω (§487.7).

929. ν *before other consonants.*

929.1 ν before π, β, φ (labials) and ψ may be assimilated to μ.

νπ, νβ, νφ, νψ > μπ, μβ, μφ, μψ

929.2 ν before κ, γ, χ (palatals) and ξ may be assimilated to γ-nasal.

νκ, νγ, νχ, νξ > γκ, γγ, γχ, γξ

929.3 ν before a liquid (λ, ρ) may be totally assimilated.

νλ > λλ

νρ > ρρ

929.4   In the hellenistic period non-assimilation was becoming common in the case of the prepositions σύν and ἐν compounded with verbs. Bl-D §19.

929.5   ν before μ is totally assimilated: νμ > μμ.

929.6   ν before ζ or σ is dropped in compounds with σύν, e.g. συζητέω, *discuss* (imperf. συνεζήτουν); συσταυρόω, *crucify together* (aor. pass, συνεσταυρώθην).

929.7   ν before σ undergoes various changes: In the dat. pl. of 3rd declension nouns with stems in ν, the ν is dropped before the ending -σι(ν) (§187). Nouns with a long final stem vowel (η or ω): αἰών (αἰών-) , gen. αἰώνος, dat. pl. αἰώσι(ν) (< αιωνσι(ν)); nouns with a short final stem vowel (ε or ο): ποιμήν (ποιμεν-) , gen. ποιμένος, dat. pl. ποιμέσι(ν) (< ποιμενσι(ν)).

929.70   In connection with nouns with short final stem vowels, the question arises why this vowel was not subject to compensatory lengthening (§914) when the ν was dropped. The answer apparently is that the ε (or ο) is not really a stem vowel and the ν was not really dropped. Rather, ποιμν̥σι represents the weak grade of the stem (§913), and ν became sonant (vocalic), producing an α in its place (§906): ποιμνσι > ποιμάσι; the α was then replaced by ε (or ο) by analogy to the other oblique cases (leveling; cf. §186). Cf. φρασί (Pindar) for φρν̥σι, which later became φρεσί by analogy to the forms φρένες, φρενῶν, etc. This is the explanation for the fact that the dat. pl. is ποιμέσι(ν) (short vowel) rather than ποιμεῖσι(ν) (as would be the case under compensatory lengthening). Smyth §250 N.

929.8   More often ν before σ disappears and the preceding vowel is lengthened in compensation (§914): ε > ει, ο > ου, α > ᾱ): e.g.

> λύουσι(ν) (3rd pl. present act. indic.) < λυ-ο-νσι
> εἷς (cardinal, one) < ἑνς
> τούς (article, ace. masc. pl.) < τονς
> μέλᾱς (adj., nom. masc. sg., black) < μελανς
> τεθείς (participle, nom. masc. sg., τίθημι) < τιθεν(τ)ς

929.9   ντ, νδ, νθ before σ: The dental is assimilated to σ and one σ is dropped (§927.2); ν then disappears before the σ and the preceding vowel lengthened in compensation (§929.8).

> πᾶσι (ν) (adj., dat. pi.) < παντ-σι
> τιθεῖσι, (ν) (participle, dat. masc.-neut. pl.) < τιθεντ-σι
> πείσομαι. (1st sg. fut. mid. indic.) < πενθ-σομαι

929.90 See §930.5 for cases where σ is lost following ν.

930. σ. The behavior of σ has been treated in part under other headings.

> For labials and palatals before σ, s. §927.1.
> For dentals before σ, s. §927.2.
> For ν before σ, s. §929.6–8.
> For ν plus a dental before σ, s. §929.9.

930.1 Interconsonantal σ (σ between consonants) is sometimes lost. This loss is to be observed in the 2nd pl. mid.-pass, of the perfect tense (§391.1) where σ is dropped between a final stem consonant and θ: τέτριφε < τέτριβ-σθε; ἔσταλθε < εσταλ-σθε; but λέλυσθε. The same applies to the perf. mid.-pass. inf. (§4660.4): πεφάνθαι, < πεφαν-σθαι; but λελύσθαι.

930.2 Intervocalic σ (σ between vowels) is lost under a variety of circumstances, causing the vowels thus brought together to contract (§917).

930.20 In the future tense of liquid verbs (verbs ending in a liquid or nasal), -εσ o/ε is added to the stem to form the future tense stem; intervocalic σ is then lost and the vowels contract (§917), e.g. μενῶ < μενεσω; στελῶ < στελέσω; ἐγερῶ < ἐγερεσω. S. §376.

930.21 In the 2nd sg. middle endings, both primary and secondary (-σαι and -σο), σ is lost between vowels (except in the perfect/pluperfect tenses and the present/imperfect of μι-verbs). The vowels thus brought together contract (§917): λύῃ < λυεσαι; τιμᾷ < τιμαεσαι; ἐλάβου < ἐλαβεσο; ἐλύσω < ἐλυσασο; ἐτιμῶ < ἐτιμαεσο; but ἵστασαι, ἵστασο (pres./imperf., μι-verb); λέλυσαι, ἐλέλυσο (perf./pluperf.).

930.22 The same phenomenon is to be observed in the inflection of neuter nouns of the 3rd declension with stems in -εσ- (nom. in -ος) (§196), and of 3rd declension adjectives in -ής, -ές (§234).

930.23 Intervocalic σ is by no means always lost. It may be retained when it is the result of phonetic change or by analogy (Smyth §120).

930.4 Initial σ before a vowel is often lost. Its former presence may be marked by rough breathing: ἑπτά, seven (Latin septem); ἅλς, salt (Latin sal); ἵστημι < σιστημι (reduplication, §3430.4).

930.40 The rough breathing (§930.4) may in turn be lost when the following syllable contains an aspirate (deaspiration, §928.2–3): ἔχω < σεχω, fut. ἕξω, aor. ἔσχον (stem σχ-, weak grade).

930.5 In the formation of the first aorist tense, σ after a liquid (λ, ρ) or nasal (ν) is lost and the preceding stem vowel lengthened in compensation (§914): ἔμεινα <

εμενσα; ἔστειλα < ἐστελσα; ἔφηνα < ἐφανσα. Cf. §928.8–9 for the loss of ν before σ On liquid aorists, s· §410.

930.6   Two σ's brought together in inflection are simplified as one, e.g. ἔθνεσι(ν) < ἐθνεσσι. Cf. §927.2.

931.   *Liquids.* Phonetic changes involving liquids (λ, ρ) are considered under other headings.

> For ν before a liquid, s. §929.3.
> For the future tense of liquid verbs, s. §930.20.
> For the aorist tense of liquid verbs, s. §930.5.
> For sonant (vocalic) liquids, s. §§906, 913, 929.70.

932.   *Consonants before* ι̯ (semivowel, §905). The combination of ι̯ with a preceding consonant produces a variety of phonetic changes that are relevant especially to the formation of the present tense stem of a certain class of verbs (§§484–4840).

932.1   δι̯ between vowels and γι̯ after a vowel becomes ζ.

> ἐλπίζω < ἐλπιδ-ι̯ω
>   Cf. ἐλπίς, ἐλπίδος (ελπιδ-)
> ἁρπάζω < ἁρπαγ-ι̯ω
>   Cf. ἁρπαγή, -ῆς, ἡ (ἁρπαγ-)
> On -ζω verbs from δι̯ and γι̯, s. §§484.1f.

932.2   κι̯, χι̯ become σσ (Attic ττ).

> κηρύσσω < κηρυκ-ι̯ω
>   Cf. κῆρυξ, -υκος, ὁ (κηρυκ-)
> ταράσσω < ταραχ-ι̯ω
>   Cf. ταραχή, ῆς, ἡ (ταραχ-)
> On -σσω verbs from κι̯, χι̯, s. §§484.2f.

932.3   γι̯ and τι̯ occasionally appear to yield σσ

> τάσσω < ταγ-ι̯ω
>   Cf. ταγή, -ῆς, ἡ (ταγ-)
> πλάσσω < πλατ-ι̯ω
>   Cf. 1. aor. ἔπλασα (§927.2)

Present tense stems in -σσω developed from verbs with stems in γ and τ by the addition of ι̯ were created by analogy to verbs with stems in κ, χ (Smyth §516).

932.4   λι̬ becomes λλ.

> βάλλω < βαλ-ι̬,ω
>> Cf. 2. aor. ἔβαλον

On -λλω verbs from λι̬, s. §484,3.

932.5   τι̬ (θι̬) after long vowels, diphthongs, and consonants becomes σ.

> πᾶσα < πανσα (§929.8) < παντ-ι̬α

932.6   ι̬ after αν, ον, αρ, op influences the preceding vowel rather than consonant: ι̬ is added to the vowel or, more accurately, the preceding vowel is assimilated to the ι-sound.

> φαίνω < φαν-ι̬ω
>> Cf. 1. aor. ἔφανα
>
> χαίρω < χαρ-ι̬ω
>> Cf. 2. aor. pass, ἐχάρην

932.7   ι̬ after εν, ερ influences the preceding vowel as in §932.6: ενι̬ > ειν, ερι̬ > ειρ.

> ἐγείρω < ἐγερ-ι̬ω
>> Cf. aor. pass, ἠγέρθην
>
> φθείρω < φθερ-ι̬ω
>> Cf. fut. φθερῶ

On verbs in –αίνω, -αίρω, -είνω, -είρω, s. §§484.4f. For adjectives exhibiting a comparable phenomenon, s. §2361.

932.8   Verbs with present stems in -πτω also appear to be derived from a labial + ι̬, e.g.

> καλύπτω < καλυπ-ι̬ω
>> Cf. 1. aor. ἐκάλυψα (§927.1)

933.   ϝ (digamma). The former presence of ϝ (§905) occasionally leaves traces.

933.1   In third declension nouns with stems in ευ, αυ, ου, ϝ is represented by υ in the nom. sg. and dat. pl. (in some nouns in the acc. sg. as well). Its former presence in the other forms accounts for some irregularity of declension.

> βασιλεύς, king, βασιλεῦσι(ν) (dat. pl.), but βασιλέως (gen. sg.)

933.2   In the augment and reduplication of certain verbs, initial ϝ, now lost, produces some irregularity.

ὁράω, *see* (ϝοράω) , imperf. ἑώρων, perf. ἑώρακα
εἶδον, *saw* (ἐ-ϝιδον), cf. *video*

For details, s. §§3371, 3372, 3430.4.

933.3   The former presence of ϝ in the stem of some verbs is marked by the presence of υ in certain tense stems.

πνέω, *breathe* aor. ἔπνευσα
ῥέω, *flow* fut. ῥεύσομαι
κλαίω, *weep* (< κλαϝ-ι̯ω) fut. κλαύσω

Note: Appendix II, The Catalog of the Nominal System, and Appendix III, The Catalog of the Verbal System, are available online only. Links to the PDFs can be found by clicking on Resources at: www.westarinstitute. org/store/a-beginning-intermediate-grammar-of-hellenistic-greek/

Appendix IV

Parsing Code

1. Cuts

/	marks the limits of primary words and word groups in S
//	stands between words and word groups in apposition
	marks a secondary cut
/	marks a tertiary cut
()	encloses conjunctions
[]	encloses sentence connectors
→ =	goes with, modifies

2. Arabic numbers

An arabic number is set over the word or head term of the subject, main (finite) verb, and each unit of the predicate, as follows:

1	= word or word group in the structure of subject
2	= main (finite) verb
3	= in predicate: word or word group with head term in nominative case
4	= in predicate: word or word group with head term in accusative case
5	= in predicate: word or word group with head term in dative case
6	= in predicate: word or word group with head term in genitive case

In addition,

A	= in predicate: any adverb not included in another word group; a word cluster headed by an adverb
I	= in predicate: any infinitive not included in another word group; a word group headed by an infinitive
S (s)	= in predicate: any included independent (dependent) sentence
P	= prefixed to any word or word group initiated by a preposition

3. Parts of speech

Lower case letters are used to designate parts of speech (except for adverbs: upper case):

b	= pronoun
d	= pronominal adjective
n	= noun
a	= adjective
g	= participle
i	= infinitive
p	= preposition
A	= adverb

A plus sign is added to the basic designation for word clusters headed by a part of speech.

+	= word cluster (e.g. 4n+, 5g+)

4. In the analysis of nominal word clusters,

t	= the article in any gender, number, case

5. Adverbs, negatives, conjunctions and particles:

A	= adverb
N	= negative particle
B	= subordinator
C	= conjunction
D	= connector
Q	= question signaling words and word groups
W	= wish signaling words and word groups
E	= exclamation signaling words and word groups
H	= nuance words, sentence modalizers
I	= attention getters

6. Additional designations

Sentence types are marked with roman numerals

P	= the passive form of a sentence type, e.g. IIIP
T	= the transformation
a^c	= comparative degree of an adjective

Appendix V

Paradigms

Paradigms which must be committed to memory and other materials which need to be consulted frequently are reproduced here for convenience. Section numbers (§§) refer to the sections of the *Grammar* where they are first presented and discussed.

1. The Article (§121)

	Singular			Plural		
	Masc.	Fem.	Neut.	Masc.	Fem.	Neut.
Nom.	ὁ	ἡ	τ ό	οἱ	αἱ	τ ά
Gen.	τ οῦ	τ ῆς	τ οῦ	τ ῶν	τ ῶν	τ ῶν
Dat.	τ ῷ	τ ῇ	τ ῷ	τ οῖς	τ αῖς	τ οῖς
Acc.	τ όν	τ ήν	τ ό	τ ούς	τ άς	τ ά

2. τίς, τί (§151)

	Singular		Plural	
	Masc.-Fem.	Neuter	Masc.-Fem.	Neuter
N	τί ς	τί	τίν ες	τίν α
G	τίν ος	τίν ος	τίν ων	τίν ων
D	τίν ι	τίν ι	τί σι (ν)	τί σι (ν)
A	τίν α	τί	τίν ας	τίν α

3. πᾶς, πᾶσα, πᾶν (§231)

πᾶς, πᾶσα, πᾶν — *every, each, all*

	Singular			Plural		
	M	F	N	M	F	N
N	πᾶς	πᾶσα	πᾶν	πάντες	πᾶσαι	πάντα
G	παντός	πάσης	παντός	πάντων	πασῶν	πάντων
D	παντί	πάσῃ	παντί	πᾶσι (ν)	πάσαις	πᾶσι (ν)
A	πάντα	πᾶσαν	πᾶν	πάντας	πάσας	πάντα

4. Personal Pronouns (§256)

	Singular		Plural	
	First Person	Second Person	First Person	Second Person
N	ἐγώ [cf. *ego*]	σύ	ἡμεῖς	ὑμεῖς
G	ἐμοῦ, μου	σοῦ, σου	ἡμῶν	ὑμῶν
D	ἐμοί, μοι	σοί, σοι	ἡμῖν	ὑμῖν
A	ἐμέ, με	σέ, σε	ἡμᾶς	ὑμᾶς

5. Structure of the Verb System (§303)

Principal Parts	I. Present	II. Future	III. Aorist
Active Voice			
Indicative	λύω	λύσω	ἔλυσα
Subjunctive	λύω	—	λύσω
Optative	λύοιμι	(λύσοιμι)	λύσαιμι
Imperative	λῦε	—	λῦσον
Infinitive	λύειν	λύσειν	λῦσαι
Participle	λύων, -ουσα, -ον	λύσων, -ουσα, -ον	λύσας, -ασα, -αν
Middle Voice			
Indicative	λύομαι	λύσομαι	ἐλυσάμην
Subjunctive	λύωμαι	—	λύσωμαι
Optative	λυοίμην	(λυσοίμην)	λυσαίμην
Imperative	λύου	—	λῦσαι
Infinitive	λύεσθαι	λύσεσθαι	λύσασθαι
Participle	λυόμενος, -η, -ον	λυσόμενος, -η, -ον	λυσάμενος, -η, -ον
Passive Voice			
Indicative	Same as Middle	See Sixth	See Sixth
Subjunctive		Principal Part	Principal Part
Optative			
Imperative			
Infinitive			
Participle			

IV. Perfect Active	V. Perfect Middle and Passive	VI. Aorist Passive
λέλυκα λελυκὼς ὦ (λελυκὼς εἴην) (λέλυκε, λελυκὼς ἴσθι) λελυκέναι λελυκώς, -υῖα, -ός		
See Fifth Principal Part	λέλυμαι λελυμένος ὦ (λελυμένος εἴην) λέλυσο λελύσθαι λελυμένος, -η, -ον	
See Fifth Principal Part	Same as Middle	ἐλύθην λυθῶ λυθείην λύθητι λυθῆναι λυθείς, -εῖσα, -έν

Tenses formed on the same stem

Principal Parts	I. Present	IV. Perfect Active	V. Perfect Middle and Passive	VI. Aorist Passive
Indicative	Imperfect Active ἔλυον	Pluperfect (ἐ)λελύκειν	Pluperfect (ἐ)λελύμην	Future Passive λυθήσομαι
	Middle and Passive ἐλυόμην			
Infinitive		——	——	(λυθήσεσθαι)
Participle		——	——	λυθησόμενος, -η, -ον

Future Perfect:
λελυκὼς ἔσομαι (active)
λελύσομαι (passive)

6. Primary Personal Endings (§318)

		Active Voice	Middle-Passive Voice
Singular	1.	-ω, -μι or #	1. -μαι
	2.	-ς	2. -η : σαι
	3.	-# (ν) or -σι (ν)	3. -ται
Plural	1.	-μεν	1. -μεθα
	2.	-τε	2. -σθε
	3.	-ουσι (ν) or -ασι (ν)	3. -νται

N.1. # indicates no ending, called a *zero* form

N.2. (ν) indicates ν-movable: §321

3180. Notes:

3180.1 First singular active -ω is really the thematic vowel o (§322) lengthened. The ending -μι occurs with a very restricted class of verbs (§327).

3180.2 The second singular active has an old alternate ending -θα (-σθα), which is rare.

3180.3 The third singular active -σι (ν) occurs with μι-verbs. An alternate form is -τι (ν).

3180.4 The third plural active ending is theoretically *-νσι. The present and future ending -ουσι (ν) derives from -ο-νσι; ν disappears before σ (§929.7), and the preceding vowel lengthened in compensation (§914). The form -ασι (ν), which appears in the present indicative of μι-verbs and in the perfect, is the same ending, except that the long form -ασι is apparently derived from -ανσι > -ᾱσι (compensatory lengthening).

3180.5 The second singular middle-passive -σαι appears in the perfect and present indicative of μι-verbs. Elsewhere it is contracted: e.g. λυ-ε-σαι > λυ-ε-αι (intervocalic σ is lost, §930.21) > λυ-ῃ (contraction). Other contractions (-ᾳ, -οι, -ῳ) occur where thematic vowel is lacking and/or the stem vowel is α or ο. Further exception to contraction: §3680.1.

7. Secondary Personal Endings (§319)

		Active Voice	Middle-Passive Voice
Singular	1.	-ν or #	-μην
	2.	-ς	-ου : σο
	3.	-#(ν)	-το
Plural	1.	-μεν	-μεθα
	2.	-τε	-σθε
	3.	-ν or -σαν	-ντο

N.1. # indicates no ending, called a *zero* form

N.2. (ν) indicates ν-movable: §321

3190. Notes:

3190.1 The original first singular ending was μ which became ν when preceded by a vowel (Smyth §133.c).

3190.2 There is an alternate second singular active ending -σθα, which is rare (originally a perfect ending, it spread to the imperfect by analogy; cf. §§3180.2, 405f.).

3190.3 Like the third singular of the primary active set (§318), the third singular of the secondary active set shows no personal ending (*zero* form). However, where the stem formative vowel in ε, ν-movable may be added (§321).

3190.4 The third plural active ending -ν, when added to tense stems such as the first aorist ελυσα-ν, gave rise to an ending -σαν, which was then employed elsewhere.

3190.5 The second singular middle-passive ending -σο appears in the imperfect indicative of μι-verbs and in the pluperfect indicative (cf. §3180.5 on -σαι). Elsewhere it is contracted, e.g. ελυ-ε-σο > λυ-ε-ο (intervocalic σ is lost) > λυ-ου (contraction). Another contraction -ω occurs when the thematic vowel is lacking and/or the stem vowel is -α.

8. Inflectional Categories in the Verb System
(Indicative Mood) (§4750)

I. Present
Present active/middle-passive
1. ω-verbs uncontracted (§§367–3670)
2. ω-verbs contracted (§§368–3691)
3. μι-verbs (§§370–3712)

Imperfect active/middle-passive
1. ω-verbs uncontracted (§§401–4010)
2. ω-verbs contracted (§§402–4031)
3. μι-verbs (§§404–4050)

II. Future
Future active/middle
1. regular (§§373–3750)
2. liquid (§§376, 377)
-ίζω verbs (§3760)
3. Doric (§3761)
4. Without tense formant (§3763)

III. Aorist
Aorist active/middle
1. second aorist (§§407–4070)
2. first aorist (§§408–409)
3. liquid aorists (§410)
4. 'root' aorists (§411)
5. κ-aorists (§§412–4121)
6. mixed (§4122)

IV. Perfect
Perfect active
1. first perfect (§§385, 386–3860)
2. second perfect (§§3850, 387–3880)

Pluperfect active
1. first pluperfect (§§415–4150)
2. second pluperfect (§§415–4150)

V. Perfect Middle-Passive

Perfect middle-passive (§§389–3922)

Pluperfect middle-passive (§§416–418)

VI. Aorist Passive

Aorist passive

    1. first aorist passive (§§421–422)

    2. second aorist passive (§§423–4241)

Future passive

    1. first future passive (§§393–3940)

    2. second future passive (§§393–3940)

9. εἰμί

Present Tense (§371)

Sg. 1.	εἰμί	Pl. 1.	ἐσμέν
2.	εἶ	2.	ἐστέ
3.	ἐστί (ν)	3.	εἰσί (ν)

Imperfect Tense (§405)

Sg. 1.	ἤμην	Pl. 1.	ἦμεν, ἤμεθα
2.	ἦς, ἦσθα	2.	ἦτε
3.	ἦν	3.	ἦσαν

Future Tense (§378)

Sg. 1.	ἔσομαι	Pl. 1.	ἐσόμεθα
2.	ἔσῃ	2.	ἔσεσθε
3.	ἔσται	3.	ἔσονται

10. Key for Identifying the Verb (§431)

431.   The key for verb identification covers the subjunctive, optative, infinitive, and participle, as well as the indicative mood.

Prefixes

431.1   *Augment*: if the verb shows augment, it must be aorist, imperfect, or pluperfect (in the order of frequency; the augment is usually omitted with the pluperfect in the New Testament). §§0335–3400.

431.11   Present tense stem augmented and secondary endings: imperfect

431.12   Aorist tense stem augmented: second aorist indicative

431.121 First will have -σα as suffix

431.13   Pluperfect will have reduplicated stem

431.2   *Reduplication*: if the verb stem is reduplicated, the form will most often be perfect (or pluperfect). §§341–3450.

431.20   There are reduplicated stems in the present and aorist tenses also (§345)

Suffixes

431.3   *Tense suffixes*

431.31   σ added to present stem: future

431.32   σα added to aorist stem: first aorist

431.33   κα added to verb stem, either first perfect or aorist of μι-verbs

431.34   θη (η) added to aorist passive stem: aorist passive

431.35   θησ (ησ) added to aorist passive stem: future passive

431.4   *Mood suffixes*

431.41   Lengthened thematic vowel (ω/η): subjunctive

431.42   ιη in place of thematic vowel: optative

431.43   Thematic vowel plus ι: optative

431.5   *Other suffixes*

431.51   -ειν or -αι attached to the tense stem: infinitive

431.52   -ντ-, -οτ-, -μενο- as part of the suffix: participle

    Note: The nominative singulars of participles are the exception.

Greek Index

Numbers refer to §§ throughout

ἀποστέλλω: transitive verb w. inf. of purpose 580, indirect obj. w. 602.3
ἅπτομαι: w. gen. obj. 596.1
ἄρα: inferential particle 634.2, used to introduce apodosis of conditional sentence 856.6, ἄρα οὖν 634.2
ἄραγε: inferential particle 634.2
ἀρήν, ἀρνός, ὁ: declension 1890.3
Ἄρης, -εως: declension 206.3
ἀρνίον, -ου, τό: 1890.3
ἁρπάζω: pluperfect 418, second aorist passive 4241, tense bases 484.10
ἄρσην, -εν: declension 2351.2
ἀρχιερεύς, -έως, ὁ: declension 201f.
ἄρχομαι: periphrasis w. and infinitive 570
ἄρχων, -οντος, ὁ: declension 166f.
ἀσθενής: comparison 242.2
-ασι(ν): personal ending 318, 3180.4, 3660, 370.1
ἆσσον: comparison 245
ἀστήρ, -έρος, ὁ: declension 183f.
ἄστυ, -εως, τό: declension 2003
αὐτός, -ή, -ό: 2561, 260, declension 261
    In simple nominal word clusters w. pronoun as head term 690.1, syntax 719–722: uses 719, pronominal adjective of identity 720, intensifying pronominal adjective 721, personal pronoun, third person 722
ἀφῆκεν: aorist of ἀφίημι 433.16
ἀφῆκα: κ-aorist 4120–4121
ἀφίημι: s. -ιημι Indirect obj. w. 602.3, in S-III 605, deletion of indirect and direct objects w. in S-IV 605, ἄφες (ἄφετε) introducing a hortatory subjunctive 821.2
ἄφρων, -ον: declension 235f.
ἄχρι(ς), ἄχρι(ς) οὗ: introducing temporal clauses 872
-άω verbs (contracted): present indicative 368–3680, tense stems 358, 374, 3791.2, imperfect, conjugation 402–4020, present subjunctive 444.1, present imperative, conjugation 457–4570, present inf. 4660.1, formation of tense bases 374, 4780.2–3, 482.3
-Β-
βάλλω: liquid future 377.2, 3791.3, imperfect and second aorist 4070, mixture of paradigms in aorist 4122, pluperfect 418
βαρύς: comparison 242.1
βασιλεῦ (voc): 205.3
βδελύσσομαι: reduplication 3430.2
βέλτιον: comparison 245
βιβρώσκω: reduplicated present 345.2
βλέπετε: introducing volitive or deliberative subjunctives 821.1
βλητέος, -α, -ον: declension 2370.5
βούλομαι: introducing a deliberative question 821.3
βοῦς, βοός, ὁ or ἡ: declension 202f.
-Γ-
γ: sound 056.1, γ-nasal 064.2, 9030.1, 925.3
γάλα, -ακτος, τό: declension 172f.
γάρ: sentence connector 630.2, 631, uses 633

γαστήρ, γαστρός, ἡ: declension 1840.1
γέρας, γέρως, τό: declension 1970.3
γεύομαι: w. gen. obj. 596.2
γήρας, γήρως (γήρους), τό: declension 1970.3
γίνομαι: reduplicated present 345.2, second perfect 3870, imperfect and second aorist 4070, pluperfect 418, μὴ γένοιτο (optative) 0445
    As copulative verb 507
γινώσκω: reduplicated present 345.2, athematic aorist 3664, root aorist, conjugation 411, pluperfect 418, athematic aorist optative 448–4480, athematic aorist imperative, conjugation 461–4610, athematic aorist inf. 4660.3 W. ptcp. in indirect discourse 585.7
Γολγοθᾶ, -ᾶν, ἡ: declension 206.4
γόνυ, γόνατος, τό: declension 172f.
γράφω: second perfect 3870, second perfect active, conjugation 387, perfect middle-passive, conjugation, 3920–3921, pluperfect active, conjugation 415–4150, pluperfect middle-passive, conjugation 4171, second aorist passive, conjugation 423, second aorist passive 4241, second aorist passive subjunctive, conjugation 443, perfect inf. 4660.4, aorist passive inf. 4660.5, perfect middle-passive participle 4687
Indirect obj. w. 602.3
γυνή, γυναικός, ἡ: declension 1621.1, γύναι voc. 205.3
-Δ-
δάκρυσιν (dat. plur.): 1990.2
δαρήσομαι: second future passive 4241
δέ: sentence connector 630.2, 631, uses 632, 635, ὁ δέ 630.2, 635.1, 712.1, μέν . . . δέ 630.2, 635.2, δ μέν ... δ δέ 712.2, other combinations 712.3, w. ἄλλος and ἕτερος 760
δεῖ: uncontracted present 3690, imperfect 4030, in deliberative questions 820.3, w. inf. as subject 832
δείκνυμι: present indicative, conjugation 3700–3701, second perfect 3870, imperfect, conjugation 4040–4041, present subjunctive 444.2, present imperative, conjugation 458–4580, present active participle 4684.1
    Indirect obj. w. 602.3
δεικνύς, δεικνῦσα, δεικνύν: declension 2470.3
δεῖνα: declension 2691
δεισιδαίμων: comparison 242.4
δέομαι: uncontracted present 3690, imperfect 4030, pluperfect 418
δέος, -ους, τό: declension 1962.2
δέρω: second aorist passive 4241
δέσποτα (voc): 205.3
δεῦρο: introducing a hortatory subjunctive 821.2
δεῦτε: introducing a hortatory subjunctive 821.2
δεύτερος: declension 274
δέχομαι: perfect middle-passive, conjugation 3920–3921, perfect middle-passive inf. 4660.4
δηλόω: present inf. 4660.1
διά: w. gen. of intermediate agent, w. articular inf. to express cause 836.2
Διδάσκαλε (voc): 205.3

διδάσκω: reduplicated base 3410, verb base 486.2 W. two accusatives in S-VI 520, 523–524

-διδράσκω: reduplicated present 345.2, second aorist 4070

δίδωμι: reduplicated present 345.2, present indicative, conjugation 3700–3701, imperfect, conjugation 4040–4041, aorist conjugation 4120–4121, pluperfect 418, present subjunctive 444.2, athematic aorist optative 448–4480, present imperative, conjugation 458–4580, athematic aorist imperative, conjugation 461–4610, present inf. 4660.1, athematic aorist inf. 4660.3, present active participle 2470.3, 4684.1, verb base and tense bases 479.2

    In active and passive forms of S-IV 510, catenative verb w. inf. 583, indirect obj. w. 602.3

διότι: introducing causal clauses 0877–877

δίς: indeclinable 274

δόξα, -ης, ἡ: declension 132.2

δόρυ, δόρατος, τό: declension 172f.

δύναμαι: augment 3360.21, present conjugation 3702.1, optative form 4471

    Catenative verb w. inf. 571–573, in deliberative questions 820.3

δυνατός: w. inf. 835

δύο: declension 269.2

-δύω: second aorist passive 4241

-Ε-

-εάγην: second aorist passive 4241

ἐάν: = ἄν 6740, used to introduce protasis of conditional sentences 855.1, w. third class condition 858, 861.1, ἐὰν καί to introduce concessive clauses 8590, καὶ ἐάν 643.3

ἑαυτοῦ, -ῆς, -οῦ: declension 257

ἑαυτῶν: 2570.3, 2580.2

ἐάω: augment 3371

ἐγγύς: comparison 245

ἐγείρω: reduplication 344, liquid future 377.2, 3791.3

ἔγνων: root aorist 411

ἔγνωσαν: aorist of γινώσκω 433.12

ἐγώ: declension 256

ἐδίδαξεν: aorist of διδάσκω 433.15

ἔδομαι: future w. ἐσθίω 376 3, 487.4

ἑδραῖος, -ον: declension 2211

ἔδραμον: second aorist 4070

-ἔδραν: second aorist 4070

ἔδυ: root aorist 411

ἔδωκα: κ-aorist 4120–4121

-ἔθανον: second aorist 4070

ἔθηκα: κ-aorist 4120–4121

ἐθίζω: reduplication 3430.4

ἔθνος, -ους, τό: declension 196f.

εἰ: 006.3, used to introduce protasis of conditional sentences 855.1, w. first class condition 856, w. second class condition 857, w. fourth class condition 859, εἰ καί to introduce concessive clauses 8590

εἰ-: augment of 3370.3

εἶδον: second aorist with ὁράω 4070, 487.6

    Catenative verb w. ptcp. 584

εἰδώς, εἰδυῖα, εἰδός: declension 2490

εἴκω: augment 3370.3

εἰκών, -όνος, ἡ: declension 188f.

εἴληφα: reduplication 3430.4, second perfect 3870

-εῖλον: second aorist 4070, mixture of paradigms 4122, aorist of αἱρέω 487.1

εἰμί: 321, 327, athematic 3664, present conjugation 371–3710, future 378, imperfect 405–4050, identification of forms 432.2, present subjunctive, conjugation 443, optative 4471, present imperative, conjugation 459–4590, present inf. 4660.1

    As copulative (equative) verb 507, 555, periphrasis w. and the participle 3910, 442.2, 568, 785 (present), 791.1, 792.5 (imperfect), 798 (perfect), 800.3 (pluperfect), w. adjectives = complex verb 835

εἶμι: present conjugation 3711.2

-ειν: suffix of inf. 431.51, 464.1, 4662

-είνω, -είρω: verbs in 484.4, 932.7, class III.4 (Appendix III)

εἶπον: augment 3371, reduplication 3430.4, second aorist 4070, mixture of paradigms 4122, aorist w. λέγω 487.2 Common in S-IV 600–602

εἴρηκα: reduplication 3430.1, perfect active w. λέγω 487.2

εἴρηται: perfect middle-passive w. λέγω 487.2

εἰς: meaning and function as structure signal 140–1471, w. πιστεύω 591.3, 6, w. acc. for indirect obj. 602.2–3, w. articular inf. to express purpose 833.2, to express result 0880, 881, w. terminal acc. 894.9

εἷς, μία, ἕν: declension 268.2f.

    In complex word clusters 706.1, εἷς ἕκαστος 751.5, correlation w. ἄλλος, ἕτερος 760, w. partitive gen. 888.3

εἴωθα: perfect for present 3880, pluperfect 418

ἐκ (ἐξ): meaning and function as structure signal 140–1471, w. partitive gen. 1120, 1121, w. ἀκούω 595.6, in ablative sense 888.3

ἑκάτερος, -α, -ον: declension 267

ἕκαστος, -η, -ον: declension 267

    In simple nominal word clusters w. pronoun as head term 690.5, in complex clusters 706.1

    Syntax 750–753: in simple word clusters 751, εἷς ἕκαστος 751.5, in complex word clusters 752, used alone 753, w. partitive gen. 888.3

ἐκεῖ: locative adverb 557–558, 560

ἐκεῖνος, ἐκείνη, ἐκεῖνο: declension 264

    Always in predicate position 6 84.3, in simple nominal word clusters 687.2, 729–731, in complex word clusters 732, as pointer 725, 727, 728, as independent grammatical item 733

ἔλαβον: second aorist 4070

ἐλάσσων, ἐλάχιστος: 245, ἐλαχιστότερος 2450.3

ἐλαύνω: reduplication 344, present base 485.40

Syntax 613–617: οὐ μή 614.2, 615.3, in emphatic negative assertions 818, 858.5, compounds w. 614.3, μηδέ 63.7.4, μήτι 617.7, question signaling 617.7, w. imperative 810, w. prohibitive subjunctive 527, 810, introducing final clauses 0878, 878.2, expressions of apprehension 879

μηδείς, μηδεμία, μηδέν: declension 269.1

μηκέτι: κ in 9220

-μην: personal ending 317, 319, 4050.2 Tied to personal pronoun, 1. sg. 534

μῆνις, μήνιος, ἡ: declension 1990.1

μήποτε: introducing expressions of apprehension 0878, 879

μήπως: introducing expressions of apprehension 0878, 879

μήτε . . . μήτε: 617.3

μήτηρ, μητρός, ἡ: declension 184f.

μι-verbs: present indicative 366, 3660, 370–3712, imperfect 400–4000, 404–4050, present subjunctive 444.2, present imperative, conjugation 458–4590, present inf. 4660.1

-μι: personal ending 318, 3180.1, 327, 3660, 370.1, in optative 446.3, 4480.1
        Tied to personal pronoun, 1. sg. 534

μιαίνω: liquid future 377.2

μικρός: comparison 245

μιμνήσκομαι: reduplication 3430.2, reduplicated present 345.2, present base 486.3, perfect = state or condition 799, w. gen. obj. 596.3

μνηστεύω: reduplication 3430.2

μόνος: in simple nominal word clusters w. pronoun as head term 690.4, modifying a demonstrative 731.3

Μύρα, Μύρων, τά: declension 206.5

Μωϋσῆς, -έως, ὁ: declension 206.3

-N-

ν: vocalic (sonant) 1840.2, 906, 929.70

-ν: personal ending 319, 3190.1, 3190.4, 393, 4000, 4050.2, in optative 4480.1
        Tied to personal pronoun, 1. sg. 534

ν-movable: 319, 3190.3, 321, 3860.1, 916.4, 920

-ναι: suffix of inf. 465, 4662

νῆστις, νήστιος, ὁ or ἡ: declension 1990.1

-ντ-: participial suffix 431.52, 433.17, 468.2, present, future, second aorist active ptcps. 4680, present and athematic active ptcps. of μι-verbs, first aorist active and passive ptcps. 4684, 4692

-νται: personal ending 318, 320.2

ναῦς, νεώς, ἡ: declension 2021.1

-ντο: personal ending 319, 320.2

νύξ, νυκτός, ἡ: declension 1621.2

νύσσω: second aorist passive 4241

-Ξ-

ξ: sound 056.3, components 083.1, 9030.5

ξηραίνω: perfect middle-passive, conjugation 391.2

-O-

ὁ, ἡ, τό: declension 120–1240, as structure signal

125–129, 713–7160, as demonstrative 263, position of modifiers w. article 684, in simple nominal word clusters 687, 688, 689, in complex nominal word clusters 695, 696, 697, 698, 6980, 699, 701, 702, 703, as head term in complex nominal word clusters 705
        Syntax of article as determiner 710–7160: the definite article 711, as pronoun 712
        W. αὐτός 719–722, w. demonstratives 729–731, w. πᾶς 740–745, 747, 748, w. ἕκαστος 750.1, w. ἄλλος and ἕτερος 755, 757–760, w. ptcp. 770.1, 774, 775–777
        W. inf. 8300, 8310, 832.4, 833.2, 836, 837.2–4, τοῦ w. inf. 830, 8300, 832.4, to express purpose 833.1, to express result 834.2, in temporal clauses 836.1
        W. voc. 886.50

ὅδε, ἥδε, τόδε: declension 2640.1

ὁδός, -οῦ, ἡ: declension 136.2

ὀδούς, -όντος, ὁ: declension 1670.1

ὅθεν: introducing local clauses 0875–875, introducing causal clauses 0877–877

οἶδα: conjugation 388, pluperfect 418, perfect subjunctive 442.2, conjugation 443, perfect imperative 455.2, confusion with εἰμί 4590.1, active participle 4686, tense bases 487.5 Present perfect 799, pluperfect = past state or condition 800.2

οἰκεῖος, -ον: 2211

οἰκοδομέω: pluperfect 418

οἰνόμελι, -ιτος, τό: declension 172f.

οἷος, -α, -ον: declension 272, correlatives 27 3

ὄλλυμι: reduplication 344, liquid future 377.2, 3791.3, second perfect 3870, present base 485.41

ὅλος: in simple nominal word clusters w. pronoun as head term 690.3, modifying a demonstrative 731.2

ὀμνύω: tense bases 485.42

ὁμοίως: correlated w. καθώς 867.2

ὀνίνημι: reduplicated present 345.2, 3450.2, present conjugation 3702.1, optative form 4481

ὄνομα, -ατος, τό: declension 171f.

ὀνομάζω: w. two accusatives in S-V 522

ὁποῖος, -α, -ον: declension 272, correlatives 273

ὁπόσος, -η, -ον: declension 272

ὅπου: w. ἄν = protasis of conditional sentence 86 0.3, introducing local clauses 0875–876

ὀπτάνομαι: new present for ὁράω 487.6

ὅπως: introducing final (purpose) clauses 0878–878.1

ὁράω: augment 3371, 3372.2, reduplication 3430.4, imperfect and second aorist 4070, pluperfect 418, tense bases 487.6
        ὅρα (ὅρατε) introducing volitive and deliberative subjunctives 821.1

ὄρνις, -ιθος, ὁ (ἡ): declension 1630.1

ὄρος, -ους, τό: declension 1962.1

ὀρύσσω: second aorist passive 4241

*ὅς, ἥ, ὅ: declension 123–1240, 270
        Relative pronoun 641–643, syntax 665–674: transformation of sentence into relative clause 666–667, adjective clauses 668–669, attraction of relative to

Subject Index

Numbers refer to §§ throughout

Abbreviations: w. = with, sing. = singular, plur. = plural, nom. = nominative, gen. = genitive, dat. = dative, acc. = accusative, voc. = vocative, inf. = infinitive, ptcp. = participle, S = sentence, further s. Parsing Code, Appendix IV.

Accent: 072–075, of nouns 1321.2, present tense of contract verbs 3680.2, interrogative pronominal adjective τίς always w. acute accent 0765.1, accent of indefinite pronominal adjective τις 0765.1

Accusative: functions 0114–1140, 0894, signals direct object 114, 508.1, 590, 894.1, internal object 114, 894.2, external object 114, two accusatives 114, 520–524, 894.3, 4, acc. retained in passive form of S-VI 894.5, 52 3.2, predicate acc. 114, 521–522, terminal 114, 894.9, of specification or respect 1140, 894.6, extent of space 1140, 894.8, extent of time 1140, 559, 894.8, adverbial 1140, 592, 894.7, subject of inf. 1140, 580, 89 4.10, prepositions w. 141.1

Active Voice: s. Voice

Adjectives: 011.2, 012.3, 101, inflectional paradigm 102, inflection of 220–2370, comparison of 240–2451, superlative in elative sense 240, double comparison 2450.3, "substantivized" 222, 688.1, 715.1, declension of comparatives 235–2351, verbal adjective 2370.5

As subject 543.4, word group headed by adjective as subject 545.5, in simple word clusters 549.4, 687.4–8, 6 88, in complex word clusters 701–703, ptcp. as 141 adjective 771, as predicate 684.4, 730.3 w. πᾶς 740.1, 741.1, followed by inf. 831.2, 835, by ἵνα-clause 658, 835.3

Also s: Pronominal Adjectives

Adjective Clauses: 643.1, relative 668–669, agnate to articular ptcp. 672, 773, temporal 868.1, local 875.1

Adverbs and Adverbials: 014.2, 101, 610, comparison of adverbs 014.2, 240

Articular adverb as subject 5470.1, in complex word clusters w. article 705.3, «substantivized» 705.4, 715.2, attributive 705.3, 732.2, adverbial acc. 1140, 592, 894.7

Common adverbials 556 –5610: adverbs 557, p-clusters 558, noun clusters 559, combinations 560, ptcps . 561 –5610, verbs as adverbs, s. Verb Chains, adverbial modifiers w. catenative verbs 574.2, negative adverbs, καί as adverb

Adverbial Clauses: 643.3, relative clauses as 674, inf. as 831.3, 836, s. further Circumstantial Participle, Conditional Sentences, Concessive, Comparative, Temporal, Local, causal, Final, and Consecutive clauses

Agnate: definition 592, agnate constructions 595.4, 595.9, 656, 658, 659, 660, 672, 776.2, 833.4, 835.3, 837

Agreement: adjectives w. nominal head 220, subject w. finite verb 533.1, 534–538, neuter plur. subject w. sing, verb 536, 56 8, two or more subjects connected by καί 537, aonstructio ad sensum 538, relative pronoun w. antecedent 667.1, in simple nominal word clusters 6 85.1, 772.1, ptcp. w. head 771, 845.1, 8460

Alphabet: 050–051, form of letters 051

Anarthrous: noun or nominal not determined by article called anarthrous 683.6, demonstratives rarely modify anarthrous noun 729, 730.2, ἕκαστος used regularly w. anarthrous nominal heads 750.1, ptcp. modifying anarthrous noun 774.1, supplementary and circumstantial ptcp. regularly anarthrous 845.4

Further s. Article, ὁ, ἡ, τό

Aorist Tense: 0301, reduplication in 342, formation of tense base, first aorist active and middle 346.1, 406, 408, second aorist active and middle 349.1, 406, 4070, first aorist passive 346.4, second aorist passive 349.3

Conjugation of active and middle 0406, 4122, types 406, second aorist active and middle 407, first aorist active and middle 408–4122, liquid first aorists 410, ‹root› aorists 411, 4120, compared w. second aorist passive 424, x-aorists 412–4120, mixture of first and second aorist paradigms 4122, aorist passive 393, 0419–4241, types 419, first aorist passive 421–422, second aorist passive 423–4241, catalogue of second aorist passives 4241, subjunctive 443, 444.3, optative 447, 448, 449, active inf. 4660.3, passive 4660,5, ptcp. 4680–4685

Present/past 786–7860, aorist indicative 787–7880: indefinite or punctiliar aspect in past time 788, complexive or constative aorist 788.1, ingressive or inceptive 788.2, periphrasis for 569, 570, effective or resultative 7 88.3, gnomic, epistolary 7880, often equivalent of English past perfect 800.4, in second class condition 857, ptcp. 849.1–2

Aspect: 309–310.1, 312.1, 788, aorist/imperfect distinguished 786, aspect of tense stem originally 7860, aorist/perfect distinguished 794

Appositives and Apposition: in nom. case 110, 886.3, in expansions of subject 547, clauses in apposition 652.1, 657, 662, explanatory (epexegetical) inf. 837

Article: as determiner in English 683.1

Syntax as determiner 710–7160: as determiner of nominal head 711, as pronoun 712, as grammatical device 713, as signaler of case 714, as «substantiv-